lonely planet

Canada's Maritime Provinces

David Stanley

LONELY PLANET PUBLICATIONS
Melbourne • Oakland • London • Paris

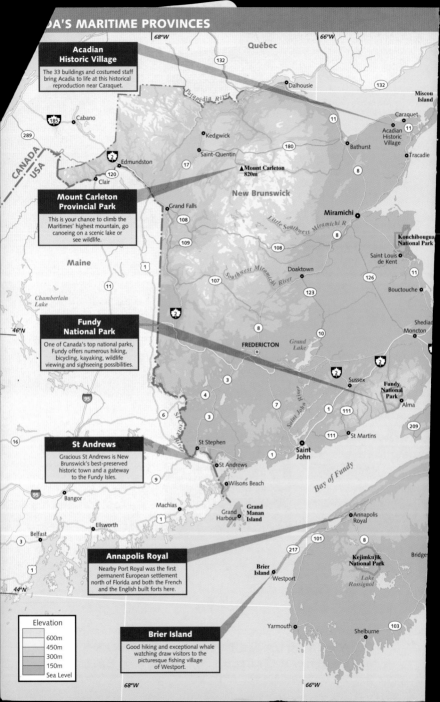

Acadian Historic Village

The 33 buildings and costumed staff bring Acadia to life at this historical reproduction near Caraquet.

Mount Carleton Provincial Park

This is your chance to climb the Maritimes' highest mountain, go canoeing on a scenic lake or see wildlife.

Fundy National Park

One of Canada's top national parks, Fundy offers numerous hiking, bicycling, kayaking, wildlife viewing and sighseeing possibilities.

St Andrews

Gracious St Andrews is New Brunswick's best-preserved historic town and a gateway to the Fundy Isles.

Annapolis Royal

Nearby Port Royal was the first permanent European settlement north of Florida and both the French and the English built forts here.

Brier Island

Good hiking and exceptional whale watching draw visitors to the picturesque fishing village of Westport.

Québec

Miscou Island

Caraquet

Acadian Historic Village

Tracadie

Bathurst

Cabano

Kedgwick

Saint-Quentin

Edmundston

Clair

Grand Falls

New Brunswick

▲ Mount Carleton 820m

Miramichi

Konchibouguac National Park

Saint Louis de Kent

Maine

Chamberlain Lake

Doaktown

Bouctouche

Southwest Miramichi River

Little Southwest Miramichi R.

Shediac

Moncton

FREDERICTON

Grand Lake

Sussex

Fundy National Park

Alma

St Croix River

Saint John River

St Martins

St Stephen

Saint John

St Andrews

Bay of Fundy

Wilsons Beach

Bangor

Machias

Grand Harbour

Grand Manan Island

Annapolis Royal

Ellsworth

Belfast

Brier Island

Westport

Kejimkujik National Park

Lake Rossignol

Bridge

Yarmouth

Shelburne

CANADA

USA

Elevation	
	600m
	450m
	300m
	150m
	Sea Level

68°W   66°W

46°N

44°N

CANADA'S MARITIME PROVINCES

64°W

62°W

60°W

48°N

Charlottetown
The birthplace of Canada, this charming provincial capital has well preserved streets and parks, plus an excellent choice of pubs.

Îles de la Madeleine

Cabot Trail
The region's most famous drive takes you past whale-watching venues, hiking trails, wildlife, quaint villages and marvelous scenery.

Gulf of St Lawrence

0   35   70 km
0   20   40 miles

Tignish

Alberton

12

Prince Edward Island

2

Cavendish

Cape Breton Island

Cabot Trail

Cape Breton Highlands National Park

Ingonish Beach

Chéticamp

11

Summerside

6

16

Cabot Trail

Souris

2

15

2

Inverness

Cabot Trail

Cape Tormentine

1

4

19

105

Borden-Carleton

Charlottetown

3

Lake Ainslie

223

4

Sydney

22

16

Montague

252

Iona

Big Pond

327

Louisbourg

Northumberland Strait

Wood Islands

1

Bras d'Or Lake

46°N

Amherst

6

Cape George

Louisbourg
This is Canada's largest historic reconstruction, 18th-century New France brought back to life.

104

4

245

104

Pictou

Antigonish

344

Isle Madame

104

Trans Canada Hwy

347

7

Truro

16

Canso

374

Nova Scotia

Sherbrooke

316

Sherbrooke Village
Nineteenth-century life is recreated in this large pioneer village of 28 authentic historic buildings.

14

Shubenacadie

olfville

Lake Charlotte

102

or

101

7

HALIFAX

ATLANTIC

OCEAN

Halifax
The only big city in the Maritimes, Halifax has a stunning waterfront and countless cafes, restaurants and pubs.

44°N

nburg

Lunenburg
This almost intact 18th- and 19th-century town is the region's only world heritage site.

64°W

62°W

60°W

Canada's Maritime Provinces
1st edition – July 2002

Published by
Lonely Planet Publications Pty Ltd ABN 36 005 607 983
90 Maribyrnong St, Footscray, Victoria 3011, Australia

Lonely Planet Offices
Australia Locked Bag 1, Footscray, Victoria 3011
USA 150 Linden St, Oakland, CA 94607
UK 10a Spring Place, London NW5 3BH
France 1 rue du Dahomey, 75011 Paris

Photographs
Many of the images in this guide are available for licensing from
Lonely Planet Images.
W www.lonelyplanetimages.com

Front cover photograph
Peggy's Cove Lighthouse in Halifax, Nova Scotia (John McInnes)

ISBN 1 74059 023 6

text & maps © Lonely Planet Publications Pty Ltd 2002
photos © photographers as indicated 2002

Printed through Colorcraft Ltd, Hong Kong
Printed in China

Contents

INTRODUCTION 11

FACTS ABOUT CANADA'S MARITIME PROVINCES 13

History 13
Geography 15
Climate 15
Ecology & Environment . . 16
Flora 17
Fauna 17

National &
Provincial Parks 18
Government & Politics . . . 20
Economy 21
Population & People 21
Education 24

Arts 24
Society & Conduct 28
Religion 28
Language 28

FACTS FOR THE VISITOR 30

The Best & Worst 30
Suggested Itineraries 31
Planning 32
Responsible Tourism 33
Tourist Offices 33
Visas & Documents 34
Embassies & Consulates . . 36
Customs 37
Money 38
Post & Communications . . 41
Digital Resources 43
Books 44
Films 46
Newspapers & Magazines 46
Radio & TV 46

Video Systems 47
Photography & Video . . . 47
Time 47
Electricity 47
Weights & Measures 47
Laundry 48
Toilets 48
Health 48
Women Travelers 50
Gay & Lesbian Travelers . . 50
Disabled Travelers 50
Senior Travelers 51
Travel with Children 51
Useful Organizations 51
Dangers & Annoyances . . 52

Emergencies 53
Legal Matters 53
Business Hours 53
Public Holidays 54
Special Events 54
Activities 55
Courses 58
Work 58
Accommodations 58
Food 62
Drinks 64
Entertainment 65
Shopping 65

GETTING THERE & AWAY 67

Air 67
Land 72
Sea 74

GETTING AROUND 75

Air 75
Bus 75
Train 76

Car & Motorcycle 76
Bicycle 79
Hitchhiking 80

Ferry 80
Local Transportation 81
Organized Tours 81

FACTS ABOUT NOVA SCOTIA 82

History 82
Climate 83
Economy 83

Population & People 83
Information 83
Activities 84

Accommodations 85

HALIFAX 86

Dartmouth 110

SOUTHWESTERN NOVA SCOTIA — 114

Prospect 114
Peggy's Cove 114
St Margaret's Bay 115
Chester 116
Tancook Islands 117
Mahone Bay 118
Lunenburg 119
Bridgewater 124
LaHave 125
LaHave Islands 126

Liverpool 126
Seaside Adjunct Kejimkujik
National Park 128
Shelburne 128
Barrington 131
Barrington to Yarmouth . 132
Yarmouth to Windsor .. 132
Yarmouth 132
Darling Lake 135
French Shore 136

Digby 137
Digby Neck 139
Bear River 142
Kejimkujik National Park 142
Annapolis Valley 144
North of Kentville 150
Wolfville 150
Grand Pré 153
Windsor 153

CENTRAL NOVA SCOTIA — 158

Shubenacadie 158
Maitland &
Shubenacadie Canal ... 159
Truro 159
Chignecto 164
Amherst 168

Sunrise Trail 170
Tidnish 170
Pugwash 170
Wentworth 171
Tatamagouche 171
Around Tatamagouche.. 172

Pictou 173
Around Pictou 175
Antigonish 177
Around Antigonish..... 178

EASTERN SHORE — 180

Lawrencetown Beach .. 180
Porters Lake
Provincial Park 180
Musquodoboit Harbour 180
Jedore Oyster Pond 181
Tangier 181

Taylor Head
Provincial Park 181
Sheet Harbour 182
Port Dufferin 182
Liscomb Mills 183
Sherbrooke 184

Port Bickerton 184
Country Harbour 184
Canso 185
Guysborough 185

CAPE BRETON ISLAND — 186

Port Hastings 186
Mabou 188
Inverness 189
Margaree Valley 190
Margaree Harbour ... 191
Belle Côte 191
Chéticamp 191
Cape Breton Highlands
National Park 194

Pleasant Bay 196
Cape North 197
Ingonish 198
St Ann's 200
Big Bras d'Or 200
North Sydney 201
Sydney 202
Around Sydney 206
Louisbourg 208

Louisbourg
National Historic Site ... 209
Baddeck 210
Around Bras d'Or Lake . 213
South of Bras d'Or Lake 213
Sable Island 215

PRINCE EDWARD ISLAND — 216

**Facts about Prince Edward
Island 216**
Charlottetown 222
**Kings Byway
Scenic Drive 233**
Orwell 233
Wood Islands 234
Murray River 234

Montague & Around ... 234
Georgetown 235
Souris 235
Basin Head 237
East Point 237
Elmira & North Lake ... 237
St Margaret's &
Naufrage 238

St Peters 238
Greenwich 238
Mount Stewart to
Tracadie 238
**Blue Heron
Scenic Drive 239**
Borden-Carleton 239
Victoria 239

Prince Edward Island
National Park & Around   240
New London 249
Park Corner 249
Malpeque Bay 250
Kensington 250

Lady Slipper
Scenic Drive 250
Summerside 251
Région Évangéline 254
Tyne Valley 254

Lennox Island
First Nation 255
Alberton 255
Tignish to North Cape . . 255
The West Coast 257

NEW BRUNSWICK   258

Facts about
New Brunswick 258
Fredericton 260
Saint John
River Valley 270
Mactaquac 270
Woodstock 271
Hartland 272
Florenceville 273
Grand Falls 273
Edmundston 274
Saint-Jacques 278
West Fundy Shore 278
St Stephen 278
St Andrews 281
Fundy Isles 287
New River
Provincial Park 298
Saint John 298
Central Fundy Shore . . . 312

St Martins 312
Fundy Trail Parkway . . . 313
Fundy National Park . . . 314
Alma 316
Cape Enrage 317
Shepody Bay
Shorebird Reserve 317
Hopewell Rocks 317
Hillsborough 318
Moncton to Sackville . . 318
Moncton 318
Saint-Joseph 327
Dorchester 327
Sackville 328
Fort Beauséjour
National Historic Site . . . 329
Northumberland Shore. . 330
Cape Jourimain 330
Shediac 331
Bouctouche 332

Saint-Louis-de-Kent   . . . 334
Kouchibouguac
National Park 334
Northeastern
New Brunswick 335
Miramichi River 336
Red Bank First Nation . . 336
Miramichi 336
Burnt Church
First Nation 341
Caraquet 341
Caraquet to Bathurst . . . 342
Bathurst 344
Petit-Rocher 344
Eel River First Nation . . . 345
Dalhousie 345
Campbellton 346
Kedgwick 347
Mount Carleton
Provincial Park 348

GLOSSARY   350

INDEX   352

MAP LEGEND   360

CANADA'S MARITIME PROVINCES MAP INDEX

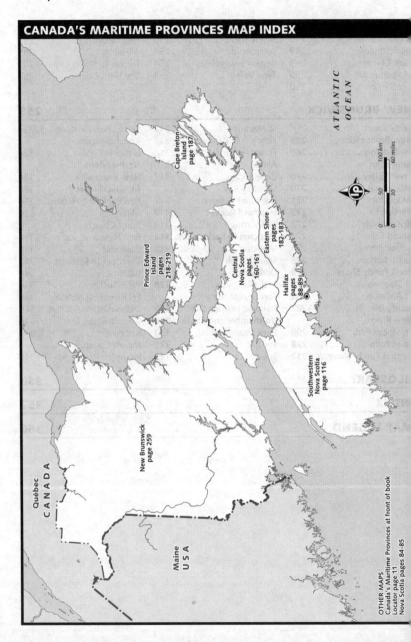

ATLANTIC OCEAN

Cape Breton Island page 181

Prince Edward Island pages 218-219

Central Nova Scotia pages 160-161

Eastern Shore pages 182-183

Halifax pages 88-89

Southwestern Nova Scotia page 116

New Brunswick page 259

Québec
CANADA

Maine
USA

OTHER MAPS:
Canada's Maritime Provinces at front of book
Locator page 11
Nova Scotia pages 84-85

0   50   100 km
0   30   60 miles

The Author

David Stanley

David Stanley studied Spanish literature at schools in Canada, Mexico and Spain, ending with an honors degree from the University of Guelph, Ontario. Stanley has spent much of the past three decades on the road, with visits to 174 of the planet's 244 countries and territories. He has crossed six continents overland.

During the 1980s, he wrote pioneering travel guidebooks to Alaska and the Yukon and the Pacific Islands. His *South Pacific Handbook,* now in its 7th edition, was the original guide to the South Seas. Just prior to the fall of the Berlin Wall, he led Lonely Planet into Eastern Europe with the first three editions of *Eastern Europe on a shoestring,* which he researched and wrote single-handed. He also prepared the first two editions of Lonely Planet's *Cuba* from scratch. Many other writers have followed in his footsteps.

FROM THE AUTHOR

I'm grateful for having been given the opportunity to introduce this memorable region of Canada to world travelers. As an Ontario boy, I'm a longstanding admirer of the gentler, friendlier lifestyle in the Maritimes, where the almighty dollar hasn't yet been crowned king. As travel destinations go, these three provinces are comparable to the best in the world.

I researched this book on my own and have no chaperons to thank. If I'm indebted to anyone, it's the provincial tourist offices whose excellent printed materials allowed me to zero in on the type of facilities travelers want. I hope Maritimers will be able to accept this book for what it is – a frank examination of their realm by a visitor. And I trust readers will find more herein than they could have got for free from the brochures.

Special thanks to Cyndi Gilbert of the Sierra Club of Canada, Sharon Labchuk of Earth Action PEI, James R Culbert of Rainbow Lodge and Geoffrey Milder of Halifax, who pointed out areas worthy of attention. However, the one person whose advice and support made it all possible for me was my wife, Ria de Vos.

This Book

This 1st edition of *Canada's Maritime Provinces* was written by David Stanley. Portions of the text originally came from the Nova Scotia, New Brunswick and Prince Edward Island chapters of the 7th edition of *Canada*, which were originally written by Mark Lightbody and more recently updated by Thomas Huhti.

FROM THE PUBLISHER

This book was edited in LP's Oakland office by Wade Fox, with lots of help from senior editor David Zingarelli. We're grateful to baby Caleb, who held off his arrival just long enough for Wade to wrap up his editorial duties on the book. Tom Valtin proofed the text, and Ken DellaPenta created the index.

Margaret Livingston created the cover (with the help of Susan Rimerman) and created the color pages and laid out the book.

Justin Marler coordinated the illustrations and drew the sidebar trim, chapter end and original illustrations for this book. Further illustrations were drawn by Mark Butler, Hugh D'Andrade, Hayden Foell and Martin Harris.

Laurie Mikkelsen was the lead cartographer for this project. Anneka Imkamp, Laurie and Rudie Watzig drew maps. Ed Turley was the cartographic data specialist, with help from Molly Green and John Spelman. Buck Cantwell, Brad Lodge, Graham Neale, Carole Nuttall, Patrick Phelan, Terence Philippe and Herman So did the base map edits. Tim Lohnes was the main cartographic technical coordinator, with help from Chris Howard. Mapping was supervised by senior cartographers Tracey Croom and Bart Wright. As always, Alex Guilbert was king of all mapworld.

Foreword

ABOUT LONELY PLANET GUIDEBOOKS

The story begins with a classic travel adventure: Tony and Maureen Wheeler's 1972 journey across Europe and Asia to Australia. Useful information about the overland trail did not exist at that time, so Tony and Maureen published the first Lonely Planet guidebook to meet a growing need.

From a kitchen table, then from a tiny office in Melbourne (Australia), Lonely Planet has become the largest independent travel publisher in the world, an international company with offices in Melbourne, Oakland (USA), London (UK) and Paris (France).

Today Lonely Planet guidebooks cover the globe. There is an ever-growing list of books, and there's information in a variety of forms and media. Some things haven't changed. The main aim is still to help make it possible for adventurous travelers to get out there – to explore and better understand the world.

At Lonely Planet we believe travelers can make a positive contribution to the countries they visit – if they respect their host communities and spend their money wisely. Since 1986 a percentage of the income from each book has been donated to aid projects and human-rights campaigns.

Updates Lonely Planet thoroughly updates each guidebook as often as possible. This usually means there are around two years between editions, although for more unusual or more stable destinations the gap can be longer. Check the imprint page (usually following the color map at the beginning of the book) for publication dates.

Between editions up-to-date information is available in two free newsletters – the paper *Planet Talk* and email *Comet* (to subscribe, contact any Lonely Planet office) – and on our Web site at www.lonelyplanet.com. The *Upgrades* section of the Web site covers a number of important and volatile destinations and is regularly updated by Lonely Planet authors. *Scoop* covers news and current affairs relevant to travelers. And, lastly, the *Thorn Tree* bulletin board and *Postcards* section of the site carry unverified, but fascinating, reports from travelers.

Correspondence The process of creating new editions begins with the letters, postcards and emails received from travelers. This correspondence often includes suggestions, criticisms and comments about the current editions. Interesting excerpts are immediately passed on via newsletters and the Web site, and everything goes to our authors to be verified when they're researching on the road. We're keen to get more feedback from organizations or individuals who represent communities visited by travelers.

Lonely Planet gathers information for everyone who's curious about the planet – and especially for those who explore it firsthand. Through guidebooks, phrasebooks, activity guides, maps, literature, newsletters, image library, TV series and Web site we act as an information exchange for a worldwide community of travelers.

Research Authors aim to gather sufficient practical information to enable travelers to make informed choices and to make the mechanics of a journey run smoothly. They also research historical and cultural background to help enrich the travel experience and allow travelers to understand and respond appropriately to cultural and environmental issues.

Authors don't stay in every hotel because that would mean spending a couple of months in each medium-size city and, no, they don't eat at every restaurant because that would mean stretching belts beyond capacity. They do visit hotels and restaurants to check standards and prices, but feedback based on readers' direct experiences can be very helpful.

Many of our authors work undercover; others aren't so secretive. None of them accept freebies in exchange for positive write-ups. And none of our guidebooks contain any advertising.

Production Authors submit their manuscripts and maps to offices in Australia, the USA, UK or France. Editors and cartographers – all experienced travelers themselves – then begin the process of assembling the pieces. When the book finally hits the shops, some things are already out of date, we start getting feedback from readers and the process begins again...

WARNING & REQUEST

Things change – prices go up, schedules change, good places go bad and bad places go bankrupt – nothing stays the same. So, if you find things better or worse, recently opened or long since closed, please tell us and help make the next edition even more accurate and useful. We genuinely value all the feedback we receive. A well-traveled team reads and acknowledges every letter, postcard and email and ensures that every morsel of information finds its way to the appropriate authors, editors and cartographers for verification.

Everyone who writes to us will find their name listed in the next edition of the appropriate guidebook. They will also receive the latest issue of *Planet Talk*, our quarterly printed newsletter, or *Comet*, our monthly email newsletter. Subscriptions to both newsletters are free. The very best contributions will be rewarded with a free guidebook.

We may edit, reproduce and incorporate your comments in all Lonely Planet products, such as guidebooks, Web sites and digital products, so let us know if you don't want your comments reproduced or your name acknowledged.

Send all correspondence to the Lonely Planet office closest to you:

Australia: Locked Bag 1, Footscray, Victoria 3011
USA: 150 Linden St, Oakland, CA 94607
UK: 10a Spring Place, London NW5 3BH
France: 1 rue du Dahomey, 75011 Paris

Or email us at: talk2us@lonelyplanet.com.au

For news, views and updates, see our Web site: www.lonelyplanet.com

HOW TO USE A LONELY PLANET GUIDEBOOK

The best way to use a Lonely Planet guidebook is any way you choose. At Lonely Planet, we believe the most memorable travel experiences are often those that are unexpected, and the finest discoveries are those you make yourself. Guidebooks are not intended to be used as if they provided a detailed set of infallible instructions!

Contents All Lonely Planet guidebooks follow roughly the same format. The Facts about the Destination chapters or sections give background information ranging from history to weather. Facts for the Visitor gives practical information on issues like visas and health. Getting There & Away gives a brief starting point for researching travel to and from the destination. Getting Around gives an overview of the transport options when you arrive.

The peculiar demands of each destination determine how subsequent chapters are broken up, but some things remain constant. We always start with background, then proceed to sights, places to stay, places to eat, entertainment, getting there and away, and getting around information – in that order.

Heading Hierarchy Lonely Planet headings are used in a strict hierarchical structure that can be visualized as a set of Russian dolls. Each heading (and its following text) is encompassed by any preceding heading that is higher on the hierarchical ladder.

Entry Points We do not assume guidebooks will be read from beginning to end, but that people will dip into them. The traditional entry points are the list of contents and the index. In addition, however, some books have a complete list of maps and an index map illustrating map coverage.

There may also be a color map that shows highlights. These highlights are dealt with in greater detail in the Facts for the Visitor chapter, along with planning questions and suggested itineraries. Each chapter covering a geographical region usually begins with a locator map and another list of highlights. Once you find something of interest in a list of highlights, turn to the index.

Maps Maps play a crucial role in Lonely Planet guidebooks and include a huge amount of information. A legend is printed on the back page. We seek to have complete consistency between maps and text and to have every important place in the text captured on a map. Map key numbers usually start in the top left corner.

Although inclusion in a guidebook usually implies a recommendation, we cannot list every good place. Exclusion does not necessarily imply criticism. In fact there are a number of reasons why we might exclude a place – sometimes it is simply inappropriate to encourage an influx of travelers.

Introduction

Canada's Maritime provinces harbor an unexpected wealth of natural and historic wonders world travelers scarcely know. While the great wildlife parks of Alberta and the jagged mountains of British Columbia are heavily promoted, the soaring cliffs, lonely coastlines and unexplored trails of Nova Scotia, Prince Edward Island and New Brunswick receive little attention. Few recognize that Halifax rivals Toronto for nightlife, or that the museum town Lunenburg is almost comparable to Québec City.

Twice a day the highest tides in the world pump water in and out of the Bay of Fundy, allowing one to walk on the ocean's floor or witness a tidal bore surge up one of the region's rivers. At the mouth of the Bay of Fundy and along the coast of Cape Breton,

great whales come to bask in summer. In recent years the Maritimes have become a mecca for adventure tourists, especially kayakers and bicyclists. On Prince Edward Island a disused railway line has been converted into Canada's finest long-distance bicycle trail.

Yet for many, the essence of the Maritimes are their unpretentious, warmhearted people. Here at least, the term 'friendly' is not just a cliché – it really fits. Maritimers are invariably eager to share their treasures with strangers. At a thousand B&Bs all across the region, local people welcome visitors into their homes, and the musical traditions run deep. You don't need to go all the way to Scotland or Ireland to experience world-class folksinging and dancing.

11

Canadians of French or First Nation ancestry are also pleased to introduce you to their cultures. And from Maritime seas come a bounty of foods guaranteed to delight even the most jaded gourmet.

Best of all, this compact region is readily accessible from the rest of Canada and abroad. If you get an early start, you can drive there in a day from Toronto or New York, and flights arrive from Europe and much of North America. There are trains from Montréal, ferries from the US and numerous buses from points west. Information is readily available, and there's so much to see and do that you'll barely scratch the surface in a single visit. A wide welcome mat awaits you down east, on Canada's Atlantic doorstep.

Facts about Canada's Maritime Provinces

The term 'Maritime provinces' refers collectively to three of Canada's four east coast provinces – New Brunswick, Prince Edward Island and Nova Scotia. Add Newfoundland and Labrador to the equation and you have what is referred to as the Atlantic provinces. Canadians living west of this region often refer to Ontario and Québec as eastern Canada, when that area is rightly central Canada.

Western Canadians tend to forget that there's anything east of the Great Lakes at all. For them, Toronto – not Halifax – is the metropolis 'back east.' Despite these slights, Maritimers are well aware that their region has often played a central role in Canada's development.

The Maritime provinces are a geographical extension of New England, a pocket-sized region rich in history and natural wonders. These shores witnessed the first contacts between Europeans and the aboriginal inhabitants of North America. Then came French colonists intent on taming the marshes of Acadia. Britain and France fought a war here to determine ownership of the continent, and subsequent masses of English-speaking immigrants changed the ethnic character of the land. First came Loyalists from the rebellious 13 Colonies, then sturdy farmers and tradespeople from the British Isles. This compact region's historical and cultural roots set it quite apart from all its neighbors.

HISTORY
Original Inhabitants

When Europeans arrived in the Maritimes in the early 1600s, they encountered the Mi'kmaq and Maliseet peoples, members of the Algonquin-speaking eastern woodlands tribes. Although less sophisticated than the Indians of Central and South America, the Maritime First Nations had developed complex customs, religious beliefs, trading patterns, arts and crafts, skills, laws and governments.

They practiced agriculture and lived in more or less permanent settlements. Hunting, fishing and gathering were also important. The main tribes were comprised of smaller bands that came together in winter or in times of celebration or hardship and when marriage partners were sought.

European explorers and pioneers, both intentionally and by accident, nearly destroyed the culture and way of life of the Mi'kmaq and Maliseet. Diseases were introduced, and the tribes were forced to side with either the French or the English in their seemingly never-ending wars. In the end they wound up losing most of their land anyway.

Treaty arrangements provided reservations (now called reserves) and a minimum of support for the survivors, but it was not until 1960 that Canada's First Nations people were finally granted Canadian citizenship. Canada never had the all-out wars and massacres that marred the clash of cultures in the USA, yet Canada's Native Indians harbor numerous grievances stemming from the many rights, freedoms and territories they lost. One need only visit a reserve and speak to anyone living there to verify this.

European Exploration

The first European visitors to Canada were Vikings from Iceland and Greenland. Whether they reached the Maritimes is a subject of debate, but there's ample proof that they settled in northern Newfoundland around AD 1000. How long they stayed, how much they explored and what became of them is unknown.

The French arrived next. After a few earlier exploratory visits by various Europeans, Jacques Cartier, a subject of Francis I of France, reached the gulf of the St Lawrence River in 1534 and claimed all the surrounding area for France. Canada probably got its name from Cartier. *Kanata*, a Huron-Iroquois word for 'village' or 'small

Jacques Cartier, early French explorer

community,' showed up in Cartier's journal, and European mapmakers later transformed it into 'Canada.' The name was used for the St Lawrence area and eventually became the official name of the new country.

The first commodities prized by the French were the fish of the Atlantic coast and furs for the fashion-conscious European market. In search of these, Samuel de Champlain, another Frenchman, began further explorations in the early 1600s. In 1604, he and his party spent the winter on St Croix Island, a tiny islet in the river on the present international border with Maine. The next year Champlain and his patron Sieur de Monts moved their small settlement to Port Royal in the Annapolis Valley, where it endured eight years before being destroyed by the English.

Large scale French colonization only got underway in 1632, with the arrival of immigrants brought by Isaac de Razilly at LaHave, followed in 1635 by others led by Charles de la Tour. French settlers colonized the Annapolis Valley and the shores of the Bay of Fundy, a region they called Acadia.

The Struggle for Power

Things changed in 1713, when the Treaty of Utrecht transferred the peninsula of Nova Scotia to the British. The French retained Cape Breton Island, Prince Edward Island and what is today New Brunswick, erecting a fortress at Louisbourg on Cape Breton Island to defend the sea routes to their main colony at Québec.

In 1745, a British colonial army from Massachusetts moved northeast and captured Louisbourg. The area was soon returned to France, but the struggle for control of the new land continued. In 1749, Halifax was founded, as capital of Britain's 14th colony in America, to counter French power. The British encouraged German Protestants to establish nearby Lunenburg in 1753, further counterbalancing the French Catholics to the northeast.

The conflict known as the French and Indian Wars began in 1754, and the following year a security-conscious British governor of Nova Scotia, Charles Lawrence, ordered the deportation of about 10,000 Acadians after they refused to swear allegiance to Britain. Excluding events involving Native Indians, the expulsion of the Acadians ranks as the darkest moment in Canadian history. In Europe, the Seven Years War began in 1756. The French held the upper hand for the first few years, but in 1758, British Generals Amherst and Wolfe recaptured Louisbourg, followed by Wolfe's capture of the French stronghold at Québec itself in 1759. These major victories signaled the end of the French colonial era, and at the Treaty of Paris in 1763, France handed Canada over to Britain. In 1769, Prince Edward Island was made a British colony separate from Nova Scotia.

Following the removal of the Acadians, their lands in the Annapolis Valley were given to 12,000 New England colonists called 'planters.' Some Acadians chose to return from exile after peace was restored, but they were forced to settle on the less favorable 'French Coast' between Yarmouth and Digby. The next wave of immigrant refugees were English-speaking 'Loyalists' set in motion by the American Revolution

(1775–83) against Britain. North of the Bay of Fundy the Loyalists were so numerous that New Brunswick was spun off as a separate colony in 1784. Cape Breton too was separated from the peninsula in 1784, but in 1820 the two portions of present-day Nova Scotia were reunited to reduce administration costs.

British naval power at Halifax was so formidable that during the War of 1812 between Britain and the United States few battles were fought in the Maritimes. All through the first half of the 19th century, shipbuilding made New Brunswick and Nova Scotia wealthy, and Nova Scotia soon boasted the world's fourth-largest merchant marine. The Cunard Line was founded at Halifax in 1840, and immigration from Scotland and Ireland flourished.

Confederation

Nova Scotia and New Brunswick achieved responsible government in 1848 and 1854 respectively, meaning that henceforth the colony's administrations required majority support in the elected legislatures. The uncertainties of the American Civil War gave further impetus to moves to reform Britain's North American colonial system. Conferences at Charlottetown and Québec City in 1864 laid the groundwork for a Confederation of the Canadian colonies, and in 1867 the British North America Act (BNA Act) was passed by the British parliament, establishing the Dominion of Canada. This initially included Ontario, Québec, Nova Scotia and New Brunswick, and in 1873 Prince Edward Island joined the lineup.

Politically and economically, Confederation reoriented the Maritime provinces away from New England and toward central Canada. In 1876 the Intercolonial Railway linked the Maritimes to Montréal, and by 1885 the ribbon of steel had crossed the continent from Atlantic to Pacific, tying the young nation together. At the time of confederation Nova Scotia was Canada's richest province, but a slow period of decline began as the economic focus shifted toward Ontario. The sudden end of the era

of the wooden sailing ships in the late 19th century was a blow from which the region has never recovered. During both world wars the Maritimes played a key role as a staging area for the convoys that supplied Britain, but even today the Atlantic provinces continue to be financially dependent on subsidies from the federal government in Ottawa.

GEOGRAPHY

The Maritimes are part of the Appalachian Region, which also includes Newfoundland and that portion of Québec south of the St Lawrence River. The land is mainly hilly and wooded. A mere 10,000 years ago the entire region was scraped clean by glaciers, and the continent's rocky mantle is visible in many places. The highest peaks are the rounded summits around Mount Carleton (820m) in north central New Brunswick. On Cape Breton Island, North Barren Mountain reaches 532m.

The distinctive feature of the region is the long coastline, with numerous bays, inlets, headlands, channels and basins. The Bay of Fundy was first mapped by the Portuguese in 1520. They called it Baie Fondo (Deep Bay), and it's well known today for its red cliffs and jack-in-the-box tides. Bucolic Prince Edward Island is not unlike the rolling English countryside, and northern New Brunswick gives a taste of the great Canadian wilderness.

CLIMATE

The Maritime provinces experience four distinct seasons. July and August are the warmest months, with temperatures usually in the mid and upper 20s Celsius. Each year there are a few days in the 30s Celsius. Maritime winters are long, and snowfall can be heavy. Deep snowbanks can remain well into April.

As most cities and towns are along the coasts, elevation doesn't play a major role in most people's daily lives. And in a pocket-sized region like this, latitude doesn't create large climatic variations. What does influence the climate is the sea, especially the warm Gulf Stream in the east.

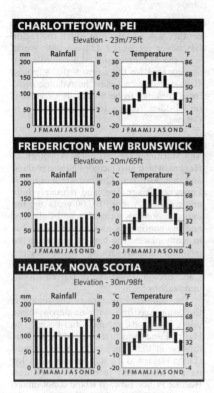

Halifax is cool even in midsummer, due to the sea breeze. This region is generally cooler than the rest of southern Canada and can have more summer rain as well. See the climate charts for more details on specific areas.

ECOLOGY & ENVIRONMENT

Successive governments have favored powerful companies more concerned about profits than the public interest, and environmental controls remain as lax as public opinion will allow. It's been an uphill fight for groups like the Sierra Club, Earth Action and the Conservation Council of New Brunswick to force government officials and private businesses to reduce pollution and clean up the messes they create.

All across the region forests are falling to the chain saws. Clearcutting is universally practiced, destroying the habitats of woodland fauna, and replanting is done using just a few commercially attractive softwood species, thereby further reducing biodiversity. Pulp mill chimneys spew thousands of tons of wastes into the atmosphere every day.

The other major contributor to air pollution is electricity generation. The Maritimes don't have many great rivers to dam, and there's only one nuclear power station, so oil, coal and coke are burned, releasing carbon into the atmosphere.

The coal mines of Cape Breton have now all closed because the soft coal brought up from their shafts is considered too dirty to burn, and the deposits themselves are too dangerous to mine. In northern New Brunswick, lead and zinc are still extracted in large quantities and processed at a smelter north of Bathurst. Sulfuric acid created at the smelter is stored at a former fertilizer plant there, and the entire area is considered so dangerous that no one is allowed to live nearby.

Oil and gas exploration off the coast of Cape Breton Island threatens fish stocks and seabird populations by releasing toxins into the environment. Overfishing has already decimated many fish species, so companies are turning to aquaculture for salvation. Huge enclosures in many bays hold salmon once caught in Maritime rivers. The salmon cages spread fish diseases to the remaining wild stocks and generate wastes. Offshore mussel farming is also a growth industry, though the mussel farms are threatened by pesticides flowing into the sea from potato fields.

On Prince Edward Island the local economy is totally dependent on potato growing and tourism. The potato fields may look quaint, but the pesticides sprayed on them present a health hazard, and huge french fry and potato chip factories create an appalling stench with their cooking oil. In eastern New Brunswick, the stink comes from pig factories where tens of thousands of hogs are held in close quarters to ensure a cheap supply of sausages. Groundwater pollution from this activity is a serious concern. And throughout the region, the red lobster is being trapped to extinction.

Nova Scotia is the site of one of North America's worst environmental nightmares, the Sydney Tar Ponds. For about a century, steel was manufactured in a careless fashion on northern Cape Breton Island, leaving contaminated soils and a vast toxic wasteland in the heart of Nova Scotia's third city. The cleanup will cost many billions, and the politicians are hoping to put it off as long as they can.

Energy

The Maritimes' only nuclear power plant is at Point Lepreau, east of Saint John; further information about it will be found in the New Brunswick chapter. Fossil fuel–burning power plants exist at Belledune, Dalhousie, Dartmouth, New Waterford, Point Aconi, Port Hastings, Saint John and Trenton. To check the emission levels of these facilities, go to W www.pollutionwatch.org. In 1984 a generating station at Annapolis Royal proved capable of harvesting power from tides in the Bay of Fundy, but the experiment hasn't been repeated because fossil fuels are still so cheap.

FLORA

The forests of New Brunswick are half softwood, a quarter hardwood and a quarter mixed. Red, white and black spruce account for half the coniferous softwoods, followed by balsam fir. Spruce is the most commercially important tree for both lumber and pulp production. Balsam fir is also fed into the pulp and paper mills, as well as being cut for Christmas trees. The less common white pine was once used to construct sailing ships.

The deciduous hardwoods are more diversified, with maples, birches and aspen the most important types. The sap of the sugar maple is collected in spring for the production of maple syrup, while the wood is used for quality furniture. The leaves of the red maple turn bright orange in fall. Aboriginal peoples once used the bark of the white birch to make canoes. The trembling aspen

gets its name for the way its leaves flutter in the wind.

Softwoods predominate in the lowlands, hardwoods in the highlands and a mixed forest thrives in between. Soil, water and weather conditions determine which species grow where. The aspen is often the first to recolonize areas devastated by fires.

Apart from the forests, there are numerous other habitats, including marshes, bogs and mudflats. Plants like skunk cabbage, orchids and pitcher plants flourish in the wetlands.

From May to July wildflowers such as lupines, violets, trilliums, lilies and tansies are abundant in the Acadian forest, and blueberries, snowberries and bunchberries yield their fruits in fall.

FAUNA

The land mammals of the Maritimes are those found throughout much of southern Canada, including the beaver, porcupine, raccoon, snowshoe hare, fox, coyote, bobcat, lynx, white-tailed deer and black bear. The moose is the largest land animal in the region.

On Prince Edward Island, foxes are being driven out onto the highways by the destruction of the last remaining pockets of forest on the island and an increase in the

The moose is the largest land animal in the Maritimes.

coyote population. People feeding the foxes also lures them out of the woods.

Nova Scotia has 440 species of bird, from great blue herons along the shorelines to sandpipers in the mudflats. The common tern nests in large colonies on beaches and islands for defense. Nova Scotia's bald eagle population is the largest east of the Rockies. Seabirds abound offshore, including puffins and shearwaters.

In spring and summer, the endangered piping plover builds its nest directly on sandy beaches along the north shore of Prince Edward Island, on the west coast of New Brunswick and on the southwest side of Nova Scotia.

In fall the birds migrate south to Florida and the Caribbean for the winter. The piping plover is highly vulnerable to disturbance by people (and dogs) sharing the same beach.

Over a dozen species of whale frequent these waters from July to October. Whales are most often seen off the islands at the mouth of the Bay of Fundy, including Deer Island and Grand Manan in New Brunswick and Brier Island in Nova Scotia. The most abundant Bay of Fundy whale is the finback, followed by the humpback, minke and endangered right whale. Off Cape Breton Island you're more likely to see smaller pilot whales, but finbacks, humpbacks and minkes also frequent the Atlantic and the Gulf of St Lawrence. On many whale-watching trips, you'll pass seals, porpoises and dolphins.

NATIONAL & PROVINCIAL PARKS

Canada's Maritime provinces contain five national parks and dozens of provincial parks. The only sizable provincial parks are Mount Carleton in north central New Brunswick and Cape Chignecto on the Bay of Fundy. All the national parks and many of the provincial parks have campgrounds. Hiking trails are found in almost all, as are picnic tables. Otherwise there's a lot of variety; the parks run by the federal government and the three provinces are managed in four quite different ways.

Of the national parks, Cape Breton Highlands is the oldest and largest. Most visitors see this park from the Cabot Trail, a paved highway, and surprisingly, there are no long hiking trails into the interior. Kejimkujik, also in Nova Scotia, is ideal for canoeing, and it gives you an idea what the entire region must have been like in pre-European times. Fundy, on the New Brunswick coast, offers something for everyone, from a variety of backcountry trails, lots of short trails and points of interest, recreational facilities and accessible wildlife. New Brunswick's other park, Kouchibouguac, is oriented toward family beach holidays, as is Prince Edward Island National Park. You might see moose at Cape Breton Highlands, Kejimkujik and Fundy, whales at Cape Breton Highlands and seals at Kouchibouguac National Park.

National park admissions average $3.50/10.50 for 1/4 days for an adult or $7/21 for a family. An excellent deal is the Atlantic Pass, which covers admission to all five Maritimes parks plus two in Newfoundland for the entire season at $38 adults, $19 children aged six to 16, $75 family, $28 seniors. For some reason this pass isn't widely promoted at the parks and you must specifically request it. The national parks only charge admission from mid-May to mid-September. Other months you can often enter for free, although the campgrounds, toilets and visitor centers may be closed. Campsite reservation policies and facilities differ; for more information turn to the individual park listings later in this book. Cape Breton Highlands, Kejimkujik and Fundy have golf courses and chalets, if that's your idea of wilderness.

As elsewhere in Canada, the national parks tend to be victims of their own success as visitors arrive in increasing numbers every year. In contrast, the provincial parks – especially those of Nova Scotia – offer some of the last easily accessible natural areas in the region where you can still be alone, even in mid-summer. For more information on Canadian national parks, check out the Parks Canada Web site at Ⓦ www.parkscanada.gc.ca.

Nova Scotia Parks

For nature lovers, the provincial parks of Nova Scotia are far and away the best in the Maritimes. You won't find any golf courses, tourist resorts, restaurants or trailer parks here. Development has been kept to a minimum, and there are only unserviced campsites with a picnic table. Because they're so simple (no electrical hookups), the Nova Scotia parks don't attract the hordes of RVs and campers you see elsewhere, a definite plus. Camping fees vary from $14 to $18 per site, depending on whether showers and flush toilets are provided. Most parks have hiking trails and picnic areas, and day use of all parks is free. Opening dates are provided in the individual listings.

Campsite reservation policies vary from park to park. Usually you can reserve a site by calling the individual park directly between 8:30am and 4:30pm and providing your credit card number. There's no additional fee for this service, but you cannot request a specific site – you must choose from whatever is available when you arrive. You'll be charged if you cancel less than 24 hours in advance or don't show up. In practice, it's unnecessary to reserve in June or September, and even in July and August you'll often get a site without a reservation, as the parks hold back four or five sites for travelers. Days when you *should* reserve are Fridays and Saturdays from mid-July to mid-August, as the parks do fill at those times. By noon Sunday lots of vacancies will have appeared as local families head home.

Noteworthy Nova Scotia provincial parks include Thomas Raddall and The Islands on the South Shore, Valleyview and Blomidon just off the Annapolis Valley, Five Islands and Cape Chignecto south of Amherst, Porters Lake and Taylor Head on the Eastern Shore and Battery at St Peters on Cape Breton. All of those except Taylor Head have campgrounds, and Cape Chignecto contains a major backcountry hiking route.

Keep in mind that only a minority of provincial parks in Nova Scotia have campgrounds. The rest of the parks resemble what might be called roadside rest areas in other provinces (the official term is 'picnic park'). The Nova Scotia Department of Natural Resources deserves credit for the way they administer their parks, and readers interested in a natural holiday should take this into consideration when allocating their time in the Maritimes. For more information, check the Nova Scotia Provincial Parks Web site (W parks.gov.ns.ca).

Prince Edward Island Parks

Unfortunately, the other two provinces haven't done as well as Nova Scotia with their parks. Many of the Prince Edward Island provincial parks are dominated by crowded tourist resorts, and over half of their campsites have multiple hookups intended for recreational vehicles. Most PEI parks open only for eight to 10 weeks in midsummer, and then they're suddenly packed, as 80% of the sites are reservable.

From early September to late June, almost all PEI provincial parks are chained shut. To use them during the off-season, you must park your car on the highway and walk in along sometimes long access roads. That's assuming you can find the park at all, as the signposting is removed in the fall. On the plus side, the parks don't charge any day-use fees, and they're rather numerous. Check the PEI provincial government site for more information on the province's parks (W www.gov.pe.ca/visitorsguide/explore/parks).

New Brunswick Parks

Many New Brunswick provincial parks have been privatized and are now run as ordinary RV resorts. Others have been converted into commercial tourist attractions where stiff entry fees are charged and camping is not allowed. The desire to turn a profit has led to golf courses and chalets being constructed in most parks still run by the government.

That said, the nine remaining parks vary greatly, and a few are outstanding. When the national park system was being extended to the Maritimes a century ago, Mount Carleton almost became the region's first national park. Instead it was made a provincial park, the closest equivalent in the Maritimes to Ontario's famous Algonquin Park. Herring Cove and The Anchorage in the Fundy Isles are the best places to stay on Campobello and Grand Manan respectively. Most of the other parks are family recreation facilities with busy campgrounds. Some New Brunswick parks charge a $5 day-use fee, though only from late May to early September as the gates are not staffed other months. For more information, contact the New Brunswick tourism Web site (W www.tourismnbcanada.com/web/english/outdoor_network).

GOVERNMENT & POLITICS

Canada is a constitutional monarchy with an appointed governor general who claims to represent the British monarch. In practice, this person is a ceremonial figurehead who presides on formal occasions but has no authority. Although Queen Elizabeth II is officially Canada's head of state and her image appears on Canadian currency, neither she nor the UK government have any say in the way the country is run. In a divided world, Canada's international prestige is enhanced by its Commonwealth membership, and most Canadians value the old British connections, as they help balance the overwhelming influence of the USA.

At the federal level, Canada has a parliamentary system with two houses. The upper house, or Senate, made up of political appointees, is deemed to be the house of review regarding potential legislation. Mostly it acts as a rubber stamp for the wishes of the elected lower house, or House of Commons. Senate reform, or its abolition, is an ongoing debate within the country.

The head of the political party with the most elected representatives in the House of Commons becomes prime minister, the leader of government. From the members of parliament within the governing party, the prime minister selects a cabinet that, in effect, runs the country and initiates legislation. Unlike in the USA, leaders can continue for as long as they enjoy political

support within their party. Governments are elected for five year terms, but elections can be called earlier by the prime minister.

The 10 provinces are essentially self-governing and are presided over by premiers. Each province has an elected provincial legislature that functions along the same lines as the federal House of Commons. The lieutenant governor of each province is appointed to the post by the federal government.

The constitution consists of written proclamations under the Constitution Acts (1867 and 1932) and unwritten conventions. Updating, changing and clarifying constitutional matters, and the division of powers between the provinces and the federal government, are ongoing contentious issues. Each of the 10 Canadian provinces has as many or more powers than the 50 American states, and a lot more authority than provinces or regions in Europe.

Political Parties

Three political parties routinely elect members in the Maritimes at both the provincial and federal levels. The Liberal Party has dominated the federal parliament through most of the country's history. Their traditional rival, the Progressive Conservative Party, espouses policies very similar to those of the Liberals, and voters happily elect them whenever the Liberals appear to have become complacent or arrogant. The third party, the left-leaning New Democratic Party (NDP), has never come close to forming a government on the federal level. It often presents itself as the conscience of the Liberals, and Canada's system of universal health care and some other social ini tiatives are a result of NDP influence.

On the provincial level, the three main parties remain the Liberals, the Conserva tives and the NDP. The provincial partie generally keep their distance from thei federal cousins and act independently fron them. The voters, too, treat them differently While the Liberals have controlled the federal parliament in Ottawa since 1993, the Conservatives currently run all three pro vincial governments in the Maritimes. Ther have also been Liberal provincial governments, but the NDP has never done better than third place in any of these provinces – despite the fact that the leader of the federal NDP is from Nova Scotia and many of her fellow NDP members in the federal parliament are from the region.

ECONOMY

The economy of the Maritimes, like that of the rest of Canada, is based on natural resources, including fish, timber, minerals, natural gas and oil. In New Brunswick and on Prince Edward Island, potato growing plays a key role. Canada's major trading partner, the USA, buys most of the Maritimes' fish and timber products.

The fishing industry has been in crisis in recent years as one species after another is terminally swept from the sea. A moratorium on cod fishing was imposed in 1992, and herring is now the species most fished in the Maritimes, followed by hake and haddock. Among the shellfish, the lobster is the most valuable by far, followed by shrimp and scallops. Nova Scotia's fishery is the most lucrative in Canada, worth double those of New Brunswick and Prince Edward Island combined.

With the region's natural salmon stocks depleted through dam construction and pollution, Atlantic salmon are now farmed in floating sea cages, between 10m and 30m in diameter, moored to the ocean floor. New Brunswick is second only to British Columbia in aquaculture. Mussel and oyster farming on Prince Edward Island are growing fast.

The forest industry is extremely important, with large pulp and paper mills throughout New Brunswick and Nova Scotia. In New Brunswick alone, 28,000 jobs depend directly or indirectly on forestry, and pulp and paper exports are worth a million dollars a year. Almost 99% of the tree harvesting involves clearcutting.

In 2001, the last coal mine on Cape Breton Island and an associated steel mill in Sydney closed down after federal subsidies were withdrawn. Elsewhere in Nova Scotia, a mine at Pugwash produces salt. In New Brunswick, large scale lead and zinc mining continues near Bathurst, and potash is mined near Sussex. Peat mining is done on the Acadian Peninsula and on western Prince Edward Island. Undersea natural gas fields off Sable Island feed pipelines bound for the USA, but the benefits received by Nova Scotia for its natural gas are small compared to the huge profits earned by the oil companies.

Manufacturing has long been a weak component of the economy, though high-tech industries and developers in the space and computer fields are playing increasing roles in the economy. By far the largest part of the economy is in services, which includes the enormous civil service. Banking, insurance, education, communications and consulting bring in foreign exchange. Tourism is also an important money earner throughout the region.

POPULATION & PEOPLE

Together the three Maritime provinces account for just 1% of Canada's landmass but 7% of the country's people live there. The population breakdown is Nova Scotia 941,000 inhabitants, PEI 138,900 and New Brunswick 756,600.

About 65% of Maritimers are of British stock, a result of immigration from Britain and the USA. People of French descent comprise 37% of the population of New Brunswick, 12% of PEI and 9% of Nova Scotia. Throughout the Maritimes, you'll immediately know you're in a French-speaking area when you see the red-white-and-blue Acadian flags painted on utility poles or fluttering in front of houses. The French regions are also recognizable for the large houses strung out along the highways, quite unlike the more compact English-speaking towns and villages.

The French-speaking parts of New Brunswick are Edmundston (85% French), the Acadian Peninsula (Caraquet, Shippagan), the coast from Miramichi to Shediac (mixed English and French) and Moncton (40% French). In Nova Scotia the Acadians originally lived in the Annapolis Valley, but those Acadians who returned after the 1755

An Empire Called Irving

In 1924, KC Irving (1899–1992) opened a garage and service station at Bouctouche, New Brunswick, that would eventually grow into Atlantic Canada's largest business empire. Today the Irving family dominates energy, home heating, pesticides, construction, shipbuilding, forestry, publishing and transportation around the region. All four of New Brunswick's leading newspapers are owned by the family, as are the largest chains of retail gas stations, convenience stores, home improvement centers and the main bus companies. On Prince Edward Island, Irving's Cavendish Farms dominates agriculture by processing the bulk of the island's potato crop. The Web site at W www.jdirving.com lists 63 major companies belonging to the conglomerate.

Initially KC Irving formed an alliance with Standard Oil to ensure a regular supply of fuel. In 1960 Irving Oil opened its own refinery at Saint John, New Brunswick, now one of the largest in North America. In the late 1980s, the company began investing in new technologies to produce low-sulfur gasoline. A billion dollars was spent in 1999 rebuilding the refinery, dramatically reducing greenhouse gas emissions, and by 2001 the sulfur levels in Irving gasoline had been brought down to standards not required by law until January 2005.

Over the years the company has made huge profits clearcutting trees on Crown land, and they own 16 sawmills. The Irving Pulp and Paper Ltd mill next to Saint John's Reversing Falls is one of the city's biggest polluters, although investments are currently being made to reduce the production of wastes at the mill. Much still needs to be done.

Perhaps inevitably, the Irvings have been at the center of public controversy more than once. In September 1970, the 82m barge *Irving Whale* sank in the Gulf of St Lawrence, 60km northeast of Prince Edward Island, with a heavy cargo of 4200 tons of fuel oil aboard. Some 80km of shoreline on the Îles de la Madeleine were contaminated, and 20 liters of oil a day continued to leak from the vessel until it was finally raised by the Canadian government in July 1996. Irving Oil concealed the presence of toxic PCB-based fluids on the *Whale* until June 1995, when it was about to be discovered and made public. The company refused to contribute to the $35 million salvage operation because the barge sank in international waters, and Canada's taxpayers were left holding the bill.

One of the world's richest men, KC Irving moved to Bermuda in 1972 to avoid paying Canadian income tax. Until his death in 1992, KC continued spending half a year plus a day in Bermuda, whereupon his $7 billion estate was placed in a trust to keep it exempt from Canadian tax.

KC Irving wasn't known for his charity, and he used his economic and media might to control politicians, break unions and eliminate competitors. The Irving companies do business with each other as much as possible to keep profits within the group, and have used the threat of moving operations elsewhere to protect their position when challenged by government. The Irvings already own much of New Brunswick, and they're steadily moving into adjacent jurisdictions, including Maine and the rest of New England.

KC's heir, JD Irving, has tried to soften the family's image by building high-profile 'ecotourism' parks near Saint John and Bouctouche, funding research at universities, publicizing the company's 'green' initiatives etc. But the harsh realities of the Irving way of making money were demonstrated in 1996 when the company suddenly commenced logging operations around Nova Nada Monastery, a retreat center deep in the woods near North Kemptville, Nova Scotia. Despite appeals by the monks to JD Irving himself, the company refused to grant the 2-mile 'silence and wilderness' buffer zone that the monks requested, and Nova Nada was abandoned in 1998 after more than a quarter century of existence. The monks have now established the Nova Nada Ecoforestry Award for those who labor to protect Canada's forests.

deportation found their ancestral lands occupied by New Englanders. They settled instead along the French Shore from Yarmouth to Digby. On Cape Breton there are predominantly French populations around Chéticamp and on Île Madame. On PEI the French speakers live from Miscouche to Mont-Carmel.

The Acadians of the Maritimes are a close-knit group who don't consider themselves part of the Québec French community. They're not obsessed with their relationship with English Canada. Until the beginning of the 20th century they lived in relative isolation, which helped them preserve their unique culture.

Over a million Maritimers are of Scottish or Irish ancestry. After the defeat of the Jacobites at the Battle of Culloden (1746) in Scotland, thousands of Highlanders immigrated to Nova Scotia to escape persecution. Some went to Prince Edward Island, and another group arrived at Pictou in 1773 aboard the *Hector*. After a failed rebellion in Ireland in 1798, large numbers of Irish immigrants also began arriving. This immigration grew larger during the depression that followed the Napoleonic wars, and about a million Gaelic-speaking Scots and Irish emigrated from the British Isles during the potato famine of 1846–51. By 1871, Scots were the largest ethnic group in Nova Scotia and Prince Edward Island. In New Brunswick, the Irish are the biggest single ethnic group in places like Saint John and Miramichi.

After 1900, the great waves of European immigrants coming to Canada bypassed the Maritimes entirely and went west by train o colonize the prairies. Instead, the Maritimes became a region of emigration. In the half century up to 1930, over a half million Maritimers left, most of them to the United States.

First Nations People

ome 23,500 Mi'kmaqs and Maliseets live n the three Maritime provinces. Just over 0,000 members of both bands live in New Brunswick, the Maliseets in the upper Saint ohn River valley in the west and the Mi'k-maqs to the east. Some 1000 Mi'kmaqs are on Prince Edward Island. About 12,500 Mi'kmaqs live in Nova Scotia in 14 communities, mostly around Bras d'Or Lake on Cape Breton and near Truro. Together First Nations people account for just over 1% of the Maritimes' total population. Included in these figures are 2000 Métis, the name used to denote those of mixed aboriginal and European blood.

Of course, the region's present political boundaries are not the same as the territories of the Mi'kmaq and Maliseet nations, which stretch well into eastern Maine and the Gaspe region of Québec. If one were to count the entire Mi'kmaq and Maliseet population in eastern North America, both on and off the reserves, they might number 200,000 including non–Native Indian husbands and wives.

Many residents of the 36 First Nations reserves in the Maritimes live in poverty, on some form of government assistance. With little education and few modern skills, many Native Indians end up on the streets of cities like Moncton and Halifax without a job or a place to live. Infant mortality, life expectancy, literacy, income and incarceration rates all compare unfavorably with those of other Canadians.

This situation is largely a result of Canadian governmental policy. When great numbers of Native Indians died from European diseases during the 18th century, the survivors were relocated on small reserves in remote, unfavorable areas. Their hereditary hunting and fishing rights were largely abolished, and their traditional beliefs were attacked by Christian missionaries. Right up until the 1960s, Native Indian children were torn from their parents and placed in 'residential schools' where they were taught English and forcibly assimilated. Traditional ceremonies were banned. Only during the past two decades has a revitalization movement appeared to encourage a return to the original spirituality, culture and language. Native Indian leaders have had to fight a running battle to right some of these historic wrongs. Compensation claims by residential school survivors are presently before the courts, and in recent years Mi'kmaq warriors have had direct physical confrontations with federal officials over fishing, logging and land rights. Each summer Native Indian roadblocks and 'illegal' fishing and logging have disrupted the status quo, and both the federal and provincial governments are finding it increasingly difficult to ignore this state of affairs.

First Nations self-government, education and social services remain dependent on federal handouts, and surprisingly little has been done to change this. Native economic developments that might impact the positions of large corporations are actively opposed by federal officials. At Burnt Church, New Brunswick, for example, despite the 1999 Marshall decision by the Supreme Court of Canada that upheld the right of Native Indians to hunt, fish and gather, the Department of Fisheries and Oceans (DFO) has refused to allow the Mi'kmaq to manage their own fishery, offering only temporary licenses to fish for ceremonial and household use. The entrenched rights of large forestry companies like Fraser and Irving to clearcut Crown land are firmly upheld over native requests to selectively log their ancestral lands on a much smaller scale. First Nation reserves often have huge polluting power plants or pulp mills just outside their boundaries, and the federal government frequently erects prisons adjacent to Native Indian communities.

EDUCATION

Under the jurisdiction of the provinces, Canada provides free education from elementary through to secondary school. Beyond that, tuition must be paid in what are known as community colleges and universities, although the true cost is subsidized through taxes.

At the early levels, there are two basic school systems, known as the public and the separate. Both are free and essentially the same, but the latter is designed for Catholics and offers some religious education along with the three 'Rs.' Anyone can join either school system, but the two do split pretty much along religious denomination.

Education in French is available right up to university level. The Université de Moncton, New Brunswick, and the Université Sainte Anne at Church Point, Nova Scotia, are the region's French cultural pillars.

ARTS
Music & Dance

The most renowned music of this region comes from Cape Breton Island. From marches to jigs and reels, this is a kind of music that's meant to be danced to. Cape Breton music originated in 18th century Scotland. Traditionally a lone bagpiper would provide rhythm for the dancers, as a fiddler and pianist usually do today. More and more, instruments like electric guitars, synthesizers and drums are being added to the lineup. To attend a Cape Breton kitchen party, or *ceilidh,* is an unforgettable experience. Ceilidhs also occur on Prince Edward Island or almost anywhere the Scots and Irish settled.

A difference between the Scottish and Irish versions of Celtic fiddle music is that the Scots favor a solo or duet fiddler/singer, while the Irish often play in ensembles. Cape Breton Scottish groups like the Rankins (now disbanded) and the Barra MacNeils were the exception. The best Cape Breton musicians, such as Ashley MacIsaac, Buddy MacMaster and Natalie MacMaster, combine concert virtuosity with dance discipline.

Acadian/Cajun music has some surprising parallels with Celtic-based music, especially in the traditional fiddling and step dancing. Notable groups include Les Mechants Macquereaux, Blou and Grand Dérangement. Blou has created a new category of Acadian 'world music' called Acadico, a mix of traditional and contemporary music.

Two Nova Scotia vocalists in more of a country vein are Anne Murray from Springhill and Rita McNeil of Big Pond, Cape Breton. Superstar Sarah McLachlan is originally from Halifax. Country singe

Natalie MacMaster, Cape Breton fiddle virtuoso

Stompin' Tom Connors of Saint John, New Brunswick, has become something of a Canadian folk icon for his many songs about issues entwined in the national psyche.

Literature

The literature of the Maritimes is a unique melange of the academic tendencies of the Loyalists, the folk traditions of the Scottish immigrants and the seductive culture of the Acadians. Early political satires were tempered by a certain understated humor, and as in the field of music, woeful Cape Breton has inspired many writers.

In *The Clockmaker* (1836), Nova Scotian Thomas Chandler Haliburton (1796–1865) coined phrases such as 'the early bird gets the worm' and 'you can't get blood out of stone,' which have become part of the language. Haliburton characters like Sam Slick rivaled those of Charles Dickens in popularity, and Mark Twain called Haliburton the 'father of American humor.'

Joseph Howe (1804–1873) is best remembered as a newspaper publisher and politician, yet his speeches, letters, poems and essays have a literary value of their own. This fierce defender of freedom of the press was also an eloquent spokesperson for the natural wonders of Nova Scotia.

Late-19th-century Fredericton was an important literary center, and the Confederation Group there included William Bliss Carman (1861–1929), Archibald Lampman and Duncan Campbell Scott, poets who used unembellished language to paint the beauty of Canada's landscape. The most prominent member of the group was Charles GD Roberts (1860–1943), the 'Father of Canadian poetry.' Childhood memories of New Brunswick's Tantramar marshes provided an inspiration for Roberts's acclaimed animal stories.

Lucy Maud Montgomery (1877–1942) may be the region's most famous writer. Though her children's classic *Anne of Green Gables* (1908) was initially rejected by five publishers, the story of the lively orphan on a farm at Avonlea has since been made into several films and a long-running musical. The book's setting and sites associated with the author around Prince Edward Island have become literary shrines.

Thomas Raddall (1903–1994) brought early Nova Scotia to life in historical novels such as *His Majesty's Yankees* (1942) and *The Governor's Lady* (1960). Raddall's experiences as a radio operator on Sable Island are narrated in *The Nymph and the Lamp* (1950). Raddall left behind a mass of short stories and several history books that are still widely read. *The Mountain and the Valley* (1952), by Raddall's contemporary Ernest Buckler (1908–1984), belongs to the same genre.

The Halifax Explosion of 1917 (see the 'A Christmas Tree for Boston' boxed text in the Halifax chapter) provided Hugh MacLennan (1907–1990) with subject matter for his first novel *Barometer Rising* (1941). In subsequent books like *Each Man's Son* (1951), which was about a Cape Breton mining community, MacLennan portrayed contemporary Canadian life with an immediacy few had previously achieved.

The best known, most widely read Maritimes poet is Milton Acorn (1923–1986) of Prince Edward Island. Called 'the people's poet,' Acorn was denied official recognition for many years due to his left-wing political activities during the 1960s. Only after the publication of *The Island Means Minago* in 1975 was Acorn finally accepted by the cultural tsars in Ottawa who confer literary awards. He later coauthored the play *The Road to Charlottetown* (1977), and his many public readings made him a cult figure of sorts.

Bouctouche novelist Antonine Maillet (born 1929) is the best known New Brunswick Acadian writer. *La Sagouine* (1971), 16 monologues by a disheveled Acadian fisherman's wife, has been adapted for the stage with great success. *Pélagie* (1982) tells the story of the return from exile in Louisiana of a group of 18th-century Acadians. Maillet is a skillful folklorist, and the 17th-century French slang used by her characters has made her writings immensely popular in French Canada and France alike. By converting everyday life into epic, Maillet has assured her place in Canadian literary history.

Mi'kmaq poet Rita Joe (born 1932) from Whycocomagh, Cape Breton Island, is a veteran of the notorious residential school system. Her poems articulate the experiences and feelings of First Nations people in a white world.

One of the region's most prolific modern poets was Alden Nowlan (1933–1983), poet in residence at the University of New Brunswick for 15 years. His book of poems *Bread, Wine and Salt* (1967) has won much praise.

The short stories about Cape Breton by Alistair MacLeod (born 1936) have found a worldwide audience. Tales like *The Lost Salt Gift of Blood* (1976) and *As Birds Bring Forth the Sun* (1986) focus on the hard life of the people. MacLeod's first novel, *No Great Mischief* (1999), traces a family from Scotland to Cape Breton over several generations. His stories convey the Gaelic melancholy and loneliness of the island.

David Adam Richards (born 1950) is author of a brilliant series of novels about life in central and northern New Brunswick. Richards's first novel *The Coming of Winter* (1973) was translated into Russian and became widely read in the former Soviet Union. *Mercy Among the Children* (2000) recounts the vilification of a Miramichi family by their neighbors after the father is falsely accused of arson during a strike and imprisoned.

Painting

Artists began painting Canada as early as the 1700s, and their work has grown to encompass a wide variety of styles and international influences. One of the earliest distinctive Canadian painters was Cornelius Krieghoff, who used the St Lawrence River area of Québec as his subject matter. The Crombie Art Gallery in New Glasgow, Nova Scotia, has a collection of Krieghoff's work.

The region's most celebrated living artist is the modernist realist painter Alex Colville (born 1920), who lives in Wolfville, Nova Scotia. Oblivious to the trendy Toronto art scene, the meticulous craftsman Colville produces only a few paintings and silk screens a year, and they hang in the world's finest galleries.

Fellow realist painter Mary Pratt (born 1935) was born and raised in New Brunswick but moved to Newfoundland in 1963. Colville taught art at Mount Allison University in Sackville, New Brunswick, while Pratt was there as a student.

As intriguing as the academic artists are the self-taught 'folk' or 'naive' artists whose work is often strikingly original and accessible. Maud Lewis (1903–1970) of Digby, Nova Scotia, overcame polio to produce delightful paintings of outdoor scenes. Maud covered the walls of her tiny home with colorful flowers, butterflies and birds, and the panels are now on permanent display at the Art Gallery of Nova Scotia. Earl Bailly (1903–1977) of Lunenburg, also stricken by polio, worked by holding his paintbrush between his teeth. Another artist of note is William deGarthe (1907–1983), whose paintings and sculptures of nautical scenes can be enjoyed at the deGarthe Gallery in Peggy's Cove. Numerous folk artists are encountered in the Acadian regions – watch for signs along the highways, especially near Chéticamp.

Aboriginal artists such as Alan Syliboy born 1952), of the Millbrook First Nation t Truro, have drawn inspiration from ncient petroglyphs found in Kejimkujik lational Park and elsewhere. Syliboy's vebsite (W www.redcrane.ca) provides an xcellent introduction to contemporary li'kmaq art.

The leading establishment galleries here you can sample the region's artistic vealth are the Art Gallery of Nova Scotia in Ialifax, the Confederation Centre of the rts in Charlottetown and the Beaverbrook Irt Gallery in Fredericton. Several univer- ities have prestigious galleries, including ne Dalhousie Art Gallery in Halifax, the Acadia University Art Gallery in Wolfville, ne Galerie d'Art de l'Université de 1oncton and the Owens Art Gallery at 1ount Allison University in Sackville. 1ore radical galleries where emerging rtists can be found include the Khyber 'entre for the Arts in Halifax and Gallery Connexion in Fredericton. Others worthy f note are the Arts Council Gallery at An- apolis Royal, the Fraser Cultural Centre at 'atamagouche and the Aitken Bicentennial xhibition Centre at Saint John.

Cinema

Canadian film is well respected abroad pri- 1arily through the work of the National ilm Board (NFB), whose productions are, erhaps surprisingly, little viewed and carcely known in Canada. Each year the lm board, formed in 1939, releases a com- ination of documentary, dramatic, and ani- 1ated films. Canadian public libraries often ave videos of National Film Board roductions.

Memorable moments in the region's film istory include the day in May 1907 when 1usicians at Saint John's Nickel Theatre ac- ompanied a silent movie for the first time 1 North America and 1913, when the first eature-length film was produced in 'anada, a movie about the Acadians based n Longfellow's poem *Évangéline*. Saint ohn, New Brunswick, is the hometown of 1ovie mogul Louis B Mayer and actors Valter Pidgeon and Donald Sutherland.

Theater

The region's theatrical offerings can be divided into two categories. Serious aca- demic or avant garde productions are gen- erally staged for local audiences during the winter season. In the summer months, the highbrow theaters are closed, or they're used for special 'folkloric' programs de- signed for tourist audiences. Several dozen summer-only theaters around the region depend almost entirely on the patronage of visitors.

The *Anne of Green Gables* musical pre- sented each summer in Charlottetown is easily the most celebrated tourist produc- tion. The French equivalent is *Évangéline* at Church Point, Nova Scotia. Other summer theaters offering this sort of dramatic fare include the Chester Playhouse, the King's Theatre at Annapolis Royal, the Ship's Company Theatre at Parrsboro, the deCoste Entertainment Center in Pictou, the Louis- bourg Playhouse, the King's Playhouse at Georgetown, the Victoria Playhouse, the Jubilee Theatre in Summerside, the Britan- nia Hall Theatre in Tyne Valley and the Live Bait Theatre at Sackville. For summer theater in French, there's the Théâtre Popu- laire d'Acadie at Caraquet, the Théâtre de la Grand-Voile at Shediac and Le Pays de la Sagouine at Bouctouche. Check any of these in July and August.

Summer festivals such as the Atlantic Theatre Festival in Wolfville and the Festi- val Antigonish bring live theater to smaller communities. In summer you can often see unstructured performances in the parks of Fredericton or along the Halifax waterfront, and Shakespeare by the Sea in Halifax's Point Pleasant Park is excellent. The musi- cals at Halifax's two dinner theaters run year-round before an audience of tourists and locals.

The region's leading conventional the- aters are the Neptune Theatre at Halifax, the Playhouse Theatre in Fredericton, the Imperial Theatre in Saint John and the Per- forming Arts Centre in Moncton. If you'll be visiting between October and April, call ahead for program information. The Sir James Dunn Theatre at Halifax's Dalhousie

University presents student theater in the winter. Also of interest is the Mermaid Theatre in Windsor, a children's theater which appears only on tour.

SOCIETY & CONDUCT
Traditional Culture
The Maliseet and Mi'kmaq had a system of beliefs in which there was no sharp division between the sacred and the secular. Europeans did their best to crush the original cultures, and together with disease and loss of land and means of livelihood, they were largely successful. Today the predominant religion among Native Indians in the Maritimes is Christianity, and English is the principal language.

A cultural rebirth, with a revival of Native Indian song and dance, language programs, healing and ritual, now accompanies the legal battles being waged across the region for fishing and timber rights and political autonomy. There's also a small but growing movement back to the traditional spiritual belief systems based on the natural world and the words of the ancestors.

RELIGION
After 1534, the Maritimes were settled by Christians, primarily French and Irish Roman Catholics, and English and Scottish Protestants. The large Irish and French ethnic elements in the Maritimes mean a high percentage of the population is Catholic. Besides Québec, New Brunswick is the only province in Canada with a Catholic majority.

Regardless, formal religion plays an ever-diminishing role in Canadian life. Attendance at the established churches has declined steadily since WWII.

LANGUAGE
There are two official languages in Canada, English and French. You'll notice both on highway signs, maps, tourist brochures and all types of packaging.

English is spoken throughout the region, and even in the French-speaking areas, tourists are expected to speak English. Only around Edmundston, near the Québec

border, will you encounter people wh don't understand English.

Many recent immigrants use thei mother tongue, as do some Native Indian (although in some First Nations commun ties though, it's only older members wh retain their indigenous language). Fe Canadians other than Native Indians spea any aboriginal language, but some word such as 'igloo,' 'parka,' 'muskeg' and 'kayak have entered the common usage.

There's also a patois slang called Chiac, mixture of French and English. The pures form of Chiac is spoken by the Méti people, who are concentrated aroun Moncton.

French
The French spoken in Canada is not, for th most part, the language of France – to Parisian it can be nearly unintelligibl Canadian schools generally teach th French of France, but local dialect persist For example, most people schooled i Parisian French would say *Quelle heure es il?* for 'What time is it?,' but on the streets c the Acadian regions you're likely to hea *Y'est quelle heure?*

Most Acadians understand the mor formal French – it will just strike them as little peculiar. Other differences betwee European and Canadian French you ma wish to remember are the terms for break fast, lunch and dinner. Rather than *petit de jeuner, déjeuner* and *diner,* you're likely t see and hear *déjeuner, diner* and *soupe* Hitchhiking is known not as *auto stop* but a *le pousse* (the thumb).

Acadian French is derived mostly fro the Poitou region of France. The people c New Brunswick's Acadian Peninsula spea an antiquated 18th-century French rathe different from that of Québec (people i Edmundston speak Québec French). Onl those with a very advanced knowledge c French will be able to hear the differenc however.

Surprisingly, New Brunswick is the onl officially bilingual province in Canad (English is not an official language i Québec, and French isn't official in th other eight provinces). Nova Scotia has a significant French population, though, and there are pockets of French on Prince Edward Island as well. The preservation of French in the Maritimes is a primary concern, and helps account for the widespread promotion of Acadian culture.

For a comprehensive guide to the language get a copy of Lonely Planet's handy pocket-sized *French phrasebook*.

Facts for the Visitor

THE BEST & WORST

In the personal opinion of the author, the following are the best and worst of the Maritime provinces:

Top 10

Acadian Historic Village With 33 buildings and a large staff in period costume, this attraction brings Acadia to life. Nearby Caraquet, New Brunswick, is a lively French Canadian community with a colorful fishing harbor.

Brier Island The quaint village of Westport, Nova Scotia, offers some of the best whale watching in the region, and the hiking around the island is great.

Cabot Trail Though somewhat overpromoted, the Cabot Trail is still Nova Scotia's finest scenic drive, and there's excellent whale watching at Chéticamp and Pleasant Bay.

Confederation Trail This conversion of a defunct 350km railway line into a bicycling route has been a resounding success and could make Prince Edward Island the ecotourism capital of Canada.

Fundy National Park Fundy is the Maritimes' top national park, with abundant hiking, bicycling, kayaking, wildlife viewing and sightseeing possibilities. There's something for everyone here.

Louisbourg Though completely rebuilt from the foundations up, Louisbourg is arguably the region's most significant historic site. It's the largest historic reconstruction of its kind ever attempted in Canada.

Lunenburg Lunenburg, Nova Scotia, on the other hand, is an almost intact 18th- and 19th-century town. As a priceless survivor of the days of sail, it's worthy of its status as a world heritage site, the only place in the region so honored by Unesco.

Mount Carleton Off the beaten track and little known outside the region, New Brunswick's Mount Carleton Provincial Park offers you the opportunity to climb the highest mountain in the Maritimes.

Parrsboro & Cape Chignecto The wild north coast of Minas Channel attracts rockhounds beachcombing for fossils and gems and backpackers bound for the 45km Bay of Fundy Coastal Hiking Trail.

St Peter's The St Peter's Canal has linked Bras d'Or Lake to the Atlantic Ocean since the 1850s. Campers at Battery Provincial Park, adjacent to the mouth of the canal, can paddle their rental kayak into the single lock and be lifted into Bras d'Or.

Bottom 10

Belledune-Noranda Lead Smelter A desolate scene awaits you in northeastern New Brunswick, including yellow smelter wastes, sulfuric acid storage facilities and a horrendous coke-burning power plant.

Cavendish In Cavendish, tourism has run wild, with a hungry pack of attractions vying for your dollars. Adjacent Prince Edward Island National Park is much diminished by the clutter.

Charlottetown Delta Hotel The city planners must have been asleep the day they approved this ugly red brick box on the Charlottetown waterfront.

Dalhousie Generating Station As elsewhere in Canada, prisons and polluting industries are the things you're most likely to find adjacent to First Nation reserves. In this case, the people of Eel River First Nation just outside Dalhousie get New Brunswick

Power's black smoke but none of the economic or employment benefits.

Dorchester Penitentiary Dorchester is to the Maritimes what Kingston is to Ontario, a baleful prison where errant inmates were systematically whipped as recently as 1966.

Imperial Oil Refinery The billowing black smoke and ugly outline of this facility are visible from all around Halifax Harbour.

Irving Pulp & Paper Mill This smelly pulp mill is adjacent to Saint John's biggest tourist attraction, the Reversing Falls, yet somehow it never manages to appear in the tourism promotion brochures.

Kimberley-Clark Pulp Mill Pictou would be one of the most picturesque towns in Nova Scotia if it weren't for this high-profile plant that dominates the skyline.

Magnetic Hill Moncton may be the best place in the Maritimes to study how to build a tourist attraction out of nothing.

Sydney Tar Ponds One of North America's worst environmental nightmares, the contaminated pools and poisoned soils of Sydney, Nova Scotia, are an object lesson in how not to run a steel mill.

SUGGESTED ITINERARIES
By Car

If you're driving your own car or willing to rent one, in a week you could easily drive a loop through Lunenburg, Shelburne, Yarmouth, Digby, Westport, Annapolis Royal, Wolfville and Windsor, with a couple of days left for Halifax. To start, fly into Halifax or take the car ferry to Yarmouth from Portland or Bar Harbor, Maine.

With two weeks, you could add Cape Breton Island to your tour. A month would give you time to include Prince Edward Island and a bit of southeastern New Brunswick, perhaps more if you drive fast. With two months, you'll be able to enjoy the entire region at leisure.

By Public Transportation

The adventuresome public transportation rider has a surprising choice of routes, though the options are fewer. See the Getting Around chapter for information on bus and train passes that can make long-distance travel more affordable.

Bus travelers can do the same one-week loop between Halifax and Yarmouth that was recommended for motorists, though stops must be planned more carefully. Lunenburg is an obvious stop, and Liverpool and Shelburne are also convenient. In Yarmouth, the bus station, ferry terminal and accommodations are all far apart, but you'll almost certainly have to change buses there. There's no bus service to Westport on the Digby Neck, but Annapolis Royal is on the route. Budget accommodations are limited in Kentville and Wolfville, so consider spending that last night in Windsor before reaching Halifax.

With two weeks you can also get to Cape Breton, though not as easily. The Eastern Shore bus service from Halifax ends in Sherbrooke, forcing you to backtrack or stick out your thumb. Acadian Lines buses run through Truro and Antigonish to Sydney, but there's no bus service around the Cabot Trail. If you're unwilling to rent a car, consider signing up for a Cape Breton tour from Halifax, such as the ones operated by the Halifax HI hostel (see Organized Tours in the Halifax chapter).

Public transportation users with a month or two at their disposal could add the other Maritime provinces to their itinerary. On Prince Edward Island, the only place easily accessible by bus is Charlottetown (via Moncton). New Brunswick cities reachable by bus include Fredericton, Grand Falls, Edmundston, St Stephen, Saint John, Moncton, Sackville, Miramichi, Bathurst, Dalhousie and Campbellton. New Brunswick has convenient bus connections from Québec via Edmundston or Campbellton and from Maine via St Stephen and Saint John. The train from Montréal to Halifax makes stops in Campbellton, Bathurst, Miramichi, Moncton, Sackville, Amherst and Truro, any of which can be used to link up with the bus network. Remember too the ferries from Maine to Yarmouth.

PLANNING
When to Go
Spring, summer and fall are all ideal for touring. Daylight hours are long in spring and summer, and many of the region's festivals are held during the summer months. If you're skiing or visiting cities, a winter visit won't present any major hurdles. Winter tourism is increasing, with some outfitters offering skiing, snowmobiling and other winter outdoor activities. Theater and symphony seasons in the main cities also run through the winter months.

The school summer holidays in Canada are from the end of June to the beginning of September. This is also when most locals take their vacations, and facilities can get crowded. University students have a longer summer break, running from some time in May to the beginning or middle of September.

Note that outside the main summer season, which runs roughly from mid-June to early September, many visitor-oriented facilities such as tourist offices, attractions, museums, parks and even accommodations may be closed. Advantages are the slower pace, lack of crowds, lower prices and decreased pressure on the people serving you.

Spring and fall make a good compromise between the crowds of peak season and the sometimes brutal cold of winter. From mid-May to mid-June and again in September, you'll enjoy mostly good weather and will have the place to yourself. For campers, though, July and August are the only reliably warm months. For more detail, see the climate charts in the Facts about Canada's Maritime Provinces chapter.

What Kind of Trip
If you'll be staying mostly in hostels and university dormitories, financially you're just as well off alone as you would be sharing expenses with other travelers. However, at motels and B&Bs, the price of a double is usually only slightly more than a single, and at campgrounds one person will always pay the same as a family of six. Public transportation is priced per person, but if you're in a car it's just as cheap to be four as a driver alone. Two or three people can tour the area by car, staying at motels, almost for the price of one.

Most national and provincial parks are inaccessible via public transportation, so if your primary interest is nature, your best bet to reach the parks is to drive (or ride a bicycle). Some organized tours go to the parks, but only for short stays. On the other hand, if history and entertainment are your thing, public transportation will get you around just fine, as the towns are full of historic sites.

Maps
Good provincial road maps are available for free from tourist offices and automobile clubs. Bookstores generally sell both provincial and city maps.

The Canada Map Office produces topographic maps of the entire country. The regional distributor in the Maritimes is the Nova Scotia Geomatics Centre (☎ 902-667 7231, fax 902-667-6008), 160 Willow St Amherst, Nova Scotia B4H 3W5.
Web site: ⓦ www.gov.ns.ca/snsmr/land product

What to Bring
In general, travelers in Canada have no real need for any special articles. Those with allergies or any particular medical ailments or conditions should bring their customary medicines and supplies. Extra prescription glasses or contact lenses are always a good idea. A small travel alarm clock is useful.

A bathing suit, which weighs next to nothing, is always good to throw in the pack. Aside from possible ocean and lake swimming in summer, there are city, hotel and motel pools, and some hotels have saunas. A collapsible umbrella is a very useful, practical accessory. A sturdy pair of walking shoes or boots is a good idea for all but the business traveler with no spare time.

Drivers traveling long distances should have a few basic tools, a spare tire that h been checked for pressure, a first-aid kit and a flashlight. A few favorite tapes may help pass the hours driving in remote areas where there's nothing on the radio but static.

Those planning nonsummer trips should bring a number of things to protect against cold. Layering of clothes is the most effective and the most practical way to keep warm. One thin and one thick sweater and a windbreaker are recommended. On particularly cool days, a T-shirt worn under a long-sleeved shirt and then a combination of the above is quite effective. Gloves, scarf and a hat should be considered and are mandatory in winter. Campers will need a warm sleeping bag and an insulation mat even in midsummer.

RESPONSIBLE TOURISM

Mass tourism has as much impact on developed countries as it does on sunspot destinations in the developing world. In the Maritimes, visitors tend to pile up at a few places during the short summer season. If you can come during the quieter shoulder seasons, or at least make an effort to get off the beaten track, you'll help reduce the overcrowding and spread the economic benefits of your stay.

Our globe is shrinking fast, and the way we produce our energy, food and consumer products has done much harm. As a visitor you should take an interest in conservation issues and perhaps gain insights you can carry home. Travel isn't only about quaint museums and trendy cafés, it's also about learning how to live.

Don't assume that being a tourist gives you any special status, and refrain from telling people how much better things work wherever you come from. Foreigners often make fools of themselves by criticizing situations simply because they're different, which is rather ironic when you think about it. It's OK to complain if something is wrong, so long as you remember that you're a guest in Canada.

TOURIST OFFICES

Tourism is a provincial responsibility and tourist information is supplied by provincial and local bodies. Canadian embassies, consulates and high commissions won't be of much help in planning a visit to Canada, so don't bother with them unless you have questions about visa requirements or customs regulations. Occasionally they have general brochures published by the Canadian Tourism Commission.

Provincial Tourist Offices

Each of the provincial tourist bureaus has a number of offices around its province, especially in the major cities and at the provincial boundaries. These supply, at no charge, excellent maps, directories, accommodation guides and attraction brochures, all of which can be requested on the Internet. They can also provide information on events scheduled for the current or upcoming year.

New Brunswick
Tourism New Brunswick (☎ 800-561-0123)
PO Box 40, Campbellton, New Brunswick E3N 3G1
Web site: w www.tourismnbcanada.com

Nova Scotia
Tourism Nova Scotia (☎ 800-565-0000)
PO Box 456, Halifax, Nova Scotia B3J 2R5
Web site: w www.explorens.com

Prince Edward Island
Prince Edward Island Tourism
(☎ 888-734-7529)
PO Box 2000, Charlottetown, Prince Edward Island C1A 7N8
Web site: w www.peiplay.com

Local Tourist Offices

In addition to the excellent provincial tourism offices, most cities and towns, and some regions, have a local office for distributing visitor information. The smaller tourist offices are clearly the best places for travelers seeking specialized information on a specific area. As a general rule, the staff there will have little knowledge of facilities outside their region, although they usually have brochures on other parts of the province.

Many roadside tourist offices are staffed by students who are only off school from June until the end of August, so that's when the offices are reliably open. Volunteers or regular staff may keep an office open into September, but if you visit between October and mid-May it's unlikely you'll find any tourist offices open at all, except perhaps the administrative headquarters of the provincial tourism organizations in the main cities.

VISAS & DOCUMENTS
Passport
Visitors from all countries except the USA need a passport. Two exceptions are people from Greenland (Denmark) and Saint Pierre & Miquelon (France), who do not need passports if they are entering from their areas of residence. All of the above do need to have good identification when visiting Canada, however.

For US and Canadian citizens, a driver's license has traditionally been all that is required to prove residency, but with security tightening up, this is no longer sufficient. A birth certificate or a certificate of citizenship or naturalization, if not a passport, will probably be required before admission is granted. US citizens arriving in Canada from somewhere other than the USA must have a passport.

If you've rented a car, trailer or any other vehicle in the USA and are driving it into Canada, bring a copy of the rental agreement for inspection by border officials. The rental agreement should stipulate that taking the vehicle into Canada is permitted.

Visas
Citizens of the following countries do not need a visa for a stay of six months or less: Andorra, Antigua and Barbuda, Australia, Austria, Bahamas, Barbados, Belgium, Botswana, Brunei, Costa Rica, Cyprus, Denmark, Dominica, Finland, France, Germany, Greece, Grenada, Hungary, Iceland, Ireland, Israel (national passport holders only), Italy, Japan, Kiribati, Liechtenstein, Luxembourg, Malaysia, Malta, Mexico, Monaco, Namibia, Nauru, Netherlands, New Zealand, Norway, Papua New Guinea, Portugal, Republic of Korea, St Kitts and Nevis, St Lucia, St. Vincent, Samoa, San Marino, Saudi Arabia, Singapore, Solomon Islands, Spain, Swaziland, Sweden, Slovenia, Switzerland, Tuvalu, United States, Vanuatu and Zimbabwe.

In addition, permanent residents of the United States, British citizens and British overseas citizens who are re-admissible to the United Kingdom, citizens of British dependent territories in the Caribbean or Holy See passport holders do not need visas. Everyone else must apply for a visa at a Canadian diplomatic mission before embarking for Canada.

Visitor visas, which cost $75/150 for single/multiple entries, are granted for a period of six months and are extendible for a fee. A different visa is required for visitors intending to work or go to school in Canada. Since the events of September 11, 2001, there's been talk of tightening up Canada's entry requirements, and since visas must be obtained before arrival in Canada, check the current situation before leaving home.

A passport or visa does not guarantee entry. Admission and duration of permitted stay is at the discretion of the immigration officer at the border. The decision is based on a number of factors, including being law abiding, in good health, having sufficient money and possibly being in possession of a ticket out of the country. This last requirement will not often be asked of any legitimate traveler, especially from a Western country.

Success in crossing the US/Canadian border in either direction can also depend on your appearance. If you're driving a late model car and are above a certain age, you'll probably be waved through after quick check of documents. But if you're driving a rent-a-wreck or are on foot with backpack, you could be questioned closely. People riding buses attract closer scrutiny than those traveling by ferry or air. The border guards are on the watch for people who look nervous or who fit certain profiles. Young travelers are checked more closely than older folks.

If you have a visa but are refused entry, you have the right of appeal at the Immigration Appeal Board at the port of entry. Travelers under 18 years old should have a letter from a parent or guardian. Single parents (especially males) accompanied by small children may require additional documentation.

Visa Extensions An application for a visa extension must be submitted one month before the current visa expires. The fee for an extension is $75. Extensions can only be obtained by mail through the Case Processing Centre in Vegreville, Alberta (applying in person at Canadian immigration centers is no longer possible). The requirements for receiving an extension include having a valid passport, an onward ticket and adequate finances. Current information and application forms are available online at W www.cic.gc.ca.

Travel Insurance
A travel-insurance policy that covers medical problems is a good idea. You may prefer a policy that pays doctors or hospitals directly, rather than requiring you to pay on the spot and claim later. If you have to claim later, make sure you keep all documentation. Most policies ask you to call back (collect) to a center in your home country, where an immediate assessment of your problem is made.

Check to see if the policy covers ambulances or an emergency flight home. If you have to stretch out you'll need two seats, and may have to pay for them.

Make sure your regular health insurance covers you during a visit to Canada, and check the precise details, limitations and exclusions of that coverage. Medical, hospital and dental care is excellent but very expensive in Canada. The standard rate for a bed in a city hospital is at least $2000 a day for nonresidents and often over $3000. The most cursory examination at a hospital outpatient department costs $200 and up. Private doctors charge much less, but many do not accept new patients.

One of the largest sellers of hospital and medical insurance for visitors to Canada is Ingle Life & Health. It offers hospital medical care (HMC) policies from a minimum of seven days to a maximum of one year, with a possible renewal for one additional year. The 30-day basic coverage costs $113 for an adult under the age of 55, $136 for ages 55 to 64 and $166 for ages 65 and up. Family rates are available. These prices are for $50,000 coverage; for $100,000 coverage the cost is slightly more. The policy includes hospital expenses, doctors' fees, extended health care, repatriation and other benefits. Visitors are not covered for conditions that existed prior to their arrival in Canada.

Ingle also offers insurance policies for foreign students (at reduced rates) and to those visiting Canada on working visas. Most insurance companies sell Ingle products, or you can order directly by phone using a credit card. The head office (☎ 416-340-8115, 800-216-3588), 438 University Ave, Suite 1200, Toronto, ON, M5G 2K8, can supply insurance information on a variety of plans to suit different needs. Read the information carefully; there are exclusions and conditions that should be clearly understood. Also check the maximum amounts payable, as different policies allow for greater payments.

There are many other companies offering travelers insurance, so consult the Yellow Pages.

Driver's License & Permits
A valid driver's license from any country is good in Canada for three months, and an international driving permit, available in your home country, is good for one year almost anywhere in the world. If your license is written in a language other than English or French, you should have an international driver's license.

Hostel Cards
A Hostelling International (HI) membership card will save you between $2 and $5 a night at the nine official HI hostels in the

Maritimes. The card will also get you a 10% discount at some businesses around Halifax. Since the card costs $35 a year in Canada, you'll need to spend at least nine nights in hostels that year to break even. Die-hard budget travelers can get a life membership for $175. You can sign up for a hostel membership online at their Web site at W www.hihostels.ca.

Student & Youth Cards

An International Student Identity Card (ISIC) will get you discounts at most museums, and reduced rates at summertime university hostels. Many transportation companies also offer student discounts. In Canada, full-time students attending secondary or post-secondary institutions can purchase the card for $16 at any Travel CUTS office, a student association office or a VIA Rail train station. Canadians can apply by mail after downloading the application form at W www.travelcuts.com. Student travel offices around the world also sell the ISIC. Proof of full-time student status is required.

An International Youth Travel Card (IYTC) is available to travelers 25 years of age or younger who are not enrolled as full-time students. This card brings many of the same benefits as the ISIC, as does the International Teacher Identity Card (ITIC), which is designed for teachers and college professors.

Copies

All important documents (passport.data page and visa page, credit cards, travel insurance policy, air/bus/train tickets, driver's license etc) should be photocopied before you leave home. Leave one copy with someone at home and keep another with you, separate from the originals.

You can also store details of your vital travel documents in Lonely Planet's free online Travel Vault in case you lose the photocopies or can't be bothered with them. Your password-protected Travel Vault is accessible online from anywhere in the world – you can create your vault at W www.ekno.lonelyplanet.com.

EMBASSIES & CONSULATES
Canadian Embassies, High Commissions & Consulates

Diplomatic representation abroad includes:

Australia
High Commission:
(☎ 02-6270-4000)
Commonwealth Ave, Canberra ACT 2600
Canadian Consulate General:
(☎ 02-9364-3000 or 02-9364-3050 for Visa Immigration Office)
111 Harrington St, Level 5, Quay West, Sydney, New South Wales 2000
Consulate:
(☎ 03-9811-9999)
123 Camberwell Rd, Hawthorn East, Melbourne, Victoria 3123
Consulate:
(☎ 08-9322-7930)
267 St George's Terrace, 3rd Floor, Perth, Western Australia 6000

France
Embassy:
(☎ 01-44-43-29-00)
35 Avenue Montaigne, 75008 Paris

Germany
Embassy:
(☎ 49-3020-3120)
Friedrichstrasse 95, 12th Floor, 10117 Berlin

Ireland
Embassy:
(☎ 353-1-418-4100)
65 St Stephen's Green, Dublin 2

Netherlands
Embassy:
(☎ 070-311-1600)
Sophialaan 7, 2500 GV The Hague

New Zealand
High Commission:
(☎ 4-473-9577)
61 Molesworth St, 3rd Floor, Thorndon, Wellington
(Note: Visa and immigration inquiries are handled by the Consulate General of Canada Sydney, Australia.)

UK
High Commission:
(☎ 020-7258-6600)
Canada House, Trafalgar Square, London SW1Y 5BJ

USA
Consulate General:
(☎ 212-596-1628)
1251 Avenue of the Americas, New York, N York 10020-1175

(Note: The Canadian Consulate Generals in Buffalo, Detroit, Los Angeles, New York and Seattle can provide visa information; and the Consulate Generals in Atlanta, Boston, Buffalo, Chicago, Dallas, Detroit, Honolulu, Los Angeles, Miami, Minneapolis, New York, San Juan and Seattle may have some tourist information. The only embassy is in Washington, DC.)

Embassies & Consulates in Canada

It's important to realize what your own embassy – the embassy of the country of which you are a citizen – can and can't do to help you if you get into trouble. Generally speaking, it won't be much help if the trouble you're in is remotely your own fault. Remember that you are bound by the laws of the country you are in. Your embassy will not be sympathetic if you end up in jail after committing a crime locally, even if such actions are legal in your own country.

You might get some assistance in genuine emergencies, but only if other channels have been exhausted. For example, if you need to get home urgently, a free ticket home is exceedingly unlikely – the embassy would expect you to have insurance. If you have all your money and documents stolen, it might assist with getting a new passport, but a loan for onward travel is out of the question.

Some embassies used to hold letters for travelers or have a small reading room with some newspapers, but these days, most mail-holding service has been stopped, and even newspapers tend to be out-of-date.

The principal diplomatic representations in Canada are in Ottawa, which are listed here. Other offices can be found in Halifax and Moncton.

Australia
High Commission:
(☎ 613-236-0841)
50 O'Connor St, Ottawa ON K1P 6L2
France
Embassy:
(☎ 613-789-1795)
42 Sussex Drive, Ottawa ON K1M 2C9
Consulate General:
(☎ 506-857-4191)
777 Main St, Suite 800, Moncton NB E1C 1E9

Germany
Embassy:
(☎ 613-232-1101)
1 Waverley St, Ottawa ON K2P 0T8
Ireland
Embassy:
(☎ 613-233-6281)
130 Albert St, Ottawa ON K1P 5G4
Netherlands
Embassy:
(☎ 613-237-5030)
350 Albert St, Suite 2020 Ottawa ON K1R 1A4
New Zealand
High Commission:
(☎ 613-238-5991)
727-99 Bank St, Ottawa ON K1P 6G3
UK
High Commission:
(☎ 613-237-1542)
80 Elgin St, Ottawa, ON K1P 5K7
Consulate:
(☎ 902-461-1381)
Secunda Marine Building, 1 Canal Street, Dartmouth NS B2Y 3YN
USA
Embassy:
(☎ 613-238-5335)
490 Sussex Dr, Ottawa ON K1N 1G8
Consulate General:
(☎ 902-429-2485)
Cogswell Tower, Scotia Square, 2000 Barrington St, Suite 910, Halifax NS B3J 3K1

CUSTOMS

How thoroughly customs will check you out upon arrival at a Canadian entry point depends on a number of things. First among them are point of departure, nationality and appearance. Arriving from countries known as drug sources or with a history of illegal immigration or refugees will add to the scrutiny. Always make sure the necessary papers are in order.

Travelers may find that different border personnel interpret the rules differently. Some are polite, others rude. Arguing is of little use. If you are refused entry and you feel it is unjust, the best course is simply to try again later (after a shift change) or at a different border crossing. Young travelers may find rules strictly enforced.

If an agent wants to frisk or strip search you, you are entitled to be given a reason for their suspicion. If you wish to refuse, you can ask for legal counsel, which may be available at airports and larger entry points.

Don't get caught bringing drugs into Canada. This warning includes marijuana and hashish, as they are termed narcotics in Canada. Sentences can be harsh.

Adults (age varies by province but is generally 19 years) can bring in 1.1L (40oz) of liquor or a case of 24 beers and 200 cigarettes, 50 cigars or 200g of tobacco (all cheaper in the USA). You can bring gifts up to $60 in value into the country (if you mention a gift worth over $60, you'll be charged duty).

Sporting goods, including cameras and film, can also be brought in without trouble. Registering excessive or expensive sporting goods, cameras etc, with customs before you leave home might save you some hassle, especially if you'll be crossing the Canadian-US border a number of times.

If you have a dog or cat with you, you'll need proof that it's had a rabies shot in the past 36 months. For US citizens this is usually easy enough; for residents of other countries there may well be more involved procedures. If you must bring a pet from abroad, check with the Canadian government or a representative before arriving at the border.

For boaters, pleasure craft may enter Canada either on the trailer or in the water and stay for up to one year. An entry permit is required and is obtainable from the customs office at (or near) the point of entry. All boats powered by motors over 10hp must be licensed.

Pistols, fully automatic weapons and any firearms less than 66cm (26 inches) in length are not permitted into the country. If you're thinking of bringing a sporting rifle or shotgun, check with a Canadian embassy or consulate beforehand, as the regulations are being tightened up.

MONEY
Currency
Canadian currency is much like that of the USA, with some noteworthy variations. Coins come in one cent (penny), five cent (nickel), 10 cent (dime), 25 cent (quarter), $1 (loonie) and $2 (twoonie) pieces. The loonie is an 11-sided, gold-colored coin known for the common loon (a species of waterbird) featured swimming on it. In 1996, the twoonie was introduced. It's a two-toned coin with a nickel outer ring and aluminum-bronze core featuring a polar bear. There is also a 50-cent coin, but this is not often seen.

Paper currency is found in $5, $10, $20 and $50 denominations. The $100 and larger bills are far less common and could prove difficult to cash, especially in smaller businesses or at night. If you're offered them when changing money, politely request notes of $50 or less. Canadian bills are all the same size but vary in their colors and images. Some denominations have two styles, as older versions in good condition continue to circulate.

All prices quoted in this book are in Canadian dollars, unless stated otherwise.

Exchange Rates
At press time, exchange rates were as follows:

country	unit		Canadian dollar
Australia	A$1	=	$0.7
euro	€1	=	$1.3
Japan	¥100	=	$1.2
New Zealand	NZ$1	=	$0.6
UK	UK£1	=	$2.1
USA	US$1	=	$1.5

Exchanging Money
Changing money is best done at banks. Hotels, restaurants, stores, attractions and service stations will often accept US dollars but the rate of exchange is unlikely to be in your favor. Other foreign currencies may be changed at banks, and excessive fees may be charged. Personal checks are rarely accepted at any commercial enterprise.

Banking hours are generally shorter than regular retail hours. Only a few banks are open on Saturday morning, so don't count on them. For more information, see Business Hours later in this chapter.

Traveler's Checks You'll make life easier for yourself if your traveler's checks are in Canadian dollars, as these are often accepted as cash without any charges by banks or businesses. Occasionally a bank will want to charge a couple of dollars to cash a traveler's check, so ask first. Traveler's checks in US dollars are easily cashed at banks and many businesses, but you may be charged a commission and will receive a poorer rate of exchange than you would have when purchasing your checks. European and other foreign traveler's checks can only be changed at large banks and exchange houses.

ATMs

Automated teller machines (ATMs) with Interac are common throughout Canada. Interac permits cardholders to withdraw money from their account at any bank machine. As well as being located at banks, they can be found in some grocery stores, service stations, variety stores, shopping centers, bus and train stations and elsewhere. Known in Canada as banking machines, these can be used day or night, any day of the week. Cards must be applied for at home, through your own bank. Ask if the cards are good for use in the Canadian banking networks and how much your bank will charge you for each transaction. Canadian ATMs will take cards from most foreign countries.

Be sure to obtain the toll-free telephone number for locating banking machines. Often tourist offices or a bank will also be able to direct you to the nearest machine. Use of the Interac card by travelers has increased dramatically and is often the quickest, most convenient way to replenish your cash. Bank cards are used now instead of cash. With 'direct payment,' the card is wiped through the retailer's scanner, and your account is instantly debited. It makes spending money almost too easy.

Credit Cards

Carrying a credit card is a good idea in Canada. Their use is widespread, and they serve several purposes. They are good iden-

tification and are more or less essential for use as security deposits when renting such things as a car or even a bicycle. They are required as a deposit when making hotel reservations over the phone, and even HI hostels will take credit card reservations and payments. Credit cards can also be used to book and purchase ferry tickets, airplane tickets or theater tickets, and they can be used at banks to withdraw cash advances.

Visa, MasterCard and American Express credit cards are honored at most establishments in larger centers and most places in smaller cities and towns. American Express offers a free mail pick-up service at its Halifax office. In tiny, out-of-the-way communities, cash or traveler's checks are safer bets.

See Emergencies later in this chapter for help with lost or stolen cards.

Costs

For many visitors, the biggest expense will be accommodations. Because the tourist season is so short – just 10 weeks in most cases or three months at best – prices tend to be high. Tourist-oriented businesses that stay open all year lose money in the winter, and the eight busy weeks of July and August are crucial to their survival. To carry themselves through the lean months of winter, many accommodations, car rental agencies and attractions increase their prices during the summer months, when demand exceeds supply. If you find the prices asked in July and August exorbitant, you should try to visit between mid-May and mid-June, when many prices are a third lower, or defer your trip until mid-September.

As a rule, accommodation prices in Canada are lower than in the US, and in the top end hotels prices are much lower. Restaurant meals are cheaper than in much of Western Europe but higher than in the USA; the exception is fast food, which is generally cheaper in Canada than in the US.

Gasoline prices vary from province to province but are always more than US rates, so remember to fill the tank before crossing the border if you're coming from the USA. Canada's gasoline prices are much lower than those in Europe, however. Also, as a rule, the more isolated the service station, the higher the prices.

Buses are almost always the least expensive form of public transportation. Train fares are moderate, but you can save money by taking advantage of special rates that are made available. Again, fares are higher than in the US and lower than in Europe.

Flying between provinces is expensive because the distances are great and competition is minimal. Again, always inquire about specials, excursion fares and last minute deals.

As an example of average costs, you'll pay around $18 for a hostel bed, $50 for a double at an average motel, $15 per person for dinner at a nice restaurant, $2 for a loaf of bread, $3 for a small glass of beer, $3 for a Big Mac, 80¢ for a liter of gasoline, $22 for 100km by train, $15 for 100km by bus, 25¢ for a local phone call and a dollar for a major newspaper. Add tax to the food and accommodations prices just quoted (see Taxes & Refunds).

The Canadian dollar remains low compared to the US greenback, so exchange rates are excellent for US citizens and some Europeans. Inflation has been negligible for several years, making prices relatively stable.

Tipping
Normal tipping is 10% to 15% of the bill. Tips are usually given to cabbies, wait staff, hairdressers, barbers, hotel attendants and bellhops. Tipping for bar service is a good idea. If you give a fat tip on the first order, you won't go thirsty all night.

A few restaurants have the gall to include a service charge on the bill. No tip should be added in these cases.

Taxes & Refunds
A 7% Goods & Services Tax (GST) is added to just about every product, service and transaction in Canada. This is applied on top of the usual provincial sales tax, which is 10% on Prince Edward Island. Thus most expenditures on PEI carry 17% tax. New Brunswick and Nova Scotia have combined their provincial taxes with the GST to make one general or Harmonized Sales Tax (HST) of 15%.

Most prices you see posted (and most quoted herein) do not include taxes, so expect 15% or 17% tax to be added to most hotel rates, restaurant meals, consumer goods, transportation fares, postage stamps and even admission prices. Gasoline prices have the tax already factored in. It's a bit more complicated than that, but you should just assume you'll be charged tax and if that bumps the price above what you're willing to pay, reconsider the purchase.

No tax is applied to groceries purchased at a supermarket (although pharmacy items, soft drinks and hot cooked foods do carry tax). Tourist homes (the small ones), guesthouses and B&Bs earning under $30,000 a year aren't required to collect these taxes.

A complicated system of partial tax rebates is available to nonresidents who export their nonconsumable purchases worth over $200 (before tax) from Canada within 60 days. You may also be able to claim back a portion of the accommodations taxes you've paid, but taxes on services, meals and transportation are nonrefundable. To apply, you must collect all the original receipts (credit card slips and photocopies are not sufficient), complete Form GST176 and send in everything by mail after you've returned home. Each receipt must be for an amount over $5 before tax and must list the company name and address, tax registration number, your name, the amount of tax paid and date. Be sure to enclose proof that you've left Canada (in the form of an original transportation ticket). If you're driving or are on a tour bus, you must stop at Canadian Customs before reentering the US to have the receipts stamped. The officers will want to inspect the goods and see two forms of photo identification. Only items for personal use are eligible. Many other conditions apply, but you've got a year to get through it. If approved, your refund check in Canadian dollars will be mailed to your address outside Canada a month or two later. Check with the provincial tour offices for information if this system interests you, though in practice, it's hardly worth the hassle unless you're spending thousands of dollars and enjoy dealing with bureaucracies. Never purchase anything just because someone tells you it's possible to claim back the tax.

POST & COMMUNICATIONS

Post

The mail service in Canada is neither quick nor cheap, but it is reliable. Canadian post offices will keep general delivery mail for 15 business days, then return it to sender. Here's an example of how such mail should be addressed:

Your Name
c/o General Delivery
Halifax, Nova Scotia
Canada
B3J 2L3

Other post offices holding general delivery mail include Fredericton, NB E3B 4Y1, Saint John, NB E2M 4X6, and Charlottetown, PE C1A 1M0. Photo identification is required to collect such mail.

If you have an American Express card or AmEx traveler's checks, you can have your mail sent c/o American Express, City Center Atlantic, Box 44, Suite 205, 5523 Spring Garden Rd, Halifax, NS B3J 1G8, Canada.

A standard 1st-class airmail letter is limited to 50g to North American destinations but can weigh as much as 500g to other international destinations. To the US, heavier mail can go by either surface or, more expensively, by air in small packet mail. Anything over 1kg to the US goes by surface parcel post.

To other international destinations, letter packages up to 2kg can be sent by air. Small packet mail up to the same weight can go by either surface or air. Packages over 2kg are sent by parcel post and different rates apply. Anything over 10kg goes surface only. For full details go to a post office; a pamphlet that explains the various options, categories, requirements and prices is available.

Some countries require a customs declaration on incoming parcels; check at the post office.

Aside from the post offices themselves, stamps and postal services are often available at other outlets such as pharmacies and some small variety stores. Finding them is a matter of asking around. Hotel concessions also often stock stamps.

Here are some postal rates:

1st-class letter or postcard within Canada: 47¢ (up to 30g)

1st-class letter or postcard to US: 60¢ (up to 30g)

1st-class letter or postcard to other destinations: $1.05 (up to 20g)

Aerogrammes (which are not common): $1.05

Bear in mind that post offices cannot accept deliveries by couriers such as UPS or Federal Express. If you need to receive a parcel by courier, visit W www.mbe.com and click Locations. There you'll find the addresses and phone numbers of 19 branches of Mail Boxes Etc in New Brunswick and Nova Scotia. Any of these can receive a courier delivery on your behalf for a fee of $3 per parcel, but you should call ahead to let them know it's coming. Mail Boxes Etc's courier rates to the US are generally lower than those of the post office, and the service is much faster.

Telephone

Public telephones are readily available in hotel lobbies, bars, restaurants, large department stores, gas stations and many public buildings. Telephone booths can be found on street corners in cities and towns. The basic rate for a local connection is 25¢ at a public telephone. All Canadian business and residential phone bills for local calls are paid at a flat monthly rate – the number of calls made is immaterial. So don't feel guilty about the cost of using a friend's telephone to make free local calls.

For those who will be using the telephone in hotels, motels, guesthouses and other such places, note that most establishments charge a service fee for the use of the phone on a per-call basis, even for local calls. At maybe 50¢ per call, this can add up to a bit of a shock on the final room bill, especially if you aren't expecting it.

Toll-Free Numbers Many businesses, ferries, hotels, hostels and tourist offices have toll-free numbers for making reservations and obtaining information. These numbers begin with '800,' '888,' '877' or '777' and must be preceded with '1.' Some of these numbers can be used from anywhere in North America; others may work within Canada only; still others may cover just one province. You won't know until you try the number. Toll-free directory assistance is available at ☎ 800-555-1212.

Many Canadian businesses, tourist attractions and information offices use the cursed touch-tone menu information system. After dialing, the caller is given a range of options and recorded messages. This can be useful in learning the hours of operation of a museum, for example, but also frustrating because it's difficult to reach someone to whom you can direct specific questions.

Dialing If you wish to speak to an operator (dial ☎ 0) you will be connected free of charge. There's also no charge for dialing ☎ 911 (emergency). Calls to ☎ 411 (directory assistance) are free from public telephones but charged from private phones.

Canada's Maritime provinces have only two area codes: 902 for Nova Scotia and Prince Edward Island and 506 for New Brunswick. The country code for Canada and the US is 1, and when dialing long distance within North America you must put a 1 before the area code. The international access code for overseas calls is 011.

Long-distance calls to anywhere in the world can be made from any phone, but rates vary depending on how and when the call is placed. A call made without the assistance of an operator is cheapest and quickest, so long as you know the area code and number of the party you are trying to reach. With operator assistance, calls in increasing order of cost are, station to station (no particular person to speak to required), collect

(reverse charge) and person to person (only a specified person can receive the call).

In Canada, regular long-distance rates are cheapest from 10pm to 8am daily. The second most economical time slot is from 6pm to 10pm daily, except Sunday when this rate runs from 8am to 10pm. The most expensive time to call is from 8am to 6pm Monday to Saturday.

The reductions also apply to calls to the USA or overseas. International codes and dialing instructions are provided in the front pages of the telephone book, but for prices you must call the operator.

Telephone Cards Paying for long distance calls with coins at a public telephone is extremely expensive, as you'll find out the first time you try it. There's a wide range of local and international phone cards, but the cards issued by the local telephone companies are definitely not the best value. Instead look for posters in the windows of convenience stores and newsstands advertising tele phone cards that let you call long distance a low per minute rates via a toll-free 80 number using a pin code.

These cards cost between $5 and $20 an are much cheaper than using coins, bu beware of the connection fees, monthly fee maintenance fees or surcharges mentione in fine print at the bottom of the poster. $1 surcharge may not matter if you're on making a couple of rather long calls, but defeats the purpose if you have to make lot of short calls. Also check to see if th card has an expiration date. Anothe problem may be that the 800 access numbe is frequently engaged.

Deutsche Telekom Canada Inc has **T-NetCall** prepaid telephone card th allows you to place long-distance calls over 200 countries at excellent rates witho any connection fees or surcharges. The NetCall card comes in denominations $10, $20 and $50, with the more expensi cards offering the cheapest rates. For ca within Canada the price is 15¢/13/10 p minute with a $10/20/50 card. From Cana to the US it's 22¢/18/15 per minute. T cards do have an expiration date, which usually three months from the time of purchase. Full details are available on the Deutsche Telekom Canada Web site at W www.telekom.de/english/regions/americas/canada, or call ☎ 877-360-5555 in Canada or ☎ 877-804-7556 in the US during business hours. It's possible to order a T-NetCall card over the phone with a credit card and begin using it immediately. Ask the operator to tell you your pin number – you don't really need the plastic card at all. Once you have a pin number, the dial-up number is ☎ 800-203-8265.

eKno Communication Service

Lonely Planet's eKno global communication service provides low-cost international calls – for local calls, you're usually better off with a local phone card. eKno also offers free messaging services, email, travel information and an online travel vault where you can securely store all your important documents. You can join online at W www.ekno.lonelyplanet.com. Once you have joined, to use eKno from Canada, dial ☎ 800-808-5773.

Fax

Fax machines available to the public can be found at major hotels, city post offices and a range of small businesses in major centers. Check under 'facsimile,' 'stationers' or 'mail box services' in the Yellow Pages. Fax messages are generally charged at $1 per page.

Email & Internet Access

Email access is available at almost every public library in Canada, usually for free or for a fee of around $2 an hour. Some libraries only extend this service to holders of local library cards. You'll generally have your best luck at smaller libraries off the beaten track, where the computers aren't in such high demand and the librarians don't receive a dozen such requests a day. Always ask at the library information desk before sitting down at a computer, as most librarians will want you to enter your name on a chart. In large cities, you can sometimes reserve a time slot for later the same day.

All three provinces have government programs designed to provide Internet access in rural areas. In Nova Scotia, you'll find Community Access Program (CAP) sites in surprisingly remote locations. On Prince Edward Island, Access PEI locations aren't quite as numerous, but they're free and almost always available when you see them. In New Brunswick, you'll usually be dependent on public libraries, although some high schools provide access in the evening at $2 an hour. All nonlibrary public Internet access facilities are prominently signposted and available to all.

You'll also find commercial Internet cafes in tourist areas, charging around $6 an hour. Large hotels may also have them. If you're comfortable with the price, you'll generally find them convenient and pleasant, with extremely helpful staffs.

If you want to use email to keep in touch, you'll need a Web-based email account. The most famous of these free services are Yahoo! Mail, Microsoft's Hotmail and Lonely Planet's eKno service. To sign up, simply click 'Check Email' at W www.yahoo.com, 'Sign Up' at W www.hotmail.com or 'email' at W www.ekno.lonelyplanet.com. Once you have an Internet email address, you'll be able to send and receive email from hundreds of Internet access points all across the Maritimes.

DIGITAL RESOURCES

The World Wide Web is a rich resource for travelers. You can research your trip, hunt down bargain airfares, book hotels, check on weather conditions or chat with locals and other travelers about the best places to visit (or avoid!).

There's no better place to start your Web explorations than the Lonely Planet Web site at W www.lonelyplanet.com. Here, you'll find succinct summaries of travel destinations, postcards from other travelers and the Thorn Tree bulletin board, where you can ask questions before you go or dispense advice when you get back. You can also find travel news and updates to many of our most popular guidebooks, and the subWWWay section links you to the most useful travel resources elsewhere on the Web.

Web sites of the provincial tourist information offices are listed under Tourist Offices earlier in this book. Many email and Web addresses are given in the text under specific accommodation listings.

Here are a few other interesting sites:

Cape Breton Music Online (W www.cbmusic.com) – This site is a fantastic resource with detailed information on just about every artist and venue on the island. You can download songs for personal use from this site.

Clearcutting Nova Scotia (W www.clearcutnovascotia.com) – For the scoop on forestry issues, visit this site and the low-impact forestry site (W www.lowimpactforestry.com).

Environment Canada (W weatheroffice.ec.gc.ca) – Check here for a weather forecast.

Mike Sack's Mi'kmaq Place (W accesswave.ca/~mtsack) – Mike Sack's Mi'kmaq Place provides lots of useful information on the history, arts & crafts, politics, spirituality, reserves, stories and language of the Mi'kmaq, in an appealing format.

New Brunswick Environmental Network (W www.web.net/nben) – This site includes a bimonthly electronic magazine and much of interest about New Brunswick.

Prince Edward Island Eco-Net (W www.isn.net/~network) – Eco-Net provides a quarterly environmental magazine called *The Networker,* with useful facts on PEI.

Sable Island (W collections.ic.gc.ca/sableisland) – The gorgeous Sable Island site provides a rare glimpse of this isolated Atlantic island.

Sierra Club (W atlantic.sierraclub.ca) – The Nova Scotia–based Sierra Club Web site provides interesting background on local environmental concerns.

Torontoalacarte.com (W www.torontoalacarte.com) – Many unknown sights of Canada are described on this Web site.

Whales of Fundy Bay (W new-brunswick.net/new brunswick/whales) – This site has information about the whales of the Bay of Fundy and even recordings of their songs.

BOOKS

Most books are published in different editions by different publishers in different countries. As a result, a book might be a hardcover rarity in one country but readily available in paperback in another. Fortunately, bookstores and libraries can search by title or author, so your local bookstore or library is best placed to advise you on the availability of the following recommended books.

Canada has a small but high quality publishing industry that is very active in promoting books by and about Canadians. Fredericton's Goose Lane Editions has a large catalog of quality books on the Maritimes, including many of those mentioned herein. Check their Web site at W www.gooselane.com. For a brief guide to Maritimes literature, see the Arts section in the Facts about Canada's Maritime Provinces chapter.

Lonely Planet

For travel beyond the Maritimes, Lonely Planet has a growing number of travel guides to Canada, including *British Columbia, Canada, Montréal, Pacific Northwest, Québec, Toronto* and *Vancouver*. Several dozen Lonely Planet travel guides are available to the US. *New England* covers Maine and five other northeastern states.

Guidebooks

Kent Thompson's *Biking to Blissville* deals with bicycling in the three Maritime provinces and the Îles de la Madeleine o' Québec. Most of the trips described ar 20km to 60km loop trips, and it's a bit out o' date, as a lot of new bike trails have bee built since 1993, when Kent's book ap peared. The personal stories and back ground notes make interesting genera reading.

Walter Sienko's *Nova Scotia & the Ma itimes by Bike* is a bit more recent an preferable for real bicycle touring, as the ʹ multiday tours cover routes of betwee 100km and 600km. The background mat rial is comprehensive.

Hiking Trails of Cape Breton, by Micha Haynes, provides 302 pages of precise info mation on Cape Breton trails, with ma and an eight-page index. Michael's *Hiki Trails of Nova Scotia* encompasses t

entire province. Also good is Marianne and
HA Eiselt's *A Hiking Guide to New
Brunswick*.

In *Sea Kayaking in Nova Scotia,* Scott
Cunningham maps, photographs and describes 42 of the best coastal paddling
routes in the province. A biologist by training, Cunningham circumnavigated Nova
Scotia in 1980 and has paddled the province's coastal waters almost continuously
ever since as the owner of a sea kayaking
company east of Halifax.

Gary Saunders' *Discover Nova Scotia,
The Ultimate Nature Guide* is a good intro-
duction to the flora, fauna, landscapes and
seascapes you'll encounter along the way.
Jeffrey C Domm's two field guides to *Nova
Scotia Birds* are also excellent.

If you're a coupon clipper, you'll want to
buy a copy of *Entertainment Halifax & Surrounding Areas* (☎ 800-374-4464). This
annual publication provides two-for-one
deals at hundreds of restaurants and some
attractions in and around Halifax. A few
upscale hotel discounts are also offered. The
coupons are really only a bargain if there
are two of you, and as usual, to 'save' money
you have to spend money. Check their Web
site at Ⓦ www.entertainment.com.

Travel

Walter Stewart's first journey on the Trans
Canada Highway was in 1964. Thirty-five
years later he did it all again, and *My Cross-
Country Checkup* is the result. Insightful
and topical, Stewart's book brings the
highway and everything he sees along it to
life. His grasp of history is firm, and he
doesn't shrink from controversies such as
the Sydney tar ponds and the Irving empire.
Moving beyond clichés, Steward explores
the Evangeline legend in Nova Scotia, the
real Lucy Maud Montgomery of Green
Gables and the living village at Kings
Landing. It's a book you'll want to read
before and after your trip.

In *Local Colour,* editor Carol Martin has
collected 24 short travel stories about
Canada by different authors, including four
from the Maritimes. We visit remote Sable
Island, meet Anne of Green Gables and

pursue the frogs of Halifax. In one story
Eugène Cloutier perceptively explains how
New Brunswick is a province of exiles –
French Acadians and English Loyalists –
who have always gotten along very well due
to this shared experience.

In the summer of 1992, Silver Donald
Cameron sailed his 8m yacht *Silversark* up
the Northumberland Strait and out into the
Gulf of St Lawrence, making frequent stops
in four provinces. In *Sniffing the Coast,*
Cameron tells about the people he met in
small ports along the way, the tales they told
and the problems they face. His account of
the destruction of Africville outside Halifax
will interest the student of minority rights in
Canada.

In *Welcome Home: Travels in Small Town
Canada,* Stuart McLean shares his impressions of Sackville, New Brunswick, in 44
readable pages. Though McLean wrote this
account more than a decade ago, places like
Mel's Tea Room and the Marshlands Inn
haven't changed much.

History

A recommended primer on the country's
history is *The Penguin History of Canada,*
by Kenneth McNaught. It ends around 1969
and much of the text relates to Québec, but
it does well in elucidating the role played by
the Maritime provinces in the formation of
Canada.

The 20 pages on the Mi'kmaqs and
Maliseets in *Native Peoples and Cultures of
Canada,* by Allan Macmillan, helps place
these nations in a historical context.

The Acadiensis Readers, edited by Phillip
A Buckner, Gail G Campbell and David
Frank, comprise a two-volume anthology of
Atlantic Canada Before Confederation and
Atlantic Canada After Confederation. Each
book contains over a dozen readable essays
on the main issues in regional history.

General

To sample the way Maritimers feel about
themselves and the rest of Canada, there's
no better book than *Down Home, Notes of
a Maritime Son*. When author Harry Bruce
left Toronto for his father's birthplace in

Nova Scotia, he soon discovered how difficult it is for outsiders to be accepted by these clannish locals. Although they can be both courteous and inquisitive, the friendliness and unsolicited assistance may change to suspicion if you say you're staying longer than two weeks. In the family-oriented world Bruce describes, there are few showoffs, and even the very wealthy lead simple lives.

Elizabeth May's *At the Cutting Edge* is a devastating examination of forest management and the timber industry in Canada. It deals with the whole country, but the Maritimes are well covered.

FILMS
In recent years the three Maritime provinces have offered tax incentives and credits to filmmakers from other parts of Canada and abroad who are willing to establish a presence in the province and hire local staff. Information is available on the Web at W www.film.ns.ca for Nova Scotia, W www.techpei.com for Prince Edward Island and W www.nbfilm.com for New Brunswick.

Partly as a result of these incentives, several notable films have been shot on location here, including *Dolores Claiborne* (1995), *Margaret's Museum* (1995), *The Scarlet Letter* (1995), *Titanic* (1997) and *Magic of Marciano* (2000). Mort Ransen's *Margaret's Museum* is doubly interesting, as it was not only filmed on Cape Breton Island but is actually about the coal miners of Glace Bay. James Cameron, the director of *Titanic*, is Canadian, and he's well remembered in Halifax.

NEWSPAPERS & MAGAZINES
The region's leading daily newspapers are the Charlottetown *Guardian* (W www.theguardian.pe.ca), Fredericton *Daily Gleaner* (W www.dailygleaner.com), Halifax *Chronicle-Herald* (W www.herald.ns.ca), Moncton *Times & Transcript* (W www.nbpub.com/timestranscript), New Brunswick *Telegraph-Journal* (W www.telegraphjournal.com) and Saint John *Times-Globe* (W www.timesglobe.com). All four New Brunswick dailies are owned by the Irving family.

The *Globe & Mail* (W www.globeandmail.com), sometimes termed Canada's newspaper, is published daily in Toronto but is available around the Maritimes and provides a well written record of national affairs from politics to the arts.

Maclean's (W www.macleans.ca) is Canada's weekly news magazine. *Canadian Geographic* (W www.cangeo.ca) is a monthly with excellent articles and photography on a range of Canadian topics from wildlife to weather.

The monthly *Mi'kmaq-Maliseet Nations News* (W cmm-ns.com/mmnn) serves the First Nations of Atlantic Canada.

A unique outdoors and cultural newspaper called *Shunpiking* (☎ 902-455-4922) is published every few months in Halifax. Copies are distributed free at universities and some tourist offices.

RADIO & TV
The Canadian Broadcasting Corporation (CBC) can be seen or heard almost anywhere around the region on radio (both AM and FM bands), television or the Web (W www.cbc.ca). It carries a lot more Canadian content in music and information than any of the private broadcasting companies. CBC Radio accepts no advertising, though there is advertising on CBC TV.

CBC Radio, in particular, is a praiseworthy service that unites listeners across Canada with many of its programs. Highly recommended is *This Morning,* broadcast between 9am and noon weekdays. It's followed by *Maritimes Noon,* with equally good coverage of regional matters. On CBC TV tune in to *The National* nightly at 10pm for sometimes controversial reports on national issues. The importance of the CBC in fostering a distinct Canadian identity cannot be overstated.

The CBC also has a French radio and TV network, both going under the name Radio Canada. These can also be received anywhere around the region and on the Internet (W radio-canada.ca/atlantique).

The other major national TV network i the Canadian Television Network (CTV) with local stations in Halifax, Moncton

Saint John and Sydney. It's the main commercial channel, broadcasting a mix of Canadian, US and national programs. Its nightly national news show at 11pm is seen across the country. Its Web site is at W www.ctv.ca.

Canadians can and do readily tune into TV and radio stations from the USA. In western New Brunswick you can listen to the fine programming of Maine Public Radio.

VIDEO SYSTEMS

When buying travel videos it's important to check whether you'll be able to actually view them back home. The NTSC system used in North America is incompatible with the PAL system used in Britain, Germany and Australia or SECAM used in France.

PHOTOGRAPHY & VIDEO

Camera shops in the major centers are generally quite good, with well-informed staff and a wide range of products in stock. All types of film are available at these outlets. Shops in larger centers also provide the freshest film (always check the expiration date) and the best prices.

To buy transparency film (slides), you'll probably have to go to a good camera shop. The same goes for digital and video camera equipment and supplies. Tapes are available at Radio Shack and other electronics retailers. Pharmacists, department stores and corner convenience shops generally carry only basic Kodak and Fuji print film. The price of film in Canada generally does not include processing.

Carrying an extra battery for your built-in light meter is a good idea, because the one you're using is likely to die at the most inopportune time.

For photographing wildlife, a 100mm lens is useful and can be handheld. To get serious, you will need a 200mm telephoto lens and a tripod. Early morning and evening are the best times of day to spy animals in the wild.

Canadian airports use X-ray scanning machines for security, which should pose no problems for most film. However, to be on the safe side, any given roll should not be scanned more than half a dozen times. With specialized film, for example film with an ASA (ISO) of 400 or higher, X-ray damage is a real threat. For those who do not want to take a chance with any film, good camera shops offer lead-lined pouches that hold several canisters of film, provide total protection, and are not unduly heavy.

TIME

Canada uses daylight saving time during summer. It begins on the first Sunday in April and ends on the last Sunday in October. It is one hour later than standard time, meaning a seemingly longer summer day.

The three Maritime provinces and Labrador all follow Atlantic standard time, which is one hour ahead of eastern standard time (used from Québec to Florida) and half an hour behind Newfoundland.

For time comparisons, if it's noon in Halifax (UST/GMT), it is 8am in Vancouver or Los Angeles, 11am in Montréal, 12:30pm in Newfoundland, 4pm in London, 1am (the following day) in Tokyo and 2am (the following day) in Sydney.

ELECTRICITY

Canada, like the USA, operates on 110V, 60-cycle electric power. Non–North American visitors should bring a plug adapter if they wish to use their own small appliances such as razors, hair driers etc. Canadian electrical goods come with either a two-pronged plug (the same as a US one) or sometimes a three-pronger with the added ground. Most sockets can accommodate both types of plugs.

WEIGHTS & MEASURES

Canada officially changed from imperial measurement to the metric system in the 1970s. Many citizens accepted this change only grudgingly, and even today both systems remain in many day-to-day uses.

All speed-limit signs are in metric – so do not go 100mph! Gasoline is sold in liters, but items such as hamburger meat and potatoes are still often sold by the pound. Radio stations will often give temperatures in both Celsius and Fahrenheit degrees.

For help in converting between the two systems, see the chart on the inside back cover of this book. Note that the US system, basically the same as the imperial, differs in liquid measurement, most significantly (for drivers) in the size of its gallons.

LAUNDRY

All cities and major towns have Laundromats with rows of coin-operated washing machines and dryers. These tend to be open every day until about 11pm. There is rarely an attendant on the premises. Many Laundromats have machines that will dispense change and soap. It's fine to go out for a coffee while the wash goes through its cycle, but if you leave a load too long it may be dumped on top of a machine when somebody takes it over for their clothes. A wash and dry costs a couple of dollars, most often in one dollar or 25¢ coins.

Also common are dry cleaners, often known simply as 'the cleaners,' where clothes can be cleaned and pressed in about a day, sometimes two or three.

Many campgrounds, hostels and some B&Bs have a washer and dryer that guests may use, generally for a fee.

TOILETS

That dirty word 'toilet' is rarely used in Canada. Canadians refer to it as the bathroom, the men's or women's room, the rest room or the washroom. Public washrooms are virtually nonexistent; instead visit a hotel, restaurant, museum, mall, government office etc.

HEALTH
Predeparture Preparations

If you are embarking on a long trip make sure your teeth are OK. If you wear glasses take a spare pair and your prescription.

No jabs are required to visit Canada, except if you are coming from an infected area. Immunization against yellow fever is a requirement if you've been to South America or Africa recently. Some routine vaccinations are recommended nonetheless

for all travelers. They include polio, tetanus and diphtheria, and sometimes measles, mumps and rubella. These vaccinations are usually administered during childhood, but some require booster shots.

It's a good idea to pack a basic medical kit (antiseptic solution, aspirin, Band-Aids etc), even when your destination is a place like Canada where first-aid supplies are readily available. Don't forget any medication you are already taking.

A number of excellent travel-health sites are available on the Internet. From the Lonely Planet home page, there are links at W www.lonelyplanet.com/weblinks/wlheal .htm to the World Health Organization and the US Centers for Disease Control & Prevention.

Obtaining Medical Care as a Foreigner

Canadians have no idea how expensive health care is in their country, because the cost comes out of general tax revenues and they receive 'free' treatment. They *do* know how high their taxes are, however! Tourist information offices will often send foreign tourists to the emergency ward at a hospital without realizing that they'll be charged hundreds of dollars to see a doctor there. For example, Halifax's Queen Elizabeth II Health Services Centre charges $300 for a basic examination and $3200 per night if you need to be hospitalized!

Federal government cutbacks to health care have left the provincial systems reeling, and they're often unable to provide proper treatment for their own citizens, much less tourists. Many private doctors aren't accepting new patients, and most general walk-in clinics have closed. At last report, after-hours clinics where appointments were not required still existed in Fredericton Moncton and Charlottetown; these are listed in this book under 'Medical Services in the introductions to those cities. None are available in Saint John or Halifax.

In non-life-threatening circumstances you should ask the manager of your accommodations to call around in search of a private doctor willing to see you. Such a ppointment will cost foreigners between 25 and $50 compared to several hundred dollars at a hospital emergency room. It's no use objecting to the price – you're expected to have travel health insurance. See Travel Insurance, in the Visas & Documents section, for details.

Basics

Water Purification Canadian tap water is usually safe to drink. The following information is for those who intend to be out in the woods or the wilds on outdoor excursions, using lake and river water. Since most extended adventure trips are taken in government parks, ask the warden about local water quality. The simplest way of purifying water is to boil it thoroughly for five minutes.

Simple filtering will not remove all dangerous organisms, so if you cannot boil water it should be treated chemically. Chlorine tablets (Puritabs, Steritabs or other brand names) will kill many pathogens, but not giardia and amoebic cysts. Iodine is very effective in purifying water and is available in tablet form (such as Potable Aqua), but follow the directions carefully and remember that too much iodine can be harmful.

Motion Sickness Eating lightly before and during an ocean trip will reduce the chances of motion sickness. If you are prone to motion sickness try to find a place that minimizes disturbance – near the wing on aircraft, close to midships on boats, near the center on buses. Fresh air usually helps, reading or cigarette smoke doesn't. Commercial motion-sickness preparations, which can cause drowsiness, have to be taken before the trip commences; when you're feeling sick it's too late. Ginger (available in capsule form) and peppermint (including mint-flavored sweets) are natural preventatives. Travel stores sell elasticized wrist bands that can also prevent motion sickness.

Pesticide Exposure On Prince Edward Island and elsewhere be aware of the spraying of pesticides on potato fields and other crops. Pesticide mist can be carried considerable distances by the wind. Avoid camping in areas where spraying might occur, and roll up the car windows if you see a vehicle with long arms lined with nozzles at work. Don't pick wild berries near farm fields. After a mild exposure symptoms are similar to the flu. The long-term impact is serious but more of a threat to local residents than travelers.

Lyme Disease

A minor threat, but still something to be aware of, is Lyme disease (doesn't it seem as though there's always something new out there to get you?). Since the late 1980s each summer sees more of this disease, although the vast majority of North American cases have occurred in the USA. The disease, which infects the skin with spirochete bacterium, is really more of a condition transmitted by a deer tick, similar to a tick found on a dog but smaller. The disease was first identified in 1975 in Lyme, Connecticut, hence the name.

Most cases still go undetected, misdiagnosed or unreported. It is difficult to diagnose because symptoms vary widely. The illness usually begins with a spreading rash at the site of the tick bite and is accompanied by fever, headache, extreme fatigue, aching joints and muscles and mild neck stiffness. If untreated, these symptoms usually resolve over several weeks, but over subsequent weeks or months, disorders of the nervous system, heart and joints may develop. Treatment works best early in the illness. Medical help should be sought.

The best way to avoid the whole business is to take precautions in areas where it has been reported. If you are walking in the woods, cover your body as much as possible, use an insect repellent containing diethylmetatoluamide (DEET), and at the end of the day, check yourself, your children and your pets for the ticks. DEET is not recommended for children, so a milder substitute will have to do. Chances are that you will not feel it if bitten. Of course, most ticks are not the right sort to pass on the disease, and most of them do not carry the harmful bacteria.

WOMEN TRAVELERS

More and more women are traveling alone in Canada. This goes for vacationers, visitors and women on business. There are no overriding differences for men and women traveling in Canada and no particular cultural or traditional pitfalls of which females need to be aware.

As in most of the world, though, women may face some sexism, and the threat of violence is certainly felt more by women than by men. The following tips to consider have been suggested by women.

When traveling alone, try to arrive at your destination before dark. If arriving at a bus or train station, consider taking a taxi to the place where you're spending the night. In Halifax, for example, the bus station is not in the best part of town. Some parts of the downtown areas of major cities should be avoided at night, particularly on a Friday or Saturday.

If driving, keep your vehicle well maintained and don't get low on gasoline. If you do break down on the highway, especially at night, a large pre-made sign placed in the window reading 'Call Police' is not a bad idea. Such a sign will quickly result in calls and a cruiser on the way. Away from busy areas, it is not advisable for women alone to get out of their car and wait beside it, especially at night. Wait inside with the doors locked.

It is rare to see women hitching alone. and it can't be recommended. Mixed sex couples are the better way for women to hitch a ride if they are determined to travel this way. For more information, see Hitchhiking in the Getting Around chapter.

Women traveling alone may be more comfortable if their room is booked before they arrive in a new town. Many women prefer to simply use an initial with their surname and not to use a title when making reservations or appointments. The phone numbers provided in this book allow for reservations to be made in advance.

Hostels and B&Bs are good, safe choices. Many Canadian B&Bs are run by couples or by women. In B&Bs and guesthouses, ask whether the rooms have locks – some do not.

When checking into a motel, ask to see the room first and make sure the doors and windows can be secured. Many motel rooms come with a telephone.

Unaccompanied women in nightclubs or bars will often find they get a lot of attention (and possibly drinks) whether they want it or not.

Women who enjoy the outdoors should be aware that the smell of perfumes and fragrant cosmetics attracts bears, so if you're in an area where bears are likely to be around, it's best not to wear any fragrance. Insects, too, are said to find perfume a pleasant lure.

GAY & LESBIAN TRAVELERS

As a generally tolerant country, Canada doesn't present any particular problem for homosexuals. Discrimination against gays and lesbians at tourist accommodations is prohibited, and proprietors face fines and revocation of their license if caught doing so.

Halifax, Moncton and Fredericton have sizable gay communities with support groups and associations. Halifax is the gay and lesbian capital of Atlantic Canada, with a number of cafés, bars and B&Bs catering to this community. *Wayves,* a free monthly newspaper published in Halifax, has a full range of information, including advertisements for gay-friendly lodgings and other businesses.

The top event on the Maritimes gay and lesbian calendar is the Halifax Pride Parade through the city center, attracting large crowds of people (both gay and straight). It is held on a Saturday afternoon in late June. The Moncton Gay Pride Parade often occurs on the same weekend. Prince Edward Island's Gay Pride Week is in mid-July. Web sites such as W www.gayhalifax .com, W www.monctongay.com and W www .gaywhitenorth.com provide information on these events.

DISABLED TRAVELERS

Canada has gone further than the vast majority of the world's countries in making day-to-day life less burdensome to the phys ically disabled, most notably the wheelchair-bound. Most public buildings are wheelchair accessible, including major tourist offices. Ditto for major museums, art galleries and principal attractions. All the above and many restaurants also have washroom facilities suitable for wheelchairs. Major hotels often have wheelchair access through ramps.

Many of the national and provincial parks have accessible interpretive centers and some of the shorter nature trails or boardwalks have been developed with wheelchairs or self-propelled transport in mind. Such areas are usually indicated on park maps. Mersey River Chalets near Kejimkujik National Park in southwestern Nova Scotia has tipis and kayaks custom designed for the physically challenged.

The VIA Rail system is prepared to accommodate the wheelchair-bound, but advance notice of 48 hours should be given. All bus lines will assist passengers and take chairs or any other aids, providing they collapse and will fit in the usual luggage compartments. And all Canadian airlines are accustomed to dealing with disabled passengers and provide early boarding and disembarking as standard practice.

In major cities, parking lots all have designated parking spots for the physically disabled, usually marked with blue paint and a white wheelchair. These spots are usually located closest to the door or access point of the place being visited.

Car-rental agencies can provide special accessories such as hand controls, but again, advance notice is required. Ask if they can give you a disabled parking permit.

SENIOR TRAVELERS

Visitors over the age of 65, and sometimes 60, should take advantage of the many cost reductions available to seniors in Canada. Seniors' discounts are offered on all means of transportation and can result in substantial savings. Most of the national and provincial parks have reduced rates, as do many of the region's attractions, even movie houses. Some hotels and motels may provide a price reduction – it's always worth asking.

Elderhostel, with branches in many countries, is also found in Canada, where it's called Routes to Learning. It specializes in inexpensive, educational packages for those over 55 years of age. The standard type of program consists of mornings of talks and lectures followed by afternoon field trips and visits to related sights. Participants stay in university dorms or the like. There is generally a full-package price that includes meals, lodging and some transportation. The courses are of varying lengths but may be several weeks long. Subject matter is drawn from a variety of interests, including history, nature, geography and art. For more detailed information contact Routes to Learning (☎ 613-530-2222, fax 613-530-2096, ⓔ information@routesto learning.ca), 300 – 4 Cataraqui St, Kingston, ON K7K 1Z7 Canada.
Web site: ⓦ www.routestolearning.ca

TRAVEL WITH CHILDREN

Almost all attractions in Canada offer child rates. Some hotels don't charge at all for young children. If you have young children, inquire about safety seats before renting a car and high chairs before booking a restaurant table.

Always fit children with lifejackets during any boating/canoeing excursions. While camping or hiking in remote areas, be aware of how quickly children can become disoriented and lost. Also do not let kids stray where wild animals are known to exist. Ask park wardens if you are in any doubt. Never let children approach stray animals, no matter how cute and tame the animal appears.

For more advice on traveling with children, see *Travel with Children,* by Lonely Planet author Cathy Lanigan.

USEFUL ORGANIZATIONS

A number of local environmental groups can provide helpful information on their areas:

New Brunswick
   Conservation Council of New Brunswick
   (☎ 506-458-8747, fax 506-458-1047)
   180 St John Street, Fredericton, NB, Canada
   E3B 4A9
   Web site: ⓦ www.web.net/~ccnb

Nova Scotia

Ecology Action Centre
(☎ 902-429-2202, fax 902-422-6410)
1568 Argyle St, Suite 31, Halifax NS B3J 2B3
Web site: Ⓦ www.chebucto.ns.ca/Environment/
EAC
Nova Scotia Public Interest Research Group
(☎ 902-494-6662)
Room 314, Student Union Building, 6136 University Ave, Halifax, NS B3H 4J2
Web site: Ⓦ www.chebucto.ns.ca/Community-
Support/NSPIRG
Sierra Club of Canada
(☎ 902-422-5091, fax 902-422-9440)
1312 Robie Street, Halifax NS B3H 3E2
Web site: Ⓦ atlantic.sierraclub.ca

Prince Edward Island

Earth Action
(☎ 902-621-0719)
81 Prince St, Charlottetown, PEI C1A 4R3
Voluntary Resource Council
(☎ 902-368-7337, fax 902-368-7180)
81 Prince St, Charlottetown, PEI C1A 4R3

DANGERS & ANNOYANCES

Check the Health section earlier in this chapter for possible health risks. See also Road Rules & Safety Precautions in the Getting Around chapter for driving tips.

Ocean Currents & Tides

It may seem unlikely to those who visit in the off-season, but people do swim in the ocean here, and if you come in July and August, you'll probably want to do just that. Before entering water more than knee deep, consider if there might be a current caused by the tide or other factors. Currents in the Bay of Fundy create an amazingly strong rip, and the undertow can be just as perilous on Atlantic beaches. The beaches at Prince Edward Island National Park can also be dangerous in this regard (those on the Northumberland Strait are safer).

If you go beach hiking along the Bay of Fundy beware of becoming cut off by a rising tide. The water level can rise as much as 30m in just over an hour, and you could become stranded on the side of a cliff with the waves lapping your feet! If you begin your hike just as the tide is going out, you'll be safe for three or four hours.

Noise

Unfortunately almost no campgrounds in the Maritimes have radio-free areas. Most have rules forbidding 'excessive noise' but what constitutes excessive is a matter of opinion. It's not such a problem if you have a motorhome with a door you can close, but campers in nylon tents are very vulnerable to noise. Keep this factor in mind when choosing your campsite and don't hesitate to complain politely to the campground manager if someone really makes a nuisance of themselves.

Blackflies & Mosquitoes

In the woods of the Maritimes, the blackflies and mosquitoes can be murder. There are tales of lost hikers going insane from the bugs. This is no joke – they can make you miserable. The effect of a bite (or sting, technically, by the mosquito) is a small itchy bump. The moment of attack is itself a very minor, passing pain. Some people are allergic to blackfly bites and will develop a fair bit of swelling, but other than the unsightly welt, there is no real danger. The potential trouble is in the cumulative effects of scores of them, and even this hazard is mainly psychological.

As a rule, darker clothes are said to attract biting insects more than lighter ones. Perfume, too, evidently attracts the wrong kind of attention. Take 'bug juice' liquid or spray insect repellents. Two recommended names are Muskol and Off; the latter also has an extra strength version known as Deep Woods Off. An ingredient often used in repellents known as DEET should not be used on children. Use a repellent without it. Try to minimize the amount of skin exposed by wearing a long-sleeved shirt, long pants and a close-fitting hat or cap.

June is generally the worst month, and as the summer wears on the bugs disappear. The bugs are at their worst deep in the woods. In clearings, along shorelines or anywhere there's a breeze you'll be safe, except for the buzzing horseflies, which are basically teeth with wings.

Mosquitoes come out around sunset; building a fire will help keep them away.

For campers, a tent with a zippered screen is pretty much a necessity.

Other Insects

In some areas you may encounter sand gnats and no-see-ums – so called because you feel their bites but you never see 'em. There is not much to be done about this; fortunately neither insect is overly common. Campers should have very finely meshed tents to prevent a possible night invasion of no-see-ums, which really isn't so bad, but it's better to be told the worst than to be caught off guard.

Campsite Pests

Campers are unlikely to encounter bears, but squirrels, chipmunks, mice and raccoons are common. All of them love human food. They will tear through any bags of food or garbage you leave out and even smack pots and pans around in the middle of the night. The best defense is never to feed them, no matter how cute they are, and to store all food securely.

EMERGENCIES

In most of the region, particularly urban areas, telephone ☎ 911 for all police, fire, accident and medical emergencies. Otherwise, call ☎ 0 and ask the operator for assistance; you will then be put through to the appropriate service. Dialing ☎ 911 gets a faster response. For nonemergency police matters, consult the local telephone book for the number of the station.

Should your passport get lost or stolen, contact your consulate. It will be able to issue a temporary replacement and inform you when and how to go about getting another – and you may not even need another, depending on your travel plans.

If you plan to make a luggage insurance claim, be sure to contact the police and have them make a record of the theft. Ask for the reference number on the police report and write it down, as the insurance company will want it.

If you lose your credit card or traveler's checks, call the appropriate emergency number for assistance : VISA (☎ 800-336-8472), MasterCard (☎ 800-361-3361) or American Express (☎ 800-221-7282).

LEGAL MATTERS

Visitors are unlikely to meet Canadian police officers, as spot checks on individuals and vehicles are not common. Drunk driving is considered a very serious offense and random checks are held at bar closing time, notably around Christmas. You could find yourself in jail overnight, followed by a further court date, heavy fine, suspended license and possibly more incarceration.

Despite possible appearances of indifference, recreational drugs are illegal, and laws may be enforced at any time. Smuggling any drug, including pot, is a serious crime. See Customs earlier in this chapter.

BUSINESS HOURS
Banks

The banks are reliably open 10am to 3pm Monday to Friday, and some remain open an hour or two later on Thursday and Friday. Very few banks are open Saturday, and all are closed on Sunday and holidays. Many banks have ATMs, known in Canada as 'banking machines,' which are accessible 24 hours a day.

Post Offices

Canadian post offices are generally open 9am to 5pm Monday to Friday. Postal outlets in retail stores have much longer hours.

Stores

Cities and their suburbs generally have the longest retail store hours. Most stores are open from about 9am to 6pm. On Friday, and sometimes Thursday, shops are open until 9pm. Shopping malls, plazas, large department stores and some downtown stores may remain open until 9pm Monday to Saturday.

Larger centers have a limited number of stores that remain open 24 hours. These are usually convenience shops that sell basic groceries, cigarettes and newspapers. Some large supermarkets and pharmacies (drugstores) also remain open 24 hours.

Shops in smaller towns generally have shorter hours, with little evening shopping and nothing much available on Sunday except for basic groceries and movies.

On major highways 24-hour service stations sell gasoline and food.

Restaurants
Few restaurants are open after midnight as Canadians do not dine particularly late, rarely eating out later than 10pm. Many of the better places are open for lunch and dinner only. Smaller eateries and coffee shops open as early as 6am and close before dinner.

Bars & Liquor Sales
Hours vary according to the province. Most bars, pubs and lounges open at 11am and close at 1am or 2am. The larger cities usually have after-hours bars that remain open for music or dancing but stop serving alcohol. In all other cases, alcohol must be bought through government retail stores.

The drinking age varies from province to province, but the norm is 19 years old.

PUBLIC HOLIDAYS
Labor Day is an important holiday, as this long weekend at the beginning of September is unofficially the end of summer. It marks the closing of many businesses, attractions and services and a change in hours of operation for many others. On Victoria Day (Queen Victoria's birthday) in late May, the places that closed on Labor Day begin opening again.

Thanksgiving (the same as the American holiday but held a month earlier) is really a harvest festival. The traditional meal includes roasted turkey.

Although not officially a holiday, Halloween (October 31) is a significant and fun celebration and a time for costume parties. Based on a Celtic pagan tradition, in larger cities gays have adopted it as a major event, and nightclubs are often the scene of wild masquerades.

The following is a list of the main public holidays:

January
  New Year's Day (January 1)
April–May
  Easter (and Good Friday and Easter Monday for government and schools)
  Victoria Day (Monday preceding May 24)
July
  Canada Day (July 1)
August
  Civic Holiday (first Monday in August)
September
  Labor Day (first Monday in September)
October
  Thanksgiving (second Monday in October)
November
  Remembrance Day (November 11; banks and government offices closed)
December
  Christmas Day (December 25)
  Boxing Day (December 26; many retailers open)

SPECIAL EVENTS
Major events are listed in the text under the city or town where they occur. The provincial governments publish annual lists of events and special attractions as part of their tourism promotion packages, with dates, locations and (sometimes) brief descriptions. Local tourist departments may print up more detailed and extensive lists of their own, including cultural and sporting exhibitions, music shows, ethnic festivals, military and historic celebrations and happenings of all kinds. Some provinces produce separate booklets for summer and winter events.

Major provincial and national holidays are usually cause for some celebration, especially in summer when events often wrap up with a fireworks display. The July 1 Canada Day festivities are particularly noted for fireworks, with the skies lit up from coast to coast.

National Aboriginal Day (June 21) is not a public holiday, but the Mi'kmaq and Maliseet communities stage powwows throughout the summer, and all visitors are welcome to attend. The dancers in full regalia present a colorful spectacle, the drumming is exciting, and there are stands offering traditional foods and handicrafts

Many powwows feature a sweat lodge, talking circle and sacred ceremonies. Alcohol and drugs are usually banned. It's a great opportunity to meet First Nations people in a friendly, open venue; approximate powwow dates are listed in this book in the sections on Eel River, Lennox Island, Mount Stewart, Panmure Island, Pictou, Red Bank, Truro and Wagmatcook. The powwows are always on a weekend, but the dates do change from year to year, and obtaining reliable information can be difficult. The best way to check the dates is to call the tourism operators in the immediate area, listed in this book; they'll probably know when the powwow will be held that year.

ACTIVITIES

Canada's greatest attribute is its natural environment, and much of the country's appeal lies in outdoor activities such as hiking, cycling, kayaking, canoeing, fishing, skiing and observing and photographing flora and fauna.

There are wilderness trips of all types, organized or self-guided. Provincial tourist offices have information on activities in their region and details on the hundreds of private businesses, operators and outfitters offering adventure tours and trips. All have information on national and provincial parks; see the individual province chapters in this book for more details.

Hiking

The Maritimes offer a range of walks and hikes that are long or short, rugged or gentle, backcountry or coastal. Many of the best trails are found in or near the provincial and national parks. The majority of parks have some type of walking path, even if it's just a short nature trail. As a rule, the larger the park, the longer the trails. Some trails require a couple nights of backcountry camping to complete.

Nova Scotia has the most trails, but a few in New Brunswick's Fundy and Mount Carleton parks are outstanding. Only short walking trails are available on Prince Edward Island. The hiking season runs from

May to October, with the best conditions from July onwards, when the trails have dried out and most of the insects are gone.

Work is continuing on the Trans Canada Trail, a 15,000km crushed-stone path winding from the Atlantic to the Pacific. When finished, it will take about 300 days to cycle, 500 days to ride on horseback and 750 days to walk. For the current status and information on completed sections visit W www.tctrail.ca.

Parks with trails are discussed throughout the text, and some individual trails are outlined. Here are some highlights:

Cape Chignecto Coastal Trail (see Chignecto in the Central Nova Scotia chapter)

Cape Mabou Highlands Trail (see Mabou in the Cape Breton Island chapter)

Cape St Lawrence Trail (see Cape North in the Cape Breton Island chapter)

Cape Split Trail (see Kentville in the Southwestern Nova Scotia chapter)

Delaps Cove Wilderness Trail (see Annapolis Royal in the Southwestern Nova Scotia chapter)

Economy Falls and Devil's Bend Trails (see Chignecto in the Central Nova Scotia chapter)

Fishing Cove Trail (see Cape Breton National Park in the Cape Breton Island chapter)

Fundy Circuit Trail (see Fundy National Park in the New Brunswick chapter)

Fundy Trail (see St Martins in the New Brunswick chapter)

Kejimkujik National Park (see the Southwestern Nova Scotia chapter)

Mount Carleton & Sagamook Trails (see Mount Carleton in the New Brunswick chapter)

Uisge Bahn Falls Hiking Trail (see Baddeck in the Cape Breton Island chapter)

Cycling

Although Nova Scotia has some excellent bicycle trails, it's here that Prince Edward Island excels. The 350km Confederation Trail along the length of the island is now complete, with feeder trails down to most towns and the Confederation Bridge. Facilities have been established along the route to provide services for trail users, many in reconditioned train stations along this old railway line.

New Brunswick is working hard to do something similar, and you'll find finished but as yet unconnected sections of the New Brunswick Trail all around the province. For more information see Bicycle in the introduction to New Brunswick.

Several companies run guided bicycle tours, including MacQueen's Island Tours in Charlottetown. Check out their Web site at ⓦ www.macqueens.com.

You can rent bicycles at numerous locations, including Baddeck, Chester, Digby, Halifax, Kejimkujik, Liverpool, Lockeport, Lunenburg, Mabou, Pictou, Shelburne, Smelt Brook, Sydney, Tangier, Tatamagouche and Wolfville in Nova Scotia; Cavendish, Charlottetown and Summerside on PEI; and Edmundston, Fredericton, Gagetown, Grand Manan and Kouchibouguac in New Brunswick.

These are some of the most famous bicycling trails:

Confederation Trail (from Elmira to Tignish; see the PEI chapter)

Fundy Parkway Trail (see St Martins in the New Brunswick chapter)

Goose River Trail (one of six bicycle trails in Fundy National Park; see the section in the New Brunswick chapter)

Kouchibouguac National Park (26km of trails; see the section in the New Brunswick chapter)

Musquodoboit Trailways (see Musquodoboit Harbour in the Eastern Shore chapter)

New Brunswick Trail (sections open in various locations)

Kayaking

The fastest growing adventure tourism activity in the Maritimes is ocean kayaking. You can now take kayaking lessons, join guided tours and rent kayaks at dozens of locations. This is the best way to see the remarkable coastlines of this region.

The prime kayaking locales of Nova Scotia are along the South Shore from Halifax to Shelburne, near Tangier on the Eastern Shore and around Bras d'Or Lake on Cape Breton. There's also good kayaking off northern and western Prince Edward Island. The places to dip a paddle in New Brunswick are the Fundy Isles from St Andrews to Grand Manan, along the central Fundy shore from St Martins to Hopewell Cape and near Kouchibouguac National Park.

Over 40 companies renting kayaks are listed in this book, the majority of them in the areas just mentioned. Nearly half also offer guided kayaking. Most are only open from late June to early September. To become an expert on what's out there browse these Web sites:

Baymount Adventures, Hopewell Rocks, NB
Web site: ⓦ www.baymountadventures.com

Cape Breton Sea Coast Adventures, Ingonish Beach, NS
Web site: ⓦ www.members.tripod.com/mike_crimp

Cape Enrage Adventures, Alma, NB
Web site: ⓦ www.capenrage.com

Coastal Adventures, Tangier, NS
Web site: ⓦ www.coastal adventures.com

Crescent Sea Kayak Tours, LaHave, NS
Web site: ⓦ www.lairdadventures.com

Eastern Outdoors, Saint John, NB
Web site: ⓦ www.easternoutdoors.com

FreshAir Adventure, Alma, NB
Web site: ⓦ www.freshairadventure.com

Kayabécano, Bouctouche, NB
Web site: ⓦ www.kayabecano.nb.ca

Kayakouch, Saint-Louis-de-Kent, NB
Web site: ⓦ www.kayakouch.com

Mahone Bay Kayak Adventures, Mahone Bay, NS
Web site: ⓦ www.mahonebaykayaks.com

Mi'kmaq Kayak Adventures, Lennox Island PE
Web site: ⓦ www.minegoo.com

Novashores Adventures, Glen Margaret, NS
Web site: ⓦ www.novashores.com

Ocean Breeze Kayak Adventures, Shelburne, NS
Web site: ⓦ www.oceanbreeze3.com

Outside Expeditions, Cymbria, PEI
Web site: ⓦ www.getoutside.com

Sea Sun Kayak School & Adventures, Halifax, NS
Web site: ⓦ www.paddlenovascotia.com

Canoeing

Canoeing is better suited to inland lakes and rivers or protected areas along the coast. It's offered in many of the same areas as ocean kayaking, plus a few inland waterways.

The most famous canoe route in the region is the old Shubenacadie Canal from Dartmouth to the Bay of Fundy. Canoeing is very popular on the Saint John River around Fredericton. The whole of Kejimkujik National Park is a prime canoeing territory, and three or four companies rent canoes in that area.

The most intriguing canoe tours offered are in central New Brunswick. The three-hour Voyageur canoe tour at Kouchibouguac National Park is excellent, and the Red Bank First Nation on the Miramichi River can provide canoe guides.

An excellent source of information on this activity is the Halifax Trading and Guide Post (☎ 902-492-1420), 1586 Granville St, Halifax. They sell detailed canoeing guidebooks and route maps and can advise on tours.

Fishing

In the Maritimes, deep sea fishing is much more common than freshwater fishing. Quite a few captains of small fishing boats earn extra revenue in July and August taking visitors out on scheduled trips. Of course, you can charter a whole boat for a couple of hundred dollars, but if you only want a taste of the activity (and some sea air) you can sign up for a three-hour fishing excursion for around $25 per head.

Places where deep-sea fishing is offered include Baddeck, Bridgeport, Chéticamp, Digby, Isle Madame and Margaree Harbour in Nova Scotia; Covehead Bridge, North Rustico, Rusticoville, Seacow Pond and St Margaret's on Prince Edward Island; and Caraquet and St George in New Brunswick. All fish caught usually belong to the boat.

The two areas famous for their freshwater fly-fishing are the Margaree Valley on Cape Breton Island and the Miramichi River in New Brunswick. The salmon fishing museums at North East Margaree and Doaktown are the best sources of information. On the Miramichi you can hire guides for salmon fishing at Red Bank First Nation. With Atlantic salmon stocks in decline, the fishing is strictly catch and release.

The provincial tourist offices will have specific information about fishing outfitters and regulations. Any required licenses can be purchased through the salmon museums previously mentioned or local fly shops.

Rock Climbing

Rock climbing has come out from under its rock and is now a possibility in the Maritimes, even for novices. Group climbs, with instructors and equipment, are available. A good place to begin is the Vertigo Climbing School (☎ 902-492-1420), 1586 Granville St, Halifax, NS B3J 1X1. Check their Web site (W www3.ns.sympatico.ca/vertigo) for details.

Scuba Diving

Occasional scuba diving trips are organized by dive shops in Charlottetown, Halifax and Lunenburg from mid-June to mid-September. These cater mostly to locals, and the shops make their money selling equipment and lessons to people who do their real diving elsewhere, but it's worth checking out if you're a scuba nut. For more information, try Black Dolphin Diving & Watersports (☎ 902-894-3483, fax 902-626-3483); see Charlottetown in the Prince Edward Island chapter later in this book.

Downhill & Cross-Country Skiing

The Maritimes aren't among Canada's leading ski destinations, though there are a couple of ski resorts in northern New Brunswick to serve the needs of local residents. The best known are Sugarloaf Provincial Park at Campbellton and Mount Farlange outside Edmundston. Check with Tourism New Brunswick (see Tourist Offices, earlier) for information about these areas.

Cross-country skiing is possible all across the region in winter, and the provincial tourist offices will have suggestions. An excellent choice here would be the Wentworth HI Hostel between Amherst and Truro, Nova Scotia. It's open year-round and the ski trails are right at the door. There's also some downhill skiing at Wentworth.

COURSES

Students wishing to study formally in Canada (for example, at a university) must get authorization within their own country. This can take six months. Information should be obtained from the Canadian embassy or other government representative in your country of residence. General information regarding studying in Canada can be found on the Internet at W www .canadianembassy.org/studyincanada. Information for those interested in studying in Nova Scotia is accessible on the Web at W www.international.ednet.ns.ca.

Major cities have privately run schools specializing in teaching English as a second language (ESL). These can be found in the Yellow Pages, and some are on the Internet. For courses lasting over three months a student visa is required. Some of these schools offer TOEFL English proficiency certificates used to gain entry into Canadian universities.

Also within the cities, a wide range of vocational and recreational courses are available, ranging from acupuncture to Web page design.

Many of the outdoor outfitters mentioned in the text offer courses in canoeing, kayaking, rock climbing and the like.

WORK

It is difficult for foreign workers to get a permit to work in Canada; employment opportunities go first to Canadians. Those wishing to obtain a work permit must get a validated job offer from an employer and take this to a Canadian consulate or embassy outside Canada. Getting a work authorization may take six months. A work permit is valid for a specific job and a specified time for a single employer.

Visitors to Canada are technically not allowed to work. However, employers hiring temporary workers in hotels, bars and restaurants, construction, farm or forestry often don't ask to see a permit. Visitors working here legally have social insurance numbers beginning with nine. If you don't have a social insurance number and get caught, you will be told to leave the country.

Many young European women come to Canada as nannies. Japan has a program called Contact Canada that includes one-year work permits with prearranged work, generally on farms. Many countries have agencies where details on these programs can be obtained.

Working Holiday Program

This program is open to all Australians and New Zealanders between the ages of 18 and 30, and they need not be enrolled in a post-secondary educational institution. There's a quota of 4000 Australians and 800 New Zealanders annually. Application forms can be obtained by contacting the Canadian Consulate General in Sydney, Australia, or the Canadian High Commission in Wellington, New Zealand. See Embassies & Consulates earlier in this chapter for the addresses or visit their Web site at W www .dfait-maeci.gc.ca/australia. The minimum processing time for these applications is 12 weeks.

ACCOMMODATIONS

The three provincial accommodations directories list most campgrounds, tourist homes, B&Bs, motels and hotels (but not hostels), with specific prices, ratings and much technical information. The directories are updated annually and can be requested free of charge via the official Web sites previously listed under Provincial Tourist Offices.

If you're not online, call or write or just ask at the first tourist office you reach. You want the *Nova Scotia Complete Guide for Doers and Dreamers,* the *Prince Edward Island Visitors Guide* and the *New Brunswick Travel Planner.* By comparing them with the listings in this book, you'll soon know where to stay.

Camping

There are campgrounds all across the Maritimes – federal, provincial and privately owned. Government campsites are nearly always better and cheaper and, not surprisingly, fill up the quickest. Government parks are well laid out, green and well treed. They are usually quiet, situated to take advantage of the local landscape, and offer a program of events and talks. Private campgrounds are generally geared to trailers (caravans) and recreational vehicles (RVs). Many have other services available, even swimming pools and entertainment facilities.

In national parks, camping fees range from $10 to $17 for an unserviced (primitive) site and up to $21 for sites with services like electricity. The park entrance fee is extra. Some parks accept reservations for an additional $7.50. See the individual park listings for more information.

Provincial park camping rates vary with each province. At Nova Scotia provincial parks unserviced sites are between $14 and $18 (there are no serviced sites). On Prince Edward Island, sites are around $17/21 unserviced/serviced. In New Brunswick, unserviced sites range from $18 to $22, serviced sites $21 to $24, depending on the park. Mount Carleton Provincial Park is cheaper, at $11 or $14. Backcountry camping in the wilderness parks can cost anywhere from $3 per person at Fundy National Park to over $16 per site at Kejimkujik. Commercial campgrounds generally cost several dollars more than those in provincial or national parks.

Government parks start closing in early September for the winter. Dates vary according to the location. Some remain open for maintenance even when camping is finished, and they might let you camp at a reduced rate. Other places are free in late autumn or early in spring, with the gate left open and not a soul around. Still other parks block the road, and entering the campgrounds is not allowed. The parks themselves can still be visited, however. So, out of the main summer season you have to investigate, but using the parks after official closing can save the hardy a fair bit of money.

Some people travel around the country camping and never pay a dime for it. If you have a car or van, using roadside rest areas and picnic spots is possible, but if there are signs indicating no overnight camping, don't set up a tent. Some cities (such as Halifax) have bylaws that prohibit sleeping overnight in vehicles on city streets, in which case it's better to drive outside city limits if you want to sleep in your car. For less chance of interruption, side roads and logging roads off the highway tend to be quiet and private.

Hostels

There are a few excellent hostels in the Maritimes similar to those found all around the world. The term 'hostel', however, has some unfortunate connotations in Canada. The term has long been used in reference to both government and private shelters for the underprivileged, sick and abused. There are, for example, hostels for battered women and hostels for recovering drug addicts. So, if you get a sideways glance when you say you are on the way to spend the night at the hostel, you'll know why. Say 'travelers hostel' or 'international hostel' if you wish to clarify.

There are two hostelling groups operating in Canada geared to low-budget visitors. They represent the cheapest places to stay in the country, and you'll probably meet the most travelers in them.

Hostelling International The oldest, best known and most established hostelling association is Hostelling International (HI) Canada, a member of the internationally known hostelling association. The hostels are no longer called 'youth hostels,' although they are sometimes still referred to in this way. Throughout the text of this book, these hostels are referred to as 'HI Hostel.' Their symbol is an evergreen tree and stylized house within a blue triangle.

Hostelling International has nine hostels in the Maritimes. Nightly costs range from $12 to $18, and nonmembers can stay for an additional $2 to $5. A membership can quickly pay for itself and has now been built into the system so that after a few stays you automatically become a member. Hostels are the best bargain for people traveling alone, as the charge is per person with no reduction for doubles. Some hostels do have family rooms set aside.

In July and August space may be a problem at popular hostels like the one in Halifax, so calling ahead to make a reservation is a good idea. Reservations must be made more than 24 hours in advance, and you'll need a credit card. Call the hostel directly at the number provided in this book. Outside July and August, traffic thins and getting a bed should not be difficult. Many of the hostels are closed in winter.

In addition to the lower nightly rates, members can often take advantage of discounts offered by businesses. Local hostels should have a list of places where discounts are available. Some hostels organize outdoor activities such as canoeing, kayaking, skiing, hiking, tours and city walks.

A yearly international membership costs $35 for an adult. Contact Hostelling International–Canada (☎ 613-237-7884, fax 613-237-7868), National Office, 400-205 Catherine St, Ottawa, Ontario K2P 1C3. More information is available on the Internet at ⓦ www.hihostels.ca.

Backpackers Hostels The second group is a network of independent hostels collectively known as Backpackers Hostels Canada. Its symbol is a circled howling wolf with a map of Canada in the background. For information, including a list of hostels, log on to ⓦ www.backpackers.ca. Aside from typical hostels, there also are campgrounds, church facilities, organic farms, motels, retreats and tourist homes that provide budget travelers with inexpensive accommodation.

Unfortunately the Web site is unreliable. Many of the 30 places in the Maritimes listed on the site no longer operate as hostels. People setting up hostels often affiliate with Backpackers Hostels Canada to avoid the stringent insurance, safety and other requirements of Hostelling International. However, many drop out when they earn little return for their hard work.

The loose network has no formal standards, so quality, atmosphere and approach vary a lot. The major benefit of Backpackers for travelers is that it offers accommodations in a range of smaller, out-of-the-way

locations where nothing else of the sort i available. Many are included in this book but those that didn't readily offer the adver tised hostel prices (let alone when they looked abandoned or had large 'for sale signs in the windows) were left out.

Many hostels are in regular contact with one another, so a stay at one may turn up leads on others. Beds in shared rooms cos anywhere from $12 to $20, and private rooms are often available beginning at $30 A membership is not required to use these facilities.

University Accommodations

Many universities in the Maritimes rent ou beds in their residence dormitories during the summer months. The season runs ap proximately from May to some time in August, with possible closures for such things as large academic conferences Singles/doubles begin around $26/38 and in crease to $48/60. Many places offer student and seniors a reduction of $7 to $11. Lower weekly rates may also be possible. Parking is usually (but not always) included.

Reservations are accepted but aren't nor mally necessary, as hundreds of rooms may be available. It's wise to call ahead to confirm that the office will be open, espe cially if you're arriving late. Many of the front desks remain open 24 hours. Breakfas is sometimes included in the price, and campus facilities, such as the swimming pool, are often available to guests.

Campus accommodations are listed in the text under Hostels in Antigonish, Char lottetown, Edmundston, Fredericton Halifax, Moncton, Sackville, Saint John Sydney and Truro. Campus residences are open to all, and they're typically excellen value. For more information check on the Internet (ⓦ www.cuccoa.org).

Guesthouses & Tourist Homes

Another lodging alternative is the simple guesthouse or tourist home. These may be just an extra room in someone's home, bu some are regular commercial lodging houses. They are found mainly in places with a large tourist trade such as Charlottetown

Rooms vary in size and in amenities. Some include private bathrooms, but many do not. The standard cost is about $40 to $65 or a double.

Some so-called tourist homes are really rooming houses that are customarily rented by the week or month and usually have shared kitchens. The biggest difference from a B&B is that tourist homes don't serve breakfast.

B&Bs

B&Bs play a central role in the tourist lodging scene in the Maritimes, and they continue to grow in number. The Canadian equivalent of the European pension, B&Bs offer a more personal alternative to the traditional motel or hotel, and quite often a B&B is the only place to stay in a small town. Some are full-time businesses while others just provide their operators with income for the summer.

Prices of B&Bs vary quite a bit, roughly from $35 for a single to over $100 for a double, with the average being $45 to $55 for two people. In popular areas where there isn't a wide range of places to stay (such as Lunenburg), prices can be much higher. Most accommodations post an official rate on the room doors.

The more expensive B&Bs provide more impressive furnishings and decor. Many B&Bs are found in classic heritage houses. Rooms are almost always in the owner's home and are clean and well kept. Note that smoking is almost always prohibited. Some places will take children, and the odd one will allow a pet. Breakfast can vary from a 'continental' of toast and coffee to a 'full' cooked breakfast including eggs. It's worth inquiring about the breakfast when booking.

While rooms at hotels and motels generally have private bathrooms, many B&Bs and tourist homes offer rooms with shared bath. In such cases, provincial licensing regulations require a bathroom for the exclusive use of guests on the same floor as the bedrooms. Annual inspections are carried out, and places that don't meet the requirements don't get a license or a listing in the provincial tourism directory. A few B&Bs rent substandard rooms not approved by the provincial authorities, but the vast majority are up to standards. Although the more upscale B&Bs offer rooms with private bath, it's safer to assume that you'll have to share the bathroom with one or two other guests. If having your own private bathroom is very important, ask about it when you call.

The average life expectancy of a B&B is five years, so it's inevitable that some of those described in this book will have closed by the time of your visit. Thus it's *essential* to call ahead to make sure a given B&B is still in business, confirm that they have a room for you before going out of your way, and see if the price is still within your budget. It's better to verify exactly what is included (breakfast, tax, parking, bathroom etc) over the phone before you arrive. That way you won't need to negotiate with your hosts on their doorstep. Most of the people running B&Bs in the Maritimes do it as much because they like meeting people as for the money. It's one of the things that makes this region special.

Motels

In Canada as in the USA, motels are ubiquitous. Mostly they are simple and clean, if somewhat nondescript. They can be found dotting the highways and clustered in groups on the outskirts of larger towns and cities. Room rates range from about $35 to $65 for singles or doubles.

Prices usually go up in summer or when a special event is on. In the off-season from mid-September to mid-June, always ask about weekly rates, which may be the equivalent of three or four nights at the daily rate. In Saint John, New Brunswick, for example, most motels have weekly rates off-season, and the city provides an excellent base from which to explore a large surrounding area.

Unlike most better hotels, many motels remain mom-and-pop operations and so retain more flexibility and often reflect more of the character of the owners. You have more privacy than at a B&B, with all the basic comforts. A private bath is always included, usually a television as well, and sometimes even a fridge.

Some motels offer 'suites.' This usually means there is a separate second bedroom (good for families with children), but it might also mean there's a sitting room with TV and chesterfield set apart from the bedroom. Housekeeping units, also called 'efficiencies,' are rooms with cooking facilities. It's often worth paying a few dollars more if you can prepare your own dinner and breakfast. Many older motels have unheated cabins or cottages in addition to rows of rooms. These often have small kitchenettes.

Hotels

Good, inexpensive hotels are not Canada's strong suit. Most new hotels are part of international chains and are designed for either the luxury market or businesspeople. A few older, cheaper hotels still exist in places well off the beaten tourist track such as Miramichi and Sydney, but virtually all of the older hotels in major centers like Halifax have been renovated and upgraded. For this reason, budget travelers are unlikely to spend many nights in hotels.

Aside from the faceless business hotels, a few grand old hotels from the first half of the 20th century have been renovated by the large chains, and they're definitely worth considering if price isn't a major consideration. What follows is a list of hotels of distinction charging between $105 and $330 a room, sometimes including a meal or two. This is much less than you'd pay for the equivalent in the US or Europe. For descriptions of these properties, turn to the relevant sections of this book.

Algonquin Hotel, St Andrews, NB

Dalvay by the Sea Hotel, Stanhope, PEI

Keltic Lodge, Ingonish Beach, NS (see Ingonish in the Cape Breton Island chapter)

Lord Beaverbrook Hotel, Fredericton, NB

Lord Nelson Hotel, Halifax, NS

Pines Resort, Digby, NS (see the Southwestern Nova Scotia chapter)

Rodd Charlottetown Hotel, Charlottetown, PEI

FOOD

Gastronomy in English-speaking Canada has, with exceptions, long been based on the British 'bland is beautiful' tradition. But while there are still no distinctive national dishes, good food is certainly not difficult to come by. Various ethnic groups continue to contribute to the Canadian table, and in most cities it's not difficult to find a Greek, Italian, Mexican or Chinese restaurant. Small bistro-type places have menus emphasizing freshness, spices and the latest trends. They tend to fill the gap between the low-end greasy spoons and the pricey, high-end restaurants. Many of these, as well as numerous soup, salad and sandwich bars provide good-value lunches as they compete for office workers' business. In the larger cities, vegetarian restaurants, although not abundant, can be found. Such places may be known as natural food or health-food restaurants. East Indian restaurants also offer a selection of vegetarian dishes.

The common 'spoons,' the equivalent of US diners, have names like 'George's' or 'Linda's Place.' Little changed since the 1930s, these small, basic places are blue-collar restaurants. Some are excellent and some are bad news, but they're always cheap. There's usually a breakfast special until 11am for about $4, followed by a couple of lunch specials. A fairly balanced, basic, meal costs around $7. In some spoons cigarette smoking is a problem.

All pubs serve food, and since there are too many of them for the population, they have to do a good job. A pub is often the cheapest place in town to get a good home-cooked meal.

Deep-fried food is all too common throughout the Maritimes. It doesn't hurt to ask for an alternative cooking method or to pick from menus carefully.

There's abundant seafood that is delicious and affordable. Freshwater Atlantic salmon is less well known than Pacific salmon, but is highly esteemed. Hake and haddock appear on most menus. The Atlantic region is also famous for lobster and scallops.

cadian Food

1e centuries-old culinary traditions of the
ench Acadians can be experienced in
shes such as rappie pie *(paté à la rapure)* –
type of meat pie topped with grated paste-
e potato from which all the starch has
en drawn.

French fries in the Acadian areas, where
ey are known simply as *frîtes* or *patates*,
e unbeatable, especially those bought at
e small roadside chip wagons. *Poutine* is a
riation with gravy and cheese curds.

ative Indian Food

ative Indian foods based on wild game
ch as deer (venison) and pheasant are
mething to sample if the opportunity
esents itself.

The fiddlehead fern is a distinctive green,
ly edible in springtime, long savored by
rst Nations people. This fern is primarily
cked in the woodlands of the Maritime
ovinces.

ast Food

he municipal authorities in a few historic
wns such as St Andrews and Lunenburg
ve enacted bylaws to prevent the fast
od chains from invading their streets.
'e've followed their example and deliber-
ely left McDonald's, KFC, Taco Bell,
urger King and the like out of this book, in
art because these outfits need no introduc-
on. This isn't to suggest they aren't there:
ou won't be able to miss them in most
aces.

Almost every town in the Maritimes has
Tim Hortons donut shop, with Moncton,
ew Brunswick, boasting the highest
umber east of Ontario. Tim Hortons (part
Wendy's International) offers a soup-of-
e-day lunch special including coffee and a
onut for around $3 – a bargain.

Irving Mainway gas stations often have
keout sections that sell cheap coffee, sand-
iches, hot dogs and cold drinks. Beware of
nvenience stores that don't post prices for
ft drinks or ice cream, as some charge un-
asonably high amounts for these items.

One homegrown chain included herein is
onderosa Steakhouse, with locations in
Bedford, Fredericton, Moncton, Saint John
and Truro. Ponderosa offers a variety of
steak, seafood and chicken meals including
an unlimited soup and salad bar for $8 to
$13. Vegetarians can order the soup and
salad bar alone for $6. The cashier may try
to inflate the price with little extras like sour
cream, but it's not necessary to take them or
order a drink – cold water is on the house.
You can even print out discount coupons at
W www.steakandsalad.com. Ponderosa fare
is definitely not gourmet food, but it will fill
you up.

Markets & Groceries

Many towns have farmers' markets offering fresh organic produce, bakery items
and cooked foods at good prices. The Saturday morning Moncton Market is probably the best single place to sample
Maritime delicacies. If you're in Charlottetown, Fredericton, Halifax, Saint John or
another sizable town on a Saturday
morning, to market you must go! Most
operate year-round, and in summer a
second market day may be added. Most of
the vendors are part-timers who will be enjoying it all as much as you are.

Roadside stands offering the crops of the
season are seen along highways and secondary roads in rural areas. Corn is plentiful
and easy to prepare. Fruit is a bargain in
summer, and locally grown apples, peaches
and cherries are superb. In June watch for
strawberries; in August, blueberries. Fresh
seafood is easily purchased at kiosks or
stores near the docks. Many items (including lobster) are available cooked, ready for
a picnic.

Large supermarkets often have deli
counters where you can get soup, coffee and
light meals at low prices. Often they have a
seating area right in the store where you can
eat. This is great for a cheap lunch or dinner
but watch what you choose as some things
may not be as fresh as others. The largest supermarket chain in the Maritimes is Sobeys.
They're great places to shop for picnic fare,
and many branches are open 24 hours a day.
The supermarket chain even has a Web site
(W www.sobeysweb.com).

Costs

Food is a bit costlier than in the US but much less expensive than in Europe. Generally, dinner for under $10 at a regular restaurant is a bargain and $15 to $25 is normal. Lunches are a lot less, almost always under $10. Most of the places mentioned in this book fit into these categories.

DRINKS
Nonalcoholic Drinks

The fruit-growing areas of the Annapolis Valley produce excellent apple and cranberry ciders, some with alcohol, most without.

In Nova Scotia, visitors may want to sample a local nonalcoholic brew called spruce beer. It's produced in small batches by individuals but is sold in some local stores. It varies quite a bit and you can never be too sure what to expect when the cap comes off, but many people love the stuff.

Canadian mineral and spring waters are popular and readily available. Bottled waters from Europe, especially France, are also stocked.

An environmental deposit of 10¢ per aluminum can or plastic beverage bottle is collected in these provinces. Supermarkets do not give refunds – you must take your cans and bottles to a recycling center if you want the money back. Few visitors do this, but many national and provincial parks have bins where these items can be left for recycling.

Quality coffee, including espresso, cappuccino and other European specialities, is served at cafés such as Second Cup. A respectable cup of brewed coffee can also be obtained at the ubiquitous Tim Hortons doughnut shops. Unlike in the US, only occasionally are you offered free coffee refills at restaurants (so tip a little more if you are given free refills).

Tea is common and is served hot, in contrast to the US where tea is often served iced with lemon. In restaurants it is always made with teabags, often served in a small pot that is impossible to pour from without spilling.

Alcoholic Drinks

Canadian beer, always served cold, is gene ally good but not great – though on th whole it's stronger and more flavorful tha the major US brands. Lagers are by far th most popular beers, but ales, light bee porters and stouts are all available. Moos head beer, brewed in Saint John, is wild popular in the Maritimes.

A welcome trend is the continuir success of small breweries and brewpul (the latter brewing beer for consumption c premises) producing real or natural bee Both types of establishments have grow rapidly around the Maritimes.

In a bar, a draft beer begins around $2.2 for a 340ml glass to $5 for a pint. Draft be by the glass or pitcher is the cheapest way t drink. In places featuring live music, pric usually go up after the entertainment star (somebody has to pay the musicians).

Wine The past two decades have see Canadian wine improve steadily and co siderably. There's now a Vintners Quali Alliance (VQA) grading and classificatic system to establish and maintain standarc for the better wines – much the same as i Europe – and wines sporting the VQA lab are recommended.

Red, white, dry and sweet wines are a produced, as are some sparkling wines, b the dry whites and the very expensive ic wines are Canada's best. Several Nov Scotia wineries have retail stores and off tours for visitors.

Spirits Canada produces its own gin vodkas, rums, liqueurs, brandies an coolers, but Canadian whiskey, general known here as rye, enjoys the biggest an best reputation. Canadian Club and VO ry whiskey are Canada's most famous drinks good stuff. The Glenora Distillery nea Mabou on Cape Breton Island also pr duces quality whiskey. Rye is generall taken with ginger ale or soda, but some lik it straight or with ice. Canadian whiske has been distilled since the mid-1800s an has been popular in the USA as well Canada since the early days of productio

Most of the high price of spirits in Canada is attributable to tax.

Liquor Laws A 'licensed' restaurant is one that serves alcohol. Drinking beer or other alcoholic beverages anywhere other than a licensed establishment or a private home is illegal – this includes your campsite, so be forewarned. It's also not allowed to carry an open bottle of beer, wine or spirits in your car, even if it's packed away in the trunk! The drinking age is 19.

ENTERTAINMENT

Entertainment in major cities like Charlottetown, Fredericton, Halifax, Moncton and Saint John is top rate. As the largest English-speaking city in the Maritimes, Halifax has a particularly noteworthy theater and dinner-theater scene. For French speakers, Moncton is the Maritimes' cultural capital.

Nightclubs and bars present nightly jazz, blues and rock of widely varying caliber. There are two widespread trends in city bars: sports bars with numerous televisions for watching live sporting events, and clubs featuring pool tables coupled with recorded music.

Watch for Celtic folk music performances called 'ceilidhs,' 'shindigs' or 'kitchen parties.' These occur regularly in summer and feature some fancy fiddling and step dancing!

For more information on regional arts, see the Arts section in the Facts about Canada's Maritime Provinces chapter.

Spectator Sports

Technically, Canada's official national sport is lacrosse, a Native Indian game similar to soccer but played with a small ball and sticks. The sticks have a woven leather basket in which the ball is caught and carried, and from which it is thrown, often at high velocity.

The sport that really creates passion, and Canada's de facto national game, is ice hockey. In the Maritime provinces, this is especially true in Nova Scotia, where the game was allegedly invented (see Windsor

in the Southwestern Nova Scotia chapter). If you're in Halifax during the winter, a hockey game at the Halifax Metro Centre is recommended. The season runs from October to April.

SHOPPING

Despite being a Western consumer society filled with the standard goods of the international marketplace, Canada does offer the discriminating shopper a number of unique and interesting things to buy.

Outdoor or camping enthusiasts may find items they haven't seen before, and some of the outdoor clothing is particularly good. Such products are not cheap, but their longevity pays off.

For edibles, Digby chicks, a pungent smoked herring, are an off-beat buy. The wines of Nova Scotia can be very good; ask for advice at liquor outlets.

Most bookstores have an Atlantic Canada section for Canadian literature or books on the Maritimes. Likewise, record shops offer CDs of Canadian music. Traditional, Celtic-based folk music from Cape Breton is especially abundant.

Wood carving has a long tradition along the French Shore of Nova Scotia. At Chéticamp, also in Nova Scotia, you'll find some fine handmade rugs.

Blankets and coats of 100% wool can be bought at MacAusland's Woollen Mill at Bloomfield on Prince Edward Island. Roots, a high-profile Canadian clothing company

with a dozen outlets across the Maritimes and products in major department stores, offers a range of fashionable, high-quality garments and accessories.

Crafts shows, flea markets and specialty shops showcase the work of Maritime artisans. Potters, weavers and jewelers turn out some fine work.

Native Indian arts and crafts are available on most First Nation reserves, and these represent some of the most 'Canadian' souvenirs. Popular items include dream catchers, jewelry, baskets and porcupine quill work.

Shops located at tourist attractions are generally not the best place to look for a meaningful keepsake. Plastic Mounties, cheap pseudo-Native Indian dolls, miniature beavers, off-color T-shirts and Anne of Green Gables kitsch are good for a smirk and nothing more.

Readers have suggested that visitors planning to stay the winter need not bring a lot of bulky, warm clothing with them since all the larger cities have secondhand clothing shops (such as Salvation Army and Value Village) where good used clothes of all sorts can be bought very cheaply.

Getting There & Away

Getting There & Away

AIR

Airports & Airlines

Halifax International Airport in Nova
Scotia is the major gateway to the Maritime
Provinces. Air Saint Pierre, American Airlines (Eagle Air), Continental Airlines and
Icelandair all fly into Halifax, as do the domestic carriers, Air Canada, Air Labrador
and Air Transat.

Air Canada arrives at Halifax from
Boston, Calgary, London-Heathrow, Mon-
tréal, Newark, Ottawa, St John's, Toronto,
Vancouver and Winnipeg.

Of the foreign airlines serving Halifax,
Air Saint Pierre arrives from Saint Pierre (a
French island off Newfoundland), Ameri-
can Airlines from Boston, Continental Air-
lines from Newark and Icelandair from
Reykjavik.

The region's second most important
airport is Moncton, in New Brunswick. Air
Canada flies to Moncton from Montréal,
Ottawa and Toronto. Westjet arrives from
Hamilton and Ottawa in Ontario.

Air Canada really dominates the region's
other four large airports. They fly to Charlottetown from Toronto, connecting with
other points via Halifax. Air Canada is the
only airline serving Fredericton and Saint
John (from Montréal, Ottawa and Toronto),
and they connect through Halifax to
Sydney. Air Saint Pierre flies between Saint
Pierre and Sydney.

Buying Tickets

World aviation has never been so competitive, making air travel a better value than
ever. But you have to research the options
carefully to make sure you get the best deal.
The Internet is an increasingly useful resource for checking airfares.

Full-time students and people under the
age of 26 (under 30 in some countries)
have access to better deals than other travelers. You have to show documentation
proving your date of birth or a valid International Student Identity Card (ISIC)

when buying your ticket and boarding the
plane.

One of the basics in air travel is that most
airlines, particularly the larger ones (including the Canadian companies flying internationally), provide greater discounts on
roundtrip tickets than on one-way fares.
Generally, one-way fares are no bargain. If
they cost less than a roundtrip ticket, it is
not by much, and it is not uncommon for
one-way tickets to cost more than
roundtrips.

Generally, there is nothing to be gained
by buying a ticket directly from the airline.
Discounted tickets are released to selected
travel agents and specialist discount agencies, and these are usually the cheapest
deals going. One exception to this rule is the
'no-frills' carriers, which sell directly to travelers. Unlike the full-service airlines, no-
frills carriers often make one-way tickets
available at around half the roundtrip fare,

Warning

The information in this chapter is particularly
vulnerable to change: prices for international
travel are volatile, routes are introduced and
canceled, schedules change, special deals
come and go, and rules and visa requirements are amended. Airlines and governments seem to take a perverse pleasure in
making price structures and regulations as
complicated as possible. You should check
directly with the airline or a travel agent to
make sure you understand how a fare (and
any ticket you may buy) works. In addition,
the travel industry is highly competitive, and
there are many lurks and perks.

The upshot of this is that you should get
opinions, quotes and advice from as many
airlines and travel agents as possible before
you part with your hard-earned cash. The
details given in this chapter should be regarded as pointers and are not a substitute
for your own careful, up-to-date research.

Air Travel Glossary

Cancellation Penalties If you have to cancel or change a discounted ticket, there are often heavy penalties involved; insurance can sometimes be taken out against these penalties. Some airlines impose penalties on regular tickets as well, particularly against 'no-show' passengers.

Courier Fares Businesses often need to send urgent documents or freight securely and quickly. Courier companies hire people to accompany the package through customs and, in return, offer a discount ticket which is sometimes a phenomenal bargain. However, you may have to surrender all your baggage allowance and take only carry-on luggage.

Full Fares Airlines traditionally offer 1st class (coded F), business class (coded J) and economy class (coded Y) tickets. These days, so many promotional and discounted fares are available that few passengers pay full economy fare.

Lost Tickets If you lose your airline ticket, an airline will usually treat it like a traveler's check and, after inquiries, issue you with another one. Legally, however, an airline is entitled to treat it like cash: if you lose it, it's gone forever. Take good care of your tickets.

Onward Tickets An entry requirement for many countries is a ticket out of the country. If you're unsure of your next move, the easiest solution is to buy the cheapest onward ticket to a neighboring country or a ticket from a reliable airline that can later be refunded if you do not use it.

Open-Jaw Tickets These are return tickets that permit you to fly into one place but return from another. If available, these tickets can save you backtracking to your arrival point.

Overbooking Because almost every flight has some passengers that fail to show up, airlines often book more passengers than they have seats. Usually excess passengers make up for the no-shows, but occasionally somebody gets 'bumped' onto the next available flight. Guess who it is most likely to be? The passengers who check in late.

Promotional Fares These are officially discounted fares, available from travel agencies or direct from the airline.

Reconfirmation If you don't reconfirm your flight at least 72 hours prior to departure, the airline may delete your name from the passenger list. Call to find out if your airline requires reconfirmation.

Restrictions Discounted tickets often have various restrictions – for example, they may need to be paid for in advance, or altering them may incur a penalty. Other restrictions include minimum and maximum periods you must be away.

Round-the-World Tickets RTW tickets give you a limited period (usually a year) in which to circumnavigate the globe. You can go anywhere the carrying airlines go as long as you don't backtrack. The number of stopovers or total number of separate flights is decided before you set off, and these tickets usually cost a bit more than a basic return flight.

Transferred Tickets Airline tickets cannot be transferred from one person to another. Travelers sometimes try to sell the return half of a ticket, but officials can ask you to prove that you are the person named on the ticket. On an international flight, tickets are compared with passports.

Travel Periods Ticket prices vary with the time of year. There is a low (off-peak) season and a high (peak) season, and often a low-shoulder season and a high-shoulder season as well. Usually the fare depends on your outward flight – if you depart in the high season and return in the low season, you pay the high-season fare.

eaning that it is easy to put together an
en-jaw ticket when you fly to one place
t leave from another.

The other exception is booking on the In-
rnet. Many airlines, both full-service and
-frills, offer some excellent fares to Web
rfers. They may sell seats by auction or
mply cut prices to reflect the reduced cost
electronic selling. Many travel agencies
ound the world have Web sites, which can
ake the Internet a quick and easy way to
mpare prices. There is also a growing
mber of online agents that operate only
the Internet.

Online ticket sales work well if you are
ing a simple one-way or roundtrip on
ecified dates. However, super-fast online
re generators are no substitute for a travel
ent who knows about special deals, has
ategies for avoiding layovers and can
er advice on everything from travel in-
rance to which airline has the best vege-
rian food.

Sales taxes and the GST may or may not
included in airline ticket prices quoted in
nada, so ask.

harters

ost charter trips with a Canadian connec-
n are between Canada and Europe.
ther Canadian charters connect to US
stinations, mostly Florida or Las Vegas
e sun spots), or to the Caribbean.

Private Canadian charter companies
erate flights to various European coun-
es. One worth inquiring about in Europe
Air Transat. In Canada or abroad, travel
encies and university student offices
ould have information on potential
arter trips.

eparture Tax

nada has a departure/airport tax that is
vied on all international flights out of
nada. Almost all tickets out of Canada,
ether purchased in Canada or abroad,
ould have this cost built in.

Virtually all airports in the Maritimes
arge departing passengers an 'airport im-
ovement fee.' This fee averages $10 and
ually must be paid separately at the gate

(although in Halifax it is included in the
ticket price).

Within Canada

Flights within Canada, including those to
the Maritimes, tend to be costly. Prices and
schedules change and fluctuate often, and
Air Canada may give you quite different information from one week to the next. The
best thing to do is shop around – directly
with the airline or through a travel agent –
and be flexible. Waiting a day or two or
avoiding a weekend flight could save you a
lot of money. If you have the time, booking
flights well in advance is usually the most
economical.

To keep the price of air travel down there
are a few general strategies to follow. Try to
plan in advance, because the best bargains
are excursion fares: pre-booked roundtrip
flights with minimum and maximum stays.
Flights booked at least seven days in
advance cost less than last-minute prices,
and booking 14 or 21 days in advance is
usually cheaper still. If possible, don't fly
during peak hours (between 7am and 7pm),
and be prepared to make stops; nonstop
flights often cost more.

Occasionally there are short-term specials for promotion of a certain flight; these
can be cheap but are irregular. Keep your
eyes open for 'seat sales' offering discounted fares. To give you a rough idea of
possible costs, a roundtrip ticket to Halifax
from Toronto/Vancouver might cost
$375/800 in the off-season, $500/870 in July
and August.

Air Canada sometimes offers fly-drive
packages that cover airfare and car rental.
The packages, only available on roundtrip
flights, sometimes include accommodations.
Other possibilities include reductions on
cars, hotels and bus tours. The hotels used
are generally expensive, however. You just
have to ask about the latest gimmicks and
offers.

Travel agencies offer economical charters
and package tours to Halifax or Prince
Edward Island. These turn up throughout
the year but especially through the summer
holiday season. Book well in advance to

take advantage of these specials. There's a varying minimum and maximum stay on charter flights.

Airfares in Canada are generally quoted as the base fare only, and all taxes, including the GST, are additional. Ticket agents will quickly total these for you, but you do need to ask. This is worth doing to avoid nasty surprises later, as taxes can add quite a bit to the bill.

Always confirm your bookings and ask for a specific seat number, as this will guarantee you a seat on the plane.

Booking At any given time, Air Canada will have as many as 13 different fare levels for each of their services, depending on the date of travel, length of stay, how far in advance tickets were purchased etc. Prices of regular economy flights go up for the high seasons of Christmas and summer. These fares change frequently, and to quote exact prices here would be meaningless. Check the Air Canada Web site at W www.aircanada.ca and call them up at ☎ 888-247-2262. Ask if any specials are available and also consult your travel agent.

Be sure to find out what Air Canada's competitor Air Transat is offering, as they may be cheaper and more convenient. You'll learn what's available by perusing the ads in the travel section of your weekend newspaper or checking their Web site (W www.airtransat.com).

Although Halifax gets the most flights by far, compare the price of flying into Moncton. It's not only more centrally located in the Maritimes than is Halifax, but Moncton Airport is a lot closer to the center of town. If you're planning to visit Prince Edward Island, Moncton is ideal.

An inexpensive way to get to Moncton is with Westjet from Hamilton, Ontario (near Toronto). This costs $349 one way the same day or as low as $149 when booked 10 days in advance. Westjet has same-day connections through Hamilton from Calgary, Edmonton, Kelowna, Ottawa, Regina, Saskatoon, Thunder Bay, Vancouver, Victoria and Winnipeg – ask your travel agent to look into this if you live near any of those

places. Check out Westjet's Web site W www.westjet.com.

Travel CUTS (☎ 800-667-2887) Canada's national student-travel agen and has offices in all major cities. Its W address is W www.travelcuts.com. If you' eligible for one of the cards mentioned the Student & Youth Cards section of t Facts for the Visitor chapter, it's wor finding out what they have to offer.

The USA

Via its hub in Toronto, Air Canada brin passengers to Halifax from points all acrc the US. Connections from the US are al possible on American Airlines (W www. .com) via Boston and on Continental A lines (W www.continental.com) via Newa Ask your travel agent to compare all thr possibilities. Fares can vary dramatically c pending on season and advance purchase

Sample roundtrip ticket prices to Halif from Boston/Newark/San Francisco a US$245/250/500 during the off-season US$345/370/700 in July and August (the fares are quoted in US dollars – all othe are in Canadian).

Discount travel agents in the USA a known as consolidators (although ye won't see a sign on the door saying 'Cons idator'). Ticket Planet is a leading tick consolidator in the USA and is recoi mended. For more information, visit its W site at W www.ticketplanet.com.

The *New York Times*, the *Chica Tribune*, the *San Francisco Chronicle* a the *LA Times* produce weekly travel se tions containing numerous ads with curre airfares. You could also try the stude travel services STA Travel or Coun Travel, which have offices in most ma cities, or their Canadian counterpart CU' (see the Getting Around chapter f details).

The UK & Continental Europe

Discount air travel is big business London. Advertisements for many tra agencies appear in the travel pages of t weekend broadsheet newspapers, in *Ti Out,* the *Evening Standard* and the fi agazine *TNT.* You're looking at roundtrip res to Halifax in the neighborhood of ₤00/660 from Amsterdam/London in pring and fall. From June to mid-August xpect to pay a third to 50% more. Shop round.

For students or travelers under the age of 5, one popular travel agency in the UK is TA Travel (☎ 020-7361-6262), W www.sta avel.co.uk, with an office at 86 Old rompton Rd, London SW7 and branches cross the country. It sells tickets to all travers but caters especially to young people nd students.

The key to cross-Atlantic flights is timing. n either direction, the season affects the rice, but the definition of high and low eason varies from airline to airline. What ay of the week you travel and the duration f your stay are also factors. Usually, the onger the stay, the higher the cost.

Many of Europe's major centers are erved by Air Canada. You can fly nonstop om London-Heathrow to Halifax on Air 'anada once a day. From other European ties, you connect through either London, 1ontréal or Toronto. Fares vary a lot deending on the time of year, with summer epartures from June 15 to August 15 and ose at Christmas being 30% more expenve. In any case, an advance booking of 21 ays is required for the best prices, and dearting midweek is cheaper than leaving on weekend.

Icelandair offers direct fares to Halifax om all across Europe via their hub in

Rekyjavik, which is often cheaper and just as fast as connecting through London.
Web site: W www.icelandair.com

If you're also thinking of visiting central Canada, consider one of the so-called open jaw roundtrip tickets, which allow you to land in one city and depart from another, sometimes (but not always) at no extra charge. For example, you could fly into Halifax and fly back home from Toronto, thus eliminating the need to backtrack. Stopover privileges in Canada for routes like London-Halifax-Toronto-Vancouver-London are offered on some fares.

Australia & New Zealand

For flights from Australia and New Zealand to North America, there are several competing airlines and a variety of airfares. Round-the-world (RTW) tickets are often real bargains. Australia and New Zealand are pretty much all the way on the other side of the world from North America, and it can sometimes save you money to keep going right around the world on a RTW ticket than to do a U-turn on a return ticket. Look for a ticket with a stop in Halifax – Montréal and Boston are the next closest choices.

Quite a few travel offices specialize in discount air tickets. Some travel agents, particularly smaller ones, advertise cheap airfares in the travel sections of weekend newspapers.

In Australia, two well-known agents for cheap fares are STA Travel and Flight

Centre. STA Travel (☎ 03-9349-2411) has its main office at 224 Faraday St, Carlton, in Melbourne, with offices in all major cities and on many university campuses. Call ☎ 131-776 throughout Australia for the location of the nearest branch, or visit their Web site at ⓦ www.statravel.com.au. Flight Centre (☎ 131-600 Australiawide) has a central office at 82 Elizabeth St, Sydney, and there are dozens of offices throughout Australia. Flight Centre's Web address is ⓦ www.flightcentre.com.au.

In New Zealand, Flight Centre (☎ 09-309-6171) has a large central office in Auckland at National Bank Towers (on the corner of Queen & Darby Sts) and many branches throughout the country. STA Travel (☎ 09-309-0458) has its main office at 10 High St, Auckland, and has other offices in Auckland, as well as in Hamilton, Palmerston North, Wellington, Christchurch and Dunedin.

Asia

Since no flights arrive in Halifax directly from Asia, you'll need to connect through another North American city. Air Canada can bring you here via Vancouver or Toronto, and there are many other possibilities.

LAND
Border Crossings

Over a dozen border crossings exist between Maine and New Brunswick, the busiest of which are Fort Kent/Clair, Madawaska/Edmundston, Houlton/Woodstock, St Croix/McAdam, Calais/St Stephen and Lubec/Campobello. The only land border crossing with public transportation is Calais/St Stephen. The larger crossings are open 24 hours a day.

During the summer months, Friday and Sunday can be very busy at Calais/St Stephen, with shoppers, vacationers and visitors all traveling at the same time. Delays can be especially long on the holiday weekends in summer. The small, secondary border points elsewhere are always quiet, sometimes so quiet the officers have nothing to do except tear your luggage

apart. If you've nothing to hide, this is mo[r]e fun than waiting in line at a busier crossin[g].

Bus

Greyhound (☎ 800-661-8747) doesn't ser[ve] the Maritime provinces, so you'll have [to] switch to another carrier in Québec [or] Maine. Through tickets are available fro[m] all Canadian cities to the Maritimes and th[e] connections are fairly seamless. US Gre[y]hound buses go to Portland, Maine, which [is] linked to Nova Scotia by ferry. Greyhou[nd] USA also has a service between New Yo[rk] and Montréal, which might be included [in] your US Ameripass. In Montréal you c[an] catch the train to the Maritimes or contin[ue] east by bus. Greyhound's Canadian We[b] site is at ⓦ www.greyhound.ca.

New Brunswick's SMT bus lines (☎ 80[0-] 567-5151) links up with Orleans Express [in] Rivière-du-Loup, Québec, three times [a] day. Direct connections from North Ba[y,] Toronto, Ottawa, Montréal and Québe[c] City right through to Moncton are possibl[e.] SMT also connects to Orleans Express [in] Campbellton daily.

On Friday and Saturday, SMT buses fro[m] Saint John go as far as Bangor, Main[e,] where they connect with Vermont Transit [to] and from Boston and New York. Eas[t]bound, a bus leaves New York just aft[er] midnight on Saturday and Sunday connec[t]ing right through to Halifax with changes [in] Bangor, Saint John, Moncton and Amhers[t,] a 24-hour trip! For information on the dai[ly] bus service between Bangor and Calais, s[ee] Getting There & Away in the St Stephe[n] section. Also, check SMT's Web site [at] ⓦ www.smtbus.com.

Bus Passes Some – but not all – of Gre[y]hound's multiday Ameripasses are valid [in] the Maritimes, and some US Ameripass[es] are accepted only in the US. If you're usin[g] a US pass, find out how close you can get [to] your Canadian destination before you hav[e] to buy a separate ticket.

Greyhound's **Canada Pass Plus** allow[s] for unlimited travel right across Canada, i[n]cluding some routes in the Maritimes (bas[i]cally, Québec to Charlottetown and Halifa[x] via Moncton). This pass comes in seven- ($279), 10- ($369), 15- ($425), 21- ($475), 30- ($529), 45- ($615) and 60-day ($685) variations, plus tax. Seniors (65 and over) can get 10% off.

Two other Greyhound passes to investigate are the **NE Seabord Pass** ($349/489 for 10/21 days) and the **Eastern Seaboard Pass** ($449/609 for 15/30 days), both of which include the Maritimes, Ontario, Québec and the northeastern US. The Greyhound passes are available all year but must be purchased at least a week before the beginning of travel.

The **Maritime Bus Pass** is valid on all SMT and Acadian Lines services in the Maritimes. It costs $201/259/380 for 7/10/14 consecutive days and can only be purchased at the bus stations in Antigonish, Campbellton, Charlottetown, Edmundston, Fredericton, Halifax, Moncton, New Glasgow, Saint John, Sydney, Truro and Yarmouth. Although the pass is valid on SMT services to/ from Rivière-du-Loup, Québec, and Bangor, Maine, it cannot be purchased in those cities. If you have time, you could order one in advance over the phone at ☎ 800-567-5151 and have it mailed to you; otherwise just take the train from Montréal to Campbellton, or a ferry from Maine to Yarmouth, and purchase your bus pass once you arrive.

Train

VIA Rail (☎ 888-842-7245), a federal government agency, operates a passenger service between Montréal and Halifax six times a week. For schedules, pick up the *National Timetable* booklet at any VIA Rail station, or check their Web site at ⊠ www.viarail.ca. Train travel is more expensive than going by bus, and reservations are important, especially on weekends and holidays.

Tickets are available from Montréal to Campbellton ($114, 11 hours), Bathurst ($127, 13 hours), Miramichi ($134, 14 ours), Moncton ($163, 15½ hours), ackville ($167, 16½ hours), Amherst ($170, 7 hours), Truro ($183, 18½ hours) and Ialifax ($197, 20 hours).

If your final destination is Charlottetown or Saint John, it's cheaper to book your bus ticket in conjunction with the train; the railway-bus connection to PEI is available at Moncton. Similarly, there are railway-bus connections in Truro to Sydney and to Newfoundland. You can save even more money by taking the train only as far as Campbellton, where the previously mentioned Maritimes Bus Pass kicks in.

The pricing policy at VIA Rail is essentially that every trip is considered a one-way fare. A roundtrip between points A and B is thus billed as two one-way fares: one from A to B, and one from B to A. There are usually no roundtrip or excursion fares, but there are other ways to reduce your costs considerably.

Between the Maritimes and Québec, travel is discounted 40% if the trip is booked seven or more days in advance. Booking well in advance can pay off because only a limited number of seats are offered at the discounted rates, and once they're gone the rest of the seats are full fare.

Children, seniors (over 60) and students with international cards are entitled to discounts any time. People with children should inquire about family fares that are offered at various times and can mean substantial savings.

The train travels overnight between Montréal and the New Brunswick border in both directions. Between Campbellton and Halifax you travel during the day. VIA offers several types of cars and different sleeping arrangements, ranging from semi-reclining seats to upper and lower pull-out berths to private roomettes of varying sizes. The price of any sleeping arrangement is added to the basic coach seat fare or Canrailpass. Discounts are available with advance purchase; reservations for sleepers should be made well in advance.

In smaller towns the station may only be open at arrival and departure times. Also, when telephoning the station, you'll probably be speaking to someone at a call center in another part of the country that handles all questions and reservations.

Train Passes For those interested in combining a visit to the Maritimes with a train trip to other parts of Canada, VIA Rail offers the **Canrailpass**. The pass is available to anyone and provides 12 days of coach-class travel throughout Canada within a 30-consecutive-day period beginning on the day that travel commences.

The pass is good for any number of trips and stopovers from coast to coast. Reserving early is recommended, as the number of seats on any given train that are set aside for pass holders is limited. Seat reservations can be made up to six months in advance. You can buy the Canrailpass in Canada or in Europe (ask a travel agent or a VIA Rail outlet), and there's no difference in cost.

The Canrailpass comes in two price versions – low season and high season. The low season extends from mid-October to May. The cost of a pass is $411 with tax, or $370 for students and those under 17 or over 60 years of age. The high season runs from June to mid-October, when the pass with tax is $658 full fare or $592 for those in the specified age categories. For all passes, up to three extra days can be purchased at additional cost.

The **North America Rail Pass** covers all of VIA Rail and Amtrak's routes in Canada and the US for 30 days. It costs $702/1004 low/high season, or $632/892 for students, youths and seniors. Neither of these passes is accepted on the weekly train from Halifax to Sydney.

Car & Motorcycle

Visitors are allowed to bring their vehicles into Canada for six months. Some form of auto or motorcycle insurance is mandatory.

For important further information see Visas & Documents and Customs in the Facts for the Visitor chapter.

SEA
Ferry

From May to October, Yarmouth, Nova Scotia, is connected with the US by ferry routes from Bar Harbor and Portland, both in Maine. See the Yarmouth section in the Southwestern Nova Scotia chapter for more details. From the south end of Deer Island, New Brunswick, in the Bay of Fundy, a ferry runs to Eastport, Maine, in July and August.

A free ferry at the north end of Deer Island runs to the New Brunswick mainland year-round.

Passenger Ships

Plenty of cruise ships visit Halifax between July and October, the majority spending only one day in port. If you're interested in something like that, travel agents are the best source of information, as most cruise lines do not sell directly to the public.

Princess Cruises (☎ 661-753-0000), 24305 Town Center Drive, Santa Clarita, CA 91355, USA, is one company with departures from New England to the Maritimes and destinations along the St Lawrence River.

Web site: W www.princess.com

Getting Around

If you're not on an organized tour, there are only two ways to get around the Maritimes: public or private transportation. Private transportation includes riding a bicycle – a credible, eco-friendly option. Driving your own car is the most common way to go. Gasoline prices are a bit higher than in the USA but considerably lower than those in Europe. Getting around by bus and train is also quite possible.

AIR

Canadians often gripe about Air Canada, a publicly owned carrier that enjoys a near monopoly that allows it to get away with asking stiff prices for variable service. Most regional flights within the Maritimes are operated by Air Canada's subsidiary, Air Nova. Look for it at airports in Charlottetown, Fredericton, Halifax, Moncton, Saint John, Sydney and Yarmouth. In practice, Air Nova's flights are meant to feed passengers into Air Canada's long-haul services, and they're not much help in getting around the region.

BUS

Buses supply the most extensive transportation routes around the region. They stop in all the main towns and are cheaper than the train. Buses are usually clean, safe and comfortable. They are also generally efficient and run on time.

The largest bus companies are Acadian Lines (☎ 800-567-5151) in Nova Scotia and SMT (☎ 800-567-5151) in New Brunswick. Both are owned by the Irving family, which explains why many of their depots are at Irving gas stations. More information is available on both companies on the SMT Web site at ⓦ www.smtbus.com. Here's a list of the main SMT and Acadian Lines routes:

Amherst, Truro, Halifax

Bangor, Saint John, Moncton

Campbellton, Miramichi, Moncton

Halifax, Kentville, Digby, Yarmouth

Halifax, Truro, Baddeck, Sydney

Halifax, Truro, St Peter's, Sydney

Moncton, Fredericton, Miramichi

Moncton, Sackville, Amherst

Moncton, Summerside, Charlottetown

Rivière-Du-Loup, Edmundston, Fredericton, Moncton

The only other important lines run along the South Shore of Nova Scotia. DRL Coachlines (☎ 888-263-1852) runs west from Halifax to Yarmouth via Lunenburg. Web site: ⓦ www.drlgroup.com

Zinck Bus Company (☎ 902-468-4342) heads east from Halifax to Sherbrooke, and Transoverland operates a bus from Sydney to Chéticamp. Private minibus shuttles run between Charlottetown and Halifax. Bus services are covered in the text.

SMT gives a 20% discount to students with an ISIC, and children aged four to 11 ride for half fare (under four free). There's no student discount on the Maritime Bus Pass previously mentioned in Getting There & Away.

Travel Tips

All bus lines (except in rare cases) use the same central bus station in any given city, so you can change bus lines or make connections at the same location. Buses are also convenient because reservations are not required. Seating is on a first-come, first-served basis.

Arrive at the station about an hour before departure to purchase your ticket. Tickets can also be purchased several days in advance if this is convenient. Be aware, though, that advance tickets do not apply to any specific bus and do not guarantee a seat. You must still arrive early and line up for your bus.

On holiday weekends, especially on Friday night or around major holidays such as Easter, the bus stations can get pretty crowded and chaotic. During these holidays arriving early or having a ticket beforehand is recommended.

On longer trips always ask if there is a direct or express bus. On some routes some buses go straight through while others stop seemingly everywhere, making the trip seem interminable. The price is generally the same, and you may save several hours by choosing an express instead of a 'local.'

In summer, air-conditioners on buses can be far too effective, so take a sweater on board. Smoking is not permitted. Most of the larger bus stations have $2 coin-operated luggage lockers if you want to store your bags.

TRAIN
The VIA Rail trains that operate between Halifax and Montréal six times a week can also be used for getting around the Maritimes. The route is Halifax to Truro, Amherst, Sackville, Moncton, Miramichi, Bathurst and Campbellton, with railway bus connections to Charlottetown and Saint John available at Moncton. From June to early October there's also a weekly passenger service from Halifax to Sydney.

Within the Maritimes, reduced fares are available year-round if you book at least five days in advance, though the number of reduced-fare seats on any given train is limited. Reservations are accepted up to six months in advance. The train is an interesting change of pace from buses for only a bit more money. See Train in the Getting There & Away chapter for more information on this service.

CAR & MOTORCYCLE
In many ways, driving is the best way to travel in the Maritimes. You can go where and when you want, use secondary highways and roads and get off the beaten track. Maritime roads are generally good and well marked, but getting hold of a decent provincial highway map is advisable before setting out. Provincial tourist offices have free roadmaps, and bookstores and variety stores have similar maps for sale.

The Trans Canada Hwy runs over 7000km from St John's, Newfoundland, to

Victoria, British Columbia. In the Maritimes, it goes from Sydney to Edmundston via New Glasgow, Moncton and Fredericton. A branch of the road loops through Charlottetown. The only toll road in the region is a 45km section of the Trans Canada between Truro and Amherst, costing $3. Some bridges also require a small payment.

Road Rules & Safety Precautions
The use of seat belts is compulsory throughout Canada, and the fines for not wearing them are heavy. All provinces require motorcyclists to drive with lights on, and for both drivers and passengers to wear helmets. You're not allowed to drive in Canada without auto insurance.

Traffic in both directions must stop when stationary school buses have their red lights flashing – this indicates that children are getting off and on. In cities with pedestrian crosswalks, cars must stop to allow pedestrians to cross.

Turning right at red lights (after first coming to a complete stop) is allowed, but take note that this practice is not legal in Québec.

All posted speed limits in Canada are metric. For those who aren't conversant with the metric system (most Americans probably fit this category), 40kph (kilometers per hour) equals 25mph (miles per hour), 50kph is 31mph, 60kph is 37mph, 70kph is 43mph, 80kph is 50mph, 90 kph is 56mph, 100kph is 62mph and 110kph is 68mph.

If you can, avoid driving in areas where there is heavy snow; if you have no choice it may mean having to buy snow tires. Many Canadian cars have four-season radial tires. If you get stuck, don't stay in the car with the engine running; every year people die of carbon monoxide suffocation by doing this during big storms. A single candle burning in the car will keep you reasonably warm.

On gravel roads the biggest problems are dust and flying stones from other vehicles. Keep a good distance back from the vehicle in front of you, and when you see an ncoming vehicle, slow down and keep well) the right (this also applies when you are eing passed). Having a spare tire, fan belt nd extra hoses is suggested.

In wooded areas, drive with caution etween dusk and dawn, as collisions with 100se and deer are tragically common long some Maritime highways. If you see n animal standing beside the road ahead, low down, as it could suddenly bolt and imp in front of you.

Most run-ins occur at night, when the nimals are active and visibility is poor. In reas with roadside signs alerting drivers to ossible animal crossings, keep your eyes canning both sides of the road and be prepared to stop. Often a vehicle's headlights vill mesmerize the animal, leaving it frozen n the middle of the road; try flashing the ghts or using the horn if they don't move ut of the way. Always slow down immediately if you see an animal standing in the oadway.

Rental

Avis, Budget, Hertz and National have carental desks at all regional airports (Dollar nd Thrifty are only at Halifax International Airport). Discount, Enterprise and Rent-A-Wreck operate out of low overhead premses in the suburbs and are usually cheaper. Enterprise has excellent monthly rates. These chains can book cars for you at any of heir outlets. To save time and be certain of inding a car, it's worthwhile making a reservation before your arrival.

Note that rates are not consistent even vithin a given company, as each outlet is run ndependently. Rates vary from city to city nd location to location. Most companies ave a daily rate of about $30 to $50 plus a ilometer fee. Others offer a flat rate that is learly always the better deal, since distances can be unexpectedly long.

Car rental prices can double in July and August, with the rates fluctuating daily according to supply and demand or who you nappen to talk to. None of the car rental companies list prices in their brochures. In ummer, it's usually essential to book head – especially in prime tourist spots like

Charlottetown – as there often just aren't enough cars to go around.

Call the toll-free reservations numbers or check the Web sites of large chains to compare prices:

Avis	☎ 800-879-2847
	W www.avis.com
Budget	☎ 800-268-8900
	W www.budget.com
Dollar	☎ 800-800-4000
	W www.dollar.com
Hertz	☎ 800-263-0600
	W www.hertz.com
National	☎ 800-227-7368
	W www.nationalcar.com

Then contact the smaller companies to see if they'll give you a better deal:

Discount	☎ 888-636-9333
	W www.discountcars.ca
Enterprise	☎ 800-325-8007
	W www.enterprise.com
Rent-A-Wreck	☎ 800-327-0116
	W www.rentawreck.ca

Enterprise has an impressive 23 locations around the region; Discount has ten; and Rent-A-Wreck has eight. Once you've found the best price, make a reservation using your credit card.

Car rentals from the airport are always more expensive than the prices charged by the same companies at their downtown offices. This is due to the exorbitant rents charged by the airport authorities. In Nova Scotia, car rentals at airport hotels carry a special 12% tax to prevent them from competing with offices inside the terminal. You may be able to compensate for this by booking in advance via an 800 number or over the Internet at a reduced rate. Otherwise, take the airport shuttle and your business into town.

Weekend rates are often the cheapest and can include extra days, so building a schedule around this can save a lot of money. 'Weekends' in car rental parlance can extend three or even four days. For example, if you pick up a car Friday morning and return it before midnight Monday it may be billed as just three days.

Once a car has been rented you may be able to extend your rental at the same rate, and negotiation is possible. Also, if renting for extended periods of time, say weeks, ask for a discount beyond the weekly rate. Weekly rates are generally 10% less than daily rates. Some Discount and Rent-A-Wreck offices give a 10% discount to those with HI cards, though only on their weekly rates.

Depending on the locations, it is sometimes possible to drop a car off at a different office than the one where you picked it up. In some cases a hefty fee is charged for this privilege, so ask for details.

Book early, especially for weekend use, and request a smaller car if you want to save money. If the agency isn't close to where you're staying, they'll often send a driver over to pick you up at no additional cost.

Prices can be deceptive. The daily rate may be an enticing $29, but by the time you factor in insurance, gasoline, the charge for kilometers driven (if applicable), taxes and other bits and pieces, the bill can easily double. Make sure you're aware of all the extra costs in order to avoid a rude surprise. Fill the tank before returning the car or you'll pay the rental company's gasoline prices plus a fee for the service.

Many car rental agencies tack an additional $1 per day 'administration fee' onto their rates to cover the cost of dealing with government bureaucracies (for permits, licenses etc).

Some companies offer vans, and with a number of people sharing the cost this can work out to be quite economical. These should be booked well in advance.

You will need a credit card as a security guarantee to rent a car in Canada. Some companies require you to be over 21 years of age, others over 26. You may be asked to buy extra insurance depending on your age, but the additional premiums are not high. Insurance is generally optional. Check to see if your car insurance at home includes rentals or a rental clause. Doing it this way is cheaper than buying the insurance from

the rental agency. Some credit cards also offer insurance covering car rentals, at least in part; call the number on the back of your card to find out.

Parents take note: Children under 18kg (40lb) are required to be in a safety car seat that is secured by a seat belt. The big-name rental companies can supply child seats at a small daily rental fee. Outside the major cities it may take a couple of days for the outlet to come up with one, but the cost is the same.

Purchase

If you plan to be driving for several months a used car can be an excellent investment especially if there are two of you. Older cars can be bought quite cheaply in Canada, and you can usually sell the car for nearly the same amount as you paid for it. A fairly decent older car should be available for under $4000. Look in the local newspaper or the weekly *Bargain Hunter Press, Auto Trader, Wheeler Dealer, Deals on Wheels,* or equivalent publications, all of which can be bought at corner variety stores. Private deals are nearly always the most economical way to buy a car. Used-car businesses must mark up the prices in order to make a profit. Generally, North American cars are less expensive than Japanese and European cars. And remember that haggling over car prices, whether at a dealership or someone's home, is the norm. Expect to knock off hundreds or even a thousand dollars depending on the value of the car.

For those who prefer a more scientific approach to car buying, take a look at Phil Edmunston's excellent *Lemon-Aid Car Guide.* His book details all the used cars on the market, rates them and gives rough price guidelines for buyers. Also check out his entertaining and informative Web site (W www.lemonaidcars.com).

You will need Canadian insurance to purchase a car. Bring a letter from your current company if you have a good driving record. In addition to making transactions easier, this might entitle you to a discount as it makes you a more credible risk. You will also need an international driver's license call a Canadian insurance broker (check the Yellow Pages), and they will find you a company offering temporary insurance, say or three months. In order to get the insurance and a license plate for the vehicle, you will need an address in Canada – the address of a friend or relative will suffice. You should also have your passport.

Insurance costs vary from province to province. As a rule, rates for women are noticeably lower than for men of comparable age with a similar driving record. If you're planning a side trip to the USA, make sure the insurance you negotiate is valid there as well. Also remember that rates are linked to the age and type of car. A newer car may cost more to insure but may also be easier to sell.

Canadian Automobile Association

Known as the CAA, this organization, like its counterpart the American Automobile Association (AAA), provides assistance to member motorists (check in your country of origin to see if there are reciprocal agreements). The services provided include 24-hour emergency roadside assistance, trip planning and advice, and free guides and maps.

If you have a decent car, the association's help may not be necessary, but if you have bought an older car to tour the country, the fee may well be invaluable; after one or two breakdowns your membership will have paid for itself, as towing charges are high. A basic annual membership costs $73 but only covers four tows of 5km or less. 'Plus' membership is $106 and lets you be towed up to 200km four times a year.

The CAA has established a network of approved auto repair services. These are indicated by signs bearing the CAA logo. They're usually smaller, independent operators who will be less likely to recommend unnecessary repairs the way some of the large chains are prone to doing. If you have to be towed, ask to be taken to a CAA-approved repair shop. Otherwise call the local CAA office or the CAA Maritimes office and ask for a few addresses.

For information contact the CAA Maritimes office (☎ 800-561-8807), 737 Rothesay Ave, Saint John, NB E2H 2H6. Their Web site is at ⓦ www.caa.maritimes.ca. Other CAA offices can be found in Charlottetown, Dartmouth, Fredericton, Halifax and Moncton. For CAA/AAA emergency road service anywhere in North America, call ☎ 800-222-4357.

Gasoline

Gasoline (petrol) varies in price across the region. Drivers arriving from the USA should try to arrive with a full tank, as US prices are considerably lower than in Canada. Gas prices are generally higher in Québec and Newfoundland than in the Maritimes, so tank up again before heading their way.

Gasoline prices on Prince Edward Island are controlled by the provincial government, and they tend to lag behind market fluctuation elsewhere. Thus when crude oil prices are rising internationally, gas will probably be cheaper at PEI pumps than in New Brunswick or Nova Scotia. In times of falling energy prices, however, gasoline on PEI may cost more. The difference can be as high as 5¢ a liter. First Nation reserves often have gas stations with the lowest prices in their area.

In general, the big cities have the best prices, so fill up in town. The more remote the gas station, the higher the price tends to be. Major highway service stations offer no bargains, and they often jack up the price on long weekends and holidays in order to fleece captive victims. Self-service pumps may be a cent or two cheaper than full service. Gasoline is always sold by the liter. On average a liter of gasoline costs about 75¢, or about $2.84 (US$1.90) per US gallon. If you use a credit card at a gas station, don't let it out of your sight for an instant.

BICYCLE

The Maritime provinces are ideal for bicycle touring thanks to the good scenery, excellent facilities and relatively short distances (for Canada). Cape Breton is hilly;

Prince Edward Island is flat; New Brunswick and Nova Scotia offer variety and towns tend to be close together so you get a good mix of country and city life.

The provincial highway maps have more detail and secondary roads than the usual tourist maps. You can pick them up for free at tourist offices. Large bookshops and some bike shops have cycling guides. Provincial tourism offices can also help find companies specializing in overnight and long-distance cycling trips, and bicycle shops are good sources of information. Major cities have well-stocked stores where all manner of supplies and cycling gear can be purchased.

VIA Rail allows passengers to take bicycles on the train between Montréal and Halifax for a flat fee of $15 plus tax. A box is included in the price, but you're required to put your bike in it yourself.

Air Canada has a flat fee of $65 to take a bicycle on a one-way flight. You must fix the handlebars sideways and remove the pedals, then place the bicycle in a plastic bicycle bag provided by the airline.

Bicycle rentals, routes and events are discussed in the text. See Cycling under Activities in the Facts for the Visitor chapter for more information.

HITCHHIKING

Readers' letters indicate few problems hitching in the Maritimes. However, hitching is never entirely safe in any country, and we can't recommend it. Travelers who decide to hitch should understand that they are taking a small but potentially serious risk.

That said, hitching is feasible in the region. It's not the UK, which is a hitchhiker's dream, but thumbing a ride is still a reasonable option. Many travelers depend on hitching for at least some portion of their trip. Public transportation can be expensive, but people generally turn to hitchhiking due to a lack of bus service, not the cost of a ticket. And of course you meet people you would otherwise never speak to. Two people hitching together, one of each gender, is ideal. If you're three or more, or a single woman, it isn't advised.

Outside the bigger cities, stay on the main highways. Traffic can be very light on the smaller roads, so try to get off where there's a service station or restaurant, not a side road or farmer's gate.

Around towns and cities, pick your spot carefully. Stand where you can be seen and where a car can easily stop. A foreign T shirt, like one with 'University of Stockholm' on it, might be useful. Some people find it helpful to have a cardboard sign with large clear letters naming their destination especially if there's a lot of local traffic in the area and you're looking for a long ride.

If you're going into a large city, make sure the ride is going all the way. If it's not ask to be dropped where you can catch a city bus, especially after dark. When leaving a city, it's best to take a bus out of town a little way if possible.

You must stay off intercity expressways, though the feeder ramps are OK.

Hitching in town is not productive. It's illegal to hitch within some city limits, and fines can be steep. Police tend to be more suspicious of scruffy-looking hitchhikers; be sure you have proper ID and documents to prove your identity in case you are questioned by police.

Around the larger centers there will be heavy traffic leaving on Friday and returning on Sunday. Despite the volume, hitching is difficult during these times because most cars are full with families. Weekdays are best, when salespeople and truckers are on the road. Many companies forbid truck drivers to pick up hitchers, though some do so anyway. Local residents are more likely to pick up hitchhikers – tourists usually can't be bothered.

Nights can be very cold as early as the end of summer, depending where you are and snow can fall in October. Don't push your luck.

FERRY

Since Nova Scotia is almost completely surrounded by water, major ferries link the province to New Brunswick, Prince Edward Island, Newfoundland and Maine. From Prince Edward Island, ferries connect with

Québec's Îles de la Madeleine in the Gulf of the St Lawrence. See the Souris entry in Prince Edward Island for information.

Nova Scotia is connected to Maine by two ferry routes and to New Brunswick, across the Bay of Fundy, by another. For information on the routes to Bar Harbor and Portland, Maine, see the Yarmouth section in the Southwestern Nova Scotia chapter. For details on the Digby to Saint John link, turn to Getting There & Away in those sections. The Caribou ferry to Wood Islands, PEI, is covered in the introduction to Prince Edward Island.

Marine Atlantic connects Nova Scotia to Newfoundland. For information and reservations write to Marine Atlantic Reservations Bureau (☎ 800-341-7981), 355 Purves St, North Sydney, Nova Scotia B2A 3V2, or check their Web site at W www.marine-atlantic.ca. Details are found in the North Sydney Getting There & Away section.

Various boat tours and local ferry services are found throughout the region, both long and short; some of these are discussed in the text.

As a rule, car ferry reservations need not be made more than two days in advance and can be booked by telephone. Walk-on passengers without motor vehicles almost never require advance reservations. Tourist information offices usually have brochures with full details on ferry services.

LOCAL TRANSPORTATION

The only cities in the Maritimes with municipal bus services are Fredericton, Saint John, Moncton, Halifax and Sydney. The Annapolis Valley has an excellent regional bus service between Wolfville and Bridgetown. Elsewhere the private car is king.

Local ferries cross the numerous rivers and harbors around the Maritimes. River ferries are almost always barges intended to carry cars, and motorists pay generally $3 per vehicle. Persons on foot can often walk aboard for free. The Halifax harbor ferry costs the same as a city bus ticket, and bus transfers are accepted.

In New Brunswick, local ferries link Deer Island and Grand Manan to the mainland year-round. The connection from Deer Island to Campobello Island only operates in summer. In Nova Scotia, ferries cross the two channels on the Digby Neck year-round.

ORGANIZED TOURS

Organized tours are offered in all major tourist centers, with the largest concentration in Halifax. Of particular interest are the tours from Halifax to Cape Breton Island, covered in the Halifax section of this book. Organized group tours are best arranged through bus companies, travel agencies or tour companies themselves. Many of the private specialized tour companies are listed in the directories available from provincial tourist offices.

Small companies offering low-cost, often nature-based, tours are discussed in the text. These can be found all around the region offering a variety of adventure trips of different lengths and difficulty. Good camping stores often carry pamphlets put out by such companies. You can also pick them up at hostels and tourist offices.

The Halifax HI Hostel runs inexpensive transportation-only minibus tours to Cape Breton and Fundy National Park. See Organized Tours in the Halifax chapter for more information.

Facts about Nova Scotia

At 55,491 sq km, Nova Scotia is about a third smaller than New Brunswick but 10 times the size of Prince Edward Island. In Nova Scotia, you're never more than 56km from the sea, a feature that has greatly influenced the character of the province.

Almost all of the towns are on the coast or within reach of tidal waters. For generations the rugged 7400km of coastline, with its countless bays and inlets, has provided shelter for small fishing villages, especially along the southern shores.

Inland, much of the province is covered with forest, and low hills roll across the north. The Annapolis Valley, famous for its apples, is gentle, bucolic farm country, resplendent in spring with lovely pink and white blossoms.

The Bay of Fundy region is dominated by the world's highest tides. Along the impressive Northumberland Strait are wide sandy beaches washed by the warmest waters around the province.

The tranquil villages with their typical Maritime scenes give way on the south-central coast to Halifax-Dartmouth, one of Canada's most attractive major metropolitan areas – a modern, cosmopolitan center that retains a historic air.

For many, a visit to rugged and mountainous Cape Breton Island, which shows another side of the province's varied topography, is the highlight of a trip to Nova Scotia.

HISTORY

When Europeans first arrived in what was to become Nova Scotia, they encountered the Mi'kmaq First Nation, the dominant people of the Maritimes.

The French created the first settlement at Port Royal in 1605, calling the region Acadia. Despite the region's changing hands with the English several times over the following 100 years, there were really no major British communities until the founding of Halifax in 1749. The first English settlers (and pirates) came here, followed by a contingent of Germans to the nearby Lunenburg area. The Highland Scots landed in familiar-looking Cape Breton in 1773, and over the next century many more Scots followed to settle Nova Scotia, which means 'New Scotland.' In the late 1700s, thousands

Highlights

Entered Confederation: July 1, 1867
Area: 55,491 sq km
Population: 941,000
Provincial Capital: Halifax

- Visit Halifax, with its well-preserved history, fine dining and lively music scene
- Enjoy the charm of villages such as Lunenburg and Peggy's Cove
- Watch the whales at Digby Neck or Pleasant Bay
- Explore Annapolis Valley, with its fascinating Acadian history
- Forage the fossil-laden shoreline of Parrsboro
- Learn what life was like 125 years ago at Sherbrooke Village
- Drive the Cabot Trail to see dramatic coastal scenery
- Experience early French Canada at Louisbourg National Historic Site

of Loyalists and a significant number of US and Jamaican blacks further swelled the population.

The 1800s brought prosperity through lumbering and shipbuilding, especially for the export markets, and coal mining followed soon after.

CLIMATE

The sea tends to keep the weather moderate. Summer and autumn are usually sunny, although the eastern areas and Cape Breton are often windy. Rain is heaviest on the east coast. The entire southern coast from Shelburne to Canso is often wrapped in a morning fog, which may take until noon or later to burn off. Winters can be very snowy.

ECONOMY

Manufacturing, mostly resource-based, is the most significant industry. Agriculture – with dairy, fruit and Christmas trees being the main products – is also a significant part of the economy.

Fishing remains important, with Lunenburg maintaining one of the east coast's major fleets. The catch includes herring, shrimp, lobster and scallops. Nova Scotia, along with Newfoundland, has been hit hardest by the decline in fish stocks and the resulting moratorium on most cod fishing.

At many points offshore you'll see the buoys and nets of the local aquaculture industry. Nova Scotia is North America's largest center of mussel-farming, and most Atlantic salmon on the market are reared in cages in the province's protected bays and inlets. Fish-farming may eventually overtake ocean fishing as the natural stocks show the effects of centuries of indiscriminate hauling.

Mining, shipbuilding, tourism and crafts are also major moneymakers. For over a century, Cape Breton produced a soft coal that was dirty to burn and dangerous to mine, as the shafts extended for miles beneath the ocean floor. The last mine finally closed in 2001, as did the steel mill at Sydney. The former industrial zone from Sydney Mines to Glace Bay is now among the most scarred and economically depressed areas in Canada.

POPULATION & PEOPLE

Many of the Mi'kmaq people remain on their original lands on Cape Breton and near the town of Truro. French culture and language live on in other areas. But the majority (about 75%) of Nova Scotia's 941,000 people are of English, Scottish and Irish descent. In a few places you can still hear Scottish Gaelic spoken.

INFORMATION
Tourist Offices

Tourism Nova Scotia (☎ 800-565-0000 in North America, 902-425-5781 from anywhere else) operates provincial information offices in Halifax and six other strategic locations across the province, plus Bar Harbor and Portland, Maine. Check their Web site at W www.explorens.com. Nova Scotia's free *Doers & Dreamers* guide is an invaluable publication. Use it to check accommodations and to find guided trip operators.

If you enjoy sightseeing, ask about the Nova Scotia Museum Pass, valid at 25 provinciallyoperated museums and historic sites around the province. It costs $30/60 adult/family and can be purchased anywhere the pass is accepted; or order one in advance at ☎ 800-632-1114 or W museum .gov.ns.ca. Numerous interesting events are scheduled at these museums throughout the summer.

There are 10 designated scenic routes on older, smaller roads (not the main highways) throughout the province. (Each is marked with roadside symbols.)

Internet Access

Service Canada, a federal government agency, provides Internet access at Community Access Program (CAP) sites in hundreds of rural communities around Nova Scotia. The CAP sites are usually staffed by students and are open during business hours on weekdays. Access is either free or a dollar or two per hour at these well-signposted facilities. Virtually all public libraries also provide Internet access, usually for free. Ask at the information counter as you enter the library.

Tax

The Harmonized Sales Tax (HST) is 15%.

ACTIVITIES

In addition to its coastline and intriguing history, Nova Scotia offers varied outdoor activities. Cycling is excellent in parts of the province, particularly around Cape Breton Island. Rentals are available provincewide.

Due to the vast number of waterways, canoeing in the province is good. Ocean kayaking is becoming increasingly popular, and outfitters are found at numerous coastal towns around the province.

The surfing here is still unheralded. The season runs from late summer to early fall, when waves generated in the tropics roll north toward Nova Scotia's Atlantic coast. Lawrencetown Provincial Park just east of Halifax is famous for its surf, and there are more possibilities along the South Shore. A full-service surf shop exists in Liverpool.

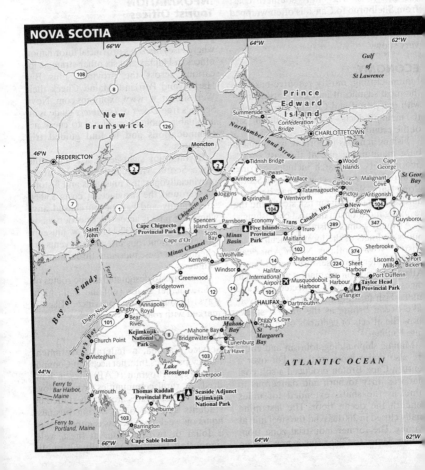

For hiking, the national and provincial parks contain both easy and strenuous trails.

Also popular is whale watching along the Digby Neck area and the north shore of Cape Breton. In peak season, making reservations up to a week in advance might be necessary.

Other outdoor pursuits include bird watching, rock hounding, fossil hunting and freshwater and deep-sea fishing.

For more information, see Activities in Facts for the Visitor.

ACCOMMODATIONS

Nova Scotia has a wide range of lodgings, from backcountry campsites to fine, historic inns. July and August are by far the busiest months, and accommodation can be scarce in much of the province.

The central and South Shore regions are not as popular as the other areas, however; finding a room each night before dark is always recommended. You should be aware that many attractions, campgrounds and guesthouses are closed from late September to late May.

Halifax

Nova Scotia's capital sits by one of the world's most extensive natural harbors, midway along Nova Scotia's south Atlantic shore. With a population of 114,000 (335,000 in the metropolitan area), Halifax is the largest Canadian city east of Montréal. The historic central district, never more than a few blocks from the water, is pleasingly compact. Modern buildings nestle among heritage structures interspersed with numerous green areas and parks.

The port is the busiest on Canada's east coast, partially because it's a year-round harbor – ice forces most others to close in winter. Canada's largest naval base is here as well. Other major industries are manufacturing, oil refining and food processing.

Halifax residents are referred to as Haligonians.

History

The area was first settled by the Mi'kmaq, and Halifax itself was founded in 1749 as a British stronghold counterbalancing the French fort at Louisbourg on Nova Scotia's far eastern tip.

The harbor was used as a British naval base during the American Revolution (1775–83) and the War of 1812. During both World Wars, Halifax was a distribution center for supply ships heading for Europe, a function that brought many people to the city.

In 1917 the *Mont Blanc,* a French munitions ship carrying a cargo of TNT, collided with another ship in the harbor. The result, known as the Great Explosion, was the biggest manmade explosion in history prior to A-bombs being dropped on Japan in 1945.

Halifax was the home of Canada's first representative government, first Protestant church and first newspaper.

Orientation

This hilly city lies on a peninsula between the harbor and an inlet called the North West Arm. The downtown area, dating from the earliest settlement, extends west from Lower Water St to the Citadel, a star-shaped fort on a hill. Cogswell St to the north and Spring Garden Rd to the south mark the other boundaries of the capital's core. Conveniently, much of what is of interest to visitors is concentrated in this area, making walking the best way to get around.

From this central area the city spreads in three directions. Main streets leading west up from the shoreline are Sackville St and Spring Garden Rd. Dartmouth, a twin city, lies east across the harbor and has business and residential districts of its own.

Two bridges span the Halifax Harbour, connecting Halifax to Dartmouth and leading to highways north (toward the airport) and east. The Macdonald Bridge at the eastern end of North St is closest to downtown. The toll for cars is 75¢. You can walk across, but bicycles cannot be ridden. Farther north is the MacKay Bridge, which also has a 75¢ toll. A $1.65 passenger ferry links the two downtown areas.

The airport is 40km northeast of town on Hwy 102.

If you'll be staying long in Halifax, you should check the dates of cruise ship arrivals. These huge ships arrive in port about 10 times a month in July and August and almost every other day in September and October. When they do, the downtown

LOCATOR

waterfront and all the main tourist sites become hopelessly overcrowded. Save Point Pleasant Park or McNabs Island for such a day.

Information

Tourist Offices You won't have any trouble getting information. At the airport, there's a Nova Scotia Visitor Information Centre (☎ 902-873-1223) between the baggage claim and check-in counters. Hours are 9am to 9pm daily year-round.

Downtown, Tourism Nova Scotia has an information office (Map 2; ☎ 902-424-4248) at 1655 Lower Water St, next to the Maritime Museum right down by the water. It's open year-round, 8:30am to 8pm daily in summer, 8:30am to 4:30pm Wednesday to Sunday mid-October to May.

Tourism Halifax has its International Visitor Centre (Map 2; ☎ 902-490-5946) on the corner of Sackville and Barrington Sts. It is centrally located and geared to the city. It's open 8:30am to 7pm daily from late May to September (until 8pm in July and August), 8:30am to 4:30pm weekdays the rest of the year. Upon request they'll play *Voyages Remembered,* a 20-minute video about the *Titanic,* in their 48-seat auditorium at the back of the office.

Other Information Offices The Ecology Action Centre (Map 2; ☎ 902-429-2202, 1568 Argyle St, Suite 31) can provide information on local environmental matters. They're open 9am to 4pm Monday to Thursday. You can check their Web site at **w** www.chebucto.ns.ca/Environment/EAC.

The Nova Scotia Public Interest Research Group (NS-PIRG; Map 1; ☎ 902-494-6662, Student Union Building, Room 314, 6136 University Ave) is a good source of information on environmental concerns provincewide. Their hours are 10am to 5pm Monday to Thursday.

Money Halifax has numerous banks, including several along Spring Garden Rd, but the only one open on Saturday (from 9am to 3pm) is TD Canada Trust (Map 1), 239 Quinpool Rd.

Casino Nova Scotia (Map 2; ☎ 902-425-7777), 1983 Upper Water St), will change foreign cash or traveler's checks 24 hours a day, but they give a lousy rate.

The exchange office at Halifax International Airport is open 6am to 9pm daily and charges a $5 fee per transaction.

American Express (Map 2; ☎ 902-423-3900), City Center Atlantic, 5523 Spring Garden Rd, Box 44, Suite 205, Halifax, NS B3J 1G8, is the only full-service American Express office east of Montréal. They'll cash traveler's checks and cardholders' personal checks and accept mail for those with American Express credit cards or traveler's checks. They can also replace lost or stolen checks. They're open 9am to 5pm weekdays.

Post The post office (Map 2; ☎ 902-494-4670) is at 1680 Bedford Row, between Sackville and Prince Sts. Mail sent c/o General Delivery, Halifax, NS B3J 2L3, is held here. It's open 7:30am to 5:15pm weekdays.

The post office inside Lawtons Drugs (Map 2; ☎ 902-429-0088), 5675 Spring Garden Rd, stays open 8am to 9pm Monday to Friday, 9am to 6pm Saturday and noon to 5pm Sunday.

Email & Internet Access The Halifax Public Library (Map 2; ☎ 902-490-5700), 5381 Spring Garden Rd, offers free Internet access, and it's possible to book a time slot. It's open 10am to 9pm Tuesday to Thursday, 10am to 5pm Friday and Saturday.

Access is also available at the North Branch Public Library (Map 1; ☎ 902-490-5723), 2285 Gottingen St. It's open 10am to 9pm Tuesday to Thursday, 10am to 5pm Friday and Saturday.

Travel Agencies Travel CUTS (Map 2; ☎ 902-482-8000), 1589 Barrington St, is a student travel agency with other offices in the Student Union Buildings at Dalhousie and St Mary's University.

For discount tickets try United Travels (Map 2; ☎ 902-422-0111) in Scotia Square, Upper Mall, 5201 Duke St.

HALIFAX – MAP 1

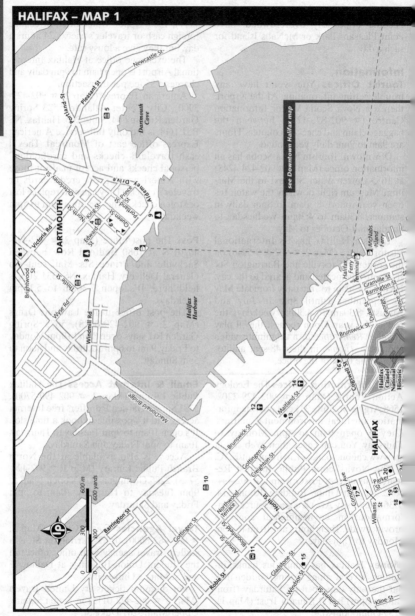

see Downtown Halifax map

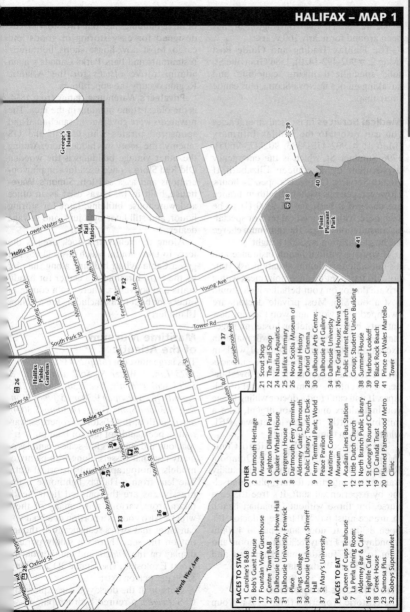

PLACES TO STAY
1 Caroline's B&B
15 Bob's Guest House
17 Fountain View Guesthouse
27 Centre Town B&B
29 Dalhousie University, Howe Hall
31 Dalhousie University, Fenwick Place
33 Kings College
36 Dalhousie University, Shirreff Hall
37 St Mary's University

PLACES TO EAT
6 Queen of Cups Teahouse
7 La Perla Dining Room; Alderney Bar & Café
16 Highlife Café
18 Greek House
23 Samosa Plus
32 Sobeys Supermarket

OTHER
2 Dartmouth Heritage Museum
3 Leighton Dillman Park
4 Quaker Whaler House
5 Evergreen House
8 Dartmouth Ferry Terminal; Alderney Gate; Dartmouth Public Library; Tourist Desk
9 Ferry Terminal Park; World Peace Pavilion
10 Maritime Command Museum
11 Acadian Lines Bus Station
12 Little Dutch Church
13 North Branch Public Library
14 St George's Round Church
19 TD Canada Trust
20 Planned Parenthood Metro Clinic
21 Scout Shop
22 The Trail Shop
24 Nautilus Aquatics
25 Halifax Infirmary
26 Nova Scotia Museum of Natural History
28 Oxford Cinema
30 Dalhousie Arts Centre; Dalhousie Art Gallery
34 Dalhousie University
35 The Grad House; Nova Scotia Public Interest Research Group; Student Union Building
38 Summer House
39 Harbour Lookoff
40 Black Rock Beach
41 Prince of Wales Martello Tower

Bookstores The Book Room (Map 2; ☎ 902-423-8271), 1546 Barrington St, has been around for nearly 160 years.

The Halifax Trading and Guide Post (Map 2; ☎ 902-492-1420), 1586 Granville St, sells specialized hiking, canoeing and kayaking guides in Nova Scotia, plus canoe route maps.

Medical Services In medical emergencies you can resort to the Halifax Infirmary (Map 1; ☎ 902-473-3383, 902-473-7605), 1796 Summer St, which is the emergency department of the Queen Elizabeth II Health Services Centre. It's open 24 hours. However, persons without health insurance are charged a basic fee of $300 (!) to be seen here, with any medical tests or specialist consultations extra. The minimum charge for hospitalization is $3200 a night.

If you are without health insurance and it's not a life threatening situation, ask your hotel to try to set up an appointment with a private doctor on your behalf, which should cost about $25. Most private doctors are swamped with work and won't accept new patients, but your hotel or hostel manager may be able to find one who will make an exception. There are no general walk-in clinics in Halifax, and healthcare cutbacks by the federal government have overburdened the entire system to the point of collapse. If you can't find a doctor willing to see you in Halifax and it's not urgent, take a minibus shuttle to Charlottetown, PEI, where walk-in clinics *do* exist.

The Planned Parenthood Metro Clinic (Map 1; ☎ 902-455-9656), 6009 Quinpool Rd, Suite 201, offers pregnancy and sexually transmitted infection testing, plus counseling by experienced staff. It's free to see a nurse, but those without Canadian health insurance must pay $20 to see a doctor. It's open 8:30am to noon and 1pm to 4:30pm Monday and Friday, 8:30am to noon and 1pm to 8pm Tuesday and Thursday, and 1pm to 4:30pm Wednesday.

The Historic Properties

The Historic Properties (Map 2) is a group of restored buildings on Upper Water St

constructed between 1800 and 1905. Many of these buildings are long two-story places, designed for easy storing of goods and cargo. Most now house shops, boutiques, restaurants and bars. Parks Canada's main administrative offices for the Atlantic Region occupy the upper floors.

Privateer's Warehouse, dating from 1814, is the oldest stone building in the area. The privateers were government-sanctioned and sponsored pirates who fed off the US 'enemy'; the booty was hidden here. Among the other vintage buildings is the wooden **Old Red Store** – once used for shipping operations and as a sail loft. **Simon's Warehouse**, built in 1854, was used as an office and warehouse building, later for storing liquor, and still later by a junk and salvage dealer.

Along the renovated dock area is the ferry to Dartmouth, which costs $1.65. The green **Cable Wharf** building along the pier by the ferry terminal is a center for handicrafts and souvenirs. There are a couple of offices for boat tours, including the McNabs Island ferry.

Maritime Museum of the Atlantic

This large museum *(Map 2; ☎ 902-424-7490, 1675 Lower Water St; $6/2 adult/child & $5/15 senior/family, free 5:30pm-8pm Tues & mid-Oct-Apr; open 9:30am-5:30pm Mon-Sat, 9:30am-8pm Tues, 10:30am-5:30pm Sun)*, south of the Historic Properties, warrants a peek, and not just for boat buffs. It's spacious and contains full-scale examples of many regional vessels, along with plenty of models, photographs and historical data. The lens from a Halifax lighthouse is impressive, as are the painted figureheads taken from various ships, many of them wrecks. Also good is a portion of a boat you can enter that sways realistically as though out on the sea. There's a wildly popular display on the *Titanic* and another on the Great Explosion. The Titanic 3D Theater is $2.50 per person extra.

Outside at the dock you can explore the CSS *Acadia,* a retired hydrographic vessel from England. Also docked here is the

WWII corvette HMCS *Sackville*, the last of 22 warships of its kind. Admission to each ship is $1, but both are free with your Maritime Museum ticket.

Often moored at the wharf by the museum is *Bluenose II*, a replica of Canada's best-known boat. The original *Bluenose* schooner was built in 1921 in Lunenburg and never lost a race in 20 years. In tribute, the Canadian 10¢ coin bears the schooner's image. The *Bluenose* has become nearly as familiar a Canadian symbol as the maple leaf.

The *Bluenose II* was launched in 1963 and now has a permanent berth at the Maritime Museum when not on display at other Canadian ports. Two-hour harbor tours are given on the schooner, but when it's docked you can walk on board to look at this beautiful piece of work for free.

Brewery Market

Also part of the restored waterfront, this complex is in the Keith's Brewery building (Map 2) at 1496 Lower Water St. Dating from 1820, the building now contains boutiques, restaurants and a couple of pubs. A farmers' market is held on the lower level on Saturday from 7am to 1pm year-round (from 8am in winter).

Keith's Brewery Tours (☎ 902-455-1474; *adult/child $9/7; every half hour from noon-9pm Mon-Thur, noon-9pm Fri & Sat, noon-4pm Sun*) are led by a costumed guide and include two mugs of beer. From October to May the tours are only on Saturday and Sunday.

Pier 21 Centre

Pier 21 (Map 2; ☎ 902-425-7770, **W** pier21 ns.ca, 1055 Marginal Rd; *adult/senior/child $6.50/5.50/3.50; open 9am-5pm daily June-Aug, 9am-5pm Tues-Sat Sept-May*) was to Canada what Ellis Island was to the US. Between 1928 and 1971 over a million immigrants entered Canada through Pier 21, including 48,000 war brides (mostly from the UK) and their 22,000 children. In addition, nearly half a million troops departed from here for Europe during WWII. In 1999 this national historic site reopened as a museum featuring a large pavilion with in-formation displays, boutiques, cafes and multimedia exhibits detailing the travails of refugees and immigrants hoping to call Canada home. Pier 21 is somewhat hidden behind the VIA Rail station (go around the side of the Westin Hotel on Terminal Rd). Better yet, follow the waterfront boardwalk a kilometer south from the Historic Properties and you'll bump right into it.

Historic Downtown Area

Government House This edifice (Map 2) is between Hollis and Barrington Sts, near the corner of Bishop St. Government House has been the residence of the provincial lieutenant-governor since 1807. It was built for Governor John Wentworth.

St Paul's Cemetery Also known as the Old Burying Ground, the cemetery (Map 2), first used in 1749, is across the street from Government House on Barrington St. By the time it closed in 1844, over 12,000 people had been buried there.

Province House Since 1819 this fine example of Georgian architecture *(Map 2; ☎ 902-424-4661, Hollis St between George & Prince Sts; free guided tours; open 9am-5pm Mon-Fri, 10am-4pm Sat & Sun July & Aug)* has been the home of Canada's oldest provincial legislature. In the off-season the staff will show you part of the building 9am to 4pm weekdays.

St Paul's Church St Paul's Anglican Church *(Map 2; ☎ 902-429-2240, 1749 Argyle St; admission free; open 9am-4:30pm Mon-Fri Sept-May, 9am-5pm Mon-Sat June-Aug)*, near Prince St, was the first Protestant church in Canada (dating from 1749). A guide is on hand to answer questions. One intriguing curiosity is the piece of metal lodged above the door in the north wall, inside the porch. This is part of a window frame from another building, which was implanted here during the explosion of the *Mont Blanc* 3km away in Halifax Harbour in 1917. (See the boxed text 'A Christmas Tree for Boston' for more information on the explosion.)

A Christmas Tree for Boston

Few cities have experienced such a sudden and unexpected turning point in their history as Halifax did with the Great Explosion. The day it occurred, December 6, 1917, was bright and clear, and WWI was raging somewhere overseas in Europe, not in Canada. At 8:30am, out in the harbor, the *Mont Blanc,* a French munitions ship, and the *Imo,* a Belgian relief ship, struck each other due to human error.

Even after the two boats collided in the Narrows, adjacent to the city, the *Mont Blanc* – filled with 300 rounds of ammunition, 10 tons of gun cotton, 200 tons of TNT, 2100 tons of picric acid (used in explosives) and 32 tons of highly flammable benzol stacked in barrels on the deck – did not immediately explode. Instead it caught fire, and its crew, only too aware of the cargo, took to lifeboats and rowed to Dartmouth. The ship then drifted unattended toward Halifax, drawing by-standers to the waterfront to watch the spectacle.

At 9:05am the ship exploded in a blinding white flash, the largest man-made explosion in history prior to the nuclear age. More than 1900 people were killed and 9000 were injured. Almost all of the northern end of Halifax, roughly 130 hectares, was leveled. Most of the buildings and homes that were not destroyed by the explosion itself later burned to the ground because of winter stockpiles of coal in their cellars.

All 2830 tons of the *Mont Blanc* were blown to pieces. The barrel of one of the guns was found 5km away, and the anchor shank, which weighed more than a ton, flew 3km in the other direction. The blast was felt as far away as Sydney on Cape Breton and could be heard on Prince Edward Island. The misery was compounded the following day, when Halifax was hit by a blizzard that dumped 40cm of snow on the city.

Relief efforts were immediate, and money poured in from as far away as New Zealand and China. But what Haligonians most remember is the generosity of the US state of Massachusetts, which donated $750,000 and instantly sent an army of volunteers and doctors to help in the recovery effort. Halifax was so grateful for the assistance in its hour of despair that the city still sends a Christmas tree to Boston every year as a token of appreciation.

City Hall Built in 1890 at the opposite end of the sunken courtyard from St Paul's Church, City Hall (Map 2) is a gem of Victorian architecture.

Old Town Clock At the top of George St, at Citadel Hill, stands one of the city's most beloved symbols, the Old Town Clock (Map 2). The inner workings arrived in Halifax in 1803 after being ordered by Prince Edward, the duke of Kent, then the military commander of Halifax.

Art Gallery of Nova Scotia

The provincial art gallery *(Map 2; ☎ 902-424-7542, W www.agns.gov.ns.ca, 1723 Hollis St; adult/student $5/2, by donation Tues; open 10am-6pm Tues-Fri, noon-5pm Sat & Sun* year-round, also noon-5pm Mon in July & Aug) is housed in the restored heritage Dominion Building of 1868 (once used as the post office) across from Province House. Provincial and other Canadian works make up much of the large collection of 5000 pieces. There are both permanent and changing exhibits and free tours Sundays at 2pm.

Other Galleries

The **Nova Scotia Centre for Craft and Design** *(Map 2; ☎ 902-424-4062, 1683 Barrington St; admission free; open 9am-4pm Mon-Fri, 10am-4pm Sat)* presents exhibitions of Nova Scotia crafts, including weaving, woodworking and jewelry.

The **Khyber Centre for the Arts** *(Map 2 ☎ 902-422-9668, W www.khyberarts.ns.ca*

1588 Barrington St; admission free; open 11am-5pm Tues-Sat, until 10pm Thurs) is more avant-garde. This artist-run center includes several galleries, plus the studio of noted potter Shana Salaff. The center's Artist's Club is worth joining ($10) if you're at all interested in the Halifax art scene, as you'll be allowed into the member's bar and invited to attend lectures, cabarets, raves and other events. Show openings are usually 8pm Mondays, accompanied by dancing to DJ music. Another DJ spins the discs from 10pm Wednesdays. All in all, the Khyber Centre is a great place to touch base with emerging artists.

Nova Scotia Sport Hall of Fame

The hall of fame *(Map 2; ☎ 902-421-1266, 1645 Granville St; admission free; open 10:30am-4pm Mon-Fri, 10:30am-3:30pm Sat)* honors provincial heroes and teams with displays of trophies and photographs. Most fun are the computer exhibits and the miniature hockey rink.

Halifax Public Gardens

The public gardens (Map 1) may be small – if seven hectares is small – but they're regarded as the finest Victorian city gardens in North America. They're found on the corner of S Park St and Spring Garden Rd. Oldies bands perform off-key concerts in the gazebo 2pm to 4pm Sundays from late June to early September.

Halifax Citadel National Historic Site

Canada's most visited national historic site, the Citadel *(Map 1; ☎ 902-426-5080, off Sackville St; adult/child & senior/family $6/3 & $4.50/$14.75 May-Oct; grounds free rest of the year but exhibits closed; open 9am-6pm daily July & August, 9am-5pm daily Sept-June)* is a huge, oddly angled fort on top of Halifax's big central hill. It has been the city's towering landmark since 1749, when construction began with the founding of Halifax. This version is the fourth, built from 1818 to 1861.

Halifax was a good location from which the British could rule Nova Scotia, as well as a strategic military base from which to deal with the French, who had forts of their own in Louisbourg and Québec City. The fort we see today was built later to defend Halifax from the Americans.

The excellent guided tours will explain the fort's shape and how, despite appearances, it was neither well designed nor well constructed. For a freebie, come by for the hourly changing of the kilted guard in ostrich feather hats.

Also in the compound is the Army Museum, with exhibits relating to Atlantic Canada's military history.

Nova Scotia Museum of Natural History

This museum *(Map 1; ☎ 902-424-7353, 1747 Summer St; adult/family $4/12, free mid-Oct-May; open 9:30am-5:30pm Mon-Sat, 9:30am-8pm Wed, 1pm-5:30pm Sun June-mid Oct, 9:30am-5pm Tues-Sat, 1pm-5pm Sun mid-Oct-May)* west of the Citadel is considered the headquarters of the provincial museum system. History, wildlife, geology, anthropology and industry are all covered. The three-dimensional animal and fish exhibits are excellent. The history section contains an old stagecoach and a working model of a late-1800s sawmill.

Gottingen Street

The neighborhood around Gottingen Street north of the Citadel hosts a significant former African Canadian community, the descendants of former US slaves who settled here in the 1840s. Their original settlement, Africville, was several kilometers north at Seaview Point. With the building of the MacKay Bridge in the 1960s, Africville was demolished and most of the residents were relocated here. (See the 'Venerable Visible Minority' boxed text in the Shelburne section of the Southwestern Nova Scotia chapter for more information.) Today a number of advocacy groups representing Canadian blacks or Native Indians have offices along Gottingen north of Cogswell St, as well as many businesses catering to this population, making it a fascinating area to explore.

Nearby is **St George's Round Church** *(Map 1; 2222 Brunswick St; admission free; open 9:30am-5pm Mon-Fri mid-June-Aug)*, the only 18th-century Canadian church built in the circular Palladian style. It was erected in 1800 under the patronage of Edward, duke of Kent, son of King George III, who served as military commander of Halifax from 1794–1800. Damaged by fire in 1994, this little-known architectural gem has been completely restored.

A long block north of St George's at the corner of Brunswick and Gerrish Sts is the **Little Dutch Church** (Map 1), built by German (Deutsche) settlers in 1755. The adjacent cemetery is among the oldest in the city.

Maritime Command Museum

This museum *(Map 1; ☎ 902-427-0550, ext 8250, 2725 Gottingen St; admission free; open 10am-3:30pm Mon-Fri)* is on the Canadian Forces Base (CFB) between North and Alman Sts. It's in a fine stone building that served as the personal residence of the commander-in-chief of the British Royal Navy in North America from 1819–1904. The grounds are protected by numerous cannons. You'll see mementos like uniforms and medals from the military past of the Maritimes. The Regional Police Museum is housed here. Seven different city bus routes pass this way.

Titanic Grave Site

Since the film *Titanic* swept through the 1998 Academy Awards like, well, an iceberg, nondenominational **Fairview Cemetery** (Map 3) has been incorporated into the tour bus circuit. Halifax, the base of rescue operations for the tragedy, is home to nearly all the residuals of the fateful voyage, and among the 121 victims buried here is a lowly coal shoveler named Jim Dawson who was transformed into Jack Dawson (Leonardo DiCaprio) by Hollywood. It's easy to find grave No 227, marked simply 'J Dawson, April 15, 1912,' as weepy adolescents have made it a pilgrimage point and there are usually flowers. Jack and Rose aside, the rows of graves themselves are worth the trek, and if you arrive around midmorning you'll be able to tag along with one of the groups and hear the whole story. Entrances to the cemetery are off Connaught and Chisholm Aves (bus Nos 9 & 17), not far from the MacKay Bridge, and admission is free.

Hemlock Ravine Park

A system of linked walking trails winds through this large wooded estate (Map 3) once called home by Edward, duke of Kent, Queen Victoria's dad. It includes a view of Bedford Basin, and amid the gardens are some very impressive 30m-tall trees. To reach it by car, drive along the Bedford Hwy (Hwy 2) and turn left on Kent Ave a few blocks north of Kearney Lake Rd (bus Nos 80 & 82).

Point Pleasant Park

Point Pleasant Park (Map 1) is highly recommended. Some 39km of nature trails, picnic spots, a restaurant, a beach and the Prince of Wales Martello Tower – a round 18th-century defensive structure – are all found within this 75-hectare wooded sanctuary. Good views are to be enjoyed all the way around the perimeter. No cars are allowed.

The park is at the far southern end of town, at the tip of the peninsula. If you're walking, the park begins 2km south of Spring Garden Rd. The No 9 bus connects Point Pleasant with the downtown Scotia Centre until 9pm, or you can drive to the park's edge. There's ample free parking at Harbour Lookoff and at another lot. Whichever way you come, check out the size of the houses along Young St.

At the city edge of the park is the Port of Halifax, a very busy terminal piled high with containers. Walk out to the lighthouse by the port for great views of the surroundings and all the shipping activity.

In early 2001, the brown spruce long horn beetle was discovered in the park. Evidently it had arrived via the adjacent container port, and federal officials ordered that all spruce trees at Point Pleasant be cut and burned in an attempt to eradicate the beetle. This outraged local residents, who feared their park would be destroyed, and the Sierra Club obtained an injunction to stop the cutting. Evidence then emerged that the beetle had been in the park for almost a decade and that it had already spread to nearby areas. Despite this, officials anxious to protect Canada's vast spruce forests (and the industries which depend on them) continue to push for a cull, so the controversy continues.

An interesting historical aside is that the park still belongs to the British government, which has rented it out on a 999-year lease at the rate of 10¢ a year.

York Redoubt
The remains of a 200-year-old fort make up this national historic site, which overlooks the harbor from a bluff just south of the North West Arm (south of the center). It was designed to protect the city from attack by sea and is built at the narrowest point of the outer harbor. The site was used in various capacities by the military from 1793 to as late as 1956.

Aside from the view, there are mounted guns, a Martello tower and historical information and displays; the underground tunnels are fun to explore.

York Redoubt (☎ 902-426-5080; admission free; grounds open 9am-8pm daily mid-May-Aug, 9am-7pm Sept, 9am-6pm Oct, 9am-5pm other months, buildings open 10am-6pm mid-June-early Sept) is off Hwy 253, 6km south of Sir Sandford Fleming Park. Bus No 15 comes directly here.

Cape Sambro
From York Redoubt, it's a pleasant 20km seaside drive south to Cape Sambro via Ketch Harbour. There's a great view of the picturesque fishing village of Sambro from the Government Wharf beyond the coast guard station in the village. Crystal Crescent Beach is 2km west. This wonderful sandy beach with clear cold water is easily accessible via a boardwalk and hiking trails beginning from the parking lot. In the past Crystal Crescent has been used for nude sunbathing, but this is officially illegal and crackdowns have occurred, so keep your pants on!

McNabs Island
Out in the harbor and easily seen from York Redoubt, this small island makes a good break from the city. There are guided walks, beaches, picnic tables and hiking, and a teahouse serves basic snacks or seafood. Between 1888 and 1892, a fort was built at the south end of the island to defend Halifax Harbour. Today, McNabs is being made into a provincial park to help defend against the rising tide of tourism.

Boats depart from the Halifax dock area at 9am and 2pm from June to mid-September, and tickets ($12.50) can be bought from Murphy's on the Water (☎ 902-420-1015) by Cable Wharf.

Mike Tilley's **McNabs Island Ferry** (Map 2; ☎ 902-465-4563, 800-326-4563, ☒ www.mcnabsisland.com) is an eight-seater open boat that will take you over upon request year-round (so long as he isn't away on another job). Mike leaves from Fisherman's Cove across the harbor in Dartmouth, charging $8 per person roundtrip to the island. To get there, take the ferry from Halifax to Dartmouth ($1.65), and request a transfer when getting on board; that will get you onto the No 60 bus to Fisherman's Cove.

Activities
Kayaking & Canoeing Ocean kayaking tours and rentals are available through **Sea Sun Kayak School & Adventures** (Map 3; ☎ 902-471-2732, ☒ www.paddlenovascotia.com, St. Mary's Boat Club, 1741 Fairfield Rd, off Jubilee Rd). Rental of a single kayak is $35/50 a half/full day, doubles $50/78. Full-day guided kayaking tours ($99 plus tax) are offered on Wednesday, Friday and Sunday from May to October. Trips of two, three and four days are also possible.

The **Trail Shop** (Map 1; ☎ 902-423-8736, 6210 Quinpool Rd; single/double kayaks $25/35 a day, $20/25 each additional day, $45/55 Fri morning-anytime Mon) has kayaks for rent.

Dragonfly Outfitters *(Map 3; ☎ 902-462-5050,* **W** *www.dragonflyoutfitters.com, Graham's Grove Park, Prince Albert Rd; open 10am-8pm July & Aug)* offers canoe, kayak and bicycle rentals at the Graham's Grove waterfront. Single kayaks or canoes are $10/30 for one/four hours, double kayaks $18/50 plus tax.

Rock Climbing The **Vertigo Climbing School** *(Map 2; ☎ 902-492-1492,* **W** *www3.ns .sympatico.ca/vertigo, 1586 Granville St)* at Halifax Trading & Guide Post, offers an introduction to rock climbing for $85. They also run rope courses, hikes and custom trips.

Scuba Diving There are about 50 wrecks at the mouth of Halifax Harbour, and more good diving is available along the coast. For information and equipment rentals, try **Nautilus Aquatics** *(Map 1; ☎ 902-454-4296, 6162 Quinpool Rd)*. From late May to early September they run dive charters every Sunday ($45 per person for the boat plus $12 per tank). If you need a wetsuit, fins, mask, etc, a complete equipment package including one tank is $50.

Cycling For bicycling information or to join a bicycle tour of the city or the Halifax region, you can contact the helpful folks at the nonprofit **Velo Bicycle Club** *(☎ 902-423-4345,* **W** *www.velohalifax.ca)*.

Bicycles can be hired from **Peddle and Seat Ventures** *(☎ 902-497-3092)*. They don't have an office, but if you call them, a pick-up point or delivery will be arranged. Hybrid bikes, helmets and locks are $22/100 plus tax per day/week, and panniers and racks are another $3 a day. Owner Dana Gallant will help with bicycle touring arrangements and can be hired as a tour leader.

Organized Tours

There's no shortage of tours in Halifax. The tourist office has a complete list, but some of the more established and interesting ones follow. Most have discounts for seniors, children or students.

Harbour Hopper Tours *(Map 2; ☎ 902-490-8687,* **W** *www.harbourhopper.com, near the Maritime Museum)* runs 55-minute tours around town and out into the harbor in a seaworthy Lark 5 tour bus/boat. It operates every 90 minutes from May to mid-October ($23 per person).

Double Decker *(☎ 902-420-1155)* offers 1½-hour city tours in London-style buses that leave from the corner of Duke and Water Sts at 10:30am and 12:30pm daily mid-June to mid-October (also at 2:30pm in July and August). A ticket costs $18/17/6 adult/senior/child, including tax.

The most reliable tours around Halifax are those run by **Atlantic Tours Gray Line** *(Map 2; ☎ 902-425-9999,* **W** *www.atlantic-tours.ca)*, which consistently delivers what is promised. They'll even run a tour when only one or two people have booked. Atlantic Tours Gray Line also has tours in winter, when most of the other operators have closed down. Their three-hour city sightseeing tour (adult/child $25/5) begins at 9am year-round. The Peggy's Cove and Lunenburg tour from May to October is $64/48 with/without lunch. From May to October, Gray Line has booking kiosks on Lower Water St outside the Maritime Museum of the Atlantic and outside the Sheraton. In winter, give them a call.

Halifax Ghost Walk *(☎ 902-469-6716 e macrev@ns.sympatico.ca; adult/senior o child $8.50/5; open July-mid-Sept)* offers a two-hour walk from the Old Town Cloc (Map 2), beginning at 8:30pm every coupl of days. The tour winds through town to the docks and features tales of pirates buried treasure and ghosts from the ol city's lore.

anging of the guard at the Citadel, Halifax

Old and new side by side in Halifax

wind fills the sails in Halifax Harbour.

Evangeline and the Commemorative Church

A bit of the sun on Nova Scotia

A reconstructed house at the Port Royal National Historic Site, near Annapolis Royal

The beauteous *Bluenose II* (Map 2), perhaps the country's best known boat, takes visitors out on **harbor sailing cruises** 1-800-763-1963, W *www.bluenose2.ns.ca, Lower Water St near the Maritime Museum)* whenever it's in town or not being worked on. If you're lucky enough to be around when it's operating, don't miss this too-cheap-to-be-true $20 cruise. Trips are usually at 9:30am and 1:30pm from June to September, but they're canceled if there's rain, wind or fog.

Murphy's on the Water *(Map 2; ☎ 920-0-1015,* W *www.murphysonthewater.com, Cable Wharf at the Historic Properties)* has as many as 17 boat tours throughout the day from May to October. The two-hour narrated trip aboard the *Harbour Queen* goes past both new and old city landmarks and is a pretty good value at $16. The boat carries 200 people and has open and closed decks, a snack counter and a bar. From mid-June through August there are three to four runs daily. Out of peak season, there are two trips daily, and in winter it closes down completely. Dinner cruises are another option ($37). Murphy's also operates the *Mar II,* a very handsome sailboat, for trips around the harbor. The 1½ hour sailing trips cost $18. There's a moonlight sail on Friday and Saturday, and other themes that may be appealing. Some trips include whale watching, but this is not a prime area for whales.

From mid-June to early October, **Peggy's Cove Express** *(Map 2; ☎ 902-422-4200, www.peggyscove.com, Cable Wharf)* has a 2-hour boat/bus tour to Peggy's Cove for $0 including a chowder lunch ($69 if you want lobster).

Also offering a Peggy's Cove tour is **Markland Tours** *(☎ 902-499-2939).* The four-hour tour is $30, and it picks up at the HI hostel (10% discount for HI cardholders). Other tours include Annapolis Valley ($62), Lunenburg ($60) and a city tour ($24). These tours are available year-round, and you book by phone.

The **Halifax Heritage House Hostel** *(Map* ☎ *902-422-3863, 1253 Barrington St)* runs minibus tours that are inexpensive because only transportation is included (meals and lodging are paid separately). There are day trips to Digby and the South Shore ($40), an overnight trip to Fundy National Park ($80) and a three-day trip to Cape Breton and the Cabot Trail ($120). The tours generally operate from mid-June to early September, depending upon demand. A reservations list is kept at the hostel reception, and you don't need to be staying there to sign up. It's a great value and a lot of fun.

Kiwi Kaboodle's Tradewind Shuttle *(☎ 902-463-4244)* offers visitors 10-hour, transportation-only tours to Chester, Mahone Bay, Lunenburg and Bridgewater at $60, picking up around Halifax at 9:30am. Peggy's Cove can be included for an additional $10. The driver will take you anywhere you like. Groups of four or more can request a discount.

For custom hiking/camping tours to Cape Breton, get in touch with Sean Drohan of **Halifax Trading and Guide Post** *(Map 2; ☎ 902-492-1420, 1586 Granville St near Sackville).* The office is opposite the Ultramar gas station, a block down from Halifax Tourism. Sean can organize a trip exactly the way you want it, charging $150 a day for the first person, then $25 for each additional person. Food is $10 per person a day. Transportation is another $125 per group for the whole trip (four persons maximum). Groups of up to 15 are welcome, but they must rent a larger vehicle. Sean's tours are a bargain if there are several of you splitting the cost, and the services of an experienced guide are included.

Special Events

Some of the major events held in Halifax in July and August include the following:

Gay Pride Parade

On a Saturday afternoon in late June gays and straights assemble in downtown Halifax for the biggest coming out of the year.

Canada Day

Canada's birthday on July 1 is celebrated in high style in Halifax, with parades, live entertainment, rock concerts and fireworks.

Nova Scotia International Tattoo

Every year this event is held in Halifax during the first week of July (or thereabouts). You'll see

DOWNTOWN HALIFAX – MAP 2

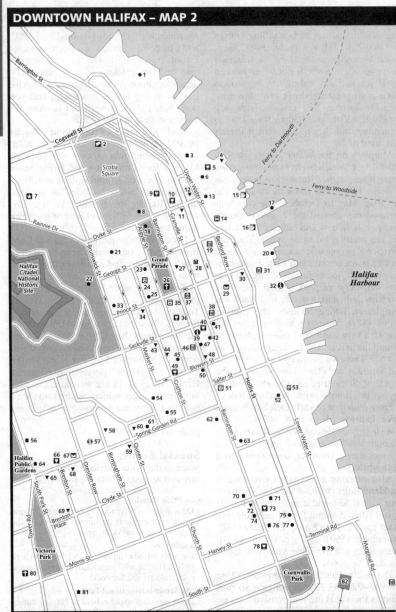

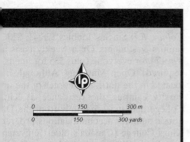

ACES TO STAY
Halifax Sheraton;
Atlantic Tours Gray Line
Kiosk; Hertz
YMCA
Lord Nelson Hotel
Dalhousie University,
O'Brien Hall
Halliburton House Inn
Waverley Inn
Halifax Heritage House
Hostel
Westin Hotel
Garden Inn B&B

ACES TO EAT
Harbourside Market
Bluenose II Restaurant
O'Carroll's Irish Pub
Café C'est Si Bon
McKelvie's
Midtown Tavern & Grill
Maxwell's Plum Tavern
Satisfaction Feast
Mediteraneo Café
Tu Do Restaurant
Thirsty Duck Pub &
Eatery
Rogues Roost Brew Pub
Mikey's Wraps
Your Father's Moustache
Curry Village
Kinh-Do

HER
Casino Nova Scotia
US Consulate; Cogswell
Tower
Lower Deck
Historic Properties
Police Headquarters
United Travel
Peddler's Pub
Split Crow
Double-Decker Tours
Start
Transit Terminal
Halifax Ferry Terminal
McNabs Island Ferry
Cable Wharf; Murphy's
on the Water; Peggy's
Cove Express
City Hall
Art Gallery of Nova Scotia
Harbour Hopper Tours

21 Halifax Metro Centre
22 Old Town Clock
23 The Dome
24 Grafton St Dinner Theatre
25 Avis Rent-a-Car
26 St Paul's Church
28 Province House
29 Post Office
31 Maritime Museum of the
    Atlantic; Atlantic Tours
    Gray Line Kiosk;
    Bluenose II
32 Tourism Nova Scotia
33 New Palace Nightclub
35 Neptune Theatre
36 Diamond Bar
37 Nova Scotia Centre for
    Craft and Design
38 Nova Scotia Sport Hall of
    Fame
39 Tourism Halifax
    International Visitor
    Centre
40 Reflections Cabaret
41 Budget Rent-a-Car
42 Halifax Trading and
    Guide Post; Vertigo
    Climbing School
45 Ecology Action Centre
46 Khyber Centre for the
    Arts
47 Travel CUTS
49 The Eagle Pub & Eatery
50 Book Room
51 Halifax Feast
52 Keith's Brewery Building;
    Brewery Market
53 Impark
54 Air Canada
55 Halifax Public Library
57 American Express
61 Second Cup
62 St Paul's Cemetery
63 Government House
66 Birmingham Bar & Grill
67 Lawtons Drugs
73 Bearly's Bar & Grill
75 Trident Booksellers &
    Café
77 Discount Car Rentals
78 Spring Brewery
80 All Saints Cathedral
82 VIA Rail Station;
    Enterprise Rent-a-Car
83 Pier 21 Centre

vast formations of Scottish bagpipers on parade. Check the Web site at W www.nstattoo.ca for more information.

Halifax Natal Day
A major event held at the end of July or early August with a parade, street parties, boat races, a bridge walk, concerts and a fireworks display.

DuMaurier Atlantic Jazz Festival
This festival takes place at the end of July. Web site: W www.jazzeast.com

Halifax Atlantic Fringe Festival
This festival in August draws hundreds of performers, from musicians and actors to comics and mimics, for a variety of events that are staged throughout the metro area. Buskers arrive in Halifax en masse around this same time.
Web site: W www.atlanticfringe.com

Places to Stay

Camping There isn't a campground in Halifax itself. Turn to Places to Stay in the Dartmouth section that follows for information on camping at Shubie Park, which is accessible by city bus from Halifax. For better campsites west of town, see Places to Stay in the Peggy's Cove section of the Southwestern Nova Scotia chapter.

Hostels *Halifax Heritage House Hostel* (*Map 2;* ☎ *902-422-3863, fax 902-422-0116,* W *www.hostellingintl.ns.ca, 1253 Barrington St*) Dorm beds $18/22 members/nonmembers, private rooms $40/47 single/double for all. Check-in 4pm-11pm Nov-Apr; 4pm-1am May-Oct. This HI hostel is perfectly located in a fine historic house erected in 1864. The hostel is an easy walk from the VIA Rail station or to downtown and the waterfront. There's room for 70 guests and amenities include cooking facilities and an outdoor patio. Double and family rooms with shared bath are also available. The maximum stay is seven nights. From the airport, the Airbus goes to the nearby Westin Hotel. From the bus depot, take the No 7 bus south from the corner of Robie and Almon to the corner of Barrington and South Sts. The hostel can be seen from this corner. No parking is available. For information on minibus tours around the province from the hostel, see Organized Tours earlier in the Halifax section.

YMCA *(Map 2;* ☎ *902-423-9622, fax 902-425-3180, 1565 S Park St)* Singles $30/130 daily/weekly. The 45-room YMCA accepts men only, and bathrooms are shared. Facilities include a gym and swimming pool. The location is excellent, across from the Public Gardens and near Citadel Hill. Free parking is available after 6pm only.

Dalhousie University *(Map 1;* ☎ *902-494-8840, fax 902-494-1219,* e *conference .services@dal.ca,* w *www.dal.ca/confserv)* Singles/doubles $39/59, students $27/46, seniors $35/53. From mid-May to late August, Dalhousie's massive summer accommodations program is your best bet for an inexpensive room in Halifax. They're available at Fenwick Place, Howe Hall, O'Brien Hall and Shirreff Hall, and the front desks of these residences are staffed 24 hours a day. You can go directly there, but it's not a bad idea to call ahead as groups sometimes reserve entire buildings.

The bathrooms are generally shared, but the rates usually include parking, taxes, breakfast and use of athletic facilities. A common fridge and microwave may be provided on your floor. Laundry services are $1. The reduced student rate doesn't include parking ($7 a night extra, if required). If you stay a week, you pay for only six nights.

Two of the residences are on the campus: **Howe Hall** *(Map 1;* ☎ *902-494-2108, 6230 Coburg Rd)* is a four-story stone building adjacent to the main campus. **Shirreff Hall** *(Map 1;* ☎ *902-494-2428, 6385 South St)* is a stone building erected in 1919 featuring a magnificent portico with four pillars. The other two residences are much closer to downtown. **O'Brien Hall** *(Map 2;* ☎ *902-494-2013, fax 902-494-6955, 5217 Morris St)* has a great location, on the corner of Barrington St just around the corner from the HI hostel. **Fenwick Place** *(Map 1;* ☎ *902-494-3886, fax 902-494-2213, 5599 Fenwick St)* is a 33-story skyscraper with 200 apartments. It's the most upscale of the Dalhousie residences and tends to be full when the others still have rooms. Singles/doubles cost $56/80 for a two-/three-bedroom unit. A large Sobeys Supermarket is right across the street.

Kings College *(Map 1;* ☎ *902-422-127.* fax 902-423-3357, w *www.ukings.ns.ca, 63. Coburg Rd)* Singles/doubles $28/41, $20/: seniors & students. On a weekly basis it $94/174 for everyone (plus $35 for linens, required). Open May-Aug. Although it located in the northwest corner of the un versity campus, the residence at King College operates separately from the Da housie summer accommodations progra: Kings College (Canada's oldest universit founded in 1789) features pleasant Englis Gothic architecture, and the cheaper pri compensates for the additional distan from town. The 94 rooms with shared ba are often fully occupied by groups, so ca ahead. The reception in Alexandra Hall open 24 hours. Parking is included (but n meals).

St Mary's University *(Map 1;* ☎ *902-42 5486, 888-347-5555, 902-420-5049 after 4pr* w *www.stmarys.ca/conferences, 5865 Gors brook Ave, near Robie St cnr Roxton R.* Singles/doubles $28/43 plus tax, studen $20 single. Open mid-May-mid-Aug. Tl rooms with shared bath in the Loyola Res dence are cheap and not far from the ci center, and groups tend to book many them for large chunks of the summer. Fr. parking is available.

Mount St Vincent University *(Map* ☎ *902-457-6286, 902-457-6788, fax 902-44. 5793,* e *conference.office@msvu.ca,* w *ww .msvu.ca/campus-information/conferenc services.htm, on Seton Rd off Bedford Hw* Singles/doubles $38/53, students & senio $33/48. Nonstudents under 65 pay $34/51 they stay seven or more nights. Open Ma late Aug. Parking, breakfast and use of tl athletic facilities are included; meals a available and there's a coin laundry. App to the conference office in Assisi Hall on tl campus. This university is a 15-minute dri west of town on the Bedford Hwy (bus N 80 and 82) and overlooks the Bedfo. Basin.

B&Bs & Tourist Homes *Fountain Vie Guesthouse (Map 1;* ☎ *902-422-416.* e *ap599@chebucto.ns.ca,* w *browser.t fountainviewguesthouse, 2138 Robie S.*

ingles/doubles/triples from $24/30/35. A
oom with two double beds for four
ersons is $50. This plain, straightforward
lace is the only inexpensive tourist home
ear town. It's the bright blue house with
hite trim between Compton Ave and
illiams St. North Common is across the
reet, and the Citadel is within walking
istance. This home is reliable and consis-
nt, and its seven rooms all have TV. It's
so quite popular, so call ahead for reser-
ations. Only three parking places are
vailable.

Garden Inn B&B (Map 2; ☎ 877-414-
577, fax 902-492-1462, ⓦ www.garden
n.ns.ca, 1263 S Park St) Doubles $109
May-Oct, $89 Nov-Apr. All 23 rooms are air
onditioned. This 1875 Victorian house with
n attached annex is well located, and
mple parking is available.

Bob's Guest House (Map 1; ☎ 877-890-
060, fax 902-454-2060, ⓦ www.sjnow.com/
obs, 2715 Windsor St) Bus Nos 82 & 17.
oubles $75-99 June-Oct, $59-79 Nov-May.
long Windsor St northwest of Quinpool
d, Bob's has a variety of rooms – the attic
ite is cozy – along with nice gardens and a
ot tub. Gays are welcome here. It's near a
rge Sobeys Supermarket and the bus
ation is within walking distance.

Centre Town B&B (Map 1; ☎ 902-422-
380, fax 902-425-0605, ⓦ www.centre
wn.com, 2016 Oxford St near Quinpool
d) Doubles $99/109 shared/private bath.
ccording to the official *Doers and Dream-
s Guide*, 95% of the clientele at Centre
own is lesbian or gay. This large white
ouse is in a good area for dining out but a
t far from town.

otels As with the B&Bs, there's a serious
ortage of budget motels around Halifax,
d the few places that do exist take advan-
ge of the scarcity by charging more than
ey're worth. The main motel strip is far
om the center along the Bedford Hwy
Hwy 2) northwest of town. Bus Nos 80 and
go into the city, a 15-minute drive away.
side from the two 'cheaper' places that
llow, there are a couple of more upscale
otels out this way.

Esquire Motel (Map 3; ☎ 800-565-3367,
fax 902-835-9507, ⓦ www.esquiremote
l.ns.ca, 771 Bedford Hwy) Rooms from $70
Apr-Oct, from $55 Nov-Mar. This long
wood and brick motel has 28 rooms.

Travellers Motel (Map 3; ☎ 800-565-3394,
fax 902-835-6887, ⓦ www.travelersmotel
.com, 773 Bedford Hwy) Cabins/units from
$45/69. The 18 simple duplex cabins are
available from May to October only. From
November to April they close the unheated
cabins but continue renting the 25 motel
rooms for $52. Travellers is owned by the
same people as the Esquire Motel and is
only a short distance down the road.

Hotels The following are some of the top
end hotels in the area.

Waverley Inn (Map 2; ☎ 800-565-9346,
fax 902-425-0167, ⓦ www.waverleyinn.com,
1266 Barrington St) Doubles $95-249 May-
Oct, $79-199 Nov-Apr, breakfast included.
For a bit of a splurge, you might try this
historic place, whose 32 rooms haven't lost
a bit of their circa-1866 charm. You're
quite close to downtown, and parking is
provided.

Halliburton House Inn (Map 2; ☎ 902-
420-0658, fax 902-423-2324, ⓦ www.hal
liburton.ns.ca, 5184 Morris St) Doubles $95-
325 May-Oct, $85-250 Nov-Apr. This hotel
is immaculately kept and finished. Built in
1823, it has antiques, a library and a pleasant
garden. There are 29 rooms but only 14
parking spaces are available, on a first-
come, first-served basis.

Lord Nelson Hotel (Map 2; ☎ 800-565-
2020, fax 902-423-7148, ⓦ www.lord
nelsonhotel.com, 1515 S Park St) Rooms
$89-199. The cost of the 174 rooms in this
grand 1920s hotel fluctuates daily, from
$89 single or double around Christmas to
$199 if a conference is on. Yet even in July
and August you should be able to get a
bed at the elegant Lord Nelson for $129 if
you call ahead and ask for the summer
special. The location at Spring Garden Rd
directly opposite the entrance to the
Public Gardens is ideal, and numerous
eating and entertainment options crowd
the surrounding streets.

Places to Eat

Halifax has a good selection of restaurants offering a variety of foods in all price ranges, and generally the quality is high. We begin near the city's historic downtown waterfront.

The *Harbourside Market* (Map 2) at the Historic Properties on Upper Water St comprises six separate cafeteria-style restaurants where you can get self-service seafood, Italian dishes, salads and deli style meals for around $10. You place your order at the counter and carry your tray out onto a deck overlooking Halifax Harbour. The Harbourside Market is cheap, convenient and reasonably good quality (not fast food).

O'Carroll's Irish Pub (Map 2; ☎ 902-423-4405, 1860 Upper Water St) Mains from $18. Open 11am-11pm daily (pub until 1am). O'Carroll's is a low-key, genteel sort of pub (away from the boisterousness of other Halifax watering holes) with superb steak and seafood. There's good traditional Maritimes music here nightly from 10pm. Dinners are pricey but nondiners can absorb the atmosphere for the price of a drink.

McKelvie's (Map 2; ☎ 902-421-6161, 1680 Lower Water St) Mains $10-12, less at lunchtime. Open 11:30am-9:30pm daily. McKelvie's is famous for its seafood, and this huge place, housed in an old firehouse, is an institution. Advance reservations are advisable.

Bluenose II Restaurant (Map 2; ☎ 902-425-5092, 1824 Hollis St at Duke) Breakfast including coffee $5-6, lunch specials under $6, dinners from $7. Open 6:30am-10pm Mon-Fri, 8am-10pm Sat & Sun. This long-established restaurant is packed with locals at lunch. The menu ranges from Greek and Italian to full lobster dinners, and there is beer on tap.

Café C'est Si Bon (Map 2; ☎ 902-425-5799, 1717 Barrington St) Lunches around $5. Open 6am-11pm Mon & Tues, 6am-2am Wed-Fri, 7am-2am Sat, 7am-11pm Sun. This cafe is a pleasantly informal place to order fettucine, quiche, salad or goulash. In the evening you can listen to local musicians

(be sure to check the notices taped to th door).

Mediteraneo Café (Map 2; ☎ 902-42. 4403, 1571 Barrington St) Breakfast und $3, mains $5-10. Open 7am-10pm Mon-Sa 7am-9pm Sun. All morning long you'll fir this place jammed with people who know good breakfast deal. It is also extreme popular for its Lebanese dishes, such cabbage rolls, grapevine leaves ar shawarma. HI cardholders get a 10% di count here.

Satisfaction Feast (Map 2; ☎ 902-42. 3540, 1581 Grafton St) Dinners from $ sandwiches $5. Open 11am-10pm daily. Th well-established vegetarian restaurant housed in a pale blue building. The India curry of the day ($10) is worth considerir for lunch or dinner.

Midtown Tavern & Grill (Map 2; ☎ 90. 422-5213, 1684 Grafton St) Meals $7 inclu ing tax. Open 11am-10pm Mon-Sat. This i national treasure – a good example of th Canadian workers' tavern. The sociab owner has been offered zillions by develo ers to sell this corner spot, but he absolute balks at the notion. It's packed with friend locals at lunch, most of them enjoyir dishes like poutine ($3), large Caesar ($5 pizza ($5 to $7), fish & chips ($7) or steak eggs ($7) and washing it down with dra beer by the glass. The steak is a great de; and a draft beer from 4:30pm until closing only $1.99.

Maxwell's Plum Tavern (Map 2; ☎ 90 423-5090, 1600 Grafton St) Meals $7. Ope 10am-2am Mon-Sat, 11am-2pm Sun. Th English-style pub a block south of th Midtown Tavern boasts the largest selectio of imported draft beer and single-ma Scotch in the Maritimes. Prices are simil to those at the Midtown, but Maxwell Plum has a better selection and they ser food long after the Midtown's kitchen h closed. The pan-fried nachos ($6) and stea & fries ($5 to $6) are good. On Saturday Sundays and holidays, come for t weekend brunch from 11am to 3pm and g a pitcher of Bloody Marys or Screwdrive for $8. There's often live blues or jazz on t weekends.

Iear the HI Hostel *Kinh-Do (Map 2; ☎ 902-425-8555, 1284 Barrington St)* Lunch pecial $5. Open 11:30am-9:30pm Tues-Fri, :30pm-9:30pm Sat & Sun. Try this casual place for Vietnamese. It offers tasty food, an xtensive menu and low prices.

Sobeys Supermarket *(Map 1; ☎ 902-422-*884, 1120 Queen St at Fenwick)* Open 24 hours from 7am Monday to midnight Saturday. Come here for splendid picnic fare or roceries to carry back to the hostel.

pring Garden Road *Tu Do Restaurant (Map 2; ☎ 902-421-0081, 1541 Birmingham t)* Mains $6-7. Open until 10pm Mon-Thurs, until midnight Fri & Sat (closed 3pm-pm daily). The good, inexpensive Vietnamese food makes this place worth seeking out. There's only one entree over $10 on the menu. You'll like the linen table-cloths, fresh ingredients and pleasing decor.

Rogues Roost Brew Pub *(Map 2; ☎ 902-92-2337, 5435 Spring Garden Rd)* Meals $7-8. Open 11am-midnight Mon & Tues, 11am-2am Wed-Sun. This place has an impressive selection of beers, including its own iles. For food there are wraps ($6 to $7), pizzas ($7 to $8), pastas ($7 to $8) and plates of mussels ($6).

Thirsty Duck Pub & Eatery *(Map 2; ☎ 902-422-1548, 5470 Spring Garden Rd)* Meals $5-8. Open 11am-11pm Mon & Tues, 11am-midnight Wed, 11am-2am Thurs-Sat, 11am-9pm Sun. To get to this place, go into the store and up the stairs to the rooftop patio. It's got burgers, fish & chips, sand-viches and salads, and draft beer at low prices. You could strike gold and get live music with your food and drink.

Mikey's Wraps *(Map 2; ☎ 902-425-6453, 5680 Spring Garden Rd)* Pita wraps $5. Open 11am-10pm daily. This spot has the widest choice of healthy wraps in town .

Your Father's Moustache *(Map 2; ☎ 902-423-6766, 5686 Spring Garden Rd)* Mains $7-14. Open 11am-midnight Sun-Wed, 11am-1am Thurs-Sat. Just up the street from Mikey's, this place features a rooftop patio and live music. The food menu includes pastas ($7 to $8), steaks and ribs ($8 to $14) and grilled haddock ($10).

Curry Village *(Map 2; ☎ 902-429-5010, 5677 Brenton Place)* Mains from $8. Open 11:30am-2pm & 5pm-10pm Mon-Sat, 5pm-10pm Sun. Tucked behind Spring Garden Rd, this highly rated East Indian restaurant has some great southern madras as well. Choices include vegetarian dishes ($5 to $8), *biryanis* ($9 to $11) and combos ($11/26 for one/two people).

Farther Afield *Highlife Café (Map 1; ☎ 902-422-7050, 2011 Gottingen St, off Cogswell St next to Staples)* Mains $9-11. Open 7:30am-5pm Mon, 7:30am-10pm Tues-Fri, 1pm-10pm Sat & Sun. The music and decor are straight out of Ghana, and the food is as authentically African or Carib-bean as anything you'll find in Accra or Kingston. Dinner entrees include jollof rice ($10), curry goat ($9 to $11) and stewed beef ($9 to $11), or you can just order roti with sauce ($4). Highlife's breakfast and lunch specials are also around $4. It's one of the only bona fide African restaurants in the Maritimes.

Samosa Plus *(Map 1; ☎ 902-425-8655, 6184 Quinpool Rd)*. Lunch specials $5, dinner specials $8/10 vegetarian/nonvege-tarian. Open 11am-8pm Mon-Sat, closing at 6:30pm Wed. For North Indian food, this is very good value, though you shouldn't expect elegant surroundings at these prices. Weekdays from 11:30am to 3:30pm there's a vegetarian buffet for $6 (or $8 with chicken). Try the spiced Indian chai ($1.65) or a cooling glass of lassi ($2).

Greek House *(Map 1; ☎ 902-422-8877, 6253 Quinpool Rd)* Specials from $7. Open 7:30am-10pm daily. This aptly named place serves good breakfasts all day, along with Greek specials like moussaka ($8), stuffed green peppers ($8) and souvlakia ($9).

Entertainment

Live Music Halifax has an astonishing number of pubs (55 at last count) and nightlife options for a city its size. Doing the 'pub pinball' is a local pastime. For a com-plete rundown of the music scene grab a copy of *The Coast*, Halifax's entertainment newspaper. Offered free at restaurants and

AROUND HALIFAX – MAP 3

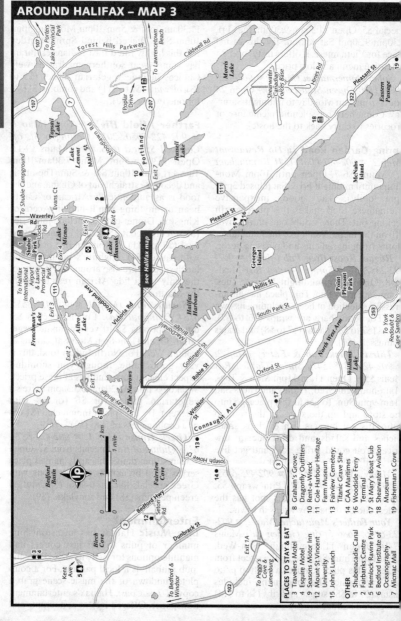

see Halifax map

PLACES TO STAY & EAT
3 Travellers Motel
4 Esquire Motel
9 Seasons Motor Inn
12 Mount St Vincent
   University
15 John's Lunch

8 Graham's Grove;
   Dragonfly Outfitters
10 Rent-a-Wreck
11 Cole Harbour Heritage
   Farm Museum
13 Fairview Cemetery;
   Titanic Grave Site
14 CAA Maritimes
16 Woodside Ferry
   Terminal
17 St Mary's Boat Club
18 Shearwater Aviation
   Museum
19 Fisherman's Cove

OTHER
1 Shubenacadie Canal
2 Fairbanks Centre
5 Hemlock Ravine Park
6 Bedford Institute of
   Oceanography
7 Micmac Mall

ubs, this publication provides a full schedule of music, film and stage performances in he city.

The information office next to the Maritime Museum has an awesome map detailing most of the pubs and clubs in town.

Lower Deck (Map 2; ☎ 902-425-1501, 869 Upper Water St) Open 11am-12:30am. On the lower level of the Privateer's Warehouse at the Historic Properties on the waterfront, Lower Deck presents Maritime olk music nightly at 9pm ($3 cover) – first-ate groups like Highland Heights, McGinty nd Clam Chowder. Every other week in ummer there's a patio party starting at 3pm on Fridays and Saturdays, with the bands olaying alternating sets inside and outside. Nothing on the food menu is over $10 (only he seafood plate is over $7). A caveat: Go early, or you won't get a seat.

Split Crow (Map 2; ☎ 902-422-4366, 1855 Granville St) Open 11am-12:30pm daily. This is the best known of the pubs in the old-fashioned Granville St Mall off Duke St. Lunch specials like clams and chips are under $5 and live Maritimes music daily rom 9pm to midnight (weekends until am). The Saturday matinee from 3:30pm to ₂:30pm also packs them in ($3 cover).

Peddler's Pub (Map 2; ☎ 902-423-5033, 1900 Granville St) Open 11am-10pm Mon-at, 11am-8pm Sun. Just down from Split Crow, Peddler's has an outdoor section. On aturdays from 4pm to 7pm there's live music and no cover charge.

Bearly's Bar & Grill (Map 2; ☎ 902-423-₂526, 1269 Barrington St) Open 11am-midnight Mon & Tues, 11am-1:30am Wed-Sun. From Thursday to Sunday live music, especially bluegrass and blues, can be enjoyed at this place near the HI Hostel.

Birmingham Bar & Grill (Map 2; ☎ 902-₄20-9622, 5657 Spring Garden Rd) Open 1am-10pm Sun-Thurs, 11am-11pm Fri & ₅at. This large bar near the Public Gardens presents hot jazz from 8pm Wednesday to ₅unday. Their list of imported beers is extensive.

Dance Clubs *The Dome (Map 2; ☎ 902-₄22-5453, 1740 Argyle St)* Open 11am-3:30am daily. Dubbed the 'Liquordome,' there are four establishments under one roof here. A single cover charge of $3 Thursday, $5 Friday and Sunday and $6 Saturday includes admission to all four venues. At *My Apartment* and *Lawrence of Oregano* a DJ spins Top 40 music nightly from 10:20pm. Upstairs in *Cheers* a live band plays cover tunes from 10:30pm Tuesday to Saturday. *The Attic (☎ 902-423-0909, 1741 Grafton St)* is the fourth and most exclusive unit at the Dome, where top rock bands cater to a smart younger crowd. Be aware of the dress code ban on athletic or camouflage wear, numbered shirts, ripped clothes, jerseys and hats. The Attic is open 10pm to 3:30am Thursday, 9pm to 3:30pm Friday and Saturday.

Reflections Cabaret (Map 2; ☎ 902-422-2957, 5184 Sackville St) Open 4pm-4am daily. Located in the basement below Tourism Halifax, Reflections began as a mainly gay disco, but it has developed into an 'in' place where plenty of straights also come. There's live music after 9pm, and the drink prices are good.

New Palace Nightclub (Map 2; ☎ 902-429-5959, 1721 Brunswick St) Live bands from 10pm Thurs-Sun, DJ on Wed from 9:30pm ($3 cover charge). For rock and blues bands and lots of grinding nightly till way, way late, try this large, loud place across from the Citadel.

Bars *Diamond Bar (Map 2; ☎ 902-423-8845, 1663 Argyle St)* Open 11am-2am daily. This is another establishment with multiple rooms, each bearing a different name. The middle room right behind the trendy sidewalk terrace is *Backstage*. To the right is gay-friendly *Diamond* and to the left *Economy Shoe Shop*, which James Cameron reportedly frequented while filming *Titanic* in Dartmouth. There's live jazz in the Shoe Shop every Monday from 9:30pm (no cover charge). The section straight back from Backstage is the *Belgian Bar* (because Belgian beer is on tap).

The Eagle Pub & Eatery (Map 2; ☎ 902-425-1889, 1565 Grafton St near Blowers St) Open 3pm-2am Mon-Fri, noon-2am Sat &

Sun. The Eagle is Halifax's most famous gay bar. Nothing on their food menu is over $9.

The Grad House *(Map 1;* ☎ *902-494-3816, 6154 University Ave next to the Student Union Building)* Open until 1am Mon-Fri during the school year. Grad House is the perfect place to go after seeing a play, movie or concert at the nearby Dalhousie Arts Center. From 7pm to 1am Monday and Thursday you can get a pitcher of beer for $7.50.

Granite Brewery *(Map 2;* ☎ *902-423-5660, 1222 Barrington St)* Dinner from $7.50. Open 11:30am-midnight Mon-Sat, noon-11pm Sun. This upmarket pub brews five kinds of beer at their in-house brewery and serves it on tap in the pub downstairs. The food's great too – try the jambalaya ($11).

Cafes *Trident Booksellers & Café (Map 2;* ☎ *902-423-7100, 1256 Hollis St)* Coffee/tea under $2. Open 8:30am-5pm Mon-Sat, noon-5pm Sun. This somewhat bohemian cafe, with its large stained-glass piece in the window, is the place to linger over a 'fair trade' coffee or a pot of herbal tea. When you've finished with the newspaper, the other half of the cafe has a fine selection of books, new and used.

Second Cup *(Map 2;* ☎ *902-429-0883, 5425 Spring Garden Rd, cnr Queen St)* Coffee just over $1. Open 7am-midnight daily. This is the largest outlet of this chain in Canada. Computers are available for free surfing on the Internet.

Classical Music & Theater *Dalhousie Arts Centre (Map 1;* ☎ *902-494-3820, 6101 University Ave)* Box office open noon-6pm Mon-Sat. This center, at the university, is a major performance venue for theater and dance. From October to April, Symphony Nova Scotia plays in the 1000-seat **Rebecca Cohn Auditorium** here. Tickets for single performances are $12 to $37 depending on the program and seat. In summer not much is happening. Between October and April four productions by the Dalhousie University Theatre Department are presented in the 250-seat **Sir James Dunn Theatre**, inside

the Dalhousie Art Centre. Each play run only one week and seats are $10 to $15.

Neptune Theatre *(Map 2;* ☎ *902-429 7070, 1593 Argyle St)* This two-stag complex was rebuilt in 1997 at a cost of $2 million, and it's now the city's leading the atrical venue, with a year-round program During the regular season from Septembe to May, you might see musicals, drama o comedy here, with tickets averaging $37 The building also contains the **du Maurie Studio Theatre**, which presents more avan garde programs from October to Apri From mid-July to mid-August the Neptun stages a musical comedy Tuesday to Sunda' with tickets varying from $15 to $30, de pending on the seat. During the winte season, many programs are sold out o weekends. Earlier in the week you've got decent chance of obtaining a ticket b asking at the box office 45 minutes befor curtain time.

Shakespeare by the Sea *(*☎ *902-422-029! Oceanside Parking Lot)* There's nothin quite like Shakespeare by the sea, and i July and August, that's exactly what you ge in performances by the Bard in Point Pleas ant Park. Performances in the Summe House (Map 1) on the east side of the par are at 7pm Tuesday to Saturday and 2pn Saturday and Sunday, with admissio costing $8.

Dinner Theaters *Grafton St Dinne Theatre (Map 2;* ☎ *902-425-1961, 174 Grafton St)* Open 6:45pm-10pm Tues-Sun. I nothing is happening at the Neptune, : dinner theater could salvage your evening Many visitors – especially those on tours consider a night out at one of these an es sential part of their vacation. At the Grafto St Dinner Theatre you get a three-cours meal and a lighthearted musical comedy fo $37 (drinks not included). Seating is at larg banquet style tables with 10 to 18 seats, s singles won't feel out of place. It's best t reserve well ahead for a Friday or Saturda night – other nights are less heavily booked

Halifax Feast *(Map 2;* ☎ *902-420-184(Maritime Center, 1505 Barrington St)* Ope 7pm-9:45pm Tues-Sat Feb-Dec. Halifa east ($40) is similar to Grafton St, although the show is different, of course. The eating here is more intimate, as the tables have 6 to 10 seats and are on three levels. The jokes are slightly more risque at Halifax Feast, whereas Grafton St is family entertainment. If you enjoyed one theater, take in the show at the other on a different night. Both venues are popular with locals as well as tourists, and the shows change three or four times a year.

Casinos *Casino Nova Scotia (Map 2; ☎ 902-425-7777, 1983 Upper Water St)* Open 24 hours year-round. So long as you can avoid the temptation to wager here, it's sort of fun to wander between the rows of slot machines and past the gaming tables. Keep in mind that everything that happens in or around the casino is carefully monitored by security cameras. You, on the other hand, are not allowed to take photos in the casino! Persons under 19 are not admitted.

Cinemas Surprisingly, there's no repertoire cinema in Halifax, and the 39 movie theaters that do exist show standard Hollywood fare. There are only two exceptions.

Dalhousie Art Gallery (Map 1; ☎ 902-494-2403, 6101 University Ave) The gallery screens a quality film at 12:30pm and 8pm every Wednesday from mid-October to May, and admission is free. Special screenings occur at other times, so it's worth giving them a call.

Oxford Cinema (Map 1; ☎ 902-423-7488, 6408 Quinpool Rd at Oxford) The Oxford sometimes shows an 'art' film on weekends (call and ask). Otherwise, it's just the usual stuff. Admission is $6.50.

Spectator Sports

Halifax Metro Centre (Map 2; ☎ 902-451-1221, 5284 Duke St at Brunswick St) Box office open 11am-5pm Mon-Fri. In winter, the Halifax Mooseheads face off frequently against visiting hockey teams at this 9000-seat center, across from the Old Town Clock. International artists and bands also perform here.

Shopping

Halifax Trading and Guide Post (Map 2; ☎ 902-492-1420, 1586 Granville St near Sackville) Open 10am-6pm Mon-Wed & Sat, 10am-9pm Thurs & Fri. This place carries quality tents and backpacking gear.

Scout Shop (Map 1; ☎ 902-429-8627, 6232 Quinpool Rd) Open 9am-5pm Mon-Fri June-Aug; 10am-6pm Mon-Wed, 10am-8pm Thurs & Fri, 10am-5pm Sat Sept-May. A good source of backpacks, tents and other camping gear. Also try *The Trail Shop* (☎ 902-423-8736, 6210 Quinpool Rd).

Getting There & Away

Air Air Canada (Map 2; ☎ 888-247-2262, open 9am-5pm Mon-Fri), 1559 Brunswick St, near Spring Garden Rd, has domestic flights from Halifax to Calgary (three daily), Edmonton (twice daily), Montréal (six daily), Ottawa (four daily), St John's (seven daily), Toronto (10 daily), Vancouver (four daily) and Winnipeg (three daily). Outside Canada, they fly directly to Boston (five times daily), London (daily) and Newark (twice daily). Their subsidiary, Air Nova, provides connections to most airports around the Maritimes, including Charlottetown, Fredericton, Moncton, Saint John, Sydney and Yarmouth.

Air Canada is not the only show in town, however. In years past, the following airlines have also flown into Halifax: Air Labrador, Air Saint Pierre, Air Transat, American Airlines (Eagle Air), Continental Airlines, Canada 3000 and Icelandair. See the Getting There & Away chapter for more information on these flights. The $10 'airport improvement fee' levied at Halifax should be included in the price of your ticket.

Bus The principal bus line is Acadian Lines, which connects with the New Brunswick SMT Lines at Amherst. There are also a couple of smaller regional lines that service the south coast. They all use the Acadian Lines bus station (Map 1; ☎ 902-454-9321) at 6040 Almon St, which runs south off Robie St, northwest of the Citadel. The station is open 6:30am to 7pm daily, plus all bus arrival times, and $2 coin lockers are provided. This station is not in the best part of town, and some care should be taken if you arrive late.

One Acadian Lines bus runs through the Annapolis Valley and down to Yarmouth. Others cover the central region, the Northumberland Shore and parts of Cape Breton. The 7am bus from Halifax connects in Moncton for Montréal daily and for New York on Friday and Saturday.

Following are the one-way fares to several destinations. To North Sydney (one express bus daily and other milk runs) it's $59, to Yarmouth $52, Moncton $45, Saint John $68 and Fredericton $75.

DRL Coachlines (☎ 902-450-1987) offers a cheaper service from Halifax to Yarmouth ($38) via Lunenburg. They run right along the South Shore, leaving Halifax at 6:25pm daily.

Zinck's bus company (☎ 902-468-4342) runs a service along the Eastern Shore from Halifax to Sherbrooke ($15), stopping at all the small villages along the way. It runs once a day (except Sunday) eastbound and Tuesday to Saturday westbound. The departure from Halifax is at 5:30pm.

Shuttles To reach Prince Edward Island by scheduled bus you must connect through Moncton. Minibus shuttles do the Halifax-Charlottetown run far more quickly and directly than the scheduled bus, completing the journey in four hours.

The Halifax-based PEI Express Shuttle (☎ 877-877-1771) and Go-Van (☎ 866-463-9660) both charge $45 one way, with front door pickups provided around Halifax between 6:30am and 7:30am.

The Charlottetown-based Advanced Shuttle (☎ 877-886-3322) and Square One Shuttle (☎ 877-675-3830) do the reverse, leaving Halifax in the afternoon. Advanced Shuttle can carry up to three bicycles at $10 each, if you let them know beforehand.

Kiwi Kaboodle's Tradewind Shuttle (☎ 902-463-4244) offers one-way transportation to Lunenburg for $30. Pick ups can be arranged anywhere in Halifax around 9:30am.

Try Town Transit (☎ 877-521-0855) als does daily van shuttles between Halifax an Lunenburg for $22 one way. They'll als pick up at your hostel door but will only g if they have at least four bookings.

Train The VIA Rail station (Map 2; ☎ 88 842-7245), 1161 Hollis St, is six blocks sout of the downtown area. It's on Terminal R by the huge Westin Hotel and is one of th few examples left in the Maritimes of monu mental Canadian train station architectur No coin lockers are available at the statio

The train is more useful for reaching ou of-province destinations than for gettin around Nova Scotia. A train to Moncton New Brunswick ($52), continuing to Mon tréal, departs at 12:55pm daily (excep Tuesday) along a route through easter New Brunswick that includes stops a Amherst, Sackville, Miramichi, Bathurs and Campbellton.

The fare to Montréal is $197, but if yo book a week in advance the price goe down to $147. You can reserve up to 33 days in advance, and it's definitely a goo idea to do so as only a limited number o cheap seats are sold for any given train.

Aside from the Montréal train, there' also a deluxe tourist train called the Bra d'Or to Sydney once a week, leavin Halifax at 7:30am Tuesday from June t early October. The fare is $219 plus tax on way, including breakfast and lunch on th train. Most people using it are on package tours, and rail passes are not accepted.

Getting Around
To/From the Airport Halifax Interna tional Airport is 39km northeast of town o Hwy 102 towards Truro.

There are no city buses to the airport, bu there is the Airbus (☎ 902-873-2091). It run between the airport and the downtow center, with stops at major central hotel such as the Westin (near the HI hostel) an the Lord Nelson. The fares are $12/20 on way/roundtrip. The bus makes 23 trips daily with the first run at 6am and the last bu leaving the airport at 11:15pm. Allow 9 minutes before flight time.

An alternative is Share-A-Cab (☎ 800-65-8669). Call at least four hours before ight time and it will find other passengers nd pick you up. The price is $24.

Remember that the Halifax-Charlotte-jwn minibus shuttles will pick up or drop ff at Halifax International Airport for an dditional $3 to $5 fee. Some pick up right t the airport door, but others make you ake a taxi to the Airport Hotel (ask). See huttles in this section for the numbers to all.

Bus Metro Transit (☎ 902-490-6600) runs he good, inexpensive city bus system. Fares re $1.65, or $30 for a 20-ticket booklet. Transfers to ferries are included. Perk's News Stand near the transit terminal at bot of George St sells booklets. Another transit terminal is on either side of Barring-on St outside Scotia Square. Call for route nd schedule information or pick up a *Metro Transit Riders' Guide* for free from Tourism Halifax.

The No 7 city bus on Robie St goes from he bus station into town. *Fred* is a free city bus running a circuit along South St, Lower Water St, Barrington St, Spring Garden Rd, South Park and back to South St. It runs every 30 minutes, 11am to 6pm daily from une to August, with 18 stops along the oute.

Hitchhikers heading north toward Truro or west toward Windsor will want to pick up bus Nos 80 or 82 to the Cobequid Terminal near the junction of Hwys 101 and 102, north of Bedford. Those heading west can use bus No 21, which terminates at the village of Timberlea on St Margarets Bay Rd (Hwy 3). Eastbound toward Sher-brooke, take bus No 62 from the Darmouth Ferry Terminal to Cherry Brook on Hwy 7 no service Sunday).

Car & Motorcycle In Halifax be on the ookout for pedestrians, who have priority at crosswalks. They'll sometimes step out into the road without looking, and the driver is held responsible should an accident occur. Pedestrians are far more abundant than elsewhere in the Maritimes, so you really do need to make a mental effort to be on guard.

The car rental companies represented at Halifax International Airport are Avis, Budget, Dollar Hertz, National and Thrifty. Due to high operating costs at the airport, car rentals from there are much more expensive than if you rent in town. To get around this, take the Airbus into town and rent your car there.

Parking in the downtown area can be a real hassle. For a central place to stash your wheels, go to Impark (Map 2; ☎ 902-423-0680), with the red signs at 1505 Lower Water St near Salter St opposite Brewery Market; they have a couple of other locations as well.

Impark has an all-day ticket for $8. After 5pm weekdays and all day Saturday and Sunday the flat rate is $5. The daily and evening flat rates are valid until 6am the next morning when a new parking period begins.

Impark will take campervans during the daytime but campers must vacate the lot by 10pm. Be aware that there's a $2000 fine for sleeping overnight in a campervan parked in a commercial parking lot or on the street.

Halifax parking meters are enforced from 8am to 6pm Monday to Friday (there's no need to feed them evenings, weekends or holidays). The fine for ordinary parking violations is around $15.

Canadian Automobile Association (CAA) Maritimes (Map 3; ☎ 902-443-5530) is at 3514 Joseph Howe Dr. It's open 8:30am to 5pm Monday to Thursday, 8:30am to 7pm Friday and 10am to 1pm Saturday.

Enterprise Rent-a-Car (Map 2; ☎ 902-492-8400), inside the VIA Rail station at 1161 Hollis St, has cars at $37 a day, including 200km (beyond that it's 14¢ per kilometer). Insurance is $19 a day (zero deductible). Their weekly rate is $200 with 1400km. Ask about reduced weekend and monthly rates.

Discount Car Rentals (Map 2; ☎ 902-423-7612), 1240 Hollis St, has four different price seasons, starting at $39/99/259 a day/weekend/week in midwinter, increasing to $50/125/320 in midsummer. Unlimited kilometers in the three Maritime provinces are included (you're not supposed to take the car to Maine, Québec or Newfoundland). Insurance is $22 a day extra ($300 deductible), and as usual, add 15% tax. If you can show a youth hostel card, you'll get a 10% discount on the weekly rate only.

Rent-a-Wreck (Map 3; ☎ 902-434-4224), 130 Woodlawn Rd, Dartmouth, has some of the lowest rates in town. Their office is way out near exit 7 off Hwy 111, but if you call they'll probably offer to pick you up. Prices start at $35 a day, with 200km free. A weekend of Friday to Monday or Saturday to Tuesday will be $100 with 800km. Weekly it's $240 with 1600km. In the off-season rates go down to $29/89/199 a day/weekend/week, and you can get a 10% discount any time by showing an HI card. In all cases, extra kilometers are 12¢ each. Insurance is $13 a day.

Other rental agencies include Avis (Map 2; ☎ 902-492-2847;open 7am to 7pm Monday to Friday, 8am to 5pm Saturday, 8am to 7pm Sunday), 1717 Grafton St; Budget (Map 2; ☎ 902-492-7541), on the corner of Hollis and Sackville Sts in the Ultramar gas station; and Hertz (Map 2; ☎ 902-421-1763), 1919 Upper Water St at the Sheraton Hotel located next to the Historic Properties.

Ferry Ferries run continuously from near the Historic Properties dock (Map 2). One boat heads across the bay to Dartmouth; the other is a peak-period service to Woodside. A ticket is $1.65 one way, and the ride provides a nice short mini-tour of the harbor. From Monday to Saturday the Dartmouth ferries run every 15 minutes at peak times, otherwise every 30 minutes. The last one is at 11:30pm. On Sunday, they run from noon to 5:30pm, but only June through September. Bicycles are welcomed.

DARTMOUTH

Founded in 1750, one year after Halifax, Dartmouth is Halifax's counterpart just across the harbor. However, the similarities end with their waterfront location. Dartmouth is a city of 65,000 people spread over

a large area and, compared with Halifax, i more residential and the city center les commercial. The downtown area lacks th history, charm and bustle of Halifax. Subur ban Dartmouth is mostly highways an shopping malls with a few beauty spot tucked away.

Having said that, Dartmouth does mak for a cheap afternoon side trip and even scenic one, thanks to the ferry. The Halifax Dartmouth ferry, operated by Metro Trans (the bus people), is said to be the oldes saltwater ferry system in North America dating back to 1752, when the ferry was jus a rowboat.

Orientation

Alderney Gate houses the ferry terminal the Dartmouth Public Library, city offices, food court and some shops. The farmer' market in the ferry complex operates 7am to 2pm on Saturdays year-round.

A number of historic sites are near the waterfront and the neighboring downtow area. You can pick up a walking-tour guide at a tourist office in either city. Buildings i old Dartmouth are primarily made of wood rather than brick or stone as in Halifax.

Beside the large ferry terminal is Ferr Terminal Park, where a walking path lead along the water and puts you in view of the Halifax-Dartmouth Industries shipyard an Dartmouth Cove, the home of Canada' largest coast guard base. The Imperial O Refinery on Pleasant St, southeast of the center beyond the Woodside Ferry Termi nal, is visible from almost everywhere around Halifax Harbour. Shearwater and Fisherman's Cove are further along.

Information

A tourist desk (☎ 902-490-4433) with brochures and staff to answer questions is a the ferry complex (Map 1; open 9am to 6pm mid-May to October). Another tourist in formation office (☎ 902-465-8009) is a Fisherman's Cove (Map 3). It's open 10am to 6pm late May to late September.

The Dartmouth Public Library (Map 1 ☎ 902-490-5745), 60 Alderney Dr, jus outside the Dartmouth ferry terminal ffers free Internet access. It's open 10am to pm Tuesday to Thursday, 10am to 5pm riday & Saturday, 2pm to 5pm Sunday.

World Peace Pavilion

Within Ferry Terminal Park (Map 1) is this unusual and touching outdoor exhibit. Metro Youth for Global Unity invited each country in the world to send in a rock or brick to symbolize the earth we all share. More than 65 countries responded, and the collection is well worth a look. The rocks range from a 127kg piece of the fallen Berlin Wall to a stone from the Great Wall of China to a block of limestone from the Bay of Pigs, Cuba, scene of the infamous 1961 invasion.

Dartmouth Heritage Museum

This museum *(Map 1; ☎ 902-464-2300, junction Alderney Drive & Wyse Rd; admission $2; open 10am-5pm Tues-Sun mid-June-Aug, 1:30pm-5pm Wed-Sat Sept-mid-June)* is adjacent to the Police Community Office and Leighton Dillman Park, about a 15-minute walk to the left (northwest) from the Halifax ferry. It houses an eclectic collection focusing on the city's natural and human history and includes some First Nation artifacts and crafts, various tools and fashions and industrial bric-a-brac. The admission fee also includes entry to the Quaker Whaler House and Evergreen House, so long as you visit all three on the same day.

Quaker Whaler House

A short walk from the ferry is the Quaker Whaler House *(Map 1; ☎ 902-464-2300, 59 Ochterloney St; admission $2; open 10am-5pm Tues-Sun mid-June-Aug)*, the oldest house in the Halifax area, built in 1786. The Quakers came to the region as whalers from New England. Guides in costume lead visitors around the house. The herb garden out back is also worth a look.

Evergreen House

Built for a judge in 1862, Evergreen House *(Map 1; ☎ 902-464-2300, 26 Newcastle St; admission $2; open 10am-5pm Tues-Sun* mid-June-Aug) is affiliated with the Heritage Museum. It's a fine example of a 19th-century house for the well-to-do. Many of the 20 rooms are open to the public and have been furnished in the style of the 1880s.

Shubenacadie Canal

From 1861–1870 the 80km Shubenacadie Canal (Map 3) connected Dartmouth (through a series of waterways, lakes and locks) with the Bay of Fundy along an old Mi'kmaq portage route. Portions of it are still used by canoeists.

For more details on the canal and a look at two of the restored locks, visit the **Fairbanks Centre** *(Map 3; ☎ 902-462-1826, 54 Locks Rd; admission free; open irregularly mid-May-mid-Sept)*, off Waverley Dr in north Dartmouth. This center is full of displays on the history of the canal, and some enjoyable hiking trails through the forest begin nearby.

Bedford Institute of Oceanography

Just outside Dartmouth is this major government marine research center *(Map 3; ☎ 902-426-2373, 1 Challenger Dr; admission free; open 9am-4pm Mon-Fri)*, Canada's leading oceanographic facility. The surprisingly interesting exhibits cover fisheries and ocean studies, and the self-guided tour is a rewarding way to spend an hour. There's also a video, an exhibit on the *Titanic* and a collection of aquarium specimens. From May to August, student guides are available. The inexpensive cafeteria is a nice place to have lunch. To get there from Dartmouth by car, take Windmill Rd to Princess Margaret Dr, which is near the MacKay Bridge. If you're coming by public transit, take bus No 51 from the Dartmouth ferry terminal.

Cole Harbour Heritage Farm Museum

This museum *(Map 3; ☎ 902-434-0222, 471 Poplar Drive; admission free; open 10am-4pm Mon-Sat, noon-4pm Sun mid-May-mid-Oct)* is away from the center off Portland Rd (Hwy 207) near the Cole

Harbour Shopping Centre. Built at the end of the 18th century, the farm has seven buildings, including the main house, a blacksmith shop, barns and a carriage shop. The farm also houses domesticated animals, and there's a tea room on the premises and walking trails nearby. It's a great place to bring children.

Shearwater Aviation Museum

South of town at Canadian Forces Base Shearwater, the aviation museum *(Map 3; ☎ 902-460-1083, Bonaventure Ave off Pleasant St near Hines Rd; admission by donation; open 10am-5pm Tues-Fri, noon-4pm Sat Apr & May, same hours June-Sept plus noon-4pm Sun)* details the history of Canadian maritime military aviation. Pictures, uniforms and other salient objects are on display, plus four aircraft: a Fairy Swordfish (the type of plane that located the elusive German warship *Bismarck* in WWII), a Tracker (combination jet and propeller plane), a Sikorsky Horse helicopter and a Harvard trainer.

The Nova Scotia International Air Show (formerly known as the Shearwater International Airshow) is held here annually, usually after Labor Day.

Fisherman's Cove

Fisherman's Cove, on the Eastern Passage 7km south of the Woodside Ferry Terminal, is a reconstructed fishing village and tourist center giving access to one of Dartmouth's most attractive areas. McCormack's Beach (opposite Lawlor Island) is here, and a ferry to nearby McNabs Island is always available; see McNabs Island in the Halifax section. There's ample parking, and bus No 60 comes straight here from the Dartmouth Ferry Terminal.

Saturday and Sunday from 6pm to 9pm mid-May to mid-September you can sign up for whale watching with **A&M Sea Charters**. Bookings are taken at Sea Side Casual Wear *(☎ 902-465-6617, 87 Fisherman's Cove; adult/senior/child $20/18/10)*. You're allowed to bring alcohol along.

Kayak rentals are offered by **Spirit of the East Kayaks** *(☎ 902-478-7330; open June-*

Oct), based at Sea Side Casual Wear, 8 Fisherman's Cove. Single kayaks are $10/ 40/70 per hour/day/two days, double kayaks $15/50/90. Canoes cost $10/40/150 per hour/ day/week. Spirit of the East also does three hour kayak tours for $30.

Special Events

Festivals include a three-day multicultural festival held in June along the Dartmouth waterfront, featuring ethnic foods and art. Other annual events are the Maritime Old Time Fiddlers' Contest in early July, th Tattoo Festival, held along the waterfront i July, and the Dartmouth Natal Day Celebration in early August.

Places to Stay

Camping *Shubie Park (Map 3; ☎ 902-435 8328,* **W** *www.shubiecampground.com Jaybee Drive off Waverley Rd)* Unserviced serviced sites $19/21. Open mid-May-mid Oct. Owned by the municipality but privately operated, Shubie Park is the onl campground accessible from Halifax via public transportation. The location near th Shubenacadie Canal is convenient, al though it's just a grassy field with littl shade. Facilities include showers and a Laundromat. Bus No 55 stops within two blocks of the entrance, but it doesn't run on Sundays, in which case head to the Micma Mall via a local trail and pick up the No 1 bus to Halifax.

Laurie Provincial Park (☎ 902-861-1623 **W** *parks.gov.ns.ca, on Hwy 2, 9km north o Hwy 102)* Sites $14. Open early June-Aug This campground is beautifully situated o Shubenacadie Grand Lake near the villag of Grand Lake, north of Dartmouth toward the airport. Seventy-one agreeable sites are available in a pleasant forest setting. Lauri does fill up on midsummer weekends, but al sites can be reserved. Call ahead if you'll be arriving on a Friday or Saturday.

See Porters Lake in the Eastern Shor chapter for an excellent camping option jus east of Dartmouth.

B&Bs *Caroline's (Map 1; ☎ 902-469-4665 134 Victoria Rd)* Singles/doubles $40/50 vith continental breakfast. Open Apr-Dec. This friendly three-room place is beyond the Dartmouth Heritage Museum and not ar from the Macdonald Bridge, a kilometer rom central Dartmouth.

Motels *Seasons Motor Inn (Map 3; ☎ 902-35-0060, fax 902-435-0060,* W *home.istar ca/~garson, 40 Lakecrest Dr, off Main St ear exit 6 from Hwy 111)* Singles/doubles 58/63 mid-June-mid-Sept, \$53/58 other months. Seasons Motor Inn offers 33 rooms n a solid two-story brick building. Facilities nclude a communal kitchen, Laundromat nd free parking. Frequent bus service is vailable to Halifax.

Places to Eat

La Perla Dining Room (Map 1; ☎ 902-469-241, 73 Alderney Dr) Meals \$10-24. Open 1:30am-9:45pm Mon-Fri, 5pm-9:45pm Sat, pm-8:30pm Sun. Go next door for outstanding but pricey Northern Italian fare. The menu is organized in pastas (\$10 to 11), chicken (\$17 \$21), veal (\$18 to \$27) nd beef (\$21 to \$24).

Alderney Bar & Café (Map 1; ☎ 902-469-787, 69 Alderney Dr) Sandwiches/mains rom around \$6/8. Open 11am-10pm Mon-Fri, 11am-3pm Sat & Sun. Opposite the erry and a little to the right, the Alderney Bar features spacious interiors and pub grub like pizza, pastas and fish & chips.

Queen of Cups Teahouse (Map 1; ☎ 902-463-1983, 44 Ochterloney St) Lunch items \$4-7. Open 10am-5pm Mon-Sat. This cozy place, more or less opposite the Quaker Whaler House, is good for a healthy lunch of soup (\$5), salad (\$4 to \$7), wraps (\$5 to \$7) or sandwiches (\$4 to \$5); you can also order tea for two (\$3). Owner Shelley Goodson will do Tarot readings if you call ahead for an appointment.

John's Lunch (Map 3; ☎ 902-469-3074, 352 Pleasant St) Mains \$8-11. Open 10am-9pm Mon-Sat, 11am-9pm Sun. This greasy spoon near the Woodside Ferry Terminal parking lot is famous for its squid & chips (\$8), clams & chips (\$10), scallops & chips (\$11) and pork chops (\$8). Rumor has it that their hamburger (\$2.25) is the best in the city, and John's portions are legendary. (Don't confuse John's Lunch with Johnny Mac's Lounge, which is in the same general area.)

Wharf Wraps (☎ 902-465-3476, 104 Fisherman's Cove) Mains \$5-9. Open 11am-8pm daily Apr-Oct. Wharf Wraps is a barn-shaped restaurant at Fisherman's Cove (Map 3), with a large outer deck where you can consume fish & chips (\$5 to \$8), scallops & fries (\$8) or shrimp & fries (\$9).

Southwestern Nova Scotia

Southwestern Nova Scotia, also called the South Shore, includes the area south and west of Halifax stretching along the coast to Yarmouth. It contains many fishing villages and several small historic towns, and the coastal scenery is typically rocky, jagged and foggy. These qualities have made the coast here and along the Eastern Shore as alluring to modern-day drug (and cigarette) smugglers as it once was to rumrunners.

The stretch of coast closest to Halifax is the city's cottage country and is quite busy. The tourist route through here is called the Lighthouse Route and is probably the most visited region of Nova Scotia. Accommodations fill up fast, thanks to all that traffic in high season, so plan to find a place to stay before dark each night.

MAP INDEX

OTHER MAPS
Southwestern Nova Scotia
page 116

Wolfville
page 151

Annapolis Royal
page 146

Lunenburg
pages 120-121

Yarmouth
page 133

DRL Coachlines buses service the area daily, leaving Halifax westbound at 6:25pm and Yarmouth eastbound at 6:25am (11:30am on Sunday). This schedule makes it more convenient for bus travelers to move east than west.

PROSPECT

Twenty-nine kilometers southwest of Halifax is the quiet and surprisingly little-visited coastal village of Prospect. The view from the top of the hill on the approach to the tiny settlement can be impressive, especially if the fog bank is obscuring some of the islands and shoreline. There's a wharf, rocks to clamber over along the shore and photogenic houses.

PEGGY'S COVE

Canada's best-known fishing village lies 43km west of Halifax on Hwy 333. It's a pretty place, with fishing boats, nets, lobster traps, docks and old pastel houses that all seem perfectly placed to please the eye. The 415-million-year-old granite boulders (known to geologists as 'erratics') littering the surroundings add an odd touch. Even the horror of Swissair flight 111 in September 1998, which crashed not far offshore, has not dimmed the quintessentially postcard feel.

The smooth shoreline rock all around the lighthouse just begs to be explored (but do not get too close – every year visitors are swept into the cold waters by unexpected swells). Count on the fog, too. It enshrouds the area at least once every three days and is present most mornings.

The village, which dates from 1811, has just 60 residents, and most of them are fishers. The lighthouse is now a small post office, which uses its own lighthouse-shaped stamp cancellation mark.

Peggy's Cove is one of the most visited places in the Maritime provinces, and its proximity to the capital means it is often crowded. The best time to visit is before

10am. Many tour buses arrive in the middle of the day and create what has to be one of the worst traffic jams in the province. When a cruise ship is berthed at Halifax – as happens a couple of times a week in summer – Peggy's Cove becomes a carnival, as passengers are bused in en masse. To help ease the problem, there's a free parking area with washrooms and a tourist information office (but no picnic tables) on the left as you enter the village. By all means stop there and walk the last few hundred meters if you're able.

DeGarthe Gallery
Across the street from the parking area is the deGarthe Gallery (☎ 902-823-2256; admission $1; open 9am-5pm daily mid-May to mid-Oct) with paintings by local artist William deGarthe (1907–1983), who also sculpted the magnificent *Fishermen's Monument* in front of the gallery. From here it's just a five-minute walk past the much-photographed fishing harbor to the rock formations and lighthouse.

Swissair Memorial
A poignant, tasteful memorial to the 229 individuals who perished aboard Swissair flight 111 has been created 1.8km north of the turnoff to Peggy's Cove. A panel at the entrance indicates the precise crash site on the horizon. After a lengthy and expensive investigation it was determined that a ceiling fire in the cockpit area led to the crash of the Geneva-bound flight an hour after it departed New York.

Kayaking
Novashores Adventures (☎ 902-449-1726, W www.novashores.com, 10295 Hwy 333, Glen Margaret), based at Wayside Camping Park, offers ocean kayaking tours on scenic St Margaret's Bay at $40/75 per half/full day in a single kayak or $60/95 for two people in tandem. A snack or lunch is included.

Boat Trips
Peggy's Cove Water Tours (☎ 902-823-1060, W www.peggys-cove.com) From mid-May to mid-October, boat trips are offered to Pearl Island, in search of puffins and minke whales. The tours leave from the village's picturesque harbor at 9am and 1pm ($35 plus tax for three hours). It's worth going even if the whales aren't cooperating, just to get out on the water. A booking table is usually set up behind the Sou'wester Restaurant.

Places to Stay & Eat
Wayside Camping Park (☎ 902-823-2271, fax 902-823-1119, 10295 Hwy 333, Glen Margaret) Unserviced/serviced sites $15/20. Open Apr-mid-Oct. This large campground 10km north of Peggy's Cove and 36km from Halifax has lots of shady tent sites up on the hill, but prime sites are snapped up quickly in midsummer.

Lover's Lane Housekeeping Cottages (☎ 902-823-2670, 8388 Hwy 333) Singles/doubles $50-75, extra persons $10. Open June-Sept. Just 500m north of the Swissair Memorial, these five attractive cottages are right on the ocean.

Cliffy Cove Motel (☎ 902-823-3178, 8444 Hwy 333) Rooms $40-75. Open May-late Oct. This motel's 11 rooms are arranged in a long block 200m north of Lover's Lane. There's one small room at $40 single or double, four with a queen bed at $69 and six larger rooms at $75.

The Sou'wester Restaurant (☎ 902-823-2561) Meals $11-22. Open 8am-9pm May-Oct, 9am-6pm Nov-Apr. Located down near the lighthouse. At this restaurant you can get anything from a 1lb lobster dinner to an order of fish & chips. The place is huge but it's still mobbed with busloads of tourists at times. There's a large gift shop brimming with tacky souvenirs.

ST MARGARET'S BAY
Just north of Peggy's Cove, the shoreline surrounding St Margaret's Bay is dotted with small towns, craft shops and small sandy beaches, with a number of motels, campgrounds and cottages. It's a developed area where many Haligonians have summer homes, and many year-round residents commute to Halifax for work. **Queensland Beach**, at the northwest corner of the bay, is extremely popular.

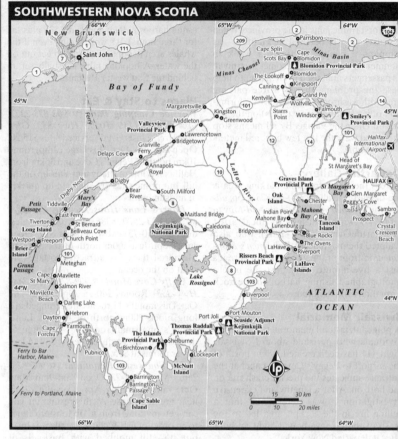

SOUTHWESTERN NOVA SCOTIA

CHESTER

Chester, an old village with 1200 residents, overlooks neighboring Mahone Bay. Established in 1759, it has h a colorful history as the haunt of pirates and Prohibition-era bathtub-gin smugglers.

The center of town is along Pleasant St between King and Queen Sts. Chester's picturesque harbor lies along Water St. A large regatta is held here in mid-August. The tourist office (☎ 902-275-4616) is in the old train depot on Hwy 3 north of town. It's open May to October.

The DRL Coachlines bus to and from Halifax ($11) and Yarmouth ($32) stops a Hammond Kwik Way (☎ 902-275-5203 3711 Hwy 3), a kilometer outside town.

Lordly House Museum

A fine example of Georgian architecture dating from 1806, Lordly House (☎ 902-275 3842, 133 Central St; admission free; open 10am-5pm Tues-Sat, 1pm-5pm Sun, mid-May to mid-Oct) contains three period rooms ex emplifying 19th-century upper class life, plu displays on the history of Chester. There's a enealogy research area you can use if any f your ancestors are from the area, and free nternet access is available to all.

Activities

Captain Evan's Wharf (☎ 902-275-2030, ₩ www.chesterahoy.com, 233 Pig Loop Rd; open mid-May-mid-Oct) At the north end f the harbor, this outlet rents watercraft at 12/35/50 for 1/4/8 hours in a single kayak, 15/40/65 in a double, canoes \$10/15/18. Captain Evan also rents bicycles at \$20 for ight hours or \$75 for a week. Hour-long arbor tours in an open boat called *Osprey 10* are \$30/45/60 for 1/2/3 people.

Places to Stay

Graves Island Provincial Park (☎ 902-275-425, ₩ parks.gov.ns.ca, 3km northeast of Chester) Sites \$18. Open mid-May-early Oct. Sixty-four wooded and open campsites re available on an island in Mahone Bay, a ilometer off Hwy 3 and connected by auseway. RVs usually park right in the iddle of the area, but some nice shady, iso-ated tent sites are tucked away on the anks of the central plateau. A hiking trail nd beach are two of the park's attractions. Graves Island is very popular in midsum-er; expect to find it full on Friday and Sat-rday nights.

Mecklenburgh Inn B&B (☎ 902-275-638, ℮ meckinn@auracom.com, ₩ www atlanticonline.ns.ca/meck, 78 Queen St) ingles/doubles \$65/75-85 with breakfast. Open mid-May-Oct. This large two-story nn next to the post office was built in 1890. here's a breezy 2nd-floor verandah, and ome rooms have private adjacent bal-onies. It's casual and full of character.

Windjammer Motel (☎ 902-275-3567, 070 Hwy 3) Singles/doubles \$60/65 mid-une-early Sept, \$50/55 other months. This otel is just 300m from the tourist office. he 18 rooms are in several long wooden locks. A restaurant is on the premises.

Places to Eat

Julien's Pastry Shop Bakery (☎ 902-275-324, 43 Queen St near Pleasant) Sand-wiches \$4. Open 8am-5pm Tues-Sun, 7am-5:30pm July & Aug. For a casual bite, Julien's features healthy sandwiches and fresh-baked croissants. Tea or coffee on their sidewalk terrace will be under \$2.

Luigi's Café (☎ 902-275-5185, 19 Pleasant St) Prices \$4-6. Across the street from the Chester Playhouse, this is the place for soups (\$2.50 to \$5.50), salads (\$4.50 to \$8.50) and sandwiches (\$4.50). Breakfast is available all day (\$4 to \$7).

Rope Loft Restaurant (☎ 902-275-3430, 36 Water St) Mains \$13-19. Open 11:30am-9pm Sun-Thurs, 11:30am-10pm Fri & Sat May-Oct. At the beginning and end of the season, they may only open from Wednes-day to Saturday. The Rope Loft upstairs serves mostly upscale seafood and steak entrees, but fish & chips (\$8 to \$11) and burgers (\$5 to \$7) are also available. When the sun is shining, meals are served on their outdoor terrace right over the water. The **Sea Deck Pub** downstairs is open until 11pm Sunday to Thursday, until 1am Friday and Saturday.

Entertainment

Chester Playhouse (☎ 902-275-3933, 22 Pleasant St) This theater stages comedies, musicals and dramas through July and August. Performances are at 8pm Wednes-day to Saturday with tickets ranging from \$13 to \$25.

Fo'c'sle Tavern (☎ 902-275-3912, cnr Queen and Pleasant Sts) Open 11am-11pm (until midnight or later on weekends). This rollicking local pub has an air of authentic-ity, and isn't as touristy as the Sea Deck Pub.

TANCOOK ISLANDS

The Tancook Islands – there's a Big and a Little Tancook – are primarily residential, but visitors are welcome to stroll around. A walking-tour brochure available at the Chester tourist office outlines the paths, which crisscross much of the island.

Big Tancook is known for its plentiful cabbage and its sauerkraut. Distinctive little cabbage storage houses can be seen around the island.

Places to Stay & Eat

Levy House B&B (☎ 902-228-2120, ℮ levyhouse@tallships.ca, ⓦ freepages.history.roots web.com/~tancook/levy.htm, Big Tancook) Singles/doubles $45/55. Open June-Sep. This is the only place to stay on the island.

Carolyn's Cafe (☎ 902-228-2749, Big Tancook) Meals $5-10. Open 11:30am-9pm Mon-Fri, 2pm-9pm Sat, 11am-9pm Sun July & Aug, around ferry time June, Sept & Oct. Just four doors down from Levy House and a four-minute walk from the ferry wharf, Carolyn's specializes in fresh seafood. The seafood chowder lunch is a good value at $7, including tea or coffee and pie, or try the fish & chips for $5 to $7. The full menu also includes scallops, clams and lobster rolls.

Getting There & Away

Both Big Tancook and Little Tancook are accessible via a 45-minute ferry ride from the Chester wharf. The ferry leaves Chester at 7:10am, 10:30am, 3:40 pm and 5:30pm Monday to Friday, 1pm and 7pm Saturday and 10am and 6pm Sunday year-round. From the Tancooks, the ferry schedule is dictated by the tides, as cars can only be loaded at high tide. A current schedule is posted at the wharf. The fare is $5 per person roundtrip; autos are $20 roundtrip.

MAHONE BAY

A little piece of eye candy, Mahone Bay, with its islands and history, has become something of a city escape. It's a popular destination for a Sunday drive from Halifax, about 100km away, or for afternoon tea. The town has antique and craft shops and is decidedly tourist-oriented. You can see fine examples of Victorian gingerbread-house architecture around town.

Along Hwy 3 on the east side of town is the tourist information office (☎ 902-624-6151, 165 Edgewater St), which is open mid-May to September. Among the many handouts are the walking tour brochures of Mahone Bay. Baywater Cemetery, behind the tourist office, contains the tombs of many early settlers of this area.

Most tourists come for the fame Wooden Boat Festival in the last week c July.

DRL Coachlines stops at the Irving ga station (☎ 902-624-6311) on Edgewater S in the center of Mahone Bay, right next t the three churches.

Things to See

In a row along Edgewater St facing the wa terfront are three historic churches belong ing to the Anglican, Lutheran and Unite denominations.

The **Settlers' Museum & Cultural Centr** (☎ 902-624-6263, 578 S Main St; admissio by donation; open 10am-5pm Tues-Sa 1-5pm Sun June-Oct) deals mainly with th first German settlers in the area. Displays i two rooms focus on the 1850s.

Amos Pewter (☎ 800-565-3369, ⓦ ww .amospewter.com, 589 Main St; admissio free), across the street from the Settlers Museum, explains and demonstrates th art of pewter making. It's open yea round (closed Sundays from January t April).

Boat Trips

The MV Summer Bay (☎ 902-521-430 adult/child $30/17 plus tax) does two-hou harbor cruises from Mahone Bay's Goverr ment Wharf four times a day in July an August.

Kayaking

Sea kayaking is excellent in island-studde Mahone Bay. **Mahone Bay Kayak Adven tures** (☎ 902-624-0334, 619 S Main St; singl double kayak rentals $58/83 per day; ope mid-May-early Oct), right on the harbor, i friendly operation with a good reputation. also has canoes and offers a shuttle servic up and down the coast.

For novice kayakers, there are half-da introductory lessons for $45. A half-da trip to Indian Point is $55/75 singl double, while full-day trips to Blue Rock and Stonehurst near Lunenburg (wher you can see seals) are $105/170. Two-da customized B&B tours, on which yo kayak from one inn to the next, can b arranged. All equipment, lodging and meals are provided.

Places to Stay

Fairmont House B&B (☎ *902-624-8089,* e *fairmonthouse@sympatico.ca, 654 S Main St*) Singles/doubles $60/85 including breakfast. Open mid-May-early Oct. This large gray wooden house near the Government Wharf has three rooms with bath.

The Red Door B&B (☎ *902-624-8479,* e *reddoor@auracom.com, 381 W Main St*) Singles/doubles/triples $55/65/75 mid-May-mid-Nov, $50 single or double other months. Breakfast is included. The three rooms (with shared bath) are in a white house opposite Mahone Bay's liquor store, 500m from the center of town. The backyard garden is nice.

Marline Spike Guest House (☎ *902-624-8664,* e *roadtotheisles@pocketmail.com, 49 Indian Point Rd, Indian Point*) Singles/doubles $40/60. Open July-Sept. Indian Point is an ideal kayaking area 7km from Mahone Bay via the road that follows the north side of the harbor. This large two-story mansion on a hill above the bay caters to those arriving by paddle or wheel. The three rooms share a bathroom.

Places to Eat

Jo-Ann's Deli Market and Bake Shop (☎ *902-624-6305, 9 Edgewater St*) Open 9am-6pm daily May-Oct. In the very heart of Mahone Bay, Jo-Ann's Deli is the place to come for organic veggies, sinfully rich cakes and pastries, and all manner of other edible goodies. There are a few tables outside where you can sit and drink 'fair trade' coffee and watch the well-to-do townfolk going about their business. For the healthiest loaves of bread you'll ever find, go next door to *LaHave Bakery* (☎ *902-624-1420, 3 Edgewater St*), in the former train station.

Salt Spray Café (*621 S Main St*) Sandwiches around $4; daily special under $8. Open July & Aug. This unpretentious cafe has a deck overlooking the harbor. There's usually a daily special like lasagna and salad.

Mimi's Ocean Grill (☎ *902-624-1342, 662 S Main St*) Lunch mains around $10, dinner $11-20. Open noon-2:30pm & 5:30pm-8:30pm Mon-Fri, noon-9pm Sat & Sun May-Oct, noon-9pm July & Aug. For nouvelle cuisine with Thai and Italian overtones, try this place. For lunch there's Tuscan panini ($10) or chicken potpie ($11), and dinner brings such dishes as ocean primavera ($17) and Atlantic potlatch ($18).

LUNENBURG

Lunenburg was officially founded in 1753 when the British encouraged Protestants to emigrate from Europe. It soon became the first largely German settlement in the country.

This attractive town of 2600 residents, partly known for the *Bluenose* sailing schooner built here in 1921, is considered the best surviving example of a planned British colonial settlement in North America. The original layout and overall appearance have endured for two and a half centuries, and Lunenburg is today the region's only UN world heritage site. Always a shipbuilding town, this well-preserved historic gem is still the linchpin of the provincial fishing industry, with one of the major fleets of the northern Atlantic seaboard. The largest fish-processing plant in North America is here, producing Highliner frozen seafood products.

Nova Scotia, like Newfoundland, has been hard hit by dwindling fish stocks and severely curtailed limits imposed by the federal government. But Lunenburg's burgeoning tourism trade has helped shore up the local economy.

Orientation & Information

The town's main street is Lincoln St, but it's Montague St, running parallel to the harbor, which is of most interest to the visitor. Many of the town's commercial enterprises are along it, including some interesting stores with gifts, crafts, antiques and prints for sale.

The Fisheries Museum of the Atlantic is one block lower, along Bluenose Drive, as are the boat tours. Farther east along Montague St are the shipyards and commercial docks for the bigger trawlers. The principal intersection is with King St, which contains several banks. Pelham St, one street back up the hill from Montague St, also has a number of shops.

Lunenburg is no Peggy's Cove, but in midseason tour buses rumble along Bluenose Drive and tourists clog the intersections. It's impossible to find a room anywhere in town for under $50 in midseason. Most of the inns and B&Bs are in the larger, gracious, historic properties around town, and that doesn't come cheap.

The Lunenburg Tourist Bureau (☎ 902-634-8100) is up on Blockhouse Hill Rd, with a great view of the surrounding area. It's open 9am to 7pm daily May to October.

The Lunenburg Branch Library (☎ 902-634-8008), 19 Pelham St, provides free Internet access. It's open 1:30pm to 5:30pm Tuesday, Wednesday & Friday, 9am to 9pm Thursday, 9am to 5pm Saturday.

Fisheries Museum of the Atlantic

This well-executed provincial museum (☎ 902-634-4794, 68 Bluenose Drive; admission $8; open 9:30am-5:30pm June-late-Oct) is housed in one building and two floating ships: a dragger and a fishing schooner. In the building are exhibits on fishing and fish processing and various films on marine life. There's also an aquarium. If you purchase your ticket after 4pm, it's good for the next day.

Knaut Rhuland House

Considered the finest example of Georgian architecture in the province, Knaut Rhuland House (☎ 902-634-3498, 125 Pelham St; admission $3; open 10am-5pm daily June-mid-Sept), erected in 1793, is the only authentic historic house in Lunenburg open to visitors (excluding B&Bs).

Bailly House

Earl Bailly (1903–1977) was one of the area's best-known seascape painters, despite having had polio, which forced him to wield his brush in his teeth. His brother Donald now lives in the family home at 134

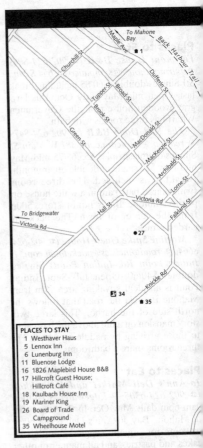

PLACES TO STAY
1   Westhaver Haus
5   Lennox Inn
6   Lunenburg Inn
11 Bluenose Lodge
16 1826 Maplebird House B&B
17 Hillcroft Guest House;
    Hillcroft Café
18 Kaulbach House Inn
19 Mariner King
26 Board of Trade
    Campground
35 Wheelhouse Motel

Pelham St, constructed in 1780, the oldest house in Lunenburg. Inside visits are no possible. Bailly's paintings can be seen a several locations around town, including the Fisheries Museum, the Lunenburg Ar Gallery and the public library. These institutions are being reorganized, however, an the fate of the city-owned collection wa unknown at press time.

Churches

For a small town, Lunenburg's churches ar impressive, and there are five of them in th downtown area. Tragically, **St John's Anglica**

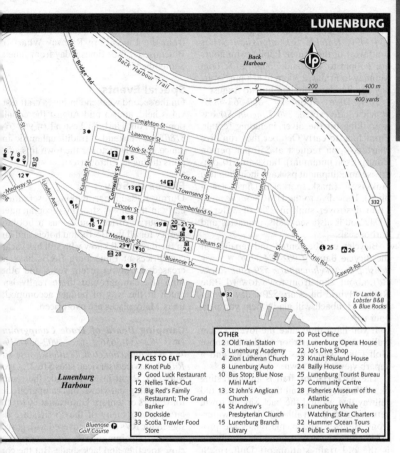

LUNENBURG

Back Harbour

Back Harbour Trail

Kissing Bridge Rd

0   200   400 m
0   200   400 yards

Creighton St
Lawrence St
York St
Duke St
King St
Prince St
Hopson St
Kempt St
Fox St
Townsend St
Cumberland St
Lincoln St
Montague St
Pelham St
Bluenose Dr
Blockhouse Hill Rd
Sawpit Rd

Starr St
Kaulbach St
Cornwallis St
Linden Ave
Medway St

332

To Lamb &
Lobster B&B
& Blue Rocks

Lunenburg
Harbour

Bluenose
Golf Course

OTHER	
2 Old Train Station	20 Post Office
3 Lunenburg Academy	21 Lunenburg Opera House
4 Zion Lutheran Church	22 Jo's Dive Shop
8 Lunenburg Auto	23 Knaut Rhuland House
10 Bus Stop; Blue Nose Mini Mart	24 Bailly House
13 St John's Anglican Church	25 Lunenburg Tourist Bureau
14 St Andrew's Presbyterian Church	27 Community Centre
15 Lunenburg Branch Library	28 Fisheries Museum of the Atlantic
	31 Lunenburg Whale Watching; Star Charters
	32 Hummer Ocean Tours
	34 Public Swimming Pool

PLACES TO EAT
7 Knot Pub
9 Good Luck Restaurant
12 Nellies Take-Out
29 Big Red's Family Restaurant; The Grand Banker
30 Dockside
33 Scotia Trawler Food Store

902-634-4994, cnr Duke & Cumberland *ts)*, one of the oldest churches in Canada, as devastated by fire in November 2001. **St ndrew's Presbyterian** (1770), on Townsend t, is the oldest Presbyterian church in the ountry.

The **Zion Lutheran** church on the corner f Fox and Cornwallis Sts has its own claim o fame. In it is one of the original bells rom the fort at Louisbourg on Cape reton Island. When the federal govern-ent briefly considered ordering the bell's eturn to the national historic site, it was emoved from the church and hidden at the bottom of Lunenburg's back harbor. The bell is still closely guarded, and the church can only be visited during the Sunday service at 11am.

Lunenburg Academy

The academy (☎ 902-634-2220, 97 Kaulback St), still a functioning school, is the huge black-and-white turreted structure on a hill seen rising above the town on your way in from Halifax. Built entirely of wood in 1895, as a prestigious high school, it is one of the few remaining survivors of the academy system of education.

Activities

The outdoor **public swimming pool** (☎ 902-634-4499, Knickle Rd; admission $4) is southwest of the center. Public swim hours are 2:30pm to 4pm and 7:30pm to 8:30pm Monday to Friday, 2:30pm to 4:30pm Saturday and Sunday from late June to August.

Jo's Dive Shop (☎ 800-563-4831, W www.jodive.ns.ca, 296 Lincoln St) has everything for the diver, including rentals. From June to early October they run dive charters upon request at $50 per person (four-person minimum). Tanks are $10; otherwise an equipment package including two tanks is $52 (mask, snorkel and fins not supplied). They dive to the HMCS Saguenay, a 112m destroyer sunk in 27m of water in 1994. You'll also see walls, pinnacles and harbor seals.

Bicycles can be rented and repaired at the **Bicycle Barn** (☎ 902-634-3426, W www.tallships.ca/bikelunenburg, 579 Blue Rocks Rd), about 2km from town toward Blue Rocks. Hybrid bikes are $20 a day. Owner Merrill Heubach will gladly help you plan your trip.

If you have time, take the lovely 1½km walk around the harbor to the Bluenose Golf Club, which has a small cafe and a superb view of the town.

The **Back Harbor Trail** is an interesting 4km hiking/cycling trail that follows an old railway line around the back side of town, returning to the trailhead via the waterfront. Benches and picnic tables are provided along the way. A good place to begin is the old train station off Dufferin St (ample free parking is available on the far side of the station).

Organized Tours

From June to mid-October **Lunenburg Whale Watching** (☎ 902-527-7175, Bluenose Dr) offers three-hour trips departing from the Lunenburg harbor for $38 per person. **Star Charters** (☎ 902-634-3535, Bluenose Dr) has four trips daily on its two-masted wooden ketch Eastern Star for $22 a person for a two-hour tour ($25 sunset tour). All trips will be running in July and August, with a reduced schedule in June and September.

Hummer Ocean Tours (☎ 902-521-0857) does coastal cruises ($25/12 adult/child) from the Lunenburg Railway Wharf of Bluenose Dr four times a day from June t September.

Special Events

On the second weekend in July, a craft festival is held, and in mid-August the equall popular **Folk Harbour Festival** (☎ 902-634-3180) is a weekend of traditional music an dance. In early October the town tips a fe pints during its Oktoberfest.

Places to Stay

During midsummer, making reservation early in the day is strongly recommended The tourist office doubles as a bookin agency for all the B&Bs and hotels, and lat in the day they'll know who still has vacar cies. Prices at Lunenburg B&Bs have in creased sharply in recent years, and othe than the campground there really isn much in the way of budget accommoda tions. Many places are overpriced.

Camping *Board of Trade Campgroun* (☎ 902-634-3656, fax 902-634-319 e LBT@auracom.com, 11 Blockhouse H Rd) Unserviced/serviced sites $16/21. Ope May-Oct. Right in town beside the touri office, with great views, this campground for trailers or tenters. Unfortunately for th latter group, many of the 55 sites are de signed for RVs and are covered with grave and the remaining grassy sites are packe close together and lack shade. But the co venient location and glories of Lunenbu make it worth putting up with these inco veniences. It does get full, so arrive earl Showers are free.

Downtown *Hillcroft Guest House* (☎ 90. 634-8031, W www.bbcanada.com/1369.htm 53 Montague St) Singles/doubles $50/6. Open May-Oct. Hillcroft offers three room with shared bath. Continental breakfast included in the price.

Mariner King (☎ 800-565-8509, fax 90. 634-8509, e marinerking@tallships.c W www.tallships.ca/marinerking, 15 King S

Doubles $75-109 mid-May-mid-Oct, $60-88 mid-Oct-mid-May, including full breakfast. This ornate three-story house (1830) is opposite the post office in the middle of the old town.

1826 Maplebird House B&B (☎ 888-595-3863, fax 902-634-3863, W www3.ns sympatico.ca/barry.susie, 36 Pelham St) Rooms $90 Mar-Oct, $75 Nov-Feb, including full breakfast. This four-room house overlooking the harbor has a lovely rear garden with a swimming pool.

Kaulbach House Inn (☎ 800-568-8818, fax 902-634-8818, W www.kaulbachhouse com, 75 Pelham St) Singles/doubles $100-130/105-135 July-Sept ($10 less other months). Open Apr-late Oct. Kaulbach House is a three-story Victorian residence with a mansard roof, dating from 1878.

Lennox Inn (☎ 888-379-7605, fax 902-634-3963, W www.skybusiness.com/lennox inn, 69 Fox St) Rooms $75/85-100 shared/private bath. Open mid-May-late Oct. This five-room, three-story wooden ex-tavern was erected in 1791. A British colonial flag flies over the building.

West of Town *Bluenose Lodge* (☎ 800-565-8851, fax 902-634-8851, e bluenose@ ox.nstn.ca, 10 Falkland St) Rooms $85-90 ($5-10 less at beginning and end of season). Open mid-May-Oct. This 125-year-old building is the big place on the corner of Lincoln St. A breakfast buffet is included.

Lunenburg Inn (☎ 800-565-3963, fax 902-634-9419, W www.lunenburginn.com, 26 Dufferin St) Singles/doubles $112-122/117-127 including breakfast ($10 less at beginning and end of season). Open Apr-Oct. This large, comfortable, historic inn is furnished with antiques.

Westhaver Haus (☎ 902-634-4937, fax 902-634-8640, 102 Dufferin St) Singles/ doubles $50-60/60-70 including breakfast. Open May-Oct (off-season by reservation). Yet another magnificent Lunenburg house, with stately columns supporting an upper deck. The lower price makes the short uphill walk worthwhile.

Wheelhouse Motel (☎ 877-997-9972, fax 902-634-7141, e dallen@tallships.ca, W www

.wheelhouse.ns.ca, 31 Knickle Rd) Rooms $85-95 July & Aug ($10 less other months). This attractive two-story motel is opposite the public swimming pool, just west of town yet still within easy walking distance.

East of Town *Lamb & Lobster B&B* (☎ 902-634-4833, fax 902-634-3195, e flower @ns.sympatico.ca, W www.bbcanada.com/ 3232.html, 619 Blue Rocks Rd) Singles/ doubles $45/55 with shared bath. Open June-Oct. This B&B is appropriately named. The owner, William Flower, is a lobster fisherman and a shepherd. In the evening, guests might observe how the family collies round up the sheep.

Places to Eat
Sampling the fish here is an absolute must, and Lunenburg offers some offbeat specialties that are worth trying. Solomon gundy is pickled herring with onions. Lunenburg pudding (pork and spices cooked in the intestines of a pig) goes well with Scotch and water. Fish cakes with rhubarb chutney are also much appreciated here. The famous Lunenburg sausage and sauerkraut reflect the town's German roots.

Nellies Take-Out (26 Lincoln St) Meals $3-7. Open 11am-6pm daily May-Sept. This converted bus parked near the Esso gas station at the west entrance to town serves some of the cheapest and best takeaway food in town. A large order of french fries is $3; fish & chips are $5 to $7; and a cheeseburger is $3. There are even two picnic tables at your disposal.

Good Luck Restaurant (☎ 902-634-8898, 15 Lincoln St) Meals $5-9. Open 11am-9:30pm daily. The $5 Chinese lunch specials include a drink (weekdays only), and the combination dinners are in the $6 to $9 range.

Knot Pub (☎ 902-634-3334, 4 Dufferin St) Meals $8. Open 11:30am-9:30pm Mon-Sat, noon-9:30pm Sun (the bar stays open later). Good pub food is on hand at this place, including pots of mussels ($4.50/8.50 small/ large), fish & chips ($8) and nachos. Happy hour with beer specials runs from 4:30pm to 7pm.

Hillcroft Café (☎ 902-634-8031, 53 Montague St) Mains from $13-20. Open 5:30pm-9pm daily mid-Apr-Oct. Lunenburg has a handful of casually upscale bistros such as this one, which provides two vegetarian options.

Big Red's Family Restaurant (☎ 902-634-3554, 80 Montague St) Mains $8-10. Open 9am-10pm Sun-Thurs, 9am-11pm Fri & Sat, 8am-11pm July & Aug. Big Red's is the name most often mentioned by locals for good, basic food. Hamburgers, subs and pizza dominate the menu, but there's also a large seafood selection with fish & chips ($8), haddock casserole ($10), surf & turf ($17) and more. The portions are typically large.

The Grand Banker (☎ 902-634-3300, rear entrance at 82 Montague St) Meals $10. Open 8am-9:30pm Sun-Wed, 8am-10pm Thurs-Sat. This pub facing the waterfront has half-price seafood during happy hour from 4pm to 5:30pm daily. Items like scallops, mussels, shrimp, calamari and Solomon gundy go for under $4 at that time (also available in winter).

Dockside (☎ 902-634-3005, 84 Montague St) Dinner $17. Open 8am-9pm daily. This is one of the more reasonable tourist places, especially when you consider the large portions. The restaurant has an outdoor patio where you can gorge on your halibut or haddock.

Scotia Trawler Food Store (☎ 902-634-4914, 266 Montague St) Open Mon-Sat. This supermarket carries local delicacies such as Lunenburg pudding and Lunenburg sausage in the meat section, Solomon gundy, sauerkraut, fresh mussels and live lobsters in the seafood section and veggie plates in the bakery. If you're camping, investigate the barbecue facilities at the campground before buying items which need to be cooked.

Entertainment
Lunenburg Opera House (☎ 902-634-4010, 290 Lincoln St) Numerous Maritimes music concerts are advertised on placards in the window, and tickets cost anywhere from $5 to $20.

Getting There & Away
DRL Coachlines buses pull in at Blue Nose Mini Mart (☎ 902-634-8845), a convenience store at 35 Lincoln St. Buses leave at 10:20am Monday to Saturday and 3:15pm Sunday for Halifax ($15), and at 8pm daily for Yarmouth ($32).

Kiwi Kaboodle's Tradewind Shuttle (☎ 902-463-4244) runs a daily van service between Halifax and Lunenburg for $3 one way. They'll pick up anywhere around Halifax at 9:30am, departing Lunenburg on the return trip at 3:30pm (or any other time if they're not busy).

Try Town Transit (☎ 877-521-0855) runs a daily van shuttle between Halifax and Lunenburg for $22 one way, although this price only applies when they have at least four bookings. They'll pick up anywhere in either town.

Parking meters in the lower town must be fed from 9am to 5pm weekdays, but they only cost 25¢ per hour. A recommended auto repair shop is Lunenburg Auto (☎ 902-634-8063), at 7 Lincoln St next to the Knot Pub.

BRIDGEWATER
Bridgewater, an industrial town with a big Michelin tire plant, is the largest center on the South Shore, with a population of over 7000. Though located right on the LaHave River, Bridgewater isn't a picture-perfect museum town like Chester, Mahone Bay or Lunenburg; rather it's the regional service center, with large shopping malls and fast food outlets. Still, quaint corners remain on the backstreets.

The South Shore Exhibition, held each July, is a major five-day fair with traditional competitions between Canadian and US teams in such events as the ox pull.

Information
The helpful Bridgewater Tourist Office (☎ 902-543-7003), 45 Aberdeen Rd, is across the highway from the Atlantic Super Store. It's open 9am to 7pm daily July and August, 9am to 5pm other months.

Aside from providing support on women's health matters, the Second Story

Women's Center (☎ 902-543-1315), 12 Dominion St, is a useful contact point for anyone interested in exploring women's issues/concerns. It's open 10am to 4:30pm Monday to Friday.

Things to See & Do

The **Desbrisay Museum** (☎ *902-543-4033, 130 Jubilee Rd; admission $2; open 9am-5pm Mon-Sat, 1pm-5pm Sun mid-May-Sept, closed Sun & Mon Oct-mid-May)*, on 10 hectares of parkland, has a small collection of goods relating to the early (mainly German) settlers of Lunenburg County. The municipal outdoor swimming pool is next-door.

The **Wile Carding Mill** (☎ *902-543-8233, 242 Victoria Rd; admission free; open 9am-5pm Mon-Sat, 1pm-5pm Sun June-Sept)* is an authentic water mill dating from 1860. Carding is the straightening and untangling of wool fibers in preparation for spinning. The Centennial Trail crosses Victoria Rd just a few meters west of the mill.

Places to Stay & Eat

Fairview Inn (☎ *877-671-0777, 25 Queen St)* singles/doubles $40/45 shared bath, $50/55 private bath, $60/65 suite. This magnificent three-story wooden hotel has been operating since 1863, and unlike the fancy B&Bs of Lunenburg, the Fairview also caters to local residents. Twenty-one rooms have shared bath; the other eight have private bath. The Fairview is brimming with atmosphere and makes a great base for touring the area.

Deluxe Delight Café (☎ *902-543-4450, 25 Queen St)* Mains $8. Open 6:30am-4pm Mon-Thurs, 6:30am-8pm Fri-Sat, 9am-8pm Sun (reduced hours in winter). This unpretentious cafe occupies the main dining room of the historic Fairview Inn. Things haven't changed much here since the 1940s, and it attracts mostly local residents ordering breakfast ($3 to $5), sandwiches ($4 to $5) or dinner (pork chops or roast beef $8, haddock $9). It's real Down East food!

Sobeys Supermarket (☎ *902-543-9244, Bridgewater Mall, Hwy 3, 349 LaHave St)* Open 24 hours Mon-Sat. This big supermar-

ket is just south of the LaHave River bridges.

Getting There & Away

DRL Coachlines uses the Irving gas station (☎ 902-543-2447) on North St, 400m south of exit 12 from Hwy 103. It's 2.3km from here to the Fairview Inn in central Bridgewater. Bus fares are $16/30 to Halifax/Yarmouth.

LAHAVE

LaHave is just a tiny village on the south bank of the LaHave River. The only HI hostel on the South Shore is here, plus an excellent bakery, a historic site and kayaking possibilities. The LaHave Ferry near the hostel is very handy for anyone driving along the coast.

Fort Point Museum

A kilometer west of the village is this national historic site. It was here, in 1632, that returning French settlers who would become known as Acadians landed, after the Treaty of St. Germain-en-Laye with England ceded Acadia to France. A fort, Sainte-Marie-de-Grâce, was built later the same year, but very little of it remains today. The site was supplanted by Port Royal in the Annapolis Valley and never became a major center. A **museum** (☎ *902-688-2696, Fort Point Rd; admission free; open 10am-5pm daily June-Aug)* in the former lighthouse keeper's house at the site tells the story of this early settlement and its leader, Isaac de Razilly.

Kayaking

Near Crescent Beach, 8km southeast of LaHave, is **Crescent Sea Kayak Tours** (☎ *902-688-2806,* W *www.lairdadventures .com, 5008 Hwy 331)*. Three-hour tours among the LaHave Islands are $35 for a single kayak and $60 for a double.

Places to Stay & Eat

LaHave Marine Hostel (☎ *902-688-2908, fax 902-688-1083,* W *www.hostellingintl .ns.ca, 3421 Hwy 331)* Members/nonmembers $12/15. Open June-Sept. This historic wooden building erected in 1900 was a warehouse back in the days when LaHave was a center for trade with the West Indies. Today it's a simple HI hostel ideal for cyclists, backpackers or any like-minded soul looking for a low-budget place to spend the night. The hostel has two double rooms, one single and one triple, and couples or even individuals can often get a room to themselves. Sheets are $2 extra. There's a well-equipped kitchen where you can prepare meals, a sitting room and a library. The riverside dock behind the hostel is a great place to linger.

LaHave Bakery (☎ 902-688-2908, 3421 Hwy 331) Lunches $4-5. Open 10am-5pm daily Sept-June, 9am-5:30pm July & Aug. The LaHave Bakery below the HI hostel is one of the best in the Maritimes, if not the whole country. When passing through LaHave, be sure to stop for a soup and sandwich lunch, or just coffee or tea. Their bread is baked daily on the premises – stock up.

Getting There & Away
The LaHave Ferry connects Hwys 332 and 331, saving motorists a 40km drive up and down the river to use the bridges at Bridgewater. The five-minute cable ferry trip goes every half hour and costs $3 per car. Pedestrians can ride back and forth as often as they like for free.

Try Town Transit (☎ 902-521-0855) operates a van shuttle between Halifax and LaHave at $31 one way.

LAHAVE ISLANDS
Just southwest of LaHave are the LaHave Islands, a handful of small, pleasant-to-look-at islands connected to the mainland by a 2km causeway along Crescent Beach and to each other by one-lane iron bridges. You're allowed to drive a car along the sands of Crescent Beach!

On Bell Island just past the Government Wharf is the **Marine Museum** (☎ 902-688-2973, 100 Bells Island; admission free; open 10am-5pm daily June-Aug). The museum is housed in St John's Anglican Church and services are occasionally still held among the marine artifacts.

Places to Stay
Rissers Beach Provincial Park (☎ 902-688-2034, ⊞ parks.gov.ns.ca, 5463 Hwy 331) Campsites $18. Open mid-May-early Oct. . kilometer west of the causeway to the islands and 10km from LaHave is Rissers Beach, which features a very busy (in July & August) campground and an excellent long sandy beach, although the water is none too warm. There's also a saltwater marsh with boardwalk trail and a good interpretive display with information on the natural environment. The 92-site campground has two sections, one along the beach and another inland. Rissers Beach is close enough to Halifax/Dartmouth to get rather crowded on midsummer weekends. Thomas Raddall Provincial Park near Port Joli to the southwest gets a lot less traffic, and the campsites are larger and more private.

LIVERPOOL
Situated where the Mersey River meets the ocean, Liverpool is another historic English-style town with an economy based on forests and fish. British privateers were active in this area in the early 1800s, protecting the British trade routes from incursions by the USA, and Liverpool's shipbuilding industry dates from those days. The many excellent free attractions in Liverpool should put the town squarely on your itinerary. Privateer Days at the end of June is a major event here.

Information
The very helpful tourist office (☎ 902-354-5421), 28 Henry Hensey Drive, just off Main St near the river bridge, has a walking-tour pamphlet and brochures of scenic drives in the area. The center is open daily mid-May to September.

Sherman Hines Museum of Photography & Galleries
This impressive museum (☎ 902-354-2667, 219 Main St; admission free; open 10am-5:30pm Mon-Sat, 10am-5:30pm Mon-Sat, noon-5pm Sun May-mid-Dec) has a name that pretty much says it all. Six – count 'em – galleries run the gamut of media

cluding the only photographic museum ast of Montréal. It's housed in the assive wooden old town hall erected in)01.

erkins House

erkins House (☎ 902-354-4058, 105 Main ; admission free; open 9:30am-5:30pm 1on-Sat, 1pm-5:30pm Sun June-mid-Oct), uilt in 1766, is now a museum with articles nd furniture from the colonial period. It's amed for well-known Loyalist Simeon erkins, whose story is told here.

ueen's County Museum

ext door, the Queen's County Museum ☎ 902-354-4058, 109 Main St; admission ee; open 9:30am-5:30pm Mon-Sat, 1pm-30pm Sun) has First Nation artifacts and arious items relating to town history, as ell as some writings by early citizens.

ort Point

cairn marks the site where Samuel de 'hamplain landed in 1604. The lighthouse ☎ 902-354-5260, 21 Fort Lane at the end of 1ain St; admission free; open 10am-6pm aily late May-early Oct) is accessible to the lambering public; you can even blow the ghthouse's hand-pumped foghorn. The dis-lays and panels in and around the light-ouse offer some fascinating insights into Jova Scotia's early history and are worthy f careful study. From Fort Point you get a ood view of the US-owned Bowater 1ersey pulp mill at Brooklyn, 3km north of .iverpool.

Jank Snow Country Music Centre

)ff Hwy 103 at exit 19 is an old train station hat has been converted into a museum ☎ 902-354-4675, 148 Bristol Ave; admission 3; open 9am-5pm Mon-Sat, noon-5pm Sun nid-May-mid-Oct), detailing the life of ocal-boy-done-good Hank Snow and also Canadian country music in general.

Hiking & Swimming

*ine Grove, a lovely park with hiking trails neandering through a large stand of white

pine, is on Hwy 8 at Milton, very near Liverpool. From the Irving gas station on Bristol Ave on the north side of Liverpool, keep straight on Milton Road. The park is on the left, some 400m beyond the Hwy 103 overpass.

There are four sandy **beaches** nearby: Beach Meadows, White Point, Hunt's Point and Summerville. All are within 11km of town, and there are others farther west.

Surfing

Rossignol Surf Shop (☎ 902-354-3733, W www.outdoorns.com/surfshop, 216 Main St; open 10am-5pm Mon-Sat), opposite the Museum of Photography, offers two-hour surfing lessons every Wednesday and Saturday morning year-round at the White Point Beach Resort. The $50 fee includes use of a board. Mid-August to November is the prime surfing season along the South Shore, and Rossignol's Web site is a good source of information.

Places to Stay

Geranium House (☎ 902-354-4484, W www.eucanect.com/tourism/geranium .html, 87 Milton Rd) Open May-mid-Oct. Doubles $40. This B&B on a large wooded property next to the Mersey River has three rooms with shared bath. It's near exit 19 from Hwy 103, only 400m from the DRL Coachlines bus stop.

Lanes Privateer Inn (☎ 902-354-3456, fax 902-354-7220, e ron.lane@ns.sympatico.ca, 33 Bristol Ave) Singles/doubles $75/87 May-Oct, $61/71 Nov-Apr, including continental breakfast. This white wooden building sits next to the bridge over the Mersey River, and the inn also runs a B&B next door with three shared bathrooms at $60/65 (available June to October only). Canoes and bicycles are for rent.

Transcotia Motel (☎ 902-354-3494, fax 902-354-3352, 3457 Hwy 3, Brooklyn) Singles/doubles $44/50 June-Sept, $39/45 Oct-May. Transcotia offers 22 tastefully designed motel rooms behind a thicket of coniferous trees a kilometer north of the Bowater Mersey pulp mill. The motel has an inexpensive restaurant.

Places to Eat

Morningside Café (☎ 902-354-2411, 236 Main St) Breakfast or lunch $5. Open 8am-3:30pm Mon-Fri, 9am-2pm Sat. This restaurant inside Home Hardware directly opposite the tourist office serves breakfast at $4 to $5, including coffee. For lunch there are sandwiches ($3 to $5), salads ($5) and quiche or potpie (both under $7).

Liverpool Pizzeria (☎ 902-354-2422, 155 Main St) Medium pizza $9, pasta $6. Open 8:30am-11pm Sun-Thurs, 8:30pm-midnight Fri & Sat. This workaday place serves standard Italian fare, including lasagna.

Lanes Privateer Inn (☎ 902-354-3456, 33 Bristol Ave) Dinner $12-16. Open 7am-10pm July & Aug, 7am-8pm other months. For an upscale dinner, order Lanes' signature dish of chowder, haddock and dessert for $20. Otherwise there's stir-fry shrimp ($16), pork chops ($12) and more. The restaurant at the Transcotia Motel serves similar fare to Lanes at noticeably lower prices.

Sobeys Supermarket (☎ 902-354-4225, 180 Bristol Ave) Open 24 hours Mon-Sat. This large grocery store is on Hwy 3 at the north entrance to town, behind the Hank Snow Country Music Centre.

Getting There & Away

DRL Coachlines buses to Halifax ($22) and Yarmouth ($27) stop at the Irving gas station (☎ 902-354-2048), corner of Bristol Ave and Milton Rd, near the Hank Snow Country Music Centre, an easy 10-minute walk from town.

SEASIDE ADJUNCT KEJIMKUJIK NATIONAL PARK

This undeveloped region of the south coast between Port Joli Bay and Port Mouton (ma-**toon**) Bay is part of a larger national park located in the interior, northwest of Liverpool. Created in 1988, the Keji Adjunct protects a beautiful wild stretch of shoreline and its fauna.

Services are nonexistent; no camping or fires are allowed, and no toilets or drinking water are available. What you will find is pristine coastline, with great beaches, coves, vistas, rock formations, wildflowers and a abundance of bird life. Admission is free.

The only access from Hwy 103 is along 6½km gravel road. From the parking lot the 3km **Harbour Rocks Trail** follows an ol cart road through mixed forest to Harbour Rocks, where seals are often seen. St Catherines Beach just beyond is closed t visitors because it's a nesting area for the endangered piping plover.

The Port Joli Basin also contains the **Point Joli Migratory Bird Sanctuary**, where birders will find waterfowl and shorebirds i great numbers, especially during migratio periods. It's at the top end of Port Jo Harbour and is only easily accessible b kayak. Liverpool's **Rossignol Surf Sho** (☎ 902-683-2550) has a beach house at 60 St Catherines River Rd on the road to the Seaside Adjunct, which they use as a base for ocean kayaking tours ($55/95 a half/fu day) from mid-May to early Octobe Kayak rentals without the tour are $30/45 half/full day.

Places to Stay

Thomas Raddall Provincial Park (☎ 902 683-2664, **W** parks.gov.ns.ca) Sites $18 Open early June-early Oct. Thomas Radda park is 4km off Hwy 103; then it's 3kr down an access road to the park gate. Th campsites are large and private, in a shad lovely forest, with showers and eight walk in sites. A 5km trail system (bikes welcom on a some trails) extends out onto awesom beaches, the real attraction here. Plenty o nesting birds and even seals are found i this area, and it's far enough away from Halifax not to be overcrowded. Across Por Joli Harbour from Keji Adjunct, Thoma Raddall makes a great base from which to visit that park.

SHELBURNE

This is one of the most attractive and in teresting towns anywhere on the South Shore. The whole place is pretty much lik a museum, with fine buildings and histori sites at every turn. In fact, Shelburne con tains Canada's largest concentration o pre-1800 wooden homes. Disney filmed

ning boats and houses in historic Lunenburg, Nova Scotia

pwreck off Cape St Mary, Nova Scotia

A strong defense, Louisbourg Fortress, Cape Breton

Take a trip to the 18th century in Louisbourg.

Tools of the trade

he *Scarlet Letter* here in 1995, and relics
om the filming include the steeple on the
andspit Artisans Cooperative on Dock St
nd the Elizabethan-style guild hall
ehind it.

Shelburne, like many towns in the
undy region, was founded by Loyalists,
nd in 1783 it had a population of 16,000,
aking it the largest community in British
orth America. Life in the USA was not
asy for those loyal to the British crown,
nd thousands left for Canada; many of
ose who came here were from the New
ork aristocracy.

This shipbuilding town with a population
f around 2200 is known as the birthplace of
achts. As well as prize-winning yachts, it
roduces several other types of boats.

Shelburne is still a major port. Clearwa-
r Continental Seafoods has a large
acking plant on the wharf, though recent
ghtening of fishing quotas has resulted in a
arked decline in fishing activity. A little
rther out are the shipyards where repairs

to regional ferries and other vessels are
carried out.

Water St, the main street, has many
houses between 100 and 200 years old, and
quite a few of the two-story wooden homes
are marked with dates.

Dock St along the harbor features
several historic buildings and museums. A
collective ticket to all four museums is $8.
The tourist office (☎ 902-875-4547) is also
on Dock St. It's open daily from mid-May to
early October. The tourist office Web site
(Ⓦ www.auracom.com/~tnshelb) has a lot
of information on Shelburne and its history.

The biggest festival is Founders' Days on
the last weekend of July.

Ross-Thompson House

Built in 1784, this house (☎ 902-875-3141, 9
*Charlotte Lane; admission $3, free until
noon Sun; open 9:30am-5:30pm daily June-
mid-Oct)*, with its adjacent store, belonged
to well-to-do merchants who arrived from
Britain via Cape Cod. It now acts as a small

A Venerable, Visible Minority

Nova Scotia's African Canadian community dates back over two centuries. Although a black man,
Mathieu da Costa, was reported at Port Royal as early as 1605, the first sizable wave of black immigration arrived from New York, Charleston and Savannah in 1782 and 1783. During the Revolutionary War the outnumbered British offered freedom to any slave of a rebel American who
would cross to their side, and toward the end of the conflict many were evacuated to Nova Scotia.

Known as Black Loyalists, these former slaves were resettled at Birchtown near Shelburne,
where many became disenchanted by the failure of the British authorities to provide the farmlands
they had promised. Thus, in 1792, some 1200 of the original 3500 Black Loyalists departed for
Sierra Leone, Africa, where they founded Freetown.

In 1796, 550 Jamaican ex-slaves were resettled at Preston east of Dartmouth, but they too left
for Sierra Leone in 1800. During the War of 1812 some 2000 refugees from Chesapeake Bay
arrived at Preston, some eventually continuing to Trinidad in the West Indies. Around the turn of
the 20th century, further groups of black laborers arrived from Alabama and the Caribbean to
work in the mines and mills of Amherst and Sydney.

By the mid-1800s a large community of blacks had formed at Africville, just north of Halifax.
Their settlement eventually became encircled by industries, and in the 1960s most residents of
Africville moved to Halifax's north end, where they currently live along Gottingen, Creighton and
Maynard Sts. Many also reside in eastern Dartmouth at Cole Harbour. Paradoxically, these tenth-
generation Canadians often suffer discrimination at the hands of people whose forebears arrived
much later than theirs.

museum where furniture, paintings, artifacts and original goods from the store can be viewed. The house is surrounded by gardens.

Shelburne County Museum

Nearby is Loyalist house (☎ 902-875-3219, 8 Maiden Lane at Dock St; admission $3, free until noon Sun; open 9:30am-5:30pm daily June-mid-Oct, 9:30am-noon & 2pm-5pm Tues-Sat other months), dating from 1787, with a collection of Loyalist furnishings, displays on the history of the local fishery and other articles from the town's past. The oldest fire engine in Canada, a wooden cart from 1740, is quite something. There's also a small collection of Mi'kmaq artifacts, including typical porcupine-quill decorative work.

Dory Shop

Shelburne has long had a reputation for its dories, small boats first used for fishing from a mother schooner and in later years for inshore fishing and as lifeboats. Many were built from the 1880s until the 1970s. At the museum (☎ 902-875-4003, 11 Dock St; admission $3, free until noon Sun; open 9:30am-5:30pm daily June-mid-Oct) you can see examples still being made in the workshop upstairs.

Muir-Cox Shipbuilding Interpretive Centre

This historic shipyard (☎ 902-875-1114, 13 George St; admission $3, free until noon Sun; open 9:30am-5:30pm Mon-Fri June-Oct) at the south end of Dock St reopened as a working museum in 2001. You'll see boats being built as they have been since the 1820s.

Kayaking

Ocean Breeze Kayak Adventures (☎ 902-875-2463, W www.oceanbreeze3.com; open Apr-Oct), inside the Muir-Cox Shipbuilding Interpretive Centre at the south end of Dock St, rents kayaks ($35/60 per half/full day) and bicycles ($20 per day including helmet). They also do half-/full-day kayak tours ($45/90) to the Islands Provincial Park.

Organized Tours

Al Keith (☎ 902-875-1333, W www.studio1 .ns.ca) offers 2½-hour guided walking tour around town whenever at least four peopl are interested. The tourist office takes book ings, or call him up. The $10 price include admission to two museums – which makes a great deal – and Al knows pretty much a there is to know about Shelburne.

Places to Stay

The Islands Provincial Park (☎ 902-875 4304, W parks.gov.ns.ca, off Hwy 3) Site $18. Open mid-May-Aug. Under 2km from the Irving gas station in Shelburne (wher the DRL bus stops), this provincial par offers a view of the Shelburne waterfror across the harbor. The 65 campsites, som quite nice, are in a mature forest, and ther is swimming nearby. It's quiet during th week but has been known to get rowdy o midsummer weekends. The campgroun has showers.

Loyalist Inn (☎ 902-875-2343, fax 902 875-1452, 160 Water St) Rooms $54 for up t four people year-round. This older three story wooden hotel right in the middle c town has 18 rooms with bath. There's some times live music in the dining room dowr stairs.

Bear's Den (☎ 902-875-3234, W ww .bearsden.ns.ca, cnr Water & Glasgow Sts Singles/doubles $45/55, including breakfas Open Apr-Nov. This small and economic: B&B is just 200m from the DRL Coachline stop. You'll pass it on the way into th center of town. The owner has lately bee considering retiring and moving to Califor nia, so be sure to call ahead.

Wildwood Motel (☎ 800-565-500 W www.wildwood.ns.ca, Minto St off Wate St) Singles/doubles from $70/85 July & Au; $55/60 other months, including continenta breakfast. This motel at the edge of tow 600m from the DRL Coachlines stop, has 2 rooms in an L-shaped block.

Places to Eat

Claudia's Diner (☎ 902-875-3110, 149 Wate St) Mains under $10. Open 8am-8pm Mor Fri, noon-7pm Sun May-Oct, 9am-3pr

Mon-Fri, noon-7pm Sun Nov-Apr. This is a low-priced restaurant with style and standard fare. The cinnamon rolls are good, and the lobster chowder ($5.50) comes in a large bowl. A full breakfast with coffee will be $4 here.

Shelburne Pastry & Tea House (☎ 902-875-1164, 151 Water St) Lunch $4-7. Open 10am-8pm Mon-Sat July & Aug, 10am-5pm Mon-Sat other months. The atmosphere here is a tad trendier than at Claudia's, but it's great for a healthy soup and omelette lunch or coffee and cakes midmorning or afternoon.

Sea Dog Saloon (☎ 902-875-2862, 1 Dock St) Mains $8-16. Open 11am-8pm Mon-Sat, noon-8pm Sun May-Sept, until 9pm in July & Aug. Lots of cheap pub snacks like wings, nachos, chowder and steamed mussels are available here for around $6, but they also prepare seafood dinners ($16), steaks ($9 to $16), haddock & chips ($8 to $10) and pork chops ($9). The Sea Dog Caesar salad ($8) is recommended. There's an outdoor terrace beside the water, and live music Saturday nights from 9pm. From October to April when the downstairs section is closed, the Wreck Room sports bar upstairs remains open with a limited menu.

Scotia Lunch (☎ 902-875-2876, 64 King St) Mains $8-9. Open 8am-11:40pm daily. This place, opposite the fire department, is rather basic, and the cigarette smoke can be a drag. Aside from hamburgers, sandwiches and pizza, you can get fish, clams, scallops and shrimp, and nothing is over $12. Check the daily special on the blackboard at the counter. There's also a half-price kids menu. All the posted prices include tax.

Getting There & Away

DRL Coachlines connects Shelburne to Halifax ($30) and Yarmouth ($16). Buses stop at the Irving gas station (☎ 902-875-5033), 41 Falls Lane at Water St, near Hwy 103, 1.3km north of town.

BARRINGTON

This small village, 32km southwest of Shelburne, dates back to 1760, when Cape Cod settlers erected their meetinghouse here. The town has four museums, all within walking distance of one another. The buses don't stop anywhere near Barrington, so you'll need to have your own transportation to visit.

The tourist office (☎ 902-637-2625) is open 10am to 5pm daily mid-May to mid-October. In recent years this office has been just across the bridge from the woolen mill, but there's been talk of moving it to a new location at the turnoff to Barrington from Hwy 103.

Things to See

The most interesting museum is the **Woollen Mill** (☎ 902-637-2185, 2368 Hwy 3; admission $1; open 9:30am-5:30pm Mon-Sat, 1pm-5:30pm Sun June-Sept), restored to represent a typical small manufacturing mill of the late 1800s. This mill continued to operate until 1962, longer than any other woolen mill in this region. Costumed guides explain the entire operation, from cleaning the raw wool to spinning it into yarn, and there's a video of the mill in operation in the 1950s.

The **Barrington Old Meeting House** (☎ 902-637-2185, 2408 Hwy 3; admission $1; open 9:30am-5:30pm Mon-Sat, noon-5:30pm Sun June-Sept) reflects the town's early Quaker influence and was used as both church and town hall. There's an old cemetery next door, and services are still held in the meetinghouse on the third Sunday of August.

The **Seal Island Lighthouse Museum** (☎ 902-637-2185, Hwy 3; admission $1; open 9:30am-5:30pm Mon-Sat, noon-5:30pm Sun June-Sept) is a replica of the lighthouse found on Seal Island, 30km out to sea. Among the historical sundries on display is the lens from the original lighthouse, and from the top there's a vista of Barrington Bay.

Across the road from the Historical Society Centre, the **Western Counties Military Museum** (☎ 902-768-2292, Hwy 3; admission free; open 9:30am-5:30pm Mon-Sat, noon-5:30pm Sun June-Aug) showcases uniforms, medals and other artifacts.

Places to Stay & Eat

Bayberry Campground (☎ 902-637-2181, 538 Hwy 309, Villagedale) Unserviced/serviced sites $15/20, open May-Oct. Secluded wooded campsites and others overlooking the ocean are available at this campground 4km from the Woollen Mill. Sites by the water cost more.

Old School House Inn (☎ 902-637-3770, fax 902-637-3867, e oldschool20@hotmail.com, w www.bmhs.ednet.ns.ca/tourism/oldschol.htm, Hwy 3) Singles/doubles $70/80. Open 7am-8pm Mon-Fri, 8am-8pm Sat & Sun May-Dec, 8am-3pm other months. This inn with a large sports bar and restaurant is in Barrington Passage, 5km from the Woollen Mill and 1½km east of the turnoff to Cape Sable Island. Good sandwiches ($3 to $5) and salads ($5) are offered, as well as more substantial meals ($8 to $16). The inn's 14 cottages provide a convenient base for exploring the area.

BARRINGTON TO YARMOUTH

Cape Sable Island and Pubnico were both once Acadian settlements, and each has a small general museum. Pubnico remains French and is considered the oldest non–First Nation village in Canada still lived in by the descendants of its founders.

Yarmouth to Windsor

This region of Nova Scotia stretches northward from Yarmouth and along the Bay of Fundy to Windsor and the Minas Basin. It consists, primarily, of two very distinct geographical and cultural regions.

The coast between Yarmouth and Digby was where many Acadians ended up after their deportation from the Annapolis Valley. The 'French Shore' and its history are still very much in evidence today.

The best-known area, however, is the scenic valley of the Annapolis River, which runs more or less from Digby to Wolfville. It's famous for apples, and in springtime the blossoming valley is at its most picturesque.

YARMOUTH

With a population of nearly 8000, Yarmouth is the largest town in western Nova Scotia. It's also a transportation hub, where ferries from Portland and Bar Harbor in Maine dock. Two tourist routes from Halifax, the Evangeline Trail through the Annapolis Valley and the Lighthouse Route through Lunenburg, also terminate here.

There's a huge provincial tourist office (☎ 902-742-5033) near the ferry docks with both local and provincial information available, along with a money exchange counter. They supply a walking-tour guide to the city with a map and some historical information. The office is open 8:30am to 5pm daily May to October, 8am to 9pm July and August.

The Yarmouth Public Library (☎ 902-742-2486), 405 Main St, provides free Internet access. It's open 10am to 9pm Monday to Friday, 10am to 5pm Saturday.

Yarmouth County Museum

The museum (☎ 902-742-5539, 22 Collins St, adult/family $2.50/5; open 9am-5pm Mon-Sat, 2pm-5pm Sun, June-mid-Oct, 2-5pm Tues-Sat mid-Oct-May) is in a gray stone building that was formerly a church. Most of the five period rooms have to do with the sea, displaying ship models and a large collection of paintings of sailing ships dating from the 1840s to 1910.

One of the highlights is a runic stone found near town in 1812, believed to have been carved by Víking Leif Eriksson some 1000 years ago. Other evidence has been discovered that suggests that the Vikings were indeed in this area, although many historians discount these claims.

Firefighters' Museum

This museum (☎ 902-742-5525, 431 Main St, adult/family $2.50/5; open 9am-4pm Mon-Fri, 1pm-4pm Sat year-round, 9am-5pm Mon-Sat, 10am-5pm Sun June-Aug) has a collection of beautiful fire engines dating from 1819 to 1935.

Yarmouth Light

The Yarmouth Light (☎ 902-742-1433, Hwy 304; admission free) is 12km from the ferry

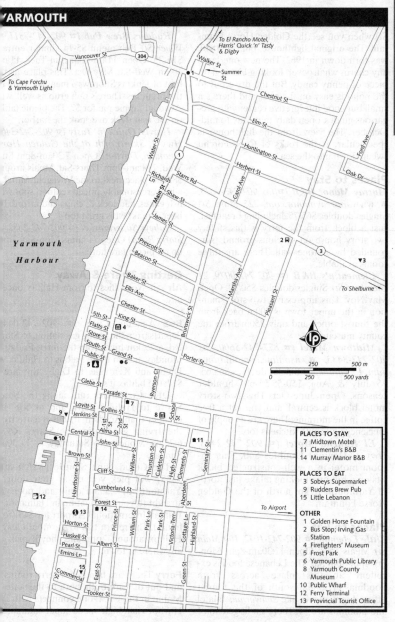

YARMOUTH

Vancouver St
304

To Cape Forchu
& Yarmouth Light

Yarmouth
Harbour

To El Rancho Motel,
Harris' Quick 'n' Tasty
& Digby

Walker St

Summer
St

1

Chestnut St

Elm St

Walter St

Huntington St

Herbert St

Ford Ave

Richards
Ln

Main St

Starrs Rd

Shaw St

Carol Ave

Oak Dr

James St

Prescott St

Beacon St

Baker St

Ellis Ave

Chester St

5th St
Flatts St
Store St
South St
Public St

King St

Grand St

Porter St

Marsha Ave

Pleasant St

Brunswick St

2

3

3

To Shelburne

Glebe St

Parade St

Collins St

1st St
2nd St

Ryerson Ct

7

8

School St

Lovitt St
Jenkins St

Central St

Brown St

John St

Cliff St

Alma St

Willow St

Thurston St

Carleton St

High St

Clements St

Seminary St

11

9

10

Hawthorne St

Cumberland St

Forest St

12

13

Horton St

Haskell St

Pearl St

Emins Ln

Commercial
St

15

East St

Tooker St

Albert St

Prince St

William St

Park Ln

Park St

Victoria Terr

Cottage Ln

Aberdeen St

Highland St

Green St

To Airport

14

0   250   500 m
0   250   500 yards

PLACES TO STAY
7 Midtown Motel
11 Clementin's B&B
14 Murray Manor B&B

PLACES TO EAT
3 Sobeys Supermarket
9 Rudders Brew Pub
15 Little Lebanon

OTHER
1 Golden Horse Fountain
2 Bus Stop; Irving Gas
   Station
4 Firefighters' Museum
5 Frost Park
6 Yarmouth Public Library
8 Yarmouth County
   Museum
10 Public Wharf
12 Ferry Terminal
13 Provincial Tourist Office

terminal at the end of Cape Forchu. From Main St, turn left on Hwy 304 (Vancouver St) when you see the Golden Horse Fountain. The original lighthouse, built in 1840, was torn down in 1962. The new one lacks any charm whatsoever, looking like a giant piece of penny candy. But the drive out to the point is easy on the eyes, and there's a small but good interpretive center with gregarious guides, open daily mid-May to mid-October. The view from the lighthouse is spectacular, as the rocks of Cape Forchu sweep down into the sea.

Places to Stay

Murray Manor B&B (*☎/fax 902-742-9625, [w] www.murraymanor.com, 225 Main St*) Singles/doubles $65/75, including breakfast. Just a block from the ferry is this stately two-story house on spacious grounds surrounded by a stone wall. There are three rooms available.

Clementin's B&B (*☎ 902-742-0079, 21 Clements St*) Singles/doubles $50/70. Open May-Nov. This impressive two-story mansion in the upper town is 700m back from the tourist office and only 250m from the county museum.

Midtown Motel (*☎ 877-742-5600, fax 902-742-3433, [w] nsonline.com/midtown .htm, 13 Parade St*) Singles/doubles $65/65-75 July & Aug, $50-55/55-60 shoulder seasons. Open June-Oct. This two-story motel block is central, and you get a free coffee in the morning. There are a couple of efficiency units with kitchens too.

El Rancho Motel (*☎ 902-742-2408, Hwy 1, Dayton*) Doubles $60. This 16-room motel in a well-constructed block sits on a hill overlooking a lake just north of Yarmouth, 1.7km north of the Golden Horse Fountain.

Places to Eat

Little Lebanon (*☎ 902-742-1042, 100 Main St*) Meals $5-7. Open 11:30am-8pm Mon-Fri, 4pm-8pm Sat. The Lebanese food is excellent at this place across from Foodmaster, 500m south of the tourist office. Light meals like *shawarma,* falafel and hummus are $4. There's a large choice of Lebanese entrees, and great desserts such as baklava or halva.

Rudders Brew Pub (*☎ 902-742-7311, 9 Water St*) Pub menu $5-14, dinner entrees $16-29. Open 11am-9pm Sun-Tues, 11am-10pm Wed-Sat May-Oct. This place at the foot of Jenkins St brews a mean ale right on the premises. There's pub grub as well, with Acadian rappie pie for $7. The picnic tables on the rear deck overlook the harbor.

Harris' Quick 'n' Tasty (*☎ 902-742-346 Hwy 1, 3km north of the Golden Horse Fountain, Dayton*) Open 7:30am-8pm Sun-Wed, 7:30am-9pm Thurs-Sat. Meals around $8. This place, next to the Voyageur Motel, a busy, reasonably priced seafood spot with fish cakes, haddock & chips and affordable beer. Breakfast is great too.

Sobeys Supermarket (*☎ 902-742-2882, 7 Starrs Road*) Open 24 hours Mon-Sat. Stock up on picnic fare here.

Getting There & Away

Air Air Nova flies to/from Halifax once day.

Bus Acadian Lines (*☎ 902-742-0440*) departs from the Irving gas station, 65 Starrs Rd, a 2½km hike from the ferry. Friday to Monday at 9am there's a bus to Halifax via Digby and Kentville. To Digby, the fare $17; to Halifax it's $52.

DRL Coachlines runs along the South Shore to Halifax daily, and at $38, it cheaper than Acadian. Its buses leave from the Irving gas station on Starrs Rd at 6:25am Monday to Saturday, at 11:30am Sunday.

The Cloud Nine Shuttle (*☎ 888-80. 3335*) will pick you up at your door in Yarmouth at 7:30am daily and take you straight to your destination in Halifax or Halifax International Airport for $45 (four hours). The return trip to Yarmouth leaves Halifax around 2pm, and they'll pick up anywhere in town.

Ferry There are two major ferry routes in and out of Yarmouth, both to the state of Maine in the USA; one connects with Bar Harbor via a high-speed super catamaran d the other connects with Portland. ares are high (for Canadians) because ey're based on US dollars, whereas mericans will comment on how cheap is cruise is for them. (The prices below ave been converted into Canadian ollars, but all fares listed in the company rochures are in US currency, a situation at isn't prominently noted in the rochures themselves.)

The Bay Ferries *Cat* (☎ 888-249-7245, fun.catferry.com) literally skates across e water in 2¾ hours to Bar Harbor; the 500 horsepower engines are truly incredi-le, as is the computerized ride-control stem. The *Cat* operates from late May rough mid-October. In July and August, vo trips a day zoom from Yarmouth, at pm and 8:45pm; the *Cat* leaves Bar Harbor t 8am and 4pm (except Wednesday after-oon). One-way fares are $85/77/39 adult/ enior/child under 13; for a day cruise, the ame fares apply. Small reductions are ffered in June and October. The fare for utomobiles is $146.

The other ferry is the *Scotia Prince,* oper-ted by Maine's Prince of Fundy Cruises ☎ 800-341-7540), and from early May to id-October, it sails back and forth to Port-nd, Maine, a journey of 320km. This is a opular trip, and for many it's as much a oliday cruise as simple ferry transporta-on. Quite a few people take the cruise ithout even bothering to leave the ship in ort. Like the Bar Harbor boat, the *Scotia rince* is well appointed and comfortable, ut the casino, complete with floor show, dds a touch of glamour.

Sailing time on the *Scotia Prince* is about 1 hours one way. Note that service is lmost every day, but there are quite a few lackout dates, so check in advance. hroughout the summer the ferry leaves armouth at 10am daily and Portland at pm daily. The basic fare is $132 from mid-une to mid-September, $102 other months, hildren under 15 half price (no senior ates). A vehicle is $162 from mid-June to id-September, otherwise $131. Monday to hursday from mid-June to mid-September pecial half-price standby vehicular fares

are offered. Bicycles are $11 to $15. Cabins range from $34 to $270 on top of the other charges, and you'll likely need to make advance reservations to get one. Americans often fly to Maine, rent a car and bring it to Nova Scotia on this ferry.

Call ahead for either trip, as vehicle reservations ($8 extra) will probably be nec-essary. Walk-on passengers should be OK any time. In Maine, a $5 departure tax is added to the prices listed above.

In Portland there's a Nova Scotia Tourist Office in the Portland Pier area, across from the old Thomas Block Building.

Getting Around

Yarmouth Airport is 3km east of downtown Yarmouth via Forest St. There's no airport bus. A taxi to or from the airport should cost $5, except for the special airport-approved taxi, which will be $8. Budget (☎ 902-742-9500) has a car rental desk, but it may be unstaffed unless someone has made a reser-vation.

DARLING LAKE

Three quite different lodging options are available in Darling Lake, 15km north of Yarmouth on Hwy 1.

Ice House Hostel (☎ 902-649-2818, 44 *Old Post Rd, Darling Lake)* Dorm beds $12. Open May-Oct. This hostel behind the Churchill Mansion Country Inn (and run by the same folks) is an old standby. It was indeed the ice house of the adjacent mansion. There are only four beds, and fa-cilities include a kitchen and shower.

Churchill Mansion Country Inn (☎ 902-649-2818, fax 902-649-2801 **w** *www.trico.ns .ca/vacation/mansion.html, off Hwy 1 in Darling Lake)* Rooms $44-140. Open May-Oct. Across the highway from Lake Breezes Campground, this magnificent Victorian country manor was built in the 1890s as a summer home for shipping magnate Aaron Flint Churchill. You can now sleep in the master bedroom with a private balcony overlooking Darling Lake. The nightly seafood buffet is good value at $13, and a full breakfast is $6. The old-world atmos-phere is a real treat.

Lake Breeze Campground & Cottages (☎ *902-649-2332, 2000 Hwy 1, Darling Lake)* Unserviced/serviced sites $15/18-20. Open mid-May-mid-Oct. Cabins $50-100. Lake Breeze is the first decent campground north of Yarmouth on Hwy 1. The serviced RV sites on the hill are gravel surfaced, but grassy tent sites are available down by the lake. Five cabins at the entrance face Darling Lake. A duplex unit will be $50 for up to four people; the three larger units with cooking are $80/90/100 for 3/5/7 people. Canoe and rowboat rentals are $5/10 an hour/day.

FRENCH SHORE

The area stretching roughly from Salmon River up the coast along St Mary's Bay toward Digby is Old Acadia, also known as the Municipality of Clare. This is where the province's largest, mainly French-speaking Acadian population lives. It's an interesting region where traditional foods and crafts are available, several historic sites can be visited and, in summer, festivals are held in some of the small villages. Because the towns are small, a visit to the area can be done quite quickly.

Among the best crafts available along the way, both in shops and private homes, are the quilts and the wood carvings, both of which have earned good reputations.

Cape St Mary

A long wide arch of fine sand, just 900m off Hwy 1, the **Mavillette Beach** is marvelous. The marsh behind the beach is good for bird watching.

Cape View Motel (☎ *902-645-2258, fax 902-645-3999,* W *nsonline.com/capeview/ index.html, off Hwy 1)* Rooms from $66. Open mid-May-early Oct. This motel just above Mavillette Beach has both regular motel rooms and self-contained cottages.

Cape View Restaurant (☎ *902-645-2519)* Dinner mains $10-18. Open 11am-8pm May-Oct; 10am-10pm July & Aug. Across the street from the motel (but under separate ownership), this place serves mainly seafood – clams are a local speciality – but also available is rappie pie ($6.50), an old

Acadian dish (for details see Church Point The beach looks great at sunset from here

Meteghan

This is a busy fishing port, and there is large commercial wharf where the boat moor. On the main street is **La Vieill Maison** (☎ *902-645-2389, 8312 Hwy Meteghan; admission free; open 11am-3p Mon-Fri June-Sept; 9am-7pm Mon-Fr 10am-6pm Sat & Sun July & Aug)*, built 1797 and one of the oldest houses in th region. It's now set up as a museum depic ing Acadian life during the 18th century. also doubles as a tourist office.

Places to Stay & Eat *Anchor Inn* (☎ *90. 645-3390,* e *anchorinnbb@hotmail.com 8755 Hwy 1)* Singles/doubles $35/45. Ope mid-May-Sept. Opposite the Esso ga station on the north side of town, this old fashioned country inn with a row of chair along the front porch rents three shared bath rooms.

Bluefin Motel (☎ *888-446-3466, fax 902 645-3003,* W *bluefinmotel.ns.ca, on Hwy 2km south of Meteghan)* Singles/double $49/59. This motel at the south entrance t Meteghan has 19 rooms in an L-shape block. It's just 500m north of Smuggler Cove, a picnic park with a pebble beach.

Seashore Restaurant (☎ *902-645-345. 8467 Hwy 1)* Meals $9. You can get loc. seafood specialities here. Otherwise, hea to the ***fish market*** near the quay for gril your-own.

Comeau's Farm Market (☎ *902-645 2342, 8711 Hwy 1; open 8am-9pm Mon-Sa 9am-9pm daily mid-Apr-Dec)* This larg store on the north side of town sells all sor of local delicacies.

Church Point (Pointe de l'Église)

The Église Sainte Marie (☎ *902-769-2808 Hwy 1; admission $2; open 9am-5pm dail mid-May-mid-Oct)* towers over the tow and most other churches too. Built betwee 1903 and 1905, it is said to be the tallest an biggest wooden church in North Americ Near the altar is a reliquary with a fragmen of the True Cross and a piece of the skull c

St Anne. The small museum in the corner by the altar contains articles from the church's history, including various vestments and chalices. A guide will show you around and answer any questions.

Adjacent is the **Université Sainte Anne**, the only French university in the province and a center for Acadian culture. Between 200 and 300 students attend classes here.

The oldest of the annual Acadian cultural festivals, Festival Acadien de Clare, is held during the second week of July. In July and August the musical *Évangéline* is presented every Tuesday and Saturday at 8pm in the **Théâtre Marc-Lescarbot** (☎ 902-769-2114) at Church Point.

Places to Stay & Eat *Belle Baie Park* (☎ 902-769-3160, fax 902-769-0065, ⓦ www .bellebaiepark.com, off Hwy 1) Unserviced/ serviced sites $18/27. Open late May-Sept. At this park just north of town, the six best sites along the shore are reserved for tenters. The rest of the campground is row upon row of RVs.

Rapure Acadienne (☎ 902-769-2172, 1443 Hwy 1) Large rappie pie for two people $6. Open 8am-5:30pm Sept-June, 8am-9pm July & Aug. A bit over a kilometer south of the church toward Yarmouth is this place with an Acadian flag outside where all the local establishments get their rappie pie *(paté à la rapure)*. Inside, several women are always busy preparing the three varieties: beef, chicken or clam. The result is difficult to describe, but it's a type of meat pie topped with grated paste-like potato from which all the starch has been drawn. They are bland, filling and inexpensive and can be bought piping hot. Weather permitting, there's a picnic table under a tree beside the building where you can gorge on rappie pie.

Belliveau Cove

Roadside Grill (☎ 902-837-5047, 3334 Hwy 1) Dishes $6-12. Open 9am-7pm daily year-round; 8am-9pm July & Aug. This pleasantly old-fashioned and comfortable local restaurant/diner has sandwiches ($3.50) and light foods but also lots of seafood – try the steamed clams ($7 to $12), a local speciality,

or the rappie pie ($5 to $7). All prices include tax. Roadside Grill rents three small cabins with fridge and microwave for $45 single or double. These unheated cabins, located behind the restaurant, are only rented from June to mid-October.

St Bernard

Here the grandest of the coast's stone churches stands – a mammoth granite Gothic-style monument that took 32 years to complete, beginning in 1910. From June to September classical music concerts are presented in St Bernard Church (☎ 902-638-8288, adult/student or senior $12/10) some Sundays at 4pm.

DIGBY

An old, attractive town with some 2200 residents, Digby was built around a hill in the Annapolis Basin, an inlet of the Bay of Fundy. It's famous for its scallop fleet and busy as the terminus for the *Princess of Acadia* ferry, which plies the waters between Digby and Saint John, New Brunswick. The town is also well known for its 'Digby chicks,' a pungent type of salty smoked herring sold at fish markets but not available in restaurants. The huge circular enclosures in the sea near the Digby ferry dock are commercial salmon farms.

The town was founded by United Empire Loyalists in 1783, and ever since then its life has centered around fishing. Up Mount St from Water St is Trinity Anglican Church and its accompanying graveyard. A couple of blocks away on Warwick St, at the south edge of downtown , is the old Loyalist cemetery (1783).

From the ferry landing, it's about 5km to Water St in downtown Digby. Water St is the main tourist draw in town; it becomes Montague Row near the tourist office.

Information

At 110 Montague Row in the center of town is the local tourist office (☎ 888-463-4429), open from mid-May to mid-October.

Along Shore Road 2½km from the ferry terminal is the much larger provincial tourist office (☎ 902-245-2201), which has information about Digby and all of Nova Scotia. It is open from 8am to 8:30pm daily May to mid-November. There's a great view of the Annapolis Basin from the parking lot opposite this tourist office.

The Western Counties Regional Library (☎ 902-245-2163), 84 Warwick St opposite the general hospital, offers Internet access. The library is open 12:30pm to 4:30pm and 6pm to 8pm Tuesday to Friday, 10am to 2pm Saturday.

Admiral Digby Museum

This small museum (☎ 902-245-6322, 95 Montague Row; adult/child $2/free; open 9am-5pm Tues-Sat, 1pm-5pm Sun June-Aug; 9am-5pm Tues-Fri Sept-mid-Oct; 9am-5pm Wed & Fri mid-Oct-May) displays articles and photographs pertaining to the town's marine history and early settlement.

At 26 Water St toward the wharf is the Lady Vanessa, an old scallop trawler that you can board and tour from June to September for $2.

Activities

For sport fishing try **Basin Charters** (☎ 902-245-8446, w www.basincharters.com, 89 Water St; open June-mid-Sept), which operates out of a tiny kiosk in the center of town. They charge $45 for four hours of fishing for cod, haddock, halibut, mackerel and pollock, starting at 8am or 5pm. At 1:30pm they run a three-hour nature tour in search of seals, seabirds and whales ($25).

Backstreet Bicycles (☎ 902-245-1989, 151 Hwy 303) is a full-service bicycle shop operating out of the basement of the Digby Venture Centre near the huge Canadian Tire Store on the way into town on Hwy 303 from Hwy 101. They rent bicycles at $25/125 per day/week and also do repairs.

Places to Stay

Digby Campground (☎ 902-245-1985, fax 902-245-1985, w www.angelfire.com/biz2/DigbyCamping, 236 Victoria St) Unserviced/serviced sites $15/18-23, overnight shelters $20. Open mid-May-mid-Oct. This campground is strategically situated between the roads to downtown Digby and Digby Neck,

4km from the Saint John ferry. Five overnight shelters are available, each holding three adults or a family of four. Basically these are just large tents, already set up, with a door and two plywood platforms (you must supply all your own bedding), but it saves you the trouble of pitching a tent and protects you from mosquitoes and the rain.

Westway House (☎ 902-245-5071, fax 902-245-5071, 6 Carlton St) Singles/doubles $40/53 shared bath, $50/54 private bath. Open mid-May-mid-Oct. This B&B on a quiet street is within walking distance of things to see. There's an outdoor barbecue.

Mary's Waterfront B&B (☎ 902-245-4949, 34 Carleton St) Singles/doubles $40/55. Open mid-June-mid-Sept. This attractive bungalow with two rooms is near downtown.

Bayside Inn (☎ 888-754-0555, w www3.ns.sympatico.ca/bayside, 115 Montague Row) Singles/doubles/triples $50/69/84, breakfast included. This renovated three-story building is opposite a park right on the Digby waterfront. The 11 rooms have private bath and TV, and there's a lounge for guests.

Thistle Down Country Inn (☎ 800-565-8081, fax 902-245-6717, w www.thistledown.ns.ca/theinn, 98 Montague Row) Rooms $85-120 including full breakfast. Open May-Oct. This inn opposite the Admiral Digby Museum has six historic rooms with private bath in the main house. The two-story motel block at the rear has another six rooms with balconies providing perfect harbor views.

Siesta Motel (☎ 902-245-2568, fax 902-245-2560, e siesta@valleyweb.com, w www.valleyweb.com/siesta, 81 Montague Row) Doubles from $53. Adjacent to the Irving gas station where the Acadian Lines buses arrive, the 15 rooms at Siesta Motel are in an L-shaped block.

Pines Resort (☎ 800-667-4637, fax 902-245-6133, e pines@gov.ns.ca, w www.signatureresorts.com, Shore Rd, 2km east of the ferry terminal toward Digby) Singles/doubles $145/160, cottages $290/300. Open May-Oct. This grand hotel erected in 1929

caters to every whim. The resort's golf course charges green fees of $27/50 for 9/18 holes.

Places to Eat

Fundy Restaurant (☎ 902-245-4950, 34 Water St) Dinner $16-20. Open 7am-10pm daily May-Nov; 11am-7pm Dec-Apr. This place is pricey but does have two outdoor balconies providing views over the harbor area. The main dining room upstairs specializes in seafood such as Digby scallops ($18), scallop stir-fry ($17) and lobster ($20). Fundy Dockside downstairs is more informal.

Kaywin Restaurant (☎ 902-245-5543, 51 Water St) Mains $7-10. Open 11am-10pm Mon-Fri, noon-10pm Sat, noon-9pm Sun. This is a cheaper place to sample the local scallops ($13), haddock ($10) and clams ($12.50). Chinese combos are under $8, and there's a $10 Chinese buffet 5pm to 7pm Friday to Sunday.

Red Raven Pub (☎ 902-245-5533, 100 Water St) Dinner $8-16. Open 11am-9pm daily May-mid-Oct. Better known as a drinking establishment, you can also order fish & chips ($8), clams & chips ($13) and scallop supreme ($16) on their outdoor patio overlooking the wharf.

Royal Fundy Fish Market (☎ 902-245-5411, on Prince William St by the docks) Open 10am-6pm Mon-Sat May-mid-Oct; 9am-9pm daily July & Aug. Half restaurant, half market, the Royal Fundy has Digby's best selection of fresh seafood. If you're camping or have cooking facilities at your motel, a bag of fresh scallops ($10 a pound) can make a remarkably delicious dinner. You can also get the scallops precooked, if you prefer.

Digby chicks, the heavily smoked herring for which the town is well known, will last up to two weeks and usually cost $1 each. There are also tables at the Royal Fundy, where you can order scallops, shrimp or clams & chips for $10, or fish & chips for $7.50. It's the best deal in town.

Sobeys Supermarket (☎ 902-245-6183, Hwy 303 near Victoria St) Open 8am-10pm Mon-Sat. Get your picnic fare here.

Entertainment

Fundy Dockside (☎ 902-245-4950, 34 Water St) This upscale pub downstairs at the Fundy Restaurant presents live music (blues, rock, folk etc) Friday and Saturday nights. *Club 98* upstairs is a glitzy disco with a DJ. It's open 10pm to 2am Wednesday to Saturday. Both places charge $3 admission.

Red Raven Pub (☎ 902-245-5533, 100 Water St) Local bands often play in this lively tavern on weekend evenings.

Getting There & Away

Acadian Lines buses stop at the Irving gas station (☎ 902-245-2048), 77 Montague Row at Warwick St, a short walk from the center of town but 6km from the ferry. There's a bus to Halifax ($38) at 10:45am daily; Thursday to Sunday there's one to Yarmouth ($17) at 10:35pm.

Bay Ferries (☎ 902-245-2116, 888-249-7245, ⓦ www.nfl-bay.com) operates year-round between Digby and Saint John, New Brunswick, with three trips daily from late June to early October, except Sunday when there are only two. Summer departure times are 5am, 1pm and 8:45pm (no 5am trip on Sunday). The crossing takes a little more than 2½ hours. Prices are steep – $35 per adult passenger and $70 per car, with bicycles an extra $25. Vehicle reservations ($5 extra) are a good idea for this trip, and you should arrive at the dock an hour before departure.

DIGBY NECK

The long, thin strip of land that protrudes into the Bay of Fundy from just north of town is known as Digby Neck. It's visible from much of the French Shore. At the far western end are Long and Brier Islands, two sections of the peninsula that have become separated from the main arm. Short ferry rides connect them, and a road links Westport (on Brier Island, at the far end) to Digby.

Whale Watching

What draws most people to the area is the sea life off Long and Brier Islands. From June to October whale- and bird-watching boat cruises run from East Ferry, Tiverton and Westport. It's a good location for whale watching; the season is relatively long, beginning in May, building up in June and remaining steady through August, with good populations of finback, minke and humpback whales, as well as dolphins, porpoises and seals. The whale-watching trips here are the best and most successful in Nova Scotia.

There are now more than half a dozen operators who run whale-watching tours, with more surely to come. Still, reservations are a good idea and can be made by phone (credit card required). Many places will give you 10% off if you're a senior or have a CAA/AAA or student card.

In East Ferry, **Petite Passage Whale Watch** (*☎ 902-834-2226, www.ppww.tsx.org, 3450 Hwy 217; 3-hour trip $38.50; open June-Sept*) operates out of a store just above the ferry landing.

In Tiverton, **Ocean Explorations** (*☎ 902-839-2417, Ⓦ www.oceanexplorations.ns.ca, 3395 Hwy 217, 100m to left of Tiverton ferry; half-day trip $45; open June-mid-Oct*) uses inflatable ocean-going Zodiacs, which being small, allow for exhilaratingly close encounters and smaller-sized tour groups. If the weather is bad, you can still take a seal-watching trip.

Pirate's Cove Whale Cruises (*☎ 902-839-2242, 3305 Hwy 217 near Tiverton post office; 3-4-hour trip $37; open June-mid-Oct*) uses a 13m vessel and offers at least two cruises daily.

In Freeport, there's **Whale & Seabird Tours** (*☎ 902-839-2177*), based at Lavena's Catch Café. Their 3½-hour tours run from mid-June to September and cost $28/25/15 per adult/senior/child.

In Westport, **Mariner Cruises** (*☎ 902-839-2346, Ⓦ www.marinercruises.ns.ca; adult/child $35/17.50; open mid-June-mid-Oct*) has a booking office just to the left of the ferry, but you board the boat 1km farther down the waterfront. Their trips can last anywhere from 2½ to five hours depending on where the whales are.

Brier Island Whale & Seabird Cruises (*☎ 902-839-2995, 800-656-3660, Westport; 4-hour tour $40*) runs five trips daily in July and August. In May, June and September they may operate only once a day, but in midseason they're often fully booked. Their office is below Brier Island Backpackers, 700m to the left as you leave the ferry.

Passengers should bring along plenty of warm clothing (regardless of how hot a day it is), sunblock, and binoculars if possible. A motion sickness pill taken before leaving the dock may not be a bad idea, either.

Tiverton

It's almost 18km between the Tiverton and Freeport ferry landings along the length of Long Island. Tiverton is a small village with a couple of whale-watching operations and a local fishing community. The **Island Museum** (*☎ 902-839-2853, 3083 Hwy 217; admission free; open 9:30am-4:30pm daily late May-mid-Oct; 9:30am-7:30pm July & Aug*), 2km west of the Tiverton ferry, also contains a tourist information desk.

The most interesting sight on Long Island is **Balancing Rock**. The trailhead is well posted along Hwy 217, 2km southwest of the Island Museum (entry by donation). The walk is close to 4km roundtrip along a trail that includes rope railings, boardwalks and an extensive series of steps down a rock bluff to the bay. (Be aware that these steps can get very slippery.) At the end there's a viewing platform that puts you within 15m of this 7m-high stone column perched precariously on the edge of a ledge just above the pounding surf of St Mary's Bay. It's such a striking sight that for years fishers have used it as a landmark to return to port.

Near the center of Long Island is **Central Grove Provincial Park**, which offers a 1km iking trail to the Bay of Fundy (2km oundtrip). This trail is not very well nown, so it won't be as crowded as others n midsummer.

Freeport

Freeport is a small fishing community most isitors drive straight through on their way o Westport. However, it offers the camping acilities that Brier Island lacks, and there's a cafe near the wharf that's worth coming back to.

Long Island Campground (☎ 902-839-327, fax 902-839-2327, 524 Hwy 217) Sites 12/15 tents/RVs. Open mid-June-mid-Sept. This campground on Hwy 217, 2½km before the Freetown ferry, has 15 sites in an open field with no shade.

Sunset Over the Bay B&B (☎ 902-839-2293, e sunset@tartannet.ns.ca, 375 Hwy 217, Freeport) Singles/doubles $50/60. Open May-Sept. This new bungalow on a hill, 2km from the Freeport ferry, has three rooms and good sea views.

Lavena's Catch Café (☎ 902-839-2517, 15 Hwy 217, Freeport) Mains $7-10. Open 9am-8pm daily mid-May-early Oct; 9am-11pm July & Aug; 11am-8pm Fri-Sun early Oct-mid-Dec. The terrace at this casual restaurant directly above the wharf at Freeport offers the best sunset views on Digby Neck. If you're staying in Westport, take the ferry over for dinner (foot passengers travel free). Lavena's Catch serves fresh seafood, such as haddock burgers ($4), scallop rolls ($5) and the haddock/scallop sampler ($7). Dinner entrees include haddock ($8) and Digby scallops ($10). Their food is all pan-fried (not deep-fried). Whale watching can be arranged, and Internet access is on a donation basis.

Westport

Brier Island has the best selection of places to stay and eat, the most whale watching cruises, the finest scenery and the longest hiking trails on Digby Neck. Westport is a quaint little fishing village still relatively unspoiled by tourism.

The tidal flows in Grand Passage between Brier and Long islands are ex-

tremely strong. Three lighthouses are on Brier Island, as well as numerous excellent, if rugged, walking trails. Columnar basalt rocks are seen all along the coast, and agates can be found on the beaches. There are countless seabirds.

Places to Stay & Eat *Brier Island Backpackers Hostel* (☎ 902-839-2273, fax 902-839-2410, e backpackers@brierislandhostel .com, w www.brierislandhostel.com, 223 Water St, Westport) Beds $12. To get there, turn left as you come off the ferry at Westport and go 700m along the waterfront to RE Robicheau Store. Above a gift shop, there are 18 brand-new beds (including one double), antiseptic washrooms, a full kitchen, an adjacent Laundromat and even Internet access in the lobby. This comfortable hostel is run by a friendly Dutchman and his wife, who's a local. They also run the large grocery store next door. It's open year-round and is one of Canada's top hostels.

Dock and Doze Motel (☎ 902-839-2601, fax 902-839-2601, e ptitus@tartannet.ns.ca, w www.canadianinnsite.com/000368.html, Westport) Doubles $60 ($10 extra with kitchen). Open May-Oct. Directly opposite the ferry landing at Westport, just to the right as you get off, are these three units – two downstairs and one above.

Westport Inn (☎ 902-839-2675, fax 902-839-2245, Westport) Singles/doubles $50/55. Open May-Oct. This place is 300m from the ferry, to the right as you get off, then left up the hill. The three rooms above the restaurant are available year-round, but the restaurant is only open mid-May to September. The restaurant serves up good home-cooked meals like fish & chips or pork chops ($11), scallops scampi ($14), a seafood platter ($19) and many other choices.

D&D Grill (☎ 902-839-2883, Westport) Mains $8-10. Open 10am-8pm May-mid-Oct, 7am-11pm July & Aug. This small lunch counter between the ferry and the hostel serves a full breakfast ($5.50), fish & chips ($8.50), clams & fries ($10) and burgers ($3 to $5).

Getting There & Away

Two ferries connect Long and Brier Islands to the rest of Digby Neck. The Petit Passage ferry leaves East Ferry on the half hour and Tiverton on the hour; they are timed so that if you drive directly from Tiverton to Freeport there is no wait for the Grand Passage ferry to Westport. The Grand Passage ferry leaves Freeport on the hour and Westport at 25 minutes after the hour.

Both ferries operate 24 hours a day year-round. In midsummer, when the traffic is heavy, the ferries run almost continuously. Return passage on each of the ferries is $3 for a car and all passengers. Pedestrians ride free.

If you've booked a whale-watching trip at Westport, you need to allow a minimum of 90 minutes to drive there from Digby, longer if you want to play it safe.

There's no public transportation along Digby Neck, so either you'll need a car or you'll have to hitchhike.

BEAR RIVER

Bear River, inland from Digby, 6km off Hwy 101 at exit 24, is a rather funky little village in the picturesque valley of the tidal Bear River. The visitor information center (☎ 902-467-3200) is in a replica Dutch windmill by the river. It's open 9am to 5pm daily mid-June to early October.

Things to See & Do

Behind the tourist office is the **Bear River Solar Aquatics Sewage Treatment Plant**, the first nonchemical sewage treatment plant of its kind in Canada. Built in 1995, the Solar Aquatics greenhouse (☎ 902-584-2188, **W** www.annapoliscounty.ns.ca) contains green leaf flora and insects used to treat the sewage. Panels around the outside of the building explain the process, and the visitor center shows a seven-minute video upon request.

Also worth a visit are the **Bear River Heritage Museum** (☎ 902-467-0902, 1890 Clementsvale Rd; admission by donation; open 10am-5pm Mon-Sat, 1pm-4pm Sun July & Aug) in the former Oldfellows Hall (1921), and the **Oakdene Centre** (☎ 902-467-3939, 1913 Clementsvale Rd; admission free), a pottery and crafts workshop. Both are on the main street in the center of the village.

Bear River First Nation

A visit to this Mi'kmaq reserve, 1½km south of the village, is worth the drive if you have time. Take the road that passes the fire department and up the hill to the left. **St Anne's Church** on the reserve dates back to 1831, and an Indian graveyard surrounds this Catholic church. **Beartown Baskets** (☎ 902-467-3060), 500m farther up the road sells handmade Indian baskets.

Places to Stay & Eat

Bear River Backpackers Hostel (☎ 902-467-0338, **e** brbackpackers@yahoo.ca, 11 Chute Rd) Dorm beds $16, private rooms $33. Open mid-May-Aug (and other months by chance if the owner happens to be present). This century-old farmhouse on a hill a kilometer north of the village has two three-bed dorms and a couple of private rooms with shared bath. There's communal cooking and a congenial atmosphere.

By the Brook B&B (☎ 902-467-3601, 1894 Clementsvale Rd) Singles/doubles $45/50. Open mid-May-Oct. Four rooms are available in this three-story Victorian edifice next to the museum.

Lovett Lodge B&B (☎ 902-467-3917, 1820 Lansdowne Rd) Singles/doubles from $42/51. Open mid-May-Oct. This quaint Victorian mansion (1892) up the hill from the post office is very atmospheric. Gays are welcome.

Rivers End Restaurant (☎ 902-467-0367, 1836 Lansdowne Rd) Mains $7-8. Open 7am-9pm July & Aug, 8am-8pm Sept-June. This country-style restaurant between the post office and Lovett Lodge serves breakfast for $4 to $6. For lunch try a large bowl of chowder ($4). Dinner choices include fish & chips ($4 to $7), clams ($7) and scallops ($8).

KEJIMKUJIK NATIONAL PARK

This park, located well away from the tourist areas of the coast, contains some of the province's most pristine wilderness and best backcountry adventures. Less than 20% of Kejimkujik's 381 sq km is accessible by car; the rest is reached either on foot or by paddle. Canoeing, in particular, is an ideal way to explore this area of glacial lakes and rolling hills, and the park is well set up for extended overnight paddles. Portage routes are well marked, and the main lake, Kejimkujik, features red navigational buoys and many primitive campsites on its islands.

Kejimkujik is 46km south of Annapolis Royal via Hwy 8. The visitor and interpretive center (☎ 902-682-2772, fax 902-682-3367, Hwy 8), where you can reserve backcountry sites and purchase maps and books, is at the main entrance, just south of Maitland Bridge. Ask about the Atlantic Pass, which allows entry to seven national parks in eastern Canada for the entire season. The visitor center is open 8:30am to 8pm daily mid-June to early September, 8:30am to 4:30pm Monday to Friday the rest of the year. The park's entrance fee is $3.25/2.50/7.50/1.75 per adult/senior/family/child for a daily pass, $9.75/7.50/22.50/5.25 for a four-day pass.

Hiking & Canoeing

There are more than 40 backcountry campsites scattered along the trails and among the lakes of Kejimkujik. The main hiking loop is a 60km trek that begins at the east end of Peskowesk Lake and ends at the Big Dam Lake trailhead. Most backpackers take three to four days to cover it, with September and early October being the prime

time for such an adventure. A shorter loop, ideal for an overnight trek, is the 26km Channel Lake Trail that begins and ends at Big Dam Lake. The Hemlocks and Hardwood Trail is the best day hike in the park.

The park also features more than a dozen lakes connected by a system of portages for flat-water paddling. Extended trips of up to seven days are possible in Kejimkujik, with portages ranging from a few meters to 2.4km in length.

Only backcountry campsites are available, and you should book them in advance by calling or stopping at the visitors center (☎ 902-682-2772). The sites are a hefty $16.25 per night plus a $4.25 reservation fee for each backcountry trip; there's a 14-day maximum, and no more than two nights in any site. Purchasing a topographical map ($5) is a good idea.

Canoes can be rented in the park at **Jakes Landing** *(☎ 902-682-2196, 8km from park entrance, open 8am-9pm daily July & Aug, 10am-6pm Mon-Thurs, 9am-7:30pm mid-May-mid-Oct; canoes $5/24/100 per hour/day/week, bicycles $24 per day)*.

You can also rent canoes at **Loon Lake Outfitters** *(☎ 902-682-2220, 902-682-2290, Hwy 8; canoes $20/100 per day/week)*, just north of the park entrance. Loon Lake also rents tents at $6 to $13 per day, depending on size. Canoe packs, stoves and other such gear can be rented at $4 per day, and a bicycle will cost you $20.

Places to Stay

Jeremy's Bay Campground (☎ 902-682-2772, ⓦ parkscanada.pch.gc.ca/keji) Sites

$14. Open year-round. Park entry fees do not include camping fees. Kejimkujik National Park has a huge campground of 360 campsites at Jeremy's Bay, including a handful of walk-in campsites near the shoreline for those who want to put a little distance between themselves and the ubiquitous RV with their generators and radios.

You can reserve a site in advance at Jeremy's Bay for an additional $7.50 fee by calling ☎ 800-414-6765 at least three days in advance, but you cannot request a specific site – you have to accept whatever is available when you arrive. Thirty percent of the sites at Jeremy's Bay cannot be booked over the phone and are assigned on a first-come, first-served basis; however, all of those will typically be taken by midafternoon Friday on any midsummer weekend.

If you have only a tent and are willing to walk three or four minutes from your car, it's possible to specifically book backcountry sites Nos A, B and D on Big Dam Lake over the phone for the usual backcountry fees ($16.25 a night, plus the $4.25 reservation fee). These three sites are secluded and perfect for nature lovers.

Whitman Inn (☎ 800-830-3855, fax 902-682-3171, e info@whitmaninn.com, w www.whitmaninn.com, 12389 Hwy 8) Singles/doubles from $55/60. Four kilometres south of the park in Caledonia is this comfortable place for noncampers. It's a restored late-19th/early-20th-century house that has an indoor swimming pool, saunas – the works – yet the simplest of the rooms are moderately priced. All meals are available.

Mersey River Chalets (☎ 902-682-2443, fax 902-682-2332, e mersey_river@bigfoot.com, w www.merseyriverchalets.ns.ca, off Hwy 8, 5km north of the national park, then 1.7km down a gravel road to a lake) Tepees $40/70 single/double July & Aug, $30/50 Apr-June, Sept & Oct. Closed Nov-March. Mersey River is an upscale resort specially designed for physically challenged persons. The chalets are pricey, but there's also a cluster of five large canvas tepees on wooden platforms with proper beds, right beside the lake. The toilets and showers are in the restaurant a few minutes away, but a shared kitchen/lounge for guests is part of the tepee complex. Use of canoes and kayaks is included in the price, and the location is lovely, with lots of paddling possibilities. The kayaks, like everything else here, are handicapped accessible; a special frame helps disabled guests get on and off. There are also special hand-powered bikes (free) and a recreational swing one can just roll into. Many of the staff speak German.

Raven Haven Hostel & Family Park (☎ 902-532-7320, fax 902-532-2096, e rec@annapoliscounty.ns.ca, w www.annapoliscounty.ns.ca, 2239 Virginia Rd, 2km off Hwy 8, near South Milford) Beds $14/16 members/nonmembers. Open mid-June-early Sept. Raven Haven is 25km south of Annapolis Royal and 27km north of the national park: From exit 22 on Hwy 101, go 17km south to Maitland, then right 2km on Virginia Rd. This community-run HI hostel is a unique combination of hostel and small family campground right on Sandy Bottom Lake. The hostel is in a cabin near the beach. There's an inexpensive canteen , five serviced RV sites ($16) and six tent sites nicely ensconced in the forest ($14). The six-bed hostel has a kitchen. It's a scenic location, and you can rent a canoe for $4/25 per hour/day.

ANNAPOLIS VALLEY

The Evangeline Trail through the valley via Hwy 1 is really not as scenic as might be expected, although it does pass through or by all the major towns and historic sites. To really see the valley and get into the countryside it's necessary to take the smaller roads parallel to Hwy 1. From these the farms and orchards, generally hidden from the main roads, come into view.

For those seeking a little work in late summer there are usually jobs available picking apples. Check in valley towns such as Bridgetown, Lawrencetown and Middleton. Line things up a couple of weeks before picking time if you can. MacIntosh apples arrive first, at the end of August, but the main season begins around the first week of September.

Annapolis Royal

Known as Canada's oldest settlement, Annapolis Royal is a picture-postcard place and one of the valley's prime attractions, with many historic sites and great places to stay and eat.

The site of Canada's first permanent European settlement, founded by Samuel de Champlain in 1605, is actually out of town at nearby Granville Ferry. As the British and French battled over the years for control of the valley and the land at the mouth of the Annapolis River, the settlement often changed hands. In 1710, the British won a decisive victory and changed the town's name from Port Royal to Annapolis Royal (in honor of Queen Anne).

Despite the town's great age (in Canadian terms), the permanent population is under 600, so it's quite a small community and easy to get around. It's a busy place in summer, with most activities and points of interest located on or near the long, curving St George St. There is a waterfront boardwalk behind King's Theatre on St George St, with views over to the village of Granville Ferry.

A farmers' market is held every Saturday morning from mid-May to mid-October, also Wednesday afternoon in July and August. Daily guided walking tours are given during the summer by the local historical society.

A Nova Scotia Tourism Information Centre (☎ 902-532-5769) is at the Tidal Power Project site by the Annapolis River Causeway. It's open mid-May to mid-October. Pick up a copy of the historic walking-tour pamphlet.

Fort Anne National Historic Site Right in the center of town, this park preserves the memory of the early Acadian settlement plus the remains of the French fort (1635), where the mounds and moats are still intact. An eight-room museum (☎ 902-532-2397, off Upper St George St; admission $2.75; open 9am-6pm daily May-mid-Oct) has replicas of various period rooms, artifacts, uniforms and weapons; the Acadian room was transferred here from an old homestead, and the four-panel tapestry is extraordinary. The admission fee is required for the museum, but entry to the extensive grounds is free.

If you're around on a Tuesday, Thursday or Sunday at 9:30pm from June to mid-September, join the fort's special Candlelight Tour of the Garrison Graveyard. Your park guide will be dressed in black, sporting an undertaker's top hat and cape, and everybody on the tour is given a candle lantern. Then you all troop through the graveyard, viewing the headstones in the eerie light and hearing tales of horror and death. The tour is $5 per person and very entertaining.

Lower St George Street St George St contains many historic buildings, with three different centuries represented. The **O'Dell Inn Museum** (☎ 902-532-7754, 136 Lower St George St; admission $2; open 10am-noon & 1pm-4pm Mon-Fri year-round, 8:30-5pm Mon-Sat, 1pm-5pm Sun July & Aug) is a mock-up of a Victorian tavern and former stagecoach stop. The **Sinclair House Inn** (☎ 902-532-7754, 220 St George St; admission free; open 10am-4pm Mon-Sat, 1pm-4pm Sun mid-June-Aug) is the former Farmer's Hotel (1710), one of the oldest buildings in English-speaking Canada. The displays deal with local history.

Design Fort Computer Museum This unexpected museum (☎ 902-532-2546, ⓦ www.computermuseum.20m.com, 302 St George St; admission free; open 9am-7pm Mon-Sat, 1pm-5pm Sun June-mid-Sept, 9am-5pm Mon-Sat rest of year), inside Emin's Store next to the Fort Anne Café, has a collection of rare vintage computers assembled by renowned Web master Herbert Eisengruber.

Historic Gardens Numerous distinct types of gardens, including Acadian and Victorian, are displayed on these green 400-hectare grounds (☎ 902-532-7018, 441 St George St; adult/child $6/5; open daily mid-May-early Oct), beyond Prince Albert Rd. There's an interpretive building, a restaurant, a gift shop and, adjacent, a bird sanctuary.

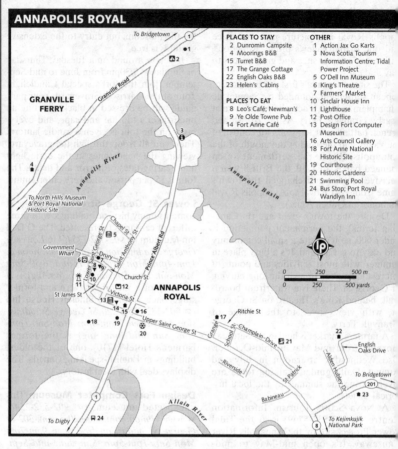

ANNAPOLIS ROYAL

To Bridgetown

GRANVILLE
FERRY

Granville Road

Annapolis River

To North Hills Museum
& Port Royal National
Historic Site

Annapolis Basin

Chapel St

Government
Wharf

Drury

Church St

Saint Anthony Rd

Prince Albert Rd

ANNAPOLIS
ROYAL

St James St

Victoria St

Ritchie St

Upper Saint George St

Champlain Drive

Grange

School St

English
Oaks Drive

Alden Hubley Dr

To Bridgetown

Riverside

St Patrick

To Digby

Allain River

Babineau

To Kejimkujik
National Park

PLACES TO STAY
2 Dunromin Campsite
4 Moorings B&B
15 Turret B&B
17 The Grange Cottage
22 English Oaks B&B
23 Helen's Cabins

PLACES TO EAT
8 Leo's Café; Newman's
9 Ye Olde Towne Pub
14 Fort Anne Café

OTHER
1 Action Jax Go Karts
3 Nova Scotia Tourism
   Information Centre; Tidal
   Power Project
5 O'Dell Inn Museum
6 King's Theatre
7 Farmers' Market
10 Sinclair House Inn
11 Lighthouse
12 Post Office
13 Design Fort Computer
   Museum
16 Arts Council Gallery
18 Fort Anne National
   Historic Site
19 Courthouse
20 Historic Gardens
21 Swimming Pool
24 Bus Stop; Port Royal
   Wandlyn Inn

0   250   500 m
0   250   500 yards

Tidal Power Project At the Annapolis River Causeway, this project (☎ 902-532-5454, 236 Prince Albert Rd; admission free; open 10am-5:45pm mid-May-mid-Oct; 8am-8pm July & Aug) offers visitors the chance to see a hydroelectric prototype that has been harnessing tidal power from the Bay of Fundy since 1984. There's an interpretive center on the 2nd floor that uses models, exhibits and a short video to explain how it works. This center also provides lots of useful information on the ecology and history of the area. Tidal power may come into its own in a few decades when cheaper fossil fuel supplies begin to run out, but a yet the cost of constructing the dams is ur economical.

Places to Stay *Dunromin Campsi* (☎ 902-532-2808, fax 902-532-2808, e dur romin@tartannet.ns.ca, w www.woodal .com/a/00124_dunromin.html, 4618 Hwy Granville Ferry) Unserviced/serviced site $18/22, cabins $45 single or double. Ope mid-Apr-mid-Oct. This is the nearest camp ground to Annapolis Royal. The tent site are in two separate areas, one well woode with nicely separated sites (Nos W1–W8 and the other just rows of sites in a field by the river (Nos T1–T16). Four camping cabins with shared bath are also available. There's a small store, Laundromat, swimming pool and kayak/canoe rentals ($10 an hour) on site.

Turret B&B (☎ 902-532-5770, 372 St George St) Doubles from $60. Open mid-May-Oct. This Victorian mansion with an actual turret has three rooms for rent.

The Grange Cottage (☎ 902-532-7993, fax 902-532-7993, e ron.marshall@ns.sympatico.ca, 102 Ritchie St) Singles/doubles $45/60. There are half a dozen upscale B&Bs and inns in historic buildings on St George St southeast of Prince Albert Rd, but for a better value (and a quieter location), check out the Grange Cottage, offering three rooms with shared bath. This three-story house with an enclosed porch stands on spacious grounds.

English Oaks B&B (☎ 902-532-2066, e engoak@tartannet.ns.ca, w www.holidayjunction.com/canada/ns/cns0025.html, 29 English Oaks Dr) Rooms from $60. Open Apr-Oct. Guests in this cool bungalow with a large shady yard facing the Annapolis River have use of a barbecue and picnic tables.

Helen's Cabins (☎ 902-532-5207, 106 Hwy 201) Singles or doubles $50. Open mid-May-Nov. These five vintage cabins built in 1950 have hot plates for cooking. The proprietors also run Tom's Pizzeria next door (pizzas $4 to $23).

The Moorings B&B (☎ 902-532-2146, fax 902-532-2146, e tileston@tartannet.ns.ca, w www.bbcanada.com/1000.html, 5287 Granville Rd, Granville Ferry) Singles/doubles $45/65. Open mid-May-Oct. This impressive three-story heritage home 2½km from the tourist office has a view straight across to Annapolis Royal.

Places to Eat Fort Anne Café (☎ 902-532-254, 298 St George St) Lunch $3-6, dinner $8-10. Open 8am-8pm daily July & Aug, 8am-3pm Mon-Sat other months. This is where the local people go (most of the other restaurants and cafés in town are just for the tourists). Breakfast is around $5 in-

cluding coffee. For lunch, there are burgers ($3 to $4), sandwiches ($3 to $6) and haddock, clams or scallops with fries ($8 to $9). At dinner you can get Digby scallops for $10 or a complete seafood platter for $14. Since they banned smoking, this place has become a lot nicer.

Leo's Café (☎ 902-532-7424, 216 St George St) Lunch under $10. Open 9am-5pm daily (closed Sundays in winter). This unpretentious little cafe serves items like sandwiches ($5 to $6), salads ($5 to $7), quiche ($8), pastas ($8) and fish cakes ($9).

Newman's (☎ 902-532-5502, 214 St George St) Dinner $12-25. Open noon-9pm Tues-Sun. This expensive and decorative restaurant has a good reputation for its varied menu, which includes haddock or pollock ($10) and vegetarian dishes ($7 to $9). Its noted scallop linguini is $14. Newman's features a dining terrace for dining outside if the weather is good.

Ye Olde Towne Pub (☎ 902-532-2244, 9 Church St) Pub meals under $10. Open 11am-11pm Mon-Fri, 10am-11pm Sat, noon-8pm Sun. Just off St George St by the wharf, this busy place is OK for lunch and a brew. The menu includes salads ($4 to $7), sandwiches ($4 to$7), burgers ($5 to $10), fish & chips ($6 to $9) and seafood ($9 to $16).

Entertainment Arts Council Gallery (☎ 902-532-7069, 396 St George St; admission free; open 10am-5pm Tues-Fri, 1pm-4pm Sat & Sun) This is an artist-run cultural resource center showcasing local, regional, and national artists' works. It also has a used bookstore.

King's Theatre (☎ 800-818-8587, 209 St George St, tickets $11-14) Across from the Fat Pheasant Restaurant is this theater that presents musicals, dramas and concerts most evenings at 8pm in July and August. Other shows are staged occasionally throughout the year, and Hollywood films are screened most weekends ($5 to $6).

Getting There & Away The Acadian Lines bus stops at the Port Royal Wandlyn Inn (☎ 902-532-2323), 3924 Hwy 1, 1.2km southwest of Annapolis Royal. Daily buses leave at 11:15am to Halifax ($33) and at 10:05pm to Digby ($6), but service to Yarmouth ($22) is only Thursday to Sunday at 10:05pm.

The highway police are especially vigilant around Annapolis Royal. The 50kph and 60kph zones extend far out from town and should be observed.

Around Annapolis Royal

Action Jax Go Karts At Action Jax (☎ 902-532-0911, 4708 Hwy 1; open 11am-10pm daily June-mid-Sept), just east of Annapolis Royal, you can drive a go-cart around the track for five minutes (5-10 laps) for $5. If you have a driver's license, you can rent a faster racer cart for $7. Those with small children can get a two-seater cart for $5.

North Hills Museum This museum (☎ 902-532-2168, 5065 Granville Rd, Granville Ferry; adult/child $2/1; open 9:30am-5:30pm Mon-Sat, 1pm-5:30pm Sun June-mid-Oct), halfway to Port Royal, has a superb collection of Georgian antiques displayed in a farmhouse dating from 1764.

Port Royal National Historic Site Some 14km from Annapolis Royal, this site (☎ 902-532-2898, 53 Historic Lane; adult/child $2.75/1.35; open 9am-6pm daily mid-May-mid-Oct) is the actual location of the first permanent European settlement north of Florida. It's a replica, reconstructed in the original manner, of de Champlain's 1605 fur-trading habitation, destroyed by the English eight years after it was begun. Costumed workers help tell the story of this early settlement.

Delaps Cove On the coast north of town is a series of typical small fishing villages, from Delaps Cove west all the way to the Minas Basin.

The **Delaps Cove Wilderness Trail**, about 24km from Annapolis Royal, is a 15km hiking trail that provides a good cross-section of the provincial coastal scenery. There are streams and waterfalls at various

places en route and an array of birds and animals. A basic campground is in the nearby fishing settlement.

Bridgetown

Further along the Annapolis Valley, Bridgetown has many fine trees and some handsome examples of large Maritime houses. A seasonal tourist office is in Jubilee Park, near the post office on Granville St. There's also the small **James House Museum** (☎ 902-665-4530, 12 Queen St; admission free; open 9am-4pm daily mid-May-early Oct), an 1835 home among the shops. The tea room in the museum is ideal for an afternoon break. Try the rhubarb sparkle ($2). Bridgetown is the western terminus of the hourly Kings Transit buses from Greenwood (connecting to Kentville and Wolfville).

Valleyview Provincial Park (☎ 902-665-2559, W parks.gov.ns.ca, north of Bridgetown) Sites $14. Open early June-Aug. Valleyview is 5km straight up Church St from Bridgetown. It's right on the northern rim of the Annapolis Valley with a fabulous view from near sites Nos 18 and 19. The sites are nicely separated with adequate shade – check No 23 if you value privacy. It would be a very steep climb up by bicycle. Valleyview is not at all as crowded as many other campgrounds around here.

Greenwood

This town near the middle of the Annapolis Valley is interesting only for the **Greenwood Military Aviation Museum** (☎ 902-765-1494 ext 5955, Ward Rd; admission free; open 10am-4pm Tues-Sat Sept-May, 9am-5pm June-Aug) at Kingston, 5km off Hwy 101 from exit 17. It's just outside the Canadian Forces Base Greenwood, and three large aircraft stand next to the parking lot. The flight simulator and aircraft restoration projects are highlights of the museum.

The hourly Kings Transit buses from Kentville and Bridgetown stop within easy walking distance of the museum. See Getting There & Away in the Kentville section for details.

Kentville

Kentville, with a sizable population of 6000, a functional town that marks the eastern end of the Annapolis Valley.

The tourist office (☎ 902-678-7170) is at 25 Park St, 1.3km west of the center. It's open 9:30am to 5:30pm daily June to early October, 9:30am to 7pm July and August.

Kentville is about a two-hour drive from Digby and about one hour from Halifax. There aren't any true budget accommodations in downtown Kentville, although a few possibilities exist in the outskirts.

Old King's Courthouse Museum This museum (☎ 902-678-6237, 37 Cornwallis Ave; admission free; open 9:30am-4:30pm Mon-Sat year-round), right in town, contains an art gallery, local artifacts and exhibits on the area's history. The courthouse was the seat of justice from 1903 to 1979. Ask to see the 30-minute Parks Canada video about the 1760 migration of New England planters to take up lands forcibly vacated by the Acadians.

Agriculture Research Station At the eastern end of town, 2km from the center, is the Agriculture Research Station (☎ 902-678-1093, off Hwy 1; admission free; open 8:30am-4:30pm daily June-Aug). The station's Blair House Museum relates the area's farming history with a focus on apples. Guided museum tours are offered during summer. The **Nature Trail Foot Path** (also known as the 'Kentville Ravine Trail') begins from the gravel parking lot immediately east of the entrance to the research station. No bicycles are allowed on this pleasant walking trail through old-growth woods, one of the few areas in the province where virgin forest still survives.

Places to Stay & Eat *Grand Street Inn* (☎ 877-245-4744, fax 902-679-1991, e grand streetinn@ns.sympatico.ca, 160 Main St) Doubles from $65, including breakfast. A kilometer out of the downtown area toward New Minas, this is a very attractive old three-story Queen Anne revival house. Guests can use the outdoor swimming pool.

Allen's Motel (☎ 902-678-2683, fax 902-678-1910, e allensmotel@ns.sympatico.ca, w www.allensmotel.ns.ca, 384 Park St) Doubles from $55. Open Feb-Dec. This attractive 10-room motel faces a small park, 2½km west of central Kentville.

Sun Valley Motel (☎ 902-678-7368, fax 902-678-5585, e rooms@svmotel.com, w www.svmotel.com, 905 Park St) Doubles from $55. Just off Hwy 101 at exit 14 toward Kentville and 2km west of Allen's Motel, Sun Valley offers a row of rooms facing the road on attractively landscaped grounds. A free continental breakfast is included.

King's Arms Pub (☎ 902-678-0066, 390 Main St) Dishes $5.25 and up. Open 11am-10pm Mon-Sat, 11am-9pm Sun. You can have a drink next to a fireplace or outside on the patio at this classic pub. Available meals include steak and kidney pie or a pot of mussels. Happy hour is from 4:30pm to 6:30 pm daily, with pints at $3.25 and half pints under $2. There's live music on weekends.

Paddy's (☎ 902-678-3199, 30 Aberdeen St) Dinners $8-15. Open 11am-9pm Sun-Wed, 11am-10pm Thurs-Sat. Near the King's Arms, this place doubles as an Irish pub and a small brewery producing such gems as Annapolis Valley Ale. Try the Paddy's Irish stew ($5.50) made with Paddy's Porter. *Rosie's* next door is part of the same complex and offers Tex-Mex favorites like chicken chimichangas ($10).

Getting There & Away Acadian Lines (☎ 902-678-2000), 66 Cornwallis St, is at the old train station in the center of town. The bus to Yarmouth only leaves Thursday to Sunday at 8:35pm ($37). To Halifax it leaves at 10:30am Monday to Friday and at 1:05pm and 6:30pm daily ($18).

Kings Transit (☎ 888-546-4442), 66 Cornwallis St (same terminal as Acadian Lines), operates an excellent regional bus service between Bridgetown and Wolfville, with a flat fare of $2. The service runs in three stages: Bridgetown to Greenwood, Greenwood to Kentville and Kentville to Wolfville, with a change of buses necessary at each stage. Free transfers are available.

Thus if you wanted to go from Bridgetown right through to Wolfville, it would cost $2, and you'd need to ask for two transfers as you boarded. The buses run hourly, leaving the transfer points on the hour. At Kentville you can catch them from 6am to 7pm Monday to Friday, 8am to 3pm Saturday (no service on Sunday).

NORTH OF KENTVILLE

The area up to Cape Blomidon, on the Bay of Fundy, makes for a fine side trip, with good scenery, a memorable view of much of the valley and a couple of beaches. At Cape Split there's a dramatic hiking trail high above the Minas Basin and Channel.

The Lookoff

From the road's edge at nearly 200m, this could well be the best view of the gentle, rural Annapolis Valley, its rows of fruit trees and farmhouses appearing like miniatures.

Look-off Family Camping Park (☎ 902-582-3022, fax 902-582-1334, e c.french@ ns.sympatico.ca, 6km north of Canning on Hwy 358) Unserviced/serviced sites $20/27. Open mid-May-mid-Oct. This place is across the street from the Lookoff. The serviced sites are in the middle of a large grassy field. The unserviced tent sites around the perimeter get some shade.

Scots Bay

The road continues north from the Lookoff to Scots Bay, which has a large pebbled beach. From the end of the road, a spectacular 13km hiking trail leads to the cliffs at Cape Split, the tip of a 100km basalt ridge running along the Bay of Fundy with cliffs 200m high. This is not a loop trail, so you must retrace your steps.

Blomidon Provincial Park

Blomidon (☎ 902-582-7319, w parks.gov.ns .ca, off Hwy 358; campsites $18; open early June-early Oct), 27km from Kentville, is on a different road than the Lookoff, beginning 3½km back toward Canning. From the junction it's 14km to the campground, dramatically set atop the red cliffs you see as you arrive. The beach and picnic area are at

the foot of the hill just before the final 2km climb to the campground. As at Kingsport sandy beach farther south, the water can get quite warm here. Blomidon's hiking trail skirt dramatic red shoreline cliffs nearl 200m high. It's a pleasant place to stay though it does fill up on summer weekend as Halifax isn't that far away. On Fridays tr to arrive by noon.

Kingsport

Halfway between Canning and Kingspor **Habitant Vineyards** (☎ 902-582-7565, 1031 Hwy 221; admission free) offers free tour year-round 9am-5pm Mon-Fri, 10am-5pm Sat and noon-5pm Sun. Inquire with th staff in their sales room.

Beach House B&B (☎ 877-562-330. 10799 Hwy 221, Kingsport) Singles/double $55/65. The two-story house in a lovel garden almost opposite Kingsport Beac provides an ideal base for touring the area

Prescott House Museum

This museum (☎ 902-542-3984, 1633 Starr Point Rd, Starr's Point; adult/child $2/1; ope 9:30am-5:30pm Mon-Sat, 1pm-5:30pm Su June-mid-Oct), 3½km east of Port William across the bay from Wolfville, occupies gracious Georgian mansion dating from 1812. The gardens and grounds around th house are a major part of its appeal.

WOLFVILLE

Wolfville (pronounced Wooffle) is a quie green university town best known as th home of artist Alex Colville. With its a gallery, comfortable inns and impressive his toric homes, there's more than a wisp c culture in the air. This is manifested by th summer-long Atlantic Theatre Festiv (☎ 902-542-4242), with four classics pe formed virtually every day June throug September.

The tourist office (☎ 902-542-7000), 1 Willow Ave, is in Willow Park, at the ea end of Main St, and is open from May t early October.

The Wolfville Memorial Library (☎ 90. 542-5760), in the former train station at 2 Elm Ave, offers free Internet access. It's ope

11am to 5pm and 6:30pm to 8:30pm Tuesday, Thursday and Friday; 11am to 5pm Wednesday and Saturday; 1pm to 5pm Sunday.

The Odd Book (☎ 902-542-9491), 8 Front St, on the street behind Acton's Café, has an intriguing collection of out-of-print books.

Waterfront Park

This viewing area (cnr Gaspereau Ave & Front St), back behind Tim Hortons, offers a stunning view of the tidal mud flats, Minas Basin and the red cliffs of Blomidon beyond. Panels provide information on the tides, dikes, flora and fauna, legends, culture,

history and ecology of the area. It's a top sight, not to be missed.

Randall House Museum

Set in a house dating from the early 1800s, this museum (☎ 902-542-9775, 171 Main St near the tourist office; admission by donation; open 10am-5pm Mon-Sat, 2pm-5pm Sun mid-June-mid-Sept) focuses on the early New England planters and colonists who replaced the expelled Acadians and the history of Wolfville up to the 1960s. Afternoon tea is served from 2:30pm to 4pm ($3) on antique China with homemade cookies – great!

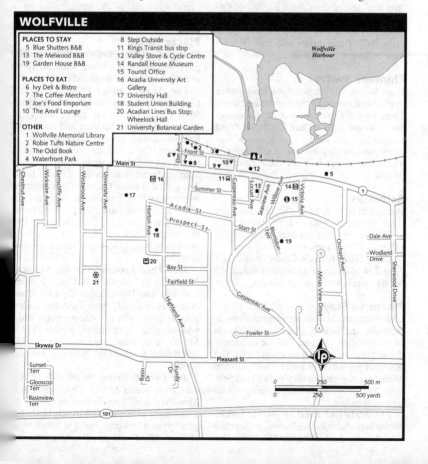

WOLFVILLE

PLACES TO STAY
5 Blue Shutters B&B
13 The Melwood B&B
19 Garden House B&B

PLACES TO EAT
6 Ivy Deli & Bistro
7 The Coffee Merchant
9 Joe's Food Emporium
10 The Anvil Lounge

OTHER
1 Wolfville Memorial Library
2 Robie Tufts Nature Centre
3 The Odd Book
4 Waterfront Park

8 Step Outside
11 Kings Transit bus stop
12 Valley Stove & Cycle Centre
14 Randall House Museum
15 Tourist Office
16 Acadia University Art Gallery
17 University Hall
18 Student Union Building
20 Acadian Lines Bus Stop; Wheelock Hall
21 University Botanical Garden

Acadia University Art Gallery

The gallery (☎ *902-585-1373; cnr Main St & Highland Ave; admission by donation; open 1pm-4pm Tues-Sun*), in the Beveridge Arts Centre building, exhibits mainly the works of Maritimes artists. It also has a collection of the work (mostly serigraphs) of Alex Colville, some of which is always on display.

University Botanical Garden

The campus of Acadia University (founded 1838), behind the art gallery, is well worth a stroll. Go past imposing University Hall to these new Botanic Gardens on University Ave. Both the gardens and the adjacent Environmental Science Research Centre were funded by the Irving family and opened in early 2002. Entry hours and fees (if any) were unknown at press time.

Chimney Swifts

From May to late August, these birds gather to glide and swoop by the hundreds at dusk. There's a full explanation of the phenomenon at **Robie Tufts Nature Centre** on Front St opposite the public library, which features outdoor displays and a tall chimney where the birds show off their acrobatic talents.

Activities

Step Outside (☎ *902-542-4327, 330 Main St*) rents mountain bikes ($25/100 per day/week) and also leads 3½-hour tours into the valley at $75 per person.

Valley Stove & Cycle Centre (☎ *902-542-7280, 234 Main St*) rents bicycles at $25/125 per day/week. They also do repairs.

Places to Stay

Unfortunately, budget accommodations in Wolfville are limited. There are no hostels or motels right in town, and the university doesn't rent rooms in their dormitories. The dozen or so B&Bs in impressive Victorian homes are superb, but they're rather expensive. You may do better pushing on to nearby Windsor.

The Melwood B&B (☎ *888-335-8588,* e *melwoodbb@hotmail.com, 6 Seaview Ave*) Singles/doubles/triples $59/74/99. This massive Victorian mansion, up the first street west of the tourist office, offers four rooms.

Blue Shutters B&B (☎ *902-542-3363,* e *blueshutters@ns.sympatico.ca,* w *www .bbcanada.com/blueshutters, 7 Blomidon Terrace*) Rooms from $60. Open May-Oct. Three hundred meters directly up the steep hill from the tourist office, this executive-style home is worth investigating. One room has a private bath.

Garden House B&B (☎ *902-542-1703,* e *gardenhouse@ns.sympatico.ca, 150 Main St*) Singles/doubles $50/65. This big old house 400m east of the tourist office has a back yard overlooking the bay.

Places to Eat

This being a college town, you'll find several pizza and sub shops along Main St. There are also a couple of good coffee shops.

The Anvil Lounge (☎ *902-542-4632, Gaspereau Ave near Waterfront Park*) Meals $6-9. Open 10am-1am daily. This large sports bar with cheap beer and occasional live music also serves gigantic portions of spaghetti ($6), vegetarian nachos ($5), steaks ($6 to $9) and some seafood entrees at prices better than anywhere else in town. The grilled chicken Caesar ($7) is fantastic. Wednesday after 5pm chicken wings are 20¢ each. The Anvil isn't noted for its haute cuisine, but it sure is filling. Be aware that the kitchen closes at 8pm (the bar stays open until late). Friday and Saturday nights there's a DJ.

Joe's Food Emporium (☎ *902-542-3033, 292 Main St*) Meals $10. Open 7:30am-midnight Sun-Thurs, 7:30am-2am Fri & Sat. A step up in quality from the Anvil, Joe's is a lively place with an outdoor patio and a wide-ranging menu including pizza ($10 to $15 for a medium), nachos supreme ($7) and quiche & salad ($6). Beer and wine are served.

Ivy Deli & Bistro (☎ *902-542-1868, Elm Ave*) Meals $10-11. Open until 8pm Mon-Wed, until 9pm Thurs-Sun. Owned by a university professor, this trendy bistro has good veggie options. The $10 specials including salad are good value (lasagna uiche, spanakopita); otherwise there's hicken Caesar ($6) and Mediterranean an-pasti ($11).

The Coffee Merchant (☎ 902-542-4315, 34 Main St cnr Elm Ave) Coffee under $2. Open 8am-10pm Mon-Thurs, 8am-10pm Fri : Sat, 8am-7pm Sun. This is a meeting place f sorts with outdoor seating in summer. Coffee, cakes and light meals are served.

Getting There & Away
Acadian Lines buses make a stop at Acadia University. Be sure to get off there, as the ext stop may be far from town. You can also board the bus in front of Wheelock Hall at the top of Horton Ave at the univer-ty. Bus tickets are available at the infor-nation counter (☎ 902-585-2110) in the tudent union building off Highland Ave. ares to Halifax are $16, to Yarmouth $39.

The easternmost terminus of the Kings ransit bus is in front of Billy Bob's Pizza, 09 Main St (note that of the four pizzerias n Wolfville, Billy Bob's is the fourth best). 'or information on this bus service, see Getting There & Away in the Kentville ection.

GRAND PRÉ
Now a very small English-speaking town, Grand Pré was the site of one of the most ragic but compelling stories in eastern Canada's history, the expulsion of the Aca-ians, detailed at the national historic site, km east of Wolfville and a kilometer north f the main highway. (See the 'Ethnic Cleansing in the 18th Century' boxed text or more information on the expulsion.)

Grand Pré National Historic Site
Grand Pré means 'great meadow' and refers o the farmland created when the Acadians built dikes along the shoreline, as they had done in northwest France for generations. There are 1200 hectares of farmland below ea level at Grand Pré. It's a beautiful area, nd you'll easily understand why the Acadi-ns didn't want to leave, especially after all he labor they'd invested. The site *(☎ 902-42-3631, 2242 Grand Pré Rd; adult/family 2.50/7; open 9am-6pm daily mid-May-Oct)*

is a memorial to the Acadians, who had a settlement here from 1675 to 1755 before they were given the boot by the British.

The historic site consists of an informa-tion center, church and gardens, and free tours are offered. Impressive views and a sense of spaciousness abound. The worth-while gift shop has a selection of books on the Acadians, among other things.

A new stone church, built in the Acadian style, sits in the middle of the site as a mon-ument to the original inhabitants. Inside, the history of those people is depicted in a series of colorful paintings done in 1987 by New Brunswick painter Claude Picard.

Walk down through the gardens to the old blacksmith's shed where there are gor-geous views of the surrounding farmlands and the air is an aromatic mix of sea breeze and worked fields.

In the gardens are a bust of Henry Wadsworth Longfellow, honored for his poem *Evangeline,* which chronicles the Aca-dians' saga, and a statue of Evangeline herself, who was born here and is now a ro-mantic symbol of her people.

Acadian Days, an annual festival held sometime toward the middle of July, con-sists of music, storytelling and arts & crafts. In winter, the site can be visited for free.

Places to Stay
Evangeline Motel (☎ 888-542-2703, e evangeline@ns.sympatico.ca, w www .evangeline.ns.ca, 11668 Hwy 1) Doubles from $59. Open May-Oct. Overlooking the turnoff to Grand Pré National Historic Site, this well-established motel is on attractive grounds. The restaurant is popular.

Blomidon View Motel (☎ 902-542-2039, 127 Evangeline Beach Rd) Doubles $48. Open mid-May-Sept. This 10-room motel right on muddy Evangeline Beach, 4km beyond Grand Pré National Historic Site, is a long wooden building with five rooms on either side. An RV-friendly campground is across the road.

WINDSOR
Windsor is a small town on the Avon River, noted for being halfway between the North

Ethnic Cleansing in the 18th Century

The story of the Acadians is one of the most interesting, dramatic and tragic in Canada's history. It was played out in what are now the country's five easternmost provinces – as well as the USA, the West Indies and Europe – and although it began in the 1600s it's not over yet.

When the French first settled the area around the Minas Basin on the southern shore of the Bay of Fundy in the early 17th century, they named the land Acadia. By the next century, these settlers thought of themselves as Acadians. To the English, however, they were always to be 'the French.' The rivalry and suspicion between these two powers of the New World began with the first landings and was only to increase in hostility and bitterness.

The population of Acadia continued to grow throughout the 17th and 18th centuries, and as a result of various battles and treaties, the region changed ruling hands from French to English and back again. Finally, in 1713, with the Treaty of Utrecht, Acadia became British Nova Scotia. The Acadians refused to take an oath of allegiance, though for the most part, they weren't much interested in France's point of view either and wanted most of all to be left alone. Things drifted along in this state for a while, and the area around Grand Pré became the largest Acadian community. By this time the total regional population was approaching 10,000, with 3500 more people in Louisbourg and still others on Prince Edward Island.

Unfortunately, tensions once again heated up between England and France, with squabbles and countermoves taking place all over the east coast. When a new hard-line lieutenant governor, Charles Lawrence, was appointed in 1754, he quickly became fed up with the Acadians and their supposed neutrality. Lawrence didn't trust them, and he demanded an oath of allegiance. As in past, the Acadians said forget it. This time, though, the rules had changed.

In late August 1755, with the crowns of France and England still locked in battle and paranoia increasing, what was to become known as the Deportation, or the Expulsion, began. All told,

Pole and the Equator. At one time it was the only British stronghold in this former bastion of French power and Acadian farmers.

Hwy 1 becomes Water St in town, and the main intersection is where it crosses Gerrish St. Just off exit 6 from Hwy 101 is the helpful tourist office (☎ 902-798-2690), open daily from mid-May to mid-October. Be sure to go up on the dike beside the tourist office for a view of the tidal river flats.

Fort Edward
National Historic Site

Off King St, there's an old wooden blockhouse and earthen mounds still intact amid portions of the British fort (☎ 902-532-2321; admission free; open 10am-6pm daily mid-June-early Sept). Dating from 1750, it was used as an assembly station during the expulsion of the Acadians, and it is thought to

be the oldest blockhouse in Canada. Th grounds are accessible year-round.

West Hants
Historical Society Museum

This museum (☎ 902-798-4706, 281 King S admission free; open 10am-6pm Tues-Sa mid-June-Aug, 10am-4pm Mon-Fri Sept), couple of blocks from Fort Edward, is in a old Methodist church. Among the exhibi are a high-wheel bicycle from the 1870s, crazy quilt from 1905 and an Acadian stov from 1911.

Haliburton House

This was the home of Judge Thomas Chan dler Haliburton (1796–1865), one of th founders of written American humor. H created the Sam Slick character, in Mar Twain–style stories. Although these aren read much now, many of Haliburton's ex

Ethnic Cleansing in the 18th Century

about 14,000 Acadians were forced out of this area. Villages were burned and the people boarded onto boats.

This sad, bitter episode was the theme for Longfellow's well-known, lengthy narrative poem *Evangeline,* which was named for its fictional heroine. Many Acadians headed for Louisiana and New Orleans, where 'Acadian' became Anglicized to 'Cajun' (a word that is often heard in songs and seen on restaurant menus). The Cajuns, some of whom still speak French, have maintained aspects of Acadian culture to this day. Other Acadians resettled in various Maritime points and New England, and still others went to Martinique, Santo Domingo or back to Europe; some even relocated as far away as the Falkland Islands. Nowhere were they greeted warmly. Some hid out and remained in Acadia. In later years many of those who had been deported returned to Acadia.

Today, most of the French people in Canada's Atlantic provinces are descendants of the expelled Acadians, and they're holding tight to their heritage. In Nova Scotia, the Chéticamp area in Cape Breton and the French Shore north of Yarmouth are strongholds. A pocket in western Prince Edward Island and the Port au Port Peninsula in Newfoundland are others. New Brunswick has a large French population stretching up the east coast past the Acadian Peninsula at Caraquet and all around the border with Québec.

There has recently been an upsurge in Acadian pride and awareness, and in most of these areas you'll see the Acadian flag proudly displayed. Museums in the Maritimes acknowledge the sorry deeds of the past and celebrate the continuing Acadian culture. The Université de Moncton, especially, is a current stronghold of Acadian culture. Festivals held in the Acadian areas provide an opportunity to see traditional dress, sample foods and hear some wonderful fiddle-based music.

ressions, such as 'quick as a wink' and 'city slicker,' are still used. Haliburton's large estate (☎ *902-798-2915, 424 Clifton Ave; adult/child $2/1; open 9:30am-5:30pm Mon-Sat, 1pm-5:30pm Sun June-mid-Oct)* is in the eastern section of town. Clifton Ave runs off Grey St, which itself runs from Gerrish St.

hand House

This small museum (☎ *902-798-8213, 389 Avon St, off Water St; admission $2; open 9:30am-5:30pm Mon-Sat, 1pm-5:30pm Sun June-mid-Oct),* on Ferry Hill overlooking the Avon River, is part of the provincial museum system. It depicts the life of a well-to-do family at the start of the 20th century.

Windsor Hockey Heritage Society

Windsor calls itself the birthplace of ice hockey, though this has created a heated

debate with Kingston, Ontario, which makes the same claim. They say the boys of King's College School here in Windsor began playing the game on Long Pond around 1800. In 1836, Haliburton even referred to 'playing ball on ice' in his book

The origins of hockey?

The Clockmaker. These tidbits and more (the first pucks were slices of a thick pine branch and the Mi'kmaq Indians supplied hand-made hockey sticks to the North American market well into the 1930s) can be gathered at this souvenir shop/museum (☎ 902-798-1800, 128 Gerrish St; admission free; open 10am-4:30pm Mon-Sat). Ask the attendant to put on the eight-minute video about Windsor's claim to have invented hockey.

Mermaid Theatre

Founded in 1972, the Mermaid (☎ 902-798-5841, 132 Gerrish St; admission free; open 9am-4:30pm Mon-Fri) is one of Canada's most famous children's theaters. The four-person troupe is on tour during winter, but the office remains open year-round.

You're welcome to peruse the large collection of puppets, costumes and sets used for previous productions, and one of the staff may offer to take you upstairs where you can see the workshop where the next batch is being made.

Howard Dill Enterprises

A bit more wacky are the Brobdingnagian pumpkins at Howard Dill Enterprises (☎ 902-798-2728, 400 College Rd; admission free; open anytime) on the south side of Windsor. Howard Dill is a four-time world champion pumpkin grower (he grew one that weighed in at 450kg!), and Dill's patch is a must from mid-August to early October, when you can have your photo taken with a pumpkin that's bigger than you are. Long Pond, just behind Dill's farm, is the place where boys from King's College, now King's Edgehill School, supposedly invented the game of ice hockey.

Activities

The outdoor **Windsor Centennial Pool** (☎ 902-798-2275, 65 Fort Edward), just below the Fort Edward blockhouse off King St, is open to the public from 2pm to 4pm daily mid-June to August ($2.50), and also from 7pm-8pm Monday to Thursday ($1.25). It's another good reason to spend a night here.

Organized Tours

The *Evangeline Express (Windsor Hantsport Railway Co;* ☎ 902-798-5667, *Water St; adults $18.50)* is a refurbished train running from here to Wolfville and back. The train leaves Windsor at 11am o Sundays in July and August, returning 3 hours later. A stop is made at Grand Pré t visit the historic site (admission to the par is extra). The train station in Windsor is o Water St near Hwy 101. In the off-seaso there are occasional weekend trips to th park at Mount Uniacke. Reservations ar recommended.

Places to Stay & Eat

Meander In B&B (☎ 877-387-6070, 15 *Albert St at Grey St)* Singles/doubles $50/6(This historic three-story mansion (1898) i the center of town has three rooms wit shared bath.

Avonside Motel (☎ 902-798-8344, 21 *Hwy 1, Falmouth)* Singles/doubles fror $44/49. This place is convenient for bus pas sengers, as it's directly across the road fror the Irving gas station where the Acadia Lines bus stops and under a kilometer nort of central Windsor. The 19 rooms are in tw long blocks.

Boegel's B&B (☎ 902-798-4183, fax 90. 798-1063, ℮ boegelbb@glinx.com, ⓦ ww .bbcanada.com/283.html, 145 Dill Rd Singles/doubles $40/50. Boegel's is only ac cessible if you have wheels. It's a large ne house renting three rooms with shared batl up the road that begins beside 'Gla Tidings' church off Hwy 14, 3km southwe: of central Windsor.

Downeast Motel (☎ 800-395-8117, 42 *Hwy 1 at the junction with Hwy 14)* Single doubles/triples $45/55/65. This first-ra motel 3km south of Windsor, near exit from Hwy 101, offers 20 spacious room with double brick walls between each un (super quiet).

Smiley's Provincial Park (☎ 902-75. 3131, ⓦ parks.gov.ns.ca, McKey Section R Sites $18. Open early June-Aug. Smiley's 20km east of Windsor, off Hwy 14. There ar nice wooded campsites, and you can swim i the river.

Getting There & Away

Acadian Lines buses from Halifax to Windsor continue on to Kentville or Digby, making stops through the Annapolis Valley. Service to Yarmouth is only Thursday to Sunday at 7:35pm. The one-way fare to

Yarmouth is $43, to Halifax $12. In Windsor the bus stops at Irving Mainway gas station (☎ 902-798-2126), 2113 Hwy 1, toward Falmouth. This station is just across the Avon River from downtown Windsor, a six-minute walk.

Central Nova Scotia

The central part of Nova Scotia, in geographic terms, essentially takes in the corridor of land from Halifax up to the New Brunswick border. For those coming by road from elsewhere in Canada, this is their introduction to Nova Scotia. But don't turn against the province because of what you see from the Trans Canada Hwy as it passes through flat, uninteresting terrain on the way to Truro. Parrsboro is a worthwhile stop southwest of Amherst, and there is some superb scenery along the shores of the Bay of Fundy.

SHUBENACADIE

Shubenacadie, or simply 'Shube,' is best known for **Shubenacadie Provincial Wildlife Park** (☎ 902-758-2040, 149 Creighton Rd off Hwy 2; adult/family $3/7.50; open 9am-7pm daily mid-May-mid-Oct, 9am-3pm Sat mid-Oct-mid-May). This unusual provincial park houses abundant examples of Nova Scotia's wildlife, including birds, waterfowl, foxes and deer, in large enclosures. Only animals that cannot be released into the wild are kept here, and you'll find it fascinating even if you're not a zoo person. The park is off Hwy 102 at exit 11, 38km south of Truro, just north of the town of Shubenacadie.

Tidal Bore Rafting

The Bay of Fundy is known for having the highest tides in the world, and an offshoot of these is a tidal wave or bore that flows up the feeding rivers when high tide comes in. The advancing tide is often pretty small, but with certain phases of the moon, it can be a meter or so in height and runs upstream, giving the impression of the river flowing backwards.

Rafting on the tidal bore is about as close as you'll come to white-water rafting in the Maritimes. The tidal bore in the Shubenacadie River creates a wave one to 3m high, and at least three adventure tourism operators load visitors into Zodiac rafts powered by outboard motors to ride the bore as it sweeps through, a real roller coaster ride. The companies are based along Hwy 215 between Shubenacadie and Maitland. These trips depart once or twice daily on a schedule dictated by the arrival of the tides, so call ahead for departure times and to reserve your seat, as each raft carries only six to eight passengers. There's no use arriving when the tide is flat.

Tidal Bore Rafting Park (☎ 902-758-4032 [W] www.tidalboreraftingpark.com, Hwy 215 13km north of Shubenacadie; 2/4-hr raft trips $50/65 a person; open May-Oct). This park is 10½km north of exit 10 from Hwy 102, Shubenacadie, then 2km down a gravel sideroad. Coming from the other direction it's 9km south of Gosse Bridge, South Maitland, on Hwy 215. If you just want to watch the tidal bore go past from shore, this park is your best bet.

Shubenacadie River Adventure Tours (☎ 888-878-8687, [W] www.shubie.com, 10061 Hwy 215, South Maitland; adult/child

MAP INDEX

OTHER MAPS
Central Nova Scotia
pages 160-161

Amherst &
Around
page 169

Truro
pages
162-163

Around
Pictou
page 175

5/60; open mid-June-mid-Oct), 2km north
Gosse Bridge, also does these trips.
Shubenacadie River Runners (☎ 800-856-
'61, W www.tidalborerafting.com, 8681
wy 215, Maitland; adult/child $65/55;
en mid-May-mid-Oct), directly opposite
wrence House in Maitland, does Zodiac
ps and several B&Bs are nearby.

laces to Stay
ild Nature Camping Ground (☎ 902-758-
31, 20961 Hwy 2) Unserviced/serviced
es $12/17. Open late May-Sept. A kilome-
r northeast of the provincial wildlife park,
is friendly, clean and well-maintained
mpground has lots of space and is not
ominated by RVs. It's over a hill from the
ghway, so there's not much traffic noise.
ots of tent sites are available at the back of
e campground, some in a forest, others in
grassy field. A lake is adjacent, and there
e hot showers.

AITLAND &
HUBENACADIE CANAL
e village of Maitland, 9km north of the
nction of Hwys 236 and 215, has an en-
anting location above the Bay of Fundy
the mouth of the Shubenacadie River.
tending south along the river through
rious locks and lakes, the Shubenacadie
anal was once a continuous navigable
ater system that led to the city of Dart-
outh and the ocean.
Opened in 1861, the canal is now a na-
onal historic site. It hasn't served as a trade
ute since 1870, but parts of it are now
opular with recreational boaters and ca-
eists. Maps available at tourist offices list
oints of interest along the route, and de-
led canoe maps and guidebooks can be
rchased at the Halifax Trading and Guide
ost in Halifax (see the Halifax chapter).

wrence House
aitland's main attraction is Lawrence
ouse (☎ 902-261-2628, 8660 Hwy 215; ad-
ssion $2; open 9:30am-5:30pm Mon-Sat,
m-5:30pm Sun June-mid-Oct), a provin-
al historical site. This grand house was
ilt in 1870 for shipbuilder William

Lawrence, who obviously did quite well for
himself. From a small room on the 2nd floor
Lawrence could watch the progress of his
vessels being built in the shipyard at the
river's edge. There's a great view of the
mouth of the Shubenacadie River from a
turnoff 100m west of Lawrence House.

Places to Stay
Terranita B&B (☎ 902-261-2102, W www
.rivercountry.ns.ca/bedandbre/terranita.htm,
8098 Hwy 215, Selma) Singles/doubles
$50/65. Open May-Oct. This magnificent
stone mansion from 1825 stands alone on a
hilltop behind the United Church in Selma,
3km west of Lawrence House.
The Cobequid Inn (☎ 902-261-2841, fax
902-261-2650, W www.bbcanada.com/cobe
quidinn, 8042 Hwy 215, Selma) Singles/
doubles $45/60. Open May-Oct. Three
rooms with shared bath are available in this
blue-and-white house with a large backyard, 200m west of the United Church.
Another B&B is across the street.

TRURO
Truro (population 12,000), with its central
position in the province, is known as the
hub of Nova Scotia. The Trans Canada Hwy
passes through the north and east of town;
Hwy 102 runs south to Halifax. The VIA
Rail line goes by, and Truro is also a bus
transfer point.
Downtown Truro is centered around the
intersection of Prince St and Inglis Place,
where some redevelopment has gentrified
the streets. Other parts of town are dominated by malls. Still, Truro offers a glimpse
of authentic Maritimes life not dominated
by tourism. Almost a tenth of the area's
population is Native Indian.
The tourist office (☎ 902-893-2922) is on
the corner of Prince and Commercial Sts.
It's open late May to October. They provide
free Internet access.

Colchester Museum
In the center of town, this large museum
(☎ 902-895-6284, 29 Young St; adult/child
$2/50¢; open 10am-5pm daily July & Aug,
10am-noon & 2pm-5pm Tues-Fri, 2pm-5pm

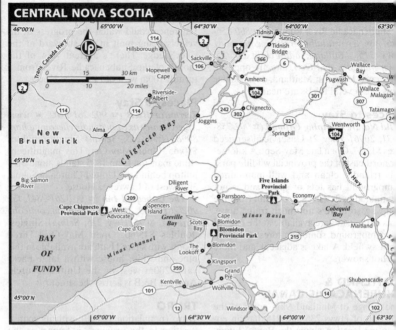

CENTRAL NOVA SCOTIA

other months) has exhibits on the founding of Truro and the history of the region. It also spotlights Elizabeth Bishop, a noted poet who grew up in the area.

Little White Schoolhouse Museum

This little museum (☎ 902-895-5170, 20 Arthur St; admission free; open 10am-6pm Mon-Sat) occupies a bona fide rural schoolhouse in use from 1868 to 1969. It was moved here in the 1970s and restored to its 1899 appearance.

Victoria Park

Located in the heart of the city, this is the gem of Truro. At nearly 1000 acres, Victoria Park is more of a rugged nature reserve than a city park. Cars must park at the entrance, leaving most of the park to walkers and cyclists. A 2km hike leads to views of Joe Howe and Waddell Falls, two small cascades set in a rocky gorge. If you're feeling

energetic, climb Jacob's Ladder, a stairwa of 173 steps.

The Victoria Park Swimming Po (☎ 902-895-7078) is another attraction, ope to the general public from 1pm to 4pm ar 6pm to 7:30pm during July and August. Th fee for swimming is $3.25.

To get to Victoria Park from the tra station on Esplanade St, head south o Young St and then turn east on Brunswic St, where the entrance to the park signposted.

Millbrock First Nation

South on James St beyond the Nova Inst tution for Women (a prison), you'll find th Millbrock First Nation, a major Mi'kma reserve. You'll get a real glimpse of co temporary Mi'kmaq life here; the rows trailers are quite a sight. The best time come is the second weekend in Augu when there's a big Mi'kmaq powwow Millbrock.

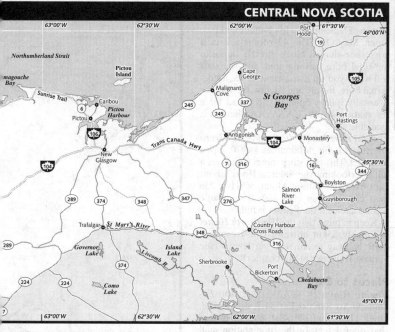

CENTRAL NOVA SCOTIA

idal Bore Viewing

ne of the most popular viewing points in
ova Scotia is the lookout on the Salmon
iver, off Hwy 236, just west of exit 14 from
wy 102 on the northwest side of Truro. A
deo on this phenomenon plays continu-
sly from May to October at the **Truro
dal Bore Interpretive Centre** *(S Tidal Bore
d opposite the Palliser Motel; admission
ee)*. The folks in the gift shop at the adja-
nt Palliser Motel will gladly tell you
actly when the next tidal bore is due to
rive. Don't expect a huge wave.

laces to Stay

ova Scotia Agricultural College (☎ 902-
3-7519, fax 902-893-6545, **e** nsacconcen@
racom.com, **w** www.nsac.ns.ca, College
d, off Main St) Singles/doubles $35/46
ily or $115/173 weekly. Just 2km north-
st of the VIA Rail station, the college
nts 126 rooms with shared bath in the
udent dorms from May to August. Apply

to the NSAC Conference Office in Fraser
House between 8:30am and 10:30pm.
There's a cafeteria on campus.

Willow Bend Motel (☎ 888-594-5569, 277
Willow St) Singles/doubles $55/69 mid-June-
mid-Sept, $45/50 other months, continental
breakfast included. Right across the street
from the Acadian Lines bus station is this
pleasant 27-room motel.

Stonehouse Motel (☎ 877-660-6638, fax
902-897-9937, 165 Willow St) Rooms $55
single or double mid-June-mid-Sept, $45
other months. This motel is halfway
between the Acadian Lines bus station and
the VIA Rail station.

Rainbow Motel (☎ 902-893-9438,
e r.cunningham@ns.sympatico.ca, 341
Prince St) Singles/doubles $46/70. Thirty-
five rooms are available in several motel
blocks on the busy road leading into Truro
from exit 14 off Hwy 102.

Palliser Motel (☎ 902-893-8951, fax 902-
895-8475, **e** palliser@auracom.com, S Tidal

NOVA SCOTIA

Bore Rd, off Hwy 236, very near exit 14 from Hwy 102) Singles/doubles $41/59, extra persons $7, including a full buffet breakfast. Open May-Oct. The 42 rooms are in a horseshoe-shaped block directly opposite the tidal bore viewing area, and the staff will wake you up if you want to see a nocturnal bore. In July and August, the Palliser is usually full by 5pm, so call ahead for a reservation. A 10% CAA/AAA discount is available.

Tidal Bore Inn (☎ 902-895-9241, 29 Truro Heights Rd) Singles/doubles $45/70. Open May-Oct. This two-story motel stands on a hill overlooking the Salmon River, about 1km from the Palliser Motel, off Hwy 236 near exit 14 from Hwy 102. It's a viable second choice if the Palliser is full.

Keep in mind that the *Wentworth Hostel* is roughly 55km northwest of Truro, not quite halfway to Amherst via Hwy 4 (see Sunrise Trail later in this chapter).

Places to Eat
Engine Room (☎ 902-895-5151, 160 Esplanade St) Sandwiches $4-7, dinners $8. Open 11am-9pm Mon-Sat, noon-8pm Sun (bar open later). In the train station mall along Esplanade St, this large sports bar also presents live music some evenings, as advertised on signs outside. Main meals include lasagna ($7) and steaks ($8 to $15).

Murphy's Fish & Chips (☎ 902-895-1275, 88 Esplanade St) Main meals $5-9. Open 11am-7pm Mon & Tues, 11am-8pm Wed-Sat, noon-8pm Sun. Opposite the ticket office at the train station, Murphy's is always packed with locals who rave about the fish & chips.

Fletcher's Restaurant (☎ 902-895-8326, 337 Prince St) All meals under $10. Open 7am-11pm Mon-Sat, 7am-10pm Sun. Friendly Fletcher's offers home cooking, including fish & chips ($5 to $7), clam or fish chowder ($4) and scallops & fries ($9). It's also very popular at breakfast.

Ponderosa Restaurant (☎ 902-895-7837, 96 Robie St) Complete meals under $10. Open 11am-9pm daily. Robie St, which leads into Truro from exit 14 on Hwy 102, has numerous fast food restaurants and

shopping malls. This glorified fast foo place, near a large Sobeys Supermarket, wi provide you with a steak and all-you-ca eat soup and salad bar for under $10. Com starved.

There's also a *farmers market* near th VIA Rail station between Havelock an Outram Sts every Saturday from June t October.

Getting There & Away
Bus The Truro Acadian Lines bus statio (☎ 902-895-3833), 280 Willow St, is one the largest in the province. The station is ju

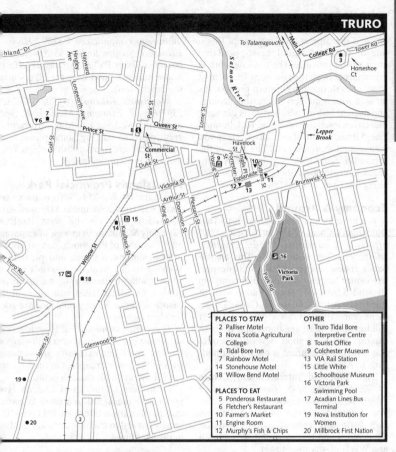

TRURO

To Tatamagouche

To Truro Rd

Salmon River

Lepper Brook

Victoria Park

Park Rd

Brunswick St

PLACES TO STAY
2 Palliser Motel
3 Nova Scotia Agricultural College
4 Tidal Bore Inn
7 Rainbow Motel
14 Stonehouse Motel
18 Willow Bend Motel

PLACES TO EAT
5 Ponderosa Restaurant
6 Fletcher's Restaurant
10 Farmer's Market
11 Engine Room
12 Murphy's Fish & Chips

OTHER
1 Truro Tidal Bore Interpretive Centre
8 Tourist Office
9 Colchester Museum
13 VIA Rail Station
15 Little White Schoolhouse Museum
16 Victoria Park Swimming Pool
17 Acadian Lines Bus Terminal
19 Nova Institution for Women
20 Millbrock First Nation

der 2km from the VIA Rail station via Willow and Arthur Sts. It's open 8am to 1pm daily. Coin lockers ($2) are available.

There are six buses a day to Halifax ($15) nd three a day, with different stops, to ydney ($48). There's an 8:20am and 2:15pm us daily to Saint John, New Brunswick 54), with a change in Amherst; two other uses go daily to Amherst ($21). There are lso four runs per day to Antigonish ($17).

rain The VIA Rail station (☎ 888-842-245) is in town at 104 Esplanade St, near e corner of Inglis Place. Trains in and out

of Nova Scotia pass through Truro, so connections can be made for Halifax, Montréal and various points in New Brunswick. Trains to Halifax ($21) run daily except Wednesday, and trains to Moncton ($35) and Montréal ($183) run daily except Tuesday. Purchasing tickets five days in advance for travel within the Maritimes or seven days in advance for travel to Québec usually saves a third or more, but these reduced seats are limited in number. A railway bus connection between Truro and Sydney can be purchased in combination with the train ticket.

CHIGNECTO

This region west of Truro is named after the bay and the cape at the western tip. This is one of the least-visited, least-populated areas of the province. The road network is minimal, although the Glooscap Trail tourist route goes through the eastern portion. It's an area with some very interesting geology and ancient history, which attracts dinosaur detectives, fossil followers and rock hounds. The Minas Basin shore has some good scenery and shoreline cliffs. The tides of the Minas Basin are high even by Fundy standards. Unfortunately, there's no bus service along this coast.

Economy & Around

If you have kids in tow, take them to **That Dutchman's Cheese Farm** (☎ 902-647-2751, off Hwy 2; admission $1.50/2 children/ adults; 9am-7pm year-round). This combination cheese shop, restaurant and interpretive center just east of Upper Economy, up Brown Rd from 4532 Hwy 2, makes some of the best Gouda cheese in Canada. The many domestic animals and pets will delight children, and there are barns and trails to explore. You get a good view of Cobequid Bay too. The restaurant is open from mid-June to August only.

The **Cobequid Interpretation Centre** (☎ 902-647-2600, 3248 Hwy 2 near River Phillip Rd, Economy; admission free; open 9am-4:30pm Mon-Fri, 9am-6pm Sat & Sun July & August) features good exhibits on the ecology and history of the area as well as a WWII observation tower

Two trail systems can be accessed near Economy. The **Economy Falls Trail** in the Cobequid Mountains begins 7km north up River Phillip Rd and leads 4km into the Kenomee Canyon, ending at a stunning 20m cascade. This is one of the best hikes in the area. The trailhead for the **Devils Bend Trail** is 3km farther up the same road. The two trails link up, as shown on the Kenomee hiking map ($2), which is available at the Cobequid Interpretation Centre. The **Thomas Cove Coastal Trail** is down Economy Point Rd, 1½km east on Hwy 2 from River Phillip Rd.

Places to Stay & Eat *Silver House B&* (☎ 902-647-2022, fax 902-647-2459, e silv .house@ns.sympatico.ca, 3289 Hwy Economy) Singles/doubles $64/69. Near t corner of River Phillip Rd, this large farm house makes a good base for hikers usir the nearby trails.

Morrisons Takeout (☎ 902-647-282 3397 Hwy 2, Economy) Meals $6-8. Ope noon-8pm Wed-Sun late May-early Sept. great place to pick up some picnic foo such as scallops, clams or fish & chips. Tax included in all posted prices.

Five Islands Provincial Park

This park (☎ 902-254-2980, w parks.go .ns.ca, 618 Hwy 2; campsites $18; open ear June-early Oct) on the west flank Economy Mountain, 9km west of Econom and 25km east of Parrsboro, 3km off Hwy offers camping, a beach and picnickin Walking trails reveal the terrain's variet some leading to the 90m-high cliffs at th edge of the Minas Basin, with views of th islands offshore. Nearby tidal flats are goo for clam digging.

The campground at Five Islands has 9 sites, most in a semi-open area with views the bay. You'll find expansive grassy cam sites in the lower area; sites in the foreste area above are a bit closer together.

From here to the Trans Canada Hw you'll pass almost a dozen small takeawa stands, all of them offering fried clams. Th locally harvested clams are among the be in the Maritimes.

Parrsboro

Parrsboro, the largest of the small tow along the north shore of Minas Basin, is good place to stay for a day or two. Ther are several museums, a fossil-laden shor line to explore and a half-dozen B&Bs an inns. In the center of town next to the tow hall is the tourist office (☎ 902-254-3266 4028 Eastern Ave. Among other things, th office has tide information for visiting roo hounds. Free Internet access is provided. It open mid-May to early October.

Next to the town hall is an 8m red fibe glass **statue of Glooscap**, principle god the Mi'kmaq people. According to a sign-board in front of the statue, 'the capricious and fun-loving spirit of these beautiful and exotic people is reflected in the Glooscap legends.' The statue was created in 1972 by a certain Reverend Tuk, but some local Mi'k-maqs have objected to the emaciated figure and the politically incorrect signboard.

The Parrsboro area is interesting geolog-ically and is known for its semiprecious stones, fossils and dinosaur tracks. People scour the local beaches and rock faces for agates and amethyst and attend the annual gem and mineral show in mid-August, a get-together for rock, mineral and fossil collec-tors which began in the 1970s and features displays, demonstrations, guided walks and boat tours.

Fundy Geological Museum At this museum (☎ 902-254-3814, 162 Two Islands Road; adult/student & senior/family $4/ 3.25/10; open 9:30am-5:30pm daily June-mid-Oct, 9am-5pm Tues-Sat mid-Oct-May) you can find out why the Parrsboro beaches have been dubbed 'Nova Scotia's own Jurassic Park.' The museum features a glit-tering collection of minerals and fossils, but also has models, hands-on exhibits and computer-aided displays that explain the fascinating geological history of the area. Naturalists on staff lead special tours to the nearby beaches.

Parrsboro Rock & Mineral Shop This shop(☎ 902-254-2981, 39 Whiteall Rd, south of the center; admission by donation; open 10am-6pm Tues-Sun May-Oct) is really the personal museum of Eldon George, who achieved international fame searching nearby shorelines for gems and fossils. He loves to talk about his collection and has some intriguing items on display, like a model of a duckbill dinosaur hatching from an egg, the world's smallest dinosaur foot-print and the world's largest crocodile footprint.

Partridge Island This is not only the most popular shoreline to search for gems (a sort of Mecca for rock hounds) but also a place

steeped in history. Among others, Samuel de Champlain landed here in 1607 and took away (what else?) amethyst rocks from the beach. The island is 4km south of town on Whiteall Rd, and there is an interpretive display explaining how the powerful Fundy tides break up the layers of rock to expose new gemstones every year. You will likely encounter a dozen or more people search-ing the pebbled shoreline or the bluffs for agate, jasper, stilbite etc.

Just before the beach is **Ottawa House Museum** (☎ 902-254-2376, 1155 Whitehall Rd; admission $1; open 10am-6pm June-mid-Sept), which preserves Sir Charles Tupper's summer home. Tupper was premier of Nova Scotia and later prime minister of Canada. The museum helps finance maintenance of the building by selling ice cream cones – a good excuse to indulge.

From the end of the beach, a hiking trail with explanatory panels climbs to the top of Partridge Island (which is actually con-nected to the mainland by an isthmus), ending at a spectacular viewpoint. The walk is about 45 minutes each way, and the views of Blomidon and Cape Split across Minas Basin are superb.

Ship's Company Theatre All the world's a stage – or in this case, an entire boat is. The MV Kipawo, built in the Saint John Ship-yard in 1926, was the last of the Minas Basin ferries. In July and August a variety of plays are performed here, most of them new works from Maritimes writers. The **box office** (☎ 902-254-3000, 198 Main St) is in town (tickets $20), but the Kipawo itself is at the south end of downtown, by the shore.

Organized Tours From May to October, **Dinatours** (☎ 902-254-3700, 237 Main St) offers three-hour guided mineral- and fossil-collecting tours for $20. Departure times vary with the tides. Numerous speci-mens from previous trips can be viewed (and purchased) at their main office.

Places to Stay Glooscap Campground (☎ 902-254-2529, fax 902-254-2313, 1380

Two Island Rd, 5km south of town) Unserviced/serviced sites $12/18. Open mid-May-Sept. This attractive municipally owned campground by the shore offers some nice secluded tent sites.

Maple Inn *(☎ 902-254-3735, 877-627-5346, W www3.ns.sympatico.ca/mapleinn, 2358 Western Ave)* Singles/doubles from $64/99. For a splurge, this magnificent Victorian house with a central tower drips with character. It has eight various rooms.

Knowlton House B&B *(☎ 902-254-2773, 2330 Western Ave)* Singles/doubles $60/65. Open mid-June-mid-Sept. Three rooms are available in this fine Parrsboro mansion.

Riverview Cottages *(☎ 902-254-2388, 3575 Eastern Ave)* Singles/doubles from $32/40 ($40/50 with a woodstove), increasing to $66 double. Open mid-Apr-mid-Nov. Riverview, a kilometer east of the center on Hwy 2, offers 18 cottages of various types. Some have light housekeeping; Others are unheated. None have telephones or televisions. Guests enjoy free use of the rowboats and canoes on the river behind the cottages. Weekly rates are possible. This is probably your best bet in Parrsboro, but it's often full.

Places to Eat *John's Café (☎ 902-254-3255, 151 Main St)* Lunches $3-8. Open 7:30am-6pm Mon-Sat, 8:30am-6pm Sun May-Nov. This unpretentious little cafe serves a variety of coffees and teas, plus healthy sandwiches, salads, soups, chili and quiche.

Berry's Restaurant *(☎ 902-254-3040, 29 Two Island Rd)* Main meals $8-9. Open 7am-9pm daily (to 10pm in summer). Try

the fish chowder ($4.25), burger plate ($6.50), flounder dinner ($8.25) or scallop dinner ($9). Berry's is right in town.

Harbour View Restaurant *(☎ 902-254-3507, 476 Pier Rd)* Mains $5-10. Open 7am-9pm May-mid-Oct (to 10pm Fri & Sat). This place at the Government Wharf has just what its name claims, along with family fare and seafood. Breakfast is $4 to $5; otherwise you can order sandwiches or burgers ($3), seafood chowder ($4 to $5), fish & chips ($5 to $7), scallops & chips ($8), fisherman's platter ($16), clam dinner ($10) or pork chops ($8). This is the only place in town with live lobster in a tank (price varies).

Diligent River
At the village of Diligent River is the **Wards Falls Hiking Trail**, a 3½km one-way hike up a river gorge. The trail is well maintained but steep in some places, and toward the end it passes the 7m cascade. The trailhead is opposite 10726 Hwy 209, 10km west of Parrsboro.

Spencers Island
The tiny village of Spencers Island, named for a small kettle-shaped island just offshore, is best known as the home port of the 31m brigantine *Mary Celeste,* which was found off the Azores in 1872 with no one aboard. The fate of the captain, his wife, daughter and the entire crew remains unknown. A plaque on the beach tells the story of the mystery ship, constructed here in 1860.

Old Shipyard Campground *(☎ 902-392-2487, fax 902-392-2226, 774 Spencer's Island)* Unserviced/serviced $15/20. Open mid-May-mid-Oct. This lovely, uncrowded site stretches along a beach and a good cafe is just opposite.

Spencers Island B&B *(☎ 902-392-2721 W www.2hwy.com/ns/s/spislabb.htm, 78 Spencer's Island)* Singles/doubles $30/45. Open June-Aug. Three rooms are for rent in this attractive two-story house just 20m up the road from Spencers Beach.

Cape d'Or
Cape d'Or Park, 5½km off Hwy 209 on a gravel road, is above the lighthouse on the

oint at the end of the peninsula. Two short iking trails provide spectacular views of ιe Minas Channel and Bay of Fundy. Three dal currents collide here, creating an xpanse of wild waters known as the Dory ips.

Lightkeeper's Kitchen & Guest House ☎ 902-670-0534, e capedor@hotmail.com) ingles/doubles $60/75. Open May-mid-Oct. he Kitchen, near the lighthouse, serves reakfast and lunch (seafood chowder 7.50) and has four rooms available.

:ape Chignecto Provincial Park

)pened in 1998, this is now the crown jewel f the peninsula, offering some of the best iking in the Maritimes. The highlight here s the very challenging yet-to-be-completed 5km **Bay of Fundy Coastal Hiking Trail**, eaturing more than three dozen wilder- ιess – nay, old growth – campsites en route. ιt the time of writing, 35km had been fin- shed, beginning and ending at Red Rocks ιn West Advocate (and they're hacking nore every day). The trail from Red Rocks o Cape Chignecto is rugged and recom- nended only for those in good physical hape, but the views are simply magnificent, vith occasional breathtaking drop-offs of '00m in some canyons.

Some hikers have tried to avoid the ups ιnd downs of the trail by taking shortcuts ιlong the beach at low tide. While it's possi- ıle to use the beach if you're only doing a hort day hike from Red Rocks, it's ex- remely dangerous to try to go from Mill 3rook toward Cape Chignecto along the ιeach; the distances between the entry and ιxit points are just too long. Hikers trapped ιy the tides have had to be rescued from the :liffs by helicopter! At the moment, hikers nust return to Red Rocks along a logging oad from Eatonville, but the last section of he trail may already have been finished, naking this unnecessary.

For a day hike, you can go halfway to Mill Brook, where a wooden staircase de- scends to the beach, which you can then use o return to Red Rocks. Double-check the ide status with the wardens before you set ›ut, though, as you could be cut off by a

rising tide while hiking the beach. All told, those in good shape should be able to com- plete this walk in around two hours. Every- one using these trails must register at the interpretive center at Red Rocks and pay a $3 hiking fee. This gives the wardens a way of controlling access to the trails, which is desirable in light of the tidal danger.

If you plan on camping in the back- country, reservations are a necessity; call the park office (☎ 902-392-2085, w www.cape chignecto.net). There are 39 wilderness campsites at six points along the coastal trail, plus 25 walk-in sites near Red Rocks. Campsites are $18, and reservations are es- sential for the wilderness sites, as only those with reservations are allowed to spend a night on the trail.. The campsites (and by ex- tension the trail) are closed from early October to mid-May.

West Advocate itself has a magnificent long sandy beach piled high with driftwood.

Places to Stay *Lands End Retreat B&B* (☎ 902-392-2835, 1219 West Advocate Rd) Singles/doubles $35/45. Open May-mid- Nov. This large two-story house near the Chignecto Variety Store is just 500m from the Red Rocks trailhead.

Reid's Century Farm Tourist Home (☎ 902-392-2592, fax 902-392-2523, 1391 West Advocate) Singles/doubles $40/50. Open June-Sept. Three rooms are available in this farmhouse on a real country farm just off Hwy 209, 1.3km from the Red Rocks trailhead.

Joggins

A short distance from Amherst on Chignecto Bay is the village of Joggins, known for its seaside cliffs full of fossils. It exposes one of the world's best Carboniferous-period fossil collections, con- sisting of trees, insects, reptiles and other fossils, some of which are 300 million years old. There's a footpath down to the beach and along the 50m-high sandstone cliffs, but it's worthwhile to first visit the **Joggins Fossil Centre** (☎ 902-251-2727, 30 Main St; admission $3.50; open 9am-5:30pm daily June-Sept). Here you'll see fossil samples, including fossilized footprints, and learn more about the site.

Fun and informative guided tours were offered until recently, but they've not been available of late due to insurance problems. Remember that this is a protected area, so do-it-yourselves beware; scavenging is OK, hacking into the cliffs is not. The museum can offer advice, if not assistance.

AMHERST

Amherst (population 10,000) is the geographic center of the Maritimes and a major travel junction. For almost anyone heading into Nova Scotia by land, passing by (or through) is a necessity. Hwy 104, which runs just outside of town, leads south toward Halifax and then cuts east for Cape Breton Island. Also from Amherst, it's not far to the Northumberland Shore and the Sunrise Trail along the north coast. Highway 16, which leads to the bridge to Prince Edward Island, is just across the border in New Brunswick.

Amherst is a pleasant town with some fine buildings, and many from the 19th century have been restored. You'll find a number of these along Victoria, the main street, whose intersection with Church St is the de facto center of town. The local tourist office has a walking tour map. Amherst is a good place to stay overnight, with some moderately priced lodgings.

Information

There are two tourist offices in Amherst. Just off exit 1 of Hwy 104 is a huge provincial welcome center (☎ 902-667-8429) that is open March to mid-December. The center features information for all of Nova Scotia, an interpretive area and gardens out front. Behind the center is the Fort Lawrence Interpretive Centre (☎ 902-667-1756), open 9am to 5pm June to mid-October, with a scale model of a British fort built near here in 1750. In those days the border between British and French territory was the Nova Scotia–New Brunswick border of today. Fort Beauséjour – clearly visible to the north – was the corresponding French fort.

The Amherst tourist office (☎ 902-667-0696), 21481 Fort Lawrence Rd, is just 400 south of the provincial welcome center of the way to downtown Amherst. Railwa buffs should certainly visit, as it's in vintage railway car actually built i Amherst in 1905. This office is open from June to mid-September.

The Nova Scotia Geomatics Cente (☎ 902-667-7231), 160 Willow St, is th central distributor of government topo graphical maps ($10.45 each) for the thre Maritime provinces. It's open 8:30am t 4:30pm Monday to Friday.

Cumberland County Museum

This museum (☎ 902-667-2561, 150 Churc St; admission $1; open 9am-5pm Mon-Sa 2pm-5pm Sun May-Sept; 9am-5pm Tues-S Oct-Apr) is in the erstwhile home (erecte 1838) of the father of confederation, R Dickey. The most interesting displays ar the articles made by prisoners of war at th Amherst Internment Camp during WW which included Leon Trotsky.

Amherst Point Migratory Bird Sanctuary

This bird sanctuary is 6km west of centra Amherst. To reach it, head west on Victori St, past the Wandlyn Inn Hotel. A few hundred meters beyond the inn veer lef toward Amherst Point when the roa divides. The poorly marked trailhea becomes apparent if you watch for parking lot in the forest on the left.

Over 200 species of bird are seen in thi 490-hectare sanctuary. A loop trail circle and crosses several ponds and lakes through fields and marsh. It's free an always open, but bicycles are prohibited.

Places to Stay

Loch Lomond Park (☎ 902-667-3890, fa 902-667-0309, off Hwy 2 just south of exit from Hwy 104) Unserviced/serviced camp sites $16/20. Open mid-May-mid-Oct. Loc Lomond has a variety of reasonably goo tenting sites near the shore of Blair Lake.

Victorian Motel (☎ 902-667-7211, 150 Victoria St) Singles/doubles $52/60. Thi

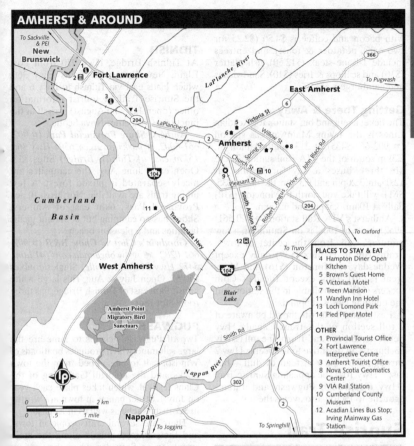

AMHERST & AROUND

PLACES TO STAY & EAT
4 Hampton Diner Open Kitchen
5 Brown's Guest Home
6 Victorian Motel
7 Treen Mansion
11 Wandlyn Inn Hotel
13 Loch Lomond Park
14 Pied Piper Motel

OTHER
1 Provincial Tourist Office
2 Fort Lawrence Interpretive Centre
3 Amherst Tourist Office
8 Nova Scotia Geomatics Center
9 VIA Rail Station
10 Cumberland County Museum
12 Acadian Lines Bus Stop; Irving Mainway Gas Station

motel offers 20 rooms in two long blocks a few minutes walk from the center of town.

Brown's Guest Home (☎ 902-667-9769, fax 902-667-2055, e dnallen@istar.ca, w home.istar.ca/~dnallen, 158 E Victoria St) Singles/doubles $45/55. Open May-Oct. The three rooms in this stately three-story house offer an alternative to the motel.

Treen Mansion (☎ 902-667-2146, 113 Spring St) Singles/doubles/triples $35/50/60. This large Victorian house with a porch and tower was built in 1907. There are three rooms; rates include breakfast in the sunroom.

Pied Piper Motel (☎ 902-667-0330, 19024 Hwy 2, 5km south of Amherst junction of Hwy 302 to Joggins) Singles/doubles $45/60. The 10 rooms are in a long block facing the road.

Places to Eat

Hampton Diner Open Kitchen (☎ 902-667-3562, 21386 Fort Lawrence Rd) Mains $10. Open 7am-9pm Tues-Sun mid-May-Sept. This classic diner, 700m south of the Amherst tourist office and 3km north of downtown Amherst, has been around since 1956. You can't miss it as you come into town. It's recommended for good, cheap food and quick, courteous service. Breakfast with bacon and coffee is $4.50 ($2.25 for two eggs, potatoes & toast), and entrees include T-bone steak ($12.50), fish platter ($10) and scallops & fries ($10). Sandwiches and hamburgers are $3.

Getting There & Away
The ticket agent and bus station for Acadian Lines is the Irving Mainway gas station (☎ 902-667-8435) at 213 South Albion St, 2.3km south of the VIA Rail station. There are three buses a day for Halifax, at 12:05am, 3:20pm and 9:35pm; the fare is $35. SMT will take you north to Moncton ($10) daily at 10am, 3:55pm and 6:35pm.

Amherst's VIA Rail station (☎ 800-561-3952), built in 1908, is on Station St, a few minutes' walk from the center of town. Trains run to Halifax ($39) daily except Wednesday, to Moncton ($16) and Montréal ($170) daily except Tuesday. Coin lockers ($1) are available in the station, but the building closes at 5pm daily.

Eastbound motorists should be aware of a toll section of the Trans Canada Hwy between Amherst and Truro. The toll is only $3, but it's an incentive to use scenic Hwy 2 through Parrsboro instead of dull – but fast – Hwy 104. The appealing Sunrise Trail (Hwy 6) through Pugwash and Tatamagouche to Pictou also avoids the toll.

Sunrise Trail

This tourist route crosses the north coastal region of the province, from the New Brunswick border to Cape Breton Island.

The Northumberland Strait is situated between Nova Scotia's north shore and Prince Edward Island and has some of the warmest waters north of the US Carolinas, with an average water temperature slightly over 20°C (68°F) in summer. Highway 6 runs along a strip of small towns and beaches on the Northumberland Shore.

This shoreline is busy, and as accommodations are not plentiful, places to stay fill quickly. In July and August it's strongly

recommended that you find a place by lunchtime.

TIDNISH
At Tidnish Bridge, Hwy 970 from Port Elgin, New Brunswick, joins Hwy 366, which leads east via Tidnish to Hwy 6 and the Sunrise Trail. A tourist information office (open July and August) is right at the junction as you enter Nova Scotia.

Amherst Shore Provincial Park (☎ 902-661-6002, W *parks.gov.ns.ca, 6596 Hwy 366, 15km east of Tidnish Bridge*) Sites $18. Open early June-Aug. The campsites are nicely separated in mixed forest. A few hiking trails are available. Northeast Beach Provincial Park, 6km east of Amherst Shore, has no camping but abundant picnic facilities and a pleasant beach.

Goodwin's Chat 'n' Chow B&B (☎ 902-661-0282, W *www.bbcanada.com/141.html, 5472 Hwy 366, Lorneville*) Singles/doubles $50/55. Open July & Aug. This large white house, 9km east of Tidnish Bridge, has three rooms for rent.

PUGWASH
Two of Pugwash's claims to fame are the large salt mine, which produces boatloads of Windsor salt to be shipped from the town docks, and the colorful Gathering of the Clans festival, which takes place each year on July 1. Street names in town are written in Scottish Gaelic as well as in English.

There are several craftspeople in town, and their wares are sold along the main street, or on Saturday when they set up tables at the former Pugwash Train Station. Built in 1888, this is one of the oldest stations in Nova Scotia and today serves as a tourist office and library. Seagull Pewter (☎ 902-243-2516, 9926 Hwy 6) has a shop and factory just west of town. Public Internet access is offered at the Pugwash CAP Site (☎ 902-243-2088), 124 Water St. It's open 8am to noon and 1pm to 4pm Monday to Friday.

Cyrus Eaton's Thinkers Lodge
Pugwash is internationally famous for this prominent white house at 247 Water St, on a point jutting into the bay. In July 1957

industrialist Cyrus Eaton (1883–1979) brought together a group of 22 leading scientists from around the world to discuss disarmament issues and science. The meeting was at the request of Bertrand Russell, Albert Einstein and others, though they themselves did not attend. The Pugwash Conference laid the groundwork for the Partial Test Ban Treaty of 1963, and since 1957 there have been over 200 Pugwash conferences at different venues. In 1995, the Pugwash Conferences on Science and World Affairs won the Nobel Peace Prize. The Pugwash Conferences still use Thinkers Lodge for occasional meetings; the building cannot be visited. For more information on the Pugwash Conferences, check the Web site at w www.pugwash.org.

Wallace Bay Nature Trail

This trail does a loop through wetlands favored by migratory birds. To get there, go ½km east of Pugwash on Hwy 6, then turn left and follow the paved road 4km toward Wallace Bay. Turn right shortly after you see a lake, and 600m along, immediately after the road cuts across the lake, you'll see the parking area and trailhead on the right. Admission is free.

Places to Stay & Eat

Hillcrest Motel (☎ 902-243-2727, fax 902-243-2704, 11054 Hwy 6, 2km east of Pugwash) Singles/doubles $38/46. Six motel-style rooms are available in a long block. The motel's restaurant (open 7am to 9pm, or until 8pm in summer) serves a full breakfast for $5. The fish & chips ($6 to $7) are better than average; for dinner try the pan-fried haddock ($11).

Caboose Café (12 Durham St) Mains $10. Open June-mid-Sept. Next to the old train station in the center of Pugwash, the Caboose Café provides lunch options such as a cabooseburger ($5), fish burger ($5) and lobster roll ($9). Dinner starts at $10 for a fish platter and rises to $23 for lobster.

WENTWORTH

The shortage of low-budget accommodations along this shore may warrant a detour

to Wentworth, 25km south of Wallace via Hwy 307 or 27km southwest of Tatamagouche on Hwy 246. Wentworth is not quite halfway between Truro and Amherst on Hwy 4.

Wentworth Provincial Park (☎ 902-548-2379, fax 902-548-2389, e wentworthhostel@ns.sympatico.ca, w parks.gov.ns.ca, 1525 Valley Rd) Sites $14. Open mid-May-early Oct. This provincial campground, just 500m off Hwy 4 between Truro and Oxford, has 49 sites scattered through the forest. The campground is managed by the same folks who run the HI hostel up on the hill behind the park.

Wentworth Hostel (☎ 902-548-2379, fax 902-548-2389, e wentworthhostel@ns.sympatico.ca, w www.hostellingintl.ns.ca, 249 Wentworth Station Rd, off Valley Rd) Beds $18. Open year-round. To reach the hostel from town, go 1.3km west on Valley Rd, then straight up Wentworth Station Rd till you see the HI hostel on the right. The last 700m are a bit steep if you're on foot carrying a backpack. This big rambling farmhouse was built in 1866 and has been used as a hostel for half a century. There are 15 dorm beds, a five-bed family room and one double room called the Livingston Room (the family and double rooms cost $2 per person extra). The hostel has kitchen facilities, showers and parking, and 75km of mountain-bike trails are accessible from a trailhead just outside the door. A good one-hour return hike from the hostel is to the Lookoff, a bluff with a great view. Downhill and cross-country skiing are practiced here in winter.

All Seasons B&B (☎ 888-879-5558, w www.bbcanada.com/1628.html, 14371 Hwy 4, Wentworth) Doubles from $45. Just 700m south of the turnoff to Wentworth Park and the hostel, this modern bungalow above the highway is another worthy option.

TATAMAGOUCHE

Despite having a population of under 1000 (and one road – the highway), Tatamagouche is something of a tourist center, as several routes converge here.

Tatamagouche's annual Oktoberfest is held at the end of September or beginning of October.

Things to See

Not to be missed is the quirky **Fraser Cultural Centre** (☎ 902-657-3285, *362 Main St; admission by donation; open 10am-4pm daily late May-mid-Sept*), a museum-cum-art gallery. The showpiece is the room dedicated to Anna Swan. Standing 2.4m tall and weighing 187kg, Swan was known as the giantess of Nova Scotia, and she rose to achieve some celebrity. Born in a nearby village in 1896, she parlayed her size into a lucrative career with Barnum & Bailey's circus and even ended up meeting the queen in London, where Anna was married. Clothes, newspaper clippings and photographs tell the big story.

The center also has some historical pieces and several galleries displaying the work of local artists. The tourist office is here in one of the many rooms.

Down the street is the less idiosyncratic **Sunrise Trail Museum** (☎ 902-657-3007, *260 Main St; admission $2; open 9am-5pm daily late June-Aug*), focusing on local history, with an emphasis on the shipbuilding industry, once of major importance here. The Acadian French settled this area in the 1700s and a display recounts their history and expulsion.

Activities

Tide and Trail Rentals (☎ 902-657-0318, ☎ 902-662-2174, *19 Main St, Tatamagouche*) operates out of a trailer by the river on the north side of Tatamagouche. They rent sea kayaks ($30/40 per half/full day), canoes ($15/30) and bicycles ($10/20). In June and September you'll only find them open on weekends.

Places to Stay

Nelson Park Campground (☎ 902-657-2730, *156 Loop of Hwy 6*) Unserviced/serviced sites $18/21-23. Open mid-May-Sept. This county-run campground is off Hwy 6, 2½km west of Tatamagouche via Tattrie Settlement Rd. You can hike into town on the

Trans Canada Trail in under half an hou Some of the 40 grassy tent sites are righ down by the bay, where you'll find shower and a beach.

Train Station Inn (☎ 888-724-5233, *fa* 902-657-9091, w *www.trainstation.ns.ca,* 2 *Station Rd*) Singles/doubles $70/90, suite from $129. This place just down the hill fror the Fraser Cultural Centre is in the (yo guessed it) old 1887 train station on the lin from Oxford Junction to Stellarton. It fea tures three rooms on the 2nd floor of th station, where the stationmaster lived, plu seven cabooses and one box car outside tha have been converted into suites, each ac commodating two to four people.

Brule Shore Cabins (☎ 902-657-2922 w *www.tata.ns.ca/businesses/brulecabin* 4261 Hwy 6, Brule*) Cabins $43/85 without with cooking facilities. Open June-Sept. Te kilometers east of Tatamagouche, Brul Shore Cabins are 500m west of the junctio with Hwy 326. The 22 units, in 11 duplexe are arranged around a horseshoe-shape driveway facing the road. Rushton's Beacl Provincial Park (no camping), 5km east o the cabins on Hwy 6, is a great place t swim.

Places to Eat

Villager Restaurant (☎ 902-657-2029, *27. Main St*) Dinner around $10. Open 11am 10pm July & Aug, 11am-9pm Tues-Sur other months. This place has daily specials seafood and quite good chowders. Try th clam strips & chips ($6), fishburger ($6) haddock dinner ($10), pan-fried scallop ($13) or seafood platter ($17).

Big Al's Acadian Beverage Room (☎ 902-657-3341, *9 Station Rd*) Meals $6-8 Open 10am-8pm Mon-Wed, 10am-9pm Thurs-Sat, noon-8pm Sun (bar open later) The unpretentious sports bar just below th Fraser Cultural Centre serves pub fare lik burgers ($4), nachos ($6), chicken finger ($6) and fish & chips ($8). Saturday an Sunday brunch (noon to 3pm) is $7.

AROUND TATAMAGOUCHE

A side trip worth taking is to the **Balmora Grist Mill Museum** (☎ 902-657-3016, *66*

Matheson Brook Rd; adult/child $2/1; open 9:30am-5:30pm Mon-Sat, 1pm-5:30pm Sun June-mid-Oct). From Tatamagouche go 5km south on Hwy 311, then 2km east on Hwy 256. This is one of the province's oldest grist mills, dating from 1874. Grinding demonstrations, held from 10am to noon and 2pm to 4pm daily during summer, show the flour (oatmeal, barley, wheat) milling process from start to finish, and the completed products are offered for sale. Note the old trees along the gorge and take a hike through the surrounding forest if you're so inclined.

From the Balmoral Grist Mill, go 5km east on Hwy 256, then 6km north on Hwy 326 to the village of Denmark. The **Sutherland Steam Mill** *(☎ 902-657-3365, 3169 Hwy 326; adult/child $2/1; open 9:30am-5:30pm Mon-Sat, 1pm-5:30pm Sun June-mid-Oct)* was built in 1894 and was run continuously by family members until 1953. The sawmill is no longer a commercial entity, but the machinery and steam engine are still operational, and they cut lumber Wednesday to Saturday from 1pm to 3pm. From here it's only 4km north to Hwy 6 and the coast.

PICTOU

Pictou (pronounced **pick**-toe), one of the most attractive and engaging towns along the North Shore, is where the Highland Scots first landed in 1773, to be followed by thousands more in the settling of 'New Scotland.' In town, among the many older structures, are several buildings and historic sites relating to the early Scottish pioneers.

Water St, the main street in town, reflects the architectural style of the early Scottish builders. Above it, Church, High and Faulkland Sts are lined with some of the old, capacious houses for which the town is noted.

Pictou, with its stone buildings and scenic waterfront, is a haven for artists. Throughout town there are various art studios and craft shops, with most of them clustering along Water and Front Sts.

Plentiful brochures are available at the large provincial tourist office *(☎ 902-485-6213)* at the Pictou Rotary (traffic circle) northwest of the town center. It's open 9am to 7pm daily May to mid-December, 8am to 9pm July and August.

Hector Heritage Quay

Part of the waterfront has been redeveloped to preserve both history and access. At the shipyard, a full-size replica of the three-masted *Hector,* the first ship to bring Scottish settlers, is being reconstructed. Begun in 1993, it will take a few more years to complete. Guides tell the story of the crossing and settlement.

The **interpretive center** *(☎ 902-485-4371, 33 Caladh Ave; adult/family $5/12 interpretive center & shipyard; 9am-6pm Mon-Sat, noon-6pm Sun mid-May-early Oct)* has displays and dioramas depicting the life of the Scottish immigrants, a blacksmith shop and a collection of shipbuilding artifacts.

Northumberland Fisheries Museum

In the old train station (1904), this museum *(☎ 902-485-4972, 71 Front St; admission $3; open 9am-7pm Mon-Sat, noon-7pm Sunday late June-early Oct)* tells the story of the area's fishing industry. A prize exhibit is the spiffy *Silver Bullet,* an early 1930s lobster boat that won three boat races.

Activities

The **Visitors Marina Centre** *(☎ 902-485-6960, 37 Caladh Ave; open late May-early Oct)* on the waterfront rents bicycles at $5 for four hours or $10 a day. The same office has kayaks at $10/35/55 an hour/four hours/day for a single, or $15/40/60 for a double. From the Marina Centre, the **Jitney Trail** runs 3km west along Pictou Harbour on a former railway line.

Special Events

The Lobster Carnival, a three-day event at the beginning of July, marks the end of the lobster season. The four-day Hector Festival in mid-August celebrates the area's Scottish heritage and includes concerts. Just across the water at Pictou Landing there's a Mi'kmaq powwow the second weekend in June.

Places to Stay

Pictou has about a dozen possibilities for spending the night, most of them upscale. Bear in mind that even though the town isn't usually particularly crowded, a steady stream of people passes through and most accommodations are full (or close to it) throughout the summer.

Hostel Pictou (☎ 902-485-8740, e alouisemacisaac@hotmail.com, 14 Chapel St) Dorm beds $17. Open June-Sept. Part of the Backpackers Hostels chain, this cozy hostel is just a block off the Pictou waterfront. It occupies a historic house dating from 1848, and the beds are in three shared double rooms. There's a large TV room/lounge and a common kitchen. Going out in the evening is no problem, as there's no curfew.

WH Davies House B&B (☎ 902-485-4864, 90 Front St) Doubles from $65. This three-room B&B is in an elegant colonial house built in 1855.

Miles Away Inn (☎ 902-485-4799, e milesaway@ns.sympatico.ca, 106 Front St) Doubles from $48. Three doors down from Davies B&B and slightly cheaper, Miles Away is in yet another heritage building.

Consulate Inn (☎ 800-424-8283, fax 902-485-1532, e consulate.inn@ns.sympatico.ca, w www.townofpictou.com/consulateinn/index.htm, 157 Water St) Rooms $59-149. This old stone building dating from 1810 once housed the American consulate in Pictou. There's a wide variety of rooms and suites, all with private bath, and the inn boasts a well-regarded dining room.

Willow House Inn (☎ 902-485-5740, e rcyr@nsis.com, 11 Willow St) Rooms from $59/69 shared/private bath including continental breakfast. This three-story wooden house dating from 1840, just up from Consulate Inn, has been fully renovated into a comfortable B&B. It features eight rooms.

Linden Arms B&B (☎ 902-485-6565, 62 Martha St) Doubles $50 including breakfast. Open June-Sept. This attractive two-story house, in a residential area seven short blocks above the waterfront, is cheaper because it isn't right in the heart of town.

The Lionstone Inn (☎ 902-485-4157, fa 902-485-4157, 241 W River Rd) Motel room $59 single or double mid-June to mid-Oct $40-49 mid-Oct-mid-June; cabins from $54 or $59-75 with cooking facilities. Away from the downtown area near the Pictou Rotary (behind KFC), the Lionstone Inn has 1 well-maintained motel units in two long wooden blocks as well as 13 older, some what austere cabins, each with its own kitchen. The unheated cabins come in various sizes and are closed in winter. At the beginning or end of the season you might be able to get one for $45.

Places to Eat

Fougere's Restaurant (☎ 902-485-1575, 89 Water St) Mains $10. Open 11:30am-9pm Tues-Sun May-mid-Nov. Lunch is less expensive, with dishes like pork schnitzel ($8) hamburgers or chicken fingers ($7) and pastas ($6 to $10). At dinner, try the seafood chowder ($7) and halibut steak ($19).

Down East Family Restaurant (☎ 902-485-4066, 12 Front St) Breakfast with coffee $4. Open 7am-7pm daily. This untouristy local favorite does some real home cooking.

Sobeys Supermarket (☎ 902-485-5841, Pictou Rotary opposite the tourist office) Open 24 hours Mon-Sat.

Entertainment

The *DeCoste Entertainment Centre* (☎ 902-485-8848, 91 Water St) Box office open 11:30am-5pm Mon-Fri. This impressive performing arts center stages a range of live shows, from plays and comedies to concerts by some of the leading Celtic musicians in Canada. For the event schedule or tickets call or stop at the box office.

Relics Public House (☎ 902-485-5577, 50 Caladh St) Open 11:30am-8pm Mon-Thurs, 11:30am-9pm Fri & Sat, noon-8pm Sun May-Oct; 11am-9pm daily July & Aug. This friendly pub on the waterfront opposite Hector Heritage Quay presents traditional Maritimes music every Saturday at 9pm ($2 cover charge). From mid-June to August there's also an open mike session on Wednesday nights and karaoke on Fridays. Typical pub food like poutine ($4), chicken fingers ($6) and nachos ($8) is available, and for bigger appetites, there's the seafood platter ($12) or the daily special advertised on the blackboard outside.

The Highlander Pub (☎ *902-485-1539, cnr Twinning & Front Sts)* Open until 2am Thurs-Sat, 11pm Sun-Wed. They promise 'warm beer and lousy food' but their pizza is said to be the best in town. The Highlander is more of a locals' place than Relics, and there's often karaoke on Saturday nights. It's just a block from the Pictou Hostel.

Getting Around

Unfortunately, Pictou has no bus service. A water taxi (☎ 902-396-8855; $10/18 one way/roundtrip) makes two runs per day to and from New Glasgow in July and August. In Pictou it leaves from beside the Salt Water Café opposite the *Hector* at 1:30pm and 6:30pm; in New Glasgow from the Riverfront Marina in town at noon and 5pm.

AROUND PICTOU
Caribou

From May to mid-December the ferry to Prince Edward Island leaves from the Caribou ferry terminal, 7km north of Pictou on Hwy 106. A provincial park is just down the road, but almost everything else here has to do with the ferry (there's no actual town). For ferry details see Getting There & Away in the introduction to the Prince Edward Island chapter. A PEI tourist information counter (☎ 902-485-6483) is inside the Servicenter at the terminal. The counter is open 10am to 8pm daily July and August.

You can do a three-hour roundtrip on the ferry as a walk-on passenger for just $11 per person (seniors $9, kids under 13 free); you pay at the cafeteria aboard ship. For departure times call ☎ 888-249-7245, and be sure not to take the last ferry of the day if you want to come right back! Free parking is available at the Caribou ferry terminal. This cheap excursion is well worth considering if you aren't planning to visit PEI.

The beach at **Caribou/Munroe's Island Provincial Park** (☎ *902-485-6134,* Ⓦ *parks .gov.ns.ca, 2119 Three Brooks Rd)*, 3.7km

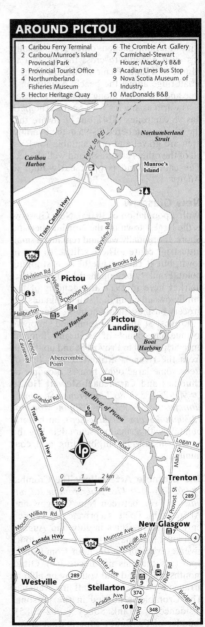

AROUND PICTOU

1 Caribou Ferry Terminal
2 Caribou/Munroe's Island Provincial Park
3 Provincial Tourist Office
4 Northumberland Fisheries Museum
5 Hector Heritage Quay
6 The Crombie Art Gallery
7 Carmichael-Stewart House; MacKay's B&B
8 Acadian Lines Bus Stop
9 Nova Scotia Museum of Industry
10 MacDonalds B&B

southeast of the Caribou ferry terminal (turn left as you leave the ferry), is sandy with water that deepens only very gradually. It's even possible to cross the sandbar to Munroe's Island. Picnic tables are along a small ridge above the beach. Admission is free and the water along this strip of ocean is as warm as any in Nova Scotia. The park has 95 campsites ($14), but be aware that the 18 sites numbered 78–95 in the overflow area are gravel and only suitable for RVs; all of the others are grassy and well shaded. The campground is open early June to August.

New Glasgow

With a population of 10,000, New Glasgow is the largest town on the Northumberland Shore. It originally was, and remains, a small industrial center. There's little to see in town, but it can be useful as a stopping point. Frank Sobey opened his first supermarket here in 1917, the genesis of the family-owned chain that still dominates the grocery business throughout the Maritimes.

Provost St, the main retail and shopping avenue, has a couple of restaurants. Temperance St, parallel to Provost St and up the hill from the river, is attractive, with lots of trees, some large older houses, a couple of churches and **Carmichael-Stewart House** (☎ 902-752-5583, 86 Temperance St, admission free; open 9:30am-4:30pm Mon-Fri, 12:30pm-4:30pm Sat June-Sep), an historic building with a small museum detailing the town's history in shipbuilding and coal mining.

The Crombie Art Gallery

The Crombie (☎ 902-755-4440, 1780 Abercrombie Rd; admission free), between New Glasgow and Abercrombie Point, is a private gallery open only on Wednesdays in July and August. You must join one of the free guided tours given every hour on the hour from 9am to 4pm (reservations not necessary). Other months, call ahead and you may be able to arrange a private visit if staff are available. The Crombie is housed in the personal residence of Frank Sobey (1902–1985), founder of the Sobey supermarket chain,

and it has an excellent collection of 19th- and early 20th-century Canadian art, including works by Cornelius Krieghoff and the Group of Seven.

Nova Scotia Museum of Industry

The most compelling New Glasgow attraction is actually in neighboring Stellarton; take exit 24 off Hwy 104. This impressive provincial museum (☎ 902-755-5425, 147 North Foord St; adult/family $7/15; open 9am-5pm Mon-Sat, 10am-5pm Sun May-Oct; 9am-5pm Tues-Sat, 1pm-5pm Sun Nov-Apr) features almost 14,000 artifacts and numerous hands-on exhibits. Several galleries display items including the Samson, the earliest standard gauge locomotive to operate in North America, the first car to drive the streets of Halifax, and articles from Stellarton's glassworks industry that produced millions of soda bottles. The museum itself is located on the site of the Albion coal mine. The tea shop in the museum has a pleasant outdoor patio.

From the museum parking lot you can pick up the **Samson and Albion Trail**, an 8km walking trail beside the East River of Pictou along an old railway line.

Places to Stay

MacKay's B&B (☎ 902-752-5889, 44 High St, New Glasgow) Singles/doubles $45/55. Open July-Aug. This large house is just three blocks from Carmichael-Stewart House, on the opposite side of St Andrews Presbyterian Church (the huge white church you can see from the museum).

MacDonalds B&B (☎ 902-752-7751, 292 Foord St, Stellarton) Singles/doubles $40/50. Open June-Sept. MacDonalds is an attractive two-story wooden house opposite Sobeys Supermarket in central Stellarton, 1.3km due south of the Museum of Industry.

Getting There & Away

Acadian Lines buses stop at the Irving Mainway gas station (☎ 902-755-5700), 5197 E River Rd, near exit 25 from Hwy 104, 2km south of central New Glasgow. Service is available three or four times a day to Truro ($10), Halifax ($25) and Sydney ($39). There's no bus to

ictou (19km) or Caribou (27km), so this
top is only convenient to those destinations
f someone is picking you up or you're
villing to continue by thumb.

ANTIGONISH

Pleasant Antigonish (pronounced An-tee-
uh-**nish**) is an agreeable stopping place
or anyone passing this way. It's a univer-
ity town (population 5000) with good
places to stay, a nearby beach and no in-
ustry. The hiking possibilities north of
own could keep you busy for a day,
perhaps more.

There are some good sandy beaches on
the coast east and north of town. For the
astern ones, take Bay St out of town.

Information

The tourist office (☎ 902-863-4921) is just
ff the Trans Canada Hwy at the Junction
with Hwy 7. It's open 9am to 6pm late June
o early October, 9am to 8pm July and
August.

The Antigonish Public Library (☎ 902-
63-4276), 274 Main St (in the town hall
building, entrance on College St), provides
public Internet access from 10am to 9pm
Tuesday and Thursday and from 10am to
pm Wednesday, Friday and Saturday.

Heritage Museum

Housed in the classic Antigonish Depot,
which was built in 1908 by the Intercolonial
Railway, this museum (☎ 902-863-6160, 20 E
Main St; admission free; open 10am-5pm
Mon-Sat July & Aug; 10am-noon & 1pm-
pm Mon-Fri other months) features displays on the early days of Antigonish. The
most interesting exhibit is the 1864 hand-
hauled fire engine the town once used to
put out blazes.

County Courthouse

In 1984 this 129-year-old building at 168
Main St was designated a national historic
ite. Restored in 1970, it still serves as the
ounty's judicial center. The design (by
Alexander Macdonald), with four massive
onic columns, is typical of many of the
province's mid-19th century courthouses.

St Francis Xavier University

The attractive campus of this 125-year-old
university is behind St Ninian's Cathedral
(1874) near the center of town. It's a pleasant place to stroll.

Activities

A 4km hiking and biking trail to the nature
reserve at **Antigonish Landing** begins just
across the train tracks from the Heritage
Museum, then 400m down Adam St. This
estuary is a good bird-watching area where
you might see eagles, ducks and osprey.

Special Events

Antigonish is known for its annual Highland Games, held in mid-July. These Scottish
games have been going on since 1861. You'll
see pipe bands, drum regiments, dancers
and athletes from far and wide. The events
last a week. For more information, check
the antigonish Highland Games Web site at
W www.grassroots.ns.ca/~highland.

Festival Antigonish is a summer theater
festival, with all performances held at one of
the university auditoriums. Its Web site is at
W festival.antigonish.com.

Places to Stay

Whidden's Campground & Trailer Court
(☎ 902-863-3736, fax 902-863-0110, e whid-
dens@ant.auracom.com, cnr Main &
Hawthorne Sts) Unserviced/serviced site/
without car $22/26/11, mobile home from
$72 plus $10 for each additional person.
Open May-Oct. This unusual accommodations complex right in town offers a real
blend of choices. It's a large place renting 16
mobile homes with complete facilities. The
grounds have a swimming pool and a Laundromat for all guests to use. Notice the
greatly reduced camping rate for persons
arriving by bicycle or on foot.

St Francis Xavier University (☎ 902-867-
2855, fax 902-867-3751, W www.stfx.ca, West
St) Singles/doubles $29/40. Office open
9am-9pm Mon-Sat, 10am-4pm Sun mid-
May-mid-Aug. Less than a kilometer from
the bus station, St Francis Xavier has 30
rooms with shared bath for rent during the
summer. Apply to Conference Services in

the side of Morrison Hall facing the Angus L Macdonald Library (after 4pm on Sunday go to the security office in the basement of MacKinnon Hall). Use of the university facilities, such as the Laundromat and pool, is included. Parking is free.

The Yellow Door B&B (☎ 902-863-1385, 38 Highland Dr) Singles/doubles $40/55. Open July & Aug. Only a few hundred meters west of the university, three rooms are available in this modern two-story house.

Bekkers (☎ 902-863-3194, 331 Clydesdale Rd) Singles/doubles $50/60 including breakfast. Open June-Oct. This modern brick bungalow with two rooms is 5km outside town in Clydesdale. Take Hawthorne St (Hwy 245) 3½km northwest, then turn left and continue another 1½km.

Places to Eat

Sunshine on Main Café (☎ 902-863-5851, 332 Main St) Mains/full dinner $9/13. Open 7am-9:30pm Sun-Thurs, 7am-10pm Fri & Sat. This café has a bistro feel. You can get creative light main courses or full dinners, and vegetarians aren't ignored. The menu includes sandwiches ($7, or $9 with soup), soup and salad ($10), gourmet burgers ($9) and pasta dishes ($11).

Wong's (☎ 902-863-3596, 232 Main St) Open 11am-10pm Tues-Thurs & Sun, 11am-11pm Fri & Sat. Full dinners $8-11. This friendly place provides the local Chinese option. Combination plates are $9 to $12, Cantonese specialties $10 to $19.

Frescoes Trattoria (☎ 902-863-4350, 76 College St) Dinner from $17. Open 11am-midnight daily. Just off Main St, this is an upscale Italian restaurant with pastas at $10 and mains in the $17 to $23 range. Thursdays at 8pm there's live jazz, and reservations are recommended.

The Piper's Pub (☎ 902-863-2590, 33 College St) Pub food $7-8. Open 11am-2pm daily. This large sports bar just down from the university is something of a student hangout. The pub grub is reasonable and there are specials on drinks. Thursday is open mike night ($2 cover charge), and live bands play most Satur-

days (cover as high as $10 if it's a real well-known group).

Sobeys Supermarket (☎ 902-863-6022) Open 24 hours Mon-Sat. This large grocer store is in the Antigonish Shopping Mall o Church St, just off the Trans Canada at th east end of town.

Getting There & Away

The Acadian Bus Lines terminal (☎ 902 863-6900) is on the Trans Canada Hwy a the turnoff for James St into town. It's o the west side of the city and within walkin distance of the downtown area. Buses ru four times daily to Halifax ($34) and thre times daily to Sydney (one midday and tw early evening trips, $31). Fares are $10 t New Glasgow and $19 to Truro. The statio is open daily until 10:30pm, and $2 coi lockers are available.

AROUND ANTIGONISH
Cape George Driving Tour

This 72km driving tour north along th coast to Cape George takes in some goo scenery, with a chance to view wildlife Points of historical note abound. From th Heritage Museum on E Main St in Antigo nish, it's 10km on Hwy 337 to the signposte **Fairmont Ridge Trail**, a 12km system rangin from leisurely 30-minute strolls aroun meadows and ponds to very challengin rough scrambles through bear country.

Shoreline Adventures (☎ 902-863-5958 at Harbor Centre is 1½km beyond the Fai mont Ridge trailhead. They offer kaya tours ($50/95 per half/full day) and renta ($15/35/55 per hour/half day/full day for single, $20/55/75 for a double). They'll onl rent to two or more persons (solitary kayak ers not accepted). Call ahead, as they don operate every day.

Another even more adventurous syster of loop and linear trails begins at the **Her itage School Museum** at Cape George 15km north of Shoreline Adventures o Hwy 337. As at Fairmont Ridge, these trail are well signposted, with maps posted at a junctions.

Just 4½km beyond the Heritage Schoo Museum is the turnoff to **Point Georg**

Lighthouse, 750m up a gravel road. There's a marvelous view of St Georges Bay from the lighthouse, with the long profile of Cape Breton Island clearly visible. If you have the time, hike down through the meadows to the shoreline below.

To make it a circle trip, drive 22km southwest on Hwy 337 to Malignant Cove, then another 19km back to Antigonish on Hwy 245. Or continue down the coast all the way to New Glasgow. This is one of the great scenic drives of the Maritimes.

Monastery

Thirty-two kilometers east of Antigonish in the village of Monastery, the Augustine Order now occupies a Trappist monastery established by French monks in 1825. The access road to **Our Lady of Grace Monastery of the Monks of St Maron** is on the right after a small bridge, just off the Trans Canada at exit 37. Two kilometers up the valley, beyond the main monastery, a trail along a stream leads to the **Shrine of the Holy Spring**. It's a palpably spiritual place.

Eastern Shore

The 'Eastern Shore' designation refers to the area between Dartmouth and Cape Canso, at the extreme eastern tip of the mainland. It's one of the least-visited regions of the province; there are no sizable towns, and the main road is slow, narrow and almost as convoluted as the rugged shoreline it follows. Marine Drive, the designated tourist route, is the only route through the area. People do live here, so you'll find scattered small stores along the highway, but east of Sheet Harbour even facilities like gas stations are rare to nonexistent. There are some campgrounds and good beaches along the coast, but the water on this edge of the province is prohibitively cold for swimming.

Getting There & Away

Zinck's Bus Co (☎ 902-468-4342) has a bus leaving the Acadian Lines terminal in Halifax for Sherbrooke, with stops all along Hwy 7, at 5:30pm Monday to Saturday. The return trip departs St Mary's River Lodge, Sherbrooke, at 8am Tuesday to Saturday and 6pm Sunday ($15 to Halifax). Other than that, you'll need a car to get around, although hitching should be no problem.

LAWRENCETOWN BEACH

Lawrencetown Beach, a wide Atlantic surfing beach, is perhaps the best beach in the vicinity of Halifax. It's on Hwy 207,

which begins in downtown Dartmouth as Portland St.

Seaboard B&B (☎ 902-827-3747, fax 902-827-3747, Ⓦ www.bbcanada.com/5112.html, 2629 Crowell Rd, East Lawrencetown) Singles/doubles from $45/60. Open June-mid-Oct. This stylish two-story house on a slope above an inlet is near the junction with Hwy 207, a kilometer from Lawrencetown Beach.

PORTERS LAKE PROVINCIAL PARK

From Lawrencetown Beach, it's just an 8km drive to Porters Lake Provincial Park along Crowell Rd.

Porters Lake Provincial Park (☎ 902-827-2250, Ⓦ parks.gov.ns.ca, 1160 Crowell Rd, 4km south of Hwy 107 from Dartmouth) Sites $18. Open early June-Aug. This campground is split between a peninsula and a small island in Porters Lake, and the 158 nicely separated campsites have lots of shade. It's best to make advance reservations for Friday or Saturday nights from mid-July to mid-August, otherwise there should be no problem getting a site. It's easily the most attractive campground around Halifax.

MUSQUODOBOIT HARBOUR

There's no real town at Musquodoboit Harbour, just a few houses and shops scattered along the highway. (The harbor's name is pronounced 'musk o **dob** it.')

The **Musquodoboit Harbour Railway Museum** (☎ 902-889-2691, 7895 Hwy 7; admission free; open June-Sept), in a former train station built in 1918, also dispenses tourist information.

The **Musquodoboit Trailway**, a 15km section of the Trans Canada Trail that follows an old rail bed to Gibraltar Rock leaves from the museum. Another trailhead is 500m up Hwy 357, off Hwy 7 not far from the museum, and ample parking is available there. It's ideal for bicycling.

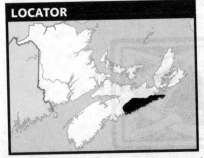

LOCATOR

Martinique Beach Provincial Park, 12km south of the village of Musquodoboit Harbour down E Petpeswick Rd from Hwy 7, boasts the longest beach in the province. The Atlantic breakers roll right in here. Camping is not allowed.

JEDORE OYSTER POND

Quite the name for a town. See the small **Fisherman's Life Museum** (☎ 902-889-2053, *58 Navy Pool Loop; adult/child $2/1; open 9:30am-5:30pm Mon-Sat, 1pm-5:30pm Sun June-mid-Oct*) – it's a model of a typical 1900s fishing family's house, with costumed guides and eternal tea time.

Golden Coast Seafood Restaurant (☎ 902-889-2386, *10320 Hwy 7, Jedore Oyster Pond*) Dinner $8-15. Open 11am-9pm daily June-Sept, 11am-7pm Sun-Thurs, 11am-8pm Fri & Sat other months. Across the street from the Fisherman's Life Museum, Gold Coast Seafood gives you the option of buying fresh fish to take away or enjoying a seafood dinner in their restaurant. The seafood chowder ($5.50), with chunks of lobster, scallops and haddock, is excellent.

TANGIER

Murphy's Camping on the Ocean (☎ 902-772-2700, **W** *www.dunmac.com/~tangiercap/murphy, Murphy's Cove, 7½km west of Tangier*) Unserviced/serviced sites $15/18. Open mid-May-mid-Oct. This campground down a sideroad 1½km off the highway has character. You should be able to find a secluded tent site, and a lounge area called 'Sailors Rest' is a cozy place to relax at night when it's raining. There's great kayaking (bring your own) among the small islands just offshore, and Murphy's rents canoes, rowboats and bicycles for $15/25 per half/full day. The owner, Brian Murphy, runs scenic boat trips at $50 an hour, plus $10 per person, for the whole boat – a good value if five or more people want to go. Brian can also drop you off on an uninhabited island where you can stay overnight in an abandoned sea shanty.

In Tangier itself, **Coastal Adventures Sea Kayaking** (☎ 902-772-2774, **W** *www.coastaldventures.com*, off Hwy 7, open mid-June-

early Oct) offers kayak courses, rentals ($35/50 per half-/full day) and guided trips. Their day trip ($100) provides a good introduction to kayaking and includes a tour to offshore islands. They also have canoes, double kayaks, and they run a small B&B called *Paddlers Retreat* next to their office. The three rooms with shared bath ($40/55 single/double) are customarily rented by people taking their trips.

TAYLOR HEAD PROVINCIAL PARK

A little-known scenic highlight of Nova Scotia, this spectacular park (☎ 902-772-2218, *20140 Hwy 7; admission free; open mid-May-early Oct*), just east of the village of Spry Harbour, occupies a skinny 6½km peninsula jutting into the Atlantic. On one side is a long, very fine sandy beach fronting a protected bay. The water doesn't get very warm here, though.

Some 17km of hiking trails cut through the spruce and fir forests. The Headland Trail is the longest at 8km and follows the rugged coastline to scenic views at Taylor Head. The trail is a three- to four-hour walk. Shorter is the Bob Bluff Trail, a 3km roundtrip to views off the end of the bluff. In spring you'll encounter colorful wildflowers, and this is a great bird-watching venue.

The main parking lot is 5km off Hwy 7 on a good gravel road, but if the gate is closed or you're on a bicycle or foot, one end of the Bull Beach Trail is just 800m from the main highway. Camping is not allowed, so stay elsewhere, but pack the picnic cooler and plan on spending a full day hiking, lounging and (if you're brave) swimming here.

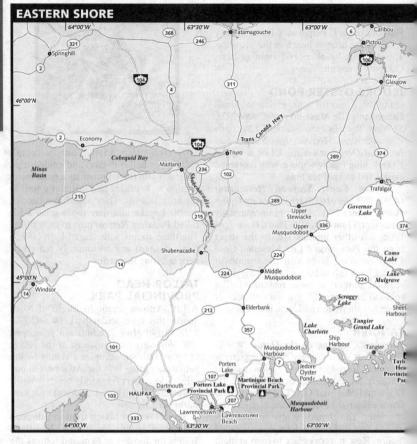

SHEET HARBOUR

Sheet Harbour, 126km east of Halifax, is one of the few small towns along this coast, a place where you could stop and spend the night. The **MacPhee House Museum** (☎ 902-885-2595, 22404 Hwy 7; admission free; open July & Aug), next to the West River bridge at the western entrance to town, contains the local tourist office. Display panels on the grounds relate local history, and a boardwalk leads down to the cascading river behind the house.

Sheet Harbour Motel (☎ 902-885-2293, W www.dunmac.com/business/shmotel.htm,

22719 Hwy 7) Singles/doubles $42/48. The 12 rooms are back-to-back in a long motel block with the restaurant in the middle.

The Manse B&B (☎ 902-885-2172, fax 902-885-2172, e the.manse@ns.sympatico .ca, 22864 Hwy 7) Doubles from $48. A large house on the hill near East River bridge.

PORT DUFFERIN

Tiny Port Dufferin, population 157, is about a two-hour drive from Halifax, Antigonish or Halifax International Airport. It offers little for the traveler

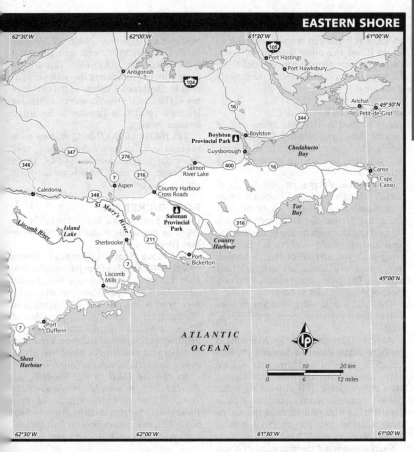

EASTERN SHORE

other than the highly regarded Marquis of Dufferin Seaside Inn.

Marquis of Dufferin Seaside Inn (☎ 902-654-2696, fax 902-654-2970, 25658 Hwy 7) Singles/doubles $60/65 in the new block, $41/47 in the old block. Open late May-mid-Oct. This inn features coastal views, sea breezes and tranquility. The nine new rooms are in a motel-like strip next to the original house, and five older rooms are in a block across the street. Larger housekeeping and family rooms are $71. The dining room (dinners $11 to $17) in the restored 1859 house serves outstanding Maritimes-style

seafood meals such as shrimp, fish casserole and haddock baked with eggs. Breakfast is $4 to $6.

LISCOMB MILLS

Several well-developed hiking trails begin near the fancy Liscomb Lodge at Liscomb Mills, 52km east of Port Dufferin on Hwy 7. The **Mayflower Point Trail** to the coast begins from the parking lot on the east side of the Liscomb River bridge. You join the nearby **Liscomb Trail** by going up the drive-way of the house at 2993 Hwy 7, then turning right. This trail follows the river's east bank for 9½km upstream through the forest to a fish ladder and a suspension bridge, which you can cross if you want to return down the other side of the river. There are many picturesque cascades along the way, and signboards explain the ecology of the area.

SHERBROOKE

Inland toward Antigonish, 26km east of Liscomb Mills, the pleasant little town of Sherbrooke is overshadowed by its historic site, which is one of the province's top attractions.

Sherbrooke Village (☎ *902-522-2400, Hwy 7; adult/family $7.25/21; open 9:30am-5:30pm daily June-mid-Oct)*, about the same size as the present-day town, recreates life 125 years ago through buildings, demonstrations and costumed workers. It's called a living museum, and all of the 28 houses, stores and workshops are original (not replicas). The green, quiet setting evokes a sense of stepping back in time.

The local tourist office is at Sherbrooke Village, open the same hours as the village itself.

About 500m away is the **Macdonald Brothers Water-Powered Sawmill** (☎ *902-522-2533; included in Sherbrooke Village admission; same opening hours)*, the former town mill, which is still in working order and has a guide to answer questions. Across the street is a nice walk through the woods along a stream to a lumber camp such as the mill workers would have lived in.

Sherbrooke is not the major center it was at the start of the 20th century, but it's one of the biggest towns in the area, so you might stop here for tourist information, groceries and gasoline.

Places to Stay & Eat

Riverside Campground (☎ *902-522-2584,* W *www.grassroots.ns.ca/~rvrcamp, 3987 Sonora Rd)* Sites $12 plus tax. Open mid-May-Oct. A hundred meters beyond the Macdonald Brothers Water-Powered Sawmill, this campground offers 26 tent sites, rather close together, by the river. There's a pool here.

St Mary's River Lodge (☎ *902-522-2177, fax 902-522-2515,* e *lodge@ns.sympatico.ca,* W *www3.ns.sympatico.ca/lodge, 21 Main St)* Singles/doubles $52/62 with bath. Breakfast is included. Open Apr-Dec. This trendy place with five rooms and two suites is adjacent to Sherbrooke Village in the center of town. The Zinck's Bus Co service to Halifax leaves here at 8am Tuesday to Saturday, 6pm on Sunday.

Vi's B&B (☎ *902-522-2042,* W *www.grassroots.ns.ca/~visbandb/visb&b.htm, 8140 Main St)* Singles/doubles $44/48. Open June-Sept. This large B&B is on the main road in Sherbrooke.

PORT BICKERTON

East of Sherbrooke along Hwy 7, then 29km to the south, is the small village of Port Bickerton.

The **Nova Scotia Lighthouse Centre** (☎ *902-364-2000, 3km from the crossroads at Port Bickerton, 2km of it on a gravel road; admission $2.50; open 9am-5pm daily mid-June-Sept)* is in a restored 1930 lighthouse. The interpretive center gives an overview of all Nova Scotia's lighthouses (great for lighthouse aficionados) and there are 3.3km of trails and boardwalks along the coast, over a bog and through the forest.

By the Sea B&B (☎ *902-364-2575, fax 902-364-2575,* W *www.bbcanada.com/3234 .html, 47 Port Bickerton Village Rd, Port Bickerton)* Singles/doubles/triples $40/60/80. This bungalow opposite Port Bickerton's post office rents three rooms.

COUNTRY HARBOUR

North of Port Bickerton, Hwy 211 is interrupted by Country Harbour. The Country Harbour ferry runs hourly 24 hours a day year-round, departing the Port Bickerton side on the half hour, the Goldboro side on the hour (in July and August the ferry runs every half hour). It's $3 per car.

Salsman Provincial Park (☎ *902-328-2999,* W *parks.gov.ns.ca, Hwy 316 between Goldboro and Goshen)* Sites $18. Open mid-May-early Oct. Near Stormont, 9km northwest of the turnoff to the Country Harbour ferry, Salsman has campsites on peninsula jutting into Country Harbour (site No 18 is nicely isolated on a point). The park has showers. It could be full the last weekend in July and the first weekend in August; otherwise you should be able to get a site.

CANSO

With a population of just 1200, this town at the edge of the mainland is the largest on the whole Eastern Shore. Since the first attempted settlement in 1518, Canso has seen it all: Native Indian battles, British and French landings and captures, pirates, fishing fleets and the ever-present difficulties of life ruled by the sea.

Things to See

The **Whitman House** museum (☎ 902-366-2170, cnr Main & Union Sts; admission free; open 9am-5pm daily late May-Sept) covers Canso's colorful history and offers a good view from the widow's walk on the roof. This 1885 house doubles as the tourist office.

An interpretive center on the waterfront tells the story of the **Grassy Island National Historic Site** (☎ 902-366-3136, Union St; site admission $2.50; open 10am-6pm daily June-mid-Sept), which lies just offshore and can be visited by boat. In 1720, the British built a small fort here to offer some protection from the French, who had their headquarters in Louisbourg. The island, however, was extremely vulnerable to military attacks and the fort was totally destroyed in 1744. There's a self-guided hiking trail amid the ruins, with eight interpretive stops explaining the history of the area. The boat to Grassy Island (included in the admission price) departs from the interpretive center upon demand.

The **Chapel Gully Trail** is a 10-km boardwalk and hiking trail along an estuary and out to the coast. It begins on the hill behind the hospital, near the lighthouse at the eastern end of Canso. A large map is posted at the trailhead and you should allow about three hours for the roundtrip.

GUYSBOROUGH

Guysborough is the county seat, and the **Old Court House Museum** (☎ 902-533-4008, 106 Church St at Queen; admission free; open 9am-5pm Mon-Fri, 10am-4pm Sat & Sun June-Sept) contains a tourist office. They have leaflets on the many hiking trails in the area.

Carritt House B&B (☎ 902-533-3855, 20 Pleasant St) Singles/doubles/triples $50/60/70. Open mid-May-mid-Oct. This two-story frame house on Hwy 16 opposite the public library in Guysborough has three rooms for rent with shared bath.

Boylston Provincial Park (☎ 902-533-3326, Ⓦ parks.gov.ns.ca, off Hwy 16) Sites $14. Open early June-Aug. Boylston is on a hilltop above Guysborough Harbour, 4km north of Guysborough village. The 36 campsites in this well-wooded park are rarely all occupied. From the picnic area on the highway below the campground, a footbridge leads to a small island. A display near the park office records the visit of a Norwegian earl, Henry Sinclair of Orkney, in 1398!

Cape Breton Island

Cape Breton, the large island adjunct at the northeast end of Nova Scotia, is justly renowned for its rugged splendor. It's the roughest, highest, coolest and most remote area of the province. The coast is rocky and rugged, the interior a blend of mountains, valleys, rivers and lakes. The Cabot Trail, the nearly 300km-long highway around Cape Breton Highlands National Park, is one of Canada's grandest and best known roads, winding and climbing to 500m between mountain and sea.

The island offers more than natural beauty – it has a long and captivating human history encompassing the Mi'kmaq, the British, the French and, especially, the Scottish, who were attracted to this part of the province because of its strong resemblance to the Scottish Highlands. A good

MAP INDEX

OTHER MAPS
Cape Breton Island
page 187

Around Sydney
page 207

Downtown
Sydney
page 203

part of Nova Scotia's Mi'kmaq community lives around Bras d'Or Lake.

Except for the struggling former coal and steel centers of Sydney and Glace Bay, most towns are small enough to be considered villages. People around Chéticamp speak French; in other areas Scottish Gaelic can still be heard. Life is hard here and unemployment is very high. Fishing, and mining, with its steel plant spin-off, have for generations been the backbones of the local economy, but all have declined sharply. While fish stocks may rebound, there is no such hope for mining and steel.

For the visitor it's a very appealing, relatively undeveloped area, with an excellent national park in the highlands and a top historic site at Louisbourg.

The Cabot Trail, understandably the most popular attraction, can be busy, even a little crowded in July and August, but it isn't difficult to get away if solitude is what you seek. The words most often used to describe the weather are 'windy,' 'wet,' 'foggy' and 'cool.' Summer days, however, can be warm and sunny. The sketchy public transportation system makes getting around Cape Breton without a vehicle difficult. Acadian Lines buses run from Halifax and Antigonish to Sydney, stopping at popular Baddeck along the way. Transoverland Ltd runs a bus route from Sydney and Baddeck to Chéticamp through the Margaree Valley. Alternatively, a variety of tours are offered from Halifax.

PORT HASTINGS

Cape Breton ceased to be a true island when the Canso Causeway was built in 1955. A big and busy provincial tourist office (☎ 902-625-4201) sits on the east side of the causeway. From here you can pick up information on all parts of Cape Breton or book rooms with the help of an agent. The office is open 8:30am to 8:30pm daily April to mid-January.

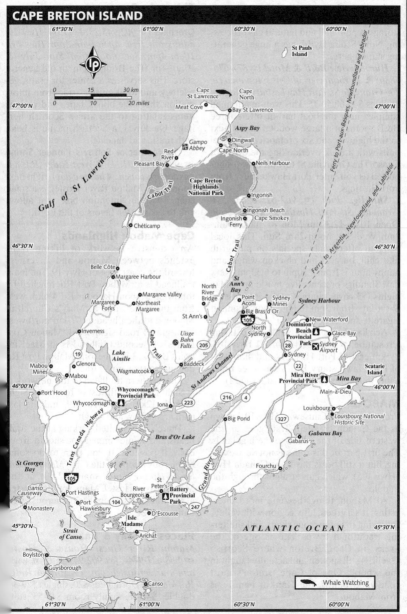

CAPE BRETON ISLAND

61°30'N · 61°00'N · 60°30'N · 60°00'N

St Pauls Island

0   15   30 km
0   10   20 miles

47°00'N

Cape St Lawrence
Cape North
Meat Cove
Bay St Lawrence

Aspy Bay

Gampo Abbey
Dingwall
Red River
Cape North
Pleasant Bay
Neils Harbour

Gulf of St Lawrence

Cape Breton Highlands National Park

Ferry to Port-aux-Basques, Newfoundland and Labrador

Ingonish

Chéticamp
Ingonish Beach
Ingonish Ferry   Cape Smokey

46°30'N

Belle Côte
Margaree Harbour

North River Bridge
St Ann's Bay

Margaree Valley
Point Aconi
Sydney Mines
Sydney Harbour

Margaree Forks
Northeast Margaree
St Ann's
Big Bras d'Or
New Waterford

Inverness
Uisge Bahn Falls
205
105
North Sydney
Dominion Beach Provincial Park
Glace Bay

Lake Ainslie
Cabot Trail
Sydney Airport
Sydney

Mabou Mines
19
Glenora
28
Mira River Provincial Park
Mira Bay
Scatarie Island

Mabou
Baddeck
Wagmatcook
22

Port Hood
252
Whycocomagh Provincial Park
St Andrews Channel
216
4
Main-a-Dieu

46°00'N

Whycocomagh
Iona
223
Big Pond
327
Louisbourg
Louisbourg National Historic Site

Trans Canada Highway
Bras d'Or Lake
Gabarus Bay

St Georges Bay
Gabarus

Fourchu

Canso Causeway
105
St Peter's
Battery Provincial Park
Grand River

Port Hastings
River Bourgeois
247

Monastery
Port Hawkesbury
104
D'Escousse

Isle Madame
ATLANTIC OCEAN
45°30'N

Strait of Canso
Arichat

Boylston

Guysborough

Canso

61°30'N · 61°00'N · 60°30'N · 60°00'N

Whale Watching

South of neighboring Port Hawkesbury is an industrial area with gypsum loading, oil storage, a pulp mill and natural gas processing. Nova Scotia Hydro has a huge generating station here.

Harbourview B&B & Motel (☎ 877-676-6886, e *harbourview.bb@ns.sympatico.ca, 209 Granville St, Port Hawkesbury*) Singles/doubles $45-60/50-75. This well-maintained complex near the boat harbor offers three B&B rooms in a large wooden house next to the highway and six prefabricated motel units with a deck overlooking the Strait of Canso. The Granville St turnoff is well signposted as you enter Port Hawkesbury from Port Hastings.

Shindigs Pub (☎ 902-625-0263, 510 *Granville St, Port Hastings*) Mains $6-9. Open 10am-12:30am Mon & Tues, 10am-2am Wed-Sat, noon-2am Sun. This local hangout offers daily specials on pub grub like chili, burgers and chicken wings, and happy hour is from 4:30pm to 6:30pm every day. Shindigs presents live music on Friday nights ($3 cover charge) and a jam session Saturdays from 3pm to 6pm. Don't come if cigarette smoke bothers you.

Acadian Lines buses stop at the Irving gas station (☎ 902-625-4304), 411 Hwy 104, 1½km east of Port Hastings and 4km west of Port Hawkesbury. Buses run three times a day to Halifax ($42) and Sydney ($22).

MABOU

From the Canso Causeway, Hwy 19, known as the Ceilidh (**kay**-lee) Trail, goes up the western side of the island to the highlands. The first part of this route is not very exciting, but it still beats the Trans Canada Hwy (Hwy 105), which cuts straight through the middle.

At Mabou, things become more interesting. It's a green, hilly region with valleys following the numerous rivers and sheltering traditional towns. This is one of the areas on Cape Breton where Scottish Gaelic is still spoken and actually taught in the schools. One of Cape Breton's most renowned bands, the Rankin Family, is from Mabou.

Things to See

Right in the center of Mabou is **An Drochaid** (☎ 902-945-2311, 11511 Hwy 19; *admission free; open 9am-5pm Tues-Fri, 10am-4pm Sat, noon-4pm Sun July & Aug*) – or 'The Bridge' – in an old general store. This serves as a center for crafts, genealogy, and local music. Aside from information, there are books, tapes and various items relating to the area's Scottish heritage. On July 1, a Scottish picnic is held, with music and dancing.

The **Mother of Sorrows Pioneer Shrine** (☎ 902-945-2221, 45 S West Ridge Rd; *admission free; open 24 hours a day*), right next door to the Mabou River Hostel, is a small chapel with an 'intention box' that allows you to ask written favors of the Lord!

Cape Mabou Highlands

An extensive network of hiking trails extends between Mabou and Inverness toward the coast west of Hwy 19. The main trailhead is at Mabou Post Rd, reached by following Mabou Harbour Rd 4½km west from the large white St Mary's Church in Mabou and then heading 7.7km northwest on a gravel road signposted 'Mabou Coal Mines.' A second trailhead is at MacKinnon's Brook, 3.8km beyond Mabou Post Rd on a narrowing gravel track.

The northern trailhead to this network is at Sight Point, southwest of Inverness. Sight Point is 12km from Hwy 19, and the last 6km are narrow and rough.

There's very limited parking at the trailheads, and in midsummer you should arrive early, if possible. If you plan to do some hiking, buy a copy of the *Cape Mabou Highlands Hiking Trails* map ($2.50) at the Mabou River Hostel. Maps are also posted at the trailheads. There are numerous alternative routes.

Places to Stay & Eat

Mabou River Guest House & Hostel (☎ 888-627-9744, fax 902-945-2605, w www.mabouriverhostel.com, 19 Mabou Ridge Rd, Mabou*) Dorm beds $20, singles $29-34, doubles $42-48, family room $45-53, suit

85-95, plus tax. Open year-round, by reservation Nov-Apr. This well-run guest house, just 100m off Hwy 19 right in town, was a boys' boarding school in the 1960s, then a home for the mentally challenged. Today the 37-bed facility with eight private rooms, two suites and five dorms is about the best budget place to stay on the whole of Cape Breton. There's a kitchen, BBQ, laundry facilities ($3 a load), Internet access ($1 per 10 minutes), game room and ample parking. The self-service continental breakfast from 8am is $3 per person. The hostel's pizzeria is open 4pm to 9pm Thursday to Sunday, with pizza from $7 to $20. Ceilidhs and step dance workshops are held in summer. Pickups can be arranged from the bus stop in Whycocomagh ($10), and the hostel offers tours of the Cabot Trail ($40) and Louisbourg Fortress ($30) if at least three people are interested. There's kayaking in the harbor near the hostel, and kayaks can be rented for $10/50 per hour/day. Bicycles are also available.

Beaton's B&B (☎ 902-945-2806, fax 902-945-2340, e bbbeaton@ns.sympatico.ca, w www.bbcanada.com/370.html, 11311 Hwy 19, Mabou) Singles/doubles/triples $40/55/70 plus tax. Three rooms are for rent in this two-story house by the road just south of Mabou.

Elmsdale Farm B&B (☎/fax 902-945-2665, e h.e.smith@ns.sympatico.ca, w www.bbexpo.com/NS/elmsdale.htm, 4680 Hwy 252, Mabou) Doubles $50-65. Open mid-May-mid-Oct. This pair of farmhouses is near Mabou United Church, 2.7km east of Hwy 19.

Shining Waters Bakery & Eatery (☎ 902-945-2728, Hwy 19, Mabou) Breakfast $4-5. Open 6:30am-7pm Mon-Sat, 9am-7pm Sun. Start the day at this healthy, inexpensive place near the Mabou River Bridge. The homemade bread is $2.75 a loaf, and you can get a full breakfast featuring thick slices of it. The salads or sandwiches are $4 to $6, and fish dishes are $5.

Mull Café & Deli (☎ 902-945-2244, 1630 Hwy 19) Dinner mains from $10. Open 11am-9pm daily (11am-7pm Nov-Apr). This cafe on the northeast side of town has an eclectic menu. Among the good choices for dinner are the pork chops or sirloin steak ($10), and the grilled haddock, stuffed sole or seafood platter ($12).

Entertainment
The Red Shoe Pub (☎ 902-945-2626, 11531 Hwy 19) Open noon-11pm Mon-Wed, noon-1am Thurs-Sun (closed Tues in winter). Thursday is chicken wing night, often with live music. There's always a group playing from 9:30pm on Saturday ($6 cover charge), and Sunday from 4pm to 8pm there's a jam session ($6 cover charge). It's Mabou's favorite venue.

Mabou Hall (☎ 902-945-2093, 11538 Hwy 19) From late June to mid-September there's a ceilidh at this hall opposite the Red Shoe Pub every Tuesday night at 7:30pm (admission $5).

INVERNESS
The first sizable town on the northern shore is this old coal-mining center. There are miles of sandy beach beginning near the fishing harbor, with some nice secluded spots and few people. Surprisingly, the water temperature is not too bad, reaching 19°C to 21°C in summer, which is about as warm as it gets anywhere around the Maritimes – cool but definitely swimmable. Pilot whales can sometimes be seen off the coast.

A boardwalk runs for a kilometer along the beach. Up closer to town, the **Inverness Miners' Museum** (☎ 902-258-3822, 62 Lower Railway St; adult/child $1/50¢; open 9am-7pm daily mid-June-early Sept) in the old train station has mementos from the former Inverness coal mines. Get there via Lower Railway Rd, which runs from Hwy 19 next to the fire department.

Places to Stay & Eat
Gables Motel (☎ 902-258-2314, fax 902-258-3104, e gables@ns.sympatico.ca, 15652 Hwy 19) Doubles from $58. This motel consists of a long block of 11 rooms facing Hwy 19 at the south entrance to town.

Cup O'Tea B&B *(☎ 902-258-2292,* e *chrismacisaac@hotmail.com, 14468 Hwy 19)* Doubles from $50. Open May-Oct. This large white house is next to the road, 6km south of Inverness.

Foot Cape B&B *(☎ 902-258-3606, Foot Cape Rd off Hwy 19)* Singles/doubles $40/50. The turnoff to this B&B is 900m north of Cup O'Tea B&B or 5km south of Inverness on Hwy 19. This modern two-story house on spacious grounds is just 600m off Hwy 19.

Ceilidh Café *(☎ 902-258-3339, 15896 Hwy 19)* Breakfast/lunch $4/5. Open 7am-11:30pm daily. This café is located on Hwy 19 toward the north end of town, next door to a Laundromat. It's a local hangout with breakfast for $4 and burgers with fries for $5, though fancier tourist food is offered in mid-summer. The cigarette smoke may be a deterrent.

MARGAREE VALLEY
Northeast of Lake Ainslie is a relatively gentle, postcard-perfect region encompassing a series of river valleys known collectively as the Margaree Valley. With a half-dozen different towns named Margaree this or Margaree that, it's an oasis of sorts in the midst of the more rugged, wild and unpopulated highlands.

The Margaree Valley is a preferred destination for folks involved in fly-fishing or horseback riding, and the tourist office at Margaree Forks should be able to provide leads on these activities. The accommodations in the valley are intended mostly for local anglers, but they're also worth check-

ing if you're simply looking for an inexpen sive place to spend the night.

This is also a good spot for local ceilidhs check the local *Inverness Oran* paper fo schedules.

Margaree Forks Public Library
Clustered around this library near the junc tion of Hwy 19 and the Cabot Trail are tourist office (open July and August only), craft shop and a CAP site with Interne access ($1 per 30 minutes). Picnic tables ar provided, and there's a marked hiking tra down to the Margaree River.

Salmon Museum
In North East Margaree, 8km east of Marga ree Forks and just off the Cabot Trail, is th **Salmon Museum** *(☎ 902-248-2848, 60 E Bi Intervale Rd; adult/child $1/25¢; open 9am 5pm daily mid-June-mid-Oct)*. It's a goo place to get information on the river, the fis that live in it and the man-made obstruction they must contend with. An aquarium con tains both salmon and trout. The fly sho across the street will interest anglers.

Places to Stay
Buckles Motel & Cabins *(☎ 902-248-2053 fax 902-248-2053, 500m south of the junction of Hwy 19 & Cabot Trail, Margaree Forks* Cabins $45 double or $70-90 for fou persons, motel rooms $50/55 single/double Open June-Oct. This place behind the Mar garee Co-op has character, and the clientel is mostly local. A variety of rustic accom modations are on a breezy hillside next t an RV park. Of the 10 self-catering cabins the four smaller double units are the bes deal. The three motel units are overpriced A Laundromat is on the premises.

Browns' Bruaich na H'Aibhne Inn & Cottages *(☎ 800-575-2935, fax 902-248-2935* w *capebretonet.com/margaree/browns, Mar garee Centre)* Single/double $35/55 motel $50/60 cottage. Browns' is in a secluded lo cation on a back road, 4½km from th Salmon Museum. Follow all signs to Marga ree Centre and ask directions. The four cot tages are good, and motel-style rooms ar available in the main building.

Ross' Housekeeping Motel (☎ *902-248-933, 1101 Egypt Rd, Margaree Valley)* singles/doubles $45/55. Open mid-May-Oct. This place offers four motel units with cooking facilities in a long block by the highway. It's 4½km from the Salmon Museum on a different road (follow signs to Margaree Valley and ask).

MARGAREE HARBOUR

Out of the valley and on the coast, celebrated Canadian writer Farley Mowat's 'boat who wouldn't float' – the *Happy Adventure*, of Burgeo, Newfoundland – has been set up on a hill just above the **Hungry Piper Café** (☎ *902-235-2839, 4031 Shore Rd; open late June-early Oct)*. Also here at the south end of the bridge over the Margaree River is the schooner *Marion Elizabeth,* once a museum but now closed after sea otters broke in and trashed the place. The café itself showcases John May's amazing collection of military miniatures depicting scenes from the Napoleonic wars. Admission to the cafe and gift shop is free, but this unusual sight may not be around much longer, as plans to build a new bridge on the site are in the pipeline.

The village of Margaree Harbour, a kilometer off the Cabot Trail from the south end of the bridge, features Lawrence's General Store, a nice beach below the lighthouse and boat cruises for deep-sea fishing or whale watching.

From June to late October canoes are for rent ($12/40 per hour/day) at the **Duck Cove Inn** (☎ *902-235-2658, Cabot Trail, Margaree Harbour)*, very near the south end of the river bridge.

Places to Stay & Eat

Harbour View Inn B&B (☎ *902-235-2314, 1020 Shore Rd, Margaree Harbour)* Rooms/chalet from $40/60. This place is directly above the Margaree River bridge at the junction of Hwy 219 and the Cabot Trail. The three rooms with shared bath are in a two-story house and an A-frame chalet.

Taylor's B&B (☎ *902-235-2652, 10038 Cabot Trail, Margaree Harbour)* Singles/doubles/triples $40/50/62. Open May-Oct.

This large farmhouse on extensive grounds is 1½km south of the Margaree River bridge (turn off beside a craft and gift shop). There are three rooms with shared bath overlooking the river.

Hungry Piper Café & Tea Room (☎ *902-235-2839, 4031 Shore Rd)* Meals under $10. This place next to the bridge serves light meals and inexpensive fish chowders. Ceilidhs with traditional Scottish Gaelic singing are held here regularly through the summer – call for times.

BELLE CÔTE

From Belle Côte, where the Cabot Trail meets the coastline, northward to Cape Breton Highlands National Park, a different cultural heritage adds another dimension to the island. The people here are predominantly French, the descendants of the Acadians who settled the area – and the area north of Yarmouth – in the 1750s after being expelled from the mainland by the British during the Seven Years' War.

The strength of this culture in Cape Breton is remarkable because of its small size and isolation from other French-speaking people. Almost everyone, it seems, speaks English as well, although an accent is often detectable. Among themselves, however, the locals switch to French, keeping the language very much alive. Aside from the language, the French food, music and dance are worth sampling.

Six kilometers north of Belle Côte watch for **Joe's Scarecrow Theatre** (☎ *902-235-2108, 11842 Cabot Trail; open mid-June-early Oct)*, by the highway next to Ethel's Takeout restaurant. It's a humorous, quasi-macabre outdoor collection of life-sized stuffed figures. Several other folk art shops are along the highway between here and Chéticamp.

CHÉTICAMP

Just before Cape Breton Highlands National Park, busy Chéticamp (population 3000) is the center of the local Acadian community and the gateway to the nearby national park. From Chéticamp the Cabot Trail becomes more scenic, with superlative vistas and lots of hills and turns as you climb to the highest point just before Pleasant Bay.

The **Church of St Pierre** dominates the town, as is so often the case in French settlements. The church dates from 1893 and has the characteristic silver spire and colorful frescoes.

Over on Île de Chéticamp, **Plage St Pierre** is a good sandy beach with camping. The island is connected by road to the mainland 4km south of town.

The Acadians have a tradition of handicrafts, but in this area one product, hooked rugs, has long been seen as particularly beautiful and valuable. Many of the local women continue this craft, and their wares are displayed and sold in numerous outlets in and around town. A good rug costs $250 to $650 or more, so they aren't cheap but they are distinctive and attractive. Each is made of wool, and to complete the intricate work takes about 12 hours per 30 sq cm.

Co-op Artisanale de Chéticamp

Don't miss this cultural center (☎ 902-224-2170, 15067 Main St; admission free; open mid-May-late Oct) near the large church in the middle of Chéticamp. The museum downstairs has a limited but fascinating display of artifacts, furniture and some older hooked rugs. Demonstrations of rug making are given. This operation is supported through the sale of quality local handicrafts at the large craft shop upstairs and by the restaurant, which closes an hour or two later than the museum and craft shop.

Les Trois Pignons

At the north end of town, this museum (☎ 902-224-2642, 15584 Main St; admission $3.50; open 8am-6pm daily July & Aug, 9am-5pm May-mid-Oct) shows, among other things, the rugs and tapestries of a number of local people, including those of Elizabeth LeFort, who has achieved an international reputation. Her detailed representational rugs and portraits in wool hang in the White House, the Vatican and Buckingham Palace. Internet access is available here at $2 an hour.

Whale Watching

Whale-watching cruises are run from Government Wharf, across and down from the church. The most common species in the area is the pilot whale, which is also called the 'pothead,' but fin whales and minkes are also seen, as are seals, bald eagles and a couple of species of seabird. Demand is high in midsummer, so reserve your whale watching cruise the day before.

The three-hour boat excursions by **Whale Cruisers** (☎ 902-224-3376, 800-81. 3376, W www.whalecruises.com, Government Wharf; adult/child $29/12) are a pretty good value. It runs three trips daily from mid-May until mid-October at 9am, 1pm and 5 or 6pm.

Acadian Whale Cruise (☎ 902-224-108 W www.whalecruise.com, Quai du Phare trips $26) arranges cruises from mid-May to September. The office is below the light house along the boardwalk near the tourist office.

Farther along the waterfront opposite Salon Le Gabriel, **Seaside Whale & Nature Cruises** (☎ 902-224-2400, ☎ 800-959-425. 15407 Main St; adult/child $27/13.50; open June-Sept) does whale watching trips on the Love Boat.

Fishing

The MV Danny Lynn (☎ 902-224-3606, Government Wharf; adult/child $30/15; open mid-June-early Sept) offers deep-sea fishing for groundfish like cod three times a day. You've got a chance of seeing eagles and whales on the 3½-hour cruise, and unlike many operators, Captain Tom lets you keep the fish – he'll even fillet them for you. He'll still go out even when only one person has booked.

Golf

Le Portage Golf Club (☎ 902-224-3338, 15582 Main St; open early May-late Oct), on Main St behind Les Trois Pignons at north end of town, is a strikingly beautiful course with the mountains in full view. Green fees are $48 (or $38 before mid-June and after mid-September). Unlike many pretentious golf courses elsewhere, pull carts ($5) are kay – power carts ($38) are not obligatory. Club rental is $12/18 half/full set. It's your chance to get in some world-class golfing without paying an arm and leg.

Organized Tours

Gaboteux Tours (☎ 902-224-2940, no office; day tour $55, not including lunch; open mid-May-mid-Oct) offers an eight-hour national park tour leaving Chéticamp at 8:30am. There's a four-person minimum, and you must book by phone. The same company also provides guides for customized hiking tours at $150/250 per half/full day per group (6 persons maximum). A 15-passenger van can be added for another $50 if the trip is to be only in the northwest part of the national park.

Places to Stay

Though there are quite a few B&Bs around town, accommodations are tight throughout July and August, so calling ahead or arriving early in the afternoon is advisable.

Plage St Pierre Camping (☎ 902-224-3112, fax 902-224-1623, e plagestpierre@auracom.com, w www.plagestpierre.com, Plage St Pierre, Île de Chéticamp, 3km off the Cabot Trail) Unserviced/serviced sites 18/23. Open June-mid-Sept. You'll see the usual hordes of RVs lined up near the entrance, but there's a tenting field farther back. You won't have a lot of privacy in July and August, but other months are less crowded. A long sandy beach is adjacent, and there's a hiking trail across the road.

Seashell Cabins (☎ 902-224-3569, 125 Chéticamp Island Rd, Île de Chéticamp) Singles/doubles $48/58. Open mid-June-mid-Oct. On the tip of the island, just 700m off the Cabot Trail, this row of three small rustic cabins is worth a try. There are basic cooking facilities, and it's near the beach. It's also gay-friendly.

Albert's Motel (☎ 902-224-2077, 15068 Main St) Singles/doubles $55/60. Open mid-May-mid-Oct. This block of four clean rooms is almost opposite the Co-op Artisanale de Chéticamp in the heart of town.

Merry's Motel (☎ 902-224-2456, fax 902-224-1786, e merrysmotel@capebreton island.com, w www.capebretonisland.com/cheticamp/merrysmotel, 15356 Main St) Singles/doubles $50/65. Open May-Oct. Merry's has eight units in a long block right in town.

Les Cabines du Portage (☎ 902-224-2822, 15660 Main St) Two-bed cabins $70 for two persons, $10 each additional person; two-bedroom cabins $80 for a double or $90 for up to four. Weekly rates are $400/450 for a small/large unit. In the off-season the units are discounted by $10 a day or $50 a week. Just outside the park, this place is ideal for a party of three or more. Each of the six two-bed cabins and four larger two-bedroom units includes a kitchen.

Auberge déjeuner de soleil B&B (☎ 902-224-1373, fax 902-224-1552, w www.cheti camp.com, 1315 Chéticamp Back Rd) Singles/doubles $44/48 July & Aug, $40/46 off-season with shared bath, $63/80 double/quad with private bath July & Aug, $48/60 off-season. Open mid-May-Oct. Up on the Belle-Marche plateau, this place has seven rooms (two with private bath). Go inland 2km on the road that begins beside the post office, then proceed another 2km to the left (stay on the paved roads). A light breakfast is included – this is one of Chéticamp's best bargains.

Places to Eat

Co-op Artisanale Restaurant (☎ 902-224-2170, 15067 Main St) Dinners under $9. Open 7am-9pm daily mid-May-end Oct, 10am-7pm toward the beginning and end of the season. This outstanding restaurant's large menu offers many fine choices, but they excel in the Acadian dishes like poulet fricot (potato and chicken soup) at $5, pâté à la viande (meat pie) at $5, blood pudding (pork custard) at $5, chiard (potato and meat stew) at $7 and fish cakes at $9. Here, as in Newfoundland, 'fish' means 'cod'; other types are called by name. For dessert, the gingerbread with hot sauce and the fruit pie are both under $3. The women who run the place do the cooking and baking in traditional dress.

Seafood Stop (☎ 902-224-1717, 14803 Main St) Mains $6-8. Open 11am-9pm daily

May-mid-Oct. This large fish market and restaurant out on the highway south of town sells all manner of takeout seafood for that special picnic. A complete lobster dinner in their dining room will be $20 with dessert and coffee, or just take the fish & chips for $6 to $8.

In July and August, *LM Chéticamp Seafoods Ltd* (☎ 902-224-1688) runs a fish market located opposite the Royal Bank on Main St.

Entertainment
Salon Le Gabriel (☎ 902-224-3685, 15424 Main St) Open 10am-11pm Mon-Fri, 10am-1am Sat, noon-11pm Sun. This family-style seafood restaurant with a lighthouse-style entrance is only open in summer, but the large sports bar attached at the back is open year-round. Saturdays from 10pm there's a DJ ($3 cover charge).

Doryman Beverage Room (☎ 902-224-9909, 15532 Main St) Open 10am-11:30pm Fri-Wed, 10am-12:30am Thurs. This place on the north side of town appears a bit rough from the outside, but inside it's friendly. Every Thursday from 9pm to midnight is open mike night and local musicians perform. Saturdays from 2pm to 6pm you can hear traditional fiddle music ($5 cover).

Getting There & Away
Chéticamp is connected to Baddeck ($10) and Sydney ($12) by Transoverland Ltd (☎ 902-248-2051). In Chéticamp their minibus departs from Cormier's Esso gas station (☎ 902-224-2315), 15437 Main St, at 7:30am Monday, Wednesday and Friday. Tickets are sold by the driver. Unfortunately, there's no bus service through or around the national park.

CAPE BRETON HIGHLANDS NATIONAL PARK
This spectacular national park includes some of the grandest terrain in the Maritimes. It stretches right across Cape Breton's noble northern finger with dramatic cliffs on one side, rocky coves and sandy beaches on the other. Established in 1936, Cape Breton Highlands was the region's first national park, and at 950 sq km it's one of the largest in eastern Canada. You stand an excellent chance of seeing moose, whales and bald eagles, and the possibilities for day hikes and car camping are many.

The Cabot Trail, one of the best-known roads in the country, gets its reputation from the 106km national park segment of it Cape Breton loop. The drive is at its best along the northwestern shore en route to Pleasant Bay. The road winds right along the shoreline, weaving through mountains crossing barren plains and valleys and climbing up to **French Mountain**, at 459m the highest point on the Cabot Trail. Along the way are lookout points, the best of which is at the very summit, where numerous interpretive geological displays complement the great views of the interior. From French Mountain the road zigzags down switchbacks to reach Pleasant Bay, just outside the park. Make sure your brakes are in good condition.

Toward Ingonish, the **Grand Anse Valley** contains virgin forest; the short **Lone Shieling Trail** leads through 300-year-old maple trees to a replica of a Scottish Highland crofter's hut, a reminder of the area's first settlers.

If possible, save the trip for a sunny day when you can see up and down the coastline. Summer conditions tend to be rather rainy, foggy and windy, even while remaining fairly warm. The driest month is generally July, with June and September the runners-up. Maximum temperatures during midsummer usually don't exceed 25°C and minimums are around 15°C.

Both of the entrances, Chéticamp and Ingonish, have information centers that are open daily during the season. Here you purchase your motor-vehicle entry permit. A one-day pass is $3.50, four days $10.50, less for seniors and children; family passes are $8 for one day, $24 for four. An Atlantic Pass, valid at seven national parks in Atlantic Canada, is also available. One-day passes are good until noon the next day.

The Chéticamp Information Centre (☎ 902-224-2306), 16646 Cabot Trail, has displays, a relief map and a 10-minute slide show. The bookstore sells maps (including topographical sheets), and the helpful staff dispenses hiking brochures and good advice. The center is open 9am to 5pm daily mid-May to mid-October, 8am to 8pm July and August.

The Ingonish Information Centre (☎ 902-285-2535), 37677 Cabot Trail, is much smaller and only hands out brochures and answers questions. Wheelchair accessible trails are indicated on the free park map available at either entrance. The Ingonish center is open 8am to 6pm daily mid-May to mid-October, 8am to 8pm July and August.

Hiking

Considering how big and rugged Cape Breton Highlands National Park is, the hiking is surprisingly limited; legitimate multiday trails are nonexistent since the Lake of Islands trail closed in 1998. The park has 25 trails and only one of them (Fishing Cove Trail) leads to backcountry campsites. Fishing Cove Trail is an 8km one-way walk that descends 330m to campsites at the mouth of rugged Fishing Cove River.

Most of the other trails are shorter and close to the road. Many of them take you to ridges for impressive views of the coast. The best is probably **Skyline Trail**, a 7km loop that puts you on the edge of a headland cliff right above the water. This trail is posted along the Cabot Trail 5½km above Corey Brook Campground. Other trails with ocean views from mountaintops include Aspy, Glasgow Lake and Franey Mountain Trail.

Cycling

Despite the effort required, the park is a popular cycling destination. Due to the steep terrain, however, it is not suggested that it be used as your inaugural trip. The riding is tough, but the views are spectacular throughout the park and on other coastal roads in the area. Despite the sometimes heavy number of tourists, considerable biking takes place here.

If you need to rent, try **Sea Spray Cycle Centre** (☎ *902-383-2732, 1141 White Point*

Rd; bicycle rentals $25/35 per half/full day; open 9am-5pm daily June-mid-Oct) in Smelt Brook. Sea Spray is an especially good out-fitter that sells maps with suggested coastal routes for self-guided tours. It also offers organized tours and does bicycle repairs.

Places to Stay

Camping (☎ *902-224-2306, fax 902-224-2445,* w *parkscanada.pch.gc.ca)* Unser-viced/serviced sites $15/21; discounts for stays over 3 days. The park entry fee is extra. There are seven campgrounds in the park, some for tenters only. Reservations are not generally accepted at any of the campgrounds – most sites are first-come, first-serve. Exceptions are the wheelchair-accessible sites, group campsites and back-country sites, which can be reserved. The park motto is 'We always have room,' but don't be surprised if it's tight on peak season weekends. The campgrounds away from the park entrances tend to be smaller, with 10 to 20 sites. In these, just pick a site, self-register and set up.

The 162-site **Chéticamp Campground** is behind the information center at the west entrance to the park, 3km north of Chéti-camp. Wheelchair-accessible sites are avail-able. When the main campground is full, they open an overflow area. However, there are no radio-free areas, so peace and quiet is not guaranteed. You register at the informa-tion center.

Self-registration applies at Corney Brook (20 sites), MacIntosh Brook (10 sites) and Big Intervale (10 sites). **Corney Brook**, 10km north of Chéticamp Campground, has only open unprotected sites around a parking area, but it's popular for its great views, sea breezes and nearby trails. **Mac-Intosh Brook**, 3km east of Pleasant Bay, offers sites in an open field with some shade (and lots of mosquitoes in spring). **Big In-tervale**, 11km west of Cape North, offers sites along a riverside, along with barbecues and a covered picnic shelter. A 9.6km hiking trail is nearby.

You must preregister for the eight back-country campsites at **Fishing Cove** at the Chéticamp Information Centre. The two access points to Fishing Cove are 4½km apart on the Cabot Trail. The more southerly trail is a gentle 8km descent along a stream, while the northern access is a steep 2.8km trail down the hillside to the beach. Either way, this area is one of the best wilderness experiences in Cape Breton Highlands National Park and is highly recommended.

On the east side of the park, you have a choice of the 256-site *Broad Cove Campground* at Ingonish or the 90-site *Ingonish Campground*, 37437 Cabot Trail near Keltic Lodge at Ingonish Beach. Special unserviced sites with a fireplace are available at both campgrounds for $17, firewood $3 extra, and both have wheelchair-accessible sites. Because these large campgrounds are near the beach they tend to be crowded with local families in midsummer and can get noisy.

From late October to early May you can camp at the Chéticamp and Ingonish campgrounds for $10, including firewood.

PLEASANT BAY
Pleasant Bay is best known for its whale tours, and various companies have kiosks along the wharf. **Pleasant Bay Whale & Seal Tour** (☎ *902-224-1316; adult/child $25/12*) has 1½-hour cruises at 9:30am, 1pm, 3pm and 5pm from June to mid-October; the 3pm and 5pm cruises are replaced by one at 4pm at the beginning and end of the season. Weather conditions and demand can alter this schedule.

Captain Mark's Whale and Seal Cruise (☎ *888-754-5112,* **W** *www.whaleandseal cruise.com; adult/child $25/12; open June-Sept)* promises a whale sighting or your money back.

Wesley's Whale Watching (☎ *902-224-1919,* **W** *www.cabottrail.com/whalewatching; adult/child $25/12; open mid-May-mid-Oct)* also guarantees a whale sighting or the tour is free. In addition to their Cape Island–style boat, they do whale watching from zodiacs for $30/15 per adult/child.

The **Whale Interpretive Centre** (☎ *902-224-1411,* **W** *www.whaleslife.com, 104 Harbour Rd; adult/family $4.50/14; open*

9am-6pm daily mid-May-Oct), 600m off the Cabot Trail next to the whale-watching boats at Pleasant Bay, opened in 2001 with informative exhibits on marine mammals. Internet access is available at the CAP site here.

Gampo Abbey
From Pleasant Bay, a paved road continues 4½km north along the coast to the small village of Red River. The road then becomes gravel and extends another 3.3km north to Gampo Abbey (☎ *902-224-2752,* **W** *www.gampoabbey.org)*. Set in a stunning location on the remote north coast, this is one of the only authentic Tibetan monasteries in North America that is intended mostly for Western followers. Students come from all across Canada and the US for extended meditation programs. The noted Buddhist author Ani Pema Chödrön spends six months of each year here.

Just beyond Gampo Abbey is the circular **Stupa for World Peace**. After another kilometer or so, the gravel road ends. Here the real adventure starts as a rough track continues 10km north to **Pollett's Cove**, an old fishing settlement, now abandoned. It's a three-hour hike each way, but the views are superb. The soaring cliffs mark another outer edge of the continent.

Places to Stay & Eat
Cabot Trail Hostel (☎ *902-224-1976,* **W** *www.cabottrail.com, 23349 Cabot Trail)* Dorm beds $20. Open mid-May-Sept. A kilometer west of the turnoff to Pleasant Bay and 700m north of the Rusty Anchor Restaurant, this eight-bed hostel is behind the Celtic Vision Café. The cafe is worth a stop for the baked goods, and Internet access is $3 for 15 minutes. Ask about the 'moose tour.' Their van does pickups at the Mabou River Hostel at $20 per person (minimum of three).

Mountain View Motel (☎ *902-224-3100,* **e** *reservation@themountainview.com* **W** *themountainview.com, 23659 Cabot Trail)* Doubles from $60, cottages $100. Open May-Oct. Mountain View is a new motel 500m east of the turnoff to Pleasant Bay with one block of 10 rooms and another of eight rooms, plus four cottages. A large restaurant is on the premises.

Rusty Anchor Restaurant (☎ 902-224-313, Cabot Trail) Seafood dinner $10-14. Open late May-late Oct. This lively tourist restaurant near the national park boundary toward Chéticamp offers locally prepared seafood, including fish & chips ($9 to $10), lobster crepe ($11), poached sole ($12), scallops & chips ($13) and fisherman's platter ($19). Breakfast (served 7am to 11am) is $5 to $7. You can sit on their patio and use the binoculars to watch for the pilot whales that are regularly seen just offshore.

CAPE NORTH

Don't confuse the village of Cape North, just outside the park, with the extreme northern finger of Cape Breton, which is also called Cape North. Cape North village, at the junction of the Cabot Trail and Bay St Lawrence Rd, has the **North Highlands Community Museum** *(☎ 902-383-2579; admission free; open 10am-6pm daily June-early Oct)*, behind Morrison's Restaurant on the corner. Local artifacts are displayed in a split-log structure of the kind built by early pioneers in this area.

North of here on Bay St Lawrence Rd, at **Cabot's Landing Provincial Park** on Aspey's Bay, is the location where John Cabot is believed to have landed in 1497. Every June 24 a reenactment is held on the beach at Sugarloaf Mountain. This long sandy beach is among the best in Nova Scotia, but there's no camping. For that, continue 8km north to Bay St Lawrence.

Places to Stay & Eat

Inlet B&B (☎ 902-383-2112, fax 902-383-2112, 462 Dingwall Main Rd) Singles/doubles $45/55. Open May-Sept. This three-room B&B is right on Dingwall Harbour, 2½km off the Cabot Trail, and whale-watching trips go out from a wharf behind the house.

MacDonald's Motel (☎ 902-383-2054, fax 902-383-2200, 2 Bay St Lawrence Rd, Cape North) Singles/doubles $55/60. Open mid-May-Oct. At the junction of Cabot Trail and Bay St Lawrence Rd opposite Morrison's Restaurant, this motel has 12 rooms in a long block, plus a few cabins behind.

Morrison's Restaurant (☎ 902-383-2051, Cabot Trail) Seafood dinner $17-21. Open 11am-8pm daily mid-May-Oct, 8am-9:30pm July & Aug. This casual cafe at the junction of Cabot Trail and Bay St Lawrence Rd offers super seafood specialities and old-fashioned atmosphere. Lunch could be a grilled salmon sandwich ($8) and for dinner consider the braised halibut, poached salmon or lobster. It's very popular.

Bay St Lawrence

Bay St Lawrence is a picturesque little fishing village where you can camp or go whale watching, and several whale-watching operators are based here. **Captain Cox** *(☎ 902-383-2981; adult/child $25/12; open July-mid-Sept)* has been doing these trips since 1986. You could see minke, pilot, fin, humpback or sei whales on your trip, plus seals, dolphins and perhaps even a moose standing by the shore. If you don't see any whales at all, he'll give you a rain check so you can try again another day. During the peak season there's also **Captain Fraser's Oshan Whale Cruise** *(☎ 902-383-2883; tours $25; open mid-July-Aug)*. They both leave at 10:30am, 1:30pm and 4:30pm and stay out between two and three hours.

Places to Stay *Jumping Mouse Campground (☎ 902-383-2914, www.cabot-trail.com/BaySt.Lawrence/DoubleCrow/camp.htm, 3360 Bay St Lawrence Rd)* Sites $15, cabin $30. Open mid-May-Sept. Directly above the harbor at Bay St Lawrence, this is one of the most spectacular campgrounds in the Maritimes, perched on a high cliff above the open sea where fin whales come up to blow. The 10 campsites are large but fully exposed to the wind. If the weather forecast is negative, ask about the storm sites in the nearby forest. There's also a bare-bones four-bed cabin with shared bath. The showers here are free and this place is quiet.

Highlands by the Sea B&B (☎ 902-383-2537, 3014 Bay St Lawrence Rd) Singles/

doubles $50-65. Open June-Oct. This large white house is adjacent to St Margaret Village Post Office, 2km before Bay St Lawrence.

Meat Cove

The northernmost road in Nova Scotia ends at Meat Cove village, 13km northwest of Bay St Lawrence (the last 7km are gravel). From Meat Cove, **hiking trails** continue west to the Cape St Lawrence lighthouse and Lowland Cove. If you're not planning to camp and want to hike to the cape, leave your car at the Meat Cove Welcome Center (☎ 902-383-2284) at the entrance to the village and walk the last kilometer, as there's no parking right at the trailhead. The center is open 8am to 7pm daily June to October.

Places to Stay *Meat Cove Campground* (☎ *902-383-2379, 902-383-2658, 2475 Meat Cove)* Sites $15. Open June-Oct. These are some of the most scenic sites in Cape Breton; you can actually watch whales from your tent perched on a grassy bluff directly above the sea. The sites aren't as far apart as they are at Jumping Mouse, and they're similarly unsheltered, but this is a great base for hiking – the trail to Cape St Lawrence begins just 200m up the road. There's an ocean beach just below the campground.

Meat Cove Lodge (☎ *902-383-2672, 2305 Meat Cove)* Doubles/quads $40/60 including breakfast. Open June-Sept. This modernistic wooden lodge nestled in a narrow valley is at the entrance to Nova Scotia's northernmost community, a kilometer before the end of the road. The Fraser Trail begins opposite the lodge. A complete lobster or crab dinner ($13 or $11) is served from 4pm to 8pm, or seafood chowder for $6.

Neils Harbour & Around

On your way down from Cape North to Ingonish, it's worth leaving the Cabot Trail and following more scenic White Point Rd via Smelt Brook to Neils Harbour, an attractive little fishing village. In fact, it's one of the nicest places you're likely to see in Nova Scotia. Down at the wharf you can buy fish and lobster.

Back on the Cabot Trail 5km south of the Neils Harbour turnoff is **Black Brook Beach** a great place to swim because a freshwater stream tumbles over the high granite cliff at the left end of the beach, allowing you to rinse off the salt water.

Places to Stay & Eat *South Harbour B&B* (☎ *902-383-2615, 210 White Point Rd, South Harbour)* Singles/doubles $35/45 Open June-mid-Oct. These two rooms with shared bath, a kilometer off the Cabot Trail on the scenic loop to Neils Harbour, include a full breakfast.

Two Tittle B&B (☎ *902-383-2817* W *www.capebretonisland.com/whitepoint 2119 White Point Village Rd, White Point)* Singles/doubles $40/60. This bungalow is directly above the harbor in the quaint fishing village of White Point. Whale-watching trips (adult/child $25/10) are offered at 10am 1:30pm and 4:30pm from July to September by your hosts. Good hiking is nearby.

Chowder House (☎ *902-336-2463, Neils Harbour)* Meals $7. Open 11am-6pm daily mid-June-Sept (11am-9pm in summer). This wildly popular place on the point next to the lighthouse just down from the harbor serves to-die-for clam or seafood chowder for under $4, and the haddock platter is just $7. The plastic plates and self-service at the counter help keep the cost down. It's just 1.2km off the Cabot Trail and worth the detour.

INGONISH

At the eastern entrance to Cape Breton Highlands National Park are Ingonish and Ingonish Beach, two small towns with accommodations and basic supplies. There are several campgrounds, both government and private, as well as motels and a park information office.

The beach at Ingonish Beach is wonderful, with a long, wide strip of sand wrapping around a bay surrounded by green hills. The water can get pleasantly warm after a few sunny days.

Kayaking

Several kayak outfitters operate tours or rent supplies for do-it-yourself kayaking, including

Cape Breton Sea Coast Adventures (☎ 902-929-2800, 877-929-2800, W www.members .tripod.com/mike_crimp, 42314 Hwy 19; half-day/day tour $49/89 plus tax; open June-mid-Oct). Tour leader Mike Crimp meets clients at a hut opposite the Muddy Rudder Seafood Shack in Ingonish Beach.

Whale Watching

Whale tours are run by **SeaQuarium** (☎ 902-285-2103, 902-285-2401, off Cabot Trail; tours $25) from North Bay, Ingonish, with three tours departing daily from mid-June to September.

SeaVisions (☎ 902-285-2628, based at Knotty Pine Cottages, 39126 Cabot Trail; adult/child $30/15) at Ingonish Ferry also does whale tours three times daily from June to early September.

Places to Stay

Sea Breeze Cottages & Motel (☎ 888-743-4443, e seabreeze.motel@ns.sympatico.ca, W ingonish.com/sea, 36104 Cabot Trail, In-gonish) Double units/cottages $55/$74 and up. Open mid-Apr-mid-Dec. This place has a dozen duplex or individual cottages of varying sizes, some better appointed than others, and six motel units in a long block.

Driftwood Lodge (☎ 902-285-2558, e driftwood.lodge@ns.sympatico.ca, 36125 Cabot Trail, Ingonish) Rooms $20-70. Open from June-Oct. This place, 100m south of Sea Breeze and 8km north of the Ingonish park entrance, is run by Wanda and Kersti Tacreiter, who are great hosts. All of the rooms in their three buildings differ in size, facilities, view and price; this can be confusing, so ask to see a few before deciding. Cheapest is the Red House, with four rooms with shared bath at $20-40 single or $30-45 double. The one apartment with kitchen and private bath is $65 double, plus $5 per extra person. The newer lodge has two rooms with shared bath at $25-40 single or $30-45 double, two rooms with private bath at $40-50 single or double, one smaller apartment with kitchen at $55 single or double, two larger apartments at $70 single or double and two basement apartments at $40-50 single

or double. There's also a large housekeeping cottage at $70 double, plus $5 per additional person. Discounts of $5-20 are offered in early June and from early September to October. A panoramic beach is just below the Driftwood.

Keltic Lodge (☎ 800-565-0444, fax 902-285-2859, e keltic@gov.ns.ca, W www .signatureresorts.com, off Cabot Trail, Ingo-nish Beach) Singles/double from $213/304 including breakfast & dinner. Open June-Oct. This is the most luxurious resort in the area, up on a hillside with commanding views. This theatrical Tudor-style complex, erected in 1940, shares Middle Head Penin-sula with the famous Cape Breton High-land Links golf course and the Ingonish Campground. Only the main lodge has any old world charm, though – the Inn at Keltic, Ceilidh Hall and the cottages are just your usual upmarket accommodation blocks. Even if you're not prepared to fork over thick wads of cash to stay here, Keltic Lodge is well worth visiting for its setting and the breathtaking hiking trail to the tip of the peninsula just beyond the resort.

The Island Inn B&B (☎ 800-533-7015, 37700 Cabot Trail) Singles/doubles/triples $45/69/79. Just outside the national park gate, this large two-story hotel-style build-ing offers a sea view from the upper deck.

Knotty Pine Cottages & Tourist Home (☎ 800-455-2058, fax 902-285-2576, e dmackinn@ns.sympatico.ca, W ingonish .com/knotty, 39126 Cabot Trail) Cottages from $50 double to $115 for four people, house rooms from $45. This place in Ingo-nish Ferry has 10 cottages with varying levels of amenities. All but one has cooking facilities, and some have balconies with views. There are also three rooms with shared bath in a house across the road.

Places to Eat

Coastal Waters Restaurant (☎ 902-285-2526, 36404 Cabot Trail, Ingonish) Mains $9-14. Open 8am-9pm daily May-Oct. A kilometer south of Driftwood Lodge, this place serves items like sandwiches ($6), burgers ($3 to $7), seafood ($13 to $14) and pastas ($9). The breakfast specials start at $4.

Muddy Rudder Seafood Shack (☎ 902-285-2280, 38438 Cabot Trail, Ingonish Beach) Appetizers $5-6, seafood dinners $15-17. Open 11am-8pm daily June-Sept. This small eatery, on the Cabot Trail just before you cross the Ingonish River, consists of a handful of tables out on a terrace. If it's rainy, you go into a shelter designed like an old fisherman's beach hut. The food is prepared with a flair by master chef Pearl and features steamed lobster, mussels, crabs and clams. It's a very original and unorthodox place, well worth checking out.

ST ANN'S

The **Gaelic College of Celtic Arts & Crafts** (☎ 902-295-3411, 51779 Cabot Trail; admission $2.50, under 12 years old free; open 8:30am-5pm daily mid-June-late Sept), at the end of St Ann's Bay, is the only Gaelic college in North America. Founded in 1938, the college offers programs in the Scottish Gaelic language, bagpiping, Highland dancing, weaving, kilt making and other things Scottish to students of all ages from across the land. Drop in any time from mid-June to early September and chances are you'll hear a student singing a traditional ballad in Scottish Gaelic or playing a Highland fiddle piece; mini-concerts and recitals are performed throughout the day. You can stroll around the grounds, see the museum with its historical exhibits or browse the giftshop for books, tapes or kilts.

Kayaking

North River Kayak Tours (☎ 888-865-2925, Murray Rd; open late May-mid-Sept), 3½km south of North River Bridge off the Cabot Trail, does half/full day kayak tours for $55/95, and 2½-hour introductory tours for $50. Day rentals are $30/50 per half/full day for a single, $40/60 for a double, and $25/40 for a canoe.

BIG BRAS D'OR

After crossing the long bridge over an arm of Bras d'Or Lake en route to Sydney, a secondary road branches off leading north to the coast and the village of Big Bras d'Or. Offshore are the cliff-edged **Bird Islands**:

Hertford and Ciboux. The islands are home to large colonies of razorbills, puffins, kittiwakes, terns and several other species.

Bird Island Tours (☎ 902-674-2384, 800-661-6680, [W] fox.nstn.ca/~birdisld, 1672 Big Bras d'Or Rd, 6km off Hwy 105; tours $32) runs 2½-hour boat tours to the islands from mid-May to mid-September. The Bird Islands are about 1½km off Cape Dauphin and take 40 minutes to reach. In the prime months of June and July up to 400 pairs of nesting puffins will be present, but plenty of birds can be seen anytime, including the bald eagles that nest in the vicinity. Binoculars (which can be rented) are handy but not a necessity, as the tour boats go to within 20m or so of the islands. Seals and occasional whales are also spotted.

Places to Stay

Mountain Vista Seashore Cottages (☎ 902-674-2384, 800-661-6680, fax 902-674-2742, [e] birdisld@fox.nstn.ca, [W] fox.nstn.ca/~birdisld, 1672 Big Bras d'Or Rd) Cottages $35-150 July & Aug, $30-130 shoulder seasons. Open May-Oct. Unserviced/serviced campsites $18/20. The same folks who run Bird Island tours rent three cottages at their base. The smaller cabin with cooking facilities but no shower is $35/30 on/off-season single or double, and the two larger

The Bird Islands are home to large colonies of puffins.

cottages can each be divided into two separate units by locking a connecting door. In that case, the rooms without cooking would start at $60/50 on/off-season single or double, and an entire two-bedroom housekeeping cottage with all facilities goes for $150/130 for up to four people. The 16 grassy campsites are a good bet in midsummer.

MacNeil's Motel (☎ 902-736-9106, fax 902-736-8070, 1408 Hwy 105) Singles/doubles $50/67 mid-June-mid-Sept, $50/55 shoulder seasons. Open Apr-early Dec. This motel, 5km from the Newfoundland ferry on Hwy 105 at Bras d'Or, exit 17, has 17 rooms in one duplex and three blocks of five units.

NORTH SYDNEY

Nondescript North Sydney is important as the Marine Atlantic terminal for ferries to Port aux Basques and Argentia, in Newfoundland. There isn't much to see here, but it makes a convenient place to put up if you're using the ferry.

In July and August, tourist information is dispensed from a kiosk (☎ 902-539-9876) on the right as you leave the ferry. It's open 9am to 5pm June to mid-October, 9am to 7pm July and August.

The main street in town is Commercial St. There's free parking behind the public library, on Commercial St near the corner of Blowers St close to the ferry terminal.

The small **North Sydney Heritage Museum** (☎ 902-794-2524, 299 Commercial St; admission free; open 10am-3pm Mon-Fri Apr-Oct, noon-4pm Mon, 10am-6pm Tues-Fri, 10am-2pm Sat June-Aug) houses a collection of historical marine detritus.

Places to Stay

If you're coming in on a late ferry it's good to have advance room reservations, as budget motels are in short supply. Three good inexpensive B&Bs are on Queen St, a southern extension of Commercial St, just over a kilometer southwest of the ferry terminal. If you decide to spend the night in the car, there's a large shopping mall up King St, where numerous RVs park for the

night. A 24-hour (except Sunday) Sobeys Supermarket is there as well.

Heritage Home B&B (☎ 902-794-4815, W www.bbcanada.com/3242.html, 110 Queen St) Singles/doubles $45/75. Heritage Home is a large two-story house surrounded by gardens on a hill overlooking the harbor.

Dove House B&B (☎ 877-550-2625, W www.capebretonisland.com/northside/dovehouse, 108 Queen St) Singles/doubles $45/75. Open May-Oct. Adjacent to Heritage Home, this large guesthouse is nicely set back from the road.

Alexandra Shebib's B&B (☎ 902-794-4876, 88 Queen St) Singles/doubles/triples $40/60/70. Just 150m south of the other two, this large house opposite the harbor is another good choice.

Places to Eat

Robena's 2000 Family Restaurant (☎ 902-794-8040, 266 Commercial St) Full breakfast $4. Open 7am-9pm daily June-Sept, 7am-7pm other months. If it's breakfast you're looking for, you'll find it here until noon weekdays, until 1pm on weekends. Lunch and dinner specials are posted in the restaurant window.

Rollie's Wharf (☎ 902-794-7774, 411 Purves St near the wharf) Mains $14-16. Open 11am-9pm daily June-Sept, 11am-7pm other months. This more upscale establishment is on the opposite (northeast) side of the ferry terminal from downtown. They offer plates like ribs, haddock, halibut and lobster ($17 to $23).

Getting There & Away

Bus There's no bus depot per se in North Sydney; the depot is in Sydney. However, the Acadian Lines bus between Sydney and Halifax via Baddeck can be picked up at the Best Western North Star Hotel (☎ 902-794-8581), 39 Forrest St, twice a day. It's $59 to Halifax. (The North Star is the long two-story hotel with a prominent red roof on the hill directly above the Marine Atlantic ferry terminal.)

The Transit Cape Breton No 5 bus runs back and forth between North Sydney and

Sydney several times a day for $3.25. It can be caught along Commercial and Queen Sts around 7:15am, 9:15am, 1:15pm, 3:15pm and 6:15pm Monday to Saturday (no 7:15am bus on Saturday). To confirm these times, call the dispatcher at ☎ 902-539-8124.

Ferry North Sydney is the terminus of all ferry crossings between Nova Scotia and Newfoundland. The service to Port aux Basques operates daily year-round, with up to four departures a day in midsummer, at $22/11 adult/child plus $67/10 per car/bicycle. To Argentia, the ferry operates three times a week from late June to mid-September, weekly from mid-September to early October, costing $60/30 adult/child plus $135/20 per car/bicycle. Cabins, dorm beds and reclining seats are extra.

Vehicle reservations are recommended in midsummer; call Marine Atlantic (☎ 902-794-8109, 800-341-7981) in North Sydney. Foot passengers can buy tickets on the spot. Combined ferry/bus/train tickets between St John's, Newfoundland, and Montréal, Québec, or anywhere in between, are available, though these must be booked well in advance.

The ferry terminal is near the center of North Sydney at Commercial and Blowers Sts. The Trans Canada Hwy (Hwy 105) leads straight into or out of the ferry terminal. If you need to make ferry reservations for a trip to Newfoundland, do it at least a few days before your planned departure. The Newfoundland tourist information counter (☎ 902-794-7433) in the ferry terminal is open from mid-May to mid-October.

SYDNEY

Sydney (population 26,000) is the only real city on Cape Breton and the embattled core of the island's collapsed industrial economy. As the heart of an old coal-mining district, this town has seen its share of grief and hardship. Long a drab, grim place with a warm, friendly, hard-drinking population, the city has managed without much money to modestly upgrade the downtown area. It is hoped that tourism will help offset the shutdown of the steel

mill and coal mines that were the region's largest employers.

The main street downtown is Charlotte St, containing many stores and restaurants. Several large malls have also popped up around town. There's a lot to do, and with the ferry to the north and Louisbourg to the south, many people pass through. The choice of accomodations is good.

Be forewarned that Sydney's parking sentinels are omniscient. They will ticket you if they get the chance. Parking meters take 50¢ an hour from 8am to 6pm weekdays; otherwise they're free.

There's a local tourist office (☎ 902-563-4636, 800-565-9464) at 320 Esplanade inside the Civic Centre on the waterfront, but it's more of a chamber of commerce. The office is open from 8:30am to 5pm weekdays year-round.

The McConnell Memorial Library (☎ 902-562-3279), 50 Falmouth St at Charlotte, provides Internet access. It's open 10am to 9pm Tuesday to Friday, 10am to 5:30pm Saturday.

Northend

The old part of town is along the Esplanade (which runs parallel to the river), Charlotte St and several adjoining streets just north of the city center. Half a dozen buildings remain from the 1700s, and many more date from the 19th century.

At 83 Esplanade across from Marine Terminal you can visit the oldest Roman Catholic Church in Cape Breton. Dating from 1828, **St Patrick's Church Museum** (☎ 902-562-8237, 87 Esplanade; admission free; open 9:30am-5:30pm Mon-Sat, 1pm-5:30pm Sun June-Aug) is in the old stone church with its three-foot-thick walls. There are various interesting artifacts inside, including the town's whipping post from the mid-19th century.

Cossit House (☎ 902-539-7973, 75 Charlotte St; admission free; open 9:30am-5:30pm Mon-Sat, 1pm-5:30pm Sun June-mid-Oct) dates from 1787. The oldest house in Sydney, Cossit House is now a museum with period furnishings. Just down the road, the **Jost Heritage House** (☎ 902-539-0366, 54

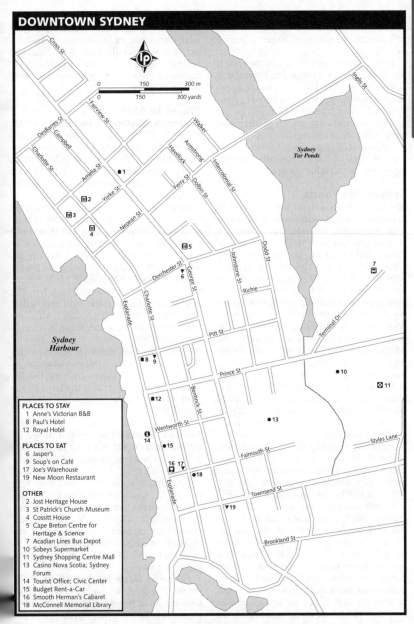

DOWNTOWN SYDNEY

Cross St
Fairview St
DesBarres St
Campbell
Charlotte St
Amelia St
Yorke St
Nepean St
Walker
Armstrong
Havelock
Intercolonial St
Ferry St
Dolbin St
Dorchester St
George St
Johnstone St
Richie
Dodd St
Terminal Dr
Pitt St
Prince St
Bentinck St
Wentworth St
Falmouth St
Styles Lane
Townsend St
Brookland St
Inglis St
Charlotte St
Esplanade
Esplanade

Sydney
Tar Ponds

Sydney
Harbour

0   150   300 m
0   150   300 yards

PLACES TO STAY
1 Anne's Victorian B&B
8 Paul's Hotel
12 Royal Hotel

PLACES TO EAT
6 Jasper's
9 Soup's on Café
17 Joe's Warehouse
19 New Moon Restaurant

OTHER
2 Jost Heritage House
3 St Patrick's Church Museum
4 Cossitt House
5 Cape Breton Centre for
   Heritage & Science
7 Acadian Lines Bus Depot
10 Sobeys Supermarket
11 Sydney Shopping Centre Mall
13 Casino Nova Scotia; Sydney
    Forum
14 Tourist Office; Civic Center
15 Budget Rent-a-Car
16 Smooth Herman's Cabaret
18 McConnell Memorial Library

Charlotte St; admission free; open 9:30am-5:30pm Mon-Sat June-Oct), built in 1790 and now also a museum, houses a marine exhibit.

In the old neoclassical Lyceum building is the **Cape Breton Centre for Heritage & Science** *(☎ 902-539-1572, 225 George St; admission free; open 10am-4pm Tues-Fri, 1pm-4pm Sat)*. The museum features an art gallery and exhibits on the human and natural history of the region.

Action Week is an annual event held in the first week of August. Festivities include music, sports and other goings-on.

Sydney Tar Ponds

Just three blocks east of the Charlotte St museums is one of North America's largest toxic waste sites, the notorious Sydney Tar Ponds. From Kia Auto Mall at the corner of Prince and Dodd Sts, go 700m north on Dodd and then Intercolonial St, keeping right toward Ferry St, which runs directly into the site (entry forbidden). From the gate at the east end of Ferry St you'll get a good view (and smell) of this poisonous pool and the now defunct steel mill, visible beyond a long hill of slag known as the 'High Dump.' The 'Tar Pond' is actually the tidal estuary of Muggah Creek, and toxic wastes are carried out to sea with every tide. A kilometer beyond the mill ruins is a 51-hectare coke oven site, now just a field of coal-black rubble contaminated to depths of 25m. It's a scene of utter desolation you'll probably only want to see once in your life.

From the founding of the Sydney steel mill in 1901, some of the world's dirtiest coal was burned here to produce coke, and wastes were simply allowed to accumulate. After the mill became unprofitable in 1967, a Crown corporation took over from Hawker Siddley. The first cleanup attempt was undertaken in 1986 with the installation of a pumping system and incinerator intended to reprocess the wastes. The system never worked, and it was abandoned after eating up $55 million in federal and provincial funds. The coke ovens closed in 1988. In 1996 a $20 million scheme to bury the Tar Ponds under a mountain of slag was canceled when alarmingly high levels of PCBs (polychlorinated biphenyls) were discovered by the contractor. In 2001 the mill was finally shut down, leaving behind 700,000 tons of sludge, including an estimated 45,000 tons contaminated with deadly PCBs.

Places to Stay

Downtown Sydney *Royal Hotel (☎ 902-539-2148, 345 Esplanade opposite the Civic Centre)* Singles/doubles/triples $40/50/60 with shared bath, singles/doubles $50/55 with private bath, $65 double suite plus $8 per extra person. This three-story wooden hotel dating from the early 20th century is nicer on the inside than the exterior suggests. There are eight rooms with shared bath, one with private bath and three two-room suites. A small communal kitchen is available for guests, and the hotel has atmosphere. Parking is provided at the rear.

Paul's Hotel (☎ 866-562-5747, 10 Pitt St) Singles/doubles $55/60 with bath (or $75 double for a larger room with two beds). This turn-of-the-19th-century two-story hotel one block from the Royal is a touch more upscale.

Ann's Victorian B&B (☎ 902-564-0921, ⓦ www3.ns.sympatico.ca/annsvictorianb_b, 115 George St) Singles/doubles $50/75. Three rooms are for rent in this large three-story heritage house in the old northern part of town.

Around Sydney *University College of Cape Breton (☎ 902-563-1792, fax 902-563-1449, ⓔ conference.services@uccb.ns.ca, ⓦ www.uccb.ns.ca, 1250 Grand Lake Rd)* Singles/doubles $33/40, students $27, parking $1. Open mid-May-mid-Aug. The college is on the highway to Glace Bay (bus No 1 hourly from Sydney). Sixty rooms with shared bath are available in a student dorm at MacDonald Residence, and the receptionist is on call 24 hours a day during the summer season.

Gathering House B&B (☎ 902-539-7172, fax 902-539-6665, ⓔ kmp38@msn.com, 148 Crescent St at Argyle St) Singles/doubles/triples $50/65/80. This large Victorian mansion stands on a hill overlooking a duck pond and park. It's only a short walk to the center.

Park Place B&B *(☎ 902-562-3518, fax 902-567-6618,* ✉ *lemcewen@cbnet.ns.ca,* ☷ *www.bbcanada.com/81.html, 169 Park St near Brookland St)* Singles/doubles $45/60. Open May-Oct. This late-19th/early-20th-century B&B is only a few blocks from the Acadian Lines bus station.

Century Manor B&B *(☎ 902-567-1300, 212 Whitney Ave)* Singles/doubles $45/60. Open May-Oct. Just two blocks from Park Place B&B, this two-story house is on an even nicer tree-lined street.

Places to Eat
Soup's on Café *(☎ 902-539-6483, 16 Pitt St)* Breakfast with coffee $3. Open 8am-5pm Mon & Tues, 8am-7pm Wed, 8am-8pm Thurs & Fri, 8am-3pm Sat, 9am-2pm Sun. Next to Paul's Hotel between Esplanade and Charlotte, this is a popular breakfast place.

Joe's Warehouse Food Emporium *(☎ 902-539-6686, 424 Charlotte St)* Mains $17-22. Open 11:30am-10pm Mon-Sat, 4pm-10pm Sun (until 11pm July & Aug). This large restaurant has a varied menu featuring steak and seafood, and there's an outdoor patio at the rear with views of the water. Joe's also includes a cozy little bar called the Front Office, with plush seating. Joe's is much nicer than the plain exterior lets on.

New Moon Restaurant *(☎ 902-539-4422, 78 Townsend St)* Meals under $10. Open 11am-11pm Mon-Thurs, 11am-1am Fri, 4pm-11pm Sat & Sun. The $7 Chinese specials are posted in the window.

Jasper's *(☎ 902-539-7109, 268 George St at Dorchester)* Meals $8-13. This reasonably priced 24-hour family restaurant has a large menu.

Entertainment
Casino Nova Scotia *(☎ 902-563-7777, 525 George St)* Open noon-4am Mon-Wed, 24hrs Thurs. The 12 table games and 370 slot machines here are heavily used. Everything that happens in and around the casino is carefully monitored by security cameras, but visitors are not allowed to take photos inside the casino.

Smooth Herman's Cabaret *(☎ 902-539-0408, Esplanade & Falmouth St)* Open 8pm-3:30am Sat-Thurs, 4:30pm-3:30am Fri. This huge bar often presents a live band Thursday through Saturday nights ($5 cover charge).

Getting There & Away
Air Air Nova flies between Sydney and Halifax year-round, and Air Canada flies to Toronto from June to mid-September only. Air St Pierre *(☎ 902-794-4800)* flies to the tiny French island of St Pierre, which is near Newfoundland.

An 'airport improvement fee' of $10 must be paid at a separate counter by all passengers (not included in the ticket price).

Bus The Acadian Lines bus depot *(☎ 902-564-5533)* is away from the center but walkable if necessary, across the street from the big Sydney Shopping Centre Mall on Terminal Drive. It can be hard to find the first time as it isn't visible from Prince St. If you're on foot, go around behind KFC at Prince Street Plaza and you'll see it next to the Ford dealer. If you're driving, turn down Terminal Dr beside the train tracks opposite the large Sobeys Supermarket at Sydney Shopping Center Mall. The infamous Sydney Tar Ponds are adjacent to the station. Coin lockers ($2) are available. The depot is open 6:30am to 11pm Monday to

Friday, 6:30am to 7pm Saturday and Sunday.

There are buses to Halifax ($60) at 7am, 8:30am and 4:30pm. The two buses that go via Baddeck stop at the ferry terminal in North Sydney. Acadian Lines sometimes has specials on the 8:30am bus to Halifax via St Peters, which brings the price down to $41.

For Charlottetown, the fare is $89 with a change of buses in Truro and Moncton. These connections only work on Friday, Saturday and Sunday. To Moncton the bus leaves daily at 7am ($72). It's also possible to buy a combined bus/train ticket to Montréal, transferring to the train at Truro.

Transoverland Ltd (☎ 902-248-2051 in Chéticamp) runs minibuses from Sydney to Baddeck, then north through the Margaree Valley and up the coast to Chéticamp ($12). They depart Monday, Wednesday and Friday at 3pm.

Getting Around

There's no city bus service to Sydney Airport (other than the hourly Glace Bay buses that pass on the highway 1½km from the terminal). A taxi to Sydney is $14, or $7.50/9 for a shared cab. Avis, Budget, Hertz and National have car rental desks at the airport, but they only open if reservations have been made. (See the Getting Around chapter for contact information.)

Transit Cape Breton (☎ 902-539-8124) operates several bus routes around the region between North Sydney and Glace Bay. Those of most interest to travelers are the No 5 bus to North Sydney (four or five a day) and hourly bus No 1 to Glace Bay via the University and Dominion. The corner of Dorchester and George Sts is the beginning point in Sydney (no buses on Sunday).

Budget Rent-a-Car (☎ 902-564-2610) is at 501 Esplanade near the Civic Centre.

AROUND SYDNEY
New Waterford

New Waterford is another old industrial town that has lost its industries. The Phalen Colliery closed in 1999. East of town is the former **Lingan Mine**, once run by the Cape

Breton Development Corporation, and 2km beyond it are the twin smokestacks of Nova Scotia Power's **Lingan Generating Station**. Coal from the mine once supplied the power plant, but now only 'cleaner' imported coal is used. The two tall smoke stacks are visible from afar.

An unexpectedly interesting sight is **Dominion Beach Provincial Park** between New Waterford and Glace Bay. Wheelchair-accessible boardwalks extend along the 1½km sandspit separating Lingan and Indian Bays. It's a good bird-watching area with a long beach for swimming in midsummer. An 1888 schoolhouse at the entrance to the park features a fascinating open-air exhibit on the history of coal mining in this area. Admission to this fascinating site is free, but there's no camping.

At west edge of New Waterford off Hwy 28 is **Colliery Lands Park**, with memorials to those who served in the old mines. Further west on Hwy 28 is **Fort Petrie**, one of seven coastal defense batteries constructed during WWII to protect Sydney Harbour. While the others have been allowed to crumble, a weird church-style roof has been mounted atop Fort Petrie's three-story concrete observation bunker to protect the structure. Museum exhibits are housed within, but the place is seldom open.

Carmel Center (☎ 902-862-3370, fax 902-862-3468, e carmel.centre@ns.sympatico.ca, 3208 Mt Carmel Ave, New Waterford) Singles/doubles/triples $34/48/58 with shared bath ($2 per person less in winter). This former convent is now run by the Carmel Center Society, a nonprofit community group. It's quite comfortable – a charming change of pace. The price includes a continental buffet breakfast, and you can order lunch from 11:30am to 2pm Wednesday to Saturday. The Sunday brunch from 11:30am to 2pm ($10) is popular.

Glace Bay

The difficulties of the Cape Bretoners are reflected in Glace Bay, part of the greater Sydney industrial region. The district has a long, bitter history of work – when there is any – with low pay, poor conditions and one

AROUND SYDNEY

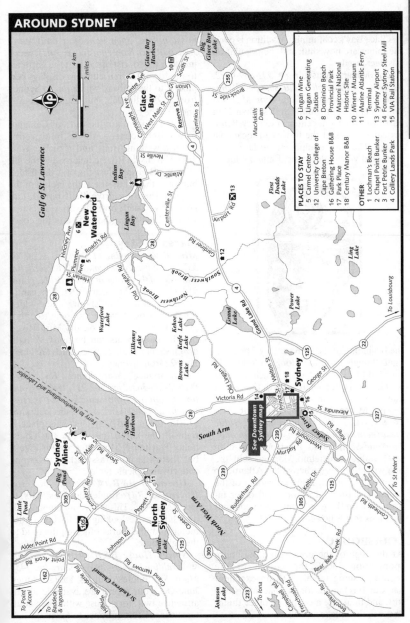

PLACES TO STAY
5 Carmel Center
12 University College of
   Cape Breton
16 Gathering House B&B
17 Park Place
18 Century Manor B&B

OTHER
1 Lochman's Beach
2 Chapel Point Bunker
3 Fort Petrie Bunker
4 Colliery Lands Park
6 Lingan Mine
7 Lingan Generating
   Station
8 Dominion Beach
   Provincial Park
9 Marconi National
   Historic Site
10 Miners' Museum
11 Marine Atlantic Ferry
   Terminal
13 Sydney Airport
14 Former Sydney Steel Mill
15 VIA Rail Station

of the highest unemployment rates in the country.

Glace Bay's coal-mining tradition is over; the mines are now shut; and the population has decreased.

The **Miners' Museum** (☎ 902-849-4522, 42 Birkley St; complete tour $8; open 10am-6pm daily June-Aug, 9am-4pm Mon-Fri other months), off South St, less than 2km east from the town center in Quarry Point, provides a look at the history of local coal mining. There are equipment displays and a recreated village depicting a miner's life at

the beginning of the 20th century. The highlight, though, is an hour-long underground tour led by a retired miner, which includes walking in the tunnel. It's worth the cost of admission.

The **Marconi National Historic Site** (☎ 902-842-2530, Timmerman St, Table Head; admission free; open 10am-6pm daily June-mid-Sept) marks the place where, in 1902, Italian Guglielmo Marconi sent the first wireless message across the Atlantic, to Cornwall, England. There's a model of the original transmitting station and other information on the developments in communications that followed.

LOUISBOURG

At the edge of the ocean sits Louisbourg (population 1300), the largest of the region's fishing towns, with an excellent harbour. It is famous for its adjacent historic fort, and there are a couple of other things to see in the village as well.

The **Sydney & Louisbourg Railway Museum** (☎ 902-733-2720, 7336 Main St; admission free; open 9am-5pm daily early June-mid-Oct, 8am-7pm July & Aug), which includes the tourist office, is at the entrance to the town. The museum has displays pertaining to the railway, which ran to Sydney from 1895 until 1968, shuffling fish one way and coal the other.

South of town are the ruins of Canada's oldest **lighthouse**, with an interpretive display, walking trails and a picnic area. Take Havenside Rd, the first road to the left after the Railway Museum, past the fishing harbor to the lighthouse at the mouth of the harbor. The 3km drive (half paved, half good gravel road) rewards you with a great view of Louisbourg Fortress and the coast.

Places to Stay

Mira River Provincial Park (☎ 902-563-3373, W parks.gov.ns.ca, off Brickyard Rd, 2km east of the bridge at Albert Bridge) Sites $18. Open mid-May-early Oct. This campground between Louisbourg and Sydney offers the closest nature camping to either place. There's a beach on the Mira River, but the motorboats can be noisy. A half-dozen small private campgrounds are along Hwy 22 from Sydney.

Louisbourg Motorhome RV Park (☎ 902-733-3631, fax 902-733-3140, W louisbourg.com/motorhomepark, 24 Harbourfront Cres) Unserviced/serviced sites $10/15. Open mid-May-Oct. This place is right on the harbor just below the Louisbourg Playhouse. Most sites are for RVers, but there's also a grassy area for tenting with covered picnic tables.

Havenhill B&B (☎ 902-733-2565, 163 Havenside Rd) Singles/doubles $40/50. Open May-Oct. This two-room bungalow is on a hilltop overlooking the harbor a kilometer from the tourist office on the road to the lighthouse.

Stacey House B&B (☎ 888-924-2242, e geraldine.beaver@ns.sympatico.ca, 7438 Main St) Singles/doubles $50/65. Open June-Oct. Four rooms are available in this attractive two-story house with green shutters near the east entrance to town.

Greta Gross B&B (☎ *902-733-2833,* e *bantama@atcon.com, 48 Pepperell St)* Singles/doubles $35/45. Open May-Oct. This two-story house is directly back from Stacey B&B.

Levy's B&B (☎ *902-733-2793, 7 Marvin St)* Singles/doubles $35/50. Open May-Oct. This B&B is just above the harbor near the fishing sheds, down the next road after Stacey House B&B.

Kathy's B&B (☎ *902-733-2264, 18 Upper Warren St)* Singles/doubles $40/45. Open June-Sept. This large two-story house with a widow's walk on the roof is just up from the post office.

The Louisbourg Manse B&B (☎ *866-733-3155,* ☎ *902-733-315,* e *jdoyle@bigfoot.com,* W *www.bbcanada.com/lsbgmanse, 10 Strathcona St)* Singles/doubles $55/65, breakfast included. Open mid-Apr-Oct. This well-maintained two-story house overlooks the harbor.

Garden Sanctuary B&B (☎ *902-733-3497, 7590 Main St)* Singles/doubles $40/45. This large yellow two-story house is at the west end of town toward the fortress.

Fortress Inn (☎ *888-367-5353, fax 902-434-2144, 7464 Main St)* Rooms from $54. This centrally located 45-room motel comes in handy when everything else is closed or full.

Places to Eat

Grubstake Restaurant (☎ *902-733-2308, 7499 Main St)* Dinner $14-20. Open noon-9pm daily mid-June-early Oct. Grubstake has been operating since 1972. They offer good seafood such as haddock or sole ($14), salmon ($15) and seafood pasta ($20).

Fortress View Restaurant (☎ *902-733-3131, 7513 Main St)* Meals $6-7. Open 8am-8pm daily mid-May-mid-Oct, 7am-9pm July & Aug. This place looks upscale from the outside but you can get fish & chips for $6-7 and hamburgers for $4-5.

Entertainment

Louisbourg Playhouse (☎ *902-733-2996, 11 Lower Warren St)* On the waterfront behind the fire station is this theater, built as a set for the Walt Disney movie *Squanto: A Warrior's Tale* in 1993. The playhouse is now Louisbourg's permanent performing arts center and hosts a variety of plays during the year. The musical *Spirit of the Island* runs weeknights at 8pm from July to mid-September (adult/senior/child $14/12/5), with various guest vocalists and other performances on weekends.

Getting There & Away

In July and August there's usually a shuttle service between Sydney and Louisbourg for $25 per person roundtrip. Contact numbers and schedules vary from year to year, but a tourist information office may know something. Otherwise you'll need to hire a taxi or rent a car for the trip.

LOUISBOURG NATIONAL HISTORIC SITE

This extraordinary historic site (☎ *902-733-2280, 259 Park Service Rd; adult/family $11/24.50, $4.50/11.25 in May & early Oct; open 9:30am-5pm daily June & Sept, 9:30am-5pm May & early Oct, 9am-7pm daily July & Aug)* is located about 50km south of Sydney on the southeast tip of Cape Breton Island and is well worth the trek. The entrance to the fortress is 2½km beyond the Railway Museum tourist office in Louisbourg.

After the Treaty of Utrecht in 1713, the French lost their bases in Newfoundland and mainland Nova Scotia. This left them Prince Edward Island, the Saint Pierre and Miquelon Islands and Cape Breton Island, which became the conduit for exporting cod to France and, later, a new military base. Louisbourg, a massive walled fort and village complex, was worked on continually from 1719 to about 1745. It looked daunting but was poorly designed, and the British took it in 46 days in 1745, when it was barely finished. It would change hands twice more. Finally in 1760, after Wolfe (the British general who led the Louisbourg onslaught) took Québec City, the walls of Louisbourg were destroyed and the city burned to the ground.

In 1961, with the closing of many Cape Breton coal mines, the federal government began a make-work project – the largest historical reconstruction in Canadian history – and Louisbourg rose from its ashes. Today the site depicts in remarkable detail what French life was like here in the 1700s. All the workers, in period dress, have taken on the lives of typical fort inhabitants. Ask them anything – what the winters are like, what that tool is for, who they had an affair with – and they'll tell you. (And Anglophones are 'harassed' as spies by the French guards at the gates!)

You'll need a lot of time to see the park properly – plan on spending a minimum of half a day at the site. The best times to visit are in the morning, when there's more going on and less of a crowd, and during June or September. Check out the movie in the interpretive center first. Free guided tours around the site are offered throughout the day, and cannons are fired four times daily.

The weather here is very changeable and often bad. Take a sweater and raincoat even if it's sunny when you start out, and be prepared for lots of walking. As well as the fort area itself, there are hiking trails around the grounds and out to the Atlantic coast.

Admission seems steep, but the fort is well worth it. This isn't just a museum or historic house but an entire town! The revenue that Parks Canada collects from visitors barely maintains the large complex.

Three restaurants on site serve food typical of the time. One place has hamburgers or sandwiches for $4, but it's worth splurging on a real 18th-century meal at the **Grandchamps House**, costing $7 to $10 including tea or coffee. The servers are dressed in period costume. In midsummer you'll likely need to wait awhile for a table. Otherwise buy a 1kg loaf of soldiers' bread at the **Destouches Bakery**. It's delicious; one piece with cheese makes a full meal.

BADDECK

An old resort town in a pastoral setting, Baddeck is on the north shore of the saltwater Bras d'Or Lakes, halfway between Sydney and the Canso Causeway. The name 'Baddeck' comes from the Mi'kmaq word

Apatakwitk, and *Bras d'Or* is French for 'Golden Arm.'

Baddeck is small, but it's a center of sorts, as nearly everyone traveling around Cape Breton spends some time here. There are some noteworthy (if upscale) places to stay and eat, and the Alexander Graham Bell Museum is well done.

Chebucto St is the main thoroughfare, but the lake is what makes Baddeck special.

An excellent tourist office (☎ 902-295-1911) sits on the corner of Chebucto and Twining Sts in the center of Baddeck. It's open 9am to 5pm daily June to mid-October, 9am to 8:30pm July and August.

The Baddeck Public Library (☎ 902-295-2055), 520 Chebucto St, offers Internet access for a donation. The library is open from 1pm to 5pm Monday, 1pm to 5pm and 6pm to 8pm Tuesday and Friday, 5pm to 8pm Thursday, 10am to noon and from 1pm to 5pm Saturday.

Alexander Graham Bell National Historic Site

Alexander Graham Bell, the inventor of the telephone, had a summer home called Beinn Bhreagh near Baddeck. It's visible to the left across the bay from the present historic site but cannot be visited, as Bell's descendants still live there. Alexander Graham himself is buried at Beinn Bhreagh.

Parks Canada operates this large museum (☎ 902-295-2069, Chebucto St; admission $4.25; open 9am-8pm daily July & Aug; 9am-6pm June & Sept; 9am-5pm Oct-May) covering all aspects of Bell's inventions and innovations. Written explanations, models, photographs and objects detail his varied works. On display are his medical and electrical devices, telegraphs, telephones, kites and seaplanes. You'll need a couple of hours to visit all three exhibit halls.

Bras d'Or Lakes & Watershed Interpretive Centre

This ecology exhibit (☎ 902-295-1675 Chebucto St; adult/child $2/1; open 1pm 3pm & 6pm-9pm daily July & Aug) jus up from the Government Wharf is in Baddeck's old stone post office.

Kidston Island

This micro-island just offshore serves as a park for Baddeck. There's a fine swimming beach, some nature trails and a lighthouse dating from 1915. In July and August the Baddeck Lions Club operates a pontoon boat at Government Wharf to make the short – and free – run to the island every 20 minutes from 10am to 6pm on weekdays and noon to 6pm on weekends. Another way to reach the island is to rent a canoe or kayak at the wharf from **Harvey's** (☎ 902-295-3318, W baddeck.com/harvey; $12/48 per hour/day; open July-mid-Sept), in a barn-shaped building near Government Wharf.

Uisge Bahn Falls Hiking Trail

This outstanding hiking area on the southern slopes of the Cape Breton Highlands is only a short drive from Baddeck. From exit 9 off Hwy 105 (Old Margaree Rd), take Baddeck Forks Rd and follow the paved highway 11.7km toward West Side Baddeck. Watch for the signposted gravel road on the right, which runs another 3½km to the park.

The Uisge Bahn Falls Picnic Park provides access to two well-marked hiking trails through a beautiful coniferous forest. One trail leads 1.3km (one way) up Falls Brook to a waterfall. There's also a 3.3km loop trail up the north branch of the Baddeck River and back through the forest. These trails intersect to create a 5.4km network. Admission is free, but camping is not allowed and the park closes at dusk.

Boat Cruises & Tours

On Water St along the waterfront, Government Wharf is lined with pleasure craft, sailing boats and tour boats offering cruises around Bras d'Or Lake. One tour organization, **Amoeba Sailing Tours** (☎ 902-295-2481; tours $20; open May-Sept), offers four tours each day on its tall-masted sailboat.

Loch Bhreagh Boat Tours (☎ 902-295-2016; adult/child $20/10; open June-mid-Oct) offers the same tour on a power boat.

Elsie Yacht Charters (☎ 800-565-5660, E elsie@capebretonresorts.com, W www.elsiecharters.com, at the Inverary Resort, 378 Shore Rd; open mid-June-mid-Oct) runs charters on inventor Alexander Graham Bell's original laboratory yacht, Elsie, for $150 an hour (six passengers maximum). Bell gave the 17-meter Elsie, built at Beinn Bhreagh in 1917, to his daughter Elsie and son-in-law Gilbert Grosvenor, editor of National Geographic magazine from 1920 to 1954. It's possible to stay overnight aboard the yacht for $250 double, including a three-hour sail, a bottle of wine and breakfast at the Inverary Resort.

You can rent kayaks ($6/10 single/double per hour) or canoes, paddle boats or bicycles at $7 per hour from the **boat house** (☎ 800-565-5660, 378 Shore Rd; open mid-June-mid-Oct). It's west of the center, down by the water beside the Lakeside Café at the Inverary Resort.

Places to Stay

KOA Kampground (☎ 800-562-7452, fax 902-295-2288, W www.koa.com/where/ns/54104.htm, off Hwy 105) Unserviced/serviced sites $19/24-26, cabins $38. Open mid-May-mid-Oct. This attractive campground 9km west of Baddeck on Hwy 105, or a kilometer east of the beginning of the Cabot Trail, is 700m off the highway. Facilities include a store, restaurant, pool and Laundromat, and there's lots of shade. The three camping cabins are a good value, but in July and August KOA will likely be full. The Silver Spruce Campground just across the highway from KOA isn't as nice and is more expensive.

Heidi's B&B (☎ 902-295-1301, 64 Old Margaree Rd) Rooms $50. Open June-Oct. Just past the hospital, this castle-like house is a long block up the hill from the tourist office.

Bain's Heritage House B&B (☎ 902-295-1069, E rgb@ns.sympatico.ca, W www.bbcanada.com/4347.html, 121 Twining St) Singles/doubles $45/75. This three-story house on the hillside is just above the tourist office in central Baddeck.

Sarah Jean's B&B (☎ *888-515-0552, fax 902-295-3162,* e *mary.macdonald@ns .sympatico.ca, 18 High St)* Rooms from $50 including a full breakfast. This large two-story house is up Twining St from the tourist office.

Restawyle Tourist Home (☎ *902-295-3253, 231 Shore Rd)* Doubles $55. Open mid-May-mid-Oct. Just west of town, this large three-story restored house with a deck in front has four rooms.

Telegraph House (☎ *902-295-1100,* e *telegraph@auracom.com,* w *baddeck .com/telegraph, 479 Chebucto St)* Singles/ doubles from $52/62, including breakfast. This 'historic motel,' right in the center of town, is very attractive, painted gray with white shutters.

Auld Manse B&B (☎ *800-254-7982,* w *www.bbcanada.com/3233.html, 1351 Baddeck Forks Rd, Baddeck Forks)* Singles/ doubles $40/55 shared bath, $60 double private bath. Open March-Nov. On the paved road just 700m before the turnoff to Uisge Bahn Park, this large house in the forest would be a good base for hiking.

Places to Eat

Village Kitchen Café (☎ *902-295-3200, 474 Chebucto St)* Breakfast/dinner $4/8. Open 7am-9pm daily June-Sept, 11am-9pm or 7pm other months. Just off the main street, this spot serves good basic breakfasts, and in the evening the 'Fish & Stein' is recommended. It's good home cooking at local prices and it's one of the few places that stays open all winter.

Highwheeler Café/Deli/Bakery (☎ *902-295-3006, 486 Chebucto St)* Open 6am-7pm daily May-mid-Oct. Deli sandwiches $5. This Baddeck eatery is inexpensive while maintaining high standards, with a mouth-watering selection of sandwiches, salads and bakery items. It's a good choice for breakfast, as they open at 6am with coffee and a vast array of baked goods.

Yellow Cello Café (☎ *902-295-2303, 525 Chebucto St)* Main meals $8-12. Open 8am-10pm daily May-Oct. This is a good choice

for an unpretentious terrace lunch with salads ($5 to $6), sub sandwiches ($4 to $6) and hot dogs ($3). They also serve pizzas, pastas and nachos, and bottled beer is available (no draft).

The *Bell Buoy* (☎ *902-295-2581, 536 Chebucto St)* Mains under $20. Open 11:30am-8:30pm Thurs-Sat, 4pm-8:30pm Sun-Wed mid-May-mid-Oct. With its terrific harbor view, soft music and pricey seafood, the Bell Buoy has a 'Fisherman's Wharf' feel. Their specialties are halibut steak ($18) and lobster in the shell ($33), but you can also order pasta ($9 to $19) or bluenose chowder ($10).

Lynnwood Inn (☎ *902-295-1995, 24 Shore Rd)* Mains $15-17. Open noon-8:30pm daily mid-June-mid-Oct; noon-10pm July & Aug. This well-regarded dining room in an elegant Victorian house is a bit cheaper than the Bell Buoy, with lake trout ($15), poached Atlantic salmon ($17), lobster platter ($26) and fish & chips ($7).

Baddeck Lobster Suppers (☎ *902-295-3307, 17 Ross St just up from the Legion Hall)* Supper $26. Open 11:30am-1:30pm & 4pm-9pm daily mid-June-mid-Oct. Lobster suppers, with a one-pounder in the shell and everything else you can eat from the buffet, are available here. They don't quite match with the value of the Prince Edward Island lobster suppers, but the food is good and plentiful. Lunch is a choice of lobster rolls ($7), seafood chowder ($4) or the mussels platter ($4).

Baddeck's finest *picnic spot* is along the boardwalk on Water St, straight down Twining St from the tourist office. None of Baddeck's fancy restaurants can match these picnic table views looking out over Bras d'Or Lake.

Getting There & Around

All buses out of town depart from the Irving gas station (☎ *902-295-1616*) on Hwy 105, 2½km west of central Baddeck via Shore Rd.

Acadian Lines buses serve Baddeck on their Halifax to Sydney run. Buses arrive from Sydney daily at 8:35am and 5:50pm continuing on to Antigonish, Truro and

Halifax. Fares are $24 to Antigonish, $13 to Sydney, $55 to Halifax.

Also from Baddeck, Transoverland Ltd buses run north through the Margaree Valley and then up the coast to Chéticamp on Monday, Wednesday and Friday. They leave for Sydney around 9:30am, toward Chéticamp around 3:30pm year-round.

AROUND BRAS D'OR LAKE
Wagmatcook First Nation

The Wagmatcook reserve, on Hwy 105 near Baddeck, is typical of the many Mi'kmaq settlements in central Cape Breton Island, but it's one of the few providing facilities for visitors. The **Wagmatcook Culture & Heritage Centre** (☎ 902-295-2999, 10751 Hwy 105; adult/child $2/free; open 9am-5pm daily July & Aug; 9am-5pm Mon-Fri other months), 5km west of the turnoff to the Cabot Trail (15km west of Baddeck), opened in 2001. The center's museum has photos and commentary on the history and culture of the Mi'kmaq people, and there's a craft shop with baskets, jewelry, children's clothes, books and compact discs of authentic Mi'kmaq music. Downstairs are health and educational facilities serving residents of the reserve. If you can, come for the Wagmatcook Powwow, held the last weekend in August since 1990.

Clean Wave Restaurant (☎ 902-295-1542, 10751 Hwy 105) Mains $9-14. Open 8am-8pm daily July & Aug; 8am-5pm Mon-Sat other months. The restaurant at the Wagmatcook Culture & Heritage Centre serves traditional Mi'kmaq foods such as a hot venison sandwich at lunch and eels supreme for dinner. A variety of soups, salads and sandwiches, meat, fish and chicken dishes are also available at normal prices.

Whycocomagh

The **Negemow Basket Shop** (☎ 902-756-3491, 9217 Hwy 105), just west of Whycocomagh on the Waycobah First Nation reserve, sells Mi'kmaq crafts. Rod's One Stop next door pumps some of the cheapest gas on Cape Breton Island.

In Whycocomagh the Acadian Lines buses stop at Vis Restaurant (☎ 902-756-

2338), at the junction of Hwys 105 and 252 opposite the Irving gas station. The Mabou River Hostel will pick you up here for $10 if you contact them in advance (the 1:30pm bus from Halifax arrives here at 7pm).

Whycocomagh Provincial Park (☎ 902-756-2448, e dnrwhy@phk.auracom.com, w parks.gov.ns.ca, 9729 Hwy 105) Sites $18. Open early June-Aug. Just 2km east of Whycocomagh, this is the only provincial park with camping facilities on this side of Cape Breton Island. There are some nice sites on the hillside above the Trans Canada Hwy, a cooking shelter and a trail to the Lookoff. Sites are usually available, even in midsummer.

Fiddler's Farm B&B (☎ 902-756-2163, fax 902-756-2163, 9519 Hwy 105) Singles/doubles $50/60. This old two-story house right next to the highway is almost opposite the Esso gas station in Whycocomagh.

Aberdeen Motel (☎ 902-756-2331, fax 902-756-3324, e motele@swiss-valley.com, w aberdeenmotelenglish.hypermart.net, 10293 Hwy 105, 4km east of Whycocomagh) Singles/doubles from $60-75 July & Aug, $50-65 rest of year. This well-maintained motel has 16 rooms in a long wing facing the highway. There's a Laundromat on premises. Prices vary according to how busy things are.

SOUTH OF BRAS D'OR LAKE

This is a little-visited, sparsely inhabited area of lakes, hills and small villages. It's a farming and forestry region where many of the roads remain unpaved, although Hwy 4 from Port Hastings to Sydney is completely paved.

Big Pond

Bald eagles can frequently be seen along the Bras d'Or Lake shoreline, particularly in the Big Pond area.

On the south shore of East Bay, *Rita's Tea Room* (☎ 902-828-2667, open 9am-7pm daily June-mid-Oct), in a converted one-room schoolhouse, is run by hometown Cape Breton singer Rita MacNeil. Adorning the walls are her music awards and records. Afternoon tea with the works is $7, otherwise a tea/coffee alone will be $2. It's an ideal place for a rest stop while driving to/from Sydney on Hwy 4. The Big Pond Concert, a sizable Cape Breton musical event, is held here every July.

MacIntyre's B&B (☎ 877-815-8663, e e.a.macintyre@ns.sympatico.ca, 7903 Hwy 4, Big Pond) Singles/doubles $50/65. This attractive two-story house is a kilometer northeast of Rita's Tea Room.

St Peter's

This bustling little town (population 731) is on a narrow peninsula separating the Atlantic Ocean and Bras d'Or Lake along Hwy 4. A variety of stores and places to eat are found along the main street. All in all, St Peter's is undervalued as a tourist destination.

Noted Canadian author Farley Mowat has a summer house at River Bourgeois near St Peter's.

The Tourism Cape Breton information office (☎ 902-535-2185) is on Hwy 4, 700m east of the St Peter's Canal. It's open 9am to 5pm daily mid-June to September.

The daily Acadian Lines bus from Sydney stops at Joe Pops Store (☎ 902-535-3349), 9982 Hwy 4 in the center of St Peter's, less than a kilometer west of the bridge over the canal.

Things to See The **St Peter's Canal** (☎ 902-535-2118, admission free), built in the 1850s, includes a 91m double-gate lock to allow vessels to move between the different water levels of the lake and the ocean. Parks Canada provides an outdoor exhibit explaining the lock's workings and the history of the canal.

The best view of the canal is from the platform opposite the **Nicolas Denys Museum** (☎ 902-535-2379, 46 Denys St; admission 50¢; open 9am-5pm daily June-Sept). The museum has old photos of the area and a few artifacts.

St Peter's is the birthplace of noted photographer Wallace MacAskill. It was MacAskill's photo of the *Bluenose* that was used for the design of Canada's 10¢

coin. The house in which he was born is now the **Wallace MacAskill Museum** (☎ 902-535-2531, Main St; admission free; open 9:30am-5:30pm daily July & Aug). It features 26 of MacAskill's hand-tinted photographs.

Activities Treasure Hollow Gift Shop (☎ 902-535-3212, 9856 Hwy 4; open 10am-5pm Mon-Sat, 1pm-5pm Sun May-Sept), in the center of town, rents sit-on-top kayaks at $7/20/35 per hour/half day/full day for a single, $10/25/40 for a double.

Places to Stay *Battery Provincial Park* (☎ 902-535-3094, w parks.gov.ns.ca, 10110 Hwy 4) Sites $14. Open early June-Aug. This uncrowded park occupies the east side of the St Peter's Canal. The park has no showers, but you'll find some nice shady sites and it's seldom full, even in midsummer. There are hiking trails and a small beach at the entrance to the canal. Battery Provincial Park makes a great base for canoeists and kayakers, who can paddle through the locks at no charge weekdays from mid-May to October. This is an excellent place to break up your trip.

MacDonald Hotel (☎ 902-535-2997, fax 902-535-3686, 9383 Pepperell St) Rooms with one bed $40 single or double ($30 off-season), two beds $50 for up to four people. Open mid-June-early Oct. This historic three-story hotel is behind the Irving gas station on Hwy 4 in the center of St Peter's, a two-minute walk from the Acadian Lines bus stop. Aside from the six rooms and nice little bar, the hotel restaurant serves lunch specials in the $7 range. At dinner there are scallops ($16), salmon ($15) and halibut ($15).

Joyce's Motel & Cottages (☎ 902-535-2404, e joyces.motel@ns.sympatico.ca 10354 Hwy 4) Cottages $50-80 mid-June-mid-Sept, $45-70 shoulder seasons. Open May-Oct. On Hwy 4 a kilometer east of the bridge at St Peter's, Joyce's has three small cabins at the bottom end of their price range and 15 cottages that are progressively more expensive. Weekly rates are the equivalent of six nights.

ABLE ISLAND

Lying south of Cape Breton, about 177km out to sea, Cape Sable Island is known as the 'graveyard of the Atlantic.' Countless ships from the 1500s to the present have gone down around the island, with its rough seas and hidden sandbars. The island, 32km long by 1½km wide, is little more than a sandbar itself, with no trees or even shrubs.

There are about a dozen inhabitants, a small herd of tough, wild ponies and lots of cranberries. The residents maintain two lighthouses, a meteorological station and a few other installations. Where the ponies came from is a source of endless debate. Output from the undersea natural gas fields off Sable Island is pumped through a pipeline to the US.

Prince Edward Island

Facts about Prince Edward Island

Known as 'the island' or PEI, Prince Edward Island is a pastoral, peaceful, wonderfully green expanse of quiet beauty. This province fits one's image of the English countryside: roads winding gently through bright red fields and manicured villages of neat wooden houses and gardens. It's very enjoyable to drive the backroads of the island, with the sea often in sight.

Away from the tourist centers, the pace of life is slow. Laws against billboards further add to the old-country flavor of the island. Indeed, in some ways it has changed little from the descriptions in the internationally known novel *Anne of Green Gables,* written here by Lucy Maud Montgomery in the early 20th century.

This is not an exciting place; there's not a lot to do, particularly after dark, and if you get a week of rain, you'll be more than a little restless. But for a really lazy holiday, take the chance.

As in the other Maritime provinces, the visiting season is short. This is perhaps even more pronounced on PEI, since many attractions, tour operations and guesthouses are open only during the two midsummer months. From early September to mid-June facilities are closed, the signs are taken down and the access roads to many parks and sights are blocked with barriers.

Yet just before mid-June and after the first week of September, room prices are discounted, the atmosphere is serene and spring or Indian summer are in the air. Then, for eight short weeks in July and August, the island is suddenly jam-packed. Toward the end of July and in early August, virtually all lodgings will be full, and reservations become almost essential.

A tenth the size of Nova Scotia, Prince Edward Island is Canada's smallest and most densely populated province. You'd

Highlights

Entered Confederation: July 1, 1873
Area: 5700 sq km
Population: 138,900
Provincial Capital: Charlottetown

- Spend time in Charlottetown, the birthplace of Canadian confederation

- Take in a *ceilidh* with traditional music and dance

- See the House of Green Gables at Cavendish, the setting for the novel *Anne of Green Gables*

- Enjoy a summer's day on one of the north coast beaches

OTHER MAPS
Prince Edward Island
pages 218-219

PEI National
Park & Around
pages 242-243

Summerside
page 251

Charlottetown
page 223

Downtown
Charlottetown
page 227

never guess this, however, as it's overwhelmingly rural and the towns aren't big at all, though countless little-used roads crisscross every segment of land. It's one of a kind in Canada.

History

Aboriginal peoples arrived here about 11,000 years ago, before the island was separated from the mainland. The Mi'kmaqs, a branch of the Algonquin nations, arrived at about the time of Christ.

Jacques Cartier of France was the first European to record seeing the island, in 1534. Settlement didn't begin for another 200 years, with a small French colony at Port La Joye, across the harbor from present-day Charlottetown. The colony grew somewhat with the British expulsion of the Acadians from Nova Scotia in the 1750s. Then in 1758, the victorious British expelled 3000 Acadians from Île St-Jean (as the French called Prince Edward Island).

After the Treaty of Paris in 1763, the island became British and was renamed Island of Saint John. In the early 1800s there was a marked rise in population due to immigration from the British Isles. In 1769 Saint John became self-governing and switched names in honor of one of the sons of King Edward III.

Prince Edward Island joined the Confederation in 1873, deciding to forgo its independence for the economic benefits. The population has remained stable at around 140,000 since the 1930s.

In 1997, after much debate and protest among the islanders themselves, PEI was linked to New Brunswick and the mainland by the Confederation Bridge, one of the world's longest at almost 13km.

Climate

Conveniently, July and August are the driest months of a fairly damp year. The warm ocean currents give the island a milder climate than most of Canada, and the sea gets warm enough for swimming in midsummer. In winter, the snow can be meters deep and can last until the beginning of May.

Economy

PEI is primarily a farming community, with the main crop, potatoes, sold all over the country. The rich, distinctively red soil is the secret, the locals say. Huge factories process the spuds. Cavendish Farms, at New Annan between Summerside and Kensington, is the biggest processor on PEI, with 850 employees. Owned by the Irvings, it makes frozen French fries. The 200-employee McCain Foods plant at Borden-Carleton processes the potatoes into specialty fries (wedges, spirals etc). Humpty Dumpty at Summerside makes potato chips, and Agrawest Foods at Souris produces potato granules for pet food additives.

At Harrington, 15km northwest of Charlottetown, Agriculture Canada has a major Crops and Livestock Center where genetically modified plants are tested. Aqua Bounty Farms on the Fortune River is a center for the development of so-called 'frankenfish' through genetic engineering. Mussel farms are common along the coast.

Traditional fishing, of course, is also important, particularly for lobsters, oysters and herring. The lobster suppers held throughout the province have become synonymous with the island life.

The quiet, gently rolling hills edged with good beaches have made tourism a reliable moneymaker. In the summer of 1997 following the opening of the Confederation Bridge, tourism increased 30% and the province now receives over a million visitors a year.

Population & People

Europeans of French, Scottish and Irish background make up nearly 90% of the population of 138,900. The Mi'kmaqs, the inhabitants at the time of colonization, now represent under 1% of the island's people.

Information

The head office of Tourism PEI (☎ 888-734-7529 free in North America, 902-368-5540 elsewhere, ⓔ tourpei@gov.pe.ca) can be contacted at PO Box 940, Charlottetown C1A 7M5, or on the Web at ⓦ www .peiplay.com. There are 11 regional tourist

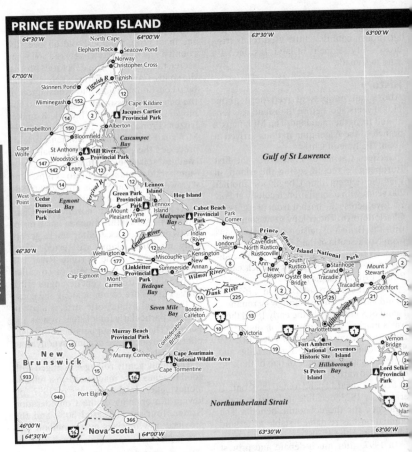

PRINCE EDWARD ISLAND

offices around the island, open 9am to 4:30 pm June to mid-October (8am to 9pm in July and August). From mid-October to May, the only ones you've got a chance of finding open are the Charlottetown tourist office and the one in an ersatz 'traditional' PEI Gateway Village complex at the foot of Confederation Bridge.

A dozen Access PEI offices around the province provide free Internet access on a first-come, first-served basis. You can obtain free Internet access at all public libraries.

The provincial sales tax is 10%, added to the 7% GST.

Activities

Cycling With its winding country roads, gently rolling hills and short distances between towns, Prince Edward Island is one of Canada's most popular destinations for cyclists. Hills rarely exceed a 30 degree incline or 1km in length, and the highest point on the island, at Springton, is only 142m.

You can rent wheels in Charlottetown and put together a multiday tour of the island. For route suggestions, ask the staff at the bike shops or obtain a copy of *Prince Edward Island Cycling Guide*, which is sold

Kayaking Ocean Kayaking has taken off around PEI in recent years, and from mid-June to mid-September kayak tours are offered at North Rustico, Cymbria, Brudenell River, Souris and Lennox Island. The leader in this field is Outside Expeditions (☎ 800-207-3899, 890 Hwy 242, Cymbria), which runs kayaking and bicycle tours lasting two to 18 days. See their Web site (W www.getout side.com) for more information.

Accommodations

The province has an automated reservation hotline (☎ 888-268-6667 in Canada) that will give you the phone numbers of accommodations with vacancies.

Prince Edward Island is covered with campgrounds – 13 provincial parks, one national park and numerous private campgrounds. The provincial parks range from $17 for an unserviced site to $23 for fully serviced ones. All accept reservations, but you must call the individual park directly (there's no central reservations number). Specific campsites cannot be reserved – you have to accept whatever site happens to be available upon arrival.

Across the province there are few hotels, but fortunately the island has an abundance of good guesthouses. The quality is generally high and the prices are excellent. PEI guesthouses and tourist homes offer some of the best lodging deals in Canada. A double room averages about $45 and rarely goes above $55, and sometimes this includes breakfast. Many places are rented by the week. Much accommodation is in beautiful old wooden homes. There are about 11 provincial tourist offices around the island, including one at the Wood Islands ferry terminal, one at the foot of the big bridge and one in Charlottetown. Any one of them can arrange accommodations anywhere on the island within an hour.

Food

There are nearly 40 outlets around the island for buying fresh seafood – good if you're camping and can cook your own food. Some guesthouses offer cooking facilities or the use of a barbecue.

or $15 at Smooth Cycles, 172 Prince St, Charlottetown.

The grandaddy of trails in the Maritimes the Confederation Trail, a 350km multiuse rail stretching from Tignish to Elmira along railway lines abandoned in 1989. The trail is now complete, with signs and shelters up. The prevailing winds on Prince Edward Island blow from the west or southwest, and you should also cycle in that direction if possible.

See the Charlottetown Getting Around and Cavendish sections later in this chapter for bike rental information.

PRINCE EDWARD ISLAND

Also look for the famous lobster suppers held in church basements, community halls or restaurants – these are usually buffet style. Restaurants offer the most reliable quality, but they're not quite as much fun (the others are sometimes hit and miss).

There are about 16 Royal Canadian Legion halls scattered around PEI, and all have good local bars where visitors are welcome. A few also serve meals. (For non-Canadians, the RCL is a veterans organization, and a Canadian flag will always be flapping prominently in front of these halls.)

Getting There & Away

Air Charlottetown has a small airport on Hwy 15 about 6km north of the center. Air Canada – actually their subsidiary link airline Air Nova – connects PEI with the major Canadian cities, usually through Halifax. Air Canada has a daily nonstop flight from Toronto.

Bus See the Charlottetown Getting There section for information on the SMT bus service from Moncton and the various van services from Halifax.

Car & Motorcycle Well, it's finally open – The Bridge (see the boxed text 'Bridge over Troubled Waters'). Whatever one's take on it, the 13km bridge is an absolute flip-out to drive across at 80kph, and it makes getting to PEI faster, easier and cheaper. Traffic can access the bridge 24 hours a day, seven days a week; sadly the 1.1m-high guardrails steal away any panorama you'd hoped for. There are two lanes and two breakdown lanes, with emergency callboxes every 750m. The fare is $37 for a car and all passengers and is only collected as you leave PEI. (Note that the ferry costs $49 if you're trying to scrimp; but if you're heading into Nova Scotia that $12 isn't worth the extra driving.)

Bicycles and pedestrians are banned from the bridge and must use a free, demand-driven shuttle service. On the PEI side, go to the Bridge Operations Building near the toll gates; on the New Brunswick side, look for the Bridge Facility Building at the junction of Hwys 16 and 955. You're not supposed to have to wait over two hours for the shuttle at any time. To hear a recording about all this, call ☎ 902-437-7300, or you can check the bridge's Web site (**W** www .confederationbridge.com) for more information.

Charlottetown is about 60km from Borden-Carleton, at the PEI end of the bridge. The drive takes about 40 minutes.

Ferry The remaining ferry service to PEI links Wood Islands (in the eastern section of PEI province) to Caribou, Nova Scotia. Seasonal, the ferry doesn't operate from mid-December to April. This 22km trip takes 1¼ hours and costs $49 for a car and all passengers, $11 per person for pedestrians or $2 for a bicycle and cyclist (tandem bikes are also $20, including both riders). In summer there are eight runs in each direction daily, dropping to seven a day in September. You only pay as you're leaving PEI; the trip over from Nova Scotia is free. There's a cafeteria on board. Contact Northumberland Ferries Ltd (☎ 888-249-7245), 94 Water St, Charlottetown, or check their Web site (**W** www.n bay.com) for information. It's first-come first-served (reservations not taken) and this route is busy – during peak season you may have a one or two-ferry wait.

The other ferry service is from Souris to the Îles de la Madeleine in Québec. For information about it, turn to Getting There & Away in the Souris section.

Getting Around

There's no public transportation to speak of on PEI. A Beach Shuttle operates between Charlottetown and Cavendish during the summer months, but otherwise you're pretty much out of luck. Almost all visitors who didn't drive here in their own car end up renting one. For a few prices, turn to Getting Around in the Charlottetown section.

Prince Edward Island is small and, with a car, easy to get around. In one day it's possible to drive from Charlottetown to the beaches for a swim, along the north coast at

Bridge over Troubled Waters

Almost nothing in the history of Prince Edward Island so divided the islanders as the building of the massive and controversial Confederation Bridge. Either they loved it or they hated it; there was virtually nobody in between.

Opened in 1997, the bridge connects Cape Jourimain, New Brunswick, with Borden-Carleton, Prince Edward Island. It's the narrowest point of the strait, yet the bridge is still nearly 13km long, allowing Canadians to claim they have the longest bridge in the world. There is a longer one in Denmark, but an island in the middle technically makes it two bridges.

At a cost of $900 million, the project included 44 spans. Each span is almost a city block long and is made from 8000 tons of steel-reinforced concrete that had to be lifted into place. Each tower is 20 stories high, measured from the waterline. Driving at posted speeds – and, with the wind behind you, going any faster is truly frightening – it takes 12 minutes to cross.

With the bridge completed, Prince Edward Island is now part of mainland Canada, and that's the source of all the ballyhoo. Those who rail against the bridge say it carries hordes of tourists, who in turn bring crime, litter and the proliferation of chain restaurants and tacky tourist attractions. Friends of the Island, an antibridge coalition, even went to court to halt construction, claiming the bridge causes ice buildup in the strait that will harm lobster and scallop stocks.

Pro-bridge forces say the link is necessary because travel to and from the island was always a nightmare for locals. During summer most of a day would be lost waiting for a ferry, and in winter boats would often get stuck for hours in the ice pack. With the bridge, proponents claim, PEI companies are able to compete more effectively with their mainland rivals. And as for kitsch – where there are tourists there is kitsch, and it preceded the bridge by decades, albeit in less overwhelming doses than today.

There is no argument that once the toll gates opened, PEI entered a new era. At least for the present, the changes haven't been too palpable – no brazen packs of hoodlums roam the streets; the tourists are as tacky as anywhere but no worse than before; and you still see contented moo-cows chewing cud pretty much everywhere. Perhaps most symbolically, PEI radio stations still broadcast incessant reminders of the Wood Islands–Caribou, NS, ferry schedule.

he way up to North Cape, then back along he western shoreline, over to Summerside nd down to Borden-Carleton to the bridge. And this is without even rushing!

Three equal-sized counties make up the sland: Prince in the west, Queens in the middle and Kings to the east. Each county has a scenic road network mapped out by he tourist bureau. Though far from the only options, these routes do take in the better-known attractions and the historical and geographical points of note. The Kings Byway circles the east side of the island; the Blue Heron loops around the center; and the Lady Slipper reaches the westernmost shores of PEI.

Thumbing around the island is fairly common and accepted by residents. The province is relatively free of violence and you can generally hitch without expecting trouble. You probably won't have to wait long for a ride. However, as is the case everywhere, your safety cannot be guaranteed, and hitching cannot be recommended without some reservations.

All accommodations and points of interest on Prince Edward Island are well indicated with neat little highway signs. In contrast, the roads themselves are often poorly marked. Good maps are freely available, but try to keep track of where you are.

Charlottetown

Charlottetown (population 33,000) – or 'Ch'town' – is an old, quiet country town that also happens to be the historic provincial capital. Established in 1763, it's named after Charlotte, Queen of Great Britain and Ireland (1744–1818). It's Canada's smallest capital, with a downtown area so compact that everything is within walking distance. The slow-paced, tree-lined colonial and Victorian streets make Charlottetown the perfect urban center for this gentle and bucolic island. In July and August the streets are bustling with visitors, but things are rather quiet out of season.

Orientation

University Ave is the city's main street; it ends at the block taken up by Province House and the Confederation Centre of the Arts complex.

A block west along Grafton St is Queen St, parallel to University Ave. This is the other main street of Charlottetown and of more interest to visitors. During summer, the first block of Richmond St east of Queen St becomes a gentrified pedestrian mall called Victoria Row.

From Richmond St south to the waterfront is Old Charlottetown. A number of buildings have plaques giving a bit of their history and the date of construction. Great George St running downhill from Province House is Charlottetown's most monumental street, lined with late-19th-century mansions.

At the foot of Great George St, south of Water St, is Peake's Wharf and Confederation Landing. This redeveloped waterfront area is often the focal point of the city festivals. The main tourist information center is nearby.

West of town is the large Victoria Park, with a broad promenade running along its edge and the bay. This is the nicest place in the city to go jogging.

Information

Tourist Offices The tourist office (☎ 902-368-4444) in Charlottetown and the main office for the whole island is in the Stone Cottage, 178 Water St, near Founders Hall at the foot of Hillsborough St. It's one of the few tourist offices in the Maritimes open year-round (8am to 10pm daily July and August, 9am to 6pm shoulder seasons, 9am to 4:30pm Monday to Friday early October to mid-May). Inside are courtesy phones to make local reservations.

There's also a tourist information office (☎ 902-629-4116) at City Hall, 199 Queen St at Kent. It's open from 8am to 4pm weekdays from May to October and specializes in Charlottetown. At one of these, pick up *The Buzz,* a free entertainment newspaper.

The Voluntary Resource Council (☎ 902-368-7337), 81 Prince St, is the headquarters of 15 environmental and human rights groups, including Earth Action (☎ 902-621-0719). It's worth dropping in if you want to find out about environmental issues the folks at the tourist offices don't address. It's open 7:30am to 4pm Monday to Friday.

Money TD Canada Trust (☎ 902-629-2265), 192 Queen St at Kent, is open 9am to 3pm Saturdays.

Post The central post office (☎ 902-628-4400), 135 Kent St, Charlottetown PE C1A 1M0, holds general delivery mail. It's open 8am to 5:15pm Monday to Friday.

Internet Access The Confederation Public Library (☎ 902-368-4642), on Queen St between Victoria Row and Grafton St, provides free Internet access, and it's possible to book a time slot. The library is open 10am to 9pm Tuesday to Thursday, 10am to 5pm Friday and Saturday and 1pm to 5pm Sunday.

Bookstores The Reading Well Bookstore (☎ 902-566-2703), 72 University Ave, has a selection of books on PEI and Anne of Green Gables.

The Bookman (☎ 902-892-8872), 177 Queen St, has an intriguing assortment of used books.

Laundry Downtown Convenience (☎ 902-368-1684), 54 Queen St, has a satellite

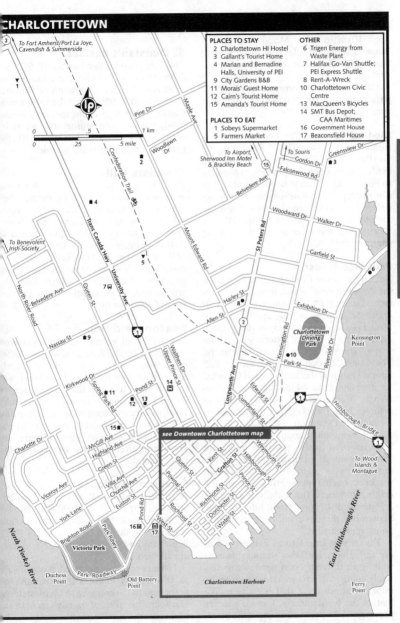

PRINCE EDWARD ISLAND

TV–equipped Laundromat in the basement. A wash or dry costs $1.25, and it's open 10am to 10pm Monday to Friday, 11am to 10pm Saturday and 11am to 9pm Sunday. Check out the 99¢ ice cream cones upstairs.

Other local Laundromats (with easier parking) are at Nos 236 and 251 University Ave.

Medical Services The Polyclinic Professional Center (☎ 902-629-8810), at 199 Grafton St, is an after-hours walk-in medical clinic open 5:30pm to 8pm Monday to Friday and 9:30am to noon Saturday. Any Canadian provincial health card will be accepted here, but foreigners must pay a $40 fee. Appointments are not required. The tourist office will know about other walk-in clinics of this kind.

Province House

Next door to the Confederation Centre of the Arts, this neoclassical, three-story sandstone building (☎ 902-566-7626, 165 Richmond St; admission free; open 9am-5pm Mon-Fri Oct-May; 9am-5pm daily June-Sept) is both a national historic site and the seat of the current provincial legislature. The Confederation Chamber on the 2nd floor is known as the 'birthplace of Canada,' for it was here in 1864 that the 23 representatives of the British North American colonies began working out the details for forming the Dominion of Canada.

This room and a couple of others have been restored to the way they looked in 1864. Inside, or perhaps outside at the entrance, you may also see costumed workers, each representing one of the original founders. Thrice daily, at 11:15am, 2:15pm and 4:15pm, from July to early September, there is a 'fathers of confederation' reenactment.

The current Legislative Chamber is also on this floor, and the summer breeze wafting in through open windows to this small, comfortable room lends an intimate, informal atmosphere that is quite unlike that of the legislatures in Canada's larger provinces. A 15-minute film about the build-

ing's place in history can be seen on the 1s floor.

St Dunstan's Basilica

This large neo-Gothic basilica (☎ 902-894-3486, 45 Great George St; admission free open 8am-5pm daily) is south of Provinc House. Built in 1898, this is the town's mai Catholic church. It is unexpectedly ornat inside, painted in an unusual style, with a lo of green trim that blends well with th green and blue tints in the marble.

Founders Hall

This new attraction (☎ 902-368-1864 w www.foundershall.ca, 8 Prince St; adul senior/youth/family $7.50/6/4/19; ope 8:30am-8pm daily June-early Oct, 10am 4pm Tues-Sat early Oct-May) opened i 2001 in a former railway building at the foo of Prince St. The multimedia exhibits show case Canada's history since the 1864 Char lottetown Conference, which laid the groundwork for the creation of the Domin ion of Canada in 1867.

Beaconsfield House

This beautiful yellow Victorian mansio (☎ 902-368-6603, 2 Kent St; admission $3.50 open 9am-5pm Tues-Sun mid-June-earl Sept, 10am-4pm the rest of the year) wa built in 1877. It is now the headquarters o the PEI Museum. There are 11 historically furnished rooms, along with a gift shop an a bookstore specializing in books abou PEI. During summer guided tours are given, and afternoon tea is served on the large veranda.

Government House

Across Kent St from Beaconsfield House i Victoria Park and Government House another beautiful old mansion. This one ha been used as the official residence of PEI' lieutenant-governor since 1835. No visitors are allowed.

From here follow the wooden boardwalk to **Old Battery Point**, where six cannons point toward the entrance to Charlottetown Harbour. This is one of the city's most beau tiful corners.

Trigen Energy from Waste Plant

The Trigen Energy from Waste Plant (☎ 902-629-3960, 40 Riverside Dr) burns a third of PEI's garbage, plus sawdust from a sawmill near Georgetown, to create energy to heat most of Charlottetown's larger buildings, including nearby Queen Elizabeth Hospital. It's done by conveying heated water through 19km of pipes to the city. No tours of this privately owned facility are offered, but you get a free whiff of the stench as you pass.

Fort Amherst/Port la Joye National Historic Site

Very close to the Rocky Point Indian Reserve is the site of the old French capital, and more recently, Fort Amherst (☎ 902-75-2220, 191 Hwy 19, Rocky Point; admission $2.25; open 10am-6pm daily mid-June-early Sept), built by the British in 1758 after they had taken over the island. There isn't really anything left to see other than foundations, but the interpretive center features exhibits and an audiovisual show. There are views of the city, various monuments and a picnic area within the park. Out of season, the grounds can be visited free.

Scuba Diving

Black Dolphin Diving and Watersports (☎ 902-894-3483, fax 902-626-3483, 106 Hillsborough St) does scuba diving charters from Covehead Wharf every Wednesday at 7pm and Sunday at 9am from mid-June to mid-September. It's $20 per person, plus $45 for gear (two tanks). If required, a mask, snorkel, fins and boots are $5 extra per set. You'll see lobster, scallops, crabs and luxuriant sea growth on all dives. Every week or two, they do an advanced dive to the wreck of the *Tunstal,* where fish are plentiful (including large cod); the *Tunstal* dive is to 35m, but the others don't go deeper than 25m.

Organized Tours

Bus trips around the island are offered by Abegweit Tours (☎ 902-894-9966) from June to early October. There are three trips: the north shore, the south shore and Charlottetown itself. The north shore trip ($60) takes about six hours. The city tour ($9) takes just an hour. The south shore trip ($60) makes a stop at Fort Amherst National Historic Park. They'll go whenever they have at least three bookings. Check their Web site at W www.peisland.com/abegweit/tours.htm.

Avonlea Tours (*Prince Edward Tours,* ☎ 902-566-9970, 18 Queen St), located inside the Delta Hotel, is a Japanese-oriented operation.

Peake's Wharf Boat Cruises (☎ 902-566-4458, 1 Great George St) depart from the marina at the wharf for a 70-minute harbor tour ($15), a 6:30pm sunset cruise ($15) or a 2½-hour tour to see the seals off Government Island ($21). They operate from June to August.

Finally, **walking tours** (☎ 902-368-1864, 8 Prince St; adults $3.50, children under 12 free) of the historic district of Charlottetown commence at Founders Hall at 10am, 11am, 1pm, 3pm and 4pm in July and August. There's also a Merchants & Mansions walking tour at 2pm and Waterfront Storytelling at 7pm (same price, same months). Alternatively, the good self-guided tour brochure available at the tourist office covers the waterfront area and Peake's Wharf.

Special Events

All across the province, look for the local ceilidhs (**kay**-lees) – mini-festivals at which there is always some music (usually of the traditional Celtic variety) and dancing. There is usually one every week during high season. Times and venues of many are listed on W www.festivalspei.com. Some of the major events held in PEI from June to September include the following:

Jazz & Blues Festival
Bigger every year, this festival (☎ 902-569-1878) in early May features major Canadian blues and jazz performers.

Charlottetown Festival
This festival is held each year from mid-June to mid-September. It's a theatrical event with drama and musicals, especially the *Anne of Green Gables* musical (see Entertainment,

PRINCE EDWARD ISLAND

which follows). The festival also includes free outdoor performances, a children's theater and dance programs.

Web site: W www.confederationcentre.com

Blue Grass Music Festival

This festival (☎ 902-569-4501) is held near Souris every July. It's a two-day camping event held at a park or campground. Tickets are not costly.

Provincial Exhibition

This event, held in the first week or two of August, features tractor pulls, a carnival with rides, harness racing, entertainment and games of chance along with the traditional horse and livestock shows.

Web site: W www.peiprovincialexhibition.com

National Milton Acorn Festival

This is a unique event worth considering. Sometimes known as Canada's People's Poet, Acorn was born and raised on PEI. The festival, held in Charlottetown during the third week of August, includes poetry readings and music.

Festival of the Fathers

Held along the historic waterfront in late August, this festival celebrates the Charlottetown Conference of 1864 with street musicians, dances, traditional food and a 10-tavern pub crawl.

Web site: W www.capitalcommission.pe.ca/festivals/fathersschedule.cfm

Places to Stay

Camping *Holiday Haven Campground* (☎ 902-566-2421, fax 902-368-3139, off Terry Rd, 3km from Cornwall on Hwy 1) Unserviced/serviced sites $21/23. Open June-early Oct. This campground is the closest real campground to Charlottetown (RV parking lots excluded). The 30 unserviced and 240 serviced sites are in several large gassy fields bordered by trees on West River. The unserviced sites numbered C56 to C75 are best for tenters.

Hostels *Charlottetown HI Hostel* (☎ 902-894-9696, fax 902-628-6424, W www.isn.net/peihostel, 153 Mount Edward Rd) Beds $15.50/18.50 members/nonmembers plus $1 for compulsory linen rental. Open June-Aug. This good, friendly HI hostel is about 3km from the downtown area and close to the university. The barn-shaped building has room for 50 people in dorms of four to seven beds, men on the upstairs floor,

Milton Acorn

Born in Charlottetown in 1923, Milton Acorn was to become somewhat the bad boy of Canadian literature. Despite living and working as a poet, he did not fit the usual academic mold and was always known for voicing his firmly held left-wing opinions. He supported a range of what were at the time considered radical causes, such as opposition to the Vietnam War and support for the Civil Rights Movement, and his poems often reflected his political biases and his unwavering support of the working person. Milton also opposed American economic and cultural domination of Canada. Spending much of his life in Montréal, Toronto and Vancouver, he became known as the People's Poet, being honored as such by fellow poets. He died in his home town in 1986.

Dig up My Heart: Selected Poems 1952–1983 is the most complete and representative collection of Acorn's poetry, offering a good sample of his subject matter and style. Many prefer his numerous nature poems and reflective poems, some of which have a wonderful, easy lyricism.

women downstairs. There's a kitchen with microwave available for light cooking. T reduce staffing costs, the hostel is close from 10am to 4pm daily. The hostel ren bicycles for $15 a day (plus $10 deposit and the Confederation Trail passes jus behind the building. You can walk int town along the trail in about 30 minute Ample parking is available.

University of PEI (☎ 902-566-0486, fa 902-566-0793, e residence@upei.ca, W ww .upei.ca/~housing, 550 University Ave Singles/doubles $34/39 shared bath, $46/4 private bath, plus $4 per person for break fast in July & Aug. Open May-Aug. The un versity offers rooms with shared bath a Marian Hall and larger rooms with twi beds in Bernadine Hall. Two-bedroor apartments suitable for up to four person are $79. Shared kitchenettes are availabl and parking is included. The office is in Bernadine Hall (open 24 hours), and reservations are a good idea in July and August.

Tourist Homes & B&Bs In Charlottetown, B&Bs that don't provide breakfast are called 'tourist homes.' Over 70 places fit into this category, and some of the less expensive homes closer to town are listed here. There are plenty of more upmarket lodgings in fine heritage homes, often decorated with antiques and collectibles. Several of the larger historic places have been converted to inns, a separate category here.

Aloha Tourist Home (☎ 902-892-9944, 866-892-9944, 234 Sydney St) Singles/doubles $35/50, 25% discount off-season. This very central, unassuming place is in a large old house opposite a park and has four rooms with shared bath. There's a large kitchen that visitors can use. The owner, Maynard MacMillan, is an affable, helpful host. Cyclists can stash their bikes in the garage.

Blanchard Tourist Home (☎ 902-894-9756, 163 Dorchester St) Singles/doubles $25/30. Open May-Oct. This authentic old wooden Charlottetown house from 1909 is

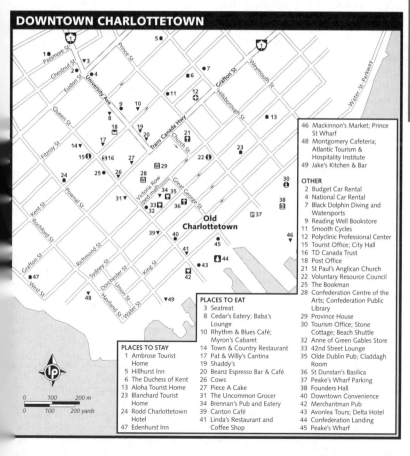

DOWNTOWN CHARLOTTETOWN

46 Mackinnon's Market; Prince St Wharf
48 Montgomery Cafeteria; Atlantic Tourism & Hospitality Institute
49 Jake's Kitchen & Bar

OTHER
2   Budget Car Rental
4   National Car Rental
7   Black Dolphin Diving and Watersports
9   Reading Well Bookstore
11 Smooth Cycles
12 Polyclinic Professional Center
15 Tourist Office; City Hall
16 TD Canada Trust
18 Post Office
21 St Paul's Anglican Church
22 Voluntary Resource Council
25 The Bookman
28 Confederation Centre of the Arts; Confederation Public Library
29 Province House
30 Tourism Office; Stone Cottage; Beach Shuttle
32 Anne of Green Gables Store
33 42nd Street Lounge
35 Olde Dublin Pub; Claddagh Room
36 St Dunstan's Basilica
37 Peake's Wharf Parking
38 Founders Hall
40 Downtown Convenience
42 Merchantman Pub
43 Avonlea Tours; Delta Hotel
44 Confederation Landing
45 Peake's Wharf

PLACES TO EAT
3   Seatreat
8   Cedar's Eatery; Baba's Lounge
10 Rhythm & Blues Café; Myron's Cabaret
14 Town & Country Restaurant
17 Pat & Willy's Cantina
19 Shaddy's
20 Beanz Espresso Bar & Café
26 Cows
27 Piece A Cake
31 The Uncommon Grocer
34 Brennan's Pub and Eatery
39 Canton Café
41 Linda's Restaurant and Coffee Shop

PLACES TO STAY
1   Ambrose Tourist Home
5   Hillhurst Inn
6   The Duchess of Kent
13 Aloha Tourist Home
23 Blanchard Tourist Home
24 Rodd Charlottetown Hotel
47 Edenhurst Inn

0   100   200 m
0   100   200 yards

also central. These two rooms, with shared bath, are a bargain. Daytime parking is limited around here, but it's okay to park overnight on the street.

Ambrose Tourist Home (☎ 902-566-5853, 800-665-6072, 17 Passmore St) Singles/doubles $32/38 ($45 with two beds). Open May-Oct. Six rooms with shared bath are available in this signposted duplex house near downtown. There's also a self-contained apartment at $65.

Morais' Guest Home (☎ 902-892-2267, 79 Spring Park Rd) Singles/doubles with shared bath $33/40, includes light breakfast ($30/35 Sept-May). This two-room home offers pickup from the airport or bus depot. The owner speaks English and French.

Amanda's Tourist Home (☎ 902-894-9909, 130 Spring Park Rd) Rooms $30. There are two rooms with shared bath in this large two-story house with ample parking.

Cairn's Tourist Home (☎ 902-368-3552, 18 Pond St) Singles/doubles $24/30. This spotless and friendly place in a modern bungalow on a residential street has three rooms with shared bath available. It's just two blocks from the SMT bus station.

City Gardens B&B (☎ 902-892-7282, fax 902-894-3937, w www.boyles-optical.com, 114 Nassau St) Singles/doubles $35/45 ($65 with private bath) including breakfast. This large two-story house on the north side of town has four rooms.

Gallant's Tourist Home (☎ 902-892-3030, fax 902-368-1713, e st.clair.gallant@pei .sympatico.ca, 196 Kensington Rd) Singles/doubles/triples $20/25/35 plus tax. Gallant's is a couple of kilometers northeast of the city center, but the four rooms with shared bath in this single-story bungalow beyond Belvedere Golf Course are attractively priced. They'll pick you up for free at the airport or bus station if you call ahead and run you into town in the morning.

Inns **The Duchess of Kent** (☎ 902-566-5826, 800-665-5826, fax 902-368-8483, w www.bb canada.com/5155.html, 218 Kent St) Doubles from $85. Open May-Nov. This central B&B is in a large 1875 heritage house with period furnishings. There are four spacious rooms or suites with private bath. A common kitchen and living room are made available to guests.

Hillhurst Inn (☎ 902-894-8004, 877-994-8004, fax 902-892-7679, w www.hillhurst .com, 181 Fitzroy St) Doubles $105-190, including breakfast. Open May-Oct (other months by advance reservation). Here you can stay in one of Charlottetown's grandest mansions, built in 1897. The nine rooms with bath and TV are usually full in midsummer, so call at least a week ahead.

Edenhurst Inn (☎ 902-368-8323, 877-766-6439, fax 902-894-3707, w www.peisland .com/edenhurst/index.html, 12 West St) Doubles $115-195, including breakfast. This seven-room inn is among the city's most impressive accommodations, both for the magnificent 1897 mansion and for the location on one of Charlottetown's most prestigious streets. The elegance of a bygone era can be gently savored here.

Motels **Sherwood Inn Motel** (☎ 902-892-1622, 800-567-1622, fax 902-892-2358, e ping@isn.net, 281 Brackley Point Rd) Rooms from $42 mid-June-mid-Sept, $35 other months. Less than a kilometer from the airport, this motel has a variety of rooms. Six rooms in an older two-story block are $42/47 for a single/double in July and August ($35 rest of year). The 20 housekeeping rooms in two long blocks are $57 in July and August ($40 other months). The 18 new rooms in the main block are $83 during high season ($50 off-season). A Laundromat is on the premises.

Hotels **Rodd Charlottetown Hotel** (☎ 902-894-7371, 800-565-7633, fax 902-368-2178, w www.rodd-hotels.ca/charlottetown/chtow .htm, 75 Kent St) Rooms $175 mid-June-mid-Sept, $105 mid-Sept-mid-June. This Charlottetown's grand old hotel, erected in 1931 by the Canadian National Railway. The four twin columns over the entrance are indicative of the elegance inside. Discounts are offered on the 115 rooms for CAA/AAA cardholders or those over 5 years of age, reducing the price to $90/1

w/high season. From mid-September to
id-June they might even throw in
reakfast.

Places to Eat

Breakfast *Linda's Restaurant and Coffee
Shop* (☎ 902-892-7292, 32 Queen St) Break-
ast $4. Open 7am-8pm Mon-Sat, 8am-4pm
Sun (closes 5:30pm Mon-Sat in winter). This
place is small and cheap, but with a certain
charm.

Town & Country Restaurant (☎ 902-892-
282, 219 Queen St) Breakfast special $4.
Open 9am-10pm daily. For breakfast or a
simple meal, this cheap and unpretentious
place fits the bill with its basic Canadian and
Lebanese menu. In summer the excellent
breakfast special is served until noon on a
small outdoor patio.

Cafes *Beanz Espresso Bar & Café* (☎ 902-
92-8797, 38 University Ave) Sandwiches or
salads under $5. Open 6:30am-6pm Mon-
Fri, 8am-6pm Sat, 9am-5pm Sun. Charlottetown is rich in pubs and poor in cafes, and
Beanz is really more of a sandwich and
salad joint. Still, it's OK for a specialty
coffee or a cup of Newfoundland tea.

Pubs *Jake's Kitchen & Bar* (☎ 902-892-
098, 1 Pownal St) Meals $9-11. Open 11am-
10pm daily mid-May-Sept. Above the
Charlottetown Yacht Club at the waterfront
end of Pownal, Jake's is a yachtie hangout
serving mussels ($7), mozzarella sticks ($8),
scallops ($9), fish & chips ($9), lobster
burgers ($11) and clams & chips ($11), plus
standbys like nachos, wings and oysters.
There's draft beer and an open-air deck
with a great view of the harbor.

Brennan's Pub & Eatery (☎ 902-892-
222, 132 Richmond St) Dinners $10-22.
Open 11am-2am Mon-Sat, 11am-midnight
Sun (in winter they open at 4pm). This
lively, gay-friendly pub boasts a menu that
ranges from fettucine primavera to steaks
and nachos. In the afternoon, folk musicians
serenade the crowd outside, and at night
there's live jazz and blues.

Pat & Willy's Cantina (☎ 902-628-1333,
19 Kent St) Dinners $8-15. Open 11am-

midnight Mon-Thurs, 11am-1am Fri & Sat,
noon-10pm Sun. For California-style
Mexican, this is the place. Cheese nachos
are $5/8 half/full.

Restaurants *Seatreat* (☎ 902-894-5678, 202
University Ave) Mains $5-13. Open 9am-
10pm daily. The most affordable seafood in
town is served at this restaurant, including
baskets of steamed mussels ($5), salmon or
haddock dinners ($13), bowls of fish
chowder ($4.25) and, of course, lobster
dinners.

Cedar's Eatery (☎ 902-892-7377, 81 University Ave) Dinners $8-14. Open 11am-
midnight Mon-Thurs, 11am-1am Fri-Sat,
4pm-11pm Sun. This fine little restaurant is
smack dab in the middle of town. The speciality is Lebanese food, ranging from
falafel ($8) to more expensive kabobs ($16),
but there's also standard Canadian fare like
salads, sandwiches and steaks, plus a
number of vegetarian dishes. Cedar's is one
of the few places to eat in Charlottetown
that stays open late.

Shaddy's (☎ 902-368-8886, 44 University
Ave) Mains $8-17. Open 8am-9pm Mon-Fri,
11am-10pm Sat & Sun. Another place for
Lebanese and Canadian fare, Shaddy's also
has vegetarian falafel ($8). Topping their
menu is the meat platter with Lebanese
salad and rice ($15-17).

Rhythm & Blues Café (☎ 902-892-4375,
151 Kent St) Mains $15-16. Open 11am-
midnight daily. This wing of Myron's
Cabaret adds a seafood section to their
menu in summer with mussels ($6),
chowder ($6), lobster roll ($10), salmon
fillet ($15), pan-fried scallops ($15) and
lobster ($16). It's cheaper than many other
places serving these dishes, and different
specials are offered nightly.

Piece A Cake (☎ 902-894-4585, 119
Grafton St) Mains from $9. Open 11am-
10pm Mon-Sat (closed Mon evening in
winter). Upstairs, next to the Confederation
Court Mall, this casual bistro in a pleasant
open locale offers salads, pastas and cre-
ative mains with detectable Asian overtones. The lunch/dinner entrees start at
$7/14, pastas $10/11.

PRINCE EDWARD ISLAND

Canton Café (☎ 902-892-2527, 73 Queen St) Lunch/dinner specials $6/7. Open 11am-2am Mon-Wed, 11:30-3:30am Thurs-Sat, 11am-12:30am Sun. Good value Chinese specials are available from 11am to 9pm, with a choice of dishes and tea or coffee included. Lobster is $19.

Montgomery Cafeteria (☎ 902-894-6857, 4 Sydney St) Three-course lunch $8. The Culinary Institute of Canada at the Atlantic Tourism & Hospitality Institute trains workers for jobs at top restaurants and resorts all around the region. The school's training cafeteria, downstairs, offers cheap self-service meals from 11:30am to 1pm weekdays. A full meal with soup or salad, entree, dessert and tea or coffee will set you back $8, or take the entree alone for under $4. On Thursday and Friday a $3.50 breakfast is served from 8am to 9am. Upstairs is the showy Lucy Maud Dining Room, open for dinner, but it's not as good a value as the cafeteria.

Ice Cream *Cows* (☎ 902-892-6969, 150 Queen St) It's not big, but it's an island institution turning out good home-made ice cream ($3 to $4). There are also outlets, open May to early October only, in Borden-Carleton, Cavendish, Summerside and North River, plus one in Charlottetown at Peake's Wharf (☎ 902-566-4886). People across Canada can be seen sporting the colorful, humorous Cows T-shirts ($22).

Self-Catering *Farmers Market* (☎ 902-626-3373, 100 Belvedere Ave) Open 9am-2pm Sat year-round, also 9am-2pm Wed July & August. This is a fun place to go for breakfast, lunch, organic vegetables, island foods and genuine handicrafts. It's right beside the Confederation Trail.

The Uncommon Grocer (☎ 902-368-7778, 123 Queen St) Lunch $4. Open 8am-6pm Mon & Tues, 8am-9pm Wed-Fri, 9am-6pm Sat. This is the only vegetarian deli on PE with five different sandwiches ($4), tw soups ($3), a choice of salads ($4) and ho meals, plus vegan items. It's the best plac on the island to get a loaf of healthy rea bread or organic vegetables. The small caf here serves specialty coffees.

Mackinnon's Market (☎ 902-894-931 Prince St Wharf) Open 8:30am-8:30pr Mon-Sat, 11am-8:30pm Sun May-Oc Down at the edge of Confederatio Landing on Charlottetown's waterfront i Mackinnon's, where you can buy fres mussels, clams and oysters, as well as live o cooked lobster.

Sobeys Supermarket (☎ 902-566-3218 679 University Ave) Open 24 hours Mon Sat. This store, opposite Canadian Tire ou well beyond the university, is a good plac to stock up on groceries.

Sobeys Supermarket (☎ 902-894-3800, Kinlock Rd, Stratford) Open 24 hours Mon Sat. This location is 4km outside Charlotte town, on Hwy 1 toward Wood Islands.

Entertainment

For a complete rundown on plays, dinne theater and what band is playing where i Charlottetown, get *The Buzz*, the free en tertainment guide for PEI.

Confederation Centre of the Arts (☎ 902 566-1267, 800-565-0278, cnr Queen & Grafton Sts) Evening shows $22-40, mati nees $20-36. The architectural style of thi large modern structure is at odds with the rest of town, making the building contro versial since construction began in 1960 Each year *Anne of Green Gables*, dubbe 'Canada's favorite musical,' is performee here. Showtimes are at 8pm Monday to Sat urday from mid-June to early September; i July and August there's also a matinee a 2pm Monday, Wednesday and Saturday Special guest appearances on Thursday an Friday nights in July and August may dis place the musical those nights.

Peake's Quay (☎ 902-368-1330, 1 Grea George St, upstairs) Open 11am-1am Mon Wed, 11am-2am Thurs-Sat, 11am-midnigh Sun mid-May-late Sept. This pub regularl presents live music – though perhaps not always of the traditional bent – at Peake's Wharf in summer. It's touristy, but locals pack the place as well.

Merchantman Pub (☎ 902-892-9150, 23 Queen St) Open 11:30am-10pm Mon-Thurs & Sat, 11:30am-11pm Fri. If you're enamored of upscale pubs, this excellent place is casually upmarket.

42nd Street Lounge (☎ 902-566-4620, 125 Sydney St) Open 4:30pm-midnight Mon-Sat. At this cocktail lounge above the Off Broadway Restaurant, you can sip a martini while relaxing on a comfy sofa. It's gay friendly, and the gregarious server behind the long bar makes everyone feel at home.

Olde Dublin Pub (☎ 902-892-6992, upstairs, 131 Sydney St) Open 11am-2am Mon-Sat, 4pm-midnight Sun (closed Sun in winter). This place has an agreeable outside deck and live Irish and Maritime music from 10pm Thursday, Friday and Saturday nights ($5 cover charge). Beers on tap include Guinness, Harp, Killkenny Cream and Smithwick's Amber Ale. Pub grub like fish & chips, shepherd's pie and striploin steak all costs $8. And if that's not good enough, the upscale *Claddagh Room* downstairs has pricey but good seafood.

Myron's Cabaret (☎ 902-892-4375, 151 Kent St) Open 11am-3am daily. Off University Ave, Myron's is the largest nightclub on the island, with two dance floors. There's live music downstairs starting around 9pm Wednesday to Saturday. The disco upstairs cranks up at 11pm Thursday to Saturday. Admission is free on Wednesday; Thursday to Saturday it's $5-6 for entry to both sections.

Baba's Lounge (☎ 902-892-7377, 81 University Ave) Cover $3-5. Open 11am-2am Mon-Sat, noon-midnight Sun. This bar above Cedar's Eatery presents live modern rock and blues nightly. It's a slightly alternative scene where you can hear local groups playing their own original music.

Benevolent Irish Society (☎ 902-963-7156, 582 North River Rd) Admission $7. Nearly every Friday at 8pm mid-May through late October the Irish Hall on the far north side of town presents a ceilidh

with traditional Irish, Scottish and PEI music and dance – and it's great fun. Arrive early, as parking and seating are limited.

Spectator Sports

Charlottetown Driving Park (☎ 902-892-6823, 46 Kensington Rd) Just north of the center, this track offers you a chance to soak up some of the excitement of the races at no cost. As elsewhere in the Maritimes, you'll see harness racing here – a horse pulling a small buggy with a driver. Races are held 7:30pm to 10:30pm every Saturday night from May to early January and also 7:30pm to 10:30pm Thursdays from June to September. Admission is free because these folks make their money on the gambling.

Shopping

Anne of Green Gables Store (☎ 902-368-2663, 110 Queen St) Open 9am-7pm Mon-Wed, 9am-8pm Thurs & Fri, 9am-5pm Sat, noon-5pm Sun Apr-Dec. Here you'll find enough Green Gables kitsch to last a lifetime.

Getting There & Away

Air Air Canada (or their subsidiary Air Nova) flies between Halifax and Charlottetown five or six times a day and directly to Montréal and Toronto at least daily. A $10 'passenger facility charge' is collected from each passenger over the age of two (not included in the ticket price). Before buying a plane ticket to Ch'town, compare the price of flying into nearby Moncton and renting a car there.

Bus SMT Bus Lines uses the Confederation Bridge to and from Moncton, New Brunswick. They also pick up and drop off passengers in Kensington and Summerside. In summer, there are two trips daily, except Friday and Sunday when there are three. For Moncton, a ticket is $35. In Moncton this service connects to numerous other buses, plus the train to Montréal. The SMT depot (☎ 902-566-9744), 330 University Ave, has $2 coin lockers. It's open 8:30am to 6pm Monday to Friday, 7am to 2:30pm and 5pm to 6pm Saturday & Sunday.

Shuttles If you're headed to Halifax or any point along the way, private van shuttles are a better bet than the bus. The seven-passenger Go-Van Shuttle (☎ 902-456-5678, 866-463-9660) operates daily upon request, leaving Halifax around 7:30am and Charlottetown at noon. In Halifax they'll pick up and drop off anywhere in the city; in Charlottetown they pick up in the parking lot between KFC and Dollarama, on University Ave near Nassau St. You must book by phone (of course, they only go when there are bookings). Between Charlottetown/Summerside and Halifax, the fare is $45 one-way (students and seniors $40), pretty standard for this route.

The Halifax-based PEI Express Shuttle (☎ 877-877-1771) works exactly the same as the Go-Van, except that they pick up at 11:30am from Burger King, at University and Belvedere Aves in Charlottetown. They operate daily year-round. Check their Web site at ⓦ www.peishuttle.com.

Two Charlottetown-based companies, the Square One Shuttle (☎ 877-675-3830) and the Advanced Shuttle (☎ 877-886-3322) do the reverse, leaving Charlottetown at 8am or 8:30am and Halifax at 2pm or 3pm. Advanced Shuttle will pick up at Halifax International Airport for an extra $3 and can carry up to three bicycles at $10 each if you let them know beforehand. Square One has a Web site at ⓦ www.square1shuttle.ca.

Getting Around

To/From the Airport The Charlottetown airport is 8km north of the city center at Brackley Point Rd and Sherwood Rd. There's no city bus service. A taxi to town will cost $10/12 for one/two persons, plus $4 per additional person. A taxi to Summerside will be $60. Car rental companies with desks at the airport include Avis, Budget, Hertz and National, although they may only be there when they have advance bookings.

Bus There's no city bus service or other public transportation on PEI, but the 15-passenger Beach Shuttle (☎ 902-566-3243) shuttles between Charlottetown and the north coast beaches of the national park.

The Beach Shuttle leaves from the PEI Tourism Office, 178 Water St, at 8:50am, 10:55am, 3:05pm and 5:05pm from early June to late September (at 9:35am and 3:10pm only early and late in the season). It stops at the HI hostel at 9am and 11:05am (9:45am only early and late in the season), then on to the Cavendish Visitor Centre at the junction of Hwys 6 and 13. It leaves Cavendish to return about an hour after the Charlottetown departure times. The fare is $10/18 one way/roundtrip.

Car A car, for better or worse, is the best and sometimes the only way to see much of the island. There are several rental outlets in the capital. The supply of cars is limited, and in summer getting a car is not easy. You may find they're all taken for the next week or two, so reserve well ahead.

National Car Rental (☎ 902-368-2228) is on the corner of University Ave and Euston St. Its least expensive compacts start at $39 per day, plus $16 insurance and 17% tax, with 200km free. In midsummer National bumps the basic price up to $72.

Budget Car Rental (☎ 902-566-5525), 215 University Ave, starts at $38 day, plus $21 insurance and tax, jumping to $75 a day in July and August.

There's also a Rent-A-Wreck (☎ 902-566-9955) at 57A St Peters Rd, where you pay $40 a day in summer, $30 in winter, 200km included (insurance $13 a day). It's open 8am to 5:30pm Monday to Friday, 8am to 1pm Saturday.

Parking meters cost 50¢ an hour from 8am to 6pm Monday to Friday, but they're free evenings, weekends and holidays. Parking at Peake's Wharf & Marina at the foot of Prince St is $6 a day ($12 for RVs). You'll find free on-street parking on the back streets of the old town if you look for it.

Traffic around Charlottetown doubles in July and August, with gridlock on University Ave all day and parking at a premium throughout the city.

Canadian Automobile Association (CAA) Maritimes (☎ 902-892-1612), 33 University Ave, is open 9am to 5pm weekdays, 10am to 1pm Saturday.

Bicycle Smooth Cycles (☎ 902-566-5530, fax 902-566-3424), 172 Prince at Kent St, rents hybrid bicycles for $24/85 a day/week. They sell the excellent *PEI Cycling Guide* for $15. All manner of bicycle repairs are done here.

Web site: W www.smoothcycle.com

MacQueen's Bicycles (☎ 902-368-2453, fax 902-894-4547), 430 Queen St, between Pond and Summer Sts, has road bikes for $25/100 a day/week. Both shops rent panniers ($25) and helmets, and MacQueen's also arranges bicycle tours.

Web site: W www.macqueens.com

Kings Byway Scenic Drive

The 374km circular sightseeing route east of Charlottetown around the eastern third of the province is known as the Kings Byway Scenic Drive. It travels through a lightly populated, rural region of farms and fishing communities. Much of this section of the province is peopled by descendants of Scottish settlers rather than by the French of the western side or the Irish of the central district. The ferry to Nova Scotia is on the south coast, and the ferry to the Îles de la Madeleine is at Souris, on the east coast. Plenty of B&Bs and tourist homes are found along the roadways.

ORWELL

Just 28km east of Charlottetown is the **Orwell Corner Historic Village** (☎ *902-651-8510, off Hwy 1; admission $4; open 9am-3pm Tues-Fri mid-May-late Oct; 9am-5pm daily mid-June-Aug)*, a restored and preserved 19th-century community. Originally settled by Scottish immigrants in 1766, the village includes a farm, a blacksmith, a post office and a store, among other buildings, still in their original settings. Concerts ($8) are held at 8pm four nights a week in July and August, on Wednesdays in September. This attraction is worth the price.

A kilometer beyond is the **Sir Andrew MacPhail Homestead** (☎ *902-651-2789, 271*

Fletcher Rd; admission free; open 10am-8:30pm Sun-Fri, 10am-6pm Sat July & Aug; 10am-6pm Mon, Tues & Thurs, 10am-8:30pm Wed, Sat & Sun, 10am-4pm Sat late June-Oct). This national historic site preserves the farm that Sir Andrew MacPhail and his brother used to start the island's seed potato industry. Now it features a restaurant on the wrap-around porch of their home. There are some nature trails here.

Places to Stay

Lord Selkirk Provincial Park *(☎ 902-659-7221, fax 902-659-7220,* W *www.gov.pe.ca/ visitorsguide/explore/parks, off Hwy 1)* Unserviced/serviced sites $17/20. Open mid-June-late Sept. This park at Eldon, just off Hwy 1 between Charlottetown and Wood Islands, offers rows of campsites in an open field along the side of the Belfast Highland Greens golf course. The nicest sites are Nos 4, 5, 6 & 7, which are on the edge of a bluff with sea views.

Rainbow Lodge B&B *(☎ 902-651-2202, 800-268-7005, fax 902-651-2002,* e *jim culbert@hotmail.com,* W *www.gaypei.com, Hwy 1 at Vernon Bridge)* Singles/doubles $65/80 May-Sept, $50/65 other months. Two rooms are available, and breakfast is included. It's impossible to miss this house painted in the colors of the rainbow; in fact, it's Prince Edward Island's best-known openly gay B&B.

Maclean's Century Farm Tourist Home *(☎ 902-659-2694,* W *www.2hwy.com/pe/ m/macefath.htm, 244 New Cove Rd)* Singles/ doubles $35/38. Just 2km off Hwy 1 at Orwell Cove, three rooms are available in a large farmhouse on a hill overlooking the sea.

Rachel's Motel & Cottages *(☎ 902-659-2874, 800-559-2874,* W *www.holidayjunction .com/canada/pei/cpe0014.html, 4827 Hwy 1, Eldon)* Doubles $50 mid-June-mid-Sept, $40 shoulder seasons. Open May-mid-Oct. Just west of the turnoff to Lord Selkirk Provincial Park, Rachel's consists of eight rooms in a long block and four cottages. It's clean and neat and a bit back from the highway.

PRINCE EDWARD ISLAND

WOOD ISLANDS

Down on the south coast, 'Woods' is where you'll find the PEI–Nova Scotia ferry terminal, and as such it's sometimes busy. Turn to Getting There & Away in the introduction to Prince Edward Island for details of this May-to-mid-December ferry service. The Nova Scotia mainland is 22km (75 minutes) across the Northumberland Strait. It's possible to do a three-hour roundtrip on this ferry as a walk-on passenger for only $11 (seniors $9, children under 13 free) – a cheap scenic cruise. Don't leave on the last ferry of the day if you want to come right back, however!

The PEI tourist office (☎ 902-962-7411, open 8am-6:30pm June-mid-Oct, 8am-10pm July & Aug) is just outside the ferry terminal (take a sharp right as you leave the terminal). At the harbor mouth beyond is the free day-use **Wood Islands Provincial Park** with a nice lighthouse (1876).

Northumberland   Provincial   Park (☎ 902-962-7418, Ⓦ www.gov.pe.ca/visitors guide/explore/parks, Hwy 4) Sites $17/20. Open mid-June-late Sept. This park, 3½km east of Wood Islands ferry wharf on Hwy 4, offers nice sheltered campsites in a coniferous forest right on the coast.

MURRAY RIVER

In Murray River, **Garry's Seal Cruises** (☎ 902-962-2494, Fox River Rd; adults $17; open May-Sept) departs three to five times daily from the town wharf to view PEI's largest seal colony, Bird Island and a mussel farm.

If you're traveling with children, don't miss **Kings Castle Provincial Park**, 3½km northeast of Murray River on Hwy 348. Large concrete statues of storybook characters are sprinkled through the forest and admission is free anytime. Leave your car in the parking area by the road and walk in.

Bay Breeze Campground (☎ 902-962-2747, Ⓦ www.2hwy.com/pe/b/bzmomarn .htm, 9 Mink River Rd) Unserviced/serviced sites $15/18. Open late May-early Oct. Bay Breeze is at Mink River Harbour, off Hwy 17 near Murray Harbour North, 10km northeast of Murray River. There are 36 nice wooded sites and a Laundromat. Beware of Seal Cove Campground next door, which is just a field full of RVs.

Panmure Island Provincial Park (☎ 902-838-0668, Ⓦ www.gov.pe.ca/visitorsguide/ explore/parks, Hwy 347 off Hwy 17, Gaspereaux) Unserviced/serviced sites $17/20. Open late June-early Sept. This well-wooded campsite is near a great beach, with ample free parking all along the sandspit leading to Panmure Island itself. Panmure Head Lighthouse (1853) is at the end of the beach. The Abegweit Powwow has been held here on the third weekend in August each year since 1992, and anyone is welcome to attend.

MONTAGUE & AROUND

Montague is a bustling little town with shopping malls, supermarkets, fast food outlets and traffic jams. Do your grocery shopping at the large Sobeys Supermarket on Main St.

A local tourist office (☎ 902-838-4778) is in the former train station on Station St adjacent to the Montague marina. It's open mid-May to October. Trains arrived here from 1906 to 1984, and now it's a terminus of the Confederation Trail.

A larger provincial tourist office (☎ 902-838-0670) can be found at Pooles Corner, at the junction of Hwys 3 and 4, 5km north of Montague. Aside from the racks of brochures and other information, there's a vacancy board that will list openings in motels and B&Bs throughout the region. There's also an extensive set of museum-quality displays and exhibits on PEI and a small video theater. The office is open 9am to 4:30pm June to early October, 8am 7pm in July and August.

Back in town, the **Garden of the Gulf Museum** (☎ 902-838-2467, 564 Main S. South; adult/child $3/free; open 9am-5pm Mon-Fri mid-June-late Sept, 9am-5pm Mon-Sat July & Aug) is just across a small bridge from the local tourist office. This museum in the ornate brick former post office and custom house (1888) was established in 1958 and is the oldest museum on Prince Edward Island.

Kayaking
Outside Expeditions *(☎ 800-207-3899,* W *www.getoutside.com)* runs kayak tours from Brudenell River Provincial Park from mid-June to mid-September. The three-hour Harbour Passage Tour ($50) operates three times a day in midsummer. They'll organize a trip as late as October if at least four people are interested.

Tourist Cruises
From the Montague marina, **Cruise Manada** *(☎ 902-838-3444, 800-986-3444; adult/child $18/9; open mid-June-Sept)* offers highly rated boat tours to PEI's largest seal colony. It departs from the wharf right in front of the local tourist office.

Cardigan Sailing Charters *(☎ 902-583-2020, in Cardigan village)* operates a schooner tour that departs at 10am daily from the end of June to late September. The 5½-hour trip ($60) sails down the Cardigan River and out into the bay; a lobster lunch is included. You should book at least a day in advance. It's run by the same people who do the Cardigan Lobster Suppers.

Places to Stay & Eat
Brudenell River Provincial Park (☎ 902-652-8966, W *www.gov.pe.ca/visitorsguide/explore/parks, off Hwy 3)* Unserviced/serviced sites $17/20-23. Open mid-June-early Oct. This provincial park is part of a well-developed resort complex with two golf courses, a golf academy, horseback riding, upscale cottages, a marina, conference center, resort and restaurants. Everything other than camping is very expensive. Happily, the RV park and campground are nicely separated, and the tent sites are well laid out in a coniferous forest. The Confederation Trail passes near the park.

Four Seasons Cottages (☎ 902-652-2780, W *www.fourseasonscottages.8k.com, 405 Morrison's Beach Rd)* Doubles $45, plus $5 per additional person. Open mid-Apr-Nov. Off Hwy 342, 4½km from Georgetown. This cluster of older cottages facing the Cardigan River is the polar opposite of the flashy golf/conference complex at Brudenell River. In contrast to the manicured affluence sur-rounding the resort, this place feels lived in. The beach is better than the one at the provincial park, and rowboats are loaned free. Four Seasons has eight cottages, all with cooking facilities, but be aware that in July and August they rent strictly by the week, charging $325 for the six two-bedroom units (four people) or $425 for the two three-bedroom units (seven people). In mid-summer you should reserve well ahead (preferably months ahead), but in the off months they should have something for you. If you get in, Four Seasons makes a great base for exploring this side of PEI.

Cardigan Lobster Suppers (☎ 902-583-2020, 5445 Hwy 321, Cardigan) Supper $28. Open 5pm-9pm daily late June-Sept. Cardigan, an old shipbuilding port north of Brudenell River Provincial Park, has a supper house where the meal includes chowder, salad bar and desserts as well as the lobster.

GEORGETOWN
Georgetown is a quaint little town with some evocative old stone buildings, fishing boats, a shipyard and a large seafood plant. A branch of the Confederation Trail ends at the harbor.

Georgetown Timber Ltd *(☎ 902-652-2893)* operates PEI's largest sawmill on Hwy 3 at the entrance to town, where you can gawk at mountains of logs, sawdust and sawn lumber.

The *Kings Playhouse (☎ 902-652-2053,* W *www.kingsplayhouse.com; admission $15-20; 65 Grafton St)* is a huge theater complex in the heart of this small town. From early July to early September they present plays, concerts and comedy acts most nights at 8pm.

SOURIS
With a population of 1300, Souris feels like a real town after you've passed through so many small villages. First settled by the Acadian French in the early 1700s, it was named Souris (meaning 'mouse') due to several plagues. It's pronounced like the English name Surrey. The town is an important fishing port and the departure point of the ferry to the Îles de la Madeleine in

Québec. Agrawest Foods has a large potato processing plant atop a hill overlooking Souris and next door is Polar Foods International, which cans lobster.

Main St, a strip with buildings from the 1920s and 1930s and some distinctive older architecture, is pleasantly slow, with cars stopping to let pedestrians cross. Shops, the newspaper office and a few restaurants are found here.

St Mary's Catholic Church, built of red island sandstone in 1901, rises above town on Longworth St up Chapel Ave from Main St. It's the dominant structure in Souris, but several other buildings, including the town hall on Main St, are worth a look on your way by.

There's a provincial tourist office (☎ 902-687-7030) next to the CIBC Banking Centre on Main St in town. It's open 9am to 5pm daily mid-June to early October, 8am to 7pm July and August.

Activities

Venture Out Cycle & Kayak *(☎ 902-687-1234,* W *www.peisland.com/ventureout, on Hwy 2; open July-Sept)* is at Souris Beach Park, the wide sweeping beach at the west entrance to town on Hwy 2. They rent kayaks at $12/25/40 for 1/3/7 hours for a single kayak or $17/35/60 for a double. Bicycles are $5/12/20. Their guided kayak tours are $30/48 for 2/3 hours.

Places to Stay

A Place to Stay Inn (☎ 902-687-4626, 800-655-7829, e *apts1@pei.sympatico.ca,* W *www.peislandstay.com, 9 Longworth St)* Dorm beds $20, singles/doubles $50/60, includes continental breakfast. Located right beside landmark St Mary's Church, this absolutely superb facility includes dorm rooms and 12 guest rooms. It has full kitchen and laundry facilities, a lounge and TV room, mountain bikes for rent at $4/12/22 an hour/half day/day and many more extras.

Church Street Tourist Home (☎ 902-687-3065, 8 Church St) Singles or doubles $35, including a light breakfast. Open Apr-Jan. This B&B, 10 minutes on foot from the ferry, is simple but good. It's an older two-story house in the center of town with three shared-bath rooms. The proprietor, Jimmy Hughes, is the mayor of Souris!

Century Home B&B (☎ 902-687-3572, 866-687-3572, 77 Main St, next door to Souris Town Hall) Doubles $45 including breakfast. Open mid-May-Dec. This large wooden house with an enclosed porch is diagonally opposite the Church St Tourist Home.

Dockside B&B (☎ 877-687-2829, fax 902-687-4141, W *www.colvillebay.ca, 37 Breakwater St)* Doubles $45/55 without/with bath, including breakfast. Open mid-June-mid-Oct. This modern two-story house directly above the ferry terminal has a wonderful sea view from the front lawn.

Souris West Motel (☎ 902-969-7347, W *www.peitourism.com/souriswest, Hwy 2)* Rooms $49-79 July & Aug, $45-60 other months. Located 2km west of Souris Beach on Hwy 2, this is the cheapest motel in these parts. There are eight housekeeping units in a long wooden block and one cottage.

Places to Eat

Bluefin Restaurant (☎ 902-687-3271, 10 Federal Ave) Mains $8-13. Open 7am-8pm Mon-Sat, 8am-8pm Sun, closing at 7pm mid-Sept-May. The Bluefin is tucked away down a side street opposite the CIBC Banking Centre in the center of town. It's a local favorite offering large portions of fish & chips ($8), pork chops ($11), halibut steak ($13) and a seafood platter ($16). The noon special is available from 11am to 1pm. The attached *Black Rafter Lounge (☎ 902-687-3271; open 11am until late, closed Sun Sept-May)* is a large sports bar worth checking in the evening.

Platter House Restaurant (☎ 902-687-2764, on Hwy 2 adjacent to the Souris River Bridge west of town) Mains $10-15. Open 11am-8pm early June to mid-Sept. The Platter House offers seafood chowder ($7) fish & chips ($10) and fettucine ($12). For a real feast have the mollusk-ular combo ($14) or the seafood combo ($15). Tourists are the target market here, whereas the Bluefin caters more to locals.

Getting There & Away

From April to September the car ferry MV *Madeleine* (☎ 888-986-3278) connects Souris with the Îles de la Madeleine in Québec, five hours and 134km north in the Gulf of St Lawrence. It leaves Souris daily at 2pm, with no Monday departure from April to June or in September. From mid-July to mid-August there's an additional 7am departure on Saturday, Sunday and Monday. The one-way adult/child passenger fare is $36/18, cars/bicycles $68/$8.50.

A branch of the Confederation Trail leads through town directly to the Souris Marine Terminal.

BASIN HEAD

Not really a village, Basin Head is the site of the **Basin Head Fisheries Museum** (☎ 902-357-7233, off Hwy 16; adult/child $3.50/free; open 9am-5pm daily June-Sept, 9am-6pm July & Aug), at the ocean's edge 3km northeast of Red Point. This provincial museum traces the history of the island's fishing industry with an interpretive center, boat sheds with vessels on display and the Smith Fish Cannery, which now houses a coastal ecology exhibit including saltwater aquariums. An excellent golden beach is just below the museum, with sands famous for the squeaking sound they make as you walk on them. At one time you could jump off a small bridge and be swept out to a sandbar by the tidal wash, but it's officially frowned upon now.

Red Point Provincial Park (☎ 902-357-3075, fax 902-902-357-3076, **W** www.gov.pe ca/visitorsguide/explore/parks, off Hwy 16) Unserviced/serviced sites $17/20. Open mid-June-Sept. Ten kilometers northeast of Souris, Red Point is a small park with a sandy beach and some pleasant shaded tent sites. Choose your site carefully, as changes are not allowed.

EAST POINT

At East Point, the northeast tip of the island, the cliffs are topped by a **lighthouse** (☎ 902-357-2106; adult/child $2.50/1; open 10am-6pm daily mid-June-Aug) that can be climbed as part of a little tour. The assistant's house nearby has a restored radio room and a gift shop. It's expected that in a few years the old house will have to be moved (as the lighthouse has been moved previously) because of the creeping erosion of the shoreline.

The north shore area of Kings County all the way to Cavendish is more heavily wooded than much of the island, but that doesn't mean the end of farms and potatoes altogether. There's a lot of fishing done along this coast – you could join a charter boat in search of tuna. Inland are a couple of trout streams worth investigating.

The people of the northeastern area have a fairly strong, intriguing accent not unlike that heard in Newfoundland.

ELMIRA & NORTH LAKE

North Lake is one of four fishing centers found along the north coast of Kings County. Although small, the dock area, with its lobster traps, storage sheds and boats, is always good for a poke around. With late summer comes the tuna season, a busy sport-fishing period that draws anglers from abroad. Some of the world's largest bluefin tuna have been caught in these waters. Indeed, the world-record catch, a 680kg behemoth, was reeled in off North Lake in 1979.

Railway buffs won't wish to miss the **Elmira Railway Museum** (☎ 902-357-7234, Hwy 16A, Elmira; adult/child $2/free; open 10am-5pm Fri-Wed mid-June-mid-Sept, 10am-6pm daily July & Aug) in the original railway terminal at this end of the island. The Confederation Trail starts right here. The museum has a scale model of the railway and outside is an old Canadian National Railways mail car.

Campbell's Cove Provincial Park (☎ 902-357-3080, **W** www.gov.pe.ca/visitors-guide/explore/parks, 7516 Hwy 16) Sites $17/20. Open late June-early Sept. Quiet and relaxing during the day, this small campground fills up by evening in July and August. The camping is right on the coast in a grassy field with some shade, directly above the beach. Campers here are mostly tenters, as there are no electric hookups;

facilities are minimal, so bring all necessary supplies. The beach, with red cliffs at either end, is excellent for beachcombing.

Campbells Guest Home (☎ *902-357-2504, 7325 Hwy 16, 7km west of North Lake)* Doubles $40 including continental breakfast. Two rooms are available in this new two-story farmhouse a kilometer east of Campbell's Cove Provincial Park.

ST MARGARET'S & NAUFRAGE

At the big church in St Margaret's, ***lobster suppers*** (☎ *902-687-3105)* are held daily from 4pm to 9pm mid-June to September and are $24. Aside from the deep-sea fishing, there are some good trout streams along the road, and one of them, the Naufrage River, is just west of town.

At the village of Naufrage, on the coast, there's another lighthouse and some colorful fishing boats around the wharf area. **Bay Watch Tours & Deep Sea Fishing** (☎ *902-961-2260 or 902-626-5216, Naufrage; adult/child $20/15)* offers three-hour fishing trips daily at 8am, 1pm and 6pm in July and August.

ST PETERS

The nets for commercial mussel farming can be seen stretched around St Peters Bay. A provincial tourist office (☎ *902-961-3540)* is beside the bridge at St Peters, just where the Confederation Trail crosses Hwy 2. It's open 9am to 4:30pm daily from June to early October and 8am to 7pm in July and August.

St Peters Park (☎ *902-961-2786,* **W** *www .isn.net/~stpeters)* Unserviced/serviced sites $15/20. Open mid-June-Sept. This is the closest campground to the national park's Greenwich section. St Peters Park is a grassy field next to Hwy 2, 1½km west of the bridge in St Peters. The Confederation Trail passes just below.

Midgell Centre (☎ *902-961-2963, 6553 Hwy 2)* Beds $15. Open mid-June-mid-Sept. Visitors are welcome to stay overnight in this complex of five dark green wooden buildings, set up principally for the guests of a Christian center, beside the highway 4km west of St Peters, but people of any denom-

ination are welcome. There are 60 beds; light cooking is possible; and there are showers and a lounge. It's a good base for visiting Greenwich but is often closed, so call ahead.

GREENWICH

In 1998, Parks Canada opened another rather incredible section of Prince Edward Island National Park along the peninsula north and west of St Peter's. Make sure you check this place out for the rare parabolic dunes – found only here and in one spot along Germany's North Sea coastline; 3% of the planet's piping plovers are found here too.

In 2001 the **Greenwich Interpretation Centre** (☎ *902-961-2514, 9km west of St Peters on Hwy 313; adult/families $6/15, open 9am-5pm daily May-Oct, 9am-8pm mid-June-Aug)* opened in a huge barn-shaped facility at the entrance to this section of the park. The national park entry fee ($3.50) is not included in the interpretation center admission charge, though you can get a combined ticket for $8/19. The center has exhibits on the park and a 12-minute audiovisual.

The 373 hectares in the national park's Greenwich section are crossed by 7km of trails from trailheads a kilometer west of the interpretation center. Of these the **Tlaqatik Trail** is the farthest west. The **Greenwich Dunes Trail** is a boardwalk, and the **Havre Saint Pierre Trail** is a rectangular loop. The beach is a kilometer north of the interpretation center. Camping is not allowed at Greenwich.

MOUNT STEWART TO TRACADIE

Mount Stewart is an important junction on the Confederation Trail, where the branch from Georgetown feeds in. The **Abegweit First Nation** has a reserve at Scotchfort between Mount Stewart and Tracadie. There's a powwow here the first full weekend in July (the weekend after Canada Day).

Trailside Inn (☎ *888-704-6595, 902-676-3130,* **e** *dbdeacon@isn.net,* **w** *www.pei island.com/trailside, 109 Main St, Mount* *tewart)* Rooms $80 mid-June-Sept, $100 July & Aug. This hip cafe adjacent to Confederation Trail in Mount Stewart village, just off Hwy 2, offers fine dining ($13-17), live music and bicycle rentals ($17/25 half/full day), as well as four rooms.

Around the Bend Tourist Grounds & Trail Side Camping *(☎ 902-676-2198, W www.auracom.com/~atbthome, Hwy 2 East, Tracadie)* Unserviced/serviced sites $15/22, rooms with bath $60. Open year-round. This grassy field right beside the Confederation Trail, 9km southwest of Mount Stewart, is suitable for tenting.

Blue Heron Scenic Drive

The area north of the capital in Queens County is where all the action is on Prince Edward Island. The national park is here, with its camping and beaches, as are many of the island's most touted attractions. To feed and house the vacationers, scores of the province's lodging and dining establishments are found not far from the north coast. The south coast is more of a local scene, where the islanders themselves go to escape the tourists in Cavendish. The Blue Heron Scenic Drive circles the center of the island, taking in all the main sights.

BORDEN-CARLETON

Gateway Village *(☎ 902-437-8570, Hwy 1; admission free; open 8am-10pm daily July & Aug; 9am-8pm June & Sept, 9am-6pm the rest of the year)* at the PEI end of the Confederation Bridge is worth visiting for free maps and brochures, washrooms and an exhibit called Our Island Home, which offers vague impressions of the island through a film, recordings of island music, videos, photos and displays. The usual assortment of shops and restaurants is here too, though most are closed outside of July and August.

The **Confederation Trail** begins near the corner of Dickie Rd and Industrial Dr, 1½km from Gateway Village. Ask someone to point you in the right direction. Staff at Gateway Village will give you a free map of this famous bicycle trail.

Duchess Gateway B&B *(☎ 902-855-2765, W www.peibedandbreakfast.com/duchess/ duchess.htm, 264 Carleton St)* Rooms with shared bath $40 mid-June-mid-Oct, $30 mid-Oct-mid-June, including a full breakfast and tax. Duchess Gateway is directly opposite the Irving gas station on Hwy 1 as you leave Borden-Carleton. Turn right at the next corner after Irving and swing around to the right to get there.

Carleton Motel *(☎ 902-437-3030, W www .bestofpei.com/carletonmotel.html, Hwy 1)* Rooms $50-60 July & Aug, $45 rest of year. This motel, on Hwy 1, just 1.3km beyond the Irving gas station in Borden-Carleton, has 24 rooms in a long wooden block facing the highway. Seven units have kitchens, and there's a coffee shop.

VICTORIA

Straddling Queens and Prince Counties is this picturesque fishing village just off Hwy 1, 35km west of Charlottetown. Victoria is something of a haven for artists and features a number of studios and art galleries, as well as Island Chocolates, a shop that produces excellent Belgian chocolates. The community center becomes the ***Victoria Playhouse*** *(☎ 902-685-2025; adult/youth & senior $17/15)* in July and August, presenting concerts on Mondays and theatrical productions other nights, always beginning at 8pm. In September, the program varies. You should call ahead.

Places to Stay & Eat
Simple Comforts B&B *(☎ 902-658-2951, 877-658-2951, e simplecomforts@cheerful .com, W welcome.to/simplecomforts, 20287 Hwy 1)* Hostel beds/B&B rooms $20/35 and up. Extra persons in the B&B $10 each; all rates include a hearty breakfast. Outside town on Hwy 1, this B&B bills itself as a 'bicycle hostel.' Indeed, the top floor is a 13-bed hostel with three hostel rooms at one end of the building and three nicer B&B rooms with shared bath at the other. A hostel card is not required. This ramshackle

complex is full of character, piled high with priceless relics from the days when it was an Anglican Church camp. The owners rent bicycles at $10/20 a day for an old/new bike ($20 for a tandem). Simple Comforts does airport pick-ups for guests at $20 per trip.

Victoria Village Inn (☎ *902-658-2483, fax 902-658-2676,* e *victoriavillageinn@pei .sympatico.ca,* w *www3.pei.sympatico.ca/ victoriavillageinn, 22 Howard St)* Doubles $65-85 June-mid-Sept, $50-70 other months, breakfast included. This lovely 19th-century home adjacent to the Victoria Playhouse has three rooms with bath.

Landmark Café (☎ *902-658-2286, 12 Main St)* Mains $11-17. Open 11:15am-9pm Thurs-Tues, 5pm-9pm Wed late June-early Sept. On the corner opposite the Victoria Playhouse, they serve items like homemade soups ($4.50), sandwiches ($4.50), salads ($7) and nachos ($6). The entire cafe including equipment is for sale at $110,000.

Morning Star Fisheries Ltd (☎ *902-658-2361, across the bridge 500m east of Victoria Wharf)* Open 10am-6pm Fri-Sun May-early October; 10am-7pm mid-June-Aug. You can purchase cooked lobster here, ready to consume at a picnic table overlooking the beach in adjacent Victoria Provincial Park.

PRINCE EDWARD ISLAND NATIONAL PARK & AROUND

Just 24km north of Charlottetown, this is one of Canada's smallest national parks, but it has 45km of varied coastline. Sand dunes and red sandstone cliffs give way to wide sandy beaches (widest at Cavendish).

A day pass to the park costs $3.50 per person or $8 per family; from mid-September to early June it's free. You can also get a combination pass for the park and Green Gables (see House of Green Gables in the Cavendish section), or even a seasonal Atlantic Pass accepted at seven national parks in eastern Canada. The park maintains an information desk and the exhibits in the Cavendish Visitor Centre (see Cavendish later in this chapter). Failing that, there's the Brackley Visitor Center (☎ 902-672-7474; open June to early October) at Brackley Beach and the Dalvay Administration

Office (☎ 902-672-6350; open 8am to 4pm Monday to Friday year-round) off Gulfshore Parkway behind the Dalvay by the Sea Hotel. The park's Web address is w www.parkscanada.gc.ca/pei.

The coverage that follows is organized from east to west, first dealing with the park and park-run facilities, then with private businesses both in and out of the park.

Beaches

There are several long stretches of beach in the park and they are all good. **Dalvay Beach** is the easternmost, and a couple of short hiking trails begin in the area. Two called Farmlands and Bubbling Springs Trails are quite good, with a small graveyard, some remnants of old stone dikes and a spring for a cool drink found along the way. They can be combined for a 4km walk.

Stanhope Beach, opposite the campground of the same name, has no cliffs or dunes – the landscape is flat and the beach wide. At the entrance to the beach are a midsummer-only snack bar and changing rooms with showers. A boardwalk leads to the beach, which has lifeguards on duty all day in season.

Brackley Beach, in the middle of the park, is more heavily used than the previous two. Long and wide, Brackley Beach is backed by sand dunes and is popular with locals and visitors alike. At the Brackley Visitor Center (open early June to early October) just inside the gate, there's a snack bar, and there are changing rooms by the boardwalk to the beach. Lifeguards are on duty in season.

Some of the park's most impressive terrain is between Rustico and Cavendish along Gulfshore West Parkway. At Cape Turner there's a good lookout area, and don't miss **Orby Head** with its trails leading along the high red cliffs and great seaside views. There are other stopping-off points along this stretch of coastal road.

Cavendish Beach, edged with large sand dunes, is the widest beach of them all. At the western end of the park, it is easily the most popular beach and gets pretty busy in peak season.

Take care while swimming off the north coast, as undertows and riptides are all too common. Every year people get sucked out by the undertow; windy days when there's surf are the riskiest. All the beaches along this coast tend to have red jellyfish, known locally as 'bloodsuckers' (they aren't). Most are smaller than a fist and are not really dangerous, although brushing against one can irritate the skin. There's virtually no shade to be had at these beaches, so for your own protection consider using an umbrella, a shirt and lots of sunscreen lotion.

Hiking

The park has around 40km of trails, most of them easy, some rated moderate. Unfortunately, none are officially wheelchair accessible. The main trail, the 8km **Homestead Trail**, starts near the Cavendish Campground and is moderate only in length.

Places to Stay

Camping The national park operates three official campgrounds, and as you might expect, all are in heavy demand during summer. Rates range from $17 for a bare-bones site to $21 for a three-way hookup. Eighty percent of the sites at all three campgrounds are reservable for an additional $7.50 fee, but you must do so at least three days in advance at ☎ 800-414-6765. You cannot request a specific site and must accept whatever is available when you arrive. Park entry fees are extra.

Only 20% of sites are first-come, first-served, and these go early in the day in summer. A waiting list of 30 names is kept, and any unoccupied sites are issued to those on the list around noon. To get an unreserved site in midsummer, you should arrive early and get on the waiting list right away. The staff will tell you at what time they'll begin issuing unreserved sites, and you have to be there in person when your name is read out to claim it.

Stanhope Campground (☎ 800-414-6765, fax 902-629-2428, off Hwy 6) Unserviced/serviced sites $17/19. Open mid-June-mid-Oct. Across the road from Stanhope Beach,

this wooded campground has showers, a kitchen shelter, laundry facilities and a well-stocked store.

Robinsons Island Campground (☎ 800-414-6765, fax 902-629-2428, off Hwy 15) Sites $15. Open July & Aug. Formerly known as the Rustico Island Campground, this relatively isolated campground is near the end of the road to Brackley Beach, 4km west of the Brackley Visitor Center. It has a kitchen shelter and showers. Sites are cheapest here.

Cavendish Campground (☎ 800-414-6765, fax 902-629-2428, off Hwy 6 at the turnoff 2½km west of Green Gables) Unserviced/serviced sites $17/21. Open late May-early Sept. This campground has facilities similar to Stanhope, and being near the center of things it is often filled by noon. 'Premium oceanview' sites are available for $2 extra, but they're cheek by jowl along a grassy strip with no privacy or shade. The regular sites among the trees are actually better.

Winter camping is available near the Dalvay Activity Centre.

Outside the park and adjacent to it are many private campgrounds.

Other Accommodations Tourist homes, motels and B&Bs are found along the length of the national park. The prices are steep compared to elsewhere on the island, and the closer to the beach you get, the higher the price. Phoning for a reservation, even if only a few days in advance, improves your chances of getting a bed for the night in summer.

If you have reservations to stay at private accommodations within the park or are going fishing at Covehead Bridge, you won't need to pay the park entry fee. However, as soon as you begin using national park facilities such as parking lots, beaches and trails, the fees do apply.

Stanhope

Stanhope is one of the major accommodation centers in the area; otherwise there's not a lot to do here. There are dozens of places renting cottages, often by the week or

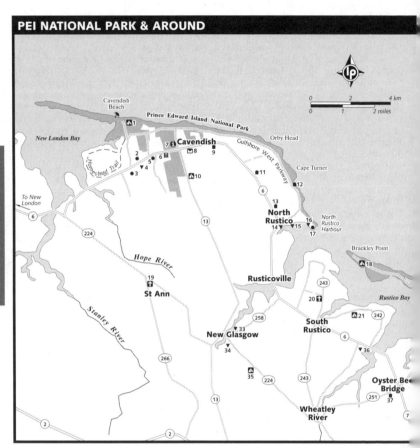

PEI NATIONAL PARK & AROUND

longer. Weekly rates vary, but most are between $400 and $700. The daily rate for most of the housekeeping units starts at $75. Near the park entrance are a couple of restaurants.

Fishing Between Stanhope Beach and Brackley Beach, at Covehead Bridge, are some deep-sea fishing operators, including **Fishy Business** (☎ 902-672-2526), **Richard's** (☎ 902-672-2376) and **Salty Seas** (☎ 902-672-3246). They all do three 3½ hour trips per day at 8am, 1pm and 6pm in July and August for around $20 per person. They'll

also go in the off-season if enough people are interested. Fish are guaranteed or there's no charge (the captain keeps the catch). Several places at Covehead Bridge sell fresh or cooked lobster by the pound during the spring.

Places to Stay *Anne's Whispering Pines Campground* (☎ 902-672-2632, 800-627-4855, 34 Harbour Rd off Hwy 6, Grand Tracadie) Unserviced/serviced sites $19/21. Open June-Sept. Only a few kilometers from the park, Anne's has 50 grassy tent sites between rows of trees and 35 serviced

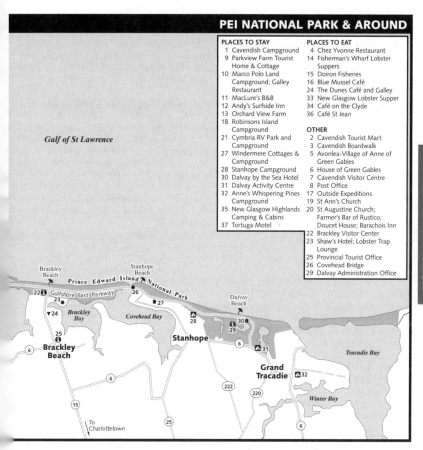

PEI NATIONAL PARK & AROUND

PLACES TO STAY
1 Cavendish Campground
9 Parkview Farm Tourist Home & Cottage
10 Marco Polo Land Campground; Galley Restaurant
11 MacLure's B&B
12 Andy's Surfside Inn
13 Orchard View Farm
18 Robinsons Island Campground
21 Cymbria RV Park and Campground
27 Windermere Cottages & Campground
28 Stanhope Campground
30 Dalvay by the Sea Hotel
31 Dalvay Activity Centre
32 Anne's Whispering Pines Campground
35 New Glasgow Highlands Camping & Cabins
37 Tortuga Motel

PLACES TO EAT
4 Chez Yvonne Restaurant
14 Fisherman's Wharf Lobster Suppers
15 Doiron Fisheries
16 Blue Mussel Café
24 The Dunes Café and Galley
33 New Glasgow Lobster Supper
34 Café on the Clyde
36 Café St Jean

OTHER
2 Cavendish Tourist Mart
3 Cavendish Boardwalk
5 Avonlea-Village of Anne of Green Gables
6 House of Green Gables
7 Cavendish Visitor Centre
8 Post Office
17 Outside Expeditions
19 St Ann's Church
20 St Augustine Church; Farmer's Bar of Rustico; Doucet House; Barachois Inn
22 Brackley Visitor Center
23 Shaw's Hotel; Lobster Trap Lounge
25 Provincial Tourist Office
26 Covehead Bridge
29 Dalvay Administration Office

RV sites. A reasonable grocery store is on premises. They take reservations.

Dalvay by the Sea Hotel (☎ 902-672-2048, fax 902-672-2741, W www.dalvay-bythesea.com, off Hwy 6) Singles/doubles $200/330 mid-June-mid-Sept, $170/210 other months, includes dinner & breakfast. This hotel, built in 1895 and looking like something out of an F Scott Fitzgerald novel, is an appealing landmark. For a splurge, the Victorian seaside lodge offers a varied menu with items like marinated lobster ($26) and grilled quail ($24). Dinner reservations are required. Dalvay by the Sea is a national historic site and among the most imposing lodgings on the island.

Windermere Cottages & Campground (☎ 902-672-2234, 800-688-2234, fax 914-612-2121 W www.windermerecottages.com, 162 Ross Lane, Stanhope Beach) Cottage $75 double, $85-95 quad, $100-110 for six or seven persons, camping $20. Open mid-June-early Sept. A kilometer east of Hwy 25 off Gulfshore East Parkway, Windermere has 15 older but comfortable cottages with full cooking facilities. There are only three double cottages (the rest are larger), so call ahead. Tent camping is available on a grassy field with some shade behind the units (no RV hookups available). Windermere is only a short walk to the beach. Three other places renting cottages are adjacent, but in midsummer everything will be packed.

Brackley Beach

There's a provincial tourist office (☎ 902-672-7474) at Brackley Beach at the junction of Hwys 6 and 15, 4km before the national park. It's open 9am to 4:30pm daily June to early October, 8am to 9pm July and August.

From June to early October **Shaw's Hotel** (☎ 902-672-2022), just outside the park at Brackley Beach, rents bicycles at $5/17 an hour/day.

The Dunes Café and Galley (☎ 902-672-2586, on Hwy 15 just outside the park) Lunch/dinner $18/30. Open 9am-9pm daily July-mid-Sept. You can't miss the striking architecture of this ceramics showroom and rather pretentious cafe.

Lobster Trap Lounge (☎ 902-672-2769, off Hwy 15) Open 8pm-midnight daily mid-June to early Sept. The only pub for miles it seems, adjoining Shaw's Hotel near Brackley Beach. It's fairly rollicking, with shindigs a couple of nights a week ($2 cover charge).

South Rustico

The Acadian settlement at South Rustico dates back to 1700, and several fine historic buildings speak of this tiny village's former importance. Most prominent is **St Augustine Church** (1830), the oldest Catholic church on PEI. The old cemetery is on one side of the church, the solid red stone **Farmer's Bank of Rustico** on the other. The bank operated here from 1864 to 1894 and was a forerunner of the credit union movement in Canada. Beside the bank is **Doucet House**, an old Acadian dwelling recently moved here. The **Barachois Inn** (1870) opposite the church is a classic Victorian mansion, now an upscale country inn.

Kayaking The world headquarters of **Outside Expeditions** (☎ 800-207-3899, Ⓦ www.getoutside.com, 890 Hwy 242, Cymbria) is just 500m west of the Cymbria RV Park and Campground. They rent single/double ocean kayaks at $43/55 a half day, $54/77 a full day. Sit-on-top kayaks are a bit cheaper. Outside Expeditions offers a broad range of kayaking, canoeing and bicycling tours, and this location is open year-round.

Places to Stay & Eat *Cymbria RV Park and Campground (☎ 902-963-2458, fax 902-894-9888, Ⓦ www.cymbria.ca, on Hwy 242 about 3km off Hwy 6)* Unserviced/serviced sites $20/25. Open mid-May-mid-Oct. Some nice tent sites are at the very back of the property, and the friendly young owner Trent Howlett will help you find one. Cymbria is a bit off the beaten track and therefore less likely to be full of campers in midsummer.

Tortuga Motel (☎ 902-621-2020, 25 Hwy 251, Oyster Bed Bridge) Rooms from $45-75. Open July & Aug. This affordable motel near the intersection of Hwys 6 & 7 has 20 rooms in a long strip with a coffee shop in the middle. It's pretty basic and far from the beaches if you don't have a car.

Café St Jean (☎ 902-963-3133, 5033 Hwy 6) Lunch under $10. Open 11:30am-10pm daily mid-June-mid-Sept. Besides all the lobster suppers, this upscale cafe at South Rustico is a consistent, creative bistro with a Cajun and regional flair. It presents live traditional music, often on Tuesdays and Fridays at 7pm (admission $3-5), and stocks more regional music CDs than most music stores. Lunch includes fare such as sandwiches or fish & chips ($9). Dinner brings chicken, beef and fish dishes ($17-21) or lobster ($25), all served on a large deck overlooking Rustico Bay.

New Glasgow & St Ann

Two famous lobster supper houses are south of Rusticoville, one in the village of New Glasgow and another 7km away in St Ann on Hwy 224. Both offer lobster plus all-you-can-eat chowder, mussels, salads, breads and desserts. You may even get some live music to help the food go down.

St Ann's Church Lobster Supper (☎ 902-621-0635, Hwy 224, St Ann) Lobster dinner $25. Open 4pm-8:30pm Mon-Sat mid-June-late Sept. The St Ann supper house is an original and still operates in the St Ann's Church basement, as it has done for the past few decades. It's busy, casual and friendly.

New Glasgow Lobster Supper (☎ 902-964-2870, Hwy 258, New Glasgow) Lobster dinner $25. Open 4pm-8:30pm June-early Oct. The supper house in New Glasgow is a bit more commercial than that in St Ann, and is open on Sunday.

Café on the Clyde (☎ 902-964-4300, at the junction of Hwys 224 & 258, New Glasgow) Breakfast $8. Open 9am-8pm daily July-mid-Sept, 9am-4:30pm June & mid-Sept–mid-Oct, 11am-2pm mid-Oct-mid-Dec. At the PEI Preserve Company in New Glasgow, this trendy tourist cafe offers a full 'country breakfast.'

New Glasgow Highlands Camping & Cabins (☎ 902-964-3232, fax 902-964-3232, W www.town.cavendish.pe.ca/newglasgow highlands, 1.7km east of the PEI Preserve Company on Hwy 224) Unserviced/serviced campsites $24/26, cabins $45/50 double/ triple. Open Apr-Oct. This is probably the nicest campground on PEI, with 15 sites properly spaced in the forest. Each campsite has a fire pit, and there are also 22 cabins, each with two bunks, a double bed, sofa and picnic table (shared bath). Light cooking facilities are provided in the lodge. A Laundromat, small store and heated swimming pool are on the premises. Canoe rentals are $15 per canoe for up to five hours, including dropoff at a nearby lake. It's all immaculately maintained; in fact, this place is so

That Crazy Mixed-Up Lobster

Unfortunately for this mottled green (or bluish or blackish) prehistoric wonder, somebody realized it tasted bloody good. This has meant that we've learned a lot about it, although the facts on this 100-million-year-old crustacean read like a joke book: It tastes with its feet, listens with its legs (of which there are 10) and has teeth in its stomach (which is found just behind the head). The kidney is in the head, the brain in the neck, and the bones (shell) are on the outside.

Lobster is widely associated with the east coast of Canada, but Prince Edward Island, with its famous lobster suppers, is perhaps most closely linked with this symbol of gourmet dining. It's hard to believe now, but there wasn't much interest on the island in the delicate meat until well into the 20th century. In fact, islanders used lobster as fertilizer for the island's farms.

There are two fishing seasons, one in the spring (ending in late June) and one in the winter. Wooden or metal traps baited with herring bits are dropped overboard to rest on the ocean bottom and then checked soon after. The trap's ingenious cage design allows the lobster's claws to narrow on the way in, but once inside the claws spread apart again and crawling back out is impossible. Traditional wooden traps are available for purchase around the island at about $5 each and will one day be museum pieces. Huge holding tanks allow fresh live lobster to be offered throughout the year.

The standard restaurant lobster in Canada weighs about a pound, or a little less than 500g. Two- and three-pounders are often available, but bigger ones are not often seen. Most people are satisfied with the standard portion, as lobster dinners are rich. The meat itself is lean, and is permitted on low-cholesterol diets (but hold the butter).

Lobster can be baked, broiled or barbecued, but the usual method is to boil them alive. They're cooked in boiling, salted fresh water for 12 to 15 minutes for the first pound, adding four minutes for every extra pound (500g). When done, the lobster has the characteristic orange-red shell, not unlike the color of some bathers at Cavendish Beach. Most of the meat is in the tail and the larger claws. The green mushy liver, known as the 'tomalley,' is summarily discarded by most people, but diners in the know consider it a delicacy and one of the choicest parts to savor.

PRINCE EDWARD ISLAND

good you should definitely call ahead to reserve if you plan to be there in July or August. Before mid-June and after early September the cabin prices drop to $30 single or double, a real bargain. Rowdy behavior is not tolerated here.

North Rustico

Whereas nearby Cavendish is purely a tourist town, North Rustico has some local life. The Rustico area is the base for one of the province's largest fishing fleets. Prince Edward Island's fishing industry is inshore (as opposed to offshore), meaning that the boats head out and return home the same day.

North Rustico Harbour is a tiny fishing community with a lighthouse that you can drive to or walk to along the beach once you're in the national park. North Rustico is also the home of probably the best-known, busiest restaurant in the province. There's a post office as well as two supermarkets and a bank.

Kayaking Kayaking trips in Prince Edward Island National Park are offered by **Outside Expeditions** (☎ 800-207-3899, 902-963-3366; Ⓦ www.getoutside.com, 374 Harbourside Dr, North Rustico Harbour), PEI's leading adventure tourism provider. The 1½-hour introductory Beginner Bay Tour ($39) begins with a lesson in kayaking techniques. Their most popular trip is the three-hour Harbour Passage Tour ($50), which operates three times daily at 9am, 1pm and 5pm from mid-June to mid-September. Before and after season they will run a trip whenever at least four people want to go. Look for their office at the end of the road by the harbor, 1½km from Fisherman's Wharf Lobster Suppers.

Fishing A few captains at North Rustico Harbour take visitors out on deep-sea fishing trips in summer. Follow the road beside Fisherman's Wharf Lobster Suppers down to the wharf, and you'll see signs for **Barry Doucette's Deep Sea Fishing** (☎ 902-963-2465), **Bearded Skipper's Deep Sea Fishing** (☎ 902-963-2334), **Aiden's Deep Sea**

Fishing Trips (☎ 902-963-2442) and **Peter Gauthier's Deep Sea Fishing** (☎ 902-963-2129). **Court Bros Deep Sea Fishing** (☎ 902-963-2322) is farther down at the end of the road near Outside Expeditions. At Rusticoville, 3km south of North Rustico, there's **Joey Gauthier's Deep Sea Fishing** (☎ 902-963-2295).

Most of these trips are offered in July and August only, although Court Bros goes from June to mid-September. The actual period when they operate depends not only on the tourist season but also on government fishing seasons. The price is usually $20/10 adults/children for three hours of fishing. On a typical trip, six to 10 people will take turns fishing for cod, mackerel and several other species, and the catch belongs to the boat.

Places to Stay *Andy's Surfside Inn* (☎ 902-963-2405, fax 902-963-2405, Gulfshore West Parkway) Doubles $45-55 July & Aug, $35 June & Sept-Nov, including a light breakfast. Inside the national park, 2.7km from North Rustico on the way to Orby Head. This large rambling house overlooking Doyle's Cove has been an inn since the 1930s. Andy's offers eight rooms with shared bath. The kitchen is open to those who want to bring home a few live lobsters. The view from the porch is simply stunning.

Orchard View Farm (☎ 902-963-2302, 800-419-4468, Ⓦ www.peionline.com/al/orchard, 7602 Hwy 6, 2km west of North Rustico) Singles/doubles $45/55, cottages $150 July & Aug, $60 other months. Open May-mid-Nov. Away from the beach on the road to Cavendish, there are four B&B rooms with shared bath and a communal kitchen in a large farmhouse, plus 12 housekeeping cottages. Prices are negotiable, especially if you stay a few nights.

MacLure's B&B (☎ 902-963-2239, Ⓦ www.2hwy.com/pe/m/metehata.htm, 7920 Hwy 6) Singles/doubles $45/50 July & Aug, $40/45 other months, breakfast included. Halfway between North Rustico and Cavendish, MacLure's offers three rooms with shared bath in a large farmhouse in lovely, peaceful surroundings.

Places to Eat *Fisherman's Wharf Lobster Suppers* (☎ 902-963-2669, 7230 Main St) Lobster dinners from $27. Open 4pm-9pm daily mid-May-mid-Oct. This place is huge, but in peak season it still gets crowded, with lines from 6pm to 8pm. This fun, casual, holiday-style restaurant offers good-value dinners. For $27 a pound you are served a lobster and can help yourself to an impressive salad bar, unlimited amounts of chowder, good local mussels, rolls and a variety of desserts. If you get really lucky you'll snag a table along the back wall with a view of the ocean.

Blue Mussel Café (☎ 902-963-2152, 312 Harbourview Dr, North Rustico Harbour) Fish/lobster dinners $15/25. Open 11am-9pm daily late June-mid-Sept. This pleasant dockside cafe has a covered outdoor deck overlooking the harbour, excellent chowder and a seafood menu that includes lobster dinners and mussels steamed in wine and garlic. They don't deep-fry their fish in batter or serve French fries; instead, everything is panfried so you see what you're getting.

Doiron Fisheries (☎ 902-963-2442, Harborside Dr) Market price. Open 8am-6pm daily May-mid-Oct. At the wharf in North Rustico you can get fresh seafood ranging from lobsters and mussels to scallops, hake and cod. If there are two of you, consider feasting on a 4- or 5lb lobster (2½kg), available live or cooked. Their prices are less than half those of the restaurants.

Cavendish

At the junction of routes 6 and 13, this tourist center is the area's commercial hub. You're in the heart of things when you see the service station, wax museum, church, cemetery and assorted restaurants.

Also situated at the junction, alongside the police station and municipal offices, is the Cavendish Visitor Centre (☎ 902-963-7830). This outlet has a wealth of information on the area, along with exhibits on the national park, a craft shop and a courtesy phone to make reservations. The visitor center is open 9am to 6pm daily late May to late October, 8am to 10pm July and August.

Cavendish is the hometown of Lucy Maud Montgomery (1874–1942), author of *Anne of Green Gables,* and the House of Green Gables here is administered by Parks Canada as a heritage site.

Lucy Maud Montgomery

East of Cavendish is a large amusement park, and close by are go-cart tracks, waterslides, golf courses, miniature golf, fairy castles, petting farms, a 'palace of the bizarre,' a planetarium, West Coast totem poles, a Ripley's Believe It or Not Museum and other tacky diversions, including a life-size replica of the space shuttle *Columbia*. The growing number of these manufactured attractions is an eyesore in this scenic region of PEI.

Numerous tourist homes, motels and cottages can be found around Cavendish. Remember that this is the busiest and most expensive area for accommodations. Almost all of the motels, restaurants, shops and 'attractions' of Cavendish are closed from November to April, and a good many open only from late June to early September. Off-season many businesses take their signs down and almost vanish from sight, but in July and August this area is inundated with tourists and price gouging goes on. Come in spring or fall and you'll easily find a cottage at 50% off.

House of Green Gables Apart from the national park, this house (☎ 902-672-6350, Hwy 6, Cavendish; adult/family $5/12; open 9am-8pm daily late June-mid-Sept, 9am-5pm May-Oct, noon-4pm Wed-Sun Nov, Dec, March & Apr) is the most popular tourist attraction in the province. The house is known as the place where Anne, the heroine of Lucy Maud Montgomery's Anne of Green Gables, lived. The surrounding property was the setting of the 1908 novel – a perennial favorite not only in Canada but around the world, having been translated into nearly 20 languages.

The warmhearted book tells the story of a young orphan, Anne, and her childhood tribulations on late 19th-/early 20th-century Prince Edward Island in a way that makes it a universal tale.

The life of the real Lucy Maud Montgomery has become thoroughly entwined with that of her fictional character Anne, and everything on the island relating to either the story or the author has now become part of the Anne of Green Gables industry.

At House of Green Gables, actually a rather attractive place, the overpopularization reaches its zenith, with busloads of visitors arriving at the door continuously. When you park you might have to deftly sidestep a golf ball whizzing by your head from the links – Green Gables Golf Course, natch – adjoining the site. Visiting first thing in the morning to avoid the crowds is highly recommended, and the home is definitely worth a visit.

There are farm demonstrations and period programs here throughout the summer, and an interpretive center has audiovisual displays. The quieter trails leading from the house through the gentle creek-crossed woods are worthwhile. 'Lover's Lane,' particularly, has maintained its idealistic childhood ambience.

Other Attractions Half a kilometer away, just past the United Church in Cavendish, you can visit the site of the **house** (☎ 902-963-2231, off Hwy 6; adult/child $2/1; open 10am-5pm daily June-early Oct, 9am-7pm July & Aug) where Montgomery lived with her grandparents and where she wrote Anne of Green Gables. The farmhouse no longer stands, just the stone foundations and surrounding gardens. From here you can walk the short path to the post office to get a Green Gables postmark.

Another Anne-related site is the **cemetery** at the corner of Hwys 6 and 13 in Cavendish, where Montgomery is buried.

There's also **Avonlea – Village of Anne of Green Gables** (☎ 902-963-3050, w www.avonlea.ca, on Hwy 6 next to the turnoff to Green Gables Golf Course; adult/child $8.50/6.50; open 9am-8:30pm daily mid-June-Aug), a theme park and model village depicting the times of Lucy Maud Montgomery and late 19th-century life on Prince Edward Island. Staff in period costume animate the scene.

Organized Tours All tour operators have an Anne-themed tour (they'd be nuts not to), including **Cavendish Tours** (☎ 902-963-2031), which has a three-hour tour ($35), conveniently scheduled to start following the arrival of the Beach Shuttle from Charlottetown. Another much longer tour ($60) starts in Charlottetown.

Places to Stay Marco Polo Land Campground (☎ 902-963-2352, 800-665-2352, fax 902-963-2384, w www.marcopololand.com, 1km south of the visitor center on Hwy 13) Unserviced/serviced sites are $24/28. Open June-early Oct. This campground near Cavendish has a range of amenities on its 100 acres, including two swimming pools. Sites numbered in the 300s and 400s are scattered in a shady forest, but most of the others are RV parking plots in an open field. They take reservations by phone. Several other large private campgrounds exist along Hwy 6 at Cavendish, though they're open for a shorter season and are less favorable for tenting.

Parkview Farm Tourist Home & Cottages (☎ *902-963-2027, 800-237-9890, fax 902-963-2935, W www.peionline.com/al/ parkview, 2km east of Cavendish on Hwy 6)* Singles/doubles/cottages $45/55/135-220. Tourist home open year-round, cottages mid-May-mid-Oct. The four B&B rooms are in a sizable farmhouse on a working dairy farm overlooking the ocean. They've also got seven two- or three-bedroom cottages across the road with kitchens, which rent for $60 outside July and August.

Places to Eat *Chez Yvonne Restaurant* (☎ *902-963-2070, 8947 Hwy 6)* Mains $8. Open 7:30am-9pm daily June-Sept. Right opposite the Cavendish Tourist Mart, Chez Yvonne has been serving upscale steak and seafood dinners to tourists since the 1970s. This place is well known for its homecooking, especially the bread and rolls baked on premises.

Galley Restaurant (☎ *902-963-2354, off Hwy 13)* Lunch $6-10, dinner $10-30. Open 8am-9pm daily June-mid-Sept. This spacious, well run operation at Marco Polo Land offers three huge meals per day at reasonable prices. Sunday features a $10 brunch. It's good for families, and the takeaway dairy bar inside the campground is also popular.

Cavendish Tourist Mart (☎ *902-963-2370, 8934 Hwy 6)* Open 8am-9pm daily mid-May-Sept. This grocery store 1½km west of Green Gables stocks all essential supplies. It also has a Laundromat ($1.25 to wash).

To the west of town, near the Cavendish Campground turnoff, *Cavendish Boardwalk* has some stores and a few places to eat, including pizza, chicken and sub outlets.

Getting Around The Cavendish Red Trolley runs from the Marco Polo Land Campground at the top of every hour from 10am to 6pm; it stops at Cavendish Country Inn, the Cavendish Visitor Centre, Cavendish Beach and Green Gables. For $3 you can use the ticket all day.

Scooters (☎ 902-963-2075), beside the Petro Canada gas station at the corner of Hwys 6 and 13 in Cavendish, rents mopeds

at $20/35/60/110 for 1/2/4/8 hours for a single or $25/45/75/125 for a double. A $100 deposit is required (minimum age 18). They also rent bicycles at $5/13/18 for 1/6/24 hours. The same outlet sells ice cream and snacks at bargain rates (for Cavendish). It's open June to early September.

NEW LONDON
New London is known as the birthplace of Lucy Maud Montgomery, author of *Anne of Green Gables*. The house where she was born in 1874 is now a **museum** (☎ *902-886-2099, cnr of Hwys 6 & 20; admission $2; open 9am-5pm daily late May-early Oct)* containing some personal belongings.

Blue Winds Tea Room (☎ *902-886-2860, 10746 Hwy 6)* Lunch under $10. Open 11am-6pm daily June-early Oct. Southwest of the Lucy Maud Montgomery birthplace in New London, this well-known cafe with a nice view is a good choice for lunch, with soup-and-salad combo ($7.25), quiche ($8.50), chicken dishes ($9.50) and desserts ($3.50). Afternoon tea is served any time at $4.50.

PARK CORNER
About 10km northwest of New London in the village of Park Corner is the **Lucy Maud Montgomery Heritage Museum** (☎ *902-886-2807, 4605 Hwy 20; admission $2.50; open 9am-5pm daily June-mid-Sept)* in the home of Lucy Maud's grandfather. The site has a list of Anne paraphernalia. Take a guided tour; they guarantee that your admission will be refunded if you're not absolutely fascinated. Two ancient linden trees stand in the yard.

At Silver Bush, 500m down the hill, is a house that was once owned by Montgomery's uncle when Lucy Maud was just a girl. This was one of her favorite places and she was married in the parlor in 1911. The home is called the **Anne of Green Gables Museum** (☎ *902-886-2884, 4542 Hwy 20; admission $2.75/6 adult/family; open 9am-5pm daily May-mid-Oct)* and it contains such items as Lucy Maud's writing desk and autographed first-edition books. There's a path leading down from the house to the famed Lake of Shining Waters.

Beds of Lavender B&B (☎ *902-886-3114,* Ⓦ *www.bbcanada.com/3367.html, 4606 Hwy 20)* Singles/doubles/triples $30/40-50/60 including breakfast. Open June-mid-Oct. This pleasant house, directly opposite the Lucy Maud Montgomery Heritage Museum, has a deck overlooking the Lake of Shining Waters. It's an ideal place for Anne aficionados to stay. Call ahead as the three rooms are often full.

MALPEQUE BAY

North of Summerside, this bay produces the world-famous oysters of the same name. About 10 million of them are harvested each year from the controlled 'farms' of the bay. Malpeque Harbour is full of lobster boats in May and June.

Cabot Beach Provincial Park (☎ *902-836-8945, fax 902-836-0431,* Ⓦ *www.gov.pe.ca/visitorsguide/explore/parks, off Hwy 20)* Sites $17/20. Open mid-June-mid-Sept. Cabot Beach, 4km north of Malpeque village, is one of the larger parks on the island. There's picnicking, a beach on Malpeque Bay, and plentiful campsites are found on a long grassy hill. Aerial pesticide spraying on nearby potato fields can be a downside when the wind is blowing the wrong way.

KENSINGTON

The lively little town of Kensington is an important stop on the Confederation Trail, and the old train station (1905) has been converted into a museum (admission free) and library.

In summer, ask about Sunday night concerts in magnificent **St Mary's Catholic Church** (1902) at Indian River. It's the largest wooden building on the island with a seating capacity of 600.

Bakin' Donuts (☎ *902-836-4524, 116 Victoria St West)* Breakfast $5. Open 6am-10:30pm daily. This place on Hwy 2 is famous for its steak-and-egg breakfasts, which are served all day.

Lady Slipper Scenic Drive

The western third of PEI is made up of Prince County. The county's northern section is pretty farm country, like so much of the province. The more southerly area along Egmont and Bedeque Bays retains some evidence of its Acadian French history. Lennox Island offers the best opportunity on PEI to learn something about the province's Mi'kmaq people.

The Lady Slipper Scenic Drive (named for the provincial flower) around Prince County is 288km long and is the marked tourist route around this portion of PEI.

A Yen for Anne

Although Prince Edward Island is generally little known internationally, up to 10,000 of the island's annual visitors are now from Japan. This makes it easily one of Canada's top destinations for the Japanese traveler. There are even direct Tokyo-Charlottetown flights.

The attraction is partly because Charlottetown has become the sister city of Ashibetsu, in northern Japan. Student exchanges have taken place, as well as a number of tourist-related activities.

The main draw, however, is the Japanese fascination with *Anne of Green Gables*. The book has been on Japanese school curricula since the 1950s, and Anne's story has found a spot in the national psyche, especially among women, who identify strongly with Anne's character.

Many Japanese also now come to PEI to get hitched. Weddings in Japan can be prohibitively expensive, and are often difficult. Young Japanese couples visit PEI to enjoy the quiet countryside, and quite a few are married here in Christian ceremonies. Many choose to be wed at Silver Bush in Park Corner, where Anne's author Lucy Maud Montgomery herself was married. Arrangements are handled by the local tourism ministry.

This is the least-visited part of the island, and for that reason, perhaps the most stimulating. Outside the camping season, budget accommodations are pretty scarce here.

SUMMERSIDE

The second largest city in the province, Summerside has a population of 15,000. At one time residents of the capital would move to this side of the island during the hot months.

The approach to 'S'side' along Hwy 1A is much like that to Ch'town, lined with motels and hamburger joints. But central Summerside is a quiet village with quaint old homes on streets trimmed with big trees. The main street, Water St, contains most of the commercial establishments. The Confederation Trail runs right through Summerside, crossing the street opposite the Ultramar gas station near the Jubilee Theatre on Harbour Dr.

The provincial tourist office (☎ 902-888-8364) is 4km east of Summerside on Hwy 1A. The office is open 9am to 4:30pm daily June to early October, 8am to 9pm July and August. Here you can pick up the walking-tour pamphlet of historic Summerside, which highlights some of the town's finer buildings.

Access PEI (☎ 902-888-8000), at 120 Harbour Dr, next to the Jubilee Theatre, provides free Internet access. It's open 8:30am to 4pm Monday to Friday. The Rotary Regional Library (☎ 902-436-7323), housed in the old Summerside train station at192 Water St, also provides free Internet access. It's open 10am to 9pm Tuesday, 10am to 5pm Wednesday to Saturday and 1pm to 5pm Sunday. It's best to go in early to reserve a time slot for later in the day. The Confederation Trail passes the back door of the library.

In early to mid-July each year there's the Lobster Festival, with contests, games, music

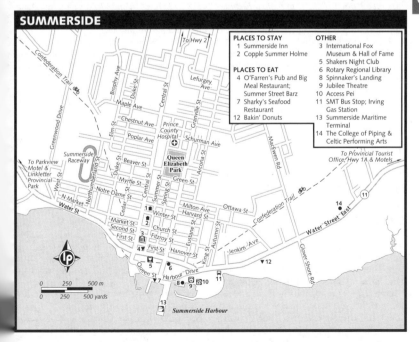

SUMMERSIDE

PLACES TO STAY
1 Summerside Inn
2 Copple Summer Holme

PLACES TO EAT
4 O'Farren's Pub and Big Meal Restaurant; Summer Street Barz
7 Sharky's Seafood Restaurant
12 Bakin' Donuts

OTHER
3 International Fox Museum & Hall of Fame
5 Shakers Night Club
6 Rotary Regional Library
8 Spinnaker's Landing
9 Jubilee Theatre
10 Access Pei
11 SMT Bus Stop; Irving Gas Station
13 Summerside Maritime Terminal
14 The College of Piping & Celtic Performing Arts

and nightly feasts. A hydroplane regatta is held at the end of the month.

Spinnaker's Landing

This boardwalk area along Summerside's waterfront includes the usual overpriced gift shops, a pub, and the **Lighthouse Lookout** (☎ 902-436-6692; admission free; open 9:30am-5:30pm daily mid-June-late Sept), which houses a tourist office on the first floor and observation platform at the top. From mid-May to late September **bicycles** are rented here at Fogarty's Cove Café (☎ 902-888-3918) for $16/24 per half/full day.

Spinnaker's Landing also contains a small outdoor stage area for free live music in summer.

International Fox Museum & Hall of Fame

The story of PEI fox farming is told at this museum (☎ 902-436-2400, 286 Fitzroy St; admission $2; open 10am-5pm daily mid-June-Aug) one block from Water St. In 1890, a Summerside resident successfully bred two wild silver foxes captured on the island – the first time wild fur-bearing animals had been bred in captivity. The principles employed are now used around the world. Through the 1920s, fortunes were made in Summerside through shipbuilding and fur farming. For a time, the latter was PEI's most important economic activity.

The museum is arranged in Holman Homestead, a beautiful historic house (1855) with a lovely garden. Holman himself was a fox breeder, and there are still fox farms on the island today.

The College of Piping & Celtic Performing Arts

The school (☎ 902-436-5377, 619 Water St E; admission free; open 11am-5pm Mon-Fri late June-Aug) provides visitors with free mini-concerts of bagpipes, singing and dancing, weekdays at 11:30am, 1:30pm and 3:30pm. There are exhibits in the main hall and a Celtic gift shop open year-round. A ticket for the special two-hour Scottish Ceilidh shows at 7pm Monday to Thursday

is $12 (shows are outdoors, so bring a sweater). Watch for the International Highland Gathering at the end of June at the college (day passes $10).

Sleeman Park

This industrial park off Hwy 2 on the north-west side of Summerside is a former air force base. There was gloom and doom over job losses when the military pulled out in 1991, but more people now live and work at Sleeman Park than were formerly employed at the base. The massive runways are largely unused, but a number of aerospace companies have branches here. There's also the Atlantic Police Academy and a huge Humpty Dumpty potato chip factory.

Places to Stay

Linkletter Provincial Park (☎ 902-888-8366, fax 902-432-2707, W www.gov.pe.ca/visitorsguide/explore/parks, 5.3km west of Summerside at the end of Linkletter Rd off Hwy 11) Sites from $17/20. Open mid-June-Sept. The 84 campsites are in an open grassy field on a ho-hum beach.

Copple Summer Holme (☎ 902-436-3100, fax 902-436-2055, e pjcopple@pei.sympatico.ca, W www.peitourism.com/copple, 92 Summer St) Singles/doubles $65/85 including breakfast. Open mid-May-Oct. Three guest rooms with bath are in an elegant antique-filled mansion built in 1880.

Summerside Inn (☎ 902-436-1417, 877-477-1417, fax 902-436-1730, W www.peisland.com/summersideinn, 98 Summer St) Doubles $75-85 June-Oct, $65-75 other months. Another huge mansion, directly across from Copple Summer Holme.

Clark's Sunny Isle Motel (☎ 902-436-5665, 877-682-6824, W www.sunnyislemotel.mainpage.net, 720 Water St E, 2½km east of the center) Rooms $46/56 for one/two beds. Open May-Oct. Summerside's motel strip starts here. The nicest rooms are at the back, facing a large garden and away from the road.

Cairn's Motel (☎ 902-436-5841, 877-224-7676, e W www.cairnsmotel.pe.ca, 721 Water St E) Doubles $46. Open May-Oct. Across the street from Sunny Isle and not quite as nice, the 12 rooms are in a long wooden block. This motel backs onto the Confederation Trail.

Baker's Lighthouse Motel (☎ 902-436-2992, 877-436-2992, 802 Water St E) Doubles $46-56 June-Sept, $36-49 Oct-May. A kilometer farther east, near the entrance to town, this motel is adequate but unexceptional. Some of the rooms are in a two-story block.

Parkview Motel (☎ 902-436-6146, e david.linkletter@pei.sympatico.ca, 161 Linkletter Rd) Doubles $42-80 July & Aug, $40-50 shoulder seasons. Open June-mid-Sept. This motel is 5km west of Summerside, just before Linkletter Provincial Park. There's a long block of nine rooms, four more rooms in a prefab block and four cottages across the road. Many of the rooms have cooking facilities.

Places to Eat

Bakin' Donuts (☎ 902-436-3201, 48 Water St E) Full breakfast $4, muffins 85¢. Open 4:30am-midnight daily. On the way into the city center from the east, this is the best place in town for breakfast. The muffins are huge and a good value, and two full breakfast specials are offered daily (served any time). Ask for the muffin of the day and pay only 60¢.

Sharky's Seafood Restaurant (☎ 902-436-8887, 240 Harbour Drive) Dishes $7-10. Open 11am-9pm daily mid-May-mid-Sept. This spot on the waterfront has fine views of the harbor and is recommended. It offers standard fare of mainly fried foods such as burgers, but there are also seafood dishes like fish & chips ($6 to $9), lobster rolls ($7), lobster burgers ($9), clam dinners ($9) and scallop dinners ($10). Fresh fish, mussels and lobster can also be purchased.

O'Farren's Pub and Big Meal Restaurant (☎ 902-888-2280, 12 Summer St) Meals $7-8. Open 7am-9pm daily. Part of the Summer Street Barz complex, O'Farren's offers popular favorites like nachos ($5 to $8), wraps ($6 to $8), burgers ($7) and fish & chips ($7).

Sobeys Supermarket (☎ 902-436-6675, 475 Granville St, between Hwy 2 and the center) Open 24 hours most of the week, but closed from midnight Saturday until 8am Monday.

Entertainment

Jubilee Theatre (☎ 800-708-6505, Harbour Dr) In July and August the Jubilee presents a dinner theater package from Tuesday to Saturday beginning at 5pm. The $50 fee includes a lobster or steak dinner with chowder, dessert and tea or coffee, plus a vaudeville-style musical program. It's guaranteed to please vacationers (shows vary from year to year).

Fogarty's Cove Café (☎ 902-888-3918, w www.summersidewaterfront.com, off Harbour Dr) Open 9:30am-5:30pm daily June-late Sept, 8am-10pm July & Aug, to 10:30pm Tues & Wed. This earthy cafe at Spinnaker's Landing presents local musicians, serves organic food and provides information on many nontouristy local events.

Tuesdays from 8pm their folk club (admission $2) is a great opportunity to hear local talent, and Wednesdays from 8pm you can join the drum circle for free. From 6pm to 8pm Friday to Sunday mid-June to early September, Spinnaker's Landing hosts free outdoor folk concerts.

Shakers Night Club (☎ 902-436-9828, 250 Water St) Open 11am-4pm Tues, 11am-2am Wed-Sat. This place is unmarked but look for the door on the corner that says 'Pro Hardware' or the sign over the entrance reading 'we know how to party.' The liveliest night here is Wednesday – ladies' night ($2.50 cover charge for men). They play a variety of music.

Summer Street Barz (☎ 902-436-7400, 12 Summer St) Open 11am-2am Mon-Sat. This is Summerside's top nightspot, with two dance floors. Bourbon Street, downstairs, pumps out high energy dance music for the 19 to 25 crowd. A slightly older clientele heads upstairs to Mustang, which plays country music and rock. Friday and Saturday are the big nights ($4 cover charge). From 8pm to 11pm Sundays there's an alcohol-free teen dance ($5 cover charge).

PRINCE EDWARD ISLAND

Spectator Sports

Summerside Raceway (☎ 902-436-7221, 477 *Notre Dame St)* Harness races are held here every Wednesday night at 7:30pm from June to mid-October. During the Lobster Festival (usually around the second or third week in July) there's racing nightly. Admission and parking are free.

Getting There & Away

The SMT bus stops at the Irving gas station (☎ 902-436-2420), 96 Water St, in the center of town. The fare to Charlottetown is $10, to Moncton $25, to Halifax $47. See Getting There & Away in the Charlottetown section for information on the Halifax van shuttles, which also pick up in Summerside upon request.

RÉGION ÉVANGÉLINE

Most of the descendants of the early French settlers on PEI live in this section of the province. Six thousand still speak French as a first language, and serious efforts are made to preserve Acadian culture, not for tourists but as a way of life. The red, white and blue flag with a single yellow star is a proud symbol of the Acadian people. (See the Southwestern Nova Scotia and New Brunswick chapters for more information on the Acadians.)

Miscouche

West of Summerside along Hwy 2, the **Acadian Museum** (☎ 902-432-2880; adult/ child $3.50/1.75; open 9:30am-5pm Mon-Fri, 1pm-4pm Sun, 9:30am-7pm daily July & Aug) in Miscouche has a collection of early Acadian memorabilia relating the engrossing history of the Acadians before and after their mass expulsion from Nova Scotia in 1755 by the British. An audiovisual exhibit provides more information, and it's worthwhile to learn something of this tragic story. It was at the Second Acadian Convention in Miscouche in 1884 that the Acadian flag and the 'Ave Maris Stella' anthem were adopted. Several monuments around the museum and the nearby Church of St John the Baptist recall these events.

Mont Carmel

From Miscouche the Lady Slipper Scenic Drive follows Hwy 11 southwest to the coast. The small French-speaking village of Mont Carmel is the site of the massive red brick **Église Notre-Dame du Mont Carmel** (1898).

Two kilometers west of the church on Hwy 11 is the **Pioneer Acadian Village** (☎ 902-854-2227, **W** *www.levillagedela-cadie.com; adult/child $2/1; open 9:30am-7pm daily June-mid-Sept),* which really is worth a look. This replica of an early-19th-century settlement has a school, store and church, among other things. There's a good beach across the road from the complex.

L'Étoile de Mer (☎ 902-854-2227; Hwy 11, 2km west of Mont Carmel) Plates $5-6. Open 8am-9pm Sun-Thurs, 8am-10pm Fri-Sat June-mid-Sept. A highlight of the Pioneer Acadian Village is the restaurant, which offers seven traditional Acadian dishes, such as *pâté acadien* (meat pie with chicken and pork), *râpure du chef* (chopped potatoes, pork and chicken, baked in an oven) and *chicken fricot* (stew). Arrive hungry.

TYNE VALLEY

The village of Tyne Valley is worth visiting for its several handicraft workshops, including a pottery studio.

Six kilometers north of Tyne Valley along Hwy 12 is Green Park Provincial Park, which includes a mediocre beach, a campground and the worthwhile **Green Park Shipbuilding Museum** (☎ 902-831-7947; admission $4; open 9am-5pm daily June-Sept). PEI's 19th-century shipbuilding industry consisted of nearly 200 small shipyards where 20-person teams built boats in six months or less. On the grounds there's an interpretive center, a recreated shipyard containing a partially constructed 200-ton brigantine (a two-masted square-rigged ship) and Yeo House, the renovated home of a wealthy 1860s shipowner.

Places to Stay & Eat

Green Park Provincial Park (☎ 902-831-7912, fax 902-831-7941, **e** *info@wavesonthe* *reen.com*, **W** *www.wavesonthegreen.com, ff Hwy 12)* Unserviced/serviced sites 17/23, cabins $35/225 a day/week. Open ate June-early Sept. The 58 campsites are in mixed forest. Inside the park beyond the camping area are 12 camping cabins with hared bath. Known as Waves on the Green, hese cabins are an excellent value.

Doctor's Inn *(☎ 902-831-3057,* **W** *www peisland.com/doctorsinn, 32 Allen Rd, Tyne alley)* Singles/doubles with shared bath 45/60 including breakfast. This is a fine country B&B whose superlative dining oom takes full advantage of its surrounding organic garden. The four-course dinner osts $50 per person including wine and is y reservation only. The inn also sells its omegrown vegetables and potatoes.

The Landing Oyster Bar *(☎ 902-831- '138, 1327 Port Hill Station Rd, Tyne Valley)* Open 11am-9pm daily, to 10pm Fri & Sat March-Dec. Meals $7-9. Between the general store and post office in the center of he village, the Landing serves seafood along with organic vegetables from the Doctors nn. Their specialty is 15 deep-fried oysters or $12. The bar stays open a couple of hours ater than the restaurant, and in July and August you can hear live Maritimes music at pm four nights a week (cover $3 to $5). In he off-season the music is only on Fridays. our local craft beers are on tap.

LENNOX ISLAND FIRST NATION

A band of about 50 Mi'kmaq families (350 or so people) live on Lennox Island in Malpeque Bay. The scenery is attractive, and the island is easily accessible by road from the west side of the bay near the village of East Bideford, north of Tyne Valley. The reserve is 7km down East Bideford Rd off Hwy 12, connected by a bridge.

The people earn a living from blueberry production and lobster fishing. There's a big powwow the last weekend in June. The main holiday here is St Ann's Day, the last Sunday in July.

Things to See

St Ann's Church, dating from 1898, can be visited. Just opposite is the **Lennox Island**

Mi'kmaq Cultural Centre *(☎ 866-831-2702; admission $3; open late June-Aug)* with exhibits on Malpeque Bay. Paintings and artifacts deal with the history of the first indigenous people in Canada to be converted to Christianity. Ask for the ecotourism walking map of the self-guiding trail.

Just down from the Cultural Center is a **craft shop** *(☎ 902-831-2653; open June-early Oct)* with a good array of items including ash-splint baskets made by the local people. Finally, there's a pottery workshop called **MicMac Productions** *(☎ 902-831-2277; open March-early Oct)* in the village.

Kayaking

Charlie Greg Sark's **Mi'kmaq Kayak Adventures** *(☎ 902-831-3131, 877-500-3131, fax 902-831-2390,* **W** *www.minegoo.com, 4 Eaglefeather Trail, Lennox Island)*, based at the craft shop, offers three-hour trips to a nearby island at 9am and 5pm ($50), sunset paddles ($50), and full-day trips to several islands ($95). A 24-hour trip (noon to noon) including camping on an island and two meals is $200. All this happens daily in July and August, or by appointment in May, June and September.

ALBERTON

The Confederation Trail branches into Alberton, leading to the old train station (1904). The tall yellow building visible from the station is the **Alberton Museum** *(☎ 902-853-4048, 457 Church St; adult/senior/family $3/2/7; open 10am-5:30pm Mon-Sat, 1pm-5pm Sun June-Sept)*, a former circuit courthouse erected in 1878.

Jacques Cartier Provincial Park *(☎ 902-853-8632,* **W** *www.gov.pe.ca/visitorsguide/ explore/parks, 16448 Hwy 12)* Sites $17/20. Open late June-early Sept. Just 6½km north of Alberton, this park has many nice sites along the beach or hidden in the bush. French explorer Jacques Cartier landed here in 1534.

TIGNISH TO NORTH CAPE

Tignish is a friendly, natural town, removed from the touristic hot spots of central PEI.

The towering **Church of St Simon and St Jude** (1859) has an impressive pipe organ built in Montréal and installed here in 1882. It employs 1118 pipes. The church itself is beautifully decorated in white and blue.

The **Confederation Trail** begins (or ends) on School St, two blocks south of the church. The **Tignish Cultural Centre** (☎ 902-882-1999, 305 School St; admission free; open 8am-4pm Mon-Fri), near the church, provides a good exhibition of old maps and photos, tourist information and a library with Internet access.

Elephant Rock

Near the village of Norway is Elephant Rock, a large eroded formation at the seashore. To find it, head 4km north of Tignish on Hwy 14, then turn right on Norway Rd (Hwy 182) and follow it 7km straight ahead via Christopher Cross and Norway to the seaside cliffs. The first 5km are paved, the rest dirt. If the way becomes too muddy or rough for your car, it's worthwhile continuing on foot.

Elephant Rock is a section of high coastal bluff that has become detached and now stands alone in the sea. The 20m red cliffs lining the shore are among the highest on PEI, and you can get down to the shore for another eerie view (but note the signs 'warning – dangerous cliffs'). The elephant's trunk was lost during a storm just before Christmas 1998, which also cut back the cliffs and washed away the parking lot. It's still a hauntingly beautiful, desolate place, and you feel you've really reached the end of PEI.

The windmills of North Cape are clearly visible from here, and a well marked trail winds north between the cliffs and Black Marsh. You could easily hike there and back in under an hour, but you can also drive around, taking a shortcut to the left on a dirt road. Check the Elephant Rock Web site (www.elephantrock.org) for more information.

North Cape

The lovely, windblown North Cape is a promontory with a lighthouse. The Atlantic Wind Test Site has been set up to study the efficacy of wind-powered generators. The **interpretive center** (☎ 902-882-2991, north end of Hwy 12; adult/senior or student $2/1, open 10am-6pm daily mid-May-early Oct, 9am-8pm July & Aug) provides information and features a small aquarium. Upstairs there's a rather pricey restaurant. North Cape's rock seabed can be explored at low tide. Look for sea life in the pools and watch for coastal birds and even seals. The cliffs here are barely half as high as those at Elephant Rock.

Boat Trips

For a bit of fun check out **Captain Mitch's Boat Tours** (☎ 902-882-2883, Hwy 12, Seacow Pond Harbour; adult/child $20/10, open July & Aug), leaving from Seacow Pond Harbour, 6½km south of North Cape.

Places to Stay

Gulf Side Park (☎ 902-882-3262, 20460 Hwy 12, Seacow Pond) Unserviced/serviced sites $14/18. Open May-mid-Oct. Here you pitch your tent in an open grassy field beside the road, 3½km south of Seacow Pond Harbour.

Murphy's Tourist Home & Cottages (☎ 902-882-2667, 325 Church St, Tignish) Cottages and rooms from $50 double. Open mid-May-early Oct. Almost adjacent to the massive red brick church in Tignish, Murphy's offers four B&B rooms in the main house at $50 single or double with continental breakfast, and five housekeeping cottages at $50 single or double with one bedroom, $60 with two bedrooms. Extra persons are $15 each. It's comfortable, welcoming and the best value west of Summerside.

Tignish Heritage Inn (☎ 877-882-2491, fax 902-882-2500, w www.tignish.com/inn, off Maple St, Tignish) Doubles from $65 ($55 at beginning and end of season). Open mid-May-mid-Oct. The four-story brick convent (1868) behind the church is now a 17-room inn. All rooms have private bath and breakfast is included.

Keefe's Farm Tourist Home (☎ 902-882-2686, 13823 Hwy 14, Skinners Pond,

eweed in Prince Edward Island National Park

n old wagon in a field along the Kings Byway, Prince Edward Island

Acadian mural in the Pioneer Acadian Village, Mont Carmel

Lobster traps and fishing boats, Prince Edward Island

Singles/doubles $30/35. The two rooms are in a farmhouse located a kilometer south of the turnoff to the fishing harbor at Skinners Pond. There's a good long beach backed by high dunes near the harbor just 1½km from Keefe's Farm. The home is open all year but visitors are advised to call at least a day or two ahead.

Places to Eat

Co-op Lunch Bar (☎ 902-882-2020, cnr of Church and Central Sts) Breakfast $3, lunch $4-5. Open 8:30am-6pm Mon-Sat (until 8pm Thurs & Fri). This lunch bar in the Tignish Co-op behind the Irving gas station in town is definitely your best bet for breakfast or lunch, with sandwiches ($2 to $3), hamburger deluxe ($4) and fish & chips ($5). It's always crowded with locals.

Royal Canadian Legion (☎ 902-882-2011, 221 Phillip St) Mains $7-11. From mid-June to September the Royal Canadian Legion at Tignish serves a full lunch from 11am to 3pm. The meals are dished out upstairs and the bar is in the basement. You're bound to find conversation here.

Cousins Diner & Restaurant (☎ 902-882-5670, 276 Phillip St) Mains $7-13. Open 7am-10pm daily (until 11pm in summer). Cousins is 1½km south of the center of town on Hwy 2. The diner side of this establishment opens at 7am daily for breakfast ($3 to $5), burgers ($6 to $7) and club sandwiches ($7). At 11am the restaurant side (where you can order alcohol) begins serving things like clam dinner ($7), nachos ($8), fish & chips ($9) and sautéed scallops ($13). The restaurant closes at 10pm, the diner at 11pm. Gunner's Pub at Cousins is a good evening venue.

THE WEST COAST

About midway down the coast on the western shore along Hwy 14 is the village of Miminegash, in one of the more remote sections of the province. The **Irish Moss Interpretative Centre** *(☎ 902-882-4313, Hwy 14; admission $1; open 10am-7pm Mon-Sat, noon-8pm Sun early June-late Sept)* was begun by local women whose families have long been involved in the collecting or harvesting of Irish moss, a type of seaweed. Almost half the world's supply comes from PEI. If you're dying to savor seaweed, the *Seaweed Pie Cafe* at the interpretative center has a standard lunch menu but also serves (you guessed it) seaweed pie for $3.25 a slice. The moss is in the middle layer of cream.

Cedar Dunes Provincial Park (☎ 902-859-8785, fax 902-859-3900, Ⓦ www.gov.pe.ca/visitorsguide/explore/parks, off Hwy 14, West Point) Unserviced/serviced sites $17/20. Open late June-mid-Sept. There's tent space in an open grassy field adjacent to West Point Lighthouse. The beach is nice.

West Point Lighthouse (☎ 800-764-6854, fax 902-859-1510, Ⓔ wplight@isn.net, Ⓦ www.peisland.com/westpoint/light.htm, off Hwy 14, West Point) Doubles $80-95 July & Aug, $70-85 June & Sept. Open late June-Sept. The lighthouse, dating from 1875, has been restored, and part of the former lightkeeper's quarters has been converted into a nine-room inn. The restaurant is famous for its clam chowder ($5/7 cup/bowl).

New Brunswick

Facts about New Brunswick

At 73,400 sq km, New Brunswick is the largest province in the Maritimes. It's quite different than bucolic Prince Edward Island or Nova Scotia with its rugged coasts. The province remains largely forested, yet few travelers visit New Brunswick's vast woodlands.

From the Québec border, the gentle, pastoral farming region of the Saint John River Valley leads to the Bay of Fundy, with its cliffs, coves and tidal flats left by the world's highest tides. The eastern shore offers warm, sandy beaches and strongholds of Acadian culture. The wooded highlands of the north contain one of the highest mountains in eastern Canada.

Saint John, the largest city, and Fredericton, the capital, both have intriguing Loyalist histories. Moncton has the largest French-speaking population of any Canadian city east of Québec.

History

What is now New Brunswick was originally the land of the Mi'kmaqs and, in the western and southern areas, the Maliseet First Nation.

The French first attempted settlement in the 1600s. The Acadians, as they came to be known, farmed the area around the Bay of Fundy using a system of dikes. In 1755, they were expelled by the English, whose numbers rose by some 14,000 with the arrival of the Loyalists after the American Revolution.

The Loyalists settled the Saint John and St Croix river valleys and established Saint John. Through the 1800s, lumbering and shipbuilding boomed, and by the start of the 20th century, other industries, including fishing, had developed. That era of prosperity was ended by the Depression of the 1930s.

Highlights

Entered Confederation: July 1, 1867
Area: 73,400 sq km
Population: 756,600
Provincial Capital: Fredericton

- Explore the Saint John River, which meanders through its province-long valley
- Visit Grand Manan, a rugged island offering hiking and whale watching
- Enjoy gracious St Andrews, one of Canada's most alluring towns
- Take a trip back in time at the Acadian Historic Village near Caraquet

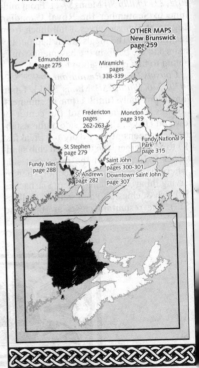

OTHER MAPS
New Brunswick page:259

Edmundston page 275
Miramichi pages 338-339
Fredericton pages 262-263
Moncton page 319
St Stephen page 279
Fundy National Park page 315
Fundy Isles page 288
Saint John pages 300-301
St Andrews page 282
Downtown Saint John page 307

258

It is only since the 1970s that New Brunswick has improved its infrastructure and further diversified its economy. Low costs combined with relatively inexpensive and bilingual labor have resulted in winning back some jobs from the rest of Canada.

Climate

Summers are usually not blisteringly hot and winters are very snowy and cold. The driest month of the year is August. Generally, there is more rain in the south.

Economy

Lumber and pulp and paper operations are two of the main industries. Manufacturing and mining are also important, as are mixed farming and fishing.

Population & People

Though a majority of the population of 756,600 has British roots, you may be surprised at how much French you hear spoken. Around 37% of the population have French ancestors, and 16% speak French only.

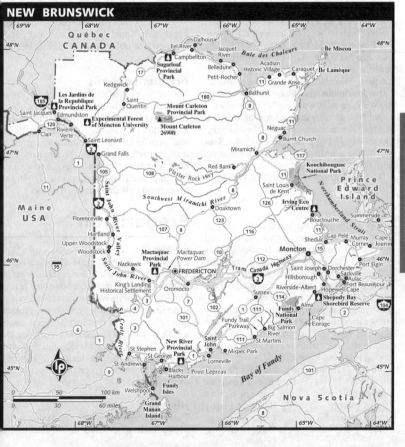

NEW BRUNSWICK

During the 1960s the Liberal provincial government of Louis Robichaud improved the prospects of New Brunswick's Acadian population by implementing an 'equal opportunity' program standardizing health and education services across the province. Previously, many public services had been supported by local taxes, which worked to the disadvantage of lower-income French-speaking areas. The establishment of the francophone Université de Moncton in 1963 was a milestone, and in 1969 New Brunswick became Canada's only officially bilingual province.

Information

Tourism New Brunswick's (☎ 800-561-0123) mailing address is New Brunswick Tourism, PO Box 40, Woodstock, NB E3N 3G1. The province has six primary visitor information centers at strategic entry points: Saint Jacques, Woodstock, St Stephen, Aulac, Cape Jourimain and Campbellton. Check the Web site at Ⓦ www.gov.nb.ca/tourism.

All New Brunswick visitor centers at the borders are open from mid-May to mid-October only. From mid-June to early Sept they're open until 9pm daily, other months until 6pm.

The Harmonized Sales Tax (HST) is 15%.

Activities

A copy of the province's *Adventures Left & Right* or *Craft Directory* may be helpful and lists useful contacts. New Brunswick has good bird and whale watching, particularly in the southern regions. In summer, booking up to a week in advance for whale tours may be necessary in some areas.

Kayaking is a popular activity in many areas, especially along the Bay of Fundy and between Bouctouche and Kouchibouguac National Park. Both kayak rentals and guided tours are available.

Fundy National Park and Mount Carleton Provincial Park have numerous hiking trails, as does the eastern Bay of Fundy region – notably the new Fundy Trail. The tourist office can help arrange canoeing trips and give advice on fishing,

especially in the province's renowned salmon rivers.

New Brunswick is a good area for cycling. The 2400km New Brunswick Trail is being built as this book goes to press; the labor is all volunteer and progress has been gradual. The section along the Saint John River from Grand Falls to Woodstock is now complete, and this portion should soon be linked to Fredericton. A respectable section of the NB Trail has been completed around Caraquet. From Edmundston you can peddle north into Québec on the Trans Canada Trail. For more information, check out the New Brunswick Trail Web site at Ⓦ www.nbtrail.com.

The two other prime cycling venues are Fundy and Kouchibouguac national parks. Helmets are obligatory for cyclists in New Brunswick.

Accommodations

The province offers a complete range of accommodations, and Tourism New Brunswick's provincial tourist offices can help with reservations. Aside from national and provincial campgrounds and motels there's a selection of B&Bs, country inns, farm vacations, sports lodges and cabins. Lodgings are required to post a sign in the room listing officially approved prices.

Fredericton

Fredericton is the queen of New Brunswick's towns. It's one of the few major cities in the Maritimes not reached by tidal waters (the city is 16m above sea level). Unlike most of its counterparts Fredericton is nonindustrial. It's a very pretty, genteel, quiet place. As the province's capital, about a fifth of its 47,000 residents work for the government. The small, tree-lined central area has some visible history to explore. Abundant benches grace the streets of this welcoming city.

History

Three hundred years ago, the Maliseet and Mi'kmaq Indians lived and fished in the area. The French followed in 1732 but were eventually burned out by the British, who brought in 2000 Loyalists fleeing the US after the American Revolution. Fredericton really came into its own the following year when the British Government decided to form a new province by splitting New Brunswick apart from Nova Scotia. Lieutenant governor Thomas Carleton visited what was then called Ste Anne's Point and was impressed with the strategic location, near the center of the province on the Saint John River, suitable for receiving large ships. In 1785, he made Fredericton the provincial capital and the base for a British garrison, renaming it 'Frederick'stown,' in honor of Sir Frederick, duke of York and the second son of King George III.

The town produced Canada's first English-speaking poet, Loyalist Jonathan Odell (1737–1818). Later, William Maxwell Aitken, Lord Beaverbrook (1879–1964), who was to rise to international prominence as a newspaper publisher, was born here.

Orientation

The city center is on a small, rounded peninsula that juts into the Saint John River. The Westmorland St Bridge connects the downtown area with the north shore residential areas. The St Mary's First Nation (Maliseet) owns a long strip of residential land in North Fredericton.

Farther east, Hwy 8 crosses the river on the Princess Margaret Bridge. Coming into town from the west on the Trans Canada Hwy, take Regent St straight down to the heart of town.

King St and parallel Queen St are the main streets, just a block from the river. The park on the corner of Queen and Regent Sts, called Officers' Square, is pretty much the center of the small downtown area.

Information

Tourist Offices The visitors center (☎ 506-460-2129) is in city hall at 397 Queen St. It's open 8am to 4:15pm Monday to Friday year-round and until 8pm during summer.

If you're driving in, the visitors center should be your first stop, as they'll give you a pass to park free at some municipal parking lots (including the one behind City Hall) and all parking meters. It's the sort of friendly gesture you remember.

The Conservation Council of New Brunswick (☎ 506-458-8747), 180 Saint John St, has information on environment-related

The Loyalists

The issue of American independence from Britain divided the American colonies into two camps: the Patriots and the Loyalists. During the American Revolution of 1775 to 1783, the Loyalists maintained their allegiance to the British Crown. About one-third of the 13 colonies' population remained loyal to Britain. Severe laws were passed against them, forcing some 200,000 to leave during and after the revolution. Of those, between 50,000 and 60,000 fled to Canada, settling in the Maritimes, the Eastern Townships of Lower Canada (Québec) and the St Lawrence–Lake Ontario region of Upper Canada (Ontario).

Not all Loyalists were of British descent. They represented a mix of ethnic backgrounds, including English, Germans, French and former African slaves. Regardless, their arrival in Canada strengthened Great Britain's hold on this part of its empire. In Nova Scotia, for example, the migration meant that the French no longer made up a majority of the population.

The Loyalists' arrival essentially resulted in the formation of the province of New Brunswick. Both the British and local governments offered clothing, rations, aid and land grants, though their promises weren't always kept. More than a few Loyalists found only disappointment in Canada, but the lucky or well-connected among them became prosperous and powerful. Today their descendants make up a significant segment of the region's population. Loyalist sites can be seen in Fredericton and Saint John, New Brunswick (particularly the latter), and Shelburne, Nova Scotia.

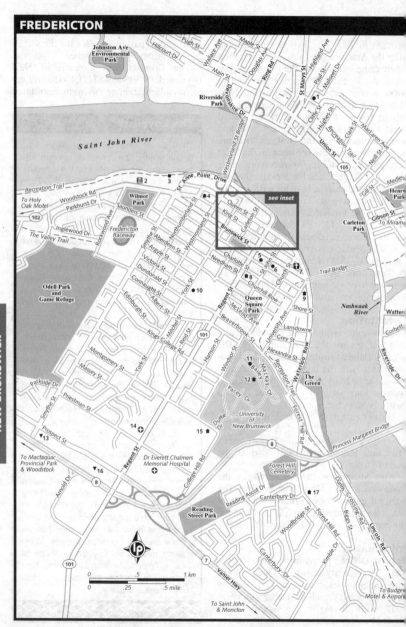

FREDERICTON

Johnston Ave
Environmental
Park

Hillcourt Dr

Pugh St

Maple St

Wallace Ave

Douglas Ave

Main St

Ring Rd

St Marys St

Highland Ave

Paul St

Maliseet Dr

Riverside Park

Westmoreland St Bridge

Devonshire Dr

Cliffe St

Hughes St

Recreation Trail

Clark St

MacLaren Ave

Union St

Neill St

Saint John River

Recreation Trail

To Holy
Oak Motel

Woodstock Rd

Parkhurst Dr

Saunders St

St Anne Point Drive

Wilmot
Park

🏛 2

3

● 4

Queen St

King St

Carleton St

see inset

105

Gill St

Medley

Henry
Park

Carleton
Park

Gibson St

To Miram

102

Inglewood Dr

Rockwood Ave

The Valley Trail

Smythe St

Aberdeen St

Northumberland St

Westmoreland St

Brunswick St

Fredericton
Raceway

Argyle St

Victoria St

Dundonald St

Connaught St

York St

Charlotte St

Needham St

Regent St

● 10

5

● 8

John St

● 6

Churchill Row

Church St

🏒 7

9

Trail Bridge

*Nashwaak
River*

Watter

Corbett

Odell Park
and
Game Refuge

Edinburgh St

Albert St

Mitchell St

Reid St

Kings College Rd

Queen
Square
Park

Beaverbrook St

McLeod Ave

University Ave

Lansdowne

Grey St

Alexandra St

Shore St

Waterloo Row

Riverside Dr

Montgomery St

York St

Hanson St

Windsor St

11
🛏 Bailey

12 ●

MacKay St

Recreation Trail

**The
Green**

Massey St

Parkside Dr

Smythe St

Priestman St

Prospect St

▼ 13

Pacey Dr

Duffie Dr

University
of
New Brunswick

Forest Hill Rd

8

Princess Margaret Bridge

14 ✛

15 ■

Dunns Crossing Rd

To Mactaquac
Provincial Park
& Woodstock

8

Arnold Dr

Regent St

Dr Everett Chalmers
Memorial Hospital
✛

College Hill Rd

**Forest Hill
Cemetery**

▼ 16

Reading
Street Park

Reading Ascot Dr

Canterbury Dr

Woodbridge St

■ 17

Forest Hill Rd

Biggs St

Lincoln Rd

Canterbury Dr

Kimble Dr

101

LP

0   .5   1 km
0   .25   .5 mile

7

Vanier Hwy

To Saint John
& Moncton

To Budget
Motel & Airport

NEW BRUNSWICK

issues. More information is available on their Web site at W www.web.net/~ccnb.

Post The main post office (☎ 506-444-8602) is at 570 Queen St. General delivery mail addressed to Fredericton, NB E3B 4Y1, is kept here. The office is open 8am to 5pm Monday to Friday.

Internet Access The Fredericton Public Library (☎ 506-460-2800), 4 Carleton St, offers free Internet access upstairs on a first-come, first-served basis. The library is open 10am to 5pm Monday, Tuesday, Thursday and Saturday, 10am to 9pm Wednesday and Friday

Bookstores Westminister Books (☎ 506-454-1442), 445 King St, has a good Atlantic life section with books on the Maritimes.

Goose Lane Editions (☎ 506-450-4251,), 469 King St, is one of the best-known specialty publishers in Atlantic Canada. They publish many excellent books about the Maritimes, including a bicycling guide. Ask the receptionist for a free catalog. And check their Web site at W www.gooselane .com for more information.

Laundry Paragon Laundromat (☎ 506-458-5852), 256 Regent St at Charlotte, charges $1.25 to wash. It's open 9am to 9pm Monday to Friday, 9am to 6pm Saturday and Sunday.

Medical Services If you need to see a doctor, there's an after-hours clinic at 1015 Regent St beside Shoppers Drug Mart. The telephone number is confidential, but no appointment is required. Canadians/foreigners without health insurance are charged $25/35. The clinic is open 6pm to 10pm Monday to Friday, 1pm to 5pm Saturday and Sunday.

Advice on birth control, sexually transmitted diseases and women's health is available at Planned Parenthood (☎ 506-454-6333), off King St next to Dimitri's Restaurant in Piper's Lane. The office is open 8:30am to 12:30pm and 2pm to 4pm Monday to Thursday.

PLACES TO STAY
4 Kilburn House
8 Fredericton International Hostel; Paragon Laundromat
9 Carriage House Inn
12 University of New Brunswick Residence Administration
15 McLeod House
17 Skyline Motel
43 Lord Beaverbrook Hotel

PLACES TO EAT
13 Ponderosa Steak House
16 Sobeys Supermarket; Fredericton Mall
22 Dimitri's Souvlaki; Dolan's Pub; Planned Parenthood
23 Piper's Lane; The G-Club; Upper Deck Sports Bar
28 Cravings Café
37 Molly's Coffee House
39 Mexicali Rosa's
41 M&T Deli
42 Regency Rose Café
46 Mei's Chinese Restaurant

OTHER
1 St Mary's First Nation
2 Old Government House
3 Small Craft Aquatic Center
5 Boyce Farmers' Market
6 Conservation Council of New Brunswick
7 Christ Church Cathedral
10 CAA Maritimes
11 Sir Howard Douglas Hall; Brydone Observatory
14 After-Hours Clinic; Shoppers Drug Mart
18 Sweetwaters Club
19 Radical Edge
20 Visitors Center; City Hall
21 Justice Building Annex; School Days Museum; Gallery Connexion
24 Justice Building
25 College of Craft & Design
26 Guard House
27 Fredericton Public Library
29 Bugaboo Creek Pub
30 Soldiers' Barracks
31 New Brunswick Sports Hall of Fame
32 York-Sunbury Historical Museum
33 Westminister Books; Goose Lane Editions
34 Officers' Square
35 Fredericton Lighthouse; Regent St Wharf
36 King's Place Mall
38 Post Office
40 Aitkens Pewter; Avis Rent-a-Car; Fine Craft Center
44 Beaverbrook Art Gallery
45 Discount Car Rentals
47 Lunar Rogue Pub
48 Playhouse Theatre
49 New Brunswick Legislative Assembly Building
50 SMT Bus Station

Officers' Square

This is the city's central park – on Queen St between Carleton and Regent Sts. The square was once the military parade ground and still sits among military buildings. At 11am and 7pm Monday to Friday from mid-July to the third week in August, you can see the full-uniform changing of the guard here.

Also in the park during summer is the Fredericton Outdoor Summer Theatre, which performs daily at 12:15pm weekdays and 2pm weekends. This free theater-in-the-square is performed by a local group known as the Calithumpians, whose skits of history are laced with a good dose of humor.

At 7:30pm on Tuesday and Thursday evenings in summer, free band concerts attract crowds. There might be a marching, military or pipe band, and sometimes classical music is performed. There is a statue of Lord Beaverbrook – the press baron and the province's most illustrious son – in the park.

York-Sunbury Historical Museum

This museum (☎ 506-455-6041, west side of Officers' Square; adult/student/family $2/1/4; open 1pm-4pm Tues-Sat Apr-mid-Dec, 10am-5pm mid-June-Aug) is in the old officers' quarters built between 1839 and 1851, an edifice typical of those designed by the Royal Engineers during the colonial period. The older section, closest to the water, has thicker walls of masonry and hand-hewn timbers. The other, newer, end is made of sawed timber.

The museum has a collection of items from the city's past spread out in 12 rooms: military pieces used by local regiments and by British and German armies from the Boer War and both world wars; furniture from a Loyalist sitting room and a Victorian bedroom; Native Indian and Acadian artifacts and archaeological finds. The prize exhibit is a stuffed 19kg frog, the pet of a local innkeeper.

New Brunswick Sports Hall of Fame

This building (☎ 506-453-3747, 503 Queen St, cnr Carleton St; admission free; open 10am-6pm daily early June-Aug, noon-4pm Mon-Fri rest of year) dates from 1881 and has been used as a post office, customs house and library. It now houses the New Brunswick Sports Hall of Fame, which focuses on the achievements of local athletes, ranging from NHL hockey players to jockey great Ron Turcotte.

Soldiers' Barracks

The barracks in the Military Compound on the corner of Carleton and Queen Sts gives you an idea of how the common soldier lived in the 1820s. The Guard House (no phone, 15 Carleton St; admission free; open July & Aug), dating from 1828, contains military memorabilia, and a well-written, interesting history of the guard house is available.

Justice Building Annex

Directly behind the Justice Building, 427 Queen St, is the School Days Museum (☎ 506-459-3738, east entrance, Justice Building Annex; admission free; open 10am-noon & 1pm-4pm Mon-Fri, 1pm-4pm Sat June-Aug), on the 1st floor of the annex. The New Brunswick Society of Retired Teachers began this classroom museum, featuring desks, textbooks and teaching aids from as far back as the early 19th century.

On the side of the annex facing the river is Gallery Connexion (☎ 506-454-1433, 356 Queen St, rear entrance; admission free; open noon-4pm Tues-Fri, until 7pm Thurs, 2pm-4pm Sun July & Aug), a nonprofit artist-run center showing contemporary and experimental art. A schedule posted on their door lists events such as poetry readings, guest speakers, video showings, receptions and dramatic performances.

Beaverbrook Art Gallery

One of Lord Beaverbrook's gifts to the town is this gallery (☎ 506-458-0970, 703 Queen St; adult/family $5/10; open Mon-Fri 9am-6pm, Sat & Sun 10am-5pm June-Sept, 9am-5pm Tues-Fri, 10am-5pm Sat, noon-5pm Sun Oct-May), opposite the Legislative Assembly Building. It houses a collection of British paintings, including works by Gainsborough, Turner and Constable. There's also a Dali and various Canadian and provincial works.

Legislative Assembly Building
Built in 1880, this government building *(☎ 506-453-2527, 706 Queen St; admission free; open 9am-7pm Mon-Fri, 10am-5pm Sat & Sun June-Aug, 9am-5pm Mon-Fri Sept-May)* is on Queen St, near Saint John St east of Officers' Square. When the legislative assembly is not in session, guides will show you around, pointing out things of particular merit like the wooden Speaker's Chair and the spiral staircase. Free tours commence every half hour. When the assembly is in session, visitors are welcome to observe the proceedings from the public gallery. Sessions run from the end of November until Christmas and from March to June, with sittings from 1pm to 6pm Tuesday and Thursday and 10am to 6pm Wednesday and Friday.

Christ Church Cathedral
Built in 1853, this is a fine early example of the 19th century revival of decorated Gothic architecture. The cathedral is interesting because it's very compact – tall for the short length of the building – yet with a balance and proportion that make the interior seem both normal and spacious.

There is some good stained glass, especially around the altar, where the walls are painted above the choir. Free tours are offered daily mid-June to Labor Day. The church is just off Queen St at Church St, by the river east of town.

Boyce Farmers Market
The farmers market *(☎ 506-451-1815, 665 George St between Regent & Saint John Sts; open 6am-1pm Sat year-round)* has nearly 150 stalls selling fresh fruit, vegetables, meat and cheese, and also handicrafts, homemade desserts and flowers. There is a restaurant, too, open for breakfast and brunch.

University of New Brunswick
The three-story **Sir Howard Douglas Hall** *(☎ 506-453-4666, 3 Bailey Dr)* on the hill in front of you as you enter from Beaverbrook St is the oldest university building still in use in Canada (1829). This institution dates back to 1785, when it was founded as Kings College; in 1857 it became the University of New Brunswick. Adjacent is the **Brydone Observatory** (1851), the first astronomical observatory in Canada.

Old Burial Ground
An easy walk from downtown, the **Loyalist cemetery** *(Brunswick St, cnr Carleton St; open 8am-9pm daily)*, dates from 1784. This area was settled by Loyalists who arrived from the 13 colonies of the US after the American Revolution, and many of them were eventually buried here. It's interesting to browse around the grounds.

Fredericton's Famous Frog

Move over, Lord Beaverbrook. Without question, Fredericton's most beloved character is not the legendary publisher but a 19kg frog. The famous frog made its first appearance in 1885, when it literally leaped into the small boat of local innkeeper Fred Coleman while he was rowing on Killarney Lake.

At the time the frog weighed a mere 3.6kg, but Coleman kept it at the inn by feeding it a steady (very steady) diet of buttermilk, cornmeal, whiskey and june bugs. Little wonder it became the world's largest frog. With the leisurely life of a gourmand, this was one frog that definitely didn't want to return to being a prince.

Today the Coleman frog is forever enshrined in a glass case at the York-Sunbury Museum. In the gift shop, Coleman frog T-shirts are the best-selling items.

NEW BRUNSWICK

Old Government House

This magnificent stone palace *(☎ 506-453-6440, ☎ 506-453-2505, 51 Woodstock Rd; admission free; open 10am-5pm daily mid-June-mid-Sept, 10am-4pm Mon-Fri other months)* was erected for the British governor in 1826. The representative of the queen moved out in 1893 after the province refused to continue paying his expenses, and during most of the 20th century the complex served as a Royal Canadian Mounted Police (RCMP) headquarters. In 2000, it was converted into a tourist attraction of the first order, and from mid-June to mid-September guided tours are led by staff in period costume (other months it's best to call ahead for tours). New Brunswick's lieutenant governor lives on the 3rd floor, and the official black limousine is often parked on the west side of the building.

Odell Park

In addition to the riverfront park and several smaller city parks, you can visit Odell Park, southwest of the downtown center off Waggoners Lane. It covers 175 hectares and contains an arboretum with examples of all of the province's tree species. There are picnic tables, a petting zoo and 9km of walking paths.

Activities

If you'd care to drift along the river, the **Small Craft Aquatic Center** *(☎ 506-460-2260, off Woodstock Rd; open mid-May-early Oct)*, near Old Government House on the Saint John River behind the Victoria Health Centre, rents canoes, kayaks and rowboats at $9 an hour. A much better deal is to pay $30 for a weekly pass that allows you to paddle up and down the river as much as you like for the entire week. The catch is, they only loan their equipment for two hours at a time, but you can report back and begin another two hours right away. The center also offers guided canoe tours from one hour to three-day river ecology trips and instruction in either canoeing or kayaking. Two-hour paddles depart upon request at $25 for the first person, $20 for the second and $15 for those under 18. They'll even go if you're

alone, but call ahead to make sure a guide will be available.

Organized Tours

Head to the information office to pick up the excellent *Tourrific Tours* brochure from the city. There are literally dozens of tours available, free or otherwise.

Throughout July and August, a member of the Calithumpian actors' group wearing a historic costume leads a good free hourlong walking tour around town, beginning at City Hall (10am & 6pm Mon-Fri, 10am Sat & Sun). The tourist office in City Hall will be able to let you know where and how to join the group. The **Haunted Hikes** ($12), given by the same, suddenly ghoulish, thespians are ultra-popular. These start at 9pm Monday, Tuesday, Thursday and Friday.

To see Fredericton from the water, the *Carleton(☎ 506-454-2628, Regent St Wharf)*, basically a houseboat, offers riverfront cruises (1-hour tour $7/3 adult/child) on the Saint John River. Tours depart in the afternoon and evening daily in July and August, 2pm and 7pm Saturday and Sunday June and September.

Special Events

Some of the major events and festivals celebrated in the city between July and September are listed here.

New Brunswick Highland Games and Scottish Festival

This two-day Scottish festival (☎ 888-368-444), featuring music, dancing and contests on the Old Government House grounds, is held in late July. Web site: **w** www.nbhighlandgames.com

New Brunswick Summer Music Festival

Four days of classical music are presented at Memorial Hall at the University of New Brunswick campus in late August. Web site: **w** www.unb.ca/FineArts/Music/festival .html

Handicraft Show

This juried craft show (☎ 506-450-8989) is held in Officers' Square on the first weekend in September. All types of handicrafts are available.

The Fredericton Exhibition

This annual six-day affair (☎ 506-458-9819) starts on the first weekend in September. It's held at the exhibition grounds on the corner of Smythe and Saunders Sts. The exhibition includes a farm show, a carnival, harness racing and stage shows.

Harvest Jazz & Blues Festival
This weeklong event transforms the downtown area into the 'New Orleans of the North' in early September when jazz, blues and Dixieland performers arrive from across North America. Web site: W www.harvestjazzblues.nb.ca

Places to Stay

The closest camping to Fredericton is in Mactaquac Provincial Park. See the Mactaquac Provincial Park heading in the Saint John River Valley section.

Hostels *Fredericton International Hostel at Rosary Hall (☎ 506-450-4417, fax 506-462-9692, 621 Churchill Row)* Rooms $20/22 members/nonmembers. Office open 7am-noon & 6pm-10pm daily. This HI-affiliated hostel is set up in a capacious older residence hall oozing with character. In summer it's fully a hostel, but even in other seasons, when students return, the management keeps rooms open for hostellers. Travelers are often pleasantly shocked to find themselves staying in a private room. A common kitchen and laundry facilities are available, and free parking is provided.

University of New Brunswick (☎ 506-453-4800, fax 506-453-3585, W www.unb.ca/housing/housing.html, 20 Bailey Dr) Singles/doubles $30/44 tourists, $19/31 students. Only students are eligible for the weekly rate of $84. From June to mid-August the university has 120 rooms available, most with shared bath (the 22 rooms with private bath are usually full). The rooms are in **McLeod House**, 81 Montgomery St, but to check in you must first go to the Residence Administration, 20 Bailey Dr, a kilometer away in the lower campus (or 1.2km southeast of the hostel). This office is open daily 8am to 11pm. Common kitchens are on the 5th and 6th floors of the residence, and there's a pool. The campus is southeast of the downtown area, within walking distance.

Tourist Homes *Kilburn House (☎ 506-455-7078, fax 506-455-8192, e kilburnb&b@*

mail.com, W www.bbcanada.com/2282.html, 80 Northumberland St) Singles/doubles from $55/70. This three-story red frame house on the west edge of downtown has three rooms.

Carriage House Inn (☎ 800-267-6068, fax 506-458-0799, e chinn@nbnet.nb.ca, W www.bbcanada.com/4658.html, 230 University Ave) Rooms $75-95. Erected in 1875, this three-story house is central but more expensive. A hot breakfast is served in the solarium of this imposing mansion.

Motels & Hotels *Skyline Motel (☎ 506-455-6683, 502 Forest Hill Rd)* Singles/doubles $46/49 ($55 with two beds), $175 a week single. This motel on the east side of town operates as a student residence from September to April. From May to August the 27 units are available to tourists.

Budget Motel (☎ 800-613-7666, fax 506-458-8784, e method@nbnet.nb.ca, 1214 Lincoln Rd) Singles/doubles $45/49 ($55 with two beds) year-round, $150/170 weekly rates available Sept-May. The 29 rooms are in a long wooden motel block facing Hwy 102, 8km west of the airport and 6km east of town.

Norfolk Motel (☎ 800-686-8555, 815 Riverside Dr) Singles/doubles $42/48 June-mid-Sept, $40/46 other months. A kilometer east of Princess Margaret Bridge in North Fredericton, the Norfolk has 20 rooms back-to-back in a long wooden block (ask for one of the quieter units on the back side). It's on the old road to Moncton, 5km from the center of town.

Holy Oak Motel & Cabins (☎ 506-459-7600, 3419 Woodstock Rd) Singles/doubles $55/65 July & Aug, $45/55 in May, June, Sept & Oct, $35/45 Nov-Apr. Cabins $65 off-season for up to four persons, $75 in July & August. This motel 10km west of the city center has 12 motel units and four cabins with cooking facilities. The proprietor, Shanti Brideau, is slowly upgrading this ramshackle assortment of units.

Lord Beaverbrook Hotel (☎ 800-561-7666, fax 506-455-1441, e lbhres@nbnet.nb.ca, W www.lordbeaverbrookhotel.com, 659 Queen St) Singles/doubles $120/130 mid-June-mid-Sept, $110/120 other months. At the top end, the venerable Lord Beaverbrook, built in 1948, is moderately priced for a place of its class. The exterior is austere, but inside it's elegant. Used mainly by businesspeople and government officials on per diems, the Lord Beaverbrook has 168 rooms with all the amenities. You may be able to get a reduced rate if you call ahead and ask about specials.

Places to Eat

There has been a small explosion of outdoor cafes and restaurants featuring outdoor decks in Fredericton. The best place to head for supper and fresh air is **Pipers Lane**, a courtyard of sorts between King and Queen Sts, west of York St. The alley between Nos 358 and 362 Queen St will take you directly there. Surrounding this open area are almost a dozen restaurants, coffee shops, pubs and ice cream parlors, half of them with outdoor seating.

Dimitri's Souvlaki (☎ 506-452-8882, 349 King St) Mains $12. Open 11am-10pm Mon-Sat. Dimitri's in Pipers Lane is good for an inexpensive Greek lunch or dinner of souvlaki, pita, brochettes, moussaka and the like. The traditional shish kebab is $12, and you can enjoy it on the restaurant's rooftop patio. Vegetarians can order a Caesar salad ($6), a deluxe Greek salad ($5) or a super vegetarian pita ($3.25).

Cravings café (☎ 506-452-7482, 384 King St, opposite Pipers Lane) Lunches under $5. Open 7:30am-6pm Mon-Fri, 8am-5pm Sat. Until 11am they serve a hearty breakfast for $3.50, then tasty lunch fare like pitas, wraps and donairs. It's self-service, but arty and informal, light-years away from the fast food places in nearby King's Place Mall.

Mexicali Rosa's (☎ 506-451-0686, 546 King St) Mains $6-12. Open 11:30am-11:30pm Sun-Thurs, 11:30am-1am Fri & Sat. Outdoor dining can be enjoyed here, with nachos ($7), cheese quesadillas ($6), chimichangas ($12) and a burrito dinner ($10).

Mei's Chinese Restaurant (☎ 506-454-2177, 74 Regent St) Full dinners $13-15. Open 11:45am-2pm Tues-Fri, 5pm-9pm Tues-Sun. Mei's is the best Chinese restaurant in town. It offers Szechuan and Taiwanese dishes and has combination plates (egg roll, fried rice and main course) for $7. A weekly event is the lunch buffet on Thursday and Friday ($11).

M&T Deli (☎ 506-458-9068, 602 Queen St) Lunch under $6. Open 7:30am-4:30pm Mon-Fri. This is a small but comfortable and casual delicatessen with an interesting notice board. It serves all the standard fare such as sandwiches, salads and bagels, as well as smoked meat from Ben's, the famous Montréal deli.

Regency Rose Café (☎ 506-455-2233, 610 Queen St) Dinners $10-19. Open 9am-9pm Mon-Sat July & Aug, 8am-4pm Mon-Wed, 11am-9pm Thurs-Sat other months. For a café au lait and more substantial fare head to this restaurant, directly opposite Officers' Square. The walls are adorned with art and the menu offers an interesting selection of salads, soups and vegetarian options.

Molly's Coffee House (☎ 506-457-9305, 554 Queen St) Dishes under $7. Open 9:30am-midnight Mon-Fri, noon-midnight Sat & Sun. For lighter fare and good coffee, Molly's has a few vegetarian options. Their specialty is baked meals such as lasagna, casserole and shepherds pie.

Ponderosa Steak House (☎ 506-458-1895, 1012 Prospect St at Smythe) Mains $8-13. Open 11am-9pm daily. The self-service steaks come with all-you-can-eat soup and salad. It's south of town, just off the Trans Canada Hwy.

Sobeys Supermarket (☎ 506-458-8891, on Prospect St West off Regent St South) Open 24 hours a day. This supermarket is at the Fredericton Mall, away from the center near the Trans Canada Hwy.

Entertainment

Playhouse Theatre (☎ 506-458-8344, 686 Queen St) Live stage performances can be enjoyed in this 763-seat theater, built in 1964. The main season is mid-September to mid-June. There are musicals, drama, dance, guest performers and concerts – the Theater New Brunswick troupe is based here. Ticket prices range from $13 to $40. Most programs begin at 8pm. Unfortunately, the theater is closed in summer.

Upper Deck Sports Bar (☎ 506-457-1475, Piper's Lane) Open 5pm-2am Mon-Thurs, noon-2am Fri-Sun. Sports freaks have their choice of sports bars in Fredericton, including this one. There are cheap pitchers of beer, lots of billiards and live music on the weekends ($4 cover).

Dolan's Pub (☎ 506-454-7474, Piper's Lane) Open 11:30am-midnight Mon-Wed, 11:30am-2am Thurs & Fri, 10am-2am Sat. Dolan's presents live Celtic music on Thursday, Friday and Saturday nights, beginning around 10pm ($5 cover).

The G-Club (☎ 506-455-7768, 377 King St off Pipers Lane) Open 8pm-2am Wed-Sun. This is Fredericton's only gay/alternative club. There's no sign. Just look for the door with the number 377 on it beside Corleone's Pizza and go up to the 3rd floor. A $3 cover charge is collected.

Sweetwaters Club (☎ 506-444-0121, 339 King St) Open 8pm-2am Thurs-Sat. This large bar and restaurant with disco dancing caters to teens and 20-somethings ($5 cover).

Lunar Rogue Pub (☎ 506-450-2065, 625 King St) Sandwiches & burgers $5-6. Open 11am-11pm Sun-Fri, 10am-1am Sat. This 'maritime pub' has British ales on tap and a nice selection of sandwiches and burgers, as well as outdoor dining. There's live music on Thursday, Friday and Saturday.

Bugaboo Creek Pub (☎ 506-453-0582, 422 Queen St) Open 8am-6pm Mon & Tues, 8am-2am Wed-Fri, 9am-2am Sat, 10am-6pm Sun. The 20s and 30s crowd comes here for live music on Friday and Saturday from 9:30pm ($3 to $7 cover, depending on who's playing). There's karaoke Tuesday and Thursday nights.

Shopping

Fredericton is a hotspot for the old craft of pewter smithing. Examples can be seen at *Aitkens Pewter (☎ 506-453-9474, 65 Regent St)*. Other craftspeople in the town do pottery and woodcarving. *The Fine Craft Center (☎ 506-450-8989, 87 Regent St)* often displays artistic pottery and sculpture.

The *College of Craft & Design of New Brunswick Community College (☎ 506-453-2305, 457 Queen St)*, behind Soldiers' Barracks, provides another chance to buy artistic pottery.

Getting There & Away

Air Fredericton is a small city, but as the provincial capital it does get a fair bit of air traffic. Many flights in and out are stopovers between other points. Air Canada or its subsidiary Air Nova has at least one nonstop flight daily from Montréal, Ottawa, Toronto and Halifax. A $12 'airport improvement fee' must be paid separately at the airport restaurant (not included in the ticket price).

Bus The SMT bus station (☎ 506-458-6000) is at 101 Regent St at Brunswick St. Coin lockers are $2. The station is open 7:30am to 8:30pm Monday to Friday, 9am to 8:30pm Saturday and Sunday. Buses leave for Moncton ($30) at 11:15am and 6pm daily; Campbellton and then Québec City ($80) at 11:30am and at 2:50pm and 8:15pm via Edmundston; Halifax ($73) and Amherst ($40) buses leave at 11:15am and 6pm daily. Buses to Summerside and Charlottetown, PEI ($61) also depart daily at 11:15am and 6pm. Buses to Bangor, Maine ($34), via Saint John, leave 11:20am Friday and Saturday.

Car Discount Car Rentals (☎ 506-458-1118), 580 King St, has compact cars with rental fees starting at $44 per day with 200km or $49 with unlimited kilometers, plus $13 per day collision insurance and 15% tax. The 'weekend special' of $123 (plus tax and insurance) gives you a car for three days with unlimited kilometers, so long as one of the days is a Saturday. In midsummer, prices could be higher.

Avis (☎ 506-454-2847), 81 Regent St, is more expensive.

Fredericton parking meters charge $1 per hour 9am to 5pm Monday to Friday. The tourist office in Fredericton City Hall distributes free parking passes (including meter parking) to visitors.

CAA Maritimes (☎ 506-452-1987) is at 418 York St.

Getting Around

To/From the Airport Fredericton Airport is 14km southeast of town on Hwy 102. A taxi to the airport is $16 for the first person, plus $1 for each additional person. Avis, Budget, Hertz and National have car rental desks at the airport.

Bus The city has a good public transportation system, Fredericton Transit (☎ 506-460-2200), and the $1.45 fare includes free transfers. Service is halved on Saturday, and no buses at all run on Sundays and holidays.

Most Fredericton city bus routes begin from King's Place Mall, on King St between York and Carleton. To facilitate connections, all buses leave together.

The university is a 15-minute walk from the downtown area; if you want to take the bus, take No 16S south on Regent St. It runs about every 20 minutes.

If you are hitching on the Trans Canada Hwy, take the Fredericton Mall bus (No 16S or 11S) out to the highway.

To head back into the city from these places catch the No 16N.

Bicycle Rentals are available at Radical Edge (☎ 506-459-3478), 386 Queen St, at $5/25 per hour/day. The tourist office or Radical Edge can clue you in to the myriad trails around the area; pick up the free multicolored *Trail Guide* brochure.

Saint John River Valley

The Saint John River winds along the western border of the province, past forests and beautiful lush farmland, through Fredericton and then around rolling hills to the Bay of Fundy. The valley's soft landscape is particularly picturesque between Saint John and Florenceville. Most of New Brunswick's Maliseet Indians live along its banks.

There are bridges and ferries across the river at various points. The Trans Canada Hwy (Hwy 2) follows the river up to Edmundston and then crosses into Québec.

Because the main highway connecting the Maritimes with central Canada runs along the river, it's a busy route in summer. Accommodations can be difficult to find in July and August – use the tourist office's toll-free reservation service to book ahead. Outside of peak season there is usually no problem at all getting a room.

There's a choice of two routes, the quicker Trans Canada Hwy, which is mostly on the west side of the river, or Hwy 105 on the east. The slower route is more scenic, passing right through many small villages.

MACTAQUAC

The **Mactaquac Power Dam**, 25km west of Fredericton on Hwy 102, has created an 84 sq km lake called Head Pond, which extends as far as Nackawic. Built in 1968, the concrete dam is 43m high, making it the tallest in the Maritimes. The six turbines generate 600,000 kilowatts of electricity in spring when the station is working at full capacity. It's possible to visit the generating station (☎ 506-462-3814, 451 Hwy 105; admission free; open 9am-4pm daily May-Sept) and take a 45-minute tour, which includes a look at the turbines and an explanation of how they work.

Fish caught in a fishway at the foot of the dam are carried by truck to a hatchery where Atlantic salmon are relieved of their eggs. Other species such as bass, gaspereau, trout and chad are released above the dam. The salmon fry are reared at a **Fish Culture Station** beside the dam, using water heated during the power generation process. Salmon are caught here in May and June, and only 10% of hatchlings ever manage to return to their birthplace.

Mactaquac Provincial Park

Mactaquac is New Brunswick's most developed provincial park. To get there from Fredericton, go 24km west on Hwy 102, cross the hydroelectric dam and continue another 6km around the lake on Hwy 105. This park (or resort) along the north side of Head Pond offers swimming, fishing, hiking, picnic sites, camping and boat rentals.

There's also a golf course where a round costs $40 (plus $15 club rentals). Day use of the park is $5 per vehicle.

The *campground* (☎ *506-363-4747,* W *www.tourismnbcanada.com/web/english/ outdoor_network, 1256 Hwy 105; open mid-May-early Oct)* is huge, with 305 sites at $21 for unserviced tent sites or $23 for sites with electricity. This place is busy and through much of the summer it will be full on Friday and Saturday nights. The lakeside campground has a swimming beach, grocery store and kitchen shelter.

King's Landing Historical Settlement

This recreated early-19th-century Loyalist village *(☎ 506-363-5090; adult/family $12/30; open 10am-5pm daily June-mid-Oct)* is 36km west of Fredericton, on the way to Woodstock. Take exit 253 off the Trans Canada Hwy. Here you can get a glimpse (and a taste) of pioneer life in the Maritimes. A community of 100 costumed staff inhabits 11 houses, a school, church, store and sawmill, typical of those used a century ago. The **King's Head Inn** serves traditional food and drink. The children's programs make King's Landing ideal for families.

A provincial tourist office (☎ 506-363-4994), 10 Prince William Rd, is at exit 253 off the Trans Canada Hwy near King's Landing. It's open 10am to 6pm daily mid-May to early October, 8am to 9pm July and August.

Woolastock Park (☎ 506-363-2959, fax 506-375-6338, on Hwy 102, 2km off Hwy 2 at exit 258) Unserviced/serviced sites $21/23. Open mid-May-mid-Sept. This large campground about 10km northeast of King's Landing has 260 secluded campsites.

WOODSTOCK

A small town set in a rich farming area, Woodstock is something of a tourist crossroads. The Trans Canada Hwy passes just outside of town, as does Hwy 95, which leads to Interstate 95 in Maine (the primary route down the eastern seaboard of the US). The center of Woodstock has some fine old Maritimes houses.

If you're arriving from the States, a large provincial tourist office (☎ 506-325-4427) is off Hwy 95, 5km east of the border crossing from Houlton, Maine, on the way to Woodstock and the Trans Canada Hwy. The office is open 10am to 6pm daily late May to early October, 8am to 9pm July and August.

A local tourist office (☎ 506-325-9049) is at the Woodstock Farm Market (see Things to See & Do). It's open 9:30am to 7:30pm daily July and August.

Things to See & Do

Downtown is **Connell House** *(☎ 506-328-9706, 128 Connell St; admission free; open 9am-5pm daily July & Aug)*, a fine Greek Revival mansion (1840) with eight Doric columns built by timber merchant and politician Charles Connell. Nearby on King St, at the junction of the Meduxnekeag and Saint John Rivers, is the **Woodstock Farm Market**, open from 8am to 2pm on Fridays.

The **Eagle Nest Gaming Palace** *(☎ 506-328-1600, 150 Hodgdon Rd; admission free; open 11am-9pm Mon-Wed, 11am-11pm Thurs-Sun)*, off the Trans Canada Hwy 6km south of the junction with Hwy 95, is a bizarre sight. This huge white 'sprung structure' was financed by a US company but is run by the Woodstock First Nation (Maliseet). The tribe's settlement is down the river directly below the gaming palace. You can play bingo here starting at 7pm Thursday to Saturday and from 3pm on Sunday. After the regular bingo finishes, there are late-night drop-in games. Video lottery terminals are available any time.

Places to Stay

Cornell Park Campground (☎ 506-325-4979, 120 Cornell Park Rd) Unserviced/serviced sites $13/20. Open May-Oct. About 2km northwest of downtown Woodstock via Kirkpatrick St, the campground has a special tenting area behind the office, with some nice grassy spots away from trailers. A large picnic area is nearby.

Riverside B&B (☎ 506-328-3094, 109 Church St) Singles/doubles from $45/55. Open Apr-Oct. This large yellow two-story wooden house is right next to the river in downtown Woodstock.

Cosy Cabins & Motel *(☎ 888-923-9009, fax 506-328-0191, 540 Hwy 103)* Singles/doubles $45/54 with one bed, $60 with two beds June-Sept, $42/49 one bed, $55 double two beds Oct-May. By the river 2km south of Woodstock on Rte 103 (2km north of the Maliseet reserve), Cosy Cabins & Motel has 11 motel units. The five cabins are rented on a weekly or monthly basis.

John Gyles Motor Inn *(☎ 506-328-6622, fax 506-328-2468,* e *gyles@nbnet.nb.ca, 11530 Hwy 2)* Singles/doubles $48/56 June-Sept, $44/52 other months. Open March-Dec. On the Trans Canada (Hwy 2), 15km south of Woodstock, this motel has 18 rooms in a long two-story block. If you're staying at the John Gyles Motor Inn, the 'Maliseet Trail' 2km south offers a good 30-minute hike up through the forest to Hayes Falls. The trailhead is well marked on the Trans Canada Hwy.

Places to Eat

There are no good independent restaurants in central Woodstock, and most of the places to eat that you will find are associated with motels.

Cosy Cabins Restaurant *(☎ 506-328-9755, 540 Hwy 103)* Lunch specials $5. Open 5pm-10pm Mon, 11:30am-10pm Tues-Thurs, 11:30am-11pm Fri, 4:30pm-11:30pm Sat, 2pm-10pm Sun. The Chinese restaurant at Cosy Cabins & Motel, 2km south of Woodstock along the river, serves inexpensive lunch specials from 11am to 2pm weekdays (open until 10pm nightly). The Sunday buffet from 4:30pm to 8pm ($9) is also good value.

Heino's German Restaurant *(☎ 506-328-6622, 11530 Hwy 2)* Mains $10-18. Open 5pm-9pm Fri-Sun Mar-Dec; 5pm-9pm daily June-Sept. At the John Gyles Motor Inn on the Trans Canada, 15km south of Woodstock, Heino's serves hearty meat dishes like pork chops, schnitzel and cordon bleu. It's real home-style cooking.

Sobeys Supermarket *(☎ 506-328-6819, Cornell Rd)* Open 8am-10pm Mon-Sat, 9am-6pm Sun. This large supermarket is

between town and Hwy 2 in Carleton Mall (opposite Canadian Tire).

Getting There & Away

The SMT bus stops at the Irving gas station (☎ 506-328-2245), 371 Cornell Rd, 3km west of town and just under a kilometer off the Trans Canada Hwy. Buses to Fredericton and Edmundston depart twice a day.

HARTLAND

Hartland is an attractive little town with a nice setting, and it's home to the grand-daddy of New Brunswick's 74 wooden covered bridges. These bridges, found scattered around the province on secondary roads, were covered to protect the timber beams used in their construction. With such protection from rain and sun, a wooden bridge lasts about 80 years. They are generally high and wide because cartloads of hay pulled by horses had to pass through.

The **Hartland Covered Bridge**, over the Saint John River, was erected in 1897 and is 390m long. The summer-only tourist office (☎ 506-375-4075) at the east end of this bridge has a complete listing of covered bridges, if you're interested. The office is open 9am to 6pm daily from late May to early October.

Northbound, instead of taking the faster Trans Canada Hwy, follow less-crowded Hwy 105, which follows the riverside for 18km from Hartland to Florenceville (continuing all the way to Grand Falls). Southbound, Hwy 105 leads to Fredericton.

Places to Stay & Eat

Ja-Sa-Le Motel *(☎ 800-565-6433, fax 506-375-8860, on the Trans Canada Hwy 2km from the bridge)* Singles/doubles $56/60 mid-June-mid-Sept, $46/50 other months. This 14-room place north of town is the only local motel. In July and August, they also rent rooms for $45/50 in a farmhouse diagonally across the highway.

21st Century B&B *(☎ 506-375-6786, 5 Monty St)* Rooms with shared bath $45 single or double year-round, including breakfast. This new two-story house is in the upper town, 1km from the bridge.

Campbell's B&B (☎ 506-375-4775, e *campbb@nbnet.nb.ca, 7175 Hwy 105*) Singles/doubles $40/50 including breakfast. This large, quaint two-story wooden house overlooks the Saint John River and is just 3km north of the famous covered bridge on Hwy 105. The New Brunswick Trail passes right by the door. It's the nicest place to stay around Hartland.

Peter's Family Restaurant (☎ 506-375-4935, 362 Main St) Meals under $10. Open 11am-10pm Mon-Fri, noon-10pm Sat & Sun. This Chinese place in an old wooden church near the covered bridge offers lunch specials from 11am to 2pm weekdays. At $7, the combination plates are a good value.

FLORENCEVILLE

There isn't much to see in Florenceville, but there are a couple of good places to stay along the Trans Canada north of town.

River Country Campground & Cabin (☎ 506-278-3700, w *www.river-country campground.com, off Hwy 2, 19km north of Florenceville*) Unserviced/serviced sites $15/18-20. Cabin $40. Open May-Sept. River Country has 80 campsites and one cabin with sink, fridge and basic cooking facilities. Most patrons here camp in their trailers, but the owners will help you find a quiet grassy campsite by the Saint John River if you're tenting. There's free firewood, a beach and one-hour boat trips for $5 per person.

Valley View Motel (☎ 506-273-2785, 20524 Trans Canada Hwy) Singles/doubles $41/46 with one bed, $53/58/63 double/triple/quad with two beds. Valley View Motel is right on the Trans Canada Hwy, 13km north of River View Campground and 7km south of Perth-Andover. The 17 rooms are in a long motel block and a two-story building across the highway from the river. It's a good place to stop between Woodstock and Grand Falls.

GRAND FALLS

A town with 7000 residents, Grand Falls consists essentially of one main street and the falls on the Saint John River that make it an interesting short stop.

The falls are best in spring or after a heavy rain. In summer, much of the water is diverted for generating hydroelectricity. The hydro dam also takes away from the rugged beauty this site must once have had. The area at the bottom of the gorge, reached by a staircase, is more scenic than the falls themselves and permits a glimpse of how things might have looked in pre-development days.

The biggest industry here is a frozen French fries factory operated by McCain Foods, on the Trans Canada Hwy north of town. The town celebrates its primary resource, the potato, with a festival each year around July 1.

Things to See

In a park in the middle of town, the falls drop about 25m and have carved out a 1½km-long gorge with walls reaching as high as 70m. Overlooking the falls is the **Malabeam Reception Centre** (☎ 877-475-7769, Madawaska Rd; admission free; open 10am-6pm daily June & Sept; 9am-9pm July & Aug) that doubles as a tourist office. Among the displays inside is a scale model of the gorge showing the extensive trail system that hugs its edge.

A 253-step stairway down into the gorge begins at **La Rochelle** (☎ 877-475-7769, 1 Chapel St; adult/family $3/7; open June-early Sept), across the bridge from the Malabeam Reception Center and left on Victoria St. You can also take a 45-minute **boat ride** (adult/family $10/25) up the gorge. They run up to eight times a day but only in midsummer when water levels are low (it's too dangerous when the river is in full flood). Buy the boat ticket first, as it includes the admission price for the stairway to the base of the gorge.

Places to Stay

Falls and Gorge Campground Lower Park (☎ 877-475-7769, fax 506-473-9091) Unserviced/serviced sites $15/22 plus tax. Open mid-May-mid-Oct. This municipal campground is near La Rochelle, at the end of Manse St. Unfortunately the gravel surface is far better suited to trailers than tents. You can book a site at La Rochelle or Malabeam. There's a free boardwalk that leads down into the gorge.

Maple Tourist Home (☎ 506-473-1763, W www.bbcanada.com/4029.html, 142 Main St) Doubles $70-90 mid-June-mid-Sept, $50-65 other months, breakfast included. This two-story house with three rooms is conveniently located right in the center of town near the SMT bus stop.

Hilltop Motel (☎ 800-496-1244, fax 506-473-4567, W www.sn2000.nb.ca/hilltop, 131 Madawaska Rd) Singles/doubles $60/65 downstairs, $66/71 upstairs mid-June-mid-Sept, $55/61 downstairs, $60/66 upstairs other months. Just up the road from the Malabeam Reception Centre, there are 28 rooms in the main block here, plus nine rooms with balcony in a new block overlooking the river. These cost $70/76 ($80 with two beds). A good restaurant is on the premises.

Places to Eat

La Bouffe Margarit's Restaurant (☎ 506-475-1818, 262 Broadway Blvd) Breakfast $5. Open 6am-9pm Mon-Sat, 7am-9pm Sun. Right in the center of town, La Bouffe serves café latte and filled croissants. It's popular with the locals.

Chinese Village Restaurant (☎ 506-473-1884, 238 Madawaska Rd) Meals $8. Open 11am-11pm daily. This place next to McDonalds on the road into town from the north lays out buffets 11am to 2pm weekdays ($8) and 5pm to 8:30pm Friday to Sunday ($12).

Entertainment

Several nightclubs are in downtown Grand Falls, including **Broadway** (☎ 506-473-2258, 246 Broadway; open 2pm-2am Tues-Sat) and **Friday's 2000** (☎ 506-473-3161, 253 Broadway; open 8pm-1am Wed-Sat), the latter of which has a DJ Friday and Saturday nights.

Grits Bar (☎ 506-473-3311, 456 Broadway Blvd) Open 6pm-2am Thurs & Sat, 4pm-2am Fri. This sports bar is on the corner of Broadway and Main Sts. There always seems to be a beer special going on, but only finger foods like chicken wings are available to eat.

Getting There & Away

The SMT bus stops at the Irving gas station (☎ 506-473-5704), 315 Broadway, right in the center of town. Daily buses to Edmundston and Fredericton depart from here.

The Plaster Rock Hwy (Hwy 108) cuts across the province to the east coast, running through forest for nearly its entire length. Deer and moose aren't much used to traffic here, so keep an eye out.

EDMUNDSTON

If you're coming from Québec, there's a good chance this will be your first town in the Maritimes, as the border is only about 20km away. From Edmunston, it's a three-hour drive to Fredericton. An international bridge on St Francois St at the south end of town connects Edmundston to Maine, just across the river.

Edmundston is an industrial pulp and paper center. The Fraser Papers Pulp Mill, founded by Archibald Fraser in 1918, is the largest employer in town.

Edmundston is pretty well split in half by the Madawaska River. The old central district on the west side of the river is built around low hills that give it some character. The population of 11,000 is 85% French-speaking, though most also speak English.

The local citizens have a whimsical notion of Edmundston as the capital of a fictitious country known as Madawaska, whose inhabitants were called Brayons. Evidently this notion has historical origins dating back to the late 1700s, when the region existed in a sort of political vacuum due to the bickering of the US and British governments over the placement of the border.

The Madawaska Maliseet First Nation has a large reserve along Queen St south of town, and Indian craft shops by the road sell wallets, belts and moccasins.

Orientation & Information

The main intersection downtown is that of Church St and Canada Rd. Within a few blocks of this corner are numerous shops, a couple of restaurants and City Hall, plus an indoor shopping mall. Most of the visitor

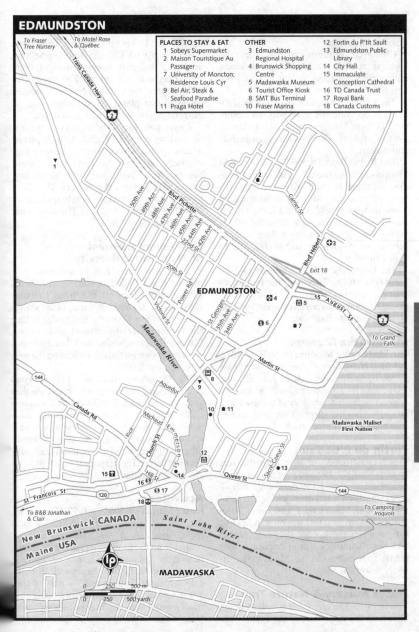

EDMUNDSTON

PLACES TO STAY & EAT
1 Sobeys Supermarket
2 Maison Touristique Au Passager
7 University of Moncton; Residence Louis Cyr
9 Bel Air; Steak & Seafood Paradise
11 Praga Hotel

OTHER
3 Edmundston Regional Hospital
4 Brunswick Shopping Centre
5 Madawaska Museum
6 Tourist Office Kiosk
8 SMT Bus Terminal
10 Fraser Marina

12 Fortin du P'tit Sault
13 Edmundston Public Library
14 City Hall
15 Immaculate Conception Cathedral
16 TD Canada Trust
17 Royal Bank
18 Canada Customs

NEW BRUNSWICK

facilities are on Victoria St, a busy commercial street running between the highway and this central section.

Clustered around exit 18 from the highway are the tourist office, a shopping mall, some fast-food restaurants and the university.

The local tourist office kiosk (☎ 506-739-2115) is opposite the university on Boulevard Hébert. You get an excellent view of town from here. The kiosk is open in July and August.

The Royal Bank (☎ 506-735-5518), 48 St Francois St, has a branch right beside Canadian customs at the border crossing. It's open 10am to 3pm Monday to Wednesday, 10am to 5pm Thursday and Friday. Otherwise TD Canada Trust (☎ 506-735-8843) is across the street. It's open 9am to 5pm Monday to Wednesday and Friday, 9am to 7pm Thursday.

The Edmundston Public Library (☎ 506-735-4714), off Queen St near the Ford dealership, offers free Internet access (identification required). It's open variable hours Tuesday to Saturday.

Madawaska Museum

The Madawaska Museum (☎ 506-737-5282, 195 Blvd Hébert, cnr 15 August St; admission $3.50; open 9am-8pm daily July & Aug, 7pm-10pm Wed & Thurs, 1pm-5pm Sun rest of year) outlines the history of the area. The museum also has displays on local industries such as the timber trade.

Fortin du P'tit Sault

This reconstruction of an old British fort (☎ 506-735-7373, 19 Saint Jean St; admission by donation; open 10am-8pm daily July & Aug) stands on a hill overlooking the junction of the Madawaska and Saint John Rivers. The original fort was built in 1841, at a time when the border between the US and New Brunswick was in dispute. A nice picnic spot is beside the Madawaska directly below the fort.

Fraser Nursery & Nature Trail

You can spend an enjoyable couple of hours hiking up the ridge behind the Fraser Tree Nursery (☎ 506-737-2220, on Second Falls Rd; admission free; always open), northeast of town. Go 1½km up Victoria St from Hwy 2, then right on Olivier Boucher St and another 13km east, keeping straight, then right over a Bailey bridge. The nursery is 500m beyond the statue of Notre Dame des forêts. Fraser plants seven million trees a year to help replace those it cuts down.

Leave your car at the nursery as there's no parking at the trailhead. A small picnic area is on the lake opposite the nursery. The marked trail into the coniferous forest begins on the right just 100m down the gravel road beyond the nursery. This 4km loop trail can be muddy in early spring and the flies arrive in June. Hunting and camping are prohibited.

Experimental Forest of Moncton University

You can easily spend half a day or more exploring this wooded upland southeast of Edmundston. Turn off the Trans Canada Hwy at exit 32, Rivière-Verte, 14km south of Edmundston. Cross the first bridge to the right soon after the turnoff and follow Chemin Rivière-Quisibis for 15km until you see a large sign on the left indicating the entrance to the forest.

The Ours Noir (Black Bear) Trail begins at a covered picnic shelter 1.5km down the gravel access road. This 3.6km trail is especially interesting since birdhouses and ponds have been built along the way to encourage the presence of wildlife. Several other well signposted and marked trails are also available. The Experimental Forest is always open and is free.

Activities

Fraser Marina (☎ 506-739-1992, Victoria St; bicycles $10 a day, boat trips $12/5 adult/child; open July & Aug) Bicycles can be rented from the kiosk marked 'L'Echassier' behind the restaurant at the marina. There's a 10km trail to the New Brunswick Botanical Garden at Saint Jacques – part of the Trans Canada Trail – but before using the trails around here you're supposed to buy a Vélo-vignette (valid only in Edmundston and Québec). This trail pass costs $5 for one day or $10 for the whole season. Rental bicycles already have the vignette. The folks in the kiosk will also have information on the two-hour boat trips from the marina to the Botanical Garden (fare includes garden admission).

Special Events
Each year on the five days preceding the first Monday in August is the Foires Festival, which celebrates the physically nonexistent republic of Madawaska. There are cultural, social and sporting events, as well as some good traditional Brayon cooking to sample.

Web site: w www.foire-brayonne.nb.ca

The Edmundston Jazz Festival (☎ 506-739-2104) is held in mid-June.

Places to Stay
Camping Iroquois (☎ 506-739-9060, 1318 Main St) Tent/trailer sites $16/21 for two people ($5 for a third person). Open mid-May-mid-Sept. Sites Nos 43 to 46 down by the river are the nicest for tents, though they are also farthest from the shower blocks. It's seldom full.

University of Moncton (☎ 506-737-5016, e admissions@cuslm.ca, w www.cuslm.ca, 171 Blvd Hébert) Singles/doubles $23/33 plus tax. Open mid-June-late August. In summer 44 rooms are available at the Residence Louis Cyr, across the street from KFC and 500m up a steep hill from the bus station. If you're lucky, you get your own washroom and fridge (a steal). No cooking facilities are provided, but a cheap Laundromat is in the building.

Praga Hotel (☎ 506-735-5567, fax 506-736-6315, w www.sn2000.nb.ca/comp/praga-hotel, 127 Victoria Rd) Singles/doubles $50/55 mid-June-mid-Sept, $40/45 other months. This three-story hotel opposite the Fraser Marina has 20 rooms. It's the closest place to the bus station.

Maison Touristique Au Passager (☎ 506-735-5781, fax 506-739-8952, 255 Power Rd) Rooms $22 per person. This place is on Power Rd, in the northern section of the city just off Hwy 2. There are six rooms with shared bath and a common kitchen. Students occupy all the rooms during the winter, but it's worth a try from June to August.

B&B Jonathan (☎ 506-739-7036, fax 506-735-5824, 556 St Francois St) Singles/doubles $50/60. Open Apr-Oct. This two-story brick house with a terrace overlooking the river is 2km west of Canada customs. It may be Edmundston's nicest B&B.

Motel Rose (☎ 506-739-9492, fax 506-739-5334, 625 Boul Acadie) One-bed rooms $35 single or double low season, $45 'when it starts getting busy.' Two-bed rooms $45/60 triple occupancy during slow/busy seasons. The nine motel rooms are in a long block facing old Hwy 2. Three small cabins are available in summer. This no-frills place is the cheapest motel in town. Motel Rose is 2km north of Edmundston and 4½km south of the New Brunswick Botanical Gardens.

Places to Eat
Bel Air (☎ 506-735-3329, 174 Victoria St) Chinese dinners $6-8, other dinners under $14, breakfast special $3. Open 24 hours. Bel Air, on the corner of Victoria St and Boulevard Hébert, has a sign that can't be missed. This place has been here since the 1950s and is something of a city landmark. The extensive menu offers Italian, Chinese, seafood or basic Canadian fare. The portions are generous.

Steak & Seafood Paradise (☎ 506-739-7822, 174 Victoria St) Meal $15. Adjoining the Bel Air is the more upmarket Steak & Seafood Paradise. This is the only place in town offering live lobster.

Praga Hotel (☎ 506-735-5567, 127 Victoria St) Lunch/dinner buffet $5.95/8.75. Chinese buffet 11:15am-2pm Mon-Fri, 5pm-9pm Tues-Sun. There's also Sunday brunch from 11am to 2pm ($8.25). The food isn't as good as that at the Bel Air, but you can take all you want.

Sobeys Supermarket (☎ 506-735-6477, 580 Victoria St) Open 8am-10pm Mon-Sat, 9am-6pm Sun. This is the place to pick up fried chicken and picnic fixings; there's free coffee at the entrance.

NEW BRUNSWICK

Getting There & Away

The SMT terminal (☎ 506-739-8309) is across the street from the Bel Air restaurant, at 169 Victoria St near the corner of Boulevard Hébert at the bridge.

You can catch buses here for Québec City, or points east such as Fredericton, Moncton and Halifax. For trips to Maine or other US destinations, departures are from Saint John.

To Moncton and Amherst, SMT Bus Lines has two buses daily, from which a transfer can be made to Halifax. One-way fares are Fredericton $42, Saint John $58, Moncton $69, Amherst $78 and Halifax $111. For Moncton, the local bus is at 7am, the express is at 2:15pm.

There are three buses daily to Québec City, which includes transferring to the Orleans Express bus line at Rivière-Du-Loup (Orleans is the company covering eastern Québec). One-way fares are Rivière-Du-Loup $19, Québec City $51.

SAINT-JACQUES

Seven kilometers north of Edmundston, about halfway to the Québec border, is the small community of Saint-Jacques. The Trans Canada Hwy runs into Québec here, becomes Hwy 185, a slender strip of bitumen linking the Maritimes with the rest of the country.

The **New Brunswick Botanical Gardens** (☎ 506-737-5383, off Hwy 2; adult/child/family $4.75/2.25/11.75; open 9am-dusk daily early June-Sept), just south of Les Jardins de la Republique Provincial Park, contain both natural and cultivated sections along the edge of the Madawaska River.

A large provincial tourist office (☎ 506-735-2747) is located right on the New Brunswick–Québec border, 9km north of Les Jardins de la Republique. It's open 10am to 6pm daily mid-May to early October, 8am to 9pm in July and August. Across the street from this office is Edmundston Airport, which has an authentic WWII Lancaster four-engine bomber on display outside the terminal. The Trans Canada Trail passes directly behind the bomber and enters Québec 20m north.

Les Jardins de la Republique Provincial Park (☎ 506-735-2525, fax 506-737-4445, W *www.tourismnbcanada.com/web/english/outdoor_network)* Unserviced/serviced campsites $20/23. Open mid-May-mid-Sept. Located between Hwy 2 and the Madawaska River, this park gets a lot of traffic noise.

West Fundy Shore

Almost the entire southern edge of New Brunswick fronts on the constantly rising and falling, always impressive waters of the Bay of Fundy. The fascinating shoreline, the resort town of St Andrews, the quiet Fundy Isles, the city of Saint John and Fundy National Park make this one of the most varied and appealing regions of New Brunswick.

ST STEPHEN

Right on the US border across the river from Calais in Maine, St Stephen is a busy entry point for US visitors. It's a small old town that forms the northern link of what is known as the Quoddy Loop – a circular tour around southeastern New Brunswick and northwestern Maine around Passamaquoddy Bay. From St Stephen the loop route goes to St Andrews, St George and then on to Deer Island and lastly to Campobello Island, which is connected by bridge to Maine. It's a popular trip that takes anywhere from a day to a week and includes some fine seaside scenery, interesting history and a number of pleasant, relaxed resort-style towns.

In St Stephen the Festival of International Cooperation, featuring concerts, parades and street fairs, is held in St Stephen every August.

Information

In the former train station at the corner of Milltown Blvd and King St is a large provincial tourist office (☎ 506-466-7390) that includes a currency exchange. It's open 10am to 6pm daily June and Sept, 8am to 9pm July and August.

International Currency Exchange (☎ 506-466-3387), 128 Milltown Blvd, two blocks from Canada customs, will cash traveler's checks in Canadian dollars at face value without charging a commission. Their rates are competitive for US/Canadian exchanges. The exchange is open 8am to 6pm daily December to April, 8am to 8pm other months.

Behind the tourist office is the St Croix Public Library (☎ 506-466-7529), which has free Internet access. It's open 9am to 5pm Wednesday, Thursday and Saturday, 1pm to 5pm and 7pm to 9pm Tuesday, 1pm to 9pm Friday.

Ganong's Chocolate Museum

St Stephen has quite a reputation as a chocolate mecca due to **Ganong**, a family chocolate business since 1873 whose products are known all around eastern Canada. It's believed that the five-cent chocolate nut bar was invented by the Ganong brothers in 1910, and they are also credited for developing the heart-shaped box of chocolates now seen everywhere on Valentine's Day. The old factory on the main street of town is now a museum (☎ 506-466-7848, 73 Milltown Blvd; adult/family $4/10; open 10am-5pm Mon-Sat) displaying everything from

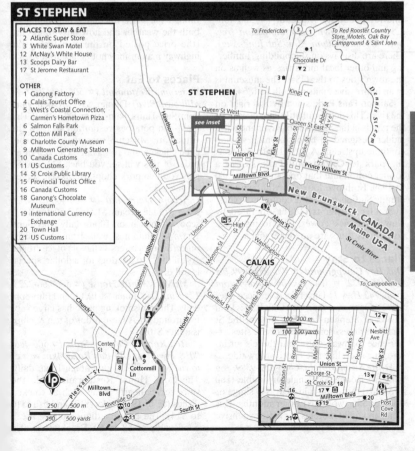

ST STEPHEN

PLACES TO STAY & EAT
2 Atlantic Super Store
3 White Swan Motel
12 McNay's White House
13 Scoops Dairy Bar
17 St Jerome Restaurant

OTHER
1 Ganong Factory
4 Calais Tourist Office
5 West's Coastal Connection;
    Carmen's Hometown Pizza
6 Salmon Falls Park
7 Cotton Mill Park
8 Charlotte County Museum
9 Milltown Generating Station
10 Canada Customs
11 US Customs
14 St Croix Public Library
15 Provincial Tourist Office
16 Canada Customs
18 Ganong's Chocolate
    Museum
19 International Currency
    Exchange
20 Town Hall
21 US Customs

NEW BRUNSWICK

boxed chocolates to bars such as Pal O'Mine, a very sweet little number. The Ganong Chocolates Store at the front of the complex can be visited free. It's open 10am to 5pm Monday to Friday, 9am to 5pm Saturday. The modern Ganong factory is on King St next to Atlantic Super Store and is not open to visitors except during the annual Chocolate Fest, which occurs in August.

Milltown

Milltown is the most monumental part of St Stephen, with many large mansions along the 3km of Milltown Blvd. About 2.5km west of the main border crossing is the **Charlotte County Museum** (☎ 506-466-3295, 443 Milltown Blvd; admission free; open 9:30am-4:30pm Mon-Sat June-Aug). There are displays on shipbuilding, lumbering and other local industries, as well as on the town's ties to the USA. The museum is in an impressive mansion built in 1864.

Salmon Falls Park is nearby and right on the river. This delightful little spot overlooks the rapids in the Saint Croix River and a fish ladder designed to help spawning salmon continue upstream. A gravel path connects the park to **Cotton Mill Park**, site of a former cotton mill that operated from 1880 to 1959. Both overlook the Milltown Generating Station, one of the continent's oldest hydroelectric plants (1881), operated by New Brunswick Power. Due to insurance constraints, tours are no longer given.

Places to Stay

Oak Bay Campground (☎ 506-466-4999, fax 506-466-5472, ⓦ www.oakbaycampground .com, 742 Hwy 1) Unserviced/serviced sites $18/21. Open mid-Apr-Oct. Oak Bay is 9km east of St Stephen and 5km west of the St Andrews access road. Many of the sites experience highway noise, but there's an interesting shoreline to explore at low tide.

White Swan Motel (☎ 888-659-9399, 186 King St) Rooms $55 single or double ($60 two beds) mid-June-mid-Sept, $49 single or double ($55 two beds) other months. This clean and quiet motel is the least-expensive place to stay close to town.

Scoodic Motel (☎ 506-466-1540, fax 506-466-9103, 241 Hwy 1, 4km east on Hwy 1) Rooms $52 single or double ($56 with two beds) mid-June-mid-Sept, singles/doubles $35/40 ($45 with two beds) other months. The price includes morning toast and coffee in the reception area. This reasonable motel is within sight of the SMT bus stop.

Busy Bee Motel & Cabins (☎ 800-890-0233, fax 506-465-8165, 419 Hwy 1) Rooms $35/43 single or double low/high season. Busy Bee is 2km east of the Scoodic and 3km west of Oak Bay Campground. The eight housekeeping cabins and 12 motel rooms are the least expensive in town, although the price fluctuates depending on both the weather and how busy things are (the price posted on the sign facing the highway may or may not be accurate).

Places to Eat

St Jerome Restaurant (☎ 506-466-3027, 73 Milltown Blvd) Dinner $9-11. Open 9am-9pm Sun-Thurs, 9am-10pm Fri & Sat. This meat-and-potatoes restaurant next to the Chocolate Museum specializes in barbecued chicken and ribs. Half a chicken or an order of ribs will set you back $11, and $9 gets you two pork chops. Breakfast, served all day, is $3.

Scoops Dairy Bar (☎ 506-466-6709, 26 King St) Ice cream $1.50/2/2.50 for 1/2/3 scoops. Open noon-10pm daily May-Sept. Just a few minutes' walk from the tourist office, Scoop's offers 48 flavors of ice cream. Ask if the 'two hot dogs for a dollar' special is still on.

McNay's White House (☎ 506-466-2223, 124 King St) Dinner $8-10. Open 11am-8pm daily. This nonsmoking place has large subs for around $6. A large order of fish & chips is under $10.

Red Rooster Country Store (☎ 506-466-0018, Hwy 1 at Old Bay Road, 4km east of town) Mains $7-14. Open 6am-10pm daily. The Cook House Restaurant inside the store serves hearty meals such as chicken dishes ($7 to $9), steaks ($12) and fish ($10 to $14). The country dinner plates are a good value at $8 to $9. Breakfast is also good, and it's worth visiting for the healthy whole-wheat bread fresh from the Homestead Bakery here. It's pleasant and friendly – as popular with the locals as it is with visitors.

Atlantic Super Store (☎ 506-465-1457, 185 King St) Open 8am-10pm Mon-Sat, 9am-6pm Sun. The deli section in this giant supermarket sells cheap fried chicken, which you can eat at the tables of the market cafe just opposite. Two large pieces with potatoes cost $3.

Getting There & Away

The SMT bus stops at Red Rooster Country Store (☎ 506-466-2121), on Hwy 1 at 5 Old Bay Rd, 4km east of town. The bus to Saint John ($19) departs daily at 4:10 pm, connecting to Moncton ($38) and Halifax ($73) on Friday, Saturday and Sunday. The bus to Bangor, Maine ($15), goes only on Friday and Saturday at 3:30 pm. In Bangor, direct connections are available to Boston and New York.

Across the border in Calais, Maine, West's Coastal Connection (☎ 800-596-2823) has a bus leaving for Bangor daily at 9:30am (US$18). The bus picks up from Marden's parking lot behind Carmen's Hometown Pizza, 63 Main St, Calais, three blocks straight ahead from US customs. In Bangor they use the Greyhound terminal and leave at 3:30pm (also making a stop at Bangor Airport). Bus passes are not accepted.

ST ANDREWS

Also known as St Andrews-by-the-Sea, this is a summer resort of some tradition and gentility. Together with a fine climate and picturesque beauty, St Andrews has a long, charming and often visible history – it's one of the oldest towns in the province and for a long period was on equal terms with Saint John.

History

The original inhabitants of this area were the Passamaquoddies, very few of whom still live in the area. European settlement began in 1783, after the American Revolu-

tion. Many British pioneers, wanting to remain loyal to Britain, left the American-controlled areas and set up house in British territory around the fort in Castine, Maine. The British-American border was subsequently changed, and these people once again found themselves on American soil. The tip of the bay across the water was scouted, and all agreed it was a place of equal beauty. The pioneers loaded up ships and headed out, some even dragging their houses on rafts behind them, and St Andrews was founded on October 3rd, 1783, back in Canada.

Prosperity came first with shipbuilding, but tourism is now the town's stock in trade. Oceanic research is now also a prominent industry. In the early part of the century, the Canadian Pacific Railway owned and ran the Algonquin Hotel, which more or less started St Andrews' reputation as a retreat. Moneyed Canadians and US citizens built luxurious summer cottages alongside the 19th-century mansions of the lumber and shipbuilding barons. This historic town attracts writers and artists from across the country.

Orientation & Information

Water St, the main street, is lined with restaurants, souvenir and craft shops and some places to stay. King St is the main cross-street; one block from Water St, Queen St is also important.

There's a local information office (☎ 506-466-4858) near the junction of Hwy 1 and Hwy 127 N. It's open 10am to 6pm daily July and August. A second tourist office (☎ 506-529-3556) is in town at 46 Reed Ave, next to the arena. Pick up the walking guide from the tourist office – it includes a map and brief description of 34 particularly interesting places. The office is open 9am to 5pm daily mid-May to early October, 8am to 8pm July and August.

Many companies offering boat trips have offices at the Adventure Destinations complex beside Market Square at the foot of King St. They're only open during the peak season from mid-June to early September.

NEW BRUNSWICK

ST ANDREWS

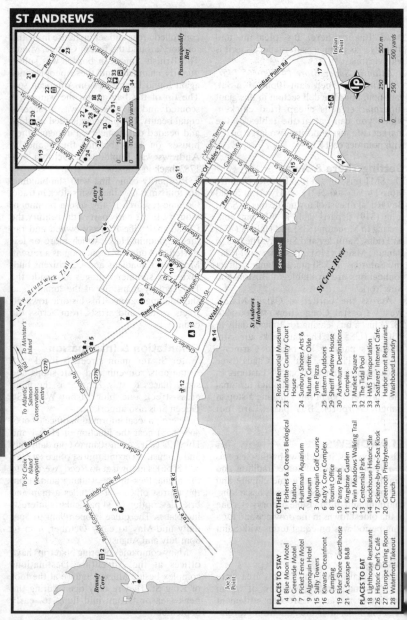

Passamaquoddy Bay

Indian Point

Indian Point Rd

St Croix River

St Andrews Harbour

Katy's Cove

New Brunswick Trail

To Minister's Island

To Atlantic Salmon Conservation Centre

To St Croix Island Viewpoint

Brandy Cove

Joe's Point

PLACES TO STAY
4 Blue Moon Motel
5 Greenside Motel
7 Picket Fence Motel
9 Algonquin Hotel
15 Salty Towers
16 Kiwanis Oceanfront Camping
19 Elder Shore Guesthouse
21 A Seascape B&B

PLACES TO EAT
18 Lighthouse Restaurant
26 Historic Chef's Café
27 L'Europe Dining Room
28 Waterfront Takeout

OTHER
1 Fisheries & Oceans Biological Station
2 Huntsman Aquarium Museum
3 Algonquin Golf Course
6 Katy's Cove Complex
8 Tourist Office
10 Pansy Patch
11 Kingsbrae Garden
12 Twin Meadows Walking Trail
13 Centennial Park
14 Blockhouse Historic Site
17 Science-by-the-Sea Kiosk
20 Greenoch Presbyterian Church

22 Ross Memorial Museum
23 Charlotte County Court House
24 Sunbury Shores Arts & Nature Centre; Olde Tyme Pizza
25 Eastern Outdoors
29 Sheriff Andrew House
30 Adventure Destinations Complex
31 Market Square
32 The Tidal Pool
33 HMS Transportation
34 Seafarers' Internet Cafe; Harbor Front Restaurant; Washboard Laundry

Seafarers' Internet Cafe (☎ 506-529-4610) 233 Water St, has five computers providing Internet access at $2 per 20 minutes. It's open 9am to 10pm daily July and August, 9am to 9pm Tuesday to Sunday the rest of the year.

Washboard Laundry (☎ 506-529-3048), 241 Water St, has new machines and charges $2 to wash or dry. It's open 8am to 11pm daily.

Sheriff Andrew House

This restored middle-class home (☎ 506-529-5080, cnr of King & Queen Sts; admission by donation; open 9:30am-4:30pm Mon-Sat, 1pm-4:30pm Sun July-Sept) dates from 1820. It has been redecorated in period style and is attended by costumed guides.

Ross Memorial Museum

This museum (☎ 506-529-1824, cnr of King & Montague Sts; admission $3; open 10am-4:30pm Tues-Sat mid-June-early Oct; 10am-4:30pm Mon-Sat July & Aug) is in a neoclassical house of some size. It features the furniture and decorative arts collections of its former owners, Mr and Mrs Ross, who lived in the house until 1945.

Algonquin Hotel

The classic 1889 resort hotel, with its veranda, gardens, tennis courts and pool, is worth a look. Inside, off the lobby, are a couple of places for a drink, be it tea or gin. In 1914, workers tarring the roof started a fire that seriously damaged the 234-room Algonquin, but it was rebuilt the next year.

Other Historic Buildings

Opposite the Algonquin Hotel, you may want to take a peek at the English-style castle-cottage called **Pansy Patch** (☎ 506-529-3834, 59 Carleton St), with its surrounding garden. Sometimes called 'the most photographed house in New Brunswick,' this is now a rather high-priced B&B.

Charlotte Country Court House (☎ 506-529-4248, 123 Frederick St; admission free; open 9am-5pm Mon-Fri June-mid-Oct, 1pm-4pm Mon-Fri mid-Oct-May), erected

1840, displays a royal coat of arms carved on the façade in 1858. The adjacent old jail is now the county archives (with a gift shop).

Greenoch Presbyterian Church (cnr of Edward & Montague Sts), dating from 1824, is named for the relief carving of a green oak on the steeple.

Katy's Cove

Katy's Cove, 400m down Acadia Rd from the east side of the Algonquin Hotel, offers a beach, snack bar and entrance to the New Brunswick Trail. This segment of the trail leads due north to Bar Rd, where it currently ends (the trail system is still being developed).

Kingsbrae Garden

Opened in 1998, this site (☎ 506-529-3335, 220 King St; adult/senior, student or child $7/5; open 9am-6pm daily June-early Oct) displays some 2000 varieties of trees, shrubs and plants over its 27 acres. The grounds include a cedar maze, ponds and streams, a functioning windmill and a woodland trail devoted to New Brunswick trees. The gardens change annually. The site also has a cafe.

Science-by-the-Sea Kiosk

This roadside exhibit showcases the scientific and historical wealth of the St Andrews area and directs you to local points of interest. It's located on Indian Point, next to the campground, and includes a telescope from which you can view much of the bay, including Minister's Island. It's open irregularly June to early October.

Blockhouse Historic Site

The restored wooden guardhouse (☎ 506-529-4270, Water St; admission free; open 9am-8pm daily June-Aug, 9am-5pm early Sept) is the last surviving guardhouse from the War of 1812, and it almost didn't survive the 20th century. In 1993, arsonists set fire to the historical structure, and the floors and ceiling were rebuilt out of white pine. The original hand-hewn walls – the darker timbers inside – survived. There are some good views through the gun holes on the

NEW BRUNSWICK

2nd floor. The park is at the northwest end of Water St. If the tide is out, there's a path that extends from the blockhouse out across the tidal flats. **Centennial Park** opposite the blockhouse has a cozy picnic pavilion.

Sunbury Shores Arts & Nature Centre

This is a nonprofit educational and cultural center *(☎ 506-529-3386, Ⓦ www.sunbury shores.org, 139 Water St; admission free; open 9am-4:30pm Mon-Fri, noon-4pm Sat year-round, also noon-4pm Sun May-Sept)* offering instruction in painting, weaving, pottery and other crafts, as well as natural science courses. Various changing exhibits run through summer. It is based in Centennial House, an old general store.

The center also maintains the 800m **Twin Meadows Walking Trail**, a boardwalk and footpath through fields and woodlands that begins opposite 165 Joe's Point Rd beyond the Blockhouse.

Huntsman Aquarium Museum

Right next to the Fisheries & Oceans Biological Station, 2km northwest of the blockhouse and past the Algonquin Golf Course, is the Huntsman Marine Science Centre, containing research facilities and labs. It's part of the Federal Fisheries Research Centre – St Andrews' most important business. Some of Canada's leading marine biologists work here.

The Huntsman lab also maintains its Aquarium Museum *(☎ 506-529-1202, 1 Lower Campus Rd; adult/child $5.75/3.75; open noon-4:30pm Mon & Tues, 10am-4:30pm Wed-Sun late May-Oct, 10am-6pm July-Sept)*, which features displays of most specimens found in local waters, including seals. There's a good seaweed display and one pool where the various creatures can be touched, even picked up, which is great for kids. The high point of the day at the aquarium is the feeding of the center's harbor seals, usually done at 11am and 4pm.

Minister's Island Historic Site

Minister's Island was purchased and used as a summer retreat by William Cornelius Van Horne, builder of the Canadian Pacific Railway across the country and the company's first president and later chairman of the board. The island, his cottage of 50 rooms and the unusual bathhouse with its tidal swimming pool can now be visited.

Minister's Island is accessible at low tide, even by car, when you can drive on the hard-packed sea floor. A few hours later, this route is under 3m of water. You can only visit the island on a guided tour through **Friends of Minister's Island** *(☎ 506-529-5081; adult/child $5/2.50, operating May-Oct)*. The two-hour tours are offered once or twice a day, depending on the tides. If you call their number, you'll hear a recording with exact departure times. You meet at the end of Bar Rd, 1½km off Hwy 127 E to Saint John, where a guide then leads the caravan across the tidal flats. You must have your own vehicle.

Atlantic Salmon Conservation Centre

In the village of Chamcook, 6km north of St Andrews and 12km off Hwy 1 via Hwy 127 E, the Salmon Centre *(☎ 506-529-4581, Ⓦ www.asf.ca; adult/student/child $4/3.50/ 2.50; open 9am-5pm daily June-mid-Oct)* tells the story of Atlantic salmon, prized by anglers and gourmets. Displays, including live fish, show the fish's history and life cycle. In recent years many additions have been opened. There's now a conservation hall of fame, waterfalls and streams right in the complex, multimedia rooms, and bucolic trails outside.

Saint Croix Island Viewpoint

On Hwy 127 N, 8km from town and 9km off Hwy 1, is a viewpoint overlooking the tiny island in the Saint Croix River where French explorer Samuel de Champlain spent his first winter in North America in 1604. The island itself is in Maine, USA, but a series of panels explain the significance of this national historic site. In 2004, there will be massive celebrations in this region to mark the 400th anniversary of the first continuous French settlement in North America.

Activities

Eastern Outdoors (☎ 506-529-4662, ❼ www
easternoutdoors.com, 165B Water St; open
mid-May-Oct) is a St Andrews-based outfit-
ter that offers three-hour kayak trips at $35.
It also has rentals of kayaks ($25/35 half/full
day single, $45/55 double), canoes ($25/35)
and mountain bikes ($7/15/25 an hour/half
day/full day).

Organized Tours

Tour Boats Several companies at the
market wharf run sightseeing cruises, which
include whale watching after the beasts
arrive in late June. Because the ideal waters
for whale watching are farther out in the
bay, it's better to take this tour from either
Deer Island or Campobello if you happen
to be visiting those places, where you'll
spend more time actually watching the
whales. Yet even without the whales, the
scenery here is lovely and seabirds are
abundant.

In St Andrews, **Fundy Tide Runners**
(☎ 506-529-4481, Adventure Destinations
complex, King St; adult/child $55/35; open
mid-May-mid-Oct) uses a 7m Zodiac to zip
you around on the bay. A couple of two-
hour tours are offered daily.

Quoddy Link Marine (☎ 506-529-2600,
Adventure Destinations complex, King St)
has a more conventional catamaran (3-hour
tour $49/45/30 adult/senior/child). They go
out at 9:30am and 1:30pm late June to September (also at 5:30pm in July and August).

The tall ship SV **Cory** (☎ 506-529-8116,
Adventure Destinations complex, King St;
adult/senior/child $50/45/35) sails about Pas-
samaquoddy Bay searching for whales two
to four times daily from June to September.

Island Quest Marine (☎ 506-529-9885,
Adventure Destinations complex, King St;
adult/child $43/25; open May-mid-Oct) uses
a 12m tour boat for their excursions.

Other Tours Heritage Discovery Tours
(☎ 506-529-4011, ❼ personal.nbnet.nb.ca/
sheilaw/hdt; adult/family $15/40) offers a
'Magical History' walking tour with costumed guides at 10am daily May to
October. There's also a 'Mysteries of the

Night Ghost Walk' at 8pm, which is great
for families with children ($10/30). All tours
begin from the Algonquin Resort, and
they're often sold out a week in advance, especially during the 'bus tour months,' September and October. Most bookings are
done by phone.

In July and August **HMS Transportation**
(☎ 506-529-4443, 260 Water St; adult/child
$12/6) has two-hour bus tours of the town
leaving the Algonquin Resort at 10am.

Places to Stay

Camping *Kiwanis Oceanfront Camping*
(☎ 877-393-7070, fax 506-529-3246, ✉ koc@
nb.sympatico.ca, ❼ www.kiwanisoceanfront
camping.com, 550 Water St) Tent site $19,
with electricity $23. Open mid-May-mid-
Oct. At the far east end of town on Indian
Point is this facility, run by the Kiwanis
Club, for tents and trailers. It's mostly a
gravel parking area for trailers, although
some grassy spots are found. There are
picnic tables and good views but no shade.

Tourist Homes & B&Bs *Salty Towers*
(☎ 506-529-4585, ✉ steeljm@nbnet.nb.ca,
340 Water St) Rooms from $30, doubles with
bath & efficiencies with kitchen $65. One
could call it a Victorian tourist home with a
hostel complex; even the proprietor dubs it
'Chateau Alternatato.' Although Salty
Towers has been an inn since 1921, it is
unlike anything in St Andrews, if not
Canada. Run by Jamie Steel, a local natural-
ist, it's a sprawling 1840s mansion turned
into an offbeat, very casual place for wan-
derers to call home – you'll also find local
students on the premises. There are 16
rooms – of every conceivable size and
fashion, so take a look at lots. Five have
private bath; the others share the baths. This
is not for those looking for gingerbread Victorian quaint. It's a funky, artsy place, like
walking into a Victorian mansion full of
junk (treasures) and becoming one of the
family. It's just a short walk from the bus
station and town.

Elder Shore Guesthouse (☎ 506-529-
4795, ✉ esgh@charlottecountyonline.com,
❼ www.charlottecountyonline.com/esgh.htm,

100 Queen St) Singles/doubles $65/80 July & Aug, $50/65 spring & fall. Open Apr-Nov. This central guesthouse is a modest but very appealing place that has been serving guests for many years.

A Seascape B&B (☎ 506-529-3872, e *mac@nbnet.nb.ca, 190 Parr St)* Singles/doubles $65/75. Open June-Sept. This place, in an 1860s Cape Cod–style home, is similar in price to Elder Shore Guesthouse.

Hotels & Motels *Picket Fence Motel* (☎ *506-529-8985, fax 506-529-8985, 102 Reed Ave)* Singles/doubles/triples from $55/65/75 July & Aug, $50/55/60 shoulder seasons. Open June-mid-Sept. This L-shaped block of 15 rooms is next to the fire department, just up the street from the tourist office.

Blue Moon Motel (☎ *877-534-5271, fax 506-529-3245,* w *www.sn2000.nb.ca/comp/blue-moon-motel, 310 Mowatt Dr)* Rooms $55 single or double July & Aug, singles/doubles from $45/50 shoulder seasons. Open May-Oct. This 39-room, single-story motel serves its purpose.

Greenside Motel (☎ *506-529-3039, fax 506-529-3039,* w *www.sn2000.nb.ca/comp/greenside-motel, 242 Mowatt Dr)* Rooms $60 and up single or double July & Aug, $50 shoulder seasons. Open June-mid-Sept. On Hwy 127 E, (also known as Mowatt Dr) and practically next door to the Blue Moon, Greenside has 17 rooms in two long blocks.

Algonquin Resort Hotel (☎ *888-460-8999, fax 506-529-7162,* e *algsales@fairmont.com,* w *www.fairmont.com, 184 Adolphus St)* Rooms from $289 single or double July-Oct, $149 April-June, $120 Nov-March. You pay for the charm and the amenities at this classic Fairmont-run hotel. A walk through the lobby or maybe a drink on the porch will give nonguests a sense of the atmosphere. Dinner in the restaurant will cost $10 to $12 for appetizers, $10 soup or salad and $18 to $33 for mains.

Places to Eat

From June to mid-October, Market Square downtown hosts a Thursday morning *farmers market*.

Waterfront Takeout (*40 King St at Wate St)* Lunch $5. Head here for cheap eats. I has fish & chips from $5 and cheeseburger from $3.

Historic Chef's Café (☎ *506-529-8888 178 Water St)* Meals $12-26. Open 6:30am 10pm daily. For a burger and a dose of Elvis there's Chef's Café, with its 1950s decor and classic jukebox. Super deluxe burgers are $8, and regular meals of chicken, steak or seafood vary.

Olde Tyme Pizza (☎ *506-529-8800, 15. Water St)* Average pizzas $8-13. Open 11am 9pm daily Mon-Sat, 4pm-9pm Sun. Olde Tyme has a large deck at the rear overlook ing the harbor.

L'Europe Dining Room (☎ *506-529-3818, 48 King St)* Mains $17-26. Open 5pm 9pm daily June-Oct; 5pm-9pm Wed-Sat Dec, Apr & May; 5pm-9pm Thurs-Sat Jan mid-Feb. For something special, consider cozy L'Europe, a German-style white stucco place. Specialties include the haddock almond ($20) and rack of lamb ($27).

Harbor Front Restaurant (☎ *506-529-4887, 225 Water St)* Mains $13. Open 11am 9pm daily May-Oct, 11am-11pm July & Aug. Right in the middle of town with a pleasant patio overlooking the boats in the harbor, is the Harbor Front. It has a bit of everything but a lot of seafood. The stuffed sole is worth trying.

Lighthouse Restaurant (☎ *506-529-3082, 1 Patrick St)* Dinners $11 and up. Open 5pm-9pm daily late May-early Oct; 11:30am-2pm & 5pm-9pm July & Aug Lobster is the main dish at this restaurant. At lunch, you can enjoy a grilled lobster and cheese sandwich for $9.

Entertainment

The Tidal Pool (☎ *506-529-4282, 248 Water St)* Open 3pm-1am Mon-Wed, noon-1am Thurs-Sun. This is the only place in town with live music, with blues and folk on weekends, and sometimes during the week. Local events are advertised on posters outside.

Getting There & Around

SMT Bus Lines departs HMS Transportation (☎ 506-529-3101) at 260 Water St at

4pm daily for the 1½ hour trip to Saint John ($14). It goes the other way toward Bangor, Maine, Fridays and Saturdays at 2:45pm ($18). Check their Web site at W www.hms trans.com.

HMS Transportation rents cars at $48 a day including 200 km, plus tax and $14 insurance.

FUNDY ISLES
St George
St George, on the Magaguadavic River 40km east of St Stephen, is a small town on New Brunswick with 1500 residents. After 1783, the United States claimed all the territory up to this river, and the matter wasn't resolved until 1842, when the current boundary was accepted.

St George is known for its granite and its water. Granite mining began in the river gorge in 1872, and a thriving industry was created that lasted for more than 60 years. Black granite and 'St George Red' were the most sought after blocks, and today St George granite is found in the Parliament Buildings in Ottawa and the American Museum of Natural History in New York City.

The town water, from deep artesian wells, is said to be the best in the country. You can see the granite and sample the water at a monument downtown in front of the post office.

St George Fishway The waterfall and gorge on the Magaguadavic River, off Brunswick St between Hwy 1 and the center of town, are a local beauty spot. By the bridge over the river is a fishway that allows fish to bypass a concrete dam built in 1928. The 43 pools in the fish ladder are used by Atlantic salmon from June to October, and by alwives in May and June. You can peer in at the migrating fish through glass windows, and there's also a fine view down the gorge.

Organized Tours All local tour operators are found in the Adventure Destinations complex adjacent to the tourist office on Hwy 770, along the Magaguadavic River just north of Hwy 1. These offices and their tours only operate from June to September, with reduced hours at the beginning and end of the season.

The **Outdoor Adventure Company** (☎ 506-755-6415, ☎ 800-667-2010, W www .havefun.net) specializes in a wildlife kayak tour ($49/95 per half/full day). Canoeing is available at the same price. Bicycle rentals are $5/20 an hour/half day.

Piskahegan River Company (☎ 506-755-6269, ☎ 800-640-8944, W www.piskahegan .com) has kayak and canoe tours ($60/95 per half/full day including a meal). They also have bases on Deer and Campobello Islands.

Interactive Outdoors (☎ 506-755-2699) offers whale watching four times a day and deep-sea fishing three times a day. Both are $40 per person.

Places to Stay & Eat Accommodations in St George are limited and expensive. You'll find better deals in St Andrews or St Stephen.

Grove Motel (☎ 506-755-3725, 30 Brunswick St) Singles/doubles $65/75 ($85 for two beds) mid-June-mid-Sept, $55/65 ($75 for two beds) other months. Open May-Dec. Just 1.2km west of the fishway, Grove Motel has 15 rooms.

Birch Grove Restaurant (☎ 506-755-3131, 34 Brunswick St) Seafood meals $10-13. Open 11am-9pm Mon-Sat, 11am-10pm Sun Apr-Dec; 7am-9pm Mon-Sat, 7am-10pm Sun June-Sept. This unusual takeaway-style place next door to Grove Motel has lobster rolls, mussels, scallops and clams, plus burgers and chips (burger platter $5). There's also a regular dining room in back. It's about the best place in town.

Blacks Harbor
The jump-off spot for Grand Manan Island is Blacks Harbor. Sardine lovers will note that this seaport is also home of Connor Brothers, one of the world's largest producers of those delectable little fish-in-a-can. Two thousand people work here. Connor Brother's trademark brand is Brunswick Sardines and the company runs a factory

NEW BRUNSWICK

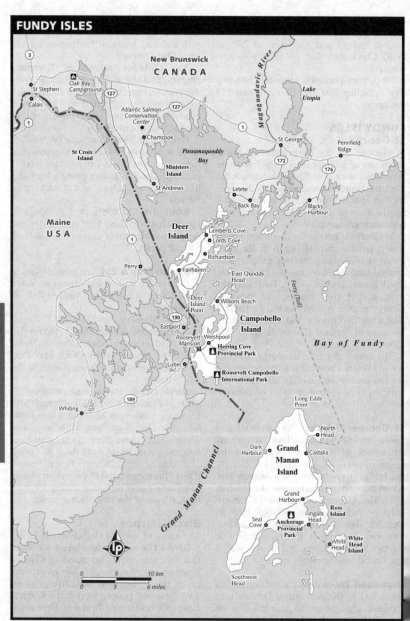

FUNDY ISLES

New Brunswick
CANADA

Maine
USA

St Stephen
Calais
3
1

Oak Bay Campground
127
127

Atlantic Salmon Conservation Center

Chamcook

St Croix Island

Ministers Island

Passamaquoddy Bay

St Andrews

1

Perry

Deer Island

Lamberts Cove
Lords Cove
Richardson
Fairhaven
East Quoddy Head

Deer Island Point
190
Eastport
Roosevelt Mansion
Welshpool
Herring Cove Provincial Park
Lubec
189
Roosevelt Campobello International Park

Whiting

Maguaguadavic River

Lake Utopia

St George
172

Pennfield Ridge
176

Letete
Back Bay

Blacks Harbour

Wilsons Beach

Campobello Island

Ferry (Toll)

Bay of Fundy

Grand Manan Channel

Long Eddy Point

North Head

Dark Harbour

Grand Manan Island

Castalia

Grand Harbour

Seal Cove

Ingalls Head

Ross Island

Anchorage Provincial Park

White Head
White Head Island

Southwest Head

NEW BRUNSWICK

0   5   10 km
0   3   6 miles

The lobster's revenge, Shediac, New Brunswick

Spring puts on a show on hiking trails around Fundy National Park, New Brunswick.

Dense, early morning mist on the Saint John River, Fredericton, New Brunswick

Making dye, Acadian Historic Village, Caraquet

East Quoddy Lighthouse, Fundy Isles

outlet store (☎ 506-456-3897) behind Silver King Restaurant in the center of town. Load up.

Bayview B&B (☎ 506-456-1982, W www.bbexpo.com/nb/bayview.htm, 391 Deadmans Harbour Rd) Singles/doubles $45/50. This family house opposite a bay, 4km from the Grand Manan ferry, offers three rooms with shared bath.

Smith's Motel (☎ 506-755-3034, W www.sn2000.nb.ca/comp/smiths-motel, 5254 Hwy 1, Pennfield Ridge) Singles/doubles $49/54 mid-June-mid-Sept, $42/47 shoulder seasons. Open Apr-Dec. Just 2½km east of the Hwy 176 turnoff to Blacks Harbor, Smith's has 27 rooms in three blocks. There's a restaurant on premises, otherwise **Pennfield Take-Out** next door has cheap takeout ice cream, hamburgers and lobster rolls.

Deer Island

Deer Island, the closest of the three main Fundy Isles, is a modest fishing community. Lobster is the main catch. Around the island are half a dozen wharves and the net systems used in aquaculture. Narrow, winding roads run down each side toward Campobello Island (drive cautiously). This 16km-by-5km island has been inhabited since 1770, and a thousand people live here year-round. It's well wooded, and deer are still plentiful. Most land is privately owned, so there are no hiking trails.

There's a summertime tourist information booth at the ferry landing. At **Lamberts Cove** is a huge (it could well be the world's largest) lobster pound used to hold live lobster. Another pound is at Northern Harbor down the road.

At the other end of the island is the 16-hectare **Deer Island Point Park** where Old Sow, the world's second-largest natural tidal whirlpool, can be seen offshore a few hours before high tide. Whales pass occasionally.

Kayaking The **Piskahegan River Company** (☎ 506-755-6269, 800-640-8944, Adventure Destinations complex, St George) offers island day tours ($60/95 a half/full day) and supper and moonlight paddles ($45 and up).

To get to their Deer Island base, take Leaman Rd to the left 1.3km from ferry. The sea kayak shack will be 500m ahead. Call ahead, as the shack is usually unstaffed unless there are reservations.

Eastern Outdoors (☎ 800-565-2925, W www.easternoutdoors.com, Brunswick Square, 39 King St, Saint John) operates Deer Island kayak tours ($59) throughout the year. Participants meet at the northern ferry wharf on Deer Island and see numerous marine mammals, seabirds, islands and beaches during the six hour tour. There's no minimum number of people required to run a tour and for an extra $10 they'll throw in return transfers from Saint John.

Whale-Watching Tours Given the island's location, the whale watching is good here. The whales arrive in large numbers in mid-July and stay right through October. **Cline Marine Inc** (☎ 506-747-0114, 800-567-5880, W www.clinemarine.com, 99 Richardson Rd) offers whale-watching tours on the 60-passenger Cathy & Trevor at 9:30am, 12:30pm and 3:30pm in July and August (2½ hours, adult/child $50/25). The 12:30pm tour is sometimes full, but you can usually squeeze on the other two. In June, only the usual 12:30pm departure goes, and in September and October, there's a special 4-hour tour at 12:30pm (adult/child $60/30). They depart from Richardson Wharf. To get there from Letete ferry, turn left after 2.8km and continue another kilometer to the office.

Lambert's Outer Island Tours (☎ 506-747-2426, 506-754-5115; adult/child/family $43/25/120) has whale-watching tours at 10am, 1pm and 4 pm in July and August. It's a smaller operation than Cline and they have a smaller boat (which is a plus or a minus, depending on your point of view). They leave from Lord's Cove, 2km straight ahead from Letete ferry.

Places to Stay Deer Island Point Park (☎ 506-747-2423, fax 506-747-1009, e dipointpark@yahoo.com, 195 Deer Island Point Rd) Tent sites $15. Open June-Sept. The best place to spend a night on the island is this park run by the Deer Island Recreational Council. You can set up your tent on the high bluff and spend an evening watching the Old Sow whirlpool. The campground includes nice grassy sites, showers, laundry facilities and even a small store. It's directly above the Campobello ferry landing.

West Isles World B&B (☎ 877-744-2946, fax 506-747-2946, ⓔ wstiswld@nb.aibn.com, ⓦ www.westislesworld.nb.ca, Lambert Rd) Singles/doubles $50/75 July & Aug, $40/65 other months. The closest lodging to the ferry is West Isles World, 800m down Lambert Rd (the first road on the right 1km from the Letete ferry). It's not far from Lamberts Cove with its huge lobster pound. This old-style house has two rooms for rent.

Gardner House B&B (☎ 506-747-2462, Lambert Rd) Singles/doubles $50/60. Open May-Sept. This large farmhouse 1½km beyond West Isles World, past Lambert's Cove, features a small but charming steak and seafood restaurant (open 11am to 10pm in summer) on the 1st floor and three rooms for rent on the 2nd floor.

Sparky Too B&B (☎ 506-747-1988, ⓦ www.angelfire.com/biz/sparkytoo, 108 Richardson Rd) Singles/doubles $60/70 July & Aug, $50/60 other months. This house on a slope overlooking the sea is just 200m south of Cline Marine.

45th Parallel Motel (☎ 506-747-2231, fax 506-747-1890, ⓦ www.angelfire.com/biz2/parallel45, 941 Hwy 772) Singles/doubles $46/60 May-Oct, $40/50 Nov, Dec, March & Apr, closed Jan & Feb. The summer rate includes breakfast. This motel in Fairhaven, 5km north of the Campobello ferry and 10½km south of Letete ferry, has a row of 10 rooms in a block behind the restaurant.

Places to Eat *Village School Diner & Takeout* (932 Hwy 772) Meals $6-10. Open daily July & Aug; Fri-Sun June & early Sept. Both places to eat on Deer Island are within sight of one another at Fairhaven. The Village School has indoor and outdoor seating. Menu items include burger platters ($6), fish & chips ($10) and ice cream ($2). They often have good fish specials ($7), and there's a pool table.

Whale Watching Galore

Whales, the great mammals of the depths, have become major attractions around the Maritimes. Tours to photograph the awesome creatures depart from ports in places ranging from New Brunswick's Grand Manan to Nova Scotia's Cape Breton. From most accounts, the trips are usually successful and well worth the $20 to $40 cost for a couple of hours.

Some of the best areas for whale watching are around the Fundy Isles in New Brunswick or from the tip of Digby Neck in Nova Scotia. Also in Nova Scotia, the north shore of Cape Breton up around the national park is excellent. Sightings are so regular in these areas that many captains offer a full refund – or at least a rain check – if no whales emerge.

Around the Bay of Fundy the most commonly seen whales are the fin (or finback), the humpback (15m), the right (18m, less commonly seen), and the minke. In addition, porpoises and dolphins are plentiful. In this area the best whale watching begins in early August and lasts until September.

From Westport, the season seems to begin a little earlier, with good sightings reported in late June, and by mid-July there are good numbers of all species.

The humpback, one of the larger whales of the Maritimes, also puts on the best show, breaching and diving, with its flukes (tail) clearly visible above the surface.

Up around Cape Breton the smaller pilot or pothead whales, also known as blackwhales, are common; sometimes they're even seen from shore. Finbacks frequent these waters as well. Operators here run trips in July and August.

Regardless of the weather or time of year, take plenty of clothing, something for seasickness and lots of film.

Research is ongoing to determine if whale watching itself is detrimental to the always vulnerable whale populations. Regulations now dictate that no boat get too close.

Whale Watching Galore

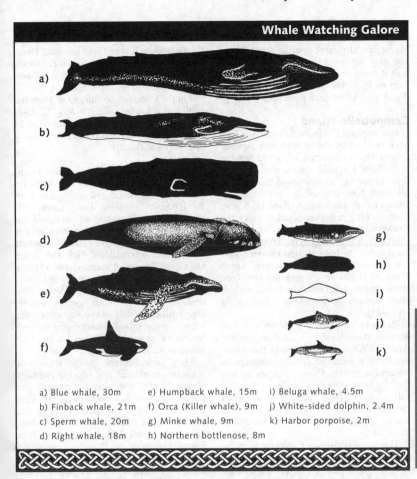

a) Blue whale, 30m
b) Finback whale, 21m
c) Sperm whale, 20m
d) Right whale, 18m
e) Humpback whale, 15m
f) Orca (Killer whale), 9m
g) Minke whale, 9m
h) Northern bottlenose, 8m
i) Beluga whale, 4.5m
j) White-sided dolphin, 2.4m
k) Harbor porpoise, 2m

NEW BRUNSWICK

45th Parallel Restaurant (☎ 506-747-2231, 941 Hwy 772) Main meals $9-14. Open noon-2pm Tues & Thurs, 5pm-10pm Fri & Sat, noon-7pm Sun mid-Sept-early June, 11am-9pm early June-mid-Sept. Their specialty is seafood, such as fish & chips ($9) and scallops & fries ($14). In summer they also serve lobster rolls ($10), clam chowder ($8) and lobster dinners ($22-25).

Getting There & Away A free 25-minute government ferry runs to Deer Island from Letete (L'Etete in French), 14½km south of St George on Hwy 172 via Back Bay. The ferries run year-round every half-hour 7am-7pm, hourly 7pm-10pm. Get in line early on a busy day.

In July and August, a privately operated ferry leaves Deer Island Point for Campobello Island. The fare is $13 for a car and driver plus $2 per passenger. It's a scenic 25-minute trip past numerous islands. During summer there are 10 trips a day between 8:30am and 6:30pm.

The same company runs another ferry that connects Deer Island Point to Eastport, Maine, an attractive seaside town where you may see freighters moored. For Eastport it leaves every hour on the hour from 9am to 6pm. The fare is $10 for car and driver, plus $2 for each passenger.

Campobello Island

Scenic, tranquil Campobello Island has long been enjoyed by the wealthy as a summer retreat. Due to its accessibility and proximity to New England – it's a stone's throw from Maine but a ways across the water to mainland New Brunswick – the island has always felt as much a part of the USA as of Canada. Like many moneyed families, the Roosevelts bought property in this peaceful coastal area at the end of the 1800s, and it is for this that the island is best known. Today you can see the 34-room 'cottage' where Franklin D Roosevelt grew up (between 1905 and 1921) and which he visited periodically throughout his time as US president (1933–45).

Roosevelt was by no means the first notable American to visit Campobello. After the American Revolution, the American 'traitor' Benedict Arnold established a warehouse at Snug Cove, which served as a base for his trading ship, the *Peggy*. Arnold's wife, a socialite from Philadelphia, no doubt thought Campobello dreadfully dull, and from 1787 to 1791 the couple resided in Saint John.

The atmosphere on Campobello is remarkably different from that on Deer Island. It's more prosperous and gentler, with straight roads and better facilities. A third of Campobello is parkland, and the golf course occupies a bit more. Most of the tourists here are Americans. There isn't even a gas station on the island; to fill their tanks, the 1200 residents of Campobello must cross the bridge to Lubec, Maine. They generally use the same bridge to get anywhere else in New Brunswick as well, since the ferry only goes to Deer Island in summer.

From the bridge at the southwestern tip of the island, it's 84km to St Stephen by road. As you cross to or from Lubec notice the lobster pond between the bridge and the lighthouse on the Canadian side. Thousands of lobsters are kept alive there awaiting shipment, and offshore sit huge salmon cages where fish are farmed.

On the Campobello side, 500m from the bridge, is a tourist office (☎ 506-752-7043) with currency exchange. It's open 10am to 6pm daily late May to early October, 9am to 7pm July and August.

Things to See The ferry from Deer Island arrives at Welshpool, which is halfway up the 16km-long island and about 3km from the Roosevelt mansion. The southern half of Campobello is almost all park, and the southernmost portion of this green area is taken up by the 1200-hectare **Roosevelt Campobello International Park**. This is the site of the Roosevelt mansion and a visitor center (☎ 506-752-2922, ⓦ www.fdr.net, Hwy 774; admission free; open 10am-6pm daily late May-Oct). Aside from an interesting photo exhibition on the Roosevelts, the visitor center proudly displays an original birchbark canoe (1890) once owned by Franklin Roosevelt himself.

Free guided tours of the Roosevelt mansion are offered, and adjacent **Hubbard House** (1898) can also be visited. The grounds around these buildings are open all the time, so you can peek through the windows even when the doors are closed. The park is just 2½km from the Lubec bridge, and from the Roosevelt mansion's front porch you can look directly across to Eastport, Maine. If you didn't know better, you'd hardly guess you were in Canada.

Unlike the manicured museum area, most of the international park has been left in its natural state to preserve the flora and fauna that Roosevelt appreciated so much. A couple of gravel roads meander through it leading to beaches and 7½km of nature trails. It's a surprisingly wild, little-visited area of Campobello Island. Deer, moose and coyote are among the mammals in the park, and seals can sometimes be seen offshore on the ledges near Lower Duck Pond, 6km from the visitor center via a gravel road. Among the many birds along the shoreline are eagles, ospreys and loons.

Along the international park's northern boundary is New Brunswick's **Herring Cove Provincial Park** (admission free). This park has another 10km of walking trails as well as a campground and a picnic area on an arching 1½km beach. It makes a fine, picturesque place for lunch.

Wilsons Beach, 10km north of Roosevelt Park, has a large pier where fish can be bought, and a sardine-processing plant with an adjacent store. There are various services and shops here in Campobello Island's biggest community.

Four kilometers north of Wilsons Beach, **East Quoddy Head**, with its lighthouse at the northern tip of the island, is the second busiest visitor spot on Campobello. Whales can often be seen from here, and many people put in some time sitting on the rocky shoreline with a pair of binoculars enjoying the sea breezes.

Kayaking From June to mid-September, the **Piskahegan River Company** (☎ 506-755-6269, 800-640-8944, Adventure Destinations complex, St George) operates out of Pollock Cove Cottages, 2455 Hwy 774, Wilson's Beach. They offer kayaking tours ($60/95 per half/full day) around Campobello, but you must call ahead for reservations, as they aren't always there.

Whale Watching The **Campobello Whale Watch Company** (☎ 506-752-2359), on North Road Wharf 3km north of Welshpool ferry, has two-hour tours (adult/child $42/25). Departures are at 10am, 1:30pm and 4pm from July to mid-September. You stand a good chance of seeing finback and minke whales, as well as porpoises.

Cline Marine (☎ 800-567-5880) will pick up passengers for their whale-watching trips at Head Harbor Wharf upon request. See the Deer Island section for details.

Places to Stay Herring Cove Provincial Park (☎ 506-752-7010, fax 506-752-7012, e herringc@gnb.ca, w www.tourismn canada.com/web/english/outdoor_network,

136 Herring Cove Rd) Unserviced/serviced sites $21.50/24. Open mid-May-early Oct. This 76-site park on the east side of the island, 3km from the Deer Island ferry, has some nice secluded sites in a forest setting. It's preferable to Deer Island Point Park and makes a good base for visiting the adjacent international park. A long sandy beach is nearby and there's ample hiking. The park also operates the golf course (☎ 506-752-7041; open May-mid-Oct) just opposite which charges $18.50 for nine holes, plus $15 club rental.

Friar's Bay Motor Lodge (☎ 506-752-2056, 802 Hwy 774; open Apr-Dec) Singles/doubles from $35/40. This simple motel 1km from the Deer Island ferry landing in Welshpool consists of a long row of basic wooden units.

Lupine Lodge (☎ 506-752-2555, e info@lupinelodge.com, w www.lupinelodge.com, 610 Hwy 774) Singles/doubles $50/70-99. Open June-Oct. This unusual hotel, 800m from Roosevelt Campobello International Park on the way from Welshpool, has 11 rooms in two large log cabin-style blocks. A third such block contains the reception area and restaurant.

Grand Manan Island

South of Campobello Island, Grand Manan is the largest of the Fundy Isles – peaceful, relaxed and engaging. The island offers a spectacular coastal setting, excellent bird watching, fine hiking trails and sandy beaches, and a series of small fishing villages are dotted along its 30km length.

On one side of the island are rock formations estimated to be billions of years old. On the other side are volcanic deposits left 16 million years ago by an underwater volcano, which draw many geologists to the area.

In 1831, James Audubon first documented the many bird species that frequent the island. About 312 species, including puffins and Arctic terns, live here or pass by each year, so the island is quite popular with bird watchers as well. It's not uncommon to see whales feeding offshore on the abundant herring and mackerel. Whales seen in the area include the humpback, finback, minke and pothead; they generally arrive in June when the waters have begun to warm up.

Despite all of this, the island's relative isolation and low-key approach to development mean there are few crowds and little obvious commercialization, making it a good place for cyclists. Grand Manan is small enough to tour in a single day by bicycle, and bikes can be rented on the island if you want to leave your car on the mainland in Blacks Harbour.

One thing many will wish to sample on the island is the dulse, an edible seaweed for which Grand Manan Island is renowned. It's a very popular snack food around the Maritime provinces, and most of it (the best, according to connoisseurs) comes from Grand Manan. Dulse is sold around the island, mostly from people's homes. Watch for signs.

Grand Manan's Visitor Information Centre (☎ 506-662-3442) is well hidden behind the Grand Manan Museum at Grand Harbour. It is open 10am to 4pm Monday to Saturday, 1pm to 5pm Sunday July and August.

North Head The ferry terminal is at North Head. There are a few craft- and tourist-oriented stores along the main drag, but of primary interest is the **Whale & Sea Bird Research Station** (☎ 506-662-3804, 24 Hwy 776; admission by donation; open 10am-4pm daily mid-May-Sept, 8:30am-5pm July & Aug), directly across the street from the ferry terminal. It provides lots of good information on the marine life in the area. Exhibits include skeletons and photographs, and there are books on whales and the island in general. The station has a harbor porpoise release program.

North End Some of the most popular of the numerous short walking trails around the island are in this area just north of North Head. Highly recommended is the somewhat pulse-quickening (especially in the fog) trail and footbridge out to the lighthouse at **Swallows Tail**, on a narrow

cliff-edged promontory. To get there, turn right as you leave the ferry – it's only a kilometer to the footbridge. The views of the coast and the sea are great.

Hole in the Wall, an unusual natural rock formation, is beyond the campground 1km from the ferry, past the turnoff to Swallows Tail. An entry fee of $4 is collected. The actual Hole in the Wall Trail is another kilometer straight ahead through the campground along a gravel road. Once you're on the trail, it's less than a 10-minute walk to reach the rock.

Grand Harbour On the north side of Grand Harbour, 11km south of North Head, is the **Grand Manan Museum** (☎ 506-662-3524, 1141 Hwy 776; adult/student $4/2; open 10am-4:30pm Tues-Sat June-Sept). Recently expanded, it has a marine section, displays on the island's geology, antiques and reminders of the Loyalist days, but the highlight is the stuffed-bird collection with examples of species seen on the island. There's a good selection of books for sale and bird checklists for Grand Manan.

Dark Harbour The only village on the west side of the island, Dark Harbour is the center of the dulse industry. The seaweed is handpicked at low tide along the shoreline. It is then dried in the sun and is ready to eat.

Seal Cove Seal Cove flourished during the epoch of the smoked herring (1870–1930), and many wooden structures remain from that time, including numerous smokehouses along the harbor. They're now used as warehouses, but their exteriors have been preserved. Purse seiners still fish for herring here, but the biggest catch is lobster.

Anchorage Provincial Park south of Seal Cove is good for bird watching – wild turkeys and pheasant are common.

Southwest Head The 9km drive south from Seal Cove to the lighthouse and a walk beyond it along the edge of the 180m cliffs should not be missed. Unlimited hiking possibilities extend in both directions.

Activities Grand Manan features more than 18 marked and maintained footpaths that cover 70km of some of the finest hiking in New Brunswick. The most extensive trail system is found at the north end of the island, where several trails can be linked for an overnight trek. Just over a kilometer to the left of the North Head ferry terminal is the beginning of Whistle Rd, which runs five paved kilometers north to **Long Eddy Point Lighthouse**. The rock formations (reaching 80m high at Seven Days Work) at Long Eddy Point offer fine seaside vistas, and whales may be seen, especially on calm days when they break the surface more conspicuously. From Long Eddy Point Lighthouse there's a marked trail east to Ashburton Head via The Bishop.

Another great view of the cliffs on the western side of the island awaits you at the bluff at the end of the road just below Long Eddy Point Lighthouse. The signposted trails to Indian Beach and Money Cove also begin here, but parking may be difficult in midsummer. The **Money Cove Trail** extends 11½km south along the west side of the island to Money Cove. From there you·can either return to North Head the way you came or continue south to Dark Harbour via the Dark Harbour North Trail. Such a trip would entail camping overnight en route.

Note that the trail access and routes may change according to the whims of local landowners; check before you go. For more information pick up a copy of *Heritage Trails and Foot Paths on Grand Manan* ($5) at the Grand Manan Museum in Grand Harbour.

Organized Tours Island Coast Boat Tour *(☎ 506-662-8181, 199 Cedar St; adult/child $44/22)* runs trips from the Fisherman's Wharf in North Head, offering four-hour whale-watching tours in a 12m vessel at 7:30am and 12pm daily July through mid-September. Whale sightings are guaranteed or your money back.

A bit different are the tours from **Sea-View Adventures** *(☎ 506-662-3211, North Head)*. They offer not only the opportunity

to see whales, porpoises etc on the surface, but divers also film life on the seafloor for those onboard, and kids have a chance to get their hands on marine life. In July and August, tours go out daily at 7:45am and 12:45pm (adult/child $43/24).

Sea Watch Tours *(☎ 506-662-8552, W www.seawatchtours.com)* in Seal Cove has been around for 25 years and knows these waters well. Most of their wildlife viewing tours are long (up to six hours), so take a lunch, an anti–motion sickness pill and a warm sweater. Peak whale watching begins in mid-July and continues through September (adult/youth/child/infant $46/36/26/16). Whale sightings are guaranteed, and you often get to see the endangered northern right whale. In midsummer these tours are often fully reserved several days in advance.

Adventure High *(☎ 506-662-3563, W www.adventurehigh.com, 83 Hwy 776, North Head; open mid-May-Oct)*, 600m to the left of the ferry wharf, does sea kayak tours for $50/95 per half/full day. Their two-hour sunset tour is $35. Adventure High also rents bicycles for $16/20 per half/full day (9am to 3pm is considered half a day).

Places to Stay There are over two dozen places to stay on Grand Manan, but prices are among the highest in the Maritimes, with no significant off-season discounts. Aside from seeing Grand Manan as a day trip by ferry, the only way to visit on a limited budget is to patronize a campground.

Hole in the Wall Park (☎ 506-662-3152, 866-662-4489, fax 506-662-3593, e hitw@ nbnet.nb.ca, W www.grandmanancamping .com, 42 Old Airport Rd, North Head) Sites $20-24. Open mid-May-Oct. The entrance to this park is a kilometer from the ferry (to the right as you exit). The 34 'cliff edge' sites are in high demand during summer. Finding your way to your site can be confusing, but the staff will guide you. Some of the sites are rather rocky for tents and they're all different, so look around before you pick one.

Anchorage Provincial Park (☎ 506-662-7022, fax 506-662-7035, W www.tourismnb canada.com/web/english/outdoor_network, between Grand Harbour & Seal Cove) Tent site $21.50, with electricity $24. Open mid-May to early October. Anchorage is 16km from the ferry, 4km north of Seal Cove and a kilometer off the island highway. If you have your own transportation, this is the best camping on the island by far, and most guests are tenters. Anchorage Provincial Park is a spacious place with 101 grassy sites that catch the ocean breeze. If you arrive early, there are some particularly nice sites edged into the woods. A kitchen shelter is provided for rainy days, and there's a playground, Laundromat and long sandy beach. It's possible to reserve in advance, but the staff never turn anyone away. Anchorage adjoins some marshes, which comprise a migratory bird sanctuary, and there are several short hiking trails, including the Long Pond Trail, the Great Pond Trail and the Red Point Trail. Noncampers are welcome to use these trails for free.

Although the lodges, inns and motels on Grand Manan are expensive, several have relatively reasonable prices.

Swallowtail Inn (☎ 506-662-1100, e *swallowtailinn_gifts@yahoo.com*, w *www .angelfire.com/nb/swallowtail, 50 Lighthouse Rd, North Head)* Singles/doubles $69/85. Open May-Sept. This B&B is the prominent white house on the point next to the lighthouse that you see from the ferry as you're arriving on Grand Manan – the erstwhile lighthouse keeper's residence. It's a kilometer to the right from the ferry and has commanding views in three directions.

Marathon Inn (☎ 506-662-8144, e *mhl@ nbnet.nb.ca*, w *www.angelfire.com/biz2/ marathon, up Marathon Lane from the post office in North Head)* Singles/doubles $94/99 July-Sept, $74/79 in June & Oct, $50 the rest of the year. Open May-Oct. With shared bath, $44/49 mid-June-mid-Sept. The Inn's three wooden Victorian-era buildings are just a few hundred meters from the ferry terminal. The original Marathon Hotel was established in 1871, and it's still impressive, although this three-story complex has obviously seen better days. The 15 rooms with bath in the first building are the best. The 13 unheated shared-bath rooms on the

top two floors of the annex are not approved by the Department of Tourism. For that reason, they're the best buy on the island, and Elderhostel groups often book them solid. Don't expect luxuries such as a lock on the door of your room at the Marathon Inn.

Shorecrest Lodge (☎ 506-662-3216, fax 506-662-3507, e *shorcres@nbnet.nb.ca*, w *www.angelfire.com/nb/shorcres, 100 Hwy 776, North Head)* Rooms with breakfast $99 in July & Aug, $65 in May, June, Sept & Oct, $50 without breakfast in March, Apr & Nov. This cozy 10-room guesthouse, 700m to the left from the ferry, is well managed.

Surfside Motel (☎ 877-662-8156, fax 506-662-9191, e *kcheney@nb.sympatico.ca, 123 Hwy 776, North Head)* Singles/doubles $70/80. This is the only motel on Grand Manan, with 24 rooms in long blocks, 900m to the left from ferry.

McLaughlin's Wharf Inn (☎ 506-662-8760, 1863 Hwy 776, Seal Cove)* Singles/doubles $69/79. Open June-Sept. This two-story wooden inn occupies a distinctive old post office built on piles right over the harbor. There's a restaurant. It's your best bet in this area.

Amble Inn Cottages (☎ 506-662-8107, 2262 Hwy 776, Seal Cove)* Singles/doubles/triples $70/75/75. The Amble Inn office, 4km south of Seal Cove, controls bookings at these six duplex cottages, 700m farther down on the road. They also handle the Spray Kist Cottages at Seal Cove itself.

Places to Eat North Head village has the widest selection of places to eat, with a couple of takeout places, two or three regular restaurants and a finer dining room in the ***Shorecrest Lodge*** serving dinner entrees at $15 to $19.

Griff-Inn (☎ 506-662-8360, 121 Rte 776, North Head)* Meals under $10. Open 7am-9pm daily year-round (until 10pm in summer). This restaurant, behind the Surfside Motel, charges a bit more than similar restaurants on the mainland, but the prices are still reasonable for breakfast ($3 to $5), sandwiches ($3 to $5), salads ($6) and fish & chips ($7 to $10). The food is good.

Farmers Market (Hwy 776, North Head) Open 10am-noon Sat late June-mid-Sept. Near the Surfside Motel, 1km to the left from the ferry, the market is always a good source of vegetables, baked goods and handicrafts.

North Head Bakery (☎ 506-662-8862, 199 *Hwy 776, North Head)* Open 6am-6pm Tues-Sat Apr-Dec, also Mon in July & Aug. Do visit this outstanding bakery opposite Grand Manan Hospital, 1.7km to the left from the ferry, for healthy rolls, pastries, cakes and pies. Coffee is served.

Fundy House Restaurant (☎ 506-662-8341, 1303 Hwy 776, Grand Harbour)* Meals $9. Open 7:30am-11pm Mon-Sat, noon-11pm Sun June-Sept; 11am-9pm Mon-Sat Oct-May. This good local restaurant beside the highway on the south side of Grand Harbour, 2km north of Anchorage Provincial Park, serves pizza as well as clams & chips.

MG Fisheries (☎ 506-662-3696, 1181 Hwy 776, Grand Harbour)* Open 8am-noon & 1pm-5pm daily. The MG Fisheries fish market has smoked pollock in July and August at around $6 a pound, plus other seasonal seafoods.

Getting There & Around Coastal Transport Ltd (☎ 506-662-3724, 506-456-3842) operates the ferry service from Blacks Harbour, south of St George on the mainland, to North Head on Grand Manan Island. Actually, there are two ferries – one old and one new. The 64-vehicle, 300-passenger MV *Grand Manan V,* built in 1990, is larger and quicker, knocking half an hour off the two-hour trip. The older MV *Grand Manan* is only used at peak periods. Both ferries have cafeterias, outdoor decks and indoor chairs. Seeing a whale is not uncommon.

For either boat the roundtrip fare is $8.75 per adult, $4.40 for children under 13 and $26.20 for a car. For campervans and trailers you pay according to their length. Bicycles are $3. The trip to Grand Manan actually requires no fare; you just board the boat in Blacks Harbour and go. A ticket is needed to return to the mainland. Advance-ticket sales are available at North Head for the first trip of the day only. Trucks with perishable cargo get priority on the ferry.

In July and August there are seven trips Monday through Saturday and six on Sunday, but there are still lines if you have a car, and there's no reservation system. For walk-ons, bicycles etc, there is never a problem. From September to the end of June the number of trips drops to three or four a day. The service is heavily subsidized by the province, and when money isn't available, crossings listed in the timetable may be cancelled.

If the line of cars at Blacks Harbour is endless or you just want to save money, consider doing Grand Manan as a day cruise. There's lots of free parking near the wharf at Blacks Harbour, though the parking lot can be crowded in midsummer. Depending on the season, you'll have between four and 10 hours on the island between ferries, plenty of time to do the Swallows Tail walk, visit the Whale & Sea Bird Research Station and explore North Head. Summer is the best time to do this, as you'll be able to stand out on deck, whales will be in the area, everything in North Head will be open and you'll have a better choice of ferries for your return.

There's no bus service, so unless you brought transportation of your own, you'll have to walk, hitch or rent a bicycle. A gas station is next to the Surfside Motel at North Head.

White Head Island

White Head is the only other inhabited island in the archipelago. A few resident families make a living fishing. There's a long sandy beach, another lighthouse to visit and some plant and animal life not found on Grand Manan.

A no-charge barge, the *Lady White Head,* makes between four and 10 30-minute trips daily from Ingalls Head, 3½km southeast of Grand Harbour, to White Head Island year-round. Note that the last ferry back leaves at 4pm on Sunday and 7pm other days. If the line of waiting cars is long, you can park free at Ingalls Head and go over on foot.

Machias Seal Island

Sixteen kilometers southwest of Grand Manan is the small island bird sanctuary of Machias Seal Island. Visitors are permitted on shore accompanied by a wildlife officer, but the number is limited to 25 people per day. The feathered residents include terns, puffins, razorbacks and several other species in lesser numbers.

Sea Watch Tours (see Organized Tours earlier in this section) offers trips to this island if the seas aren't rough. These tours operate from mid-June to mid-August. The price is $75 if you wish to land on Machias. Sea Watch begins taking advance reservations as soon as their annual license is approved in January, and by April all departures involving island visits will be fully booked for the season. You can see the birds just as well without getting off the boat, however, and tickets for just the boat trip may still be available as late as a few days before departure (adult/child $55/35).

NEW RIVER PROVINCIAL PARK

Just off Hwy 1, about 35km west of Saint John on the way to or from St Stephen, this large park has one of the best beaches along the Fundy Shore, a wide stretch of sand bordered on one side by the rugged coastline of Barnaby Head.

You can spend an enjoyable few hours hiking Barnaby Head along a 6km network of nature trails. The **Chittick's Beach Trail** leads you through coastal forest and past four coves, where you can check the catch in a herring weir or examine tidal pools for marine life. Extending from this loop is the 2½km **Barnaby Head Trail**, which hugs the shoreline most of the way and at one point puts you on the edge of a cliff 15m above the Bay of Fundy. Be careful, as some spots can be wet and slippery.

During the camping season the park charges $5 per vehicle for day use, which includes parking at the beach and the Barnaby Head trailhead.

The park *campground* (☎ 506-755-4042, fax 506-755-4063, w www.tourismnbcanada .com/web/english/outdoor_network, 78 New River Beach Rd; open late May-early Oct) is across the road from the beach and features 100 secluded sites, both rustic and serviced, in a wooded setting. Camping is $21.50 for tents and $24 for sites with electricity. Drawbacks are the gravel emplacements and traffic noise from the nearby highway. Many sites are reserved but some are kept open on first come basis.

Saint John

Historic Saint John (whose name is never abbreviated, to avoid confusion with St John's, Newfoundland) is the province's largest city (population 73,000) and leading industrial center. Sitting on the bay at the mouth of the Saint John River, the city is a major year-round port. The dry dock is one of the world's largest. The huge JD Irving conglomerate is headquartered here.

As well as a refurbished downtown area, Saint John has a proud past. It's known as the Loyalist City for the thousands of late-18th-century royalist refugees who settled here, and evidence of this background is plentiful. The central city and surrounding residential side streets have some very fine architecture, and a stroll past the impressive façades is well worthwhile.

Fog very often blankets the city, particularly in the morning. This helps to keep the area cool even when the rest of the province is sweating it out in midsummer.

History

The Maliseet were here when the British and French began squabbling about furs. Samuel de Champlain had landed in 1604; however, the area remained pretty much a wilderness until 1783, when about 7000 people loyal to Britain arrived from the United States.

The Loyalists were the true founders of Saint John, turning a fort site into Canada's first legal city, incorporated in 1785. Between 1844 and 1848 some 35,000 Irish immigrants fleeing famine in Ireland passed through Saint John, and today they comprise the city's largest ethnic group.

By the mid-19th century Saint John was a prosperous industrial town, important particularly for its shipbuilding enterprises. Though now iron and steel are used rather than wood, shipbuilding is still a major industry here. In 1877, two-thirds of the city, including most of the mercantile district, was reduced to ashes by fire. It was soon rebuilt.

Orientation

Downtown Saint John sits on a square peninsula between the mouth of the Saint John River and Courtenay Bay. King's Square marks the nucleus of town. Its pathways duplicate the pattern of the Union Jack. Brunswick Square, a modern shopping mall, is on the corner of King and Germain Sts. One block farther west at Water St is the redeveloped waterfront area and Market Square. Don't confuse Market Square with the Old City Market three blocks away.

The district below King's Square is known as the South End, with Queen Square at its heart. On Courtenay Bay, to the east, are the dry dock, shipbuilding yards and much heavy industry. North of town is Rockwood Park, a recreational area with a campground.

West over the Harbour Bridge (25¢ toll) is the neighborhood of Saint John West. Many of the street names in this section of the city are identical to those of Saint John proper, and to avoid confusion, they end in a west designation, such as 'Charlotte St W.'

Saint John West has the landing for ferries to Digby, Nova Scotia, and the city container terminals. The famous Reversing Falls are just to the north. Farther west going out of town is the motel district, with the Irving Nature Park to the south.

Information

Tourist Offices The visitor and convention bureau (☎ 506-658-2990, 888-364-4444) in Market Square has knowledgeable, friendly staff and all the printed matter you'll need. Ask for the self-guided walking tours. The bureau is open 9am to 6pm daily year-round (until 8pm mid-June to August).

There's another information office, the Reversing Falls Visitor Centre (☎ 506-658-2937) at the falls. It's in Saint John West on Hwy 100 and is open 8am-7pm daily mid-May to early October.

A third information office (☎ 506-658-2940) is located on Hwy 1 (the Saint John

A Touch of Tinsel in Saint John

No one would ever confuse Saint John with Hollywood, but it is uncanny how this east coast Canadian city is connected to that Tinsel Town on the US western coast. Louis B Mayer, founder of Metro-Goldwyn-Mayer (MGM) studios, immigrated to Saint John with his parents as a boy and eventually became one of Hollywood's most powerful men. His mother is buried in Saint John's Shaarie Zedek cemetery, whose chapel was donated by Mayer.

Actor Walter Pidgeon, one of Hollywood's leading men in the 1940s and known to most Baby Boomers as Grandpa in the television show *The Real McCoys*, was born here in 1898. So was Donald Sutherland, who had leading roles in such hits as *M.A.S.H.* and *JFK*.

Saint John was also the filming location of the movie *Children of a Lesser God* during the summer and autumn of 1985, and many of the residents played bit parts or were used as extras. The film starred William Hurt and Marlee Matlin, who went on to win an Oscar for Best Actress for her performance.

The province has formed Film New Brunswick, a consortium of government agencies designed to convince filmmakers from around Canada, if not North America, to relocate here. Given New Brunswick's francophone population, it's already become a haven for Montréal filmmakers looking for a French-speaking population and, as a bonus, living in the original home of the Acadians.

Throughway) between exits 101 and 104 in Saint John West. It's handy if you're coming from St Stephen or Fredericton and has a panoramic ocean view. It's open from 9am to 6pm daily mid-May to early October (until 8pm in July and August).

Money The American Express representative is McGinn Travel (☎ 888-632-4060), 715 Millidge Ave (near University Ave), on the far north edge of town.

Post The main post office with general delivery is in Saint John West (☎ 506-672-6704) at 41 Church Ave W, Postal Station B, E2M 4X6. It's open 8am to 5pm Monday to Friday.

Internet Access The Saint John Library (☎ 506-643-7220), 1 Market Square, provides free Internet access. The library is open 9am to 5pm Monday and Saturday, 10am to 5pm Tuesday and Wednesday, 10am to 9pm Thursday and Friday.

Laundry Princess St Laundromat (☎ 506-652-7064), 106 Princess St, has a remarkably pleasant atmosphere with comfortable chairs and TV. They charge $1.50 a wash. The Laundromat is open 8am to 7:30pm Monday to Friday, 8am to 4:30pm Saturday and Sunday.

Medical Services There aren't any after-hours walk-in medical clinics in Saint John. If you need to see a doctor, you'll have to go to the emergency room at one of the two hospitals, Saint Joseph's Hospital (☎ 506-632-5555), 130 Bayard Dr on the north side of downtown, or the Saint John Regional Hospital (☎ 506-648-6000), 400 University Ave, off Sandy Point Road 6km north of the center.

Unless you have valid travel health insurance, you should approach these facilities with caution, as absurdly high fees are asked of non-Canadians. The fee just to register at Saint Joseph's Hospital is $200, and any treatment will be extra. Saint John Regional collects a $110 hospital charge, plus $90 to see a doctor. In non-life-threatening

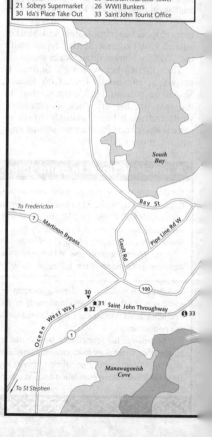

PLACES TO STAY
4 Park Plaza Motel
7 Sir James Dunn Residence
11 Fundy Line Motel
14 Rockwood Park Campground
23 Carleton House B&B
27 Balmoral Court Motel
28 King's Motel; Hillside Motel
29 Hillcrest Motel
31 Regent Motel
32 Terrace Motel & Cottages

PLACES TO EAT
10 Mediterranean Family Restaurant
12 Ponderosa Steak House
21 Sobeys Supermarket
30 Ida's Place Take Out

OTHER
1 Sandy Point Landing
2 Cherry Brook Zoo
3 CAA Maritimes
5 Discount Car Rentals
6 Exhibition Park Raceway
8 Aquatic Driving Range
9 Saint John Regional Hospital
13 American Express; McGinn Travel
15 Rent-a-Wreck
16 Fort Howe Lookout
17 Toll Booths
18 Fallsview Park; Reversing Falls Jet Boat Rides
19 Post Office
20 Moosehead Brewery; Moosehead Country Store
22 Reversing Falls Visitor Centre
24 Bay Ferries Terminal
25 Carleton Martello Tower
26 WWII Bunkers
33 Saint John Tourist Office

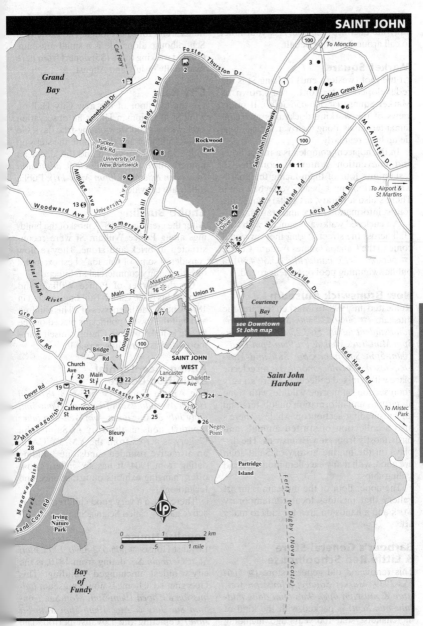

To Moncton

Grand Bay

Car Ferry

Foster Thurston Dr

Kennebcasis Dr

Sandy Point Rd

1
2

3
4 5
Golden Grove Rd
6
McAllister Dr

Tucker Park Rd
7
8

Rockwood Park

University of New Brunswick

9

Millidge Ave

University Ave

Churchill Blvd

10
11
12

Woodward Ave
13

Somerset St

14
Lake Drive

Westmoreland Rd

Rothesay Ave

Loch Lomond Rd

To Airport & St Martins

Saint John River

Magazine St

15
Station St

16
Union St

Courtenay Bay

Bayside Dr

Green Head Rd

Main St

17

see Downtown St John map

Bridge Rd
18
Douglass Ave

Church Ave
20
Main St
21
22

Dever Rd
19

Catherwood St

Lancaster Ave

SAINT JOHN WEST

Lancaster St
Charlotte Ave

23
25
City Line
24

Saint John Harbour

Red Head Rd

To Mistec Park

27
28
29

Manawagonish Rd

Manawagonish Creek

Bleury St

26
Negro Point

Partridge Island

Ferry to Digby (Nova Scotia)

Sand Cove Rd

Irving Nature Park

0   1   2 km
0   .5   1 mile

Bay of Fundy

NEW BRUNSWICK

circumstances, it's better to try to persuade a private doctor to see you. Ask your hotel to call around on your behalf.

Market Square

At the foot (western end) of King St is the redeveloped waterfront area known as Market Square (☎ 506-658-3600). It offers views of the working dockyards and container terminals along the river. Cruise ships tie up here regularly.

In the adjacent complex is a major hotel and convention center. It contains 15 restaurants, four of them facing the boardwalk overlooking a beach volleyball area. There's also a library, art gallery, museum, tourist information office and craft shop.

An enclosed walkway connects with City Hall across the street. Along the way you'll come to the Canada Games Aquatic Centre (☎ 506-658-4715; adult/child $5.50/4.50), a public swimming pool open year-round.

New Brunswick Museum

Relocated in 1998 to Market Square, the museum (☎ 506-643-2300, Market Square; adult/student/family $6/3.25/13; open 9am-5pm Mon, Tues, Wed, & Fri, 9am-9pm Thurs, 10am-5pm Sat, noon-5pm Sun mid-May-Oct, closed Mon other months) is an eclectic place with a mixed collection. There's a very good section on marine wildlife, with some aquariums and information on lobsters, and an outstanding section on whales. There's also a collection of stuffed animals and birds, mostly from New Brunswick. The displays on the marine history of Saint John are good, with many excellent models of old sailing ships.

The upper floor of the museum is an art gallery that includes local contemporary work and a hands-on area for kids to make art.

Barbour's General Store & Little Red Schoolhouse

This renovated old general store (☎ 506-658-2939, Market Square; admission free; store & museum open 9am-6pm daily mid-June-mid-Sept) is packed with the kind of merchandise sold 100 years ago, including old stoves, drugs, hardware and candy. Most items aren't for sale, though. The Little Red Schoolhouse alongside is a small museum. Guided walking tours ($5) depart from here twice daily in July and August.

City Hall

On the top floor of the new City Hall on King St at Chipman Hill is an observation deck with a good view on fog-free days. Go to the 15th floor and then climb the steps up to the 16th, where you'll find the 'deck,' an unused office (☎ 506-649-6000; admission free; open 8:30am-4:30pm Mon-Fri). Public toilets are provided.

Chubb Building

After the great fire of 1877, most of the buildings along Prince William St were reconstructed in brick and stone. They're now considered some of Canada's best examples of 19th-century commercial architecture.

On the corner of Prince William and Princess Sts is the Chubb Building, erected in 1878. Chubb had likenesses of all his children and half the town's politicians placed on the façade in little rosettes. Chubb himself is immortalized as a grinning gargoyle.

Aitken Bicentennial Exhibition Centre

The Aitken Centre (☎ 506-633-4870, 20 Hazen Ave; admission free; open 10am-5pm daily July & Aug; noon-4pm Wed-Sun other months), housing the City of Saint John Gallery, is across from the YM-YWCA in an attractive rounded sandstone building dating from 1904. It has six galleries that offer changing exhibits on art, science and technology.

There's also a very good children's interactive gallery called ScienceScape.

Loyalist House

Loyalist House (☎ 506-652-3590, 120 Union St at Germain St), dating from 1810, is the city's oldest unchanged building. This Georgian-style home is now a museum (admission $3; open 10am-5pm Mon-Sat, 1pm-5pm Sun July & Aug, 10am-5pm Mon-Fri June) depicting the Loyalist period. The house contains some fine carpentry, and the monument to the Loyalists next to the house is striking.

Old City Market

On Market St between Germain and Charlotte Sts, this colorful, interesting market (☎ 506-658-2820, 47 Charlotte St; open 7:30am-6pm Mon-Thur, 7:30am-7pm Fri, 7:30am-5pm Sat) has been in this building since 1876. Outside the door on Charlotte St, see the plaque outlining the market's history. The heavy old roof beams show shipbuilding influences in their design.

Inside, the atmosphere is friendly but busy. Apart from the fresh produce stalls, which are most active on Saturday when local farmers come in, there are several good eating spots, a deli and some antique stores. Good bread is sold, and dulse and cooked lobster are available.

An underground walkway leads to Brunswick Square.

Loyalist Burial Ground

This attractive site is just off King's Square, in a park-style setting in the center of town. Here you can see tombstones dating from as early as 1784.

Old Courthouse

The County Court of 1830, which faces King's Square on the corner of Sydney and King Sts, is noted for its spiraling stone staircase, rising three stories without any support.

No 2 Old Engine House Museum

This partially restored 1840 firehouse (☎ 506-633-1840, 24 Sydney St; admission free; open 9:30am-5pm Mon-Sat, 1pm-5pm Sun July & Aug) overlooks King's Square. Inside are old alarm systems, firefighting artifacts and, most interesting, historical photos that retell the story of the Great Saint John Fire of 1877.

Trinity Church

Trinity Church (☎ 506-693-8558, 115 Charlotte St; admission free; open 9am-5pm Mon-Fri July & Aug, 1pm-3:45pm Mon, 9am-3:45pm Tues-Fri rest of year), founded in 1783, is known as 'the church of the Loyalists.' It's a huge stone English neo-Gothic structure. The smaller Charlotte St entrance is open all year; you can only enter through the main entrance facing Germain St in summer, when a guide is present.

Fort Howe Lookout

The Fort Howe Lookout, off Magazine St, provides one of the best views of the city. A small wooden fort was erected here in 1777 to defend the settlement against American privateers active during the Revolutionary War, and it was used again during the War of 1812. You can have your photo taken in wooden stocks adjacent to the reconstructed fort.

Tea with the Mayor

Most politicians are only seen for a few weeks before election day, only to disappear until the ballot boxes are hauled out again. Not Shirley McAlary, who changed the rules upon becoming mayor of Saint John. Every Wednesday during July and August she serves tea at the Loyalist House on Union St from 2 to 3:30 pm.

'Milk or sugar,' McAlary dutifully asks a group of tourists, who are stunned to learn that the mayor of this large city is personally handing them a tea cup and offering a plate of sweets. The tradition has caught on in other cities of Atlantic Canada, but most observers agree that McAlary has taken political tea to new heights, arriving in period costume reflecting the 185-year history of this Loyalist home and serving the tea herself. 'Sometimes I serve as many as 150 cups in an afternoon,' the mayor says.

McAlary was reelected in May 2001, and whether she'll run again is anybody's guess. But whoever takes over the office, one thing seems certain – they'll be serving tea on Wednesday. 'It would be political suicide if they didn't,' says one city council member, quietly sipping his tea.

Reversing Falls

The Bay of Fundy tides and their effects (see Tidal Bore Park under Moncton later in this chapter) are unquestionably a predominant regional characteristic. The falls here are part of that phenomenon and are one of the best known sites in the province. However, 'reversing falls' is a bit of a misnomer. When the high Bay of Fundy tides rise, the current in the river reverses, causing the water to flow upstream. When the tides go down, the water flows in the normal way.

The **Reversing Falls Visitor Centre** (☎ 506-658-2937, 200 Bridge Rd; open 8am-7pm daily mid-May-early Oct) next to the bridge over the falls can supply a *Reversing Falls Tide Table* brochure, which will explain where in the cycle you are. You can also watch a film at the touristy observation deck (admission $2) above the tourist office. The frequent buses from King's Square stop here.

You'll get a better view of it all from **Fallsview Park**, reached on the east side of the bridge, at the end of Fallsview Rd off Douglas Ave. This park puts you right above the river's narrowest gorge but, unfortunately, also right across from a horrendous pulp mill. If you hang around for a few hours, what you'll see is the river rush through in one direction, become calm during slack tide and then begin flowing in the other direction. Seen in its entirety, this is a remarkable display of nature's power. At high tide, this spot is a wild scene of rapids, whitewater and huge whirlpools with both waterfowl and harbour seals playing in the wicked current. Large numbers of cormorants and gulls congregate on small islands right in front of Fallsview Park.

Moosehead Brewery

Moosehead Brewery used to claim it was the country's oldest independent beer maker, dating back to 1867, the year of Confederation. Now it also bills itself as the largest Canadian-owned brewery. This is due to the 1995 purchase of Labatt by a Belgian conglomerate and the fact that Carlton & United Breweries of Australia (producers of Foster's Lager) and Miller Brewing of the USA own a hefty slice of Molson. The Oland family (owners of Moosehead) take pride in having defied all takeover bids – a recurring theme throughout the tour of the Moosehead plant, just up the road from the Reversing Falls center.

Public tours are offered at 1pm and 3pm daily mid-June through August, and they're so popular it's wise to book them a day in advance. You can do this at any tourist office or by calling the Moosehead Country Store (☎ 506-635-7020, 49 Main St West; admission free; open 9am-5pm Mon-Wed, 9am-9pm Thurs & Fri, 10am-5pm Sat year-round). Tours include a movie and beer tasting. The country store has great logo attire for all you mooseheads.

Carleton Martello Tower

In Saint John West, the national historic site Carleton Martello Tower (☎ 506-636-4011, 545 Whipple St cnr Fundy Drive; adult/family $2.50/6.25; open 9am-5pm daily June-early Oct) is just off Lancaster Ave, which leads to the Digby ferry terminal. Look for the signs at street intersections. A Martello tower is a circular two-story stone coastal fortification. They were first built in England and Ireland at the beginning of the 19th century. In North America, the British built 16 of them during the early 1800s, including several at Halifax. Inside you can explore the restored powder magazine, barracks and the upper two levels that were added during WWII for the defense of Saint John Harbour. Guides will show you around and provide background information. Go when there's no fog, because the promontory sits on one of the highest points in the city and the view is outstanding.

Partridge Island

Out in the bay just off the Digby ferry terminal, Partridge Island was once a quarantine station for the Irish who were arriving after fleeing their homeland's potato famine. There are the remnants of some houses and a few old gun placements on the island.

At the south end of City Line, not far from the terminal of the Digby ferry, are a series of abandoned and crumbling WWII bunkers and gun emplacements on Negro Point. A stone breakwater crosses from the point to Partridge Island, though the use of it to reach Partridge Island isn't encouraged, as you'd have to clamber over rough rocks. The view from Negro Point is great.

Irving Nature Park

For those with vehicles and an appreciation of nature, this park (*☎ 506-653-7367, west end of Sand Cove Rd; admission free; open 8am-dusk early May-early Nov*) is a must (well worth the 15-minute drive southwest from the center) for its rugged, unspoiled coastal topography. It's also a remarkable place for bird watching, with hundreds of species regularly reported. Seals may be seen on rocks offshore.

Though the park is said to be on Taylors Island, this is not an island at all but a 245-hectare mountainous peninsula protruding into the Bay of Fundy. Seven trails of varying lengths lead around beaches, cliffs, woods, mudflats, marsh and rocks. Good footwear is recommended. Also be careful along the ocean side on the rocks, as very large waves can catch you off-guard. The perimeter can be driven on a 6½km dirt road.

To reach the park take Hwy 1 west from town and turn south at Exit 107, Bleury St. Then turn right on Sand Cove Rd and continue for 2km to the entrance. The No 11 Fundy Heights bus from Simms Corner comes close to the park (no service on Sunday). Maps are posted throughout the park and toilets are provided. Other facilities include free gas barbecues, picnic tables, observation decks and binoculars. Worthwhile free tours are given on weekends.

Rockwood Park

On the northeast edge of the city center, is Canada's largest park contained wholly within a city (870 hectares). Recreational facilities include picnic spots, wooded hiking trails, swimming areas, a campground, an interpretive center, a golf course, canoe rentals, horse stables and a children's farm.

The park is open 8am to 8pm and admission is free.

An offbeat feature of Rockwood Park worth checking out is the **Aquatic Driving Range** (*☎ 506-634-1676, open 11am-9pm daily mid-May-mid-Sept*), just below the golf course on the way to the zoo. Customers practice hitting golf balls out into Crescent Lake, many of which carom off the well-protected tugboat used to collect the floating balls. Balls are $5/6.50 per small/large bucket and clubs can be rented for $1. It's great fun.

Cherry Brook Zoo (*☎ 506-634-1440, 901 Foster Thurston Dr; adult/student/child/family $6/4.50/3/15; open 10am-dusk daily*) has about 35 animal species, including several which are endangered. It's at the far northern edge of Rockwood Park in the north of the city, about 6km from the Rockwood Park campground.

Mispec Park

Along the east side of Saint John Harbour stands a whole row of huge, often dirty industrial facilities. There's a shipyard, a thermal power plant, a paper mill, an oil refinery and a storage tank park for Irving Oil. Nevertheless, it's worth following Red Head Rd 15km down this way to Mispec Park (admission free), where you'll find a broad sandy beach, picnic facilities and hiking trails through the forest. It's less visited than Irving Nature Park and remarkably unspoiled considering the industrial zone you pass on the way there. The sea views are superb and it feels like Saint John is far away.

Activities

Eastern Outdoors (*☎ 800-565-2925, W www .easternoutdoors.com, 3rd floor, Brunswick Square, 39 King St; open 10am-6pm Mon-Sat, until 9pm Thurs & Fri*) rents bicycles ($25 a day), kayaks ($35) and canoes ($35). This is great if you're up for a day of peddling around Rockwood Park or the Irving Nature Park, or a paddle out to Partridge Island. Don't risk paddling over the Reversing Falls, however. Eastern Outdoors also runs daily kayaking tours to Dipper

Harbour and Deer Island for $59, plus $10 for transfers from Saint John.

North out of the city is a green rural area interspersed with deeply indented bays, rivers and islands, eventually leading to Grand Lake and Fredericton. The Saint John River flows south through here to its mouth at the Bay of Fundy and the ferries connecting roads in the area are all free.

The **Kingston Peninsula**, not far from Saint John, has scenery typical of the river valley landscapes and is particularly beautiful in autumn with the leaves changing color. Every half hour from mid-April to mid-December the free ferry *Romeo & Juliette* crosses to the peninsula from Sandy Point landing, a kilometer north of Cherry Brook Zoo in Saint John.

Organized Tours

Many vistors are surprised to find that whale watching is not an attraction in Saint John, save for an occasional wayward minke.

The **Saint John Transit Commission** (☎ *506-658-4700*) offers 2½-hour bus tours (adult/child $16/5) of the city from mid-June to early October. Departures and tickets are from Reversing Falls Visitor Centre, Barbour's General Store at Market Square and Rockwood Park Campground. Two tours daily depart. At 9:30am the bus leaves Reversing Falls, and it takes 15 minutes to get to each of the other two stops. The trip is reversed from 12:30pm to 1pm.

Also from Barbour's, in July and August, are guided walking tours around the historic portions of downtown offered by **Aquila Tours** (☎ *506-633-1224; tickets $5; depart 2pm daily*). Similar walking tours are offered by **Helyar Productions** (☎ *506-657-5244; adult/family $5/15*), leaving from the Atrium Fountain at Market Square Monday to Saturday at 7pm from June to August.

Reversing Falls Jet Boat Rides (☎ *506-634-8987*, **W** *www.jetboatrides.com; adult/child $26/20*) offers two types of trips from June to mid-October. An hour-long slow boat trip to the Reversing Falls and around the harbor departs from Market Square,

and there's also a 20-minute jet boat ride through the whitewater at the Reversing Fall that leaves from Fallsview Park. Count on getting soaked on either tour (rain gear and life jackets are provided).

Special Events

Loyalist Days (☎ 888-364-444), an eight-day event held annually during the third week of July, celebrates the city's Loyalist background. Featured are a reenactment of the Loyalists' first arrival, period costumes, parades, arts and crafts, music recitals, lots of food and fireworks on the last night of the festival.

Each August the city hosts the very popular, highly regarded Festival by the Sea. For 10 days (the exact dates change) this performing arts event presents hundreds of singers, dancers and other performers from across Canada in concerts and shows put on throughout the city night and day. Many of the performances staged in parks and along the harbor front are free. Web site: **W** www.festivalbythesea.com/intro.html

The Grand Ole Atlantic National Exhibition (☎ 506-633-2020) is held annually at the end of August in Exhibition Park and includes stage shows, livestock judging, harness racing and a large midway.

Places to Stay

Camping *Rockwood Park* (☎ *506-652-4050, fax 506-642-6304,* **W** *www.sn2000nb.ca/comp/rockwood-park-campground, Crown St*) Campsites $15/20 without/with electricity, less for stays of a week or more. Open mid-May-early Oct. Just north of Rothesay Ave, a couple of kilometers north of the downtown area, is huge Rockwood Park, with its small lakes, picnic area, golf course and a part of the University of New Brunswick's campus. It's an excellent place to camp, with pleasant campsites and a view of the city. Bus No 6 to Mount Pleasant from King's Square comes within a few blocks of the campground Monday to Saturday.

Hostels *YM-YWCA* (☎ *506-634-7720, fax 506-634-0783,* **W** *www.saintjohny.com, 19-25*

DOWNTOWN SAINT JOHN

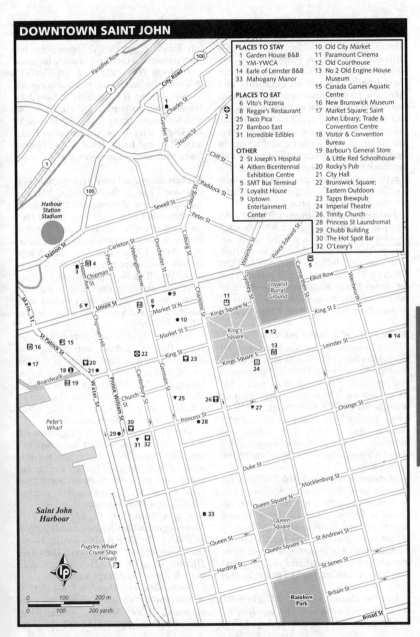

PLACES TO STAY
1 Garden House B&B
3 YM-YWCA
14 Earle of Leinster B&B
33 Mahogany Manor

PLACES TO EAT
6 Vito's Pizzeria
8 Reggie's Restaurant
25 Taco Pica
27 Bamboo East
31 Incredible Edibles

OTHER
2 St Joseph's Hospital
4 Aitken Bicentennial
   Exhibition Centre
5 SMT Bus Terminal
7 Loyalist House
9 Uptown
   Entertainment
   Center

10 Old City Market
11 Paramount Cinema
12 Old Courthouse
13 No 2 Old Engine House
   Museum
15 Canada Games Aquatic
   Centre
16 New Brunswick Museum
17 Market Square; Saint
   John Library; Trade &
   Convention Centre
18 Visitor & Convention
   Bureau
19 Barbour's General Store
   & Little Red Schoolhouse
20 Rocky's Pub
21 City Hall
22 Brunswick Square;
   Eastern Outdoors
23 Tapps Brewpub
24 Imperial Theatre
26 Trinity Church
28 Princess St Laundromat
29 Chubb Building
30 The Hot Spot Bar
32 O'Leary's

NEW BRUNSWICK

Hazen Ave) Singles $35/30/25 adult/student/HI member, no additional tax. The weekly rate of $100 is available to all. The HI-affiliated YM-YWCA features 16 single rooms with a single bed and use of a clean shared bath. (There's no dormitory and there are no doubles – couples must rent two rooms.) Each occupant gets a room key and has full use of facilities such as the swimming pool, common room and exercise rooms. A free washer and drier are in the bathroom. The lobby is always open and the snack bar is inexpensive. Parking is free except from 8am to 6pm weekdays, when it's 50¢ an hour. It's all a little threadbare, but you can't beat the price.

University of New Brunswick Saint John Campus (☎ 506-648-5755, fax 506-648-5762, e hfs@unbsj.ca, w www.unbsj.ca/hfs, off Sandy Point Rd near the Rockwood Park Golf Course) Singles/doubles $29.50/43.50 (students $18.75/35.65). The 71 rooms at the Sir James Dunn Residence, 6km north of the city center, are available from May to August. Take bus No 12 from King's Square.

B&Bs *Earle of Leinster B&B* (☎ 506-652-3275, e leinster@nbnet.nb.ca, 96 Leinster St) Singles/doubles $61/70 with one bed, $74 double with two beds. There's $5 discount if you pay cash. This inn, a short walk from King's Square, is in a three-story Victorian town house (1878) with seven rooms, all with a private bath. Rates include laundry facilities and a VCR with videos and popcorn. It's strictly nonsmoking. Calling ahead is a good idea as the place tends to fill up in summer.

Mahogany Manor (☎ 800-796-7755, fax 506-636-8001, e mmanorbb@nbnet.nb.ca, w www.sjnow.com/mm, 220 Germain St) Doubles $85-95. Not far from Queen Square just out of the center is Mahogany Manor, a magnificent three-story Victorian mansion with five rooms. It's one of province's best-known gay-friendly lodgings, and they have special lesbian and gay weekends in the off-season.

Garden House B&B (☎ 506-646-9093, e ghouse@nbnet.nb.ca, 28 Garden St) Singles/doubles $60/85 July & Aug, $50/60

other months. From King's Square walk north on Coburg St to Garden St, on the left. This large wooden Victorian home has four rooms, and there are laundry facilities.

Carleton House B&B (☎ 506-672-7458, e chouse@nbnet.nb.ca, w www.bbcanada.com/4173.html, 213 Lancaster St, Saint John West) Doubles/triples $65/80. This old wooden house dating from 1845 is close to the Digby ferry. It's at the corner of Charlotte St W and Lancaster St, not to be confused with nearby Lancaster Ave.

Motels Saint John may have more motels than any place in the Maritimes. Many of them are along Manawagonish Rd and its continuation Ocean West Way, the old Hwy 100 west of town, parallel to and north of Hwy 1. A few more motels are on Rothesay Ave (Hwy 100 eastbound), and though slightly more expensive, they're closer to town. Yet all of these places cost less than what you might pay elsewhere in the Maritimes, and outside the busy period from mid-June to mid-September prices tend to fall even further.

Many of these motels offer low weekly rates, though perhaps not in July and August. Even if you only intend to stay five or six nights, it's well worth considering taking a weekly as Fredericton and much of the coast is within commuting distance by car, and you won't need to worry about finding accommodations every night.

The main problem with Manawagonish Rd is that it's 7km west of the downtown area and Ocean West Way is another 4km west of that. Yet the No 14 Fairville bus comes and goes into town from this strip (last bus back at 6:07pm weekdays), and in a car it's just a 15-minute trip.

King's Motel (☎ 506-672-1375, 1121 Manawagonish Rd) Singles/doubles/triples $42/46/51. King's has six units in a long block overlooking the highways. The larger *Hillside Motel* (☎ 888-625-7070) next-door is a few dollars more expensive.

Balmoral Court Motel (☎ 888-463-3779, e ferry@nbnet.nb.ca, w www.sjnow.com/balmoral, 1284 Manawagonish Blvd) Singles/doubles/triples $45/50/55 ($5 more mid-summer). Balmoral Court has several neat little individual cabins, though almost half of the 22 rooms are in duplex or triplex blocks.

Hillcrest Motel (☎ 506-672-5310, 1315 Manawagonish Rd) Singles/doubles/triples $42/46/51. Almost opposite the Balmoral, Hillcrest has 17 rooms in a long wooden block. It's closer to the road and thus a bit noisier than any of the other places.

Regent Motel (☎ 506-672-8273, 2121 Ocean West Way) Singles/doubles $50/58 July & Aug, $45/48 shoulder seasons. Open May-Oct. Regent consists of two blocks of rooms.

Terrace Motel & Cottages (☎ 506-672-9670, 2131 Ocean West Way) Rooms $49-79 single or double, cabins $40-59, depending on how busy they are. In winter the six motel rooms with fridge and microwave are rented at $150 a week, and in summer the seven duplex cabins go for $175 a week.

Fundy Line Motel (☎ 506-633-7733, fax 506-633-1680, 532 Rothesay Ave) Singles/ doubles $48 June-Sept, $45 Oct-May. The 51 rooms are in a two-story block, 5km east of town. No weekly rates are offered.

Park Plaza Motel (☎ 800-561-9022, fax 506-648-9494, 607 Rothesay Ave) Singles/ doubles $52/62 mid-June-mid-Sept, $52/58 other months (all rooms contain only one bed). A kilometer east of Fundy Line Motel, the 84 units are in two single-story buildings and one two-story block. Weekly rates of $160 single or double are available year-round.

Places to Eat

The *Old City Market* between Charlotte and Germain Sts is a good place to be when hunger strikes. Aside from the produce, there are numerous small restaurants and takeout counters and a delightful solarium eating area along South Market St.

Reggie's Restaurant (☎ 506-657-6270, 26 Germain St) Dinners under $7, most sandwiches under $4. Open 6am-6pm Mon & Tues, 6am-7pm Wed-Fri, 6am-5pm Sat & Sun. This place for cheap eats has been around since 1969. Near the Loyalist House, it's a classic downtown no-nonsense diner

that specializes in smoked meat from Ben's, the famous Montréal deli. Chowders are a good deal at $4.25 or less. or breakfast you can have Reggie's Favorite – three sausages, an egg, home fries, toast and hot mustard – for $4 (coffee extra), served all day. Place your order at the counter when you arrive.

Vito's (☎ 506-634-3900, 1 Hazen Ave) Mains $6-9. Open 11:30am-midnight Mon-Fri, 11am-1am Sat, noon-11pm Sun. Vito's, on the corner of Hazen Ave and Union St, is a longtime Italian favorite. Consider the spaghetti dinner, or try other pasta dishes like Tortelline a la Vito's – tortellini stuffed with green peppers and mushrooms. Large pizzas start at $16.

Incredible Edibles (☎ 506-633-7554, 42 Princess St) Pasta $10, specials $10, dinner for two from $50. Open noon-9:30pm Mon-Sat, 5pm-9:30pm Sun. This is a nice spot for a bit of a splurge. It offers crepes, curries, pastas, seafood and a few vegetarian choices. Friday from 6:30pm to 9:30pm you can get the amazing hip of beef dinner special for $13. Specialities are the local desserts such as blueberry cobbler – a tasty fruit-based dessert with a crispy cake crust, usually topped with milk or cream.

Taco Pica (☎ 506-633-8492, 96 Germain St) Mains $10-17. Open 10am-10pm Mon-Sat. Perhaps the best ethnic cuisine in Saint John is this fusion of Guatemalan and Mexican at Taco Pica, a respected cooperative restaurant. An economical introduction to the cuisine is the *pepian* ($9), a simple but spicy beef stew that is as good as you'll find in any Guatemalan household.

Bamboo East (☎ 506-634-1661, 136 Princess St) Weekday lunch buffet ($8) noon-2pm, weekend diner buffet ($12) 5pm-8pm. Open 11am-11pm Mon-Fri, 4:30pm-11pm Sat & Sun. The best way to sample a variety of Chinese dishes at Bamboo East is the buffet.

Ponderosa Steak House (☎ 506-642-1008, 370 Rothesay Ave) Mains $8-13. Open 11am-9pm daily (to 10pm in summer). Bring a hearty appetite because an all-you-can-eat soup and salad bar comes with the steak, chicken and fish entrees. Vegetarians can get the soup and salad bar alone for $6.

The cashier who takes your order will try to add on extras like sour cream, so beware. Ponderosa isn't for gourmets, but it's cheap and substantial.

Mediterranean Family Restaurant (☎ 506-634-3183, 419 Rothesay Ave) Mains $10. Open 10am-10:30pm Mon-Sat, 11am-8pm Sun. A kilometer east of Ponderosa, Mediterranean serves better food for only a little more money. The fish, tenderloin steak and rib specials include salad, potatoes, dessert and tea or coffee. There's live music Friday nights.

Ida's Place Take Out (2112 Ocean West Way) Meals under $7. Open 11am-9pm daily. Across the road from the Terrace Motel west of town, this place features cheap grub like fish & chips ($5), hamburgers ($3) and ice cream ($2).

Sobeys Supermarket (☎ 506-674-1460, 107 Catherwood St just off Hwy 1 at exit 107) Open 24 hours a day. This is the place to stock up on picnic/snack/cooking supplies.

Entertainment

Imperial Theatre (☎ 506-674-4100, 24 King's Square S) Box office open 10am-7pm Mon-Fri, noon-4pm Sat. This performing arts center reopened in 1994 after being restored to its original 1913 splendor. Performances range from classical music to live theater. Call for the schedule and ticket information.

Paramount Cinema (☎ 506-652-7100, King's Square N) Admission $8.50; matinees $2 cheaper. Check here for Hollywood movies.

The Hot Spot Bar (☎ 506-657-9931, 112 Prince William St) Open 9pm-2am Thurs, 7pm-2am Fri, 8pm-2am Sat. Most of the action at night is near the intersection of Princess and Prince William Sts; the Hot Spot is right on the corner and it's usually hopping. The live entertainment and cheap drinks make it very popular with the youth set.

O'Leary's (☎ 506-634-7135, 46 Princess) 11:30am-11pm Tues, 11:30am-1:30am Wed-Fri, 11am-1:30am Sat. This is a good old-fashioned Irish pub with plenty of English and Irish brews as well as live music on

Thursday, Friday and Saturday evenings. On Wednesday it's open-mike night. Take a stab, you could be a star.

Tapps Brewpub (☎ 506-634-1957, 78 King St) Open 11am-midnight Mon-Thurs, 11am-2am Fri & Sat, 4pm-10pm Sun. On King St between Germain and Charlotte Sts, this spot serves decent India pale ale and a *weissbier* made on the premises. It also has sandwich-style pub grub ($7), steaks ($9 to $14) and live music during the week.

Rocky's Pub (☎ 506-652-5452, 59 St Patrick St) Open 7:30am-1am Mon-Sat, 7:30am-midnight Sun. This sports bar in Market Square, reached via a stairway, has a lively clientele, daily drink specials, reasonably priced food and 19 TV screens.

Uptown Entertainment Center (☎ 506-634-7940, 144 Union St) Bingo from 5pm Fri & Sat, noon-5pm Sun. This unpretentious place is an amusing change of pace and you'll get to meet local people.

Spectator Sports

Harbour Station Stadium (☎ 800-267-2800, 99 Station St) Harbour Station is the city's most important sporting venue, on the site of the former train station, just north of the center. During the winter hockey season from early October to early April the Saint John's Flames play here (tickets $13 to $18).

Exhibition Park Raceway (☎ 506-636-6934, 66 McAllister Drive) Harness racing can be enjoyed from 1:30pm to 4:30pm every Saturday year-round at this racetrack, off Rothesay Ave (Hwy 100) on the east side of the city. You won't see jockey racing here, only trotters pulling a small cart and driver around an oval track. Parking and admission are free – they make their money from patrons betting on races here and at other tracks.

Getting There & Away

Air Air Canada or their subsidiary Air Nova has flights to Montréal, Toronto and Halifax three or four times a day. A 'passenger facility charge' of $10 must be paid at the gate by all passengers over two years old (not included in the ticket).

Bus SMT Bus Lines (☎ 506-648-3500) has a large station at 300 Union St on the corner of Carmarthen St, a five-minute walk from the town center. It's open 7:30am to 9pm Monday to Friday, 8am to 9pm Saturday and Sunday, and $2 coin lockers are available.

To Fredericton, there are two trips daily at 9:30am and 6:15pm ($18). That same bus is used for passengers continuing on to Québec City ($80). The bus to Moncton leaves at 8:30am and 3:15pm ($24); you'll have to go there to get to Charlottetown, for which the fare is $55. The same schedule holds for buses to Halifax ($66).

SMT Bus Lines connects with Orleans Express lines in Rivière-du-Loup, Québec, for all Québec destinations. For cities in Nova Scotia, SMT connects with Acadian Bus Lines. There's also a direct service to Bangor, Maine, on Friday and Saturday.

Always ask the staff at the station which bus is quickest – you could save yourself lots of time and stops on longer trips.

Buses also run to Moncton, where VIA trains can be caught for Québec or Nova Scotia. Combination road-and-rail tickets can be purchased at the SMT bus terminal but first you have to reserve with VIA (☎ 888-842-7245), then deal with the bus. To Québec City, daily except Tuesday, the bus/train fare is $136, sometimes less, depending on how far in advance you purchase the ticket. Direct train service between Montréal and Saint John was suspended in 1994.

Car & Motorcycle There are several choices for car rentals. Discount Car Rentals (☎ 506-633-4440), 622 Rothesay Ave, is opposite the Park Plaza Motel. Rent-a-Wreck (☎ 506-672-2277), 2 Seaton St, is near the junction of Rothesay and Thorne Aves. Call and they may send a driver to pick you up. Avis, Budget, Hertz and National all have car rental desks at the airport.

Motorists should note that west of the town center, Hwy 1 crosses over the Saint John River via a toll bridge where you pay 25¢. The bridge on Hwy 100, which crosses the river at the Reversing Falls, is free. Farther west, connections can be made with Hwy 7 (north) for Fredericton.

Parking meters in Saint John take $1 an hour from 8am to 6pm weekdays only. You can park free at meters on weekends, holidays and after 6pm, but note the time limits, which may be enforced. The parking meters on Sydney St south of King's Square allow up to 10 hours free parking on weekends and holidays. You can park free any time on back streets such as Leinster and Princess Sts, east of King's Square. The city parking lot at 11 Sydney St is free on weekends. From 8am to 6pm Monday to Friday you can park at the YM-YWCA, 19-25 Hazen Ave, just up the hill from Market Square, for 50¢ an hour, though there's a three-hour maximum.

CAA Maritimes (☎ 506-634-1400) is at 737 Rothesay Ave, just off Hwy 1 at exit 117. It's open 8:30am to 5pm Monday to Thursday, 8:30am to 7pm Friday, 10am to 1pm Saturday.

Hitchhiking Hitching toward Moncton on Rothesay Ave is a bummer, as the traffic's so heavy – a destination sign may help. Take the frequent Nos 1 & 2 buses from King's Square to the corner of Rothesay Ave and McAllister Dr to get started. It's easier to hitch north or west, as you can take the No 14 Fairville bus out Manawagonish Rd to a ramp leading onto Hwy 7 for Fredericton, or a little farther to Hwy 1 to St Stephen. For St Martins, take the No 22 Loch Lomond bus out past the airport.

Ferry Bay Ferries' (☎ 506-649-7777, 888-249-7245) *Princess of Acadia* sails between Saint John and Digby, Nova Scotia, year-round. Depending on where you're headed, this can save a lot of driving around the Bay of Fundy through Moncton and then Amherst, Nova Scotia, but the ferry isn't cheap. Adult/child fares are $35/15 one way from late June to mid-October, $20/10 other months. The all-season fare for cars/motorcycles/bicycles is $70/45/25. There's a passenger-only roundtrip fare ($35) if you want to make a day cruise out of it.

Crossing time is about three hours. From late June to mid-October there are three services daily from Digby: 5am, 1pm

NEW BRUNSWICK

and 8:45pm. On Sunday there is no 5am crossing. From Saint John, times are 12:45am, 9am and 4:45pm, with no 12:45am trip on Sunday. Other months they go once or twice a day. Arrive early or call ahead for vehicle reservations ($5 additional fee), as the ferry is very busy in July and August. Even with a reservation, arrive an hour before the ferry sails or your space may be given away. Walk-ons and cyclists should be OK any time. There's a restaurant and a bar on board. For more information, contact the Bay Ferries Web site at W www.nfl-bay.com.

Getting Around

To/From the Airport The airport is east of town on Loch Lomond Rd between Saint John and St Martins. There's an airport shuttle (☎ 506-648-8888) costing $10 that leaves approximately 1½ hours before all flights, from top hotels like the Hilton on Market Square and the Delta Brunswick on Brunswick Square. For a taxi call Vets (☎ 506-658-2020); it costs $25 for the first person plus $2 for each additional passenger. City bus No 22 goes to the airport from King's Square at 6:25am, 7:50am, 9:25am, 12:35pm, 2:30pm, 4:10pm and 5:30pm weekdays (buses from the airport into town leave around 30 minutes after these times).

Bus Saint John Transit (☎ 506-658-4700) has 30 routes around the city. The most important are Nos 1 & 2 eastbound to McAllister Dr and Nos 3 & 4 westbound to near the ferry terminal in Saint John West. They stop at King's Square in the city center every 10 or 15 minutes from 6am to 7pm, every half hour from 7pm to midnight, Monday to Saturday. On Sunday it's every 45 minutes from 10am to 6pm. Another frequent bus is Nos 15 & 16 to the University. It leaves from King's Square 6:10am to 9:10am and 2:25pm to 5:55pm weekdays. At other times you catch it on Metcalfe St. On Saturdays all of the University buses leave from Metcalfe St, but on Sunday they all leave from King's Square. The bus fare is $1.75.

Central Fundy Shore

The Central Fundy Shore from Saint John to Hopewell Cape has only recently been discovered by tourism. It's still not possible to drive along the coast from St Martins to Fundy National Park – that road has yet to be built – and a detour inland through Surrey is necessary unless you're prepared to hike. Indeed, hikers, cyclists and nature lovers will all be enchanted by this coast. Kayakers can put in from several points along here, and the cliffs and tides are a big attraction.

ST MARTINS

A one-hour hour drive east of Saint John will take you to the worthy destination of St Martins, one of the province's historic towns on the Bay of Fundy. It's a small, pretty, out-of-the-way place that was once the center of the wooden ship building trade. The two covered bridges date back to 1935. Now, with the opening of the Fundy Trail Parkway, St Martins is becoming a hot spot once again.

Things to See & Do

At the east end of town you'll see a quintessentially Maritimes scene: **Old Pejepscot Wharf**, edged with beached fishing boats waiting for the tide, two wooden covered bridges and a lighthouse. (If the tide is in, however, the boats will likely be out, working.)

The tiny **Quaco Museum** (☎ 506-833-4740, 236 Main St; admission $2; open 1pm-5pm Fri-Sun mid-May-Oct, 10am-5pm daily July & Aug) depicts the shipbuilding period.

Cross one of the covered bridges and head around the corner, where a dramatic expanse of beach opens up. At the far end there are a couple of caves cut into the shoreline cliffs that are worth exploring. At the parking lot, right by the beach, is the Seaside Restaurant.

If you'd like to do some sea kayaking here, arrange it beforehand with Mike Carpenter at **River Valley Adventures** (☎ 888-

871-4244). His three-day Fundy Trail Coastline Tour from St Martins to Alma is $300.

Places to Stay & Eat

Century Farm Family Campground (☎ *506-833-2357,* e *cenfarcg@nbnet.nb.ca,* w *www .sn2000.nb.ca/comp/century-farm-camp ground, 67 Ocean Wave Dr)* Unserviced/ serviced sites $14/18, cabins $35/40 without/ with bath. Open May-mid-Oct. Near the center of St Martins, Century Farm hosts the usual rows of trailers, but there are also grassy sites for tents. There's no shade but there is a beach. Call ahead if you want a camping cabin. Four of the five cabins are without bath, but they hold up to four people; the other cabin has a toilet and sink.

Seaside Tent & Trailer Park (☎ *506-833-4413, fax 506-833-9816,* e *mikegill@ nbnet.nb.ca,* w *www.sn2000.nb.ca/comp/ seaside-trailer-park, 234 Main St)* Tent sites $18. Open mid-May-mid-Oct. This park is directly behind the Quaco Museum. It looks crowded around the entrance, but there's a grassy field where you can pitch your tent and it's a little more wooded than Century Farm, as it's been around longer.

Nostalgia's Nook B&B (☎ *506-833-4957,* w *www.bbcanada.com/3999.html, 16 West Quaco Rd)* Rooms $65 mid-June-mid-Sept, $50 other months. This B&B is in an old house just down the coastal road to the right as you enter St Martins.

Maple Miniatures Minihorse Farm B&B (☎ *506-833-6240,* e *minihorse@sprint.ca,* w *www.worldis.com/kathi, 280 West Quaco Rd, 2½km west of Nostalgia's Nook)* Rooms $55 including breakfast. Open May-Oct. Two rooms are for rent in this wooden house. Pony rides can be arranged for kids.

Seaside Restaurant (☎ *506-833-2394, 81 Macs Beach)* Main meals $8-13. Open 11am-8pm daily. Right on the beach near the caves just east of the covered bridge, Seaside serves dishes like fish & chips, scallops, seafood dinners and seafood casseroles. Lobster in the shell is $25.

FUNDY TRAIL PARKWAY

The cliff-edged coastal region between St Martins and Fundy National Park and inland toward Sussex is a rugged and gorgeous undeveloped section of the province that is said to be the only remaining coastal wilderness between Florida and Newfoundland. Late 1998 saw the culmination of years of effort by local promoters, when this jewel in New Brunswick's crown was opened to the public.

Plans are to have the drivable parkway and its adjoining littoral hiking/biking trail stretch all the way to Fundy National Park, an ambitious stretch of nearly 40km. Eventually, a triangular hiking region will link St Martins, Sussex and Alma at the edge of the national park, but this is years off.

Currently, the road and trails are open as far as Big Salmon River, a lovely (and easy) 11km stretch specially designed for hiking and bicycling. Ten viewpoints and picnic areas have been built between the entrance and the interpretive center at Big Salmon River, but camping is not allowed on the developed portion of the parkway.

At Big Salmon River is an interpretive center with exhibits and a 10-minute video presentation. Remains of a sawmill that existed here from the 1850s to the 1940s can be seen at low tide in the river directly below the interpretive center.

A suspension bridge leads to a vast wilderness hiking area beyond the end of the road. It's possible to hike from Big Salmon River to Goose River in Fundy National Park in three to five days, and at last report no permits or permissions were required to do so. Beyond Big Salmon River, you'd better be prepared for wilderness, rocky scree and even a rope ladder or two. Some beach sections are usable only at low tide and the cliffs are unsafe to climb.

The entrance to the parkway (☎ *506-833-2019,* w *www.fundytrailparkway.com; admission $5.75 per car; open 6am-8pm daily mid-May-Oct)* is 8½km west of the campgrounds in St Martins. Pedestrians and cyclists can enter free. In the off-season the main gate is closed, but you can always park at the entrance and hike or peddle in. On Saturdays, Sundays and holidays an hourly shuttle bus operates from noon to 6pm ferrying hikers up and down the trail between the parkway entrance and Big Salmon River. The shuttle is free if you paid the vehicle entrance fee and $2 if you didn't. The coast of Nova Scotia is visible across the bay.

FUNDY NATIONAL PARK

Fundy National Park (☎ 506-887-6000; entry permit $3.50/10.50 per person 1 day/4 days, family $7/21) is one of the country's most popular parks. Aside from the world's highest tides, this park on the Bay of Fundy has an extensive network of hiking trails. Irregularly eroded sandstone cliffs and the wide beach at low tide make a walk along the shore interesting. There's lots of marine life to observe and debris to pick over. The park even has a covered bridge.

Fundy is home to one of the largest concentrations of wildlife in the Maritimes, including black bears, moose, beavers and peregrine falcons. The ocean is pretty bracing here, so there's a heated saltwater swimming pool (☎ 506-887-6014; admission $2/1.50 adults/children; open 11am-6:30pm daily late June-early Sept) not far from the eastern entrance to the park where you can have a dip.

You can reach the park, 129km east of Saint John and about halfway to Moncton, by following Hwy 114. Entering from the north you first reach the Wolfe Lake Information Centre (☎ 506-432-6026, Hwy 114; open 10am-6pm daily late June-early Sept). At the south entrance is the park's visitor center (☎ 506-887-6000; open 10am-6pm daily mid-June-early Sept, 9am-4pm other months). Both have bookstores and information counters where you can purchase your entry permit. If you'll be visiting other national parks in the Maritimes and Newfoundland ask about the Atlantic Pass, which covers entry to all seven parks for the entire season.

Hiking & Biking

The park features 120km of walking trails where you can enjoy anything from a short stroll to a three-day backpacking trip. The most popular backpacking route is the Fundy Circuit, a three-day trek of 48km through the heart of the park. Hikers generally spend their first night at Marven Lake and their second at Bruin Lake, returning via the Upper Salmon River. Stop at the visitors center to reserve your wilderness campsites ($3 per person per night; call ahead for reservations if possible).

Another overnight trek is the Goose River Trail, an old cart track that extends 7.9km from Point Wolfe to the mouth of Goose River, where there's backcountry camping. The Goose River Trail links up with the Fundy Trail, which is accessible by road from St Martins. This three-day trek is one of the most difficult in the province; don't expect the trail to be as well developed as in the national park. Note that while you can cycle to Goose River, the trail beyond is for foot traffic only. For information on the section from Goose River to the suspension bridge over the Big Salmon River, see the Fundy Trail Parkway section earlier in this chapter.

Enjoyable day hikes in Fundy National Park include Coppermine Trail, a 4.4km loop to an old mine site, as well as Third Vault Falls Trail, a challenging one-way hike of 3.7km to the park's tallest falls. Note that several of the park's trails require river fordings, so be prepared.

The only wheelchair-accessible trail is the 500m boardwalk portion of the Caribou Plain Trail in the center of the park, 10½km from the visitor center. The boardwalk passes a beaver pond and is a good nocturnal hike.

From the park, Dobson Trail, another long-distance trek, leads north to the town of Riverview near Moncton. For more information, turn to the Moncton section.

Mountain biking is allowed on six trails: Goose River, Marven Lake, Black Hole, Bennett Brook (partially), East Branch, and Maple Grove. Surprisingly, at last report there were no bicycle rentals in Fundy National Park or in nearby Alma! Call the visitor center for current information on this.

Fundy has a popular Fundy Night Life Hike with a ranger; it's great – if spooky - fun. It takes place Saturdays at 8pm in July

FUNDY NATIONAL PARK

To Sussex & Moncton

114
Wolfe Lake Information Centre

Wolfe Lake Campground

Wolfe Lake

Shepody Rd

Haley Brook

Dobson Trail

To Riverview

Broad River

Forty-Five Rd

Laverty Brook

Forty-Five River

Bruin Lake
Bruin Lake Campsite

Tracey Lake
Tracey Lake Campsite

Upper Vault Brook

Black Hole Trail

Lake Brook

To Moncton

Bennett Lake

Third Vault Falls Trail

Lower Vault Brook

Upper Salmon River

To Cape Enrage

114

915

East Branch Trail

East Branch River

Bennett Brook

Bennett Brook Trail

Caribou Plain Trail

114

Kinnie Brook

Chignecto Campground

Alma

Owls Head

Headquarters Campground

Visitors Centre

Joel Head

Point Wolfe River

Rat Brook

Tail Brook

Foster Brook

Maple Grove Trail

Fundy Park Chalets

Fundy HI Hostel

Marven Lake Campsite
Marven Lake

Chambers Lake Campsite
Chambers Lake

Point Wolfe River Campsite

Marven Lake Trail

Point Wolfe Rd

Devils Half Acre Trail

Herring Cove Rd

Matthews Head

Mile Brook

Point Wolfe Campground

Covered Bridge

Goose River

Goose River Trail

Coppermine Trail

Point Wolfe

Bay of Fundy

0   1.5   3 km
0   1   2 miles

Fundy Trail to Big Salmon River

Goose Creek

Goose River Campsite

Fundy Circuit
Trail
Biking Allowed

and August (3 hrs, $8/12/33 child/adult/family) and reservations should be made well in advance at the visitor center.

Places to Stay & Eat

The park has four campgrounds with individual sites and a fifth for groups; there are also 13 wilderness sites. Reservations can be made via the national park hotline (☎ 800-414-6765). A reservation fee of $7.50 is charged. You must reserve at least three days in advance and you cannot request a specific site. The park entry fee is separate and is paid upon arrival.

Arriving from the Trans Canada Hwy, you first reach the **Wolfe Lake Campground**, which is just an open field at the northwest entrance to the park. Wolfe Lake has the advantages of a covered cooking area and few other campers. You could have it almost to yourself even in midsummer. The 20 tent sites are $10; there are no showers.

In the interior, 16km from the Wolfe Lake entrance and 3½km northwest of the visitor center, is the 264-site **Chignecto Campground**, with serviced ($17 to $19) and unserviced ($12) sites.

The 131-site *Headquarters Campground* is near the visitor center and has serviced ($19) and tent sites ($12). Along the coast, 8km southwest of the visitor center down Point Wolfe Rd, is the *Point Wolfe Campground* with 181 tent sites ($12). Expect sea breezes and cooler temperatures at the coastal campgrounds.

The 13 backcountry campsites consist of one at Chambers Lake, two at Marven Lake, four at Goose River, three by the Point Wolfe River, one at Tracey Lake and two at Bruin Lake. Only one tent per site is allowed, which means only 13 groups of one to four persons can camp in the backcountry on any given night. To reserve a backcountry site, call the visitor center at ☎ 506-887-6000. There is no additional reservation fee.

Fundy HI Hostel (☎ 506-887-2216, fax 506-887-2226, 129 Devils Half Acre Rd) Members/nonmembers $12/17, plus $1 for sheets (if required). Open June-Sept, closed 11am-5pm daily. In addition to the camping possibilities there's this HI hostel, near the golf course just off Point Wolfe Rd, 1½km from the park visitor center. It's just past the Devil's Half Acre Trail. There are two eight-bed dorms, a family room with two double beds separated by a partition, and a separate group dorm. Something is usually available but call to be sure. There are excellent cooking facilities, a lounge area and ample parking. The hostel is in five wooden buildings that were once part of an art school.

Fundy Park Chalets (☎ 506-887-2808, www.fundyparkchalets.com, off Hwy 114) Chalets $78 ($50 off-season). Open May-Oct. These nice little cottages are in a small forest between the golf course and the visitor center. Each accommodates up to four people.

ALMA

In the village of Alma, just east of the park on Hwy 114, are a motor inn, hotel and restaurants, along with a small food market, liquor store and Laundromat. Most facilities close in winter and Alma becomes a ghost town.

Fresh Air Adventure (☎ 800-545-0020, www.freshairadventure.com, 16 Fundy View Dr; open late May-mid-Sept), just up the street that begins by the bridge at the entrance to the park in Alma, offers myriad kayaking tours in and around Fundy, including the estuary and harbor (2 hrs, $45) and four-hour bay tours ($55). It also runs multiday trips in July and August, including a three-day coastal paddle to the Big Salmon River ($390).

Places to Stay & Eat

Parkland Hotel (☎ 506-887-2313, e parkland@fundyweb.com, w www.fundyweb.com/parkland, 8601 Hwy 114) Singles/doubles/triples $65/75/85 mid-June-mid-Sept, $50/60/65 beginning and end of season. Open mid-May-early Oct. This three-story hotel is a two-minute walk from the park entrance. It has a restaurant, takeout and a Laundromat.

Alpine Motor Inn (☎ 506-887-2052, e alpinegroup@auracom.com) Rooms $75. Open June-mid-Sept. On Hwy 114, 200m from the park entrance, Alpine has 34 rooms in three motel blocks, two of which have a second story.

Amber Brook B&B (☎ 877-454-4400, fax 506-887-1083, w www.amberbrook.net, 17 Butland Lane) Doubles $70-80/90 shared/private bath mid-June-mid-Sept, $10 less rest of year, full breakfast included. Just off Hwy 114 near the junction with Hwy 915, a kilometer east of Fundy National Park, this two-story house has three rooms for rent year-round.

Tides Restaurant (☎ 506-887-2313, 8601 Hwy 114) Mains $11-18. Open 11:30am-9pm Mon-Fri, 8:30am-9pm Sat & Sun mid-May-early Oct. At the Parkland Hotel, choose from the pricey main dining room, where they serve chowder ($4 to $6), mussels ($11), trout ($13), haddock($16), salmon ($18) and a seafood platter ($19), or the adjacent takeout section, also pricey at $8 to $9 for fish & chips, $10 for a clam dinner and $11 for a scallop dinner. If these prices put you off, the small grocery store across the street has fancy sandwiches and coffee.

Kelly's Bake Shop (☎ 506-887-2460, 8587 Hwy 114). Open 10am-5pm Mon-Fri, 9am-6pm Sat & Sun May-early Oct, 7am-8pm July & Aug. The sticky buns are legendary here. They cost about a dollar each, and one is enough for breakfast – maybe even lunch. There are also sandwiches and subs ($3 to $6).

Collins Seafood Lobster Shop (☎ 506-887-2054, 20 Ocean Dr) Collins Seafood, behind Kelly's, sells live or cooked lobsters, plus fresh scallops, shrimp and mussels. Smoked salmon may also be available. For the price of a meal at any of Alma's over-priced eateries you can buy the makings of a real feast here.

CAPE ENRAGE

Heading east to Moncton, take the smaller road, Hwy 915, as it detours closer to the coast, offering some fine views. At Cape Enrage, out on the cliffs at the end of the peninsula, the power of the elements is often strongly in evidence. The cape gets its name from the strong rip tide at the point.

Cape Enrage is 6½km off Hwy 915, 22km from Fundy National Park. An admission fee of $2/5 per person/car is collected as you arrive. The old lighthouse keeper's house at Cape Enrage has been converted into a *cafe*.

Cape Enrage Adventures (☎ 506-887-2273, 506-856-6081 in Moncton, W www .capenrage.com) offers a variety of adventure activities from mid-May to August. There's rock-climbing ($50), rappelling (2½ hrs $50) and they give kayak tours ($55). Call ahead or ask at the gift shop.

SHEPODY BAY SHOREBIRD RESERVE

At Mary's Point on the Bay of Fundy, another 22km east of Cape Enrage on Hwy 915, is the Shepody Bay Shorebird Reserve *(Mary's Point Rd, off Hwy 915; admission free)*. From mid-July to mid-August this is a gathering place for literally hundreds of thousands of shorebirds, primarily sandpipers. The beach is often covered with birds.

Nature trails and boardwalks have been built along the dikes and marsh. The inter-pretive center is only open from late June to early September, but you can use the 6½km of trails any time. The village of Harvey and small town of Riverside-Albert are just north of here.

Places to Stay

Sandpipers Rest B&B (☎ 506-882-2744, @ marshsp@nbnet.nb.ca, W www.sandpipers rest.nb.ca, 15 Mary's Point Road, Harvey) Singles/doubles $45/50 shared bath, doubles $60 private bath. Open May-Oct. This quiet two-story house with a nice garden is 4km south of Riverside-Albert via Hwy 915.

Cailswick Babbling Brook B&B (☎ 506-882-2079, W bay-of-fundy.com/cailswick, 5662 Hwy 114, Riverside-Albert) Singles/doubles/triples $45/55/65. This imposing two-story farmhouse stands on spacious grounds.

Peck Colonial House B&B (☎ 506-882-2114, W www.peckcolonial.com, 5566 Hwy 114) Singles/doubles/triples $45/55/65. Less than a kilometer east of Cailswick Babbling Brook, this two-story colonial-style house next to the highway contains three rooms for rent. If you're just passing by, meals (seafood chowder, clam chowder, chili) are served and baked goods (breads and pies) are sold in their tea room (open noon to 8pm).

Broadleaf Too B&B (☎ 506-882-2803, fax 506-882-2075, W www.bbcanada.com/ 4028.html, 5465 Hwy 114) Doubles $50. A kilometer east of Peck Colonial House and 12km west of Hopewell Cape, this bungalow by the highway has three rooms. Don't confuse this place with Broadleaf Guest Ranch just down the road.

HOPEWELL ROCKS

The **Hopewell Rocks Ocean Tidal Exploration Site** *(☎ 877-734-3429, off Hwy 114; admission $5/12 adult/family, shuttle $1 extra; open 9am-5pm daily mid-May-early Oct; 8am-8pm late June-mid-Aug)* is at Hopewell Cape, where the Petitcodiac River meets the Fundy waters in Shepody Bay. The 'rocks' are unusual eroded formations known as 'flowerpots.' The shore is lined with these irregular geological forms, as well as caves and tunnels, all created by erosion from the great tides.

This former provincial park is being heavily promoted as a tourist attraction, and it can be extremely crowded in mid-summer. An exploratory walk along the beach at low tide is still worthwhile, though – check the tide tables at any tourist office. You can't walk on the beach at high tide, but the rock towers are visible from the trails above. Morning is the best time for shutterbugs.

From late June to early September **Baymount Adventures** (☎ 506-734-2660, **W** www.baymountadventures.com, adult/child $45/40) offers two-hour kayak tours. Their office is 100m beyond the cafe inside the exploration site.

Pollock's Heritage Farm (☎ 506-734-1094, fax 506-734-2110, **e** hightide@nbnet.nb.ca, **W** www.hopewellrocksmotel .com/bedbreakfast.htm, 4158 Hwy 114, Hopewell Cape) Singles/doubles $55/65. Open May-Oct. This two-story blue farmhouse is just 100m north of the entrance to Hopewell Rocks.

HILLSBOROUGH
Hillsborough, 14km north of Hopewell Rocks and 20km southeast of Moncton, is a small town overlooking the Petitcodiac River. From here a restored steam engine from the **Salem-Hillsborough Railroad** (☎ 506-734-3195, off Hwy 114) pulls antique coaches 8km up the river to Salem and back (adult/child $8.50/4.50; roundtrip 1 hour). The train departs at 2pm every Wednesday, Saturday and Sunday in July and August.

Spelunking adventures through the White Caves are offered by **Baymount Adventures** (☎ 506-734-2660; $45 per person; open late June-early Sept). Reservations must be made by phone, although participants often meet at the tourist office next to the train station. The trail through the wetlands behind the tourist office is worth a wal (admission free).

Rose Arbor B&B (☎ 877-972-7276, 2835 Main St, Hillsborough) Singles/doubles $55/65. Two doors down from the train station, this large two-story building is right

on Hwy 114 and thus a little noisy, with trucks and RVs roaring up the hill.

Victoriana Steves Homestead B&B (☎ 506-734-2156, fax 506-734-2942, 57 Pleasant St) Singles/doubles $50/65. Minutes from Rose Arbor B&B, this impressive two-story house is on spacious grounds on a quiet sidestreet. The five rooms are nicely decorated.

Moncton to Sackville

This corner of New Brunswick is the geographical heart of the Maritimes, a transportation crossroads most visitors to the region will transit at least once. At the center of it all is Moncton, whose principa attractions are places where nature appears to defy gravity. Southeast of the city is a memorial to the Acadians, and a forbidding prison where Eastern Canada's worst felons are held. Almost on the Nova Scotia border the small town of Sackville will appeal to travelers from a university milieu.

MONCTON
Moncton, with a population of 60,000, is the second city of the province and a major transportation and distribution center for the Maritimes. It's only 96km west of the Confederation Bridge to Prince Edward Island, and the train to Nova Scotia passes through. Next to Halifax, Moncton has the region's busiest airport by far. A couple of odd attractions – Magnetic Hill and a tidal bore – make it worth at least a brief stop on your way by.

History
The present city of Moncton is at the southwestern end of an old Mi'kmaq portage route from Shediac. In the 1740s, the firs Acadians settled at this strategic bend in the Petitcodiac River, which they called Le Coude (The Elbow). Their situation became precarious in 1755 after troops led by Lieutenant Colonel Robert Monckton captured Fort Beauséjour to the southeast, and ir

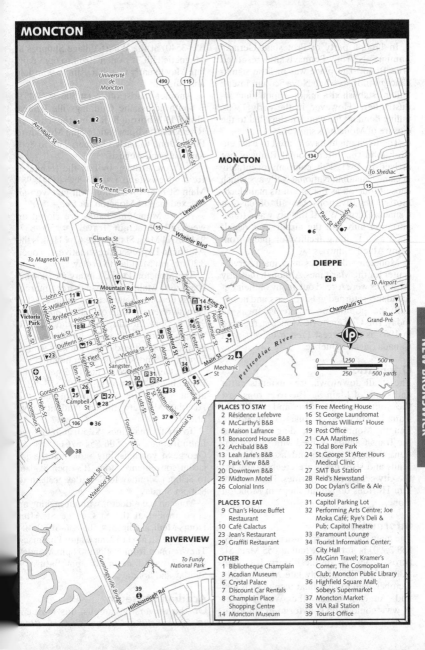

MONCTON

PLACES TO STAY
2 Résidence Lefebvre
4 McCarthy's B&B
5 Maison Lafrance
11 Bonaccord House B&B
12 Archibald B&B
13 Leah Jane's B&B
17 Park View B&B
20 Downtown B&B
25 Midtown Motel
26 Colonial Inns

PLACES TO EAT
9 Chan's House Buffet
   Restaurant
10 Café Calactus
23 Jean's Restaurant
29 Graffiti Restaurant

OTHER
1 Bibliotheque Champlain
3 Acadian Museum
6 Crystal Palace
7 Discount Car Rentals
8 Champlain Place
   Shopping Centre
14 Moncton Museum

15 Free Meeting House
16 St George Laundromat
18 Thomas Williams' House
19 Post Office
21 CAA Maritimes
22 Tidal Bore Park
24 St George St After Hours
   Medical Clinic
27 SMT Bus Station
28 Reid's Newsstand
30 Doc Dylan's Grille & Ale
   House
31 Capitol Parking Lot
32 Performing Arts Centre; Joe
   Moka Café; Rye's Deli &
   Pub; Capitol Theatre
33 Paramount Lounge
34 Tourist Information Center;
   City Hall
35 McGinn Travel; Kramer's
   Corner; The Cosmopolitan
   Club; Moncton Public Library
36 Highfield Square Mall;
   Sobeys Supermarket
37 Moncton Market
38 VIA Rail Station
39 Tourist Office

1758 the British deported all Acadians from the area.

In 1766, a party of Protestant German immigrants from Pennsylvania resettled 'The Bend.' The place was of little significance until 1846, when Nova Scotian Joseph Salter established a major shipbuilding industry here. However, in the early 1860s, falling demand for wooden ships led to the closure of Moncton's shipyards.

The town might have ceased to exist entirely had the Intercolonial Railway not arrived in 1871. This company eventually became Canadian National Railways, which chose Moncton as the site of its main locomotive repair shops for all of eastern Canada. During WWII the city was a transportation hub, and the airport was developed as a training facility for pilots from many Allied countries.

Moncton still thrives as a main service center for the Maritimes. Although the early Acadians were forced out, many of their descendants returned in later years, and nearly half the population is French-speaking today. The Université de Moncton, founded in 1963, is the largest French university in Canada outside Québec.

Orientation

The small downtown area extends north and south of Main St. The river runs past the south side of town and the Trans Canada Hwy passes just to the north. Lengthy Mountain Rd, leading west toward the Trans Canada, is lined with service stations, chain restaurants and fast-food joints. Malls and strip malls are creeping toward the city center from all sides. There are 26 Tim Hortons doughnut shops in Moncton alone.

Information

The main tourist information center (☎ 506-853-3590) is in the city hall at 655 Main St, across from the public library. It's open 8:30am to 4:30pm daily late May to early October, 9am to 7pm June, 9am to 8pm July and August. Check the Web site at w www.gomoncton.com for more information on Moncton.

If you are coming in on the Trans Canada Hwy, there's a seasonal tourist office (☎ 506-853-3540) at the Wharf Village Shoppes at Magnetic Hill. It's open 10am to 6pm daily late May to early October, 8am to 9pm July and August.

Another tourist office (☎ 506-387-2053) is south across the Gunningsville Bridge, along Hillsborough Rd by the river in Riverview. It's open 9am to 5pm Monday to Friday June to early October, 9am to 8pm daily July and August.

If you're arriving by bus, the cashier at Reid's Newsstand (☎ 506-382-1824), 985 Main St near the station, will give you an indexed map of Moncton for free.

All of Moncton's banks are closed on weekends. McGinn Travel (☎ 506-857-9545), 644 Main St opposite City Hall, is the American Express representative. It's open 8:30 to 7pm Monday to Friday.

The Moncton Public Library (☎ 506-869-6037), 644 Main St, provides free Internet access upstairs (identification required). Go early to reserve a time, or call. It's open from 9am to 5pm Monday and Friday, 9am to 8:30pm Tuesday to Thursday July and August, 9am to 8:30pm Tuesday to Thursday, 9am to 5pm Friday and Saturday other months.

You can also access the Internet at the Bibliotheque Champlain (☎ 506-858-4012) at the Université de Moncton, near the Acadian Museum, though students have priority.

To use the machines ($1.50) at St George Laundromat (☎ 506-854-6761), 64 St George St, you must buy a token at the adjacent convenience store. It's open 8:30am to 8:30pm Monday to Saturday, 9:30am to 8:30pm Sunday.

You can see a doctor without making an appointment at the St George St After Hours Medical Clinic (☎ 506-856-6122), 404 St George St, next to Jean Coutu Pharmacy. They're open from 5:30pm to 8pm Monday to Friday and noon to 3pm Saturday, Sunday and holidays.

Acadian Museum

On the university campus, this museum (☎ 506-858-4088, Clement Cormier Bldg;

admission $2/1 adults/students, Sun free; open 10am-5pm Mon-Fri, 1pm-5pm Sat & Sun July & Aug; 1pm-4:30pm Tues-Fri, 1-4 pm Sat & Sun rest of year) has displays offering a brief history of the Acadians. The museum chronicles aspects of the day-to-day life of these first European settlers in the Maritimes. The Galerie d'Art de l'Université is also at this museum. Parking is 50¢ an hour during the week but free on Saturday and Sunday. Bus No 5 Elmwood serves the University from Main St every 50 minutes from Monday to Saturday.

Moncton Museum

This museum *(☎ 506-856-4383, 20 Mountain Rd near Belleview St; admission free; open 10am-8pm daily July-Aug, 9am-4:30pm Mon-Sat, 1-5pm Sun rest of year)* outlines local history from the time of the Mi'kmaq Indians and early settlers to the present. Displays show the influence of shipbuilding and the railway on the area and an old-style street scene has been recreated. Next-door is the oldest building in town, the **Free Meeting House** dating from 1821, used by numerous religious congregations over the years.

Tidal Bore Park

The tidal bore is a twice-daily incoming wave caused by the tides of the Petitcodiac River, which are in turn related to the tides in the Bay of Fundy – known as the world's highest tides. The bore rushes upstream and sometimes raises the water level in the river by 6m in a few minutes. The wave itself varies in height from a few centimeters to over 30cm.

A good place to watch for it is in Tidal Bore Park at the east end of Main St, where a large clock displays the time of the next bore. The pleasant park is filled with old men sitting on the benches until close to bore time, when the water's edge gets really crowded with expectant visitors. Don't anticipate anything spectacular though. The wave is usually not too impressive, but the troop of street performers on hand help make this an entertaining event. It's also not unknown to see porpoises swimming here.

Note that there's no free parking right at Tidal Bore Park, so allow some time to find a spot elsewhere. The unsightly, litter-filled parking lots adjacent to Tidal Bore Park are owned by the RCMP, which has posted large 'no parking' signs.

Moncton Market

This is a year-round food market *(120 Westmorland St south of Main St; open 7am-1pm Sat)*. The weird sign outside says 'Degen Deli,' but the market is through the door. Although some organic fruits and vegetables are sold, it's not really a farmers market, as most items are ready to eat. The array of food items, mostly local specialties sold in small packages, is mind-boggling, and it's always packed with locals who come every week. Plan on having your breakfast or lunch here. It's a must if you're in Moncton on a Saturday morning.

Thomas Williams' House

Built in 1883, this 12-room Gothic-style house *(☎ 506-857-0590, 103 Park St; admission free; open 9am-5pm Mon-Sat, 1pm-5pm Sun July & Aug)* in the downtown area remained in the family as a private home until 1983, when it was bequeathed to the city as a heritage house. Much of the fine original work remains intact both inside and out, and the furnishings add to the overall effect. The tea room on the veranda is fun.

Magnetic Hill

Incredibly, this is said to be Canada's third-most-visited natural tourist attraction *(☎ 506-858-8841, corner of Mountain Rd and the Trans Canada Hwy; $3 per car; open 8am-8pm open mid-May-mid-Sept)*. Gravity here seems to work in reverse – start at the bottom of the hill in a car and you'll apparently drift upward. It looks like uphill, but it's actually downhill, an optical illusion. The car fee may be worth it if there are several of you in the vehicle, otherwise you can park free at the adjacent Wharf Village Shoppes and walk over to watch the paying customers coast back. Late at night and in the off-season it's free. The fact that hundreds of thousands of tourists a year could

NEW BRUNSWICK

The Tides of Funnel-Shaped Fundy

The tides of the Bay of Fundy are the highest in the world. This constant ebb and flow is a prime factor in the life of the bay, the appearance of the shoreline and even how residents set shipping and fishing schedules.

An old Mi'kmaq legend relates how the demigod Glooscap was looking for somewhere to take a bath. To be helpful, his friend Beaver built a massive dam across the mouth of a river, creating a huge pool. Yet just as Glooscap was stepping in, Whale appeared from the sea demanding to know why water was being withheld from her realm. Glooscap quickly returned to dry land, and at that, Whale demolished the dam with a swipe of her mighty tail, sending saltwater surging up the river. So powerful was her blow that the water has continued sloshing back and forth ever since.

A more prosaic scientific explanation for these record tides is in the length, depth and gradual funnel shape of the bay itself. As the high tide builds up, the water flowing into the narrowing bay has to rise on the edges. It is pushed still higher because the seabed gets progressively shallower. A compounding factor is called 'resonance,' which refers to the rocking back and forth from one end to the other of all the water in the bay, as if in a giant bathtub. When a massive swell on its way out of the bay meets a more powerful incoming tide head on, the volume of water increases substantially.

The contrasts between the high and ebb tide are most pronounced at the eastern end of the Bay of Fundy and around the Minas Basin, where tides of 10 to 15m occur twice daily, about 12½ hours apart. The highest tide ever recorded anywhere was 16.6m, the height of a four-story building, at Burncoat Head near the village of Noel, Nova Scotia. The times and heights of the tides vary from location to location around the bay; local schedules are available at many tourist offices in the region.

All tides, large and small, are caused by the rise and fall of the oceans due to the gravitational pull of the Sun and the Moon. Consequently, the distance of the Moon and its position relative to

be attracted by this gimmick is the most impressive part of it all.

In recent years the hill has spawned various other attractions, including the city-operated **Magnetic Hill Zoo** (☎ 506-384-0303, 100 Worthington Ave; adult/family $6.50/20, open 10am-6pm Mon-Fri, 9am-7pm Sat & Sun May-Oct; 10am-5pm Sun Nov-Apr), with over 400 animals. There's also a rather expensive **water park** (☎ 800-331-9283; adult/family $19.50/64; open mid-June-early Sept) featuring a variety of slides, as well as restaurants, stores and even a golf course. A mini-train links the different diversions in midsummer.

Dobson Trail

Just south of Moncton in Riverview, this 58km hiking trail leads you through the Albert County hills and maple forests down to Fundy National Park. Hiking the full length of the trail one way to its connection with the Laverty Falls Trail in the national park is a three-day endeavor for most people.

To reach the northern trailhead, take the causeway across the Petitcodiac River to Riverview, then turn east on Hwy 114. Turn south on Pine Glen Rd, and after 3km, you'll reach the trailhead marked by a white sign and a parking area. The first section of the trail is the 9.4km trek to Beaver Pond, where you'll find a hut and areas to make camp.

For more information get in touch with the Trailmaster, Edwin Melanson (☎ 506-855-5089), in Riverview.

Special Events

The Festival international du cinéma francophone en Acadie in late September showcases filmmaking in France, Belgium, Africa and Canada.
Web site: **w** www.ficfa.com

The Tides of Funnel-Shaped Fundy

Earth and the Sun determine tidal size. When the Moon is full or new, the gravitational forces of the Sun and the Moon are working in concert, not at cross-purposes, and the tides at these two times of the month are higher than average. When one of these periods coincides with the time (perigee, once every 27½ days) when the Moon is closest to Earth the tides are at their most dramatic.

Throughout the centuries various methods have been used around the bay to tap the tides as an energy source. Simple but successful powering of gristmills spurred dreams of grandiose generating stations feeding the eastern seaboard. There is still no commercial electricity production, but there is a working experimental tidal power plant that can be visited at Annapolis Royal, Nova Scotia.

Extremely Boring

A feature related to the tides is the tidal bore, a daily occurrence in some of the rivers flowing into the Bay of Fundy, most notably the Saint John River running through Saint John, the Petitcodiac River in Moncton and the Salmon River in Truro, Nova Scotia.

As the tide advances up a narrowing bay it starts to build up on itself, forming a wave. The height of this oncoming rush can vary from just a few centimeters to about 1m. The power behind it forces the water up what is normally a river draining down to the sea. This upstream-flowing wave is called a 'tidal bore.'

The size and height of the tidal bore is determined by the tide, which itself is regulated by the gravitational pull of the Moon. In the areas where the tidal bore is most interesting it is not difficult to get a bore schedule. As with ocean tides, there are two tidal bores a day, which are roughly 12 hours apart. While a large bore is fascinating to observe, smaller bores can be considerably less gripping.

Places to Stay

Camping *Camper's City* (☎ 877-512-7868, fax 506-855-5588, ⓦ *www.sn2000.nb.ca/comp/camper_city, 138 Queensway Dr at the Mapleton Rd exit from Hwy 2)* Unserviced/serviced sites $20/26. Open June-Sept. This is the nearest campground to the city. They cater mostly to RVs but have some nice grassy sites for tents at the back of the campground. In midsummer it will be packed, with little space between you and your neighbors.

Stonehurst Trailer Park (☎ 506-852-4162, ⓦ *www.sn2000.nb.ca/comp/stonehurst, 47915 Hwy 128)* Sites $20. Open late May-early Oct. Across the street from the Scenic Motel at Berry Mills, Stonehurst is less well known than the various campgrounds around Moncton and is seldom crowded. The usual rows of RVs are at the bottom of the hill next to the golf course, but there's a

separate tenting area on the slope back toward the highway with lots of nice shady sites.

Hostels *Université de Moncton* (☎ 506-858-4008, fax 506-858-4620, ⓦ *www.umoncton.ca; off Archibald St)* Singles/doubles $48/60 adult, $34/48 student & senior. From May to late August, the university rents rooms in two of its student residences. The 170 rooms in the 11-story *Maison Lafrance* near the Acadian Museum have private bath, microwave and refrigerator.

There are cheaper rooms with shared bath in the *Résidence Lefebvre* up the hill at $32 single ($19 for students), but they don't like to give them to tourists and you may have to beg. All bookings are handled by Housing Services at Résidence Lefebvre (open 8am to midnight).

NEW BRUNSWICK

Tourist Homes & B&Bs *Park View B&B* (☎ *506-382-4504, 254 Cameron St)* Singles/doubles/triples $45/55/65. Three rooms are available in an elegant modernistic brick house facing Victoria Park.

Bonaccord House B&B (☎ *506-388-1535, fax 506-853-7191,* **w** *www.bbcanada.com/ 4135.html, 250 Bonaccord St)* Singles/doubles $45/55. This four-room house is within walking distance of the center. It's the appealing yellow-and-white house with stately Doric columns on the porch and a yard surrounded by a white picket fence.

Archibald B&B (☎ *877-389-0123, fax 506-857-9188,* **e** *info@archibaldbedbreak fast.com,* **w** *www.archibald-breakfast .com, 194 Archibald St)* Singles/doubles/triples $75/85/95 mid-June-mid-Sept, $49/59/69 other months. Two blocks from Bonaccord House, Archibald B&B also has a large covered porch.

Leah Jane's B&B (☎ *506-854-9207, fax 506-389-9329,* **w** *www.bbcanada.com/leah janes, 146 Church St)* Singles/doubles both $75 mid-June-mid-Sept, $50/55 other months. Four rooms are for rent in this large two-story building with a pool in the rear garden and on-site parking.

Downtown B&B (☎ *506-855-7108,* **e** *lglenx@nbnet.nb.ca,* **w** *www.bbcanada .com/1994.html, 101 Alma St)* Singles/doubles both $60 mid-June-mid-Sept, $45/50 other months. This B&B has four rooms in a two-story stone mansion convenient to town.

McCarthy's B&B (☎ *506-383-9152, 82 Peter St)* Singles/doubles $45/55 mid-June-mid-Sept, $35/45 shoulder seasons. Open May-Oct. This place, also with four rooms for rent, is a longtime favorite of travelers. Peter St is near the university, just under 2km north of downtown. It's often full, so call ahead. Smoking is not permitted.

Motels *Midtown Motel* (☎ *506-388-5000, fax 506-383-4640,* **w** *www.atyp.com/midtown, 61 Weldon St)* Rooms $69/79 one/two beds mid-June-mid-Sept, $59/69 other months, extra persons $5. This two-story motel is right in the center of town, within walking distance of the bus and train stations.

Colonial Inns (☎ *800-561-4667, fax 506-858-8991,* **w** *www.colonial-inns.com, 42 Highfield St)* Singles/doubles $76/88 mid-June-mid-Sept, $68/76 other months. This two-story motel complex is also near the bus and train stations.

Scenic Motel (☎ *506-384-6105, 47910 Hwy 128)* Singles/doubles $55/60 mid-June-mid-Sept, $30/35 other months. Open May-Oct. This motel's 20 rooms face the highway in a two-story block, 3.3km west of Magnetic Hill. Go up the hill on Ensley Dr (Hwy 126 North), which begins next to McDonalds.

Restwell Motel (☎ *506-857-4884,* **w** *www.restwellmotel.com, 12 McFarlane Rd)* Singles/doubles $45/55 mid-June-mid-Sept, $35/45 other months, $195 single weekly. The Restwell, 600m west of the Scenic Motel on Hwy 128, has 12 rooms in one back-to-back block, with a few rooms upstairs above the office. All rooms have a fridge, and the weekly rooms above the office have kitchenettes. It's a little hard to see this motel from the road, as it's hidden behind a hill.

Atlantic Motel (☎ *877-958-1988, fax 506-858-1988, 8 Brown Rd, Berry Mills, on Hwy 128)* Singles/doubles $52/58 ($61 double with two beds) mid-June-mid-Sept, $45/50 ($53 two beds) other months. This no-frills place has 22 rooms in a two-story block and motel wing, 3½km west of the Restwell Motel. The Atlantic's restaurant is a popular breakfast stop.

Places to Eat

Café Calactus (☎ *506-388-4833, 179 Mountain Rd at Robinson)* Lunch $5-6. Open 10am-2pm Mon, 10-8pm Tues-Sun. This colorful cafe offers healthy California-style vegetarian food, such as flutes made with tortillas ($5), pelizzas – a type of pizza ($6), burritos ($6), soup ($2 to $4), salads ($3 to $7), whole-grain bread and metaphysical teas and coffees. It's a good place to touch base with the local counter-culture scene.

Rye's Deli & Pub (☎ *506-853-7937, 785 Main St)* Specials from $6. Open 8am-9pm Sun-Thurs, 8am-midnight Fri & Sat. This deli, on Main St near Westmorland St, has great bagels and nightly specials listed on a blackboard on the wall, such as spaghetti on Monday and steak on Thursday. It also has a happy hour from 4pm to 9pm featuring tall 20oz glasses of draft beer for $3.50, pitchers for $7.75 and shots for $2.75. There's live music Saturday from 7pm to 11pm.

Joe Moka Café (☎ 506-852-3070, 837 Main St) Open 8am-5pm Mon-Sat, 9am-5pm Sun. This cafe is a popular spot to have a café au lait ($2.25) and carrot cake. Enjoy your treats at one of the tables outside on Robinson St.

Graffiti Restaurant (☎ 506-382-4299, 897 Main St) Mains $8-12. Open 11am-11pm Sun-Thurs, 11am-midnight Fri & Sat. Graffiti is upscale in everything but price. The French-speaking staff offer tastefully presented dishes with a Mediterranean or 'new Greek' flair, including seafood ($8 to $12), grilled items ($9 to $11), moussaka ($8) and daily specials ($8 to $11).

Jean's Restaurant (☎ 506-855-1053, 371 St George St) Mains $9. This '50s-style diner is a Moncton institution, and locals really pack Jean's stools and booths. It's great for breakfast until 11am ($3 including coffee); for lunch try the fish & chips ($8), fried clams ($9) or fried scallops ($9).

Chan's House Buffet Restaurant (☎ 506-858-0112, 80 Champlain St) Lunch/dinner $8/11. Open 11am-midnight Mon-Thurs, 11am-1am Fri & Sat, 11am-11pm Sun. Chan's continuous Chinese and Vietnamese buffet continues all day every day from 11am to 9pm, with the dinner price kicking in at 3:30pm. It's just east of the Champlain Place Shopping Centre.

Ponderosa Steak House (☎ 506-384-7174, 956 Mountain Rd, opposite Club Mystique) Mains $8-13. Open 11am-9pm daily. The steaks here come with an all-you-can-eat soup-and-salad bar. It's west of town on Mountain Rd, toward Magnetic Hill.

Sobeys Supermarket (☎ 506-855-0546, Highfield Square Mall, 1100 Main St) Open 8am-9:30pm Mon-Sat, noon-6pm Sun. This supermarket is convenient to downtown. Other Sobeys supermarkets are on Mountain Rd and opposite Champlain Place Shopping Centre.

Entertainment

Look for a free copy of *Action* magazine, which gives a lengthy rundown on Moncton's vibrant nightlife. Central Main St has several bars catering to the younger set, with live bands and dancing.

Performing Arts Centre (☎ 506-856-4379, 811 Main St, Mon-Fri 9am-5pm, Sat 9am-1pm) The impressive Capitol Theatre, a 1920s vaudeville house, has been restored and is now the city's Performing Arts Centre. Call the theater box office for a schedule of performances. Theatre New Brunswick and Symphony New Brunswick both perform here on a regular basis throughout the year. The Acadian group Grand Dérangement also plays here from time to time.

The Cosmopolitan Club (☎ 506-857-9117, 702 Main St) Open 8:30pm-2am Wed-Sun. Cosmopolitan is the largest dance club in Moncton with a capacity of 1100. It's mostly the 19-to-25 crew that patronizes this disco ($4 cover charge). Friday from 4pm to 10pm there's jazz downstairs and the crowd tends to be over 30.

Kramer's Corner (☎ 506-857-9118, 702 Main St) Open 11:30am-midnight Mon & Tues, 11:30am-2am Wed-Fri, 4pm-2am Sat, 4pm-midnight Sun. In the same complex as Cosmopolitan, Kramer's has live music Saturday after 9:30pm. This is your best bet for a nice wine or scotch.

Paramount Lounge (☎ 506-860-6927, 800 Main St) Open 8pm-2am Tues-Thurs, 4pm-2am Fri, 8pm-midnight Sat. Paramount is more of a sitdown scene than 'the Cosmo,' but it can also be loud, danceable and packed with gyrating bodies. It's Moncton's gay-friendly venue. The cover charge varies.

Doc Dylan's Grille & Ale House (☎ 506-382-3627, 841 Main St) Open 11:30am-2am Mon-Fri, 10:30am-2am Sat & Sun. More live music can be enjoyed at Doc Dylan's, on the corner of Main & Foundry Sts. The pub features live music two or three times a week.

VooDoo Nightclub (☎ 506-858-8844, 938 Mountain Rd) Open 8pm-2:30am Wed-Sat,

4pm-2:30am Fri. Moncton's most renowned dance club catering to the over-25 crowd; their slogan is 'be nice or leave.' When guest performers appear, the cover charge could be between $7 and $15, but usually it's $3.75, plus $1.25 to check your coat. It's on Mountain Rd out toward Magnetic Hill.

Club Mystique (☎ 506-858-5861, 939 Mountain Rd) Open 8:30pm-2am Wed-Sat, 6pm-10pm Sun. Club Mystique, on the other side of Mountain Rd, is similar but a tad rougher. Sunday night there's a teen dance with no alcohol served.

Crystal Palace (☎ 506-859-4386, Paul St) Open noon-8pm Mon-Fri, 10am-9pm Sat, 10am-8pm Sun. If you have kids, this is the place to take them. There's a whole hall full of amusement park–style rides and games. A ride pass is $13/46 per person/family, or pay $1 a ride. Parking is free.

Moncton Coliseum (☎ 506-857-4100, 377 Killiam Dr) The coliseum is home to major shows, concerts and sporting events. It's in a remote location beyond the railway yards on the west side of the city.

Getting There & Away

Air Greater Moncton Airport is New Brunswick's busiest airport by far, and flights to other parts of Canada tend to be cheaper here than those out of Halifax. You can fly Air Canada to Halifax, Montréal, Ottawa and Toronto.

A possibility worth investigating if you want to save money is Westjet to and from Hamilton, Ontario. They have many connections to cities all across central and western Canada from there, and Westjet's one-way Hamilton-Moncton fare varies from $349 plus tax to as little as $149 if you book at least 10 days ahead. Check for specials.

An 'airport improvement & reconstruction fee' of $10 must be paid by all passengers departing from Moncton (not included in the ticket price).

Bus SMT Bus Lines (☎ 506-859-5060) has a large station at 961 Main St, on the corner of Bonaccord St between downtown and the train station. Some schedules with one-way ticket prices are as follows:

destination	departure	fare
Charlottetown, PEI	2:25pm daily & 8:40pm Fri, Sat, Sun	$35
Fredericton, NB	11:45am, 5:40pm	$30
Halifax, NS	11am, 2:15pm, 8:30pm	$43
Saint John, NB	11:30am, 6pm	$24

The bus station itself is open from 7:30am to 8:30pm Monday to Friday, 9am to 8:30pm Saturday and Sunday. There's a good little cafe in the bus station and $2 coin lockers.

Train The VIA Rail station (☎ 506-857-9830) is southwest of the downtown area near Cameron St, 200m off Main St. Look for it behind the building at 1234 Main St or behind Sobeys Supermarket at the Highfield Mall. The station is open 9am to 6pm daily, and luggage storage is $2.50 per piece.

The *Ocean* goes through northern New Brunswick, including Campbellton and Québec, on its way to Montréal, departing Moncton at 5:45pm daily, except Tuesday. The train to Halifax departs at 11:35am daily, except Wednesday. Regular one-way fares are $52 to Halifax and $163 to Montréal. If you purchase your ticket a week in advance you save 25% (provided that discount seats are still available).

There's no train service to Saint John. Instead, a railway bus to Saint John departs at 11:20am and 6:20pm. The fare is $30, or $23 if the ticket is purchased five days in advance. The railway bus to Charlottetown is at 1:30pm daily ($35).

Car & Motorcycle Discount Car Rentals (☎ 506-857-2323), 566 Paul St, opposite Champlain Place Shopping Centre, has cars for $39 daily with unlimited kilometers, plus $19 collision insurance and tax. This price may be higher in midsummer. It's open 8am to 6pm Monday to Friday, 9am to 1pm Saturday.

Parking can be a hassle in Moncton, as parking meters ($1 an hour) and no parking zones extend far out from downtown. Parking meters are free evenings and weekends, although this isn't posted. The municipal parking lot at Moncton Market on Westmorland St charges $1/7 per hour/day 7:45am to 6pm Monday to Friday and is free on Saturday, Sunday and evenings after 6pm. Capitol Parking Lot, between Main and Queen Sts from Church to Lutz Sts, charges the same rates weekdays. During the evening Capitol is $2 from 6pm to closing, but you can park there for free until 5pm on Saturday. Highfield Square Mall, on Main St between the train and bus stations, provides free parking for their clients, and who's to say you aren't one?

CAA Maritimes (☎ 506-857-8225), 60 King St, is conveniently located downtown.

Hitchhiking Hitching north or east from Moncton is a hassle, as there are numerous diverging roads and lots of local traffic. Hitching west to Saint John or Fredericton is a bit easier. In either case, the No 5 Elmwood bus from Main St will take you to the corner of Elmwood Dr and Hennessey Rd, very near the Elmwood Road exit from the Trans Canada Hwy. A destination sign will be helpful. To hitch to Fundy National Park, take the No 12 Riverview East bus to the corner of Hiltz and Hillsborough Sts (this bus is infrequent, but one leaves Highfield Square Monday to Saturday at 8:25am).

Getting Around

Greater Moncton Airport, 6km east of Champlain Place Shopping Centre via Champlain St, is served by the No 20 Champlain bus from Champlain Place nine times on weekdays. A taxi to the center of town should cost $12. Avis, Budget, Hertz and National have car rental desks at the airport.

Codiac Transit (☎ 506-857-2008) is the local bus system, running daily except Sunday. The fare is $1.50. There's no bus right to Magnetic Hill and some services are infrequent, so try to check bus schedules beforehand.

SAINT-JOSEPH

Saint-Joseph is in the Memramcook Valley, the only area near the Bay of Fundy where descendants of the early Acadians live on the same land their forebears settled before the mass deportations.

Here, 25km southeast of Moncton, is the **Monument Lefebvre National Historic Site** (☎ 506-758-9783, 480 Central St; adult/senior/child/family $2/1.50/1/5; open 9am-5pm June-mid-Oct), which tells the story of the Acadians, most of whom were expelled by the British in 1755. The exhibits, which include paintings, crafts and life-size models, are well done, and attention is given to the lives of the Acadians and their descendants right up to the present.

Memramcook Valley Learning & Vacation Resort (☎ 506-758-2511, fax 506-758-2149, 488 Centrale St) Singles/doubles $70/80 year-round. The historic site is actually on the grounds of this resort, housed in the former Université Saint-Joseph. All the amenities of a spa are here, including a golf course, massage, an Acadian restaurant and meeting and banquet rooms.

DORCHESTER

Dorchester is a historic town with many colonial relics, including the **Bell Inn**, the oldest stone structure (1811) in New Brunswick..

Dorchester Penitentiary (☎ 506-379-2471, 4902 Main St), 17km south of Saint Joseph on Hwy 106, is the oldest and largest federal prison in the Maritimes, erected on a hilltop overlooking the Memramcook River in 1881. Only prisoners serving sentences of over two years are held here, and the menacing fortress-like walls and observation towers of this Gothic institution dominate the area. There's a splendid view of the Memramcook Valley from here, but photography is prohibited. You can still see where the Acadian farmers built dikes to farm the tidal flats along the valley prior to their expulsion in 1755.

The penitentiary cannot be visited, but you're welcome at **Keillor House Museum** (☎ 506-379-6633, w www.keillorhousemuseum.com, 4974 Main St; adult/child $2/1; open 10am-5pm Mon-Fri, 1pm-5pm Sun mid-June-mid-Sept), 600m south of the prison. This is the former residence (1812) of Judge John Keillor, whose father-in-law originally owned the land on which the prison was later built. A collection of old photos of the penitentiary are on display, and you can see the original whipping bench used until the 1960s. Ankle shackles called 'Oregon boots' and other implements of torture once employed at Dorchester are also exhibited, along with daggers and bar springers fashioned by would-be escapees. Adjacent to Keillor House is a smaller provincial prison, built around the turn of the century, which closed in the 1990s. Eight prisoners were hanged within its walls.

SACKVILLE

Sackville is a small university town that's in the right place for a pit stop. In Octagon House (1855) at 6 King St, just off East Main St, is a tourist office (☎ 506-364-4967) with the usual brochures. It's open 9am to 5pm daily late May to mid-October. A few picnic tables are here.

Mount Allison University

This top-rated small university features monumental buildings on a compact parklike campus in the center of town. Mount Allison was the first Canadian university to accept a female student (in 1862), and the first in the British Empire to award a bachelor's degree to a woman (in 1875). Among the facilities open to the public is a swan pond, a library and the Owens Art Gallery (☎ 506-364-2574, 61 York St; admission free; open 10am-5pm Mon-Fri, 1pm-5pm Sat & Sun), founded in 1984. This is one of the best-known small art galleries in eastern Canada.

Sackville Waterfowl Park

Across the road from the university, off E Main St, is the Sackville Waterfowl Park. The park is on a major bird migration route. Boardwalks have been built over portions of it, and there's another trail and some interpretive signs. The Wildlife Service (☎ 506-364-5044, 17 Waterfowl Lane off East Main St; admission free; open 8am-4pm Mon-Fri) has a wetlands display in their office at one of the entrances to the park and information for those wishing to see more.

Radio Canada International Shortwave Transmitting Station

South of town toward Nova Scotia on the Trans Canada Hwy, halfway between Sackville and Aulac, you go right past this radio station (☎ 506-536-2690, accessible only from the northbound lanes of Hwy 2; admission free; open 10am-6pm July & Aug). You definitely won't be sorry if you take in one of the free, chatty guided tours offered here. It's great fun and highly educational. In the off-season, the regular staff will show you around if they're not too busy. From here Radio Canada International broadcasts around the world (although the station's studios are in Montréal). The towers are clearly visible from Fort Beauséjour on the Nova Scotia border.

Places to Stay

Marshview Trailer Park (☎ 506-536-2880, fax 506-536-4916, **W** www.sn2000.nb.ca/comp/marshview, 2 Stephens Dr) Unserviced/serviced sites $18/20. Open June-mid-Sept. Marshview offers a grassy field with picnic tables, adjacent to Hwy 2. It's on the north side of the highway very near the Cattail Ridge exit, and the traffic noise is considerable.

Mt Allison University (☎ 506-364-2250, fax 506-364-2688, **e** conferences@mta.ca, **W** www.mta.ca/conference, 155 East Main St) Singles/doubles $26/46, students $20. Open May-Aug. The university, right in the center of town, offers rooms to overnight guests. To get a room go to the Conference Office in Windsor Hall between 8:30am and 4:30pm Monday to Friday. After hours, call ☎ 506-364-7546. The dormitories have shared bathrooms and cooking facilities.

Different Drummer (☎ 877-547-2788, fax 506-536-8116, **e** drummer@nb.aibn.com, 7 Main St) Singles/doubles $65/75 mid-June-mid-Sept, $55/65 other months. This good B&B is in a large white house on a low hill opposite Sackville Memorial Hospital, 600m from the VIA Rail station. Each of the four rooms is furnished with antiques and has a bath. Breakfasts include homemade muffins and bread.

Marshlands Inn (☎ *800-561-1266, fax 506-536-0721,* ⓔ *marshlds@nbnet.nb.ca,* Ⓦ *www.marshlands.nb.ca, 55 Bridge St)* Singles/doubles/triples $60-89/69-109/99-129 May-Oct, $50-79/59-89/94-104 Nov-Apr. Near downtown Sackville, Marshlands Inn is a Victorian mansion built in 1850 and operated as an inn since 1935. Queen Elizabeth II stayed here during her 1984 trip to New Brunswick. Aside from renting 20 rooms furnished with antiques, Marshlands Inn serves upscale dinners ($14 to $24) from 5:30pm to 8pm.

Harbourmaster's House B&B (☎ *506-536-0452, 30 Squire St)* Singles/doubles/triples $60/70/85 mid-June-mid-Sept, $40/50/60 other months. This two-story house in a nice neighborhood is just up Squire St from Marshlands Inn, 400m from the center of town via Bridge St.

Tantramar Motel (☎ *800-399-1327, fax 506-364-1306,* Ⓦ *www.tantramar.com/motel, 4 Robson Ave)* Singles/doubles from $45/49 mid-June-mid-Sept, $42/45 other months. Just off Hwy 2 at the Cattail Ridge exit, 20 rooms are available in a V-shaped motel with the office in the middle. The eight-room ***Bordens Motel*** (☎ *506-536-1066),* a few hundred meters away at 146 Bridge St, 1½km east of the center, is under the same management and charges exactly the same prices.

Places to Eat
Mel's Tea Room (☎ *506-536-1251, 17 Bridge St)* Meals $6-9. Open 8am-midnight Mon-Sat, 10am-11pm Sun. The favorite among locals is this 'tea room' in the center of town, which has the charm of a 1950s diner with a jukebox and prices to match. Operating since 1919, Mel's has ice cream, pies, sandwiches and breakfast specials for $2 to $3. Major a la carte dishes include fish & chips ($6), pork chops ($7) and T-bone steaks ($9).

Patterson's Family Restaurant (☎ *506-364-0822, 16 Mallard Dr)* Mains $7-12. Open 7am-10pm daily. Patterson's is well hidden down the road that runs between the Irving gas station and Tim Horton on Main St, near the Main St exit from Hwy 2.

The locals line up here for big breakfast specials, which cost $5 to $6 with coffee, or hamburger lunches for under $7. A seafood dinner or a steak shouldn't be over $12, and there are several inexpensive vegetarian choices.

Entertainment
If you stay the night, consider a show at ***Live Bait Theatre*** (☎ *506-536-2248),* Sackville's professional stage company, which often performs comedies in summer. Performances are usually at the Tantramar Regional High School, just off Main St north of Hwy 2 at the Main St exit. Call the box office for tickets ($17) and schedule information.

Dooly's Pub (☎ *506-536-2837, 26 Bridge St)* Open 11am-2am daily. This large billiard hall and sports bar presents live music Saturdays from 10:30pm (no cover charge).

Getting There & Away
The SMT bus stops at the Irving gas station (☎ *506-364-4383)* at E Main St and Mallard, 800m north of the university. Buses between Moncton and Amherst with connections to Halifax stop here three times a day.

The VIA Rail station (☎ *888-842-7245)* is on Lorne St, 1.3km south of the university. One-way, same-day adult fares from Sackville are $17 to Moncton, $43 to Halifax and $167 to Montréal. Advance booking can reduce these prices.

FORT BEAUSÉJOUR NATIONAL HISTORIC SITE
Right by the Nova Scotia border, this park (☎ *506-536-0720, 1½km west of the provincial tourist office at Aulac; adult/child $2.50/1.50; interpretive center open 9am-5pm daily June-mid-Oct)* preserves the remains of a French fort built in 1751 to hold the British back. It didn't work. Later the fort was used as a British stronghold during the American Revolution and the War of 1812. There are good displays inside the fort and some evocative pictures set in the surroundings. Only earthworks and stone foundations remain, but the view is excellent, vividly illustrating why this crossroads of

the Maritimes was fortified by two empires. A visitor center tells the tale.

The New Brunswick Visitor Centre (☎ 506-364-4090), 158 Aulac Rd, off Hwy 2, Aulac, is at the junction of roads leading to all three Maritime provinces. It's open 10am to 6pm daily mid-May to early October, 9am to 9pm July and August.

Northumberland Shore

New Brunswick's half of the Northumberland Shore stretches from the Confederation Bridge to Kouchibouguac National Park – in Nova Scotia this coast is called the Sunrise Trail. Folks here, like those farther north on the Acadian Peninsula and in northern Prince Edward Island, claim their waters are the warmest north of either Virginia or the Carolinas in the USA, having been warmed by spin-off currents of the Gulf Stream.

This is the closest vacation area to Moncton, and in summer the beaches and campgrounds can be crowded with local families having a happy time. A good part of the population of this coast is French speaking, and Bouctouche especially is an Acadian stronghold. Farther north, Kouchibouguac National Park protects a variety of littoral environments and their natural flora and fauna.

CAPE JOURIMAIN

The opening of the Confederation Bridge at Cape Jourimain in 1997 coincided with the closing of the ferry terminal at nearby Cape Tormentine. These days most motorists zip straight onto the bridge from Hwy 16, and the nearby coast is relatively quiet.

If you are coming from Prince Edward Island, it's worth stopping at the New Brunswick Visitor Centre (☎ 506-538-2133) at the New Brunswick end of the Confederation Bridge for their free brochures. The visitor center is open 9am to 6pm daily mid-May to early October, 8am to 9pm July and August.

Also here is the **Cape Jourinain Nature Centre** where you pay $4.50 to see the exhibits and use four trails through the adjacent Cape Jourimain National Wildlife Area. You can walk to Cape Jourimain Lighthouse and back in under an hour, enjoying great views of the bridge and the strait. Environment Canada allows seasonal hunting in the marshes just behind the so-called 'national wildlife area,' so don't expect to see many ducks, geese or other birds around here.

Places to Stay

Murray Beach Provincial Park (☎ 506-538-2628, answered 8am-4:30pm Mon-Fri, fax 506-538-2107, e murraybeach@gnb.ca, w www.tourismnbcanada.com/web/english/outdoor_network, 1679 Hwy 955, Murray Corner) Unserviced/serviced sites $22/24. Open mid-May-mid-Sept. This pleasant beach park, 12.3km west of the Confederation Bridge, has 111 nice grassy sites overlooking the Northumberland Strait. Because it's a bit off the beaten track it's usually not overcrowded. However, you can call ahead to reserve a site at no additional fee. The facilities are good, with showers and a Laundromat provided.

Chapman's Store Motel (☎ 506-538-2567, fax 506-538-2636, 150 Bayfield Rd, Bayfield) Rooms $45/55 single or double without/with cooking facilities, extra persons $5. Just 2km east of Hwy 16 on Hwy 960, this is a convenient place to stay near the New Brunswick end of the bridge. The row of motel rooms is behind a well-stocked grocery store. From November to April one room is available at $35.

C&O Coastal Cabins (☎ 506-538-1983, fax 506-538-1983, e mpwatson@nbnet.nb.ca, 113 Dixon Loop Rd, Cape Tormentine) Cabins $45/55 one/two beds. Open May-Oct. These six cozy duplex cottages are 2½km further toward Cape Tormentine from Chapman's.

Getting There & Away

If you're headed for PEI, there's no charge to use the Confederation Bridge eastbound – you pay when you come back. If you're on a bicycle or walking, you must pick up the free shuttle across the bridge at the Bridge Facility Building at the junction of Hwys 16 and 955. It leaves every two hours upon request.

Nova Scotia–bound, there's a shortcut along Hwy 970 from Port Elgin to Tidnish Bridge, which is useful if Cape Breton is your destination.

SHEDIAC

Just 22km northeast of Moncton on the coast, Shediac is a popular summer resort town with a population descended mainly from the Acadian French. The beaches are blessed with warm waters due to sand bars and shallow depths. Most popular are Parlee Beach (east of Shediac) and Pointe du Chêne, with water temperatures of around 20°C all summer.

The area also is a lobster center of some repute, and Shediac is home to the annual lobster festival in July. You can even have lobster on pizza.

The SMT bus stops at Wilson's gas station (☎ 506-532-2066), 700m west of the lobster statue and tourist office. The bus to and from Campbellton stops here daily.

Things to See

Beside the Scoudouc River bridge as you enter Shediac on Main St from the west, you'll see what is said to be the **world's largest lobster**, measuring 10.7m by 5m. It's actually a statue of the popular crustacean apparently menacing a small fisherman. In July and August, tour operators and kayak rental companies work out of the Adventure Destinations complex next to the lobster (the rest of the year the place is dead). The local tourist office (☎ 506-532-7788) is also here. It's open 8am to 10pm July and August, 8:30am to noon and 1pm to 4:30pm June and September.

In July and August, **Shediac Island Nature Park**, in Shediac Bay just north of town, is accessible by tour boat from beside the giant lobster (adult/child $20/10). A better bet is to head for the **Shediac Island Interpretation Centre** (☎ 506-532-7000, 164 Pleasant St; admission free; open 10am-6pm Wed-Sun mid-June-Aug), at the Shediac Marina, which has interesting displays on the environment of the region and an elevated observation platform. In July and August, the center runs boat shuttles to the park at $2 per person. Get there via Weldon and Belliveau Sts from near the Shediac Hotel.

Places to Stay

Parlee Beach Provincial Park (☎ 506-532-1500, 506-533-3363, fax 506-533-3312, e parlee@gnb.ca, w www.tourismnbcanada .com/web/english/outdoor_network, Belliveau Beach Rd) Unserviced/serviced sites $22/24. Open June-mid-Sept. The best spot to unroll the tent is this grassy 165-site park 6km east of the lobster statue in Shediac. Reservations are not accepted, but to get a spot for the weekend, arrive as early as possible on Friday. The campground offers some shade but is several hundred meters back from the high sandy sea beach. Parlee Beach is known for its clear water. A day-use fee of $5 per car is collected in summer. From mid-Sept to May you can use the beach for free via Gould Beach Road.

Hotel Shediac (☎ 506-532-4405, fax 506-532-4994, w www.hotelshediac.com, 15 Weldon St just off Main St) Singles/doubles $87/95 mid-June-mid-Sept, $45/48 other months. This old-fashioned hotel dates from 1853. It's convenient and central, if somewhat overpriced. The locals meet for coffee at the hotel cafe in the morning.

Seely's Motel (☎ 800-449-4141, fax 506-533-8089, w www.sn2000.nb.ca/comp/seely's-motel, 21 Bellevue Heights) Singles/doubles $69/80 in July & Aug, $48/58 other months. This well constructed two-story motel between Shediac and Parlee Beach is not visible from the highway as it's around the corner behind the China Garden Restaurant, 529 Main St. The 35 rooms are nice.

Morgan's Place B&B (☎ 506-532-8570, e gmorgan@nbnet.nb.ca, w www.sn2000 .nb.ca/comp/morgan-place, 578 Main St) Singles/doubles $62/67. Open July & Aug. This guesthouse has three rooms above Monty's Barber Shop, next to the Irving gas station 1km west of Parlee Beach.

Neptune Motel (☎ 506-532-4299, 691 Main St) Singles/doubles $60/70 July & Aug, $40/45 June & Sept. This motel is across the street from Parlee Beach Park, with free beach access available 1.3km down Belliveau Beach Rd (no parking near the beach). The 34 rooms are in a long two-story block, and there's an old-fashioned drive-in movie theater behind the motel.

Places to Eat

East of town toward Parlee Beach is a strip of eateries. You'll find clams and lobsters, cooked or fresh, dead or alive.

Fisherman's Paradise (☎ 506-532-6811, 772 Main St near Parlee Beach) Mains $16-18 at lunch, $18-23 at dinner. Open mid-May-mid-Sept. The nautical decor provides a hint that seafood is available at this upscale restaurant.

Lobsters can be bought at various outlets and at the wharves. The largest is the *Shediac Lobster Shop (☎ 506-532-4302, 261 Main St)* on the right east of the Scoudouc River, across the water from the lobster statue. Expect to pay $7 to $8 a pound for lobster and $9 a pound for scallops.

BOUCTOUCHE

This small town is a cultural focal point with several unique attractions. You can learn about Acadian and Native Indian culture, hike or kayak along a dune, go bicycling or just enjoy the beach. KC Irving (1899–1992), founder of the Irving Oil empire, was from Bouctouche, and there's a large bronze statue of the gentleman in a park beside Hwy 475 in town.

The Visitor Information Centre (☎ 506-743-8811), on Hwy 134 at the south entrance to Bouctouche, features a boardwalk that explains the oyster industry of this area. The visitor center is open 10am to 5pm Wednesday to Sunday June to September, 9am to 9pm daily July and August.

The SMT bus stops at the Irving gas station (☎ 506-743-6047), 130 Irving Blvd, 700m west of center of Bouctouche. The daily Moncton-Campbellton bus stops here.

Le Pays de la Sagouine

Dedicated to Acadian writer Antonine Maillet, Le Pays de la Sagouine is an immersion course in Acadian history and culture. This appealing attraction (☎ 800-561-9188, **W** www.sagouine.com, 57 Acadie St; adult/senior/student/family $8/6/4/20; open 10:30-4pm daily mid-June-Sept, 10am-6pm July & Aug), a kilometer south of the center of Bouctouche, consists of a cluster of buildings on a small island in the Bouctouche River. The admission is valid for two days. In July and August there's a supper theater at 7pm daily, except Sunday, with a variety of musical programs ($40 including dinner). In June and September, the dinner show is usually on Saturday only (most programs are in French).

A Micmac Experience

This center (☎ 506-743-9000; adult/child $10/5; open July & Aug) presents the legends and lore of the Mi'kmaq people through a tour of 'life ways.' It's on the territory of the Bouctouche First Nation, 3½km west of Bouctouche on Hwy 515, then 1km south on Reserve Dr to the center beside the Bouctouche River. Call ahead to ensure they're open.

Kent Museum

The Kent Museum (☎ 506-743-5005, 150 Hwy 475; adult/child $3/1; open 9:30am-noon & 1pm-4pm Mon-Fri mid-June-mid-Oct, 9am-5pm Mon-Fri, noon-6pm Sat & Sun July & Aug) is in the former Convent of the Immaculate Conception (1880), 2km east of the center of Bouctouche. The exhibits cover Acadian culture, and the chapel can also be visited.

Irving Eco Center

The Irving Eco Center (☎ 506-743-2600, 1932 Hwy 475; admission free; interpretive center open noon-5pm Mon-Thurs, noon-6pm Fri, 10am-6pm Sat & Sun mid-May-Oct, 10am-8pm daily July & Aug), on the coast 9km northeast of Bouctouche, opened in 1997. La Dune de Bouctouche is a long sandspit pointing out into the Northumberland Strait. The interpretive center has displays on the flora and fauna, but the highlight here is a 2km boardwalk above the dunes. The peninsula itself is 12km long and four to six hours are required to hike to its end and back over the loose sand. Few visitors venture beyond the boardwalk, so even a short walk farther on will leave the crowds behind.

To reduce the impact of the large numbers of visitors in July and August, only the first 2000 people to arrive each day are allowed onto the boardwalk. It reopens to everyone after 5pm. Otherwise, the boardwalk is accessible any time year-round. Saturdays at 8am there's a free bird-watching tour. Bicycles are not allowed on the dunes, but there's a separate 12km hiking/cycling trail that begins at the Eco Center parking lot and leads through a mixed forest to Bouctouche town. The excellent facilities here are sponsored by the Irving Oil Company as a public relations gesture.

A broad sandy beach with shallow, brownish water extends about 8km north along the coast from the Irving Eco Centre. A better beach is north of **Chockpish Harbour**. There's ample parking on the wharf. A large fleet of scallop boats is based at Chockpish.

Kayaking
KayaBéCano (☎ 888-529-2232, W www.kaya becano.nb.ca, 1465 Hwy 475; open mid-May-early Sept), 2½km south of Irving Eco Centre, runs two-hour kayak trips (adult/child $25/10) that explore the cultured oyster industry of the area. Three-hour kayak trips out to the dunes are $30/15. KayaBéCano rents trimarans for sailing on the Bay of Bouctouche at $35 for the first 1½ hours, plus $10 each additional hour and $10 per extra person after the first. You can also enjoy the oyster trip by trimaran for $25.

Places to Stay & Eat
Bouctouche Bay Campground (☎ 888-530-8883, fax 506-743-8883, W www.sn2000.nb .ca/comp/bouctouche-bay-camping, 2239 Hwy 475) Sites $20. Open May-Sept. This

place 1½km north of the Irving Eco Centre is typical of the many small private camp-grounds along this coast. The scarce shady sites are usually occupied by seasonal RVs, and overnighters generally end up in a crowded open field divided into sites.

Bouctouche Bay Inn (☎ 506-743-2726, fax 506-743-2387, W www.new-brunswick .com/bay-inn.htm, 206 Hwy 134) Rooms in the older single-story wing away from the highway are $65 single or double ($90 with two beds for up to four people) from mid-June to mid-September, $45 ($60 two beds) other months. The newer two-story wing has air-conditioned rooms at $80 single or double ($105 two beds) high season, $50 ($60 two beds) low season. This colorful inn overlooks the bridge and bay at the south end of Bouctouche, 2km south of Le Pays de la Sagouine. It has a degree of old world charm best expressed in its restaurant. There's a large selection of steaks ($10 to $20) and seafood ($10 to $26). Daily specials are in the $7 to $8 range.

Aux P'tits Oiseaux B&B (☎ 506-743-8196, fax 506-743-8197, e oiseau@nbnet .nb.ca, 124 Hwy 475) Single/double $50/55 plus $10 per additional person in the family room, or $50 single or double in the smaller room. Both have shared bath. Breakfast is included, and no tax is charged. This friendly B&B near the Kent Museum features a collection of 500 carved birds mounted through the house. Book ahead, as they're full all summer.

Gîte du Passant Belliveau B&B (☎ 506-743-2776, 489 Hwy 475) Singles/doubles $45/55. Open June-Sept. This new wooden house facing the bay is 2km northeast of the center of Bouctouche.

Au Bord de la Baie B&B (☎ 506-743-9626, 860 Hwy 475) Singles/doubles/triples $50/60/75 mid-June-mid-Sept, $45/55/65 other months. This new bungalow is right beside the water, 4km from central Bouctouche.

Jalbert B&B (☎ 800-338-2755, W www .sn2000.nb.ca/comp/jalbert-b&b, 2309 Hwy 475) Doubles $55. Jalbert is just across the road from the beach, 2km north of the Irving Eco Centre.

Les Pins Maritimes B&B (☎ 506-743-8450, fax 506-743-8450, W www.sn2000 .nb.ca/comp/pins-maritimes, 320 Cote Ste Anne Rd, Chockpish Harbour) Singles/doubles/triples $60/80/100 mid-June-mid-Sept, $50/70/80 other months. Open March-Nov. The large house hidden among trees right on the beach is just a few minutes' walk from the scallop boats at Chockpish Harbour.

Restaurant Le Vieux Presbytère de Bouctouche (☎ 506-743-5568, opposite the Kent Museum on Hwy 475) Lobster dinner $35. Open 5:30pm-8:30pm daily June-early Oct. This large restaurant in an old religious residence does PEI-style lobster suppers. Reservations are required.

SAINT-LOUIS-DE-KENT

This small village provides a few services, including kayak rentals and tours, for those visiting nearby Kouchibouguac National Park.

Kayakouch (☎ 506-876-1199, W www .kayakouch.com, 10617 Hwy 134; open mid-June-Aug), just 4km south of the national park, rents single kayaks at $18/28/45 for 2/5/24 hours, or $30/45/75 for a double. They also offer guided kayaking tours at $50 per person. Upon request, Co-owner Nicole Daigle will arrange two-night women-only kayak camping trips.

Places to Stay & Eat

Daigle's Park (☎ 506-876-4540, fax 506-876-3399, e parcdaig@nbnet.nb.ca, W www .campingdaigle.com, 10787 Hwy 134) Unserviced/serviced sites $17/20-26. Open mid-May-mid-Sept. If the national park campgrounds are full, a good alternative is this private campground, 2½km south of the park entrance. There are some well-wooded sites for tenters.

Kouchibouguac Motel (☎ 506-876-4317, fax 506-876-4318, e kouch@nbnet.nb.ca, W www.kouch.com, 10983 Hwy 134) Rooms from $60 single or double with one bed in the seven-room motel block, or $95 and up for one of the 16 chalets ($10 less in the off-season). This motel, located 400m south of the national park entrance, has a restaurant serving a $6 lunch special on weekdays.

Oasis Acadienne B&B (☎ 506-876-1199, fax 506-876-1918, e kayak@nbnet.nb.ca, W www.kayakouch.com, 10617 Hwy 134) Singles/doubles $39/75 including full breakfast. Open May-Oct. In the off-season rooms are $5 cheaper. This six-room B&B, 4km south of Kouchibouguac National Park, is run by the local Kayakouch people. They do kayak rentals and tours from their wharf on the Kouchibouguasis River, right in their own backyard.

KOUCHIBOUGUAC NATIONAL PARK

The highlights of this park are the beaches, lagoons and offshore sand dunes stretching for 25km. The sands are good for strolling, bird watching and clam digging. At the south end of the main beach, seals are often seen offshore.

Kouchibouguac (**koosh**-e-boo-gwack), a Mi'kmaq word meaning 'river of long tides,' also has populations of moose, deer, black bear and some smaller mammals. Other features are the birdlife around the salt marsh and a bog where there is an observation platform.

The water is warm enough for swimming. The lagoon area is shallow and safe for children, while adults will find the deep water on the ocean side more bracing. Many local families spend their annual holidays camping in the park, which explains why the campgrounds are in such high demand. There's also a 'gay beach' in the park, a 45-minute walk to the right from the end of the boardwalk at Kellys Beach.

The park is 100km north of Moncton, with an entrance just off Hwy 11. The visitor center (☎ 506-876-2443), 186 Hwy 117, features interpretive displays and a small theater as well as an information counter and gift shop. The center is open 9am to 5pm daily mid-May to mid-October, 8am to 8pm July and August. Park admission is $3.50/7 per adult/family for one day, $10.50/21 for four days. Before buying a day pass, remember that you can also get an Atlantic Pass valid at seven national parks for the entire season.

Check with the center for information on the various programs offered at the park: there's a popular three-hour tour in a large Voyageur canoe where you paddle to off-shore sandbars to view birds and possibly seals. The tours are offered four times a week from late June to early September and are $25 per adult, $15 for children.

The visitor center has a special all-terrain wheelchair with oversized wheels that is available free upon request. Thus equipped, physically challenged visitors can cover most of the trails in the park. Otherwise, the 600m boardwalk to Kellys Beach is wheelchair accessible.

The excellent **Bog Trail** is a boardwalk beyond the observation tower (the first few hundred meters from the parking lot are crushed gravel). This trail tends to be crowded around the middle of the day and is best done early or late. The **Cedars Trail** is less used.

Cycling

Kouchibouguac features hiking trails and canoe routes, but what really sets it apart from other national parks is the 40km network of bikeways – crushed-gravel paths that wind through the heart of the park's backcountry. From Ryan's day-use area, where bikes can be rented, it's possible to cycle a 23km loop and never be on the park road. In July and August, the **Ryan Rental Center** (☎ 506-876-3733) rents bicycles at $5.50/28 per hour/day and canoes/kayaks at $30/48 per day.

Places to Stay

Kouchibouguac has two drive-in campgrounds and three primitive camping areas, totaling 359 sites. The camping season is from mid-May to mid-October, and the park is very busy throughout July and August, particularly on weekends. Reservations ($8 extra fee) are taken for 60% of the sites; call ☎ 506-876-1277. Otherwise, you'll have to get on a very lengthy 'roll call' waiting list – which can take two or three days to clear.

South Kouchibouguac is the largest campground, located 13km inside the park near the beaches and featuring 311 sites along with showers and a kitchen shelter. The rate is $16.25 to $22 per night during summer. The park entry fee is extra.

Cote-a-Fabien is on the north side of Kouchibouguac River, away from the bike trails and beaches, and does not have showers. A site here is $14 per night.

The three primitive campgrounds in the park have only vault toilets and a pump for water and are $10 per night for two people. **Sipu** is located midway along the park's longest trail, the 14km Kouchibouguac River Trail. **Petit Large** is on a bike path, and **Pointe-a-Maxime** is along the shore and can be reached only by canoe.

Northeastern New Brunswick

North of Fredericton and Moncton lie vast forests. Nearly all of the province's towns are along the east coast or in the west by the Saint John River near the US border. The interior of northern New Brunswick is almost inaccessible rocky, river-filled timberland.

Inland, highways in this area can be quite monotonous, with thick forest lining both sides of the very straight roads. In the eastern section, the coastal roads are where pretty well everything of interest lies.

The Acadian Peninsula, with its Baie des Chaleurs shoreline and French population, is one of New Brunswick's most appealing regions. The peninsula's Acadian Historic Village is a major historic attraction, and Caraquet, the area's main town, is lively. Campbellton, at the edge of the northern uplands, is an access point to the neighboring province of Québec.

Aside from its thriving French cultural heritage, northeastern New Brunswick is a Mi'kmaq stronghold, with important First Nation communities at Red Bank, Eel Ground, Burnt Church and Eel River. The militancy of these people in defending their ancestral rights has placed the region at the center of the national political agenda more than once.

NEW BRUNSWICK

MIRAMICHI RIVER

Between Fredericton and Miramichi, the Southwest Miramichi River passes Doaktown. The river runs for 800km, and the waters are crystal clear. This entire area, and in particular the main river, is renowned for Atlantic salmon fishing.

Together with the Restigouche and Saint John Rivers, the Miramichi River has gained the province an international reputation among serious anglers. England's Prince Charles has fished the Miramichi. Residents and visitors both need fishing licences, although there are special regulations for nonresidents.

Doaktown

Doaktown has become the unofficial fishing center for the region. In town is the **Atlantic Salmon Museum** (☎ 506-365-7787, 236 Main St; admission $5; open 9am-5pm daily June-mid-Oct), which is actually pretty interesting and includes pools of live salmon ('king of the freshwater game fish') on the 1½-hectare grounds.

One of Canada's best fly-fishing shops, **WW Doak & Sons** (☎ 506-365-7828, 331 Main St), is next to Doaktown's post office. It sells about 60,000 flies a year, many tied on the premises.

Doak Historic Park (386 Main St; admission free; open 9am-5pm Mon-Sat, 1pm-5pm Sun mid-June-Aug) is built around the well-preserved home (1820) and farm of Robert Doak, an early Scottish immigrant. Through the summer costumed interpreters demonstrate weaving with flax and wool, and the old schoolhouse serves as a crafts school for local residents.

Taylor's Motel (☎ 506-365-4617, e tay lorsmotel@yahoo.com, w www.angelfire .com/biz/taylorsmotel, 180 Main St) Singles/doubles $45/55, campsites $12/20 unserviced/serviced. The 10 motel rooms are in a long block facing Hwy 8 at the south end of town. The campsites are in back. The motel office is in Glendella Mansion, a Disney-like structure dating from 1938 filled with incredible dolls and fancy decorations. The ornate pillared façade was added in the 1980s. You can't miss it.

The daily SMT bus stops at the Irving gas station (☎ 506-365-4666), 339 Main St. Fares are $8 to Miramichi, $9 to Fredericton.

RED BANK FIRST NATION

Red Bank sits on the banks of the Little Southwest Miramichi River, just across the bridge from Sunny Corner on Hwy 425. This sizable Mi'kmaq reserve calls itself 'the oldest village in New Brunswick.' It's worth coming to see the **Heritage Exhibit** (☎ 506-836-6179, 46 Shore Rd; adult/child $2/1; open 9am-4:40pm Mon-Sat June-Oct), which outlines the history and culture of the Mi'kmaq people.

Weekdays from June to mid-September the staff operate a three-hour 'day adventure' featuring a guided tour of the exhibit, a canoe trip and a salmon feast for $40. Reservations are necessary.

Red Bank celebrates a trout derby on the Victoria Day weekend in late May. The Metepenagiag Powwow has been celebrated at Red Bank on the last weekend in June for over a decade and is one of the largest in the Maritimes.

MIRAMICHI

In late 1995, the towns of Chatham and Newcastle, the villages of Douglastown, Loggieville and Nelson, and several 'local service districts' along a 12km stretch of the Miramichi River were amalgamated to form the city of Miramichi, with a combined population of around 20,000. Like Bathurst, Miramichi is an English-speaking enclave in the middle of a predominantly French-speaking region. It's an interesting yet seldom visited locale where the facilities are uncrowded and the people are friendly and helpful. In fact, it's one of the most undervalued tourist destinations in the Maritimes.

Each summer in early August the Miramichi Folk Song Festival, which was begun in the 1960s and is the oldest folk festival in North America, is held here. Through traditional song, the local history and culture are preserved. The largest Irish festival in the province also takes place here, in mid-July.

Information

Miramichi is 50km northwest of Kouchibouguac National Park via Hwy 11. As you approach Chatham from the south, you pass a tourist office (☎ 800-459-3131), open daily from 9am to 9pm late May to early October (9am to 6pm early and late season).

Another tourist office (☎ 506-623-2152) is in downtown Newcastle at Murray House, an 1826 edifice that was moved to Ritchie Wharf in 1993. It is only open June to August.

Free Internet access is provided at the Newcastle Public Library (☎ 506-623-2450), 100 Fountain Head Lane, just down from Ritchie Wharf, and the Chatham Public Library (☎ 506-773-6274), 30 King St, next to Elm Park. Both open from 1pm to 8pm Tuesday and Wednesday and 10am to 5pm Thursday to Saturday.

Chatham

This portion of Miramichi was prosperous during the wooden shipbuilding era, but the development of steel ships put an end to all that. The Canadian Forces base just south of Chatham closed in the early 1990s. The revamped downtown area by the Miramichi River along Water St is pleasant enough in a quiet way.

The **Natural History Museum** (☎ 506-773-7305, 149 Wellington St cnr of University Ave; admission free; open 10am-6pm Mon-Sat, noon-4pm Sun mid-June-mid Aug) has a small idiosyncratic collection.

Somewhat more interesting is **St Michael's Basilica** (☎ 506-778-5150, 10 Howard St; admission free; open 8am-4pm), which stands on a hill overlooking town. The towering brown sandstone structure has numerous colorful stained glass windows.

Douglastown

Halfway between the Chatham bridge and Newcastle is the **Rankin House Museum** (☎ 506-773-3448, 2224 King George Highway; admission free; open 9am-5pm Mon-Fri June-mid-Sept) with three floors of artifacts relating to life in early New Brunswick. A tunnel in the basement once led down to Alexander Rankin's store by

the river. Rankin House also serves as a tourist office and an anchor for the Lower Town Walk, a signposted route past other historical buildings along Douglastown's waterfront.

Newcastle

Though surrounded by two huge paper mills and a couple of sawmills, central Newcastle is pleasant – a good place to break up a trip. Around the attractive town square are some fine old wooden buildings and shops.

In the central square park is a **memorial to Lord Beaverbrook** (1879–1964), one of the most powerful press barons in British history and a statesman and philanthropist of no small reputation. Among the many gifts he lavished on the province are the 17th-century English benches and the Italian gazebo in this square. His ashes lie under the statue erected as a memorial to him by the town.

Beaverbrook spent most of his formative years in Newcastle. **Beaverbrook House** (☎ 506-624-5474, 518 King George Hwy; admission free; open 9am-5pm Mon-Fri, 10am-5pm Sat, 1pm-5pm Sun mid-June-Aug), his boyhood home (erected 1879), is now open to the public as a museum.

Ritchie Wharf, a riverfront boardwalk park nearby, has playgrounds for kids, cafes, a lighthouse, an information center and summer boat tours to **Beaubears Island**. This island in the river has been a Mi'kmaq campsite, a refugee camp for Acadians during the expulsion and a shipbuilding site. Today it's a little-known national historic site. Boat tours to the island ($8) leave between noon and 3pm on Tuesday and Thursday in July and August when at least five paying passengers are present.

Nelson

The **Beaubears Island Interpretive Center** (☎ 506-622-8526, 26 St Patricks St; admission free; open 9am-8pm Mon-Sat, noon-5pm Sat, 1pm-4pm Sun mid-June-Aug) in the Nelson Rural School displays a collection of artifacts and old photos relating to Beaubears Island, which lies just across the river. From mid-June to August the center

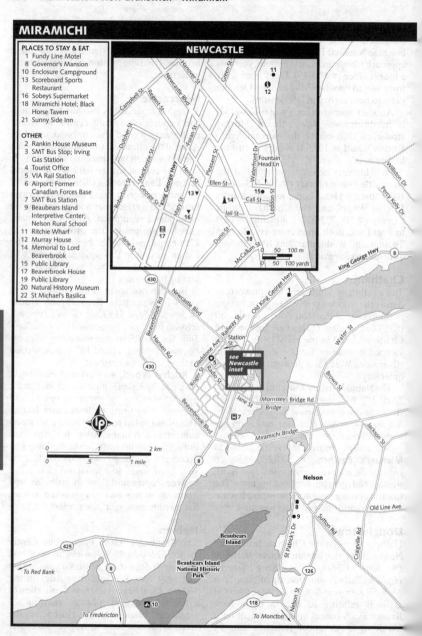

MIRAMICHI

NEWCASTLE

PLACES TO STAY & EAT
1 Fundy Line Motel
8 Governor's Mansion
10 Enclosure Campground
13 Scoreboard Sports
   Restaurant
16 Sobeys Supermarket
18 Miramichi Hotel; Black
   Horse Tavern
21 Sunny Side Inn

OTHER
2 Rankin House Museum
3 SMT Bus Stop; Irving
   Gas Station
4 Tourist Office
5 VIA Rail Station
6 Airport; Former
   Canadian Forces Base
7 SMT Bus Station
9 Beaubears Island
   Interpretive Center;
   Nelson Rural School
11 Ritchie Wharf
12 Murray House
14 Memorial to Lord
   Beaverbrook
15 Public Library
17 Beaverbrook House
19 Public Library
20 Natural History Museum
22 St Michael's Basilica

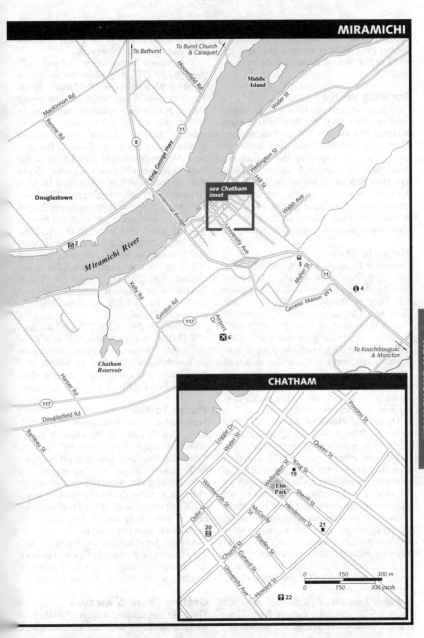

MIRAMICHI

To Bathurst

To Burnt Church
& Caraquet

Moorefield Rd

Middle
Island

Water St

MacKinnon Rd

Rennie Rd

King George Hwy

11

8

Wellington St

Hill St

Walsh Ave

see Chatham
inset

Douglastown

Centennial Bridge

University Ave

Water St

2

Miramichi River

3

4

Mather St

11

Kelly Rd

Gordon Rd

General Mason Wy

117

Airport Dr

6

To Kouchibouguac
& Moncton

Chatham
Reservoir

Harper Rd

117

Douglasfield Rd

Barrieau Rd

CHATHAM

Princess St

Loggie Dr

Water St

Queen St

Wellington St

King St

19

Elm
Park

Sheriff St

Wentworth St

McCurdy St

Henderson St

Duke St

21

Stanley St

20

Church St

Gunard St

University Ave

Howard St

0   150   300 m

0   150   300 yards

22

NEW BRUNSWICK

also runs boat trips to the island at 7pm Tuesday and Thursday and at 1:30pm Sunday ($8). Internet access is available upstairs in the Nelson Rural School at $1 an hour.

Bartibog Bridge

Fifteen kilometers northeast of Douglastown on Hwy 11 is the **MacDonald Farm Historic Site** (☎ 506-778-6085; admission $2.50; open 9:30am-4:30pm daily late June-early Sept). Overlooking the Miramichi River, this farm dating from the 1820s is typical of Scottish farms in the Maritimes. Also on the site are a barn, net shed and spring house. Costumed guides engage in the traditional activities of cooking over an open hearth, soap and rug making and so on.

Places to Stay

Enclosure Campground (☎ 506-622-8638, fax 506-622-8638, W www.sn2000.nb.ca/comp/enclosure-campground, 8 Enclosure Rd) Sites $15/19-24 unserviced/serviced. Open May-Oct. Southwest of Newcastle off Hwy 8 is another of Lord Beaverbrook's bequests – a former provincial park called the Enclosure. This riverside park is now privately run, and a nice wooded area with spacious 'wilderness' sites is available for tenters. A $3 fee per group is collected from noncampers wishing to use the park's day-use area or swimming pool.

Miramichi Hotel (☎ 506-622-1201, 83 Newcastle Blvd, Newcastle) Singles/doubles $25/30. The massive four-story Miramichi Hotel was erected just off Newcastle's central square in 1905. Most guests in the 26 rooms are permanent residents who pay by the month, and the Miramichi doesn't go after the tourist trade. For male backpackers and budget-conscious couples, however, it's great, as the SMT bus station is only 900m away. Lone women travelers might feel uncomfortable here, as the mostly male residents aren't necessarily the cream of society. A huge bar called the Black Horse Tavern is downstairs.

Fundy Line Motel (☎ 506-622-3650, fax 506-622-8723, 869 King George Hwy, Newcastle) Singles/doubles $45/55 mid-June-mid-Sept, $40/49 other months. The three long rows of rooms at the Fundy Line are 2km east of central Newcastle.

Governor's Mansion (☎ 877-647-2642, fax 506-662-3035, e govnorin@nbnet.nb.ca, W www.bbcanada.com/3947.html, 62 St Patrick's St, Nelson) Singles/doubles with shared bath begin at $40/50, increasing to $85 double for the master bedroom with private bath, or $75 for another room almost as nice. On the south side of the river near Nelson-Miramichi Post Office is the large Governor's Mansion, without a doubt one of the most intriguing inns in New Brunswick. This magnificent Victorian mansion (1860), with three floors full of antique furnishings, model ships and history, was the home of J Leonard O'Brien, the first Irish lieutenant governor of the province. The nine bedrooms are on the 2nd and 3rd floors. A continental breakfast is included. The former 'Beaubear Youth Hostel' in an adjacent building has been converted into a B&B, and hostel beds are no longer offered.

Sunny Side Inn (☎ 506-773-4232, fax 506-773-4333, e crawford@nbnet.nb.ca, W www.bbcanada.com/sunnysideinn, 65 Henderson St, Chatham) Singles/doubles $48/68. This large house with a three-story turret is 300m south of Elm Park in downtown Chatham.

Places to Eat

Scoreboard Sports Restaurant (☎ 506-622-6556, 295 Pleasant St, Newcastle) Mains under $10. Open 11am-11pm Mon-Fri, 9am-11pm Sat, 9am-7pm Sun. Just off Newcastle's main square, the unpretentious Scoreboard serves items like cheeseburgers ($4), fish & chips ($6 to $9), chicken wings ($10) and sirloin steak ($17). From September to early May there's live music on Friday from 9pm to midnight.

Sobeys Supermarket (☎ 506-622-2098, 261 Pleasant St, Newcastle) Open 24 hours a day. The picnic fare you purchase here can be eaten at the tables at Ritchie Wharf.

Getting There & Away

The SMT bus station (☎ 506-622-0445) is at 60 Pleasant St in downtown Newcastle, a kilometer from Ritchie Wharf. There are no coin lockers. Daily buses leave here for Fredericton ($17), Saint John ($35), Moncton ($14) and Campbellton ($21), with the latter two requiring a change in Chatham. The station is open 8:30am to 5pm Monday to Friday, 1pm to 3pm Saturday and Sunday.

The SMT buses also stop in Chatham at the Irving gas station (☎ 506-773-5515) on Hwy 11, 2km south of town. One bus a day arrives from Saint John at 2:15pm, making the return trip at 2:35pm. The buses north to Campbellton and south to Moncton are both daily at 2:35pm.

The VIA Rail station (☎ 800-561-3952) in Newcastle is on Station St at George St, 600m up the hill from Sobeys Supermarket. Trains from Montréal and Halifax stop here.

Unfortunately there's no longer a municipal bus between Newcastle and Chatham, although efforts are being made to obtain funding to bring the service back.

BURNT CHURCH FIRST NATION

The Mi'kmaq Nation at Burnt Church on Miramichi Bay, 40km east of Miramichi city, has witnessed violent clashes in recent years between Mi'kmaq warriors and federal fisheries officials seeking to restrict access to the lucrative lobster fishery. These events have made this small reserve a household word across Canada, and the struggle is ongoing. The name itself harks back to the destruction of an Acadian village here by the British in 1758.

Prospect Tourist Home *(☎ 506-776-3217, fax 506-776-8441, 451 Bayview Dr, Burnt Church)* Singles/doubles $25/35. Open May-Oct. This stately three-story house facing Miramichi Bay is 4½km off Hwy 11 via Church River Road. It's just outside the Mi'kmaq reserve.

CARAQUET

The Acadian Peninsula, which extends from Miramichi and Bathurst out to two islands at the edge of the Baie des Chaleurs, is a predominantly French area that was first settled by the Acadians who had been expelled from their settlements near the Bay of Fundy by the British in the 1700s. These descendants of Canada's earliest French settlers now proudly fly the Acadian flag around the region, and many Acadian traditions live on in the music, food and language, which is slightly different from the French spoken in Québec.

The oldest of the Acadian villages in this area, Caraquet was founded in 1757 by refugees from Nova Scotia, and it's now the main center of the peninsula's French community. Caraquet's colorful fishing port off Boulevard Saint-Pierre Est bustles with activity and a large variety of ships. There are ample accommodations here and lots to see and do, including the Acadian Festival (Ⓦ festival.acadie.net) in August.

The tourist office (☎ 506-726-2676), 51 Boulevard Saint-Pierre Est, is at the Day Adventure Center, on the waterfront near the fishing harbor. It's open daily mid-June to mid-September.

Acadian Museum

In the middle of town, with views out over the bay from the balcony, this museum *(☎ 506-726-2682, 15 Boulevard Saint-Pierre Est; adult/student $3/1; open 10am-6pm Mon-Sat, 1pm-6pm Sun June-mid-Sept; until 8pm July & Aug)* contains a neatly laid out collection of artifacts donated by local residents. Articles include household objects, tools, photographs and a fine woodstove in the corner. Most impressive

The Acadian tradition lives on in Caraquet.

is the desk that folds down and converts into a bed when exhaustion strikes. It belonged to a superior at the Caraquet Convent in 1880.

Activities

All the local tour operators are at the Day Adventure Center, down on the waterfront near the fishing harbor.

Sea of Adventure (☎ 800-704-3966; open July & Aug) offers three-hour whale-watching tours in 12-passenger rigid-hull Hurricane zodiacs at $50 plus tax.

The boat *Île Caramer* (☎ 506-727-0813) runs deep-sea fishing trips ($20) from Caraquet three times a day June to mid-October, departing the fishing harbor at 5:45am, 1pm and 6pm. They need a minimum of six people to go out, so call ahead.

Places to Stay

Camping Caraquet (☎ 506-726-2696, fax 506-727-3610, [w] www.sn2000.nb.ca/comp/camping-caraquet, 619 Boulevard Saint-Pierre Ouest) Unserviced/serviced sites $15/19-22. Open mid-June-mid-Sept. This former provincial park overlooking the sea is just west of the Sainte Anne du Bocage sanctuary. The core of the campground is now a solid phalanx of RVs, but there are plenty of tent sites around the perimeter.

Gîte Chez Rita (☎ 506-727-5334, 10 Des Patriotes St) Doubles $50. Open July & Aug. Just off Boulevard Saint-Pierre Ouest, this pleasant two-story house is a few minutes' walk from the center of Caraquet.

Gîte Chez ma Tante Estelle (☎ 506-727-7879, 70 Boulevard Saint-Pierre Est) Doubles $50. Open June-Sept. This modern bungalow overlooks the fishing port.

Gîte à Rita (☎ 506-727-2841, 116 St Pierre Boulevard Est) Doubles $40. Open June-Aug. This characteristically Acadian house is only a few hundred meters from the fishing harbor.

Pascal et Des Neiges Tourist Home (☎ 506-727-5493, 8286 St-Paul St, Bas-Caraquet) Singles/doubles $35/45. Open June-Sept. This modern bungalow 8km east of Caraquet offers two basement rooms with shared bath, fridge and sitting room.

Motel Landry (☎ 506-727-5225, 11665 Hwy 11, Pokemouche) Singles/doubles $45/50. This six-room motel is 12km south of Caraquet.

Places to Eat

Restaurant Maribel (☎ 506-727-4747, 3 Portage St) Mains $7-11. Open 8am-10pm Mon-Fri, 9am-10pm Sat & Sun. This unpretentious place offers a weekday lunch special for under $6 including coffee and dessert. Otherwise they have hamburgers ($3 to $7), chicken ($5 to $7) and seafood ($3 to $11).

Restaurant Le Caraquette (☎ 506-727-6009, 89 Boulevard Saint-Pierre East) Mains $6-25. Open 6am-11pm Mon-Sat, 7am-11pm Sun. Next to the Shell gas station directly above the port, La Caraquet is extremely popular with the locals. It's a good choice for breakfast ($3 to 4), and for dinner there's chicken ($6 to $8) and a large seafood selection ($7 to $25). Smoking is not allowed at La Caraquette or Maribel.

Carapro Fish Market (☎ 506-727-3462, 60 Boulevard Saint-Pierre Est) Open 10am-6pm Apr-Dec, 9am-9pm July & Aug. Opposite the dock area is this big fish market with fresh, salted and frozen seafood for sale.

Entertainment

Behind the Acadian Museum is the **Théâtre Populaire d'Acadie** (☎ 506-727-0922, 11 Boulevard Saint-Pierre Est), which puts on shows in French from mid-July to mid-August. Admission is $16.

Getting There & Away

Public transportation around this part of the province is very limited, as SMT buses don't run here. A couple of van shuttles do exist, but these are used mostly by locals wishing to connect with the bus or train in Miramichi or Bathurst and they're unlikely to be of much use to other travelers.

CARAQUET TO BATHURST
Sainte Anne du Bocage

Six kilometers west of Caraquet is Sainte Anne du Bocage (☎ 506-727-3604, 579 Boulevard Saint-Pierre Ouest; admission *free; open 8am-9pm daily May-Oct)*, one of the oldest religious shrines in the province. On this spot Alexis Landry and other Acadians settled following the infamous expulsion of 1755. The graves of some of these early Acadians are on the sanctuary grounds. Down a stairway by the sea is a sacred spring where the faithful come to fill their water bottles.

Places to Stay *Motel Bel-Air (☎ 506-727-3488, fax 506-727-3065, ⓦ www.sn2000.nb .ca/comp/motel-bel-air, 655 Boulevard Saint-Pierre Ouest)* Doubles/quads $40/50. This block of back-to-back rooms opposite an Irving gas station, a kilometer west of Sainte Anne du Bocage, is probably the least expensive motel you'll find around here.

Maison Touristique Dugas (☎ 506-727-3195, fax 506-727-3193, ⓔ mtdugas@nb.sym patico.ca, ⓦ www.maisontouristiquedugas .ca, 683 Boulevard Saint-Pierre Ouest) Singles/doubles $35/40 with shared bath, $50-60 double with cooking facilities, cabins $50 double, unserviced/serviced campsites $10/19. This large red wooden house with a rear annex, 1½km west of Sainte Anne du Bocage, dates back to 1926. A variety of accommodations are available, including 11 rooms with shared bath and two apartments with private cooking facilities in the main house, and five cabins with private bath and cooking facilities in the back yard. Breakfast and tax are extra.

Acadian Historic Village

The Acadian Historic Village *(Village Historique Acadien; ☎ 506-726-2600, 14311 Hwy 11; adult/senior/child/family $12/10/ 6/30; open 10am-6pm daily early June-Sept)*, 15km west of Caraquet, is a major historic reconstruction with 33 buildings and workers in period costumes reflecting life from 1780 to 1880. The museum depicts daily life in a typical post-expulsion Acadian village and makes for an intriguing comparison to the obviously prosperous British King's Landing historic village west of Fredericton.

A good half day is required to see the site, and you'll want to eat as well. For that

there are five choices: two snack bars, two restaurants and the *Dugas House*, the last serving Acadian dishes.

The village is on Hwy 11 between Bertrand and Grande-Anse. There's a program for kids ($30) that provides costumes and seven hours of supervised historical 'activities.' If you don't have time to see everything, ask the receptionist to stamp your ticket for reentry the next day. In September only five or six buildings will be open and admission is reduced to $6/15 adult/family. Facing the village parking lot is a **wax museum**, which costs an additional $7 to visit (audio guide included).

Grande-Anse

This small town boasts a unique **Popes Museum** *(☎ 506-732-3003, 184 Hwy 11; adult/family $5/10; open 10am-6pm daily mid-June-Aug)*, which houses images of 262 popes from St Peter to the current John Paul II, as well as various religious articles. There is also a detailed model of St Peter's Square and Basilica in Rome.

A beach and picnic spot are at the foot of the cliffs behind the large church in Grande-Anse. To get there, go down the road marked 'Quai' beside the church to the fishing port.

Auberge de l'Anse B&B (☎ 506-732-5204, 317 Hwy 11) Singles/doubles from $38/45. Open June-Aug. Ten rooms are available in this two-story building in the center of Grande-Anse.

Motel Baie des Chaleurs (☎ 506-732-2948, 480 Hwy 11, Grande-Anse) Doubles $48, camping $18. Open June-mid-Oct. This motel 7km west of the Acadian Historic Village offers 10 rooms in a back-to-back block. You can also camp here. A swimming pool is provided, and there's an ocean view from the back yard.

West of Grande-Anse

The rugged shoreline cliffs are dramatic along the route from Grande-Anse to Bathurst, and across Baie des Chaleurs you can easily see the outline of the Gaspé Peninsula, in the province of Québec. There are some beaches and picnic sites along this road.

At **Pokeshaw Community Park**, 5½km west of the Popes Museum, you can witness a rare sight. Atop an isolated sea stack created by coastal erosion, thousands of double-crested cormorants nest in summer. In late fall, the birds fly south to their winter home in Maryland. From the parking lot you can look straight across at the birds, which are at eye level, although a fair distance away. It's a terrific place to photograph the coastal cliffs, and you can picnic and swim here. Admission is $1 per car.

Chapman's Tent & Trailer Park (☎ 506-546-2883, fax 506-546-8884, W www.sn2000 .nb.ca/comp/chapmans, 5249 Cape Rd) Unserviced sites $15. Open June-Sept. This facility, between Janeville and Salmon Beach, 14km east of Bathurst off Hwy 11, has open sites overlooking the beach and ocean. A small store is on the premises and the staff is friendly.

BATHURST
Bathurst is an English-speaking enclave of about 14,000 people in a predominantly French region. It's an industrial town, with an economy based on some extremely rich lead and zinc mines and buttress lumber. The town is split into three sections – South, East and West Bathurst – by the Nepisiguit River and the Bathurst Basin. The principal street is Main St, in South Bathurst.

St Peter Ave has a range of fast food chains and service stations, as well as the **War Museum** (☎ 506-546-3135, 575 St Peter Ave; admission free; open 9am-7pm daily July & Aug). This museum, in the basement of the Canadian Legion, displays weapons, uniforms, photos and a reproduction of a WWI trench.

On the coast northeast of the harbor is the **Daly Point Reserve**, off Carron Dr, a mix of woods and salt marshes with 6km of trails that can be followed for bird watching. An observation tower provides views to the Gaspé Peninsula.

Places to Stay & Eat
Harbour Inn B&B (☎ 506-546-4757, 262 Main St) Singles/doubles $35/45. Three rooms are available in this large two-story

house in the center of town. Call ahead, as the owners aren't always around.

West-Side Motel (☎ 506-546-4846, fax 506-548-5753, 1958 St Peter Ave) Doubles $62 mid-June-mid-Sept, $48 other months. This two-story motel is at the north entrance to Bathurst on Hwy 134.

Papa Joe's & Evy's Restaurant (☎ 506-546-6179, 296 St George St at Murray) Mains $8-14. Open 7am-9pm daily July & Aug, 7am-7pm Mon-Wed, 7am-8pm Thurs-Sat, 8am-7pm Sun other months. This place is popular for breakfast ($4 to $8 including coffee). At dinner there are chicken dishes ($8), fish ($9), pork chops ($9) and steaks ($13 to $14).

House of Lee Dining Room (☎ 506-548-3019, 315 Main St) Lunch/dinner buffets $7.50/10.50. Open 11am-11pm Mon-Thurs, 11am-midnight Fri & Sat, 3pm-8pm Sun (shorter hours in winter). Just across from Papa Joe's & Evy's, the House of Lee lays out Chinese buffets from 11:30am to 2pm weekdays and from 4:30pm to 7:30pm Friday to Sunday.

Getting There & Away
The VIA Rail station (☎ 800-561-3952) is at 690 Thornton Ave on the corner of Queen St, just a kilometer from the old downtown section of Bathurst at the end of Nepisiguit Bay. The station is open 7:30am to noon daily except Wednesday, and 4pm to 9pm daily except Tuesday.

The SMT bus station (☎ 506-546-4380) is at 15 St Peter Ave on the corner of Main St. It's right in the center of town (the tourist office is just behind). There are no coin lockers. A bus heads north at 3:45pm daily for Campbellton ($12) and south at 1pm daily for Moncton ($25). The station is open 8:30am to 5pm Monday to Friday, 12:15pm to 1:15pm and 3pm to 4pm Saturday and Sunday.

PETIT-ROCHER
Some 20km north of Bathurst in Petit-Rocher is the **New Brunswick Mining & Mineral Interpretation Centre** (☎ 506-542-2672, 397 Hwy 134; admission $5.50; open 10am-6pm daily late June-Aug). This mining

museum has various exhibits on the local zinc-mining industry. The tour includes a simulated descent in a mining shaft and takes about 45 minutes.

Le Vieux Couvent (☎ 506-783-0587, fax 506-783-5587, w www.sn2000.nb.ca/comp/auberge-d'anjou, 587 Hwy 134, Petit-Rocher) Rooms from $40 including breakfast. This place is part of the upscale Auberge d'Anjou, and the 11 cheaper rooms are in an old convent behind the main building. It's near the large church in the center of town, on the corner of the road to the wharf.

Motel Château Maritime (☎ 506-783-4297, fax 506-783-7363, w www.sn2000.nb.ca/comp/chateau-maritime, 495 Hwy 134, Petit-Rocher) Singles/doubles $40/45. The 22 attractive rooms are in a well-constructed brick block between the highway and the beach. When things are slow, the price drops to $35 single or double.

Jacquet River Park (☎ 506-237-3239, fax 506-522-3704, e bell002@nbnet.nb.ca, 3712 Hwy 134) Unserviced/serviced sites $15/19. Open June-Sept. On Hwy 134 in the middle of Jacquet River village, 18km north of Belledune, this former provincial park is now run by the village. You can camp near the shore, and noncampers can use the beach for $1 per car. A supermarket and pizzeria are adjacent to this attractive park.

EEL RIVER FIRST NATION

The people of the Eel River First Nation have created an **Aboriginal Heritage Garden** at Eel River Crossing, just southeast of Dalhousie. This botanical garden has two greenhouses displaying regional plants, especially native herbs. The garden opened in the spring of 2002, and admission fees and hours were still unknown at press time. The garden is just south of Eel River First Nation, straight up Hwy 280 (Cove Road) from Chaleur Beach on Hwy 134 at the south end of the causeway along the sandbar. The Eel River Bar Powwow is held on the reserve the last weekend of July.

The barrage on Eel River just below the garden was built in the 1960s to supply water to the Dalhousie pulp mill, but it's no longer used for that purpose. What it has done instead is destroy the aboriginal clam fishery on the nearby sandbar by restricting water flows in and out of the bay.

On the north side of the reserve New Brunswick Power has erected a huge oil-burning power-generating plant that creates the black smoke visible from most parts of Dalhousie. The Mi'kmaqs of Eel River get more than their share of the fallout but none of the employment or economic benefits.

DALHOUSIE

Dalhousie is a small industrial town on the northeast coast of New Brunswick, on the Baie des Chaleurs opposite Québec. Dalhousie is about half the size of nearby Campbellton. William St and parallel Adelaide St near the dock are the two main streets.

On the corner of Adelaide St is the **Restigouche Regional Museum** (☎ 506-684-7490, 115 George St; admission free; open 9am-5pm Mon-Fri, 9am-1pm Sat, 1-5pm Sun), with local artifacts and history.

From mid-May to September the cruise boat *Chaleur Phantom* (☎ 506-684-4722) departs from the marina at the west end of Adelaide St on a nature cruise in the bay at 9am ($15), and a scenic cruise along the Restigouche River at 2pm and 7pm ($15). The cruises spot birds, seals and porpoises.

Places to Stay & Eat

Inch Arran Park (☎ 800-576-4455, fax 506-684-7613, 125 Inch Arran Ave) Unserviced site $16. Open June-mid-Sept. A kilometer east of town at the end of Victoria St is Inch Arran Park, right on the water with fine views of the bay and a few small islands with seabird colonies just offshore. There's a swimming pool, tourist office, lighthouse and beach, plus a Laundromat across the street. However, the campsites are in an open field with droves of RVs and little shade. You'll find much better tenting possibilities at Sugarloaf Provincial Park in nearby Campbellton.

Art's Motor Inn (☎ 506-684-3336, fax 506-684-4629, 657 Hwy 134) Singles/

doubles $53/58. Art's offers a long row of 10 rooms facing the highway opposite a stone quarry, 3km west of Dalhousie toward Campbellton.

Anne's Restaurant (☎ 506-684-2276, 109 Brunswick St) Mains $5-14. Open 7am-6pm Mon-Fri, 9am-11pm Sat. Anne's is known for its large portions and friendly staff. Breakfast with coffee is $2.25 to $4.25, and for lunch there are hamburgers ($4), sandwiches ($2 to $6) and a good daily special. The *Golden Eagle Pub (☎ 506-684-4511)* adjacent to Anne's, generally has live music Friday and Saturday from 10pm to 2am with a cover charge of $2 to $14 depending on who's appearing.

Getting There & Away

The former car ferry from Dalhousie to Miguasha, Québec, was discontinued in 2000 when government subsidies were withdrawn.

The daily SMT bus stops at the Irving gas station (☎ 506-684-3046), 173 Renfrew St at Goderich, about a kilometer from either the Inch Arran Campground or the center of town. Fares are $5 to Campbellton, $8 to Bathurst, $16 to Miramichi and $31 to either Fredericton or Moncton.

CAMPBELLTON

Campbellton, on the Québec border, is the second biggest highway entry point to the Maritimes from the rest of Canada. It's in the midst of a scenic area on the edge of the Restigouche Highlands. The Baie des Chaleurs is on one side and rolling hills encompass the town on the remaining sides. Across the border is Matapédia and Hwy 132 leading to Mont Joli, 148km into Québec.

The last naval engagement of the Seven Years' War was fought in the waters off this coast in 1760. The Battle of Restigouche marked the conclusion of the long struggle for supremacy in Canada between Britain and France.

Main streets in this town of 9,000 are Water St and Roseberry St, around which the downtown clusters. Campbellton is a truly bilingual town with store clerks fluent in both French and English.

Information

A large provincial tourist office (☎ 506-789-2367) is located at 56 Salmon Blvd next to the City Center Mall, near the bridge from Québec. The office is open 10am to 6pm daily mid-May to early October, 8am to 9pm July and August. A park opposite the office features a huge statue of a salmon surrounded by man-made waterfalls.

The Campbellton Public Library (☎ 506-753-5253), 2 Aberdeen St at the corner of Andrew St, provides free Internet access weekdays. It's open 10am to 5pm Monday to Friday July and August, 10am to 5pm Tuesday to Saturday other months.

Things to See

Sugarloaf Provincial Park *(☎ 506-789-2366, 596 Val d'Amours Rd; admission free; open year-round)*, off Hwy 11 at exit 415, is dominated by Sugarloaf Mountain, which rises nearly 400m above sea level and looks vaguely like its namesake mountain in Rio de Janiero. From the base, it's just a half-hour walk to the top, and you're rewarded with excellent views of the town and the Restigouche River. Another trail leads around the bottom of the hill.

A unique attraction of Sugarloaf Provincial Park is the **Alpine Slide**, which involves taking a chairlift up a neighboring hill and sliding back down a track on a small sled. The slide operates from late June to early September and costs $3.50 a ride. It closes down if there's been any rain, as the brakes on the sleds won't hold when they're wet. A nearby office rents mountain bikes at $15/25 per half/full day. In winter you can ski here.

About 12km west of Campbellton towards Matapédia, on Hwy 11 North, 4km west of Tide Head, is **Morrisey Rock**, a roadside picnic area with a sweeping view of the scenic river valley.

Places to Stay

Sugarloaf Provincial Park (☎ 506-789-2366, ⓔ bob.gerrard@gnb.ca, ⓦ www.tourismnbcanada.com/web/english/outdoor_network, 596 Val d'Amours Rd) Unserviced/serviced sites $18/21-24. Open from mid-May-early Oct. There are 76 sites in a pleasant wooded setting at this park 4km from downtown Campbellton.

Campbellton Lighthouse Hostel (☎ 506-759-7044, fax 506-759-7403, e julie.jardine@ campbellton.org, 1 Ritchie St) Tent site $5 per person, dorm beds $12/15 members/ nonmembers. Blankets are $1 extra (no sheets available). Open mid-June-Aug. This distinctive HI hostel is in a converted lighthouse by the Restigouche River, just up from the provincial tourist office. There are 20 beds in two large dorms, one with 12 beds, the other with eight. You can only check in between 4pm and midnight, but there's ample parking and the SMT bus stop is just 200m away.

McKenzie House B&B (☎ 506-753-3133, w www.bbcanada.com/4384.html, 31 Andrew St) Singles/doubles from $50/60. This large two-story house with an impressive verandah is four blocks south of the tourist office.

Sanfar Cottages (☎ 506-753-4287, e ern@nbnet.nb.ca, w www.sanfar.biz land.com, 35 Restigouche Dr, Tide Head) Cottages $46/50 for two/four people, $54/58 for three/six people, with cooking facilities. Open June-Sept. Sanfar is at Tide Head on Hwy 134, 7km west of Campbellton. The 11 neat little cottages vary in size and number of beds, and not all include cooking facilities. The cafe here doesn't generally serve breakfast, but you can get lunch from 11am to 2pm weekdays and dinner nightly from 5pm. This cozy complex is recommended.

Places to Eat

Little Saigon (☎ 506-753-2501, 144 Water St) Mains $7-10. Open 11am-8:30pm Tues-Fri, noon-8:30pm Sat-Sun. Little Saigon has friendly owners and good Vietnamese-Chinese food.

Something Else (☎ 506-753-7744, 65 Water St) Mains $12. Open 11am-2pm & 5pm-9pm Mon-Fri, 5pm-9pm Sat & Sun. For a casually upscale meal, Something Else is a good bet. The eclectic regional cuisine includes pastas ($7/9 small/large), stir-fry chicken ($12), a seafood platter ($16) and filet mignon ($18). The four vegetarian choices are $10 to $13. Weekdays there's a lunch special for $8.

Getting There & Away

The SMT bus stop is at the Pik-Quik Convenient Store (☎ 506-753-3100) on Water St near Prince William St. The SMT bus departs Campbellton daily at 11am for Fredericton and Moncton ($33 to either). Twice a day (once in the morning and once in the afternoon) an Orleans Express bus leaves Campbellton for Gaspé ($52), Québec City ($61) and Montréal ($95).

The VIA Rail station (☎ 800-561-3952) is conveniently central at 113 Roseberry St. There's one train daily, except Wednesday, going south to Moncton and Halifax, and one daily, except Tuesday, heading the other way to Montréal ($114). The station is open from 5:45am to 10:30am and 5:45pm to 10pm (closed Tuesday afternoon and Wednesday morning). No coin lockers are available.

If you'll be driving southwest toward Saint-Léonard on Hwy 17, beware of moose and deer on the road. Collisions with these animals are an almost daily occurrence here.

KEDGWICK

To the north toward Campbellton, pinhead-sized Kedgwick has a **Forestry Museum** (☎ 506-284-3138, 7989 Hwy 17; adult/family $7/18; open 9am-6pm daily mid-June-mid-Sept) that showcases the timber industry of the region. A large sawmill is in Kedgwick.

To get in a bit of canoeing on nearby rivers, call **Arpin Canoe Restigouche** (☎ 877-259-4440, w www.canoerestigouche.ca) in Kedgwick River, 14km off Hwy 17. They rent canoes for $30 a day, and offer a variety of guided canoe trips whenever at least four people are interested.

Forestry Museum Campground (☎ 506-284-3138, fax 506-284-2194, e musee@ nbnet.nb.ca, w www.multimania.com/muse forest, 7989 Hwy 17, Kedgwick) Unserviced/ serviced sites $10/17. Open mid-June-mid-Sept. This clean, fresh campground behind the museum at the north end of town offers shady, grassy sites. Be prepared for cool conditions in this high plateau region even in midsummer.

Mom's B&B (☎ *506-284-2586, 8760 Hwy 17, White Brook*) Singles/doubles $40/50. Just 8km northeast of Kedgwick, Mom's offers three rooms; the two upstairs share a bathroom and sizable kitchen. It's clean and comfortable, and the price includes a cooked breakfast.

À la Belle Étoile B&B (☎ *506-284-2270, 107 St Jean Baptist St, Kedgwick*) Doubles $60 mid-June-mid-Sept, $40 other months. This large two-story house with a restaurant downstairs is opposite a large rest area on Hwy 17, at the southwest end of town near the IGA grocery store.

MOUNT CARLETON PROVINCIAL PARK

This 17,427-hectare park is the Maritime's only truly remote, sizable nature park, offering visitors mountains, valleys and rivers in a wilderness setting. It's the New Brunswick equivalent of Ontario's famous Algonquin Park, and it's the best place in the region for seeing large mammals (moose, deer, bear) in the wild. Because it's not a national park, Mount Carleton is little known and relatively unvisited, even in midsummer.

The main feature of the park is a series of rounded glaciated peaks and ridges, including Mount Carleton, which at 820m is the highest peak in the Maritimes. This range is actually an extension of the Appalachian Mountains, which begin in the US state of Georgia.

Access to Mount Carleton Provincial Park is via Hwy 180 from Saint Quentin, between Campbellton and Saint-Léonard. The park is 41km east of Saint Quentin, all but the last 8km of it paved. Saint Quentin is your last chance to purchase gasoline and food.

At the entrance to the park is a visitors center (☎ 506-235-0793), off Hwy 385, with maps and information. The center is open 8am to 8pm Monday to Friday, 10am to 10pm Saturday and Sunday May to October. In the past an entry fee of $5 per car was charged, but in 2001 the park staff

decided the fee wasn't worth the trouble it took to collect and allowed free entry. What they'll do in future is unknown. Hunting and logging are prohibited in the park, and all roads are gravel.

Hiking

Day hiking is the best way to explore Mount Carleton. The park has a 62km network of trails, most of them leading to a handful of rocky knobs that are the highest summits.

Mount Bailey Trail, a 7½km loop to the 564m hill, begins near the day-use area and climbs the area's easiest peak. Most hikers can walk this route in three hours.

The highest peak is reached from the **Mount Carleton Trail**, a 10km route that skirts over the 820m knob, where there's a fire tower. Along the way is a backcountry campsite, located near three beaver ponds and in full view of the mountain. Plan on three to four hours for the trek and pack your parka. The wind above the treeline can be brutal at times.

The most scenic hike is the **Sagamook Trail**, a 6km loop to a 777m peak with superlative vistas of Nictau Lake and the highlands to the north of it. Allow three hours for this trek. The **Mount Head Trail** connects the Mount Carleton and Sagamook Trails, making a long transit of the range possible.

All hikers intending to follow any of these long trails must register at the visitor center or park headquarters before hitting the trail. Outside the camping season, roughly from mid-May to mid-September, you should call ahead to make sure the main gate will be open, as the Mount Carleton trailhead is 13½km from the park entrance. Otherwise, park your car at the entrance and walk in – the Mount Bailey trailhead is only 2½km from the gate.

Other Activities

Canoeing and kayaking on the chain of lakes in the center of the park is very popular. If you don't have your own equipment, you can try renting from **Nictau Lodge** (☎ *506-356-8353, fax 506-356-8354,* e *tobnor@nbnet.nb.ca,* w *www.tobique nordic.com; open mid-Apr-Nov),* inside the park on the south side of Nictau Lake. Rates for one/three days are $30/55 for a bicycle, $30/75 for a single kayak or $40/100 for a canoe or double kayak. The lodge also has five cabins with shared bath at $80 double and three lodges with bath at $150 for up to six. A bunkhouse with 11 beds is $30 per person. Reservations are essential as staff are not always there.

Places to Stay

Armstrong Brook Campground (☎ *506-235-0793, fax 506-235-0795,* e *claude .labrie@gnb.ca,* w *www.gnb.ca/0078/ carleton, off Hwy 385)* Campsites $11 Sun-Thurs, $14 Fri-Sat. Open mid-May-Sept. This large campground on the north side of Nictau Lake, 3km from the park entrance, has toilets, showers and a kitchen shelter, but no serviced sites. Because of this, the RV drivers often have their noisy generators running, so camp well away from them.

Check the eight tent-only sites along Armstrong Brook on the north side of the campground, where you're unlikely to be bothered by the noise. This campground is never full.

Aside from Armstrong Brook, there are two walk-in campgrounds and one back-country spot. The *Williams Brook Campground*, just a few kilometers beyond Armstrong Brook on the north side of Nictau Lake, has eight walk-in sites, each with a wooden tent platform. It's great if you're looking for solitude. The *Franquelin Campground* on the south shore of the lake has nine walk-in campsites and is better situated for hiking, as it's just 1½km from the Mount Bailey trailhead (10km from Mount Carleton). The *Headwaters Campsite* up on Mount Carleton itself has just three sites, and it's a good idea to call ahead and try to reserve one if you're sure you want to sleep there. Camping at Williams Brook and Franquelin costs $9 a night; at Headwaters it's $5 a night.

Glossary

Acadians – the first settlers from France who lived in the Maritimes

Atlantic provinces – Newfoundland and Labrador, Nova Scotia, Prince Edward Island and New Brunswick; see *Maritime provinces*

Bluenose II – a well-known, widely traveled replica of Canada's famous sailing vessel

Bluenoses – a common nickname for Nova Scotians

CAA – Canadian Automobile Association

ceilidh – (pronounced '**kay** lee') an informal gathering for song, dance and story, sometimes known as a kitchen party; especially popular on Prince Edward Island and Cape Breton Island

clearcut – an area where loggers have cut every tree, large and small, leaving nothing standing

dulse – an edible seaweed that is picked and sun-dried

fiddlehead – a fern collected by First Nations people as it sprouts in May and consumed after boiling for its purported medicinal qualities

First Nations – a term used to denote Canada's aboriginal or indigenous peoples

flowerpots – unusual rock formations created by wave erosion

Haligonians – residents of Halifax, Nova Scotia

interior camping – backcountry camping in sites that are accessible only by foot or canoe

Loyalists – residents of American colonies who maintained their allegiance to Britain during the American Revolution and fled to Canada

Maliseet – the second-largest Native Indian tribe in the Maritimes, found mostly in western New Brunswick

Maritime provinces – New Brunswick, Nova Scotia and Prince Edward Island; also known as the Maritimes

Métis – a person of mixed French and Native Indian ancestry

Mi'kmaq – also spelled Micmac; the largest Indian tribe in the Maritimes

Mounties – Royal Canadian Mounted Police (RCMP)

no-see-um – any of various tiny, difficult-to-see biting insects that can annoy travelers in the woods or along some beaches

PEI – Prince Edward Island

petroglyphs – ancient paintings or carvings on rock

portage – the process of transporting boats and supplies overland between navigable waterways; can also refer to the overland route used for such a purpose

poutine – french fries topped with melted cheese curds and gravy

tattoo – a military parade featuring piping and drumming; comes from the 17th-century Dutch *taptoe* (turn off the tap), a nightly march by drummers recalling troops from the taverns

trailer – in Canada, as well as in the USA, this refers to a caravan or a mobile home (house trailer); can also refer to the type of vehicle used for transporting goods

Wabanaki – literally 'the people who dwell at the sunrise,' a confederacy of Algonquin-speaking tribes in the northeastern United States and the Maritime provinces

LONELY PLANET

You already know that Lonely Planet produces more than this one guidebook, but you might not be aware of the other products we have on this region. Here is a selection of titles which you may want to check out as well:

Montréal
ISBN 1 86450 254 1
US$15.99 • UK£9.99

Canada
ISBN 1 74059 029 5
US$24.99 • UK£14.99

New England
ISBN 1 74059 025 2
US$19.99 • UK£12.99

Québec
ISBN 1 74059 024 4
US$16.99 • UK£10.99

Available wherever books are sold.

Index

Abbreviations

NB – New Brunswick   NS – Nova Scotia   PEI – Prince Edward Island

Text

A

Abegweit First Nation (PEI) 238
Acadia University Art Gallery (NS) 152
Acadian Historic Village (NB) 30, 343
Acadians
  art 26
  crafts 192
  food 63
  history 14, 132, 153, 154–5, 217, 258, 327, 341
  language 28–9
  museums 254, 320–1, 341–2, 343
  music 24
  population 21, 23, 191, 254, 259–60
accommodations 58–62. *See also individual locations*
  B&Bs 61
  camping 52–3, 58–9
  costs 39
  guesthouses 60–1
  hostels 35–6, 59–60
  hotels 62
  motels 61–2
  tourist homes 60–1
  university 60
Acorn, Milton 25–6, 226
activities 55–7. *See also individual activities*
Admiral Digby Museum (NS) 138
African Canadians 93, 129
air travel 67–72, 75
Alberton (PEI) 255

alcoholic drinks 54, 64–5
Alexander Graham Bell National Historic Site (NS) 210
Alma (NB) 316–7
Amherst (NS) 168–70, **169**
Amherst Point Migratory Bird Sanctuary (NS) 168
Annapolis Royal (NS) 145–8, **146**
Annapolis Valley (NS) 144–50
Anne of Green Gables 25, 27, 45, 216, 230, 231, 247, 248, 249, 250
Antigonish (NS) 177–8
art
  galleries 27, 92–3, 115, 126–7, 152, 176, 264–5, 328
  history 26–7
ATMs 39

B

B&Bs. *See* accommodations
Baddeck (NS) 210–3
Bailly, Earl 26, 120
Balmoral Grist Mill Museum (NS) 172–3
banks 38, 39, 53
Barrington (NS) 131–2
bars 54, 64, 65
Basin Head (PEI) 237
Basin Head Fisheries Museum (PEI) 237
Bathurst (NB) 344
Bay of Fundy 11, 15, 17, 52, 278, 304, 322–3
Bay St Lawrence (NS) 197–8

beaches
  NB 298, 331, 333
  NS 115, 127, 136, 175–6, 180, 198, 206
  PEI 240–1, 244
Beaconsfield House (PEI) 224
Bear River (NS) 142
Bear River First Nation (NS) 142
Beaverbrook, Lord 264–5, 337
Bedford Institute of Oceanography (NS) 111
beer 64, 91, 304
Bell, Alexander Graham 210
Belle Côte (NS) 191
Belliveau Cove (NS) 137
bicycling 44, 55–6, 79–80
  NB 260, 276–7, 305–6, 313, 314–5, 333, 335
  NS 84, 96, 117, 122, 138, 152, 177, 195
  PEI 218–9, 236, 239, 252
Big Bras d'Or (NS) 200–1
Big Pond (NS) 213–4
Bird Islands (NS) 200
bird watching 18
  NB 260, 293, 298, 305, 317, 328, 344
  NS 85, 128, 136, 139–40, 152, 168, 171, 177, 200, 206
blackflies 52
Blacks Harbor (NB) 287, 289
Blomidon Provincial Park (NS) 150
Blue Heron Scenic Drive (PEI) 239–50
boat tours

NB 285, 295
NS 97, 115, 118, 122, 211
PEI 225, 235, 256
books 44–6. See also litera-
ture
Borden-Carleton (PEI) 239
border crossings 34, 72
Bouctouche (NB) 332–4
Brackley Beach (PEI) 244
Bras d'Or Lakes (NS) 210–1,
213–4
Bridgetown (NS) 148
Bridgewater (NS) 124–5
Brier Island (NS) 30, 141–2
British North America Act 15
Burnt Church First Nation
(NB) 341
buses 72–3, 75–6, 81
business hours 53–4

C

Cabot, John 197
Cabot Trail (NS) 30, 186,
194
Campbellton (NB) 346–7
camping. See accommoda-
tions
Campobello Island (NB)
292–3
Canadian Automobile Associ-
ation (CAA) 79
canoeing 56–7
NB 260, 266, 305–6,
348–9
NS 84, 95–6, 117, 143
Canso (NS) 185
Cape Breton Highlands
National Park (NS) 194–6
Cape Breton Island (NS)
186–215, **187**
Cape Chignecto Provincial
Park (NS) 30, 167
Cape d'Or (NS) 166–7
Cape Enrage (NB) 317
Cape George (NS) 178–9
Cape Jourimain (NB) 330–1
Cape Mabou Highlands (NS)
188

Cape North (NS) 197
Cape Sambro (NS) 95
Cape St Mary (NS) 136
Caraquet (NB) 341–2
Caribou (NS) 175–6
Carleton Martello Tower (NB)
304
cars 76–9
border crossings 34, 72
Canadian Automobile
Association (CAA) 79
driver's license 35
gasoline 79
insurance 74, 78–9
purchasing 78–9
renting 77–8
road rules 76–7
scenic drives 178–9, 186,
194, 233–57, 313–4
Cartier, Jacques 13–4, 217
casinos 107
Cavendish (PEI) 30, 247–9
caves 318
ceilidhs 24, 65, 190, 225
Central Fundy Shore (NB)
312–8
central Nova Scotia 158–79,
160–1
Champlain, Samuel de 14,
127, 145, 148, 284, 298
Charlottetown (PEI) 222–33,
223, 227
accommodations 226–9
entertainment 230–1
restaurants 229–30
shopping 231
transportation 231–3
charters 69
Chatham (NB) 337, **339**
Chester (NS) 116–7
Chéticamp (NS) 191–4
Chiac 28
Chignecto (NS) 164–8
children, traveling with 51
chocolate 279–80
Christ Church Cathedral (NB)
265
Church Point (NS) 136–7
cinema. See films
climate 15–6
climbing 57, 96

clothing 33, 48
coal 16, 21, 83, 189, 204
Colchester Museum (NS)
159–60
Cole Harbour Heritage Farm
Museum (NS) 111–2
Coleman frog 265
The College of Piping &
Celtic Performing Arts
(PEI) 252
Colville, Alex 26
Confederation 15, 224
Confederation Bridge (NB,
PEI) 217, 220, 221
Confederation Trail (PEI) 30,
256
consulates 36–7
Co-op Artisanale de Chéti-
camp (NS) 192
costs 39–40
Country Harbour (NS) 184–5
courses 58
covered bridges 272
crafts 65–6, 92, 200, 269
credit cards 39, 53
The Crombie Art Gallery (NS)
176
cruises 74, 97, 211
Cumberland County Museum
(NS) 168
currency 38
currents 52
customs 37–8
cycling. See bicycling

D

Dalhousie (NB) 30–1, 345–6
dance 24
Darling Lake (NS) 135–6
Dartmouth (NS) 110–3
Dartmouth Heritage Museum
(NS) 111
Deer Island (NB) 289–92
deGarthe, William 26, 115
Delaps Cove (NS) 148
Digby (NS) 137–9
Digby Neck (NS) 139–42
Diligent River (NS) 166
disabled travelers 50–1
diving 57, 96, 122, 225
Doaktown (NB) 336

Bold indicates maps.

documents 34–6
Dorchester (NB) 31, 327–8
Douglastown (NB) 337
drinks 54, 64–5
driving. See cars
drugs 38, 53

E

East Point (PEI) 237
Eastern Shore (NS) 180–5,
    182–3
Eaton, Cyrus 170–1
economy 21. See also individual provinces
Economy (NS) 164
Edmundston (NB) 274–8,
    275
education 24, 58
Eel River First Nation (NB)
    345
eKno communication service
    43
electricity 47
Elephant Rock (PEI) 256
Elmira (PEI) 237–8
email 43
embassies 36–7
emergencies 53
    credit cards 53
    embassies 37
    hospitals 48, 53
    police 53
employment 58
energy 17, 146, 225, 270
entertainment 65
environmental groups 51–2
environmental issues 16–7,
    22, 30–1, 204
Evangeline 27, 153, 155
Evergreen House (NS) 111
exchange rates 38
Experimental Forest of
    Moncton University (NB)
    276

F

farmers' markets 63
fauna. See wildlife
faxes 43
ferries 74, 80–1
films 27, 46, 299

First Nations. See also individual tribes
    arts & crafts 27, 65–6, 213
    food 63
    history 13, 23–4, 45, 217,
        258
    lacrosse 65
    language 28
    population 23, 24
    powwows 54–5
    reserves 142, 160, 213,
        238, 255, 336, 345
    traditional culture 28,
        332
Fisheries Museum of the
    Atlantic (NS) 120
Fisherman's Cove (NS) 112
fishing, recreational 57
    NB 260, 336, 342
    NS 85, 138, 190, 192
    PEI 237, 238, 242, 246
fishing industry 21, 83, 217,
    237
Five Islands Provincial Park
    (NS) 164
flora. See plants
Florenceville (NB) 273
food 62–4
    Acadian 63
    costs 64
    fast 63
    health issues 49
    markets & groceries 63
    Native Indian 63
forest industry 16, 21, 44,
    235, 347
Fort Amherst/Port la Joye
    National Historic Site (PEI)
    225
Fort Anne National Historic
    Site (NS) 145
Fort Beauséjour National
    Historic Site (NB) 329–30
Fort Edward National Historic
    Site (NS) 154
Fort Point (NS) 127
Fort Point Museum (NS) 125
Fortin du P'tit Sault (NB) 276
fossils 165, 167–8
Founders Hall (PEI) 224
foxes 17–8, 252

Fraser Cultural Centre (NS)
    172
Fraser Nursery & Nature Trail
    (NB) 276
Fredericton (NB) 260–70,
    262–3
    accommodations 267–8
    entertainment 268–9
    history 260–1
    restaurants 268
    shopping 269
    transportation 269–70
Freeport (NS) 141
French and Indian Wars 14
French language 28–9
French Shore (NS) 136–7
Fundy Geological Museum
    (NS) 165
Fundy Isles (NB) 287–98, **288**
Fundy National Park (NB) 30,
    314–6, **315**
Fundy Trail Parkway (NB)
    313–4

G

Gaelic College of Celtic Arts
    & Crafts (NS) 200
Gampo Abbey (NS) 196
Ganong's Chocolate Museum
    (NB) 279–80
gardens 93, 145, 152, 278,
    283, 345
gasoline 79
gay & lesbian travelers 50
geography 15
Georgetown (PEI) 235
Glace Bay (NS) 206, 208
golf 192–3, 305
Goods & Services Tax (GST)
    40–1
government 20–1
Grand Falls (NB) 273–4
Grand Manan Island (NB)
    293–7
Grand Pré (NS) 153
Grande-Anse (NB) 343
Grassy Island National Historic Site (NS) 185
Great Explosion 25, 86, 92
Greenwich (PEI) 238
Greenwood (NS) 148

guesthouses. *See* accommodations
guidebooks 44–5
Guysborough (NS) 185

H

Haliburton, Thomas Chandler 25, 154–5
Halifax (NS) 86–110, **88–9, 98–9, 104**
    accommodations 99–101
    entertainment 103, 105–7
    history 86, 92
    restaurants 102–3
    shopping 107
    transportation 107–10
Halifax Citadel National Historic Site (NS) 93
Halifax Public Gardens (NS) 93
Hartland (NB) 272–3
health 35, 48-49
Hector Heritage Quay (NS) 173
Heritage Museum (NS) 177
hiking 44–5, 55
    NB 260, 298, 313, 314–5, 322, 333, 348
    NS 85, 122, 127, 143, 164, 166, 167, 171, 177, 181, 183–4, 185, 188, 195, 198, 211
    PEI 238, 241
Hillsborough (NB) 318
The Historic Properties (NS) 90
history 13–5, 45. *See also individual locations*
hitchhiking 80
hockey 65, 107, 155–6
holidays 54
Hopewell Rocks (NB) 317–8
horse racing 231, 254
horseback riding 190
hostels. *See* accommodations
hotels. *See* accommodations
House of Green Gables (PEI) 248
Howe, Joseph 25

Huntsman Aquarium Museum (NB) 284

I

immunizations 48
Ingonish (NS) 198–200
insects 49, 52–3
insurance
    car 74, 78–9
    travel 35
International Fox Museum & Hall of Fame (PEI) 252
Internet access 43. *See also* Web sites
Inverness (NS) 189–90
Irish moss 257
Irving Eco Center (NB) 332–3
Irving family 22
Irving Nature Park (NB) 305
itineraries, suggested 31–2

J

Jedore Oyster Pond (NS) 181
Joe, Rita 26
Joggins (NS) 167–8

K

kayaking 45, 56
    NB 260, 266, 285, 289, 293, 305–6, 316, 333, 334, 348–9
    NS 84, 95–6, 112, 115, 117, 118–9, 125, 130, 181, 198–9, 200, 214
    PEI 219, 235, 236, 244, 246, 255
Kedgwick (NB) 347–8
Kejimkujik National Park (NS) 128, 142–4
Kensington (PEI) 250
Kentville (NS) 149–50
Kidston Island (NS) 211
Kings Byway Scenic Drive (PEI) 233–9
King's Landing Historical Settlement (NB) 271
Kingsport (NS) 150
kitchen parties. *See* ceilidhs
Knaut Rhuland House (NS) 120

Kouchibouguac National Park (NB) 334–5
Krieghoff, Cornelius 26

L

lacrosse 65
Lady Slipper Scenic Drive (PEI) 250–7
LaHave (NS) 125–6
LaHave Islands (NS) 126
language 28–9
laundry 48
Lawrence, Charles 14, 154, 159
Lawrencetown Beach (NS) 180
Le Pays de la Sagouine (NB) 332
legal matters 53, 65
Lennox Island First Nation (PEI) 255
Les Trois Pignons (NS) 192
lesbians. *See* gay & lesbian travelers
Lewis, Maud 26
lighthouses
    NB 293, 295, 297, 330
    NS 127, 131, 132, 134, 141, 179, 184, 185, 208, 215
    PEI 234, 237, 238, 256, 257
Liscomb Mills (NS) 183–4
literature 25–6. *See also* books
Liverpool (NS) 126–8
lobster 17, 21, 173, 217, 245, 289, 331
lobster suppers 220, 238, 244–5
Longfellow, Henry Wadsworth 27, 153, 155
The Lookoff (NS) 150
Lordly House Museum (NS) 116–7
Louisbourg (NS) 208–9
Louisbourg National Historic Site (NS) 30, 209–10
Loyalists 14–5, 83, 129, 137, 258, 261, 271, 298, 302–3, 306

Bold indicates maps.

Lunenburg (NS) 30, 119–24, **120–1**
Lunenburg Academy (NS) 121
Lyme disease 49

M

Mabou (NS) 188–9
MacAskill, Wallace 214
Machias Seal Island (NB) 298
MacLennan, Hugh 25
MacLeod, Alistair 26
MacMaster, Natalie 24, 25
Mactaquac (NB) 270–2
Mactaquac Provincial Park (NB) 270–1
magazines 46
Magnetic Hill (NB) 31, 321–2
Mahone Bay (NS) 118–9
mail 41, 53
Maillet, Antonine 26, 332
Maitland (NS) 159
Maliseet 13, 23, 28, 45, 54–5, 258, 260, 271, 298
Malpeque Bay (PEI) 250
maps 32
Marconi National Historic Site (NS) 208
Margaree Harbour (NS) 191
Margaree Valley (NS) 190–1
Maritime Command Museum (NS) 94
Maritime Museum of the Atlantic (NS) 90–1
markets 63
McAlary, Shirley 303
McNabs Island (NS) 95
measurements 47–8
Meat Cove (NS) 198
Mermaid Theatre (NS) 156
Meteghan (NS) 136
Métis 23, 28
Mi'kmaq
   art 27
   communities 23, 24, 83, 142, 160, 213, 250, 255, 335, 336, 341, 345
   history 13, 45, 82, 86, 156, 217, 258, 260, 318
   traditional culture 28, 44, 54–5, 165, 173, 332

Millbrock First Nation (NS) 160
Milltown (NB) 280
Miminegash (PEI) 257
mining 16, 21, 83, 189, 206, 208, 287, 314, 344–5
Minister's Island Historic Site (NB) 284
Miramichi (NB) 336–41, **338–9**
Miramichi River (NB) 336
Miscouche (PEI) 254
Mispec Park (NB) 305
Monastery (NS) 179
Moncton (NB) 318–27, **319**
   accommodations 323–4
   entertainment 325–6
   history 318, 320
   restaurants 324–5
   transportation 326–7
Moncton Museum (NB) 321
money 38–41
Mont Blanc 92
Mont Carmel (PEI) 254
Montague (PEI) 234–5
Montgomery, Lucy Maud 25, 45, 216, 247, 248, 249, 250
moose 17
Moosehead Brewery (NB) 304
mosquitoes 52
motels. *See* accommodations
motion sickness 49
motorcycles 74, 76–9
Mount Allison University (NB) 328
Mount Carleton Provincial Park (NB) 15, 30, 348–9
Mount Stewart (PEI) 238–9
Muir-Cox Shipbuilding Interpretive Centre (NS) 130
Murray River (PEI) 234
museums
   Acadian Museum (PEI) 254
   Admiral Digby Museum (NS) 138
   Alexander Graham Bell National Historic Site (NS) 210

Balmoral Grist Mill Museum (NS) 172–3
Basin Head Fisheries Museum (PEI) 237
Colchester Museum (NS) 159–60
Cole Harbour Heritage Farm Museum (NS) 111–2
Dartmouth Heritage Museum (NS) 111
Fisheries Museum of the Atlantic (NS) 120
Fort Point Museum (NS) 125
Fundy Geological Museum (NS) 165
Ganong's Chocolate Museum (NB) 279–80
Heritage Museum (NS) 177
Huntsman Aquarium Museum (NB) 284
International Fox Museum & Hall of Fame (PEI) 252
Les Trois Pignons (NS) 192
Lordly House Museum (NS) 116–7
Louisbourg National Historic Site (NS) 209–10
Maritime Command Museum (NS) 94
Maritime Museum of the Atlantic (NS) 90–1
Moncton Museum (NB) 321
New Brunswick Museum (NB) 302
Northumberland Fisheries Museum (NS) 173
Nova Scotia Museum of Industry (NS) 176
Nova Scotia Museum of Natural History (NS) 93
Prescott House Museum (NS) 150
Queen's County Museum (NS) 127
Salmon Museum (NS) 190

Shearwater Aviation Museum (NS) 112
Shelburne County Museum (NS) 130
Sherbrooke Village (NS) 184
Sherman Hines Museum of Photography & Galleries (NS) 126–7
West Hants Historical Society Museum (NS) 154
Yarmouth County Museum (NS) 132
York-Sunbury Historical Museum (NB) 264
music 24–5
Musquodoboit Harbour (NS) 180–1
mussels 16, 21, 83, 238

N

national parks 18, 59
Cape Breton Highlands National Park (NS) 194–6
Fundy National Park (NB) 30, 314–6, **315**
Kejimkujik National Park (NS) 128, 142–4
Kouchibouguac National Park (NB) 334–5
Prince Edward Island National Park (PEI) 238, 240–1, **242–3**
Native Indians. See First Nations; *individual tribes*
Naufrage (PEI) 238
Neils Harbour (NS) 198
Nelson (NB) 337, 340
New Brunswick 258–349, **259**
accommodations 260
activities 260
climate 259
economy 259
highlights 258
history 258–9
parks 19–20
population 259–60
tourist offices 33, 260
New Brunswick Museum (NB) 302
New Brunswick Sports Hall of Fame (NB) 264
New Glasgow (NS) 176
New Glasgow (PEI) 244–6
New London (PEI) 249
New River Provincial Park (NB) 298
New Waterford (NS) 206
Newcastle (NB) 337, **338**
newspapers 46
noise 52
North Cape (PEI) 256
North Lake (PEI) 237–8
North Rustico (PEI) 246–7
North Sydney (NS) 201–2
Northumberland Fisheries Museum (NS) 173
Northumberland Shore (NB) 330–5
no-see-ums 53
Nova Scotia 82–215, **84–5**
accommodations 85
activities 84–5
climate 83
economy 83
highlights 82
history 82–3
parks 19
population 83
tourist offices 33, 83
Nova Scotia Museum of Industry (NS) 176
Nova Scotia Museum of Natural History (NS) 93
Nova Scotia Sport Hall of Fame (NS) 93
Nowlan, Alden 26

O

Odell Park (NB) 266
Old Government House (NB) 266
Orwell (PEI) 233
Ottawa House Museum (NS) 165
overfishing 16, 21
oysters 21, 217, 250

P

packing 32–3
painting 26–7
Park Corner (PEI) 249–50
Parrsboro (NS) 30, 164–6
Partridge Island (NB) 304–5
Partridge Island (NS) 165
Passamaquoddies 281
passports 34, 53
Peggy's Cove (NS) 114–5
Perkins House (NS) 127
pesticides 49
Petit-Rocher (NB) 344–5
pets 38
phones 41–3
photography 47
Pictou (NS) 173–5, **175**
planning 32–3
plants 17
Pleasant Bay (NS) 196–7
Point Pleasant Park (NS) 94–5
Pointe de l'Église (NS) 136–7
police 53
politics 20–1
pollution 16, 17, 30–1, 204
population 21, 23–4
Port Bickerton (NS) 184
Port Dufferin (NS) 182–3
Port Hastings (NS) 186, 188
Port Royal National Historic Site (NS) 148
Porters Lake Provincial Park (NS) 180
postal services 41, 53
potatoes 16, 21, 217, 233
powwows 54–5
Pratt, Mary 26
Prescott House Museum (NS) 150
Prince Edward Island 216–57, **218–9**
accommodations 219
activities 218–9
climate 217
economy 217
highlights 216
history 217

Bold indicates maps.

parks 19
population 217
tourist offices 33, 216–7
transportation 220–1
Prince Edward Island National
    Park (PEI) 238, 240–1,
    242–3
Prospect (NS) 114
Province House (PEI) 224
provincial parks 18–20, 59.
    See also individual parks
pubs 62, 64
Pugwash (NS) 170–1
pumpkins 156

Q

Quaker Whaler House (NS)
    111
Queen's County Museum
    (NS) 127

R

Raddall, Thomas 25
radio 46–7, 328
rafting 158–9
Red Bank First Nation (NB) 336
Région Évangéline (PEI) 254
religion 28
restaurants 54, 62–3. *See
    also individual locations*
Reversing Falls (NB) 304
Richards, David Adam 26
Roberts, Charles GD 25
rock climbing. *See* climbing
rock hounding 164–5
Rockwood Park (NB) 305
Roosevelt, Franklin D 292
Ross-Thompson House (NS)
    129–30

S

Sable Island (NS) 215
Sackville (NB) 328–9
safety
    driving 76–7
    swimming 52
Saint Croix River 284

Bold indicates maps.

Saint John (NB) 298–312,
    300–1, **307**
    accommodations 306,
        308–9
    entertainment 310
    history 298–9
    restaurants 309–10
    transportation 310–2
Saint John River Valley (NB)
    270–8
Sainte Anne du Bocage (NB)
    342–3
Saint-Jacques (NB) 278
Saint-Joseph (NB) 327
Saint-Louis-de-Kent (NB)
    334
sales tax 40
salmon 16, 21, 57, 62, 83,
    190, 270, 284, 287, 336
Salmon Museum (NS) 190
Scots Bay (NS) 150
scuba diving. *See* diving
seals 234, 235
Seaside Adjunct Kejimkujik
    National Park (NS) 128
senior travelers 51
Shearwater Aviation Museum
    (NS) 112
Shediac (NB) 331–2
Sheet Harbour (NS) 182
Shelburne (NS) 128–31
Shelburne County Museum
    (NS) 130
Shepody Bay Shorebird
    Reserve (NB) 317
Sherbrooke (NS) 184
Sherbrooke Village (NS) 184
Sherman Hines Museum of
    Photography & Galleries
    (NS) 126–7
shopping 53–4, 65–6
Shubenacadie (NS) 158–9
Shubenacadie Canal (NS)
    111, 159
Shubenacadie Provincial
    Wildlife Park (NS) 158
skiing 57
Sleeman Park (PEI) 252
Snow, Hank 127
Souris (PEI) 235–7
South Rustico (PEI) 244

southwestern Nova Scotia
    114–57, **116**
special events 54–5
Spencers Island (NS) 166
sports 65, 93, 264. *See also
    individual sports*
St Andrews (NB) 281–7, **282**
St Ann (PEI) 244–6
St Ann's (NS) 200
St Bernard (NS) 137
St Dunstan's Basilica (PEI) 224
St Francis Xavier University
    (NS) 177
St George (NB) 287
St Margaret's (PEI) 238
St Margaret's Bay (NS) 115
St Martins (NB) 312–3
St Paul's Church (NS) 91
St Peter's (NS) 30, 214
St Peters (PEI) 238
St Stephen (NB) 278–81, **279**
Stanhope (PEI) 241–4
students 36, 58
Summerside (PEI) 250–4, **251**
Sunbury Shores Arts &
    Nature Centre (NB) 284
Sunrise Trail (NS) 170–9
surfing 84, 127
Sutherland Steam Mill (NS)
    173
swimming 52, 122, 127, 156.
    See also beaches
Sydney (NS) 202–6, **203**, **207**
Sydney Tar Ponds (NS) 17,
    31, 204
Syliboy, Alan 27

T

Tancook Islands (NS) 117–8
Tangier (NS) 181
Tatamagouche (NS) 171–2
taxes 40–1
Taylor Head Provincial Park
    (NS) 181
telephones 41–3
television 46–7
theater 27–8
Thinkers Lodge (NS) 170–1
ticks 49
tidal bore 158–9, 161, 321,
    323

tides 52, 146, 322–3
Tidnish (NS) 170
Tignish (PEI) 255–6
time zones 47
tipping 40
Titanic 94
Tiverton (NS) 140–1
toilets 48
tourism, responsible 33
tourist homes. *See* accommodations
tourist offices 33–4
tourist seasons 32
tours, organized 81
Tracadie (PEI) 238–9
trains 73–4, 76
transportation
    air travel 67–72, 75
    bicycling 79–80
    buses 72–3, 75–6, 81
    cars 74, 76–9
    cruise ships 74
    ferries 74, 80–1
    hitchhiking 80
    motorcycles 74, 76–9
    trains 73–4, 76
travel insurance 35
traveler's checks 39, 53
trees 17
trekking. *See* hiking
Trigen Energy from Waste
    Plant (PEI) 225

Trinity Church (NB) 303
Truro (NS) 159–63, **162–3**
TV 46–7
Tyne Valley (PEI) 254–5

U

Uisge Bahn Falls (NS) 211
University of New Brunswick
    (NB) 265

V

vaccinations 48
VIA Rail 73–4
Victoria (PEI) 239–40
Victoria Park (NS) 160
video 47
visas 34–5

W

Wagmatcook First Nation
    (NS) 213
Wallace Bay (NS) 171
water 49
Web sites 43–4
Wentworth (NS) 171
West Fundy Shore (NB)
    278–98
West Hants Historical Society
    Museum (NS) 154
Westport (NS) 141–2
whale watching 18, 44,
    290–1

NB 260, 289, 293, 295, 342
    NS 85, 112, 122, 139–40,
    192, 196, 197, 199
White Head Island (NB)
    297
Whycocomagh (NS) 213
wildlife 17–8, 348. *See also
    individual species*
Windsor (NS) 153–7
Windsor Hockey Heritage
    Society (NS) 155–6
wine 64, 150
Wolfville (NS) 150–3, **151**
women travelers 50
Wood Islands (PEI) 234
Woodstock (NB) 271–2
work 58
World Peace Pavilion (NS)
    111

Y

Yarmouth (NS) 132–5, **133**
Yarmouth County Museum
    (NS) 132
York Redoubt (NS) 95
York-Sunbury Historical
    Museum (NB) 264
youth cards 36

Z

zoos 158, 266, 305, 322

Boxed Text

Air Travel Glossary 68
Bridge over Troubled Waters 221
A Christmas Tree for Boston 92
An Empire Called Irving 22
Ethnic Cleansing in the 18th Century 154–5
Fredericton's Famous Frog 265
The Loyalists 261
Milton Acorn 226
Tea with the Mayor 303

That Crazy Mixed-Up Lobster 245
The Tides of Funnel-Shaped Fundy 322–3
A Touch of Tinsel in Saint John 299
A Venerable, Visible Minority 129
Warning 67
Whale Watching Galore 290–1
A Yen for Anne 250

MAP LEGEND

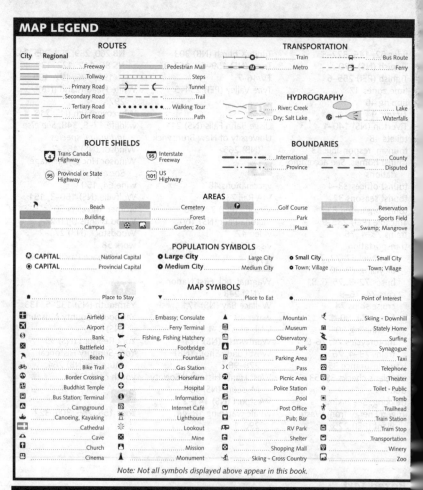

ROUTES

City	Regional	
		Freeway
		Tollway
		Primary Road
		Secondary Road
		Tertiary Road
		Dirt Road

	Pedestrian Mall
	Steps
	Tunnel
	Trail
	Walking Tour
	Path

TRANSPORTATION

Train	Bus Route
Metro	Ferry

ROUTE SHIELDS

Trans Canada Highway

Interstate Freeway

Provincial or State Highway

US Highway

HYDROGRAPHY

River; Creek	Lake
Dry; Salt Lake	Waterfalls

BOUNDARIES

International	County
Province	Disputed

AREAS

Beach	Cemetery	Golf Course	Reservation
Building	Forest	Park	Sports Field
Campus	Garden; Zoo	Plaza	Swamp; Mangrove

POPULATION SYMBOLS

CAPITAL ... National Capital	Large City ... Large City	Small City ... Small City
CAPITAL ... Provincial Capital	Medium City ... Medium City	Town; Village ... Town; Village

MAP SYMBOLS

Place to Stay	Place to Eat	Point of Interest

Airfield	Embassy; Consulate	Mountain	Skiing - Downhill
Airport	Ferry Terminal	Museum	Stately Home
Bank	Fishing, Fishing Hatchery	Observatory	Surfing
Battlefield	Footbridge	Park	Synagogue
Beach	Fountain	Parking Area	Taxi
Bike Trail	Gas Station	Pass	Telephone
Border Crossing	Horsefarm	Picnic Area	Theater
Buddhist Temple	Hospital	Police Station	Toilet - Public
Bus Station; Terminal	Information	Pool	Tomb
Campground	Internet Café	Post Office	Trailhead
Canoeing, Kayaking	Lighthouse	Pub; Bar	Train Station
Cathedral	Lookout	RV Park	Tram Stop
Cave	Mine	Shelter	Transportation
Church	Mission	Shopping Mall	Winery
Cinema	Monument	Skiing - Cross Country	Zoo

Note: Not all symbols displayed above appear in this book.

LONELY PLANET OFFICES

Australia
Locked Bag 1, Footscray, Victoria 3011
☎ 03 8379 8000 fax 03 8379 8111
email talk2us@lonelyplanet.com.au

USA
150 Linden Street, Oakland, California 94607
☎ 510 893 8555, TOLL FREE 800 275 8555
fax 510 893 8572
email info@lonelyplanet.com

UK
10a Spring Place, London NW5 3BH
☎ 020 7428 4800 fax 020 7428 4828
email go@lonelyplanet.co.uk

France
1 rue du Dahomey, 75011 Paris
☎ 01 55 25 33 00 fax 01 55 25 33 01
email bip@lonelyplanet.fr
www.lonelyplanet.fr

World Wide Web: www.lonelyplanet.com *or* AOL keyword: lp
Lonely Planet Images: lpi@lonelyplanet.com.au